AFRICAN HISTORICAL DICTIONARIES
Edited by Jon Woronoff

Historical Dictionary
of South Africa

Second Edition

Christopher Saunders
Nicholas Southey
bibliography by Mary-Lynn Suttie

African Historical Dictionaries, No. 78

The Scarecrow Press, Inc.
Lanham, Maryland, and London
2000

SCARECROW PRESS, INC.

Published in the United States of America
by Scarecrow Press, Inc.
4720 Boston Way
Lanham, Maryland 20706
http://www.scarecrowpress.com

4 Pleydell Gardens, Folkestone
Kent CT20 2DN, England

British Library Cataloguing in Publication Information Available

Library of Congress Cataloging-in-Publication Data

Saunders, Christopher C.
    Historical dictionary of South Africa / by Christopher Saunders and
Nicholas Southey ; with bibliography by Mary-Lynn Suttie. — 2nd ed.
        p.   cm. — (African historical dictionaries ; no. 78)
    (Includes bibliographical references.)
    ISBN 0–8108–3646–7 (cloth : alk. paper)
    1. South Africa—History—Dictionaries.   I. Southey, Nicholas. II. Title.
III. Series.   IV. Series: Includes bibliographical references.
    DT1772.S38   2000   99–18963
    968′.003—dc21   CIP

㊞™ The paper used in this publication meets the minimum requirements of
American National Standard for Information Sciences—Permanence of
Paper for Printed Library Materials, ANSI/NISO Z39.48–1992.
Manufactured in the United States of America.

Contents

Editor's Foreword

The "new" South Africa is distinctly different from the old. It is ruled by the African majority, not the white minority. The African National Congress, once proscribed and suppressed, now heads the government. The economy is being adapted to the needs of the mass of the population. Socially, the races are learning to live with one another and cooperate as necessary. Most impressive, the changes have taken place so calmly and peacefully that one can merely wonder why they were not made earlier. Obviously, problems remain in every sphere: political, economic, and social. But they are nothing compared with those faced before. Given this far-reaching transformation, a new edition of the *Historical Dictionary of South Africa* is most welcome.

What is particularly welcome about this new edition is that, in addition to the "new" South Africa and the former regime run by Afrikaners, the previous phases are amply covered as well, among them the period of British domination, early encroachments by the Boers and the British, and, most important, the peopling of the region by Africans. This is presented generally in the introduction, with the more salient aspects expanded upon in the dictionary. Although the bulk of the entries cover history and politics, the economy, society, and culture are considered as well. South Africa's long and complicated history is also traced in the chronology, and a list of abbreviations pinpoints the bodies referred to in the text. For readers who want to know more, the bibliography lists further sources of information, both general and specialized.

This book was written by Christopher Saunders, author of the first edition, now associate professor in history at the University of Cape Town and formerly head of the department. He was assisted by Nicholas Southey, senior lecturer in the History Department of the University of South Africa, Pretoria. The bibliography was revised for this edition by Mary-Lynn Suttie of the Library of the University of South Africa.

This "new" historical dictionary on the "new" South Africa is a significant contribution to our knowledge of one of Africa's most important countries.

Jon Woronoff
Series Editor

Preface

This is a revised and expanded version of the *Historical Dictionary of South Africa* published in 1983. The first edition was dedicated "to the hope that within the near future apartheid will be merely a subject for historians to study." Happily that is now the case, though apartheid's baneful legacy will long remain.

This postapartheid edition was compiled after the final constitution took effect on 4 February 1997, an event that signaled the end of a process of constitutional transformation heralded seven years earlier. The dictionary follows the guidelines set out by the general editor for the series as a whole. Common abbreviations and acronyms are listed after this preface. The length of entries does not necessarily reflect the historical importance of the subject. From the entry on the African National Congress (ANC), for example, one can move to associated entries on Umkhonto weSizwe, Nelson Mandela, and so on, entries that help to flesh out the history of the ANC. We realize that this book will inevitably be criticized both for what is included and for what is left out. We nevertheless hope that the final product will be useful, and we welcome comments from readers.

Christopher Saunders
Cape Town

Abbreviations and Acronyms

AAC	Anglo American Corporation
AIDS	Acquired Immune Deficiency Syndrome
AMEC	African Methodist Episcopal Church
ANC	African National Congress
APLA	Azanian People's Liberation Army
APO	African People's Organization
AWB	Afrikaner Resistance Movement
BOSS	Bureau of State Security
BPC	Black People's Convention
BSA	British South Africa Company
CA	Constitutional Assembly
CAAA	Comprehensive Anti-Apartheid Act (United States)
CCB	Civil Cooperation Bureau
CLPP	Coloured Labour Preference policy
CNE	Christian National Education
CODESA	Convention for a Democratic South Africa
COSAG	Concerned South Africans Group
COSATU	Congress of South African Trade Unions
CP	Conservative Party
CRC	Coloured Persons' Representative Council
DP	Democratic Party
FOSATU	Federation of South African Trade Unions
GDP	Gross domestic product
GEAR	Growth, Employment, and Redistribution Strategy
GNP	Gross national product
GNU	Government of National Unity
HNP	Herstigte Nasionale Party
ICU	Industrial and Commercial Workers' Union
IFP	Inkatha Freedom Party
IP	Independent Party
LMS	London Missionary Society

LP	Liberal Party
MDM	Mass Democratic Movement
MK	Umkhonto weSizwe
M.P.	Member of Parliament
MPLA	Movement of the People for the Liberation of Angola
NDM	National Democratic Movement
NEUM	Non-European Unity Movement
NGK	Nederduits Gereformeerde Kerk
NIC	Natal Indian Congress
NOCSA	National Olympic Committee of South Africa
NP	National Party
NRC	Natives Representative Council
NSMS	National Security Management System
NUSAS	National Union of South African Students
OPEC	Organization of the Petroleum Exporting Countries
PAC	Pan Africanist Congress of Azania
PAGAD	People against Gangsters and Drugs
PFP	Progressive Federal Party
PLAN	People's Liberation Army of Namibia
PWV	Pretoria–Witwatersrand–Vereeniging (Gauteng)
RDP	Reconstruction and Development Programme
RENAMO	Mozambican National Resistance
SAAF	South African Air Force
SAAN	South African Associated Newspapers
SACP	South African Communist Party
SADC	Southern African Development Community
SADCC	Southern African Development Coordination Conference
SADF	South African Defence Force
SAIC	South African Indian Congress
SAIRR	South African Institute of Race Relations
SANC	South African Native Convention
SANDF	South African National Defence Force
SANNC	South African Native National Congress
SANROC	South African Non-Racial Olympic Committee
SAR	South African Republic
SASO	South African Students' Organization
SASOL	South African Coal, Oil, and Gas Corporation
SSC	State Security Council
SWAPO	South West African People's Organization
TEC	Transitional Executive Council

TRC	Truth and Reconciliation Commission
TUCSA	Trade Union Congress of South Africa
UDF	United Democratic Front
UDM	United Democratic Movement
UN	United Nations
UNISA	University of South Africa
UNITA	National Union for the Total Independence of Angola
UP	United Party
VOC	Verenigde Ooste-Indische Compagnie (Dutch East India Company)

Chronology

2.5–3 million B.P.   Beginning of early Stone Age

1–3 million B.P.   *Australopithecus africanus* lives in southern Africa

90,000–1 million B.P.   *Homo erectus* lives in southern Africa, mastering the use of fire and shaping stone implements

30,000–100,000 B.P.   Middle Stone Age; *Homo sapiens* lives in southern Africa

26,000 B.P.   Earliest dated rock art

20,000 B.P.   Late Stone Age begins

15,000 B.P.   San hunter-gatherers widely distributed in southern Africa

2200 B.P.   Some San in northern Botswana acquire domestic livestock and move south, becoming known as Khoikhoi hunter-herders

3d century   Iron-using cultivators establish themselves south of the Limpopo River; beginning of early Iron Age

6th century   Lydenburg heads indicate ritual practices among early Iron Age people

7th century   Early Iron Age sites stretch along southeastern coast as far south as Mpame in Transkei

10th century   Beginnings of late Iron Age and more concentrated settlement on the high veld interior

1250–1400   Mapungubwe the dominant power in the Limpopo River valley

1300–1500   Sotho-Tswana speakers settle widely across high veld interior; Nguni speakers settle along southeastern coast and in the Drakensberg; Khoisan established as dominant society in southern and southwestern Cape

1488   Portuguese navigator Bartolomeu Dias rounds the Cape, opening sea route from Europe to the East

1497   Portuguese fleet under Vasco da Gama sails along South African coast on its way to India; first detailed information on the indigenous inhabitants transmitted to Europe

1510   Portuguese viceroy Bernardo d'Almeida killed in skirmish with Khoikhoi in Table Bay

1590s   Dutch and English ships begin to put in regularly in Table Bay and trade with Khoikhoi

1652   (6 April) Dutch East India Company (VOC) refreshment station founded on the shores of Table Bay by Jan van Riebeeck

1657   First free burghers exempted from VOC service to farm along the banks of the Liesbeek River

1658   First party of slaves arrives at the Cape

1659   First Dutch–Khoikhoi war

1673–77   Second Dutch–Khoikhoi war

1679   Land granted to white farmers in Stellenbosch district

1688   Arrival of Huguenots from France

1690s   Trekboer movement into the Cape interior begins

1702   Whites traveling east from the Cape first meet Bantu-speaking Africans near Somerset East

1713   Smallpox epidemic decimates Khoikhoi

1717   VOC decides not to grant further freehold land, only loan farms

1745   District of Swellendam established

ca. 1775   Death of chief Phalo; Xhosa divided between Gcaleka and Rharhabe

1775   Upper Fish and Bushman's Rivers declared Cape's eastern border

1778   Fish River proclaimed Cape's eastern border

1779   First Cape–Xhosa frontier war

1786   Graaff-Reinet district established

1793   H. C. D. Maynier appointed *landdrost* (chief local offical) of Graaff-Reinet; second Cape–Xhosa war

1795   First British occupation of the Cape; Maynier driven out of Graaff-Reinet

1799–1802   Khoisan rebellion in Cape eastern districts

1803–6   Cape under Batavian regime

1806   (January) Second British occupation

1808   Abolition of slave trade

1809   Caledon Code instituted to regulate Khoisan labor

1811–12   War to expel Xhosa from Zuurveld

1812   Apprenticeship ordinance

1814   Netherlands cedes Cape to Britain

ca. 1817   Ndwandwe under Zwide defeat Mthethwa; Dingiswayo killed

1817   Cape governor Charles Somerset's alliance with Ngqika

1818   Battle of Amalinde; Ndlambe defeats Ngqika

1819   Cape–Xhosa war; Somerset demands the "ceded territory"

ca. 1819   Shaka's Zulu defeat the Ndwandwe at Gqokoli Hill

1820   Almost 5,000 British settlers arrive in Algoa Bay

ca. 1822   Ngwane crosses Drakensberg and enters Caledon River valley

ca. 1823   Mzilikazi moves north of the Vaal River

1823   (June) Griqua and Tlhaping defeat the Kololo at battle of Dithakong; slave conditions at the Cape ameliorated

1824   Cape traders settle at Port Natal

ca. 1824   Moshoeshoe moves to Thaba Bosiu

1825   Slave revolt in Worcester district

1827   Cape Charter of Justice

1828   Ngwane defeated by the British and Thembu at Battle of Mbholompo; Ordinance 50; death of Shaka

1829   Establishment of the Kat River Settlement

1833   French missionaries join Moshoeshoe

1834   First legislative council at the Cape; (December) slaves emancipated; beginning of four-year "apprenticeship"; war on Cape eastern frontier

1835   Hintsa, Xhosa paramount, held captive by British army and murdered when he tries to escape; beginning of Great Trek; Mfengu move into Cape Colony; D'Urban's annexation of Queen Adelaide Province

1836   Battle of Vegkop; Voortrekkers defeat Mzilikazi's Ndebele

1836   Queen Adelaide Province is given up

1837   Ndebele leave Transvaal; Voortrekkers enter Natal under Piet Retief

1838   The "apprenticeship" of former slaves ends; the Zulu ruler Dingane massacres Retief's party; the establishment of the Republic of Natalia; the battle of Blood River; Andries Potgieter founds Potchefstroom

1840   Mpande and the Voortrekkers overthrow Dingane

1841   Cape Masters and Servants Ordinance; the Natal Volksraad resolves to move "surplus" Africans south of Natal

1843   British annexation of Natal; Napier signs treaties with Adam Kok III and Moshoeshoe; the Napier line defines Moshoeshoe's territory

1844   Potgieter founds Ohrigstad

1845   Theophilus Shepstone appointed diplomatic agent in Natal

1846–47   War of the Axe on the Cape frontier

1847   Annexation of British Kaffraria

1848   Annexation of Transorangia (the Orange River Sovereignty)

1849   Founding of Lydenburg

1850–53   War of Mlanjeni on the Cape frontier; Kat River Settlement rebellion

1852   Sand River Convention

1853   Grant of representative government to the Cape

1854   Bloemfontein Convention; creation of the Orange Free State; first meeting of the Cape Parliament; Boer commandos lay siege to Ndebele community, who take refuge in a cave under Makopane

1856   Cape Masters' and Servants' Act; representative government granted to Natal; Zulu civil war

1856–57   Xhosa cattle killing; famine follows mass slaughter of cattle and burning of crops

1858   First Orange Free State–Sotho war

1860   First indentured Indian laborers arrive in Natal

1861   Griqua leave Philippolis to cross Drakensberg

1864   J. H. Brand president of the Orange Free State

1865   Death of Mswati of Swaziland

1865–66   Second Free State–Sotho war

1866   British Kaffraria joined to Cape Colony

1867   Boers abandon Schoemansdal; discovery of diamonds in Griqualand West

1868   High Commissioner Philip Wodehouse annexes Basutoland

1869   Treaty of Aliwal North sets Basutoland's boundaries; diamond digging begins at what is to become Kimberley

1870   Death of Moshoeshoe; diamond rush

1871   British annexation of Griqualand West

1872   Cape granted responsible government; death of Mpande; pass laws on diamond fields

1873   Langalibalele Rebellion in Natal

1874   Lord Henry Carnarvon becomes secretary of state for colonies

1875   Formation of Die Genootskap van Regte Afrikaners in Paarl to campaign for recognition of Afrikaans; Carnarvon proposes confederation

1876   War between the South African Republic and the Pedi; Carnarvon's conference on confederation in London

1877   Sir Henry Bartle Frere appointed governor and high commissioner; Shepstone proclaims British annexation of the Transvaal; the South Africa Act provides for confederation

1877–78   Cape–Xhosa frontier war

1878   Resignation of Lord Carnarvon as secretary of state for colonies

1879   Anglo–Zulu War; battles of Isandlwana and Ulundi; British army moves to conquer Pedi; defeat of Sekhukhune, Pedi ruler

1880   Transkeian rebellion; Gun War in Basutoland; Britain abandons attempt to bring about a confederation; annexation of Griqualand West to Cape Colony

1880–81   Transvaal War of Independence

1881   Defeat of British forces at Majuba; Pretoria Convention grants Transvaal limited self-rule

1882   Imbumba yama Nyama formed in eastern Cape

1883   Paul Kruger elected state president of the Transvaal

1884   Britain assumes direct rule of Basutoland; London Convention; *Imvo Zabantsundu* started by J. T. Jabavu

1885   Annexation of Bechuanaland

1886   Discovery of main gold reef on Witwatersrand on the farm Langlaagte; founding of Johannesburg

1887   British annexation of Zululand; King Dinuzulu deported; Cape Parliamentary Voters' Registration Act declares that Africans who own land communally do not qualify for the franchise

1888   De Beers Consolidated Mines controls all diamond mining in Kimberley; Brand succeeded by F. W. Reitz as president of the Orange Free State

1890   Cecil Rhodes becomes prime minister of Cape

1892   Cape Franchise and Ballot Act raises property qualifications for franchise; Ethiopian church founded; railway reaches Johannesburg

1893   Natal granted responsible government; Mohandas Gandhi arrives in South Africa

1894   Passage of Glen Grey Act at Cape; Cape annexation of Pondoland; Natal Indian Congress founded

1895   British Bechuanaland added to Cape; (December) Jameson crosses border of Transvaal with an armed force

1896   (January) the fiasco of the Jameson Raid causes Rhodes' resignation as prime minister; M. T. Steyn elected president of the Orange Free State; Ethiopian church joins African Methodist Episcopal Church

1896   Indians in Natal disqualified from voting and a limit set on future immigration of Indians

1896–97   Rinderpest epidemic spreads through southern Africa

1897   Annexation of Zululand to Natal; Alfred Milner appointed high commissioner; Enoch Sontonga writes "Nkosi Sikelel' iAfrika"

1899   Bloemfontein conference between Milner and Kruger fails; (October) Transvaal and Orange Free State declare war on Britain; Boer victories

1900   (January) Battle of Spion Kop; (February) surrender of Cronje at Paardeberg, relief of Ladysmith; (March) capture of Bloemfontein; (May) relief of Mafeking; annexation of Orange Free State, renamed Orange River Colony; Lord Frederick Roberts captures Johannesburg; (June) Roberts captures Pretoria; (October) Kruger sails for France; formal proclamation of annexation of Transvaal; (November) H. H. Kitchener succeeds Roberts as commander in chief in South Africa

1901   (January) Jan Smuts captures Modderfontein; massacre of Africans; (February) Christiaan De Wet's "invasion" of Cape Colony; abortive Middelburg peace talks between Kitchener and Louis Botha; (March) Cape Town's Africans moved forcibly to Uitvlugt (Ndabeni); (August) Kitchener's proclamation of banishment for captured Boer leaders

1901–2   Tens of thousands of Boers and Africans die in concentration camps

1902   (March) Death of Rhodes; (April) Boer peace delegates meet at Pretoria; (May) meeting of Boer delegates at Vereeniging; (31 May) surrender terms signed in Pretoria

1904–7   Importation of Chinese labor to the gold mines

1905   South African Native Affairs Commission (the Lagden Commission) reports; strike of Chinese laborers at the North Randfontein mine; School Boards Act segregates Cape schools; Africans permitted to buy land in Transvaal; much of Zululand given to white farmers; poll tax introduced in Natal

1906   Bambatha Rebellion in Natal crushed brutally; passive resistance in Transvaal by Indians

1907   Transvaal and Orange River Colony granted responsible government; white miners' strike on Witwatersrand

1908–9   National Convention meets to consider terms of unification

1909   South Africa Bill passed by British Parliament; Indian passive resistance in Transvaal; (white) Labour Party founded

1910 (31 May) Union of South Africa comes into being; Louis Botha becomes first prime minister

1911 Mines and Works Act provides for mine job reservation

1912 (January) South African Native National Congress (SANNC) formed, with John Dube first president; South African Races Congress formed under Jabavu; (December) J. B. M. Hertzog ousted from Botha's cabinet

1913 (June) Natives Land Act: Africans not allowed to own or rent land outside designated reserves (7 percent of land), sharecropping illegal; white miners' strike on Witwatersrand; Indian passive resistance; African women demonstrate against passes in Free State

1914 Strike by white miners; National Party (NP) founded in Bloemfontein; SANNC delegation goes to England to protest against the Natives Land Act; Gandhi returns to India; Afrikaner Rebellion

1915 South African forces occupy German South West Africa

1916 South African Native College opened; (July) Battle of Delville Wood; report of the Natives Land (Beaumont) Commission

1917 Industrial Workers of Africa founded; the birth of Anglo American Corporation

1918 Strike by African sanitation workers in Johannesburg; Afrikaner Broederbond founded; epidemic of Spanish flu

1919 Industrial and Commercial Workers' Union (ICU) formed; Botha dies; Smuts becomes prime minister; Union Parliament accepts mandate for South West Africa

1920 African mine workers' strike; African demonstrators shot in Port Elizabeth

1921 (May) 183 Israelites shot at Bulhoek, near Queenstown in the Cape; (July) formation of Communist Party of South Africa

1922 (January) White miners' strike; (March) Rand Revolt; Stallard Commission reports

1923 SANNC changes name to African National Congress (ANC); Natives (Urban Areas) Act provides for locations for Africans in urban areas

1924 NP and Labour pact wins election; Hertzog becomes prime minister; Industrial Conciliation Act provides for job reservation

1925   Wage Act; South Africa on gold standard; Afrikaans replaces Dutch as official language; Hertzog's Smithfield speech

1926   Mines and Works Amendment Act provides for color bar in employment; Balfour Declaration defines relations with Britain; Hertzog's "Native Bills" published; Communists expelled from ICU

1927   Nationality and Flag Act; mass ICU protests of various kinds; Immorality Act prohibits sexual relations between whites and others; Native Administration Act

1928   Communist Party told to work for a "native republic"; iron and steel industry established by act of Parliament

1929   NP wins 81 seats in election, after "black danger" campaign

1930   Pixley Seme replaces Josiah Gumede as ANC president; pass-burning campaign launched by Communist Party; white women get the vote; Natives (Urban Areas) Amendment Act

1931   Property and literacy qualifications removed for white voters; Statute of Westminster; pass-burning campaign and violence in Durban

1932   Depression reaches its peak; report of the Carnegie Commission on Poor Whites; Report of the Native Economic Commission; South Africa leaves gold standard

1933   Severe drought; Hertzog and Smuts agree on coalition; coalition wins overwhelming victory in general election; Smuts becomes deputy prime minister

1934   NP and South African Party form United Party (UP); D. F. Malan forms Purified NP; Dominion Party established

1935   All-African Convention formed to resist disfranchisement of Africans; National Liberation League established

1936   Representation of Natives Act, passed by 169 votes to 11, removes Africans from Cape voters' roll; Natives Trust and Land Act

1938   (May) UP wins general election; (December) Great Trek centenary celebrated

1939   (4 September) Smuts defeats Hertzog in vote on South African participation in the war and (6 September) becomes prime minister; pro-Nazi Ossewabrandwag formed

1940   (January) Hertzog and Malan form Herenigde Nasionale Party; (December) A. B. Xuma elected president of the ANC

1941   African Mine Workers' Union formed; South African troops enter Addis Ababa, Ethiopia

1942   Influx control relaxed; draft constitution for South African republic published; (June) South African division captured at Tobruk, North Africa

1943   UP wins election; ANC releases "African Claims"; Non-European Unity Movement founded

1944   First meeting of ANC Youth League, A. W. Lembede elected president; Mpanza and followers squat in Orlando location; antipass campaign

1945   Consolidated Urban Areas Act tightens up influx control restrictions; end of World War II

1946   Asiatic Land Tenure and Indian Representation Act provokes Indian passive resistance campaign; strike by 60,000 African mine workers brutally suppressed; adjournment of the Natives Representative Council

1948   Report of the Native Laws (Fagan) Commission; (May) Herenigde Nasionale Party wins general election on a platform of apartheid; suburban railroad apartheid in the Cape peninsula; death of Jan Hofmeyr

1949   Prohibition of Mixed Marriages Act; Zulu-Indian riots in Durban; (December) "Programme of Action" adopted at ANC congress; Xuma replaced by Moroka as president of ANC

1950   (May) Stay-away in Transvaal; (June) Communist Party dissolves itself before passage of Suppression of Communism Act; (26 June) national day of protest and mourning; Immorality Act amended; Population Registration Act; Group Areas Act

1951   Beginning of attempt to remove Coloured vote; Doctors' Pact for cooperation between ANC, Natal Indian Congress, and Transvaal Indian Congress; Bantu Authorities Act provides for tribal, regional, and territorial authorities in reserves; Torch Commando holds rallies in support of Coloured voters

1952   (March) Separate Representation of Voters Act is declared illegal by Supreme Court; (6 April) Van Riebeeck tercentenary festival; (26 June) beginning of countrywide Defiance Campaign, which leads to mass arrests and mass protests; Abolition of Passes Act provides that all Africans must carry passes, and under the terms of Section 10 of the act none are to remain more than 72 hours in urban area without permission

1953   South African Communist Party (SACP) formed underground; (April) NP wins election; Liberal Party formed; Congress of Democrats formed; Separate Amenities Act provides for segregated public facilities; Bantu Education Act provides for inferior education for Africans; Public Safety Act allows for declaration of a state of emergency, banning of meetings; Criminal Law Amendment act makes civil disobedience punishable by a three-year jail sentence

1954   Federation of South African Women formed; J. G. Strijdom succeeds Malan as prime minister

1955   Formation of South African Congress of Trade Unions; (June) Freedom Charter adopted by Congress of the People; Sophiatown destroyed

1956   ANC conference approves Freedom Charter; (9 August) 20,000 women march to the Union Buildings, Pretoria; treason trial of 156 begins; Senate act enables Separate Representation of Voters Act to be passed to remove Coloureds from common voters' roll; Industrial Conciliation Act provides for job reservation

1957   Alexandra bus boycott

1957–58   Peasant uprising in Sekhukhuneland

1958   (April) NP wins 103 of 163 seats in National Assembly election; (August) H. F. Verwoerd succeeds Strijdom as prime minister; Africanists walk out of Transvaal ANC conference

1959   (April) Pan Africanist Congress (PAC) formed under R. M. Sobukwe; (November) Progressive Party founded; Promotion of Bantu Self-Government Act provides for transforming reserves into independent bantustans; Extension of University Education Act extends apartheid to higher education

1960   Representation for Africans in Parliament abolished; (February) Wind of Change speech by British prime minister Harold Macmillan to South African Parliament; (21 March) police open fire at Sharpeville, killing 69; two killed in Langa in Cape Town; Sobukwe sentenced to three years; (26 March) Albert Luthuli burns his pass and declares 28 March a day of mourning; (27 March) Oliver Tambo leaves country to set up exile mission; (28 March) national stay-away; (30 March) Philip Kgosana leads 30,000 marchers to Caledon Square police station, is promised that a delegation would be received later, and crowd returns peacefully; state of emergency declared; beginning of revolt in Pondoland; (April) Unlawful Organizations Act passed; (8 April) ANC and PAC banned; attempted assassination of Verwoerd; (June) 11 killed when police open fire in Pondoland; end of state of emergency; (October) white referendum on whether South Africa should become a republic: 52.3 percent of white voters in favor

1961   (March) Verwoerd withdraws South Africa's application to remain in the Commonwealth; (March) treason trial ends with acquittal; (March) All-in conference, Pietermaritzburg, addressed by Mandela; (May) Luthuli awarded Nobel Peace Price; (31 May) South Africa leaves the Commonwealth when it becomes a republic; B. J. Vorster appointed minister of justice and police; ANC adopts armed struggle, Umkhonto weSizwe (MK) formed, with Mandela as chief of staff; (October) NP wins election; (16 December) launch of armed struggle with beginning of MK's sabotage campaign

1962   (January–June) Mandela visits African and European countries to gain support for armed struggle; (August) Mandela arrested near Howick, Natal; (November) Mandela sentenced to five years' imprisonment; (November) Paarl uprising; United Nations (UN) General Assembly votes for economic and diplomatic sanctions against South Africa; Sabotage Act provides for harsh penalties for sabotage; house arrest introduced and the state's banning powers extended

1963   (March) Potlako Leballo of PAC announces that a general uprising is imminent; his office in Maseru is raided and membership lists are seized; (May) General Law Amendment Act provides for detention for up to 90 days and for further detention of persons convicted of political offenses (the Sobukwe clause); foundation of Christian Institute by Beyers Naudé; (July) arrest of MK High Command at Lilliesleaf farm, Rivonia; (October) Rivonia trial begins; (December) Transkei self-government

1964   Armscor established; (11 June) eight Rivonia accused sentenced to life imprisonment; (July) John Harris of African Resistance Movement sets off bomb in Johannesburg railway station; numerous sabotage and other political trials

1965   Detention without trial for 180 days introduced; Bram Fischer goes underground, is recaptured after 10 months

1966   (August) First clash between the South West African People's Organization (SWAPO) guerrillas and South African police in Ovamboland; General Law Amendment Act provides for detention of suspected "terrorists" for up to 14 days; (6 September) Tsafendas stabs Verwoerd to death in House of Assembly; Vorster becomes prime minister; District Six is proclaimed white area; (October) South Africa's mandate for Namibia is revoked by the UN General Assembly

1967   Terrorism Act provides for indefinite detention without trial on authority of policemen; Wankie campaign by MK, and South African police enter Rhodesia; death of Luthuli; formation of University Christian Movement; diplomatic relations established with Malawi

1968   English cricket tour is canceled because of the D'Oliveira affair; Prohibition of Political Interference Act prohibits nonracial political parties, and Progressive Party becomes all-white; Liberal Party dissolves itself; Coloured representation in Parliament abolished; PAC forms Azanian People's Liberation Army (APLA), its armed wing

1969   Bureau of State Security created, accountable to the prime minister; ANC holds first conference since banning, at Morogoro, Tanzania, where it adopts program entitled Strategy and Tactics and opens membership to whites; South African Students' Organization formed by Biko; Albert Hertzog forms Herstigte Nasionale Party

1970   Bantu Homelands Citizenship Act; NP wins election and no Herstigte Nasionale Party candidates are returned; Connie Mulder of NP says that aim of policy is that there should be no black South African citizens

1971   International Court of Justice rules that South Africa's occupation of Namibia is illegal

1972   Black People's Convention formed; establishment of State Security Council; Africans in urban areas brought under Bantu Affairs Administration Boards

1973   (January–March) Strikes by 61,000 black workers in Durban–Pinetown area; reemergence of independent trade unionism; formation of Afrikaner Resistance Movement (AWB); South African Defence Force (SADF) takes over from police in Northern Namibia

1974   Affected Organizations Act provides for declaration of organizations that are not able to solicit foreign funds; (April) coup in Lisbon, Portugal

1975   (August) SADF enters Angola; (November) SADF troops close to Luanda encounter resistance from Cubans; television introduced; Inkatha movement formed; Breyten Breytenbach sentenced to nine years for "terrorism"

1976 (March) South African forces withdraw from Angola; Theron Commission report released; (16 June) police open fire on march of school children to Orlando West secondary school, and widespread resistance follows in which hundreds are killed and others stream into exile; (October) Transkei declared "independent"; MK resumes operations inside South Africa; SWAPO and ANC begin to open military bases in Angola

1976–77 Continuous protest; more than 700 deaths by police; many detentions, stay-aways, and school boycotts

1977 Demolition of Cape Town squatter camps; (June) shooting in central Johannesburg leads to arrest of two MK cadres; (September) Steve Biko murdered in detention; (October) 17 organizations and three newspapers banned; (November) United Nations imposes compulsory arms embargo against South Africa; "independence" of Bophuthatswana; disintegration of UP

1978 (April) South Africa accepts Western plan for transition to independence in Namibia; (4 May) Cassinga massacre in Angola: more than 600 killed when SADF attacks SWAPO camp; Information scandal (Muldergate) breaks; (September) Vorster resigns and P. W. Botha becomes prime minister; UN Security Council passes Resolution 435 for transition to independence in Namibia; Robert Sobukwe dies; at Sobukwe's Graaff-Reinet funeral, Buthelezi is attacked by youths

1979 (April) Reprieve for Crossroads squatters; formation of Federation of South African Trade Unions; formation of civic organizations in Port Elizabeth, Soweto, and Cape Town, of the Congress of South African Students for high school students, and of the Azanian Students' Organisation; (August) P. W. Botha visits Soweto; (September) Frederik van Zyl Slabbert becomes leader of the parliamentary opposition; "independence" of Venda bantustan; Industrial Conciliation Act embodies recommendations of Wiehahn commission, including the official recognition of black trade unions; meeting between ANC and Inkatha in London ends in acrimony; Solomon Mahlangu executed

1980 Gold price soars, creating economic boom; (January) Silverton bank siege in which MK operatives take hostages, followed by shoot-out; Release Mandela campaign launched; school and consumer boycotts; (June) Sasol refinery and Sasol plants at Secunda and Sasolburg bombed by MK; Senate abolished, replaced with multiracial President's Council of nominated members to discuss new constitution

1981   (January) 14 killed in SADF raid on Matola outside Maputo, including commander of attack on Sasol; (January) abortive UN conference at Geneva on Namibia; (August) Operation Protea launched against SWAPO in Angola; (November) Griffiths Mxenge killed by Vlakplaas hit squad; (December) Ciskei declared "independent"; MK attack on main military base at Voortrekkerhoogte

1982   (February) Trade unionist Neil Aggett dies in detention at John Vorster Square; (March) right-wing NP members of Parliament, under leadership of Andries Treurnicht (Transvaal leader of the party), ousted and form Conservative Party; gold price drops and country enters recession; (July) NP federal congress approves proposals for new constitution providing for a strong executive president and tricameral parliament; (August) Ruth First assassinated by parcel bomb in Maputo; (9 December) SADF raid on Maseru and 42 killed; (December) Koeberg nuclear plant sabotaged by MK, causing millions of rands in damage

1983   (20 May) Car bomb outside South African Air Force building on Church Street, Pretoria, kills 19; (23 May) retaliatory attack on Maputo kills six, five of whom are Mozambican civilians; (June) inauguration of National Forum at Hammanskraal, near Pretoria; (August) launch of United Democratic Front (UDF) at Mitchell's Plain; (November) in a referendum, two-thirds of white voters approve the new constitution, providing for a tricameral parliament, with separate houses for whites, Coloureds, and Indians, a distinction between general and "own" affairs, and a strong executive president; at a meeting at Howick in Natal, the Coloured Labour Party decides to participate in the new Parliament

1984   (January) South African troops withdraw from Angola after Operation Askari; (February) Lusaka agreement with Angola providing for Joint Military Commission to monitor South African troop withdrawal; (16 March) Nkomati Accord signed by Botha and Samora Machel; (May) the administrator-general of South West Africa and Namibian parties meet in Lusaka, Zambia; after mutiny of MK soldiers in Pango, Angola, camp, the mutineers are sent to detention camp Quatro, and seven are executed; (June) Botha's tour of Europe; (July) Cape Verde talks between the administrator-general and Sam Nujoma of SWAPO; (3 September) firebombing of black policeman's home in Sharpeville begins township revolt in Vaal Triangle, which soon spreads to East Rand, Soweto, and other areas; the SADF is sent into townships, but the revolt spreads from the Vaal Triangle to other parts of the country; (3 September) Botha inaugurated as first executive state president, and the first tricameral Parliament is opened; Bishop Desmond Tutu awarded Nobel Peace Prize

1985   (February) Mandela's daughter reads a statement from him in Soweto in which he refuses conditional freedom and says he will return; (March) on anniversary of Sharpeville and Langa massacres, police open fire on a march near Uitenhage; (June) 13 killed in SADF raid against suspected ANC houses in Gaborone, Botswana; (June) at Kabwe, Zambia, the ANC holds its second consultative conference, which calls for the intensification of the armed struggle, and says civilians may be caught in crossfire; security police murder the Cradock Four; (20 July) partial state of emergency in 36 magisterial districts; vast powers given to police and minister of law and order; (August) killing of UDF's Victoria Mxenge sparks protest in Durban and many die; (August) Botha's failure to make concessions in his "Rubicon" speech in the Durban City Hall leads to crisis of confidence; planned march to Pollsmoor prison to demand the release of Mandela is stopped by police; (September) the Kairos Document supports struggle against injustice; Anglo American Corporation head leads delegation to meet ANC in Zambia; (November) Minister of Justice Kobie Coetsee meets Nelson Mandela at Volks Hospital, Cape Town; (December) formation of Congress of South African Trade Unions in Durban; (December) nine killed in SADF raid on Lesotho

1986   (February) Van Zyl Slabbert resigns from Parliament; (March) end of partial state of emergency; (May) SADF raid on Botswana, Zambia, and Zimbabwe results in collapse of the Eminent Persons Group mission; (May–June) destruction of satellite squatter camps and then Kakaza Trading Centre camp on Cape Flats by *witdoeke* vigilantes, aided by police; (June) nationwide state ef emergency declared under terms of Public Safety Act; regulations prevent publication of information concerning police conduct or "unrest incidents"; the security forces are indemnified for unlawful acts carried out in "good faith"; many thousands are detained; Mixed Marriages Act, Section 16 of Immorality Act, and Prohibition of Political Interference Act repealed; pass laws and influx control abolished; (August) Johannesburg headquarters of the South African Council of Churches destroyed by a bomb, later revealed to have been planted by the police; NP federal congress approves the idea of participation of all in government to highest levels; (September) the U.S. Congress passes the Comprehensive Anti-Apartheid Act, overriding President Ronald Reagan's veto; (19 October) death of all people on a plane carrying President Machel of Mozambique, which crashes just within South African territory; a camp in Caprivi is established for training 200 Inkatha members (Operation Marion)

1987 (January) 12 people die in an attack on a house in kwaMakhutha in Natal; (February) the government approves the Mossgas oil-from-gas project; (May) the Conservative Party replaces the Progressive Federal Party as the official opposition in Parliament; (June) the state of emergency is renewed; (July) 61 Afrikaners meet ANC representatives in Dakar, Senegal; (September) in a prisoner-of-war exchange in Maputo, the SADF's Wynand du Toit is exchanged; (October) Stella Sigcau becomes prime minister of Transkei; (November) Govan Mbeki is released unconditionally and confirms his allegiance to the ANC and the SACP

1988 (January) ANC declares 1988 the year of united action for people's power; (February) Bophuthatswana president Lucas Mangope is ousted in a coup, then restored to power by the SADF; 18 organizations, including the UDF and COSATU, are restricted; (July) widespread celebrations of Mandela's 70th birthday; (July) Ellis Park bomb kills two in Johannesburg; (August) the End Conscription Campaign is effectively banned; (October) all races in municipalities go to polls in local government elections for the first time; (November) former policeman Barend Strydom kills many blacks in shooting spree in the center of Pretoria; Natal police captain Brian Mitchell organizes massacre at Trust Feed

1989 (18 January) P. W. Botha suffers mild stroke; (2 February) Botha announces his resignation as leader of the NP; F. W. de Klerk elected as NP leader; (4 February) Democratic Party formed; (16 February) UDF distances itself from Winnie Madikizela-Mandela; hunger strike achieves release of political detainees; (5 July) meeting between P. W. Botha and Nelson Mandela at Tuynhuis in Cape Town; (12 July) Mandela's statement affirming desire to contribute to climate that will promote peace; (August) Tambo suffers stroke; (August) Harare Declaration outlines ANC's conditions for negotiations; Defiance Campaign for desegregation of hospitals, beaches, and public transport; (14 August) P. W. Botha resigns; (15 August) F. W. de Klerk sworn in as acting state president; (6 September) white election; nationwide protests are met with police violence, especially in western Cape; de Klerk interprets election result as mandate for reform; (September) meeting between members of National Intelligence Service and ANC in Switzerland; (20 September) de Klerk is sworn in as state president; (October) peaceful march in Cape Town by 30,000; National Security Management System dismantled; (15 October) eight long-term political prisoners, including Walter Sisulu, are released on the eve of a Commonwealth heads-of-government meeting in Kuala Lumpur; convicted murderer Almond Nofomela confesses to hit-squad activity and is supported by former police captain Dirk Coetzee; (29 October) Soweto rally in support of ANC addressed by Sisulu; (November) Namibian elections; Berlin Wall falls; bathing beaches open to all; last SADF troops in Namibia return to South Africa; (13 December) de Klerk meets Mandela for the first time

1990   (2 February) de Klerk speech opening Parliament legalizes ANC, SACP, and other opposition parties, lifts restrictions on listed people; de Klerk announces that Mandela is to be released unconditionally; (11 February) Mandela walks through gates of Victor Verster prison a free man; (March) Ciskei government is overthrown in military coup; preliminary talks between government and ANC; Sebokeng killings by police, and ANC calls off talks; (21 March) Namibian independence; (April) resumption of talks about talks; (April) Venda government overthrown in military coup; (4–5 May) ANC and government meet at Groote Schuur, Cape Town, and agree on a framework for the release of political prisoners, indemnity for exiles, and commitment to end violence; (June) the state of emergency is lifted except in Natal; Separate Amenities Act is repealed; Mandela visits the United States; (July) ANC–COSATU stay-away in protest against violence in Natal; arrests of ANC and SACP members in connection with Operation Vula; ANC–Inkatha clashes spread from Natal to Reef, and hundreds are killed; beginnings of train violence; relaunch of SACP; (8 August) at a Pretoria meeting with the government the ANC suspends the armed struggle; (August–September) escalation of violence on Reef and in Natal; (September) de Klerk visits Washington; (October) state of emergency lifted in Natal; (November) attempted coup in Transkei does not succeed; (November) Harms Commission reports and absolves security police at Vlakplaas of hit-squad activities but uncovers a covert SADF unit known as the Civil Cooperation Bureau; (December) ANC consultative conference held in Johannesburg

1991   (1 February) de Klerk announces that the pillars of apartheid are to be repealed; (12 February) D. F. Malan Minute is signed by government and ANC; (April) ANC demands dismissal of Ministers Adriaan Vlok and Malan, dismantling of hit squads, suspension of police implicated in massacres, the transformation of hostels into family units, and the establishment of an independent commission of inquiry into the violence; (June) repeal of Natives Land Act, Separate Amenities Act, Group Areas Act, and Population Registration Act; the Further Abolition of Racially Based Measures Act removes racial distinctions in other laws; (July) at ANC congress in Durban, Mandela is elected president of the ANC; (July) Inkathagate scandal reveals government funding of Inkatha and of anti-SWAPO parties in Namibia; (August) clash at Ventersdorp, where the AWB is dispersed by police outside a hall in which de Klerk spoke; (September) the National Peace Accord is signed by the ANC, the government, the Inkatha Freedom Party (IFP), and others; the introduction of value-added tax leads to massive protests against the levying of the tax on basic foods and services; (October) South Africa signs the Nuclear Non-Proliferation Treaty; a commission of enquiry is established under Justice Richard Goldstone to investigate public violence and intimidation; (November) agreement to start talks; (20 December) 19 parties attend Convention for a Democratic South Africa (CODESA) at the World Trade Centre in Kempton Park; two-day meeting ends with agreement on a Declaration of Intent by 17 parties

1992 (17 March) a whites-only referendum gives de Klerk a mandate to continue negotiations: 68.6 percent of voters approve of continuing the reform process, aimed at agreement on a new constitution through negotiations; (April) former police captain Brian Mitchell and others are sentenced for Trust Feed massacre in 1988; (15 May) CODESA 2 deadlocks; (16 June) ANC begins mass action campaign to force government to speed up reform process; (17 June) Inkatha supporters from KwaMadala hostel kill 43 in Boipatong massacre near Vanderbijlpark and provoke an international outcry; (19 June) Mandela accuses the government of complicity in the Boipatong massacre and suspends talks; (July) rolling mass action is launched to topple anti-ANC bantustan leaders; South Africa is to attend the Olympics for the first time since 1960; (August) a COSATU-sponsored stay-away involves more than four million workers; (7 September) 28 die in massacre at Bisho, when unarmed ANC supporters march to oust Oupa Gqozo, and Ciskei troops open fire; (September) Record of Understanding reached between ANC and government to break deadlock in negotiations, includes agreement to release further political prisoners, fence and patrol hostels, and prohibit carrying and display of dangerous weapons; (October) amnesty legislation passed; political prisoners released; formation of Concerned South Africans' Group (COSAG); (November) the ANC agrees to power-sharing after Joe Slovo proposes "sunset" clauses; Goldstone uncovers campaign by Directorate of Covert Collection to discredit the ANC; (December) de Klerk suspends or retires 23 senior SADF officers for involvement in illegal activities; year of severe drought and economic depression

1993 (January) European Economic Community announces that sanctions will be lifted; (March) Multi-Party Negotiating Forum planning conference attended by 26 parties, now including the Conservative Party and PAC; government delegation meets PAC in Botswana to negotiate a suspension of its armed struggle; de Klerk announces that six nuclear weapons built in the 1980s have been dismantled; (April) negotiations resume at the World Trade Centre; (10 April) Chris Hani, secretary-general of the SACP and former MK chief of staff, is assassinated; (May) 200 PAC members are arrested in a countrywide predawn swoop; (June) decision to agree on an election date leads to IFP and Conservative Party walkout, and they form Freedom Alliance; (25 June) armed right-wingers break through gates and enter World Trade Centre, occupying the building and causing damage; (3 July) election set for 27 April; (25 July) eleven churchgoers shot dead in Kenilworth, Cape Town, a crime for which APLA members are later found guilty; (August) much violence on East Rand; Amy Biehl is killed in Guguletu, Cape Town; report of Motsuenyane Commission into alleged human rights abuses against ANC detainees; (October) announcement that Mandela and de Klerk have jointly been awarded the Nobel Peace Prize; (October) UN lifts sanctions except for arms and oil embargoes; Janusz Waluz and Clive Derby-Lewis are given death sentences for the murder of Hani; SADF raid on APLA house in Umtata; (18 November) agreement reached at World Trade Centre on an interim constitution providing for a nonracial, multiparty democracy with justiciable Bill of Rights and nine provinces; (December) APLA attack on tavern in Observatory, Cape Town, kills four; Parliament approves legislation to establish a Transitional Executive Council (TEC) with seven subcouncils, an Independent Electoral Commission, and an Independent Broadcasting Authority; TEC installed; (18 December) Parliament approves interim constitution; government and ANC involved in talks with Freedom Alliance concerning its participation in the election

1994   (March) Rioting in Bophuthatswana, then TEC ousts Mangope and brings the bantustan under Pretoria's control; (28 March) battle of Shell House, when IFP marchers attack ANC headquarters in downtown Johannesburg and over 50 are killed; (31 March) State of Emergency declared in KwaZulu; General Viljoen of the Freedom Front agrees to participate in the election; (19 April) Buthelezi agrees to call off election boycott and allow IFP to be included on ballots; (26–29 April) first democratic election; (27 April) interim constitution takes effect, providing for reincorporation of Transkei, Ciskei, Bophuthatswana, and Venda into South Africa; (2 May) Mandela proclaims that South Africa is free at last; (10 May) Mandela is inaugurated President at the Union Buildings, Pretoria; (24 May) the Constitutional Assembly begins work on a final constitution; (1 June) South Africa rejoins the Commonwealth after 33 years; it also joins the Non-Aligned Movement; (16 June) the United States lifts its embargo on arms sales to South Africa; (24 June) South Africa reclaims its seat in the UN General Assembly; launch of Reconstruction and Development Programme and Masakhane ("let us build together") campaign to end rent and bond boycotts

1995   (January) Death of Joe Slovo; (June) Constitutional Court in first judgment rules the death penalty to be unconstitutional; (July) passage of National Unity and Reconciliation Act, providing for the establishment of Truth and Reconciliation Commission (TRC); (November) draft of the final constitution is released; (December) TRC appointed by President Mandela

1996   (February) Bafana Bafana, the national soccer team, wins Africa Cup of Nations; (March) beginning of trial of General Magnus Malan and others; (April) TRC begins to hear accounts of human rights abuses from victims; (8 May) final constitution sent to the Constitutional Court for certification; National Party announces it is to leave the Government of National Unity at the end of June; (July) RDP redeployed to line ministries; agreement in principle on Armscor dispute between South Africa and the United States; Bantu Holomisa sacked as deputy minister of environmental affairs; *Sarafina 2* anti-AIDS play fiasco; (September) Constitutional Court refers constitution back to Constitutional Assembly; Nelson Mandela becomes chairperson of Southern African Development Community (SADC); (October) Malan and others found not guilty; Eugene de Kock convicted and sentenced for atrocities as commander of Vlakplaas; TRC begins to hear from perpetrators and issues its first subpoenas; (November) Labour Relations Act comes into effect; (10 December) final constitution signed by Mandela at Sharpeville; extension of amnesty date to 10 May 1994; Bishop Stanley Mogoba elected president of PAC

1997   (January) Proposed arms deal with Syria put on hold; (4 February) final constitution brought into effect; National Council of Provinces inaugurated; (March) Cape Town chosen as one of the short-listed cities of 2004 Olympic Games; TRC revelations concerning apartheid murders continue; de Klerk accused of participating in decision to set up a third force in the mid-1980s; (May) South Africa mediates in the Zairean crisis; Winnie Madikizela-Mandela re-elected president of the ANC's Women's League; last amnesty applications presented to TRC; extensive mismanagement of the Independent Broadcasting Authority confirmed; (September) de Klerk resigns as NP leader and from parliament; Cape Town not chosen for 2004 Olympic Games; Mathole Motshekga elected Gauteng ANC chairman and successor to Tokyo Sexwale; United Democratic Movement led by Roelf Meyer and Bantu Holomisa founded; (November) Winnie Madikizela-Mandela testifies to the TRC at the end of a nine-day hearing on the activities of the Mandela United Football Club in the late 1980s and denies charges of murder leveled against her; Western Cape constitution approved by Constitutional Court; (December) in Ottawa, Foreign Minister Alfred Nzo signs the convention banning landmines; commercial farming sector hit by a further spate of murders of white farmers; P. W. Botha refuses to attend TRC hearings despite subpoena; 50th annual congress of ANC at Mafikeng in Northwest Province; Mandela hands over presidency of the ANC to Thabo Mbeki; Jacob Zuma chosen as ANC deputy president

1998   (January) Full diplomatic relations established with Beijing; (March) U.S. President Bill Clinton's state visit; centenary of the Kruger National Park celebrated; foreign affairs official Robert McBride arrested in Maputo and held in solitary confinement; (May) the rand begins to fall against the dollar and the pound; warlord and United Democratic Movement secretary-general Sifiso Nkabinde acquitted on charge of murder in Richmond, Natal, leading to further acts of political violence in Richmond; (June) the value of the rand falls further; Mandela and Mbeki critical of Communist Party at its conference; the TRC hears evidence of preparations for chemical and biological warfare in the 1980s and early 1990s; (July) Tito Mboweni, minister of labour, appointed governor-designate of the Reserve Bank; his appointment worsens an economic crisis brought on by a fall in the value of the rand against the dollar; former Law and Order Minister Adriaan Vlok implicates F. W. de Klerk in evidence before the Amnesty Committee of the TRC; on his 80th birthday, Mandela marries Graça Machel, former first lady of Mozambigue; (August) P. W. Botha is fined R10,000 for refusing to give evidence before the TRC; a pipe-bomb explodes at a Planet Holly-wood restaurant on the Cape Town waterfront, killing two and threatening tourism; the financial crisis deepens, with the rand falling to almost seven to the dollar and high interest rates likely to cause economic recession; (September) South African forces under the umbrella of the SADC invade Lesotho in an attempt to restore political stability to that country; (October) Anglo American announces that it will merge with its offshore arm, Minorco, and relocate its head office to London; the ANC admits that its macroeconomic policy, GEAR, will not meet its targets and will need to be adjusted

South Africa's Population, 1904–1991 (in thousands)

Year		Asians	Blacks	Coloureds	Whites	Total
1904	M	82	1,737	227	635	2,681
	F	40	1,753	218	482	2,493
	T	122	3,490	445	1,117	5,174
1911	M	96	2,023	265	685	3,069
	F	56	1,996	260	591	2,903
	T	152	4,019	525	1,276	5,972
1921	M	96	2,382	275	783	3,536
	F	67	2,315	270	738	3,390
	T	163	4,697	545	1,521	6,926
1936	M	119	3,312	387	1,017	4,835
	F	101	3,284	382	986	4,753
	T	220	6,596	769	2,003	9,588
1946	M	149	3,996	466	1,194	5,805
	F	136	3,834	462	1,178	5,610
	T	285	7,830	928	2,372	11,415
1951	M	190	4,369	551	1,323	6,433
	F	177	4,191	552	1,319	6,239
	T	367	8,560	1,103	2,642	12,672
1960	M	242	5,512	751	1,539	8,044
	F	235	5,416	758	1,549	7,958
	T	477	10,928	1,509	3,008	16,002
1970	M	314	7,543	1,008	1,882	10,747
	F	316	7,797	1,043	1,891	11,047
	T	630	15,340	2,051	3,773	21,794
1980*	M	406	8,407	1,289	2,264	12,367
	F	412	7,876	1,327	2,279	11,894
	T	818	16,283	2,617	4,543	24,261
1991*	M	489	10,865	1,606	2,820	15,480
	F	498	10,781	1,680	2,548	15,507
	T	987	21,646	3,286	5,068	30,987

M = Male
F = Female
T = Total

*Figures given are according to the 1991 boundaries (and therefore exclude the bantustans). Official estimates place the population of the bantustans in 1991 at 6,957,000 people (3,268,000 males and 3,698,000 females). The 1980 and 1991 figures have been officially adjusted to allow for undercounts on the figures that were enumerated.

South Africa's Population, by Province and Gender
October 1996 (in thousands)

Province	Males	Females	Total	Percentage
KwaZulu-Natal	3,583	4,089	7,672	20,3
Gauteng	3,651	3,520	7,171	18,9
Eastern Cape	2,703	3,162	5,865	15,5
Northern Province	1,878	2,250	4,128	10,9
Western Cape	1,982	2,135	4,118	10,9
North West	1,493	1,550	3,043	8,0
Mpumalanga	1,288	1,357	2,646	7,0
Free State	1,219	1,251	2,470	6,5
Northern Cape	366	380	746	2,0
Total	18,163	19,695	37,859	100,0

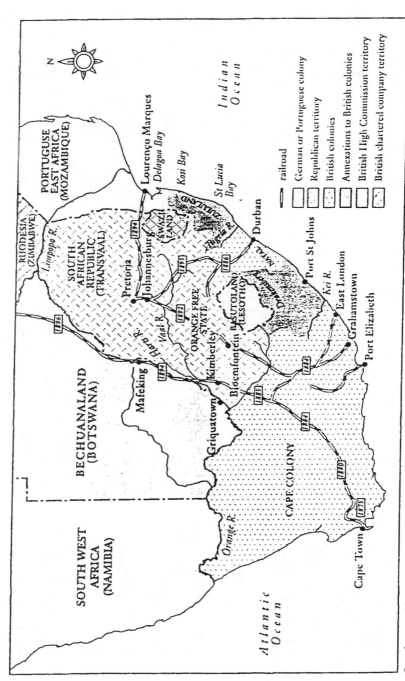

Southern Africa in the 1890s

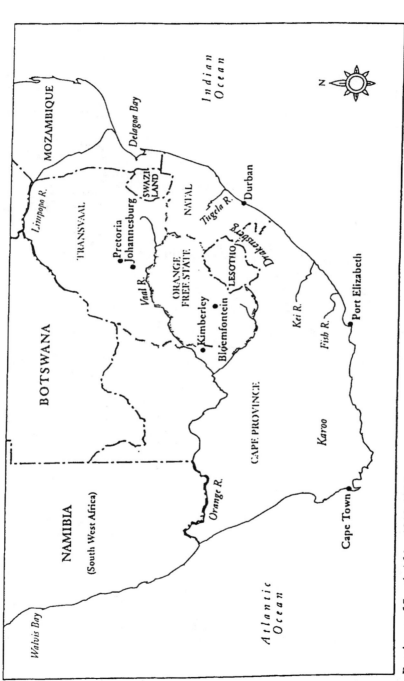

Provinces of South Africa 1910-1994

Bantustans

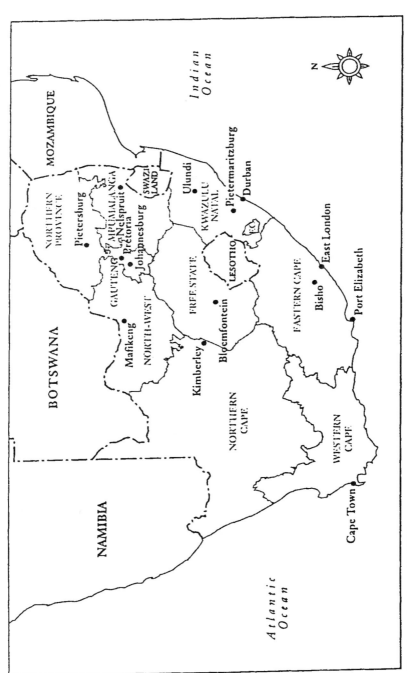

Provinces in the mid-1990s

Introduction

Dictionary entries are unable to provide the kind of context that satisfies historians. Many general histories of South Africa (the most important of which are listed in the bibliography) both provide such context and offer interpretations of how and why the history of South Africa developed as it did. This introduction merely presents a brief overall narrative; the bibliography is a guide to literature on the themes introduced here.

We know from the work of archaeologists that the location of some of the earliest human settlements anywhere in the world are to be found in South Africa. Hunter-gatherers, later called San by their Khoikhoi neighbors, lived in many parts of South Africa for hundreds of thousands of years and left behind evidence of their activities in rock art. About 2,000 years ago, former San people who had acquired sheep arrived from the north and began to expel the hunters from the areas most suitable for grazing their livestock, which came to include cattle as well as sheep. Some San speakers, retreating into the more remote areas, remained quite distinct from the Khoikhoi pastoralists, but in some places there was intermixing between them. The Dutch found it difficult to distinguish between San and Khoikhoi, and modern historians have often used the term *Khoisan* to reflect this difficulty.

About 1,500 years ago, Bantu-speaking pastoralists who also grew crops and worked iron began settling in the northern parts of what is now South Africa, initially in the river valleys. Growing their own crops, they rapidly increased in numbers and began to develop small kingdoms, some of which had brief periods of relative wealth. Trading routes began to link the coastal areas with the interior, and over time, the Bantu speakers spread southward into what is now the Eastern Cape province and the Free State. In the early 19th century, a process of political centralization led to the emergence, in what is today KwaZulu-Natal, of the relatively large Zulu state. The rise to power of its ruler, Shaka, had repercussions far and wide in the subcontinent.

In the 15th century, Portuguese seafarers first rounded the Cape of Good Hope, after which the Dutch, the French, and the English all saw the Cape as a valuable stopping place on the way to the East. It was the Dutch who established the first permanent settlement on the shores of Table Bay in 1652, to provide passing ships with refreshments. The Khoikhoi tried in vain to resist Dutch encroachment on their land. Officials of the Dutch East India Company soon brought in slaves, from both Africa and Asia, to help work the farms at the Cape, and the Dutch colony became rigidly stratified, with whites at the top, a small group of "free blacks" in the middle, and slaves and Khoikhoi at the bottom. During the 18th century the colony expanded, to the east in particular, and when the British ousted the Dutch in 1795 they took over a relatively large possession.

The new British rulers were initially as authoritarian as their Dutch predecessors, but new settlers arrived in 1820, and missionaries were influential in pushing for reforms regarding the treatment of slaves and the Khoikhoi. The Khoikhoi were granted civil liberties in 1828, and the slaves were freed in 1838 after a four-year period of apprenticeship, though without land their socioeconomic status remained much as it had been before. The British gave the Cape representative government in 1853, but relatively few people who were not white obtained the vote. A series of wars were fought with the Xhosa on the Cape's eastern frontier, as a result of which large numbers of Africans began to be incorporated into the colony from the 1850s, but they, too, remained a dominated population, though new voices began to emerge in the late 19th century to protest their inferior status.

From the beginning, the British were reluctant to extend their responsibilities. As white settlers moved into the interior, however, they carried the northern border of the Cape to the Orange (Gariep) River. From 1843, the British found themselves ruling a new colony, Natal—created by a large party of Voortrekkers who had moved into the interior, and then toward Port Natal, to escape British rule in the late 1830s—because Britain feared the Voortrekkers might link up with another European power and threaten its control of the seas. After the British took over Natal, the trekkers moved back onto the high veld, and after six years of British rule of the land between the Orange and Vaal Rivers, the Boers were able to establish new republics south and north of the Vaal. These were organized on strictly racial lines, with small white minorities dominating large African populations.

The discovery of diamonds near the confluence of the Orange and the Vaal, in 1867, and of gold—first in the Tati area, then in the eastern Transvaal in the 1870s, and in 1886 on the Witwatersrand—was to transform the country in the long run. Large numbers of new settlers arrived from Europe, and larger numbers of black migrant workers traveled great distances to work in the mines. Railways began to connect the various parts of the country. Britain, having taken over the diamond areas known as Griqualand West, wished to confederate the states in South Africa, but efforts to achieve this—which included British annexation of the South African Republic in 1877—did not succeed. In the process, however, the remaining powerful African kingdoms, those of the Zulu and Pedi, were defeated by British troops. In the 1880s the lands of the Tswana were brought under British rule, as was Zululand itself. By the end of the century, all African chiefdoms south of the Limpopo River had come under white rule.

The Boers of the Transvaal rebelled against the British in 1880, and their independence was largely restored to them, but the rich gold fields found on the Witwatersrand in 1886 soon upset the balance of power in the region. Fearing that its dominance might be in jeopardy, Britain tried to weaken the South African Republic. Cecil Rhodes, prime minister of the Cape from 1890, sought to encircle Kruger's republic but was discredited when he plotted a coup that failed in 1895–96 (the Jameson Raid). The new British high commissioner, Alfred Milner, then increased pressure on Kruger until war broke out in October 1899.

The British expected the war to be over by Christmas, but the Boers scored a number of military successes before the British captured the republican capitals by mid 1900, after which Boer guerrillas continued the war until May 1902. By then large numbers of Boer women and children, as well as Africans, had died in concentration camps. In some places Africans were able to regain control of their lands. But even though the Boers lost the war, they won the peace. The British imposed generous terms to secure their continuing influence in the region. Africans were excluded from political power and again fell under Boer dominance. When an Afrikaner-dominated National Convention decided upon a constitution for a new Union of South Africa based on white supremacy, the British welcomed it.

Afrikaners dominated the new Union. For some time the government, led by the first two prime ministers, Louis Botha and Jan Smuts, was in the hands of advocates of conciliation, who were happy to be subjects of the British monarch. But the imperial connection remained unacceptable to some Afrikaners, and a new republicanism was urged by General J. B. M. Hertzog. The Afrikaner poor were increasingly mobilized into the nationalist movement, but in 1939 Hertzog broke with Smuts over the issue of South African neutrality in World War II. Dr. D. F. Malan and his "purified" nationalists, who had broken away from Hertzog in 1934, now seized the chance to oppose Smuts, again prime minister, and in 1948, Malan's Nationalist Party gained a majority of seats, though a minority of votes. Under successive leaders, most notably, Hendrik Verwoerd, B. J. Vorster, and P. W. Botha, the National Party held power until 1994. For more than forty years, it implemented the policy of apartheid.

The National Party built on an earlier racial segregation dating back to the Reconstruction era under Milner and before. Land and urban legislation in 1913 and 1923 had set out the framework of a segregationist society, and further legislation to segregate Natal Indians was passed in 1943 and 1946. The color bar, which dated from before the Union, had been extended by Hertzog in 1926. Those who came to power in 1948 believed they had a formula to ensure the survival of white minority rule. It involved removing Coloureds from the common voters' roll, which was done in 1956, after a constitutional battle; creating bantustans for Africans, which Verwoerd decided might be led to "independence"; and forcing everyone into racially defined "group areas." The color bar was tightened, and Africans were kept in their place through an inferior educational system.

To achieve this absurd dream, the apartheid state engaged in massive social engineering (including the forced removal of millions of people), gradually rescinded almost all civil liberties, even for whites, and made extraparliamentary opposition illegal. The international community challenged the regime, in effect forcing it out of the Commonwealth in 1961, and increasingly South Africa became a pariah state on the international scene. After the murder of black consciousness leader Steve Biko in 1977, a mandatory arms embargo was approved by the United Nations. In the mid-1980s, countries and institutions began to impose trade and financial sanctions, at a time when a massive internal revolt was being crushed. Nevertheless, the state retained a large measure of its power. But by then, the body that had begun life as the South African Native National Congress and changed its name to the African National Congress (ANC) had acquired new strength both in exile, from where it launched sabotage attacks, and internally, as more and more opponents of apartheid rallied behind its banner. While the breakaway Pan Africanist Congress (PAC) suffered from internal factionalism and was regarded by many as too extreme, the ANC gained much new support after the Soweto revolt of 1976, as black consciousness supporters went into exile and joined the ANC because it was sending guerrillas back into South Africa.

P. W. Botha, realizing that some modification of apartheid policies was needed, allowed trade unions to organize and implemented a new constitution in 1983, which brought Coloureds and Indians into the central legislature. This provoked new resistance, which helped sap white morale, as did the imposition of sanctions. In Angola, the regime became embroiled in what threatened to become a major war with the Cubans, and so in 1988 it decided to withdraw from both Angola and Namibia, which had been a South African colony since 1915.

Fortunately for the National Party, changes in superpower relations from about 1986, and in Eastern Europe in 1989, enabled it to take the initiative. By the late 1980s it was clear that the bantustan policy had been a disastrous failure and that the only way to move forward was to negotiate with the ANC. In February 1990, President F. W. de Klerk announced the unbanning of the ANC, the PAC, and the Communist Party and his decision to release the imprisoned ANC leader, Nelson Mandela, unconditionally.

The government and the ANC soon found that, despite ongoing tensions and difficulties, they could work together to forge a new nonracial constitutional democracy, and the continuing political violence in the country helped convince both that they must cooperate. Between December 1991 and November 1993, negotiations were held at the World Trade Centre near Johannesburg, which resulted in the drafting of an interim constitution, under the terms of which a general election was held in April 1994. This occurred relatively peacefully, after Mangosutho Buthelezi, the leader of Inkatha, agreed to participate at the last moment. The ANC emerged the clear winner, with close to two-thirds of the parliamentary seats, and under the terms of the constitution a government of National Unity was formed. The Constitutional Assembly, formed by the new Parliament, then drafted a final constitution, which was approved by the Constitutional Court and took effect in 1997. The government embarked first on a Reconstruction and Development Programme and then, in 1996, adopted the Growth, Employment, and Redistribution (GEAR) strategy. It was clear that the success of the new democracy would depend on how long it would take to deal with the socioeconomic problems which apartheid had left the country.

The Dictionary

-A-

ABDURAHMAN, ABDULLAH (1872–1940). The most important Coloured (q.v.) political leader of the early 20th century, Abdullah Abdurahman served as president of the African People's Organization (q.v.) from 1905 until his death. The grandson of freed slaves (q.v.), he trained as a medical doctor in Glasgow, Scotland, before returning to Cape Town (q.v.) to practice medicine and participate in political life. The first Coloured person to serve on the Cape Town City Council (1904–40) and on the Cape Provincial Council (1914–40), he was much criticized in the late 1930s by a new, more militant generation of Coloured activists.

AFRICAN METHODIST EPISCOPAL CHURCH (AMEC). In 1896 the Ethiopian Church, the first important African independent church (q.v.), founded by Mangena Mokone in Pretoria in 1892, decided to become part of the AMEC, the leading African American church. Bishop Henry Turner of the AMEC made a highly successful six-week visit to South Africa in 1898, and by the end of that year the AMEC in South Africa boasted more than 10,000 adherents in 73 congregations. From the late 1890s the American church constituted the major link between black South Africans and African Americans. A number of black South Africans were educated at the AMEC's Wilberforce Institute in the United States, and the AMEC sent a succession of ministers to South Africa. For its South African members, the AMEC symbolized freedom from white control in a segregated society. It did not, however, engage politically, and it tended to remain aloof from other independent churches.

AFRICAN NATIONAL CONGRESS (ANC). Founded in January 1912 in Bloemfontein as the South African Native National Congress (SANNC), the African National Congress (a name adopted in 1923) is

1

today the oldest national political organization in the country. For almost 50 years it worked within the law against racial discrimination, and in 1956 it committed itself to a South Africa that belongs to all. Banned in 1960, the ANC was forced underground and into exile for three decades. From exile, it conducted an armed struggle for liberation. In its exile years it opened its membership to whites and other non-Africans. Unbanned in 1990, it entered formal negotiations with the government and gradually dropped the socialist policies it had earlier espoused. The negotiations eventually produced a compromise settlement that allowed the ANC to take power as a result of the election of April 1994.

The successor to a number of provincial African congresses formed by Africans in the aftermath of the South African War (q.v.), the SANNC was a response to the establishment of the Union (q.v.) of South Africa in 1910. The initiative for its formation came largely from a group of young overseas-trained lawyers, of whom the most important was Pixley Seme (q.v.). In its early years the ANC was an extremely moderate organization that believed in petitioning the government and acting responsibly as a pressure group for the promotion of African interests. Its first main concern was the Natives Land Act (q.v.), against which protest delegations were sent to Cape Town (q.v.) and London, in vain. Another delegation was sent to Versailles and London in the aftermath of World War I (q.v.). For a brief period the Transvaal (q.v.) section of Congress adopted a militant stance, and in the late 1920s a new president, Josiah Gumede, tried to persuade the organization to challenge the pass (q.v.) system more directly, but he was voted out in 1930. (*See* PASS LAWS.) In the Western Cape (q.v.), the ANC split, and an Independent ANC briefly adopted a more militant line, but by the mid-1930s the ANC had reached a low point in its fortunes.

It was in the 1940s, under the presidency of Alfred Bitini Xuma (q.v.), that there began the transformation of the ANC into a mass movement. This was in large part under the influence of the African National Congress Youth League (q.v.), formed by Fort Hare (q.v.) graduates in 1944. In 1949, in the aftermath of the 1948 victory of the National Party (NP) (q.v.) and its adoption of apartheid (q.v.) policies, the Youth League was able to get the ANC to adopt a Programme of Action, which called for new methods of struggle, including boycotts (q.v.), strikes (q.v.) and civil disobedience. In 1952, the ANC launched a Defiance Campaign (q.v.), which helped swell its membership from 20,000 to 100,000. It then took the lead in the Congress Alliance (q.v.) and the movement for a Freedom Charter. Drawn up in 1955 and adopted by the ANC the following year, the charter committed the organization to a multiracial, social democratic future for South Africa. Those of an Africanist persuasion within the organization rejected this, and in 1958 they broke away. By the end of the 1950s it was clear that little had been achieved by the ANC's attempts to resist the implementation of apartheid, attempts that included protest campaigns against Bantu education (q.v.), passes for women (q.v.), and the destruction of Sophiatown.

Instead, apartheid had intensified. A major turning point for the ANC came in April 1960, when it was banned in the aftermath of the Sharpeville massacre (q.v.). In October of that year its president, Albert Luthuli (q.v.), went to Oslo to collect the Nobel Peace Prize, which he was awarded for the nonviolent struggle he had led, but Nelson Mandela (q.v.) and others, working closely with members of the South African Communist Party (SACP) (q.v.), decided to adopt the strategy of armed struggle and launched Umkhonto weSizwe (MK) (q.v.). This was announced publicly on 16 December 1961, and a campaign of sabotage began. The ANC suffered a massive blow when its key internal leaders were arrested and given life sentences in the Rivonia trial (q.v.) in 1964. In exile, the organization was led by Oliver Tambo (q.v.), who established its headquarters in Lusaka, Zambia, and worked to win international support. A consultative conference held at Morogoro, Tanzania, in 1969 adopted a new program, Strategy and Tactics of the ANC, agreed to admit non-Africans to membership for the first time, and created a Revolutionary Council, which strengthened the influence of the SACP within the exile movement. Meanwhile, the ANC's armed wing, Umkhonto weSizwe, had sent detachments into Rhodesia in 1967 and 1968, en route to South Africa, but they were soon routed. Although the ANC played no significant role in the Soweto uprising (q.v.), most of those who fled the country as a result of that revolt joined the ANC in exile, and many of them returned to the country as members of MK. From the late 1970s, MK was increasingly active in mounting attacks on targets in South Africa, including the Sasol oil refinery, the Koeberg nuclear power plant, and the defense force base at Voortrekkerhoogte. A car-bomb attack on the headquarters of the South African Air Force in Pretoria in 1983 killed 19 people.

Support for the banned organization escalated in the townships. Many of those who had been sent to Robben Island (q.v.) as supporters of black consciousness joined the ANC because of the remarkable moral influence of Mandela and his colleagues at the island prison. Although the ANC could not organize effectively within the country, it gained great influence within the United Democratic Front (UDF) (q.v.) from 1983, and from late 1985 its legitimacy grew dramatically among whites in South Africa and in the international community. It began to be seen as a possible alternative government. At its conference in Kabwe, Zambia, in June 1985, the ANC opened its top structures to non-Africans and resolved that the armed struggle should be intensified and that the risk of civilians being caught in the crossfire should no longer impede such intensification.

The imprisoned Mandela, icon of the struggle, was widely seen as the key to its resolution. In 1985 he began to enter into discussions about talks with the government. The exile leadership started to explore ideas about a future South Africa with delegations from South Africa in Dakar (Senegal), the United Kingdom, and elsewhere. Although the ANC–SACP alliance was broadened to include the newly established Congress of South African Trade Unions (COSATU) (q.v.), the ANC's adherence to socialist rhetoric began to be modified, and as it moved to power after 1990, it slowly abandoned talk of nationalization and became increasingly pragmatic in outlook.

When F. W. de Klerk (q.v.) unbanned the ANC and the SACP in 1990, he probably hoped that the ANC or the alliance would split, but in neither case did that happen. The released Mandela soon took over the leadership from an ailing Tambo. The ANC began formal talks with the government in May 1990, agreed to suspend its armed struggle in August of that year, and in December 1991 entered formal multiparty negotiations with the government and other parties on a new constitution to provide for a democratic order. It is generally agreed that in these negotiations the ANC, whose chief negotiator was Cyril Ramaphosa (q.v.), outmaneuvered the NP and got the better of the compromise deal providing for the establishment of a new democratic order. *See also* CONVENTION FOR A DEMOCRATIC SOUTH AFRICA; MULTI-PARTY NEGOTIATING FORUM.

Under Mandela's inspirational leadership, the ANC successfully held together a number of different constituencies: those who had gone into exile, those who had been on Robben Island, and those who had worked in the UDF and the Mass Democratic Movement (q.v.). The alliances with COSATU and the SACP held firm, and in the first democratic election, in April 1994, the ANC won 62.6 percent of the votes, just short of the two-thirds that would have allowed it to write the final constitution on its own. From May it governed as the majority party in the government of National Unity (q.v.). After the withdrawal of the NP from that government in 1996, some political commentators began to talk of a one-party dominant system, as there was no effective alternative to the ANC on the political scene.

Once in power, the ANC championed the Reconstruction and Development Programme (q.v.), but by 1997 this had effectively been replaced by a Growth, Employment, and Redistribution (GEAR) (q.v.) strategy, which emphasized the need for fiscal discipline and measures to encourage foreign investment to promote economic growth; this meant cutbacks in social spending. COSATU was critical of GEAR and other policies of the ANC-led government, but it did not break away. The popular Bantu Holomisa (q.v.) was expelled from the organization for indiscipline, and Winnie Madikizela-Mandela (q.v.) proved difficult to handle, but the party emerged from its 50th congress, held at Mafikeng (formerly Mafeking [q.v.]) in December 1997, seemingly as strong as ever, with Thabo Mbeki (q.v.), its new president, committed to do what he could to increase delivery of what had been promised to the electorate: houses, running water, electricity, and, above all, jobs.

AFRICAN NATIONAL CONGRESS YOUTH LEAGUE. The Youth League was founded in 1944 to represent the interests of younger, more militant members of the African National Congress (q.v.). It probably had most influence on the parent organization in its first decade of life. Its early leaders, many educated at Fort Hare (q.v.), included its first president, Anton Lembede (q.v.), Oliver Tambo (q.v.), Nelson Mandela (q.v.), and Walter Sisulu (q.v.). In the early 1990s, the Youth League gained a new lease on life under the presidency of Peter Mokaba, then a fiery politician.

AFRICAN PEOPLE'S ORGANIZATION (APO). Founded in 1902 as the African Political Organization, the African People's Organization was the leading Coloured (q.v.) political formation during the first three decades of the 20th century. Seeking equality with whites for its members, it represented mostly the Coloured elite and was closely identified with Abdullah Abdurahman (q.v.) and the newspaper he edited, the *APO*. In the late 1930s the importance of the APO declined as a more radical generation challenged its conservatism.

AFRICAN RESISTANCE MOVEMENT. *See* LIBERAL PARTY.

AFRICANS. In the late 19th century, the term *Kaffir*, most commonly used to that time for people of Bantu-speaking origin, began to acquire increasingly pejorative connotations, and it was gradually replaced in general use by *native*. By the 1950s, whites began to realize that *native* meant indigenous to the country, and the government, wishing to assert the legitimacy of the white presence in South Africa, adopted first *Bantu* and then *black*. If *black* is used in this narrower sense, however, there is no satisfactory general term for those not classified as white (q.v.) in South Africa's apartheid (q.v.) racial terminology. In this book, *black* (q.v.) is therefore used to refer to Africans of Bantu-speaking origin, Coloureds (q.v.), and Indians (q.v.).

This book follows usual practice in scholarly writing in English on South Africa and uses the term *African* for people of Bantu-speaking (q.v.) origin. The use of the term *African* in this sense is, however, unsatisfactory from several points of view. It may suggest that people not of Bantu-speaking origin are not African in the sense of not belonging to the continent. Khoisan (q.v.) people lived in many parts of the country before the arrival of Bantu-speaking people. By the 1960s many whites had come to see themselves as Africans. After the establishment of the Republic (q.v.) of South Africa in 1961, government spokespersons often referred to whites as people of Africa, that is, people with no other home country, an interpretation accepted by leaders of African countries to the north in the Lusaka Manifesto of 1969.

AFRIKAANS. From the time of the earliest white settlement at the Cape, in the late 17th century, the form of Dutch spoken there developed differences in pronunciation and accidence, and, to a lesser extent, in syntax and vocabulary, from that of Holland. Settlers who arrived speaking German and French soon converted to Dutch. The process of creolization was influenced by the languages spoken by slaves (q.v.), Khoikhoi (q.v.), and people of mixed descent, as well as by Malay and Portuguese. Although the Dutch of Holland remained the language (q.v.) of officialdom, by the 19th century the new creolized form, Afrikaans—often known as Cape Dutch or belittled as "kitchen Dutch"—had developed into a separate language.

The first book published in Afrikaans appeared in 1856, but it was not until the 1870s that the language was used as a vehicle for cultural expression, in opposition to British imperialism. S. J. du Toit (q.v.), a clergyman of the Dutch Reformed Church (q.v.) who lived in Paarl, near Cape Town (q.v.), produced a journal, *Die Afrikaanse Patriot* (1876), a concise grammar (1876), and a history (1877), all of which aided the growth of Afrikaans as a written as well as a spoken language.

A second phase of the Afrikaans language movement began after the South African War (q.v.), partly as a response to the attempts of Sir Alfred

Milner (q.v.) to anglicize the white Afrikaans speakers of the Transvaal (q.v.). Newspapers and periodicals published in Afrikaans began to appear more regularly. One of the central figures in the language movement, J. D. du Toit (1877–1953), son of S. J. du Toit, wrote poetry under the name Totius. Other prominent poets and writers early in the century include Eugène Marais, C. Louis Leipoldt, and Jan F. Celliers. In 1909 an academy was founded to promote the language and its scientific study, and in the early 1920s the influential Cape Town newspaper, *De Burger*, and the journal of the Dutch Reformed Church, *De Kerkbode*, both changed from Dutch to Afrikaans. In 1925, Afrikaans was recognized as one of the two official languages of the Union (q.v.) of South Africa.

Usage of Afrikaans among whites was aggressively promoted from the late 1920s, mainly by the Afrikaner Broederbond (q.v.) and the (Purified) National Party (q.v.), both instruments of Afrikaner nationalism (q.v.). An Afrikaans translation of the Bible was published early in the 1930s; the language was strongly encouraged in white schools; and bodies such as the Federasie van Afrikaanse Kultuurvereniginge (Federation of Afrikaans Cultural Organizations) and the Afrikaanse Taal en Kultuurvereniging (Afrikaans Language and Cultural Organization) were established. The work of the poet N. P. van Wyk Louw (1906–70) helped give the language standing as a literary medium.

Although the majority of Coloureds (q.v.) continued to use the language, from 1948 it became closely associated with apartheid (q.v.) and Afrikaner (q.v.) domination. White Afrikaans speakers took control of the civil service, ousting English speakers (q.v.), and Afrikaans became the language of the apartheid government. A large Taalmonument (language monument) was erected in Paarl in 1976, the year in which the Soweto uprising (q.v.) was sparked by the insistence of the authorities that Africans (q.v.) be taught in high school through the medium of Afrikaans. A strongly dissident literary tradition had begun in the 1960s, associated with such writers and poets as Etienne Leroux, Ingrid Jonker, André Brink, and Breyten Breytenbach (q.v.). Brink and Breytenbach gained international reputations as their work became available in other languages. Breytenbach went so far as to reject the language for a time because of its association with apartheid. No significant proapartheid literature emerged in Afrikaans.

With the collapse of apartheid, Afrikaans, as the first language of only five million of the country's people, lost status and became one of 11 official languages. Some white Afrikaners sought constitutional protection for the language in the new political dispensation, and others, having rejected Coloureds in the apartheid era, now rediscovered kinship with them on the basis of a shared language.

AFRIKANER. In the 20th century the term usually meant a white Afrikaans-speaker (*see* AFRIKANERS). After the transition to democracy in the 1990s there was a new attempt to change the meaning of the term to include all Afrikaans-speakers, whether white or not.

AFRIKANER, JONKER (ca. 1790–1861). Jonker Afrikaner was leader of the Afrikaners, an Oorlam (q.v.) group founded by his grandfather, Klaas Afrikaner, and built up by his father, Jager Afrikaner (d. 1823). Jonker Afrikaner exercised wide power on the Cape (q.v.) northern frontier in the 1820s and 1830s. From his base on an island in the Orange River (q.v.) he subjugated Khoisan (q.v.) people in the region in return for arms and ammunition from whites, but at times he also assisted Khoisan to resist Cape Colony (q.v.) encroachment on their hunting grounds. In the 1840s he moved a long way north of the Orange, into what is now Namibia (q.v.), and there carried out extensive and brutal raids on the Herero people, plundering large herds of cattle and destroying numerous villages.

AFRIKANER BOND (LEAGUE OF AFRIKANERS). The first and most important political party in the Cape (q.v.) before creation of the Union (q.v.) of South Africa, the Afrikaner Bond was established in 1880 to further the interests of Afrikaner (q.v.) white farmers in the southwestern Cape. Under Jan Hendrik Hofmeyr (q.v.), it entered an alliance with Cecil Rhodes (q.v.) and gained some black support, including that of the influential John Tengu Jabavu (q.v.). With the advent of the Union, the Bond was dissolved in 1911.

AFRIKANER BROEDERBOND (LEAGUE OF AFRIKANER BROTHERS). Formed in 1919 to spearhead the movement for an Afrikaner republic (q.v.), the Afrikaner Broederbond was a highly influential secret society that promoted the interests of Afrikaner nationalism (q.v.). It worked to secure Afrikaner (q.v.) control in government, the economy, and culture and did much to promote the cause of the National Party (q.v.). Beginning in the 1960s, a series of revelations about its membership began to erode its power, but most influential male Afrikaners continued to be members. By the mid-1980s, under Professor Pieter de Lange, it was ahead of the government of the day in promoting the idea of moving away from apartheid (q.v.). In the new order that arose after 1990, it came to accept that its ranks should be opened to Afrikaans-speaking males who were not white, but by then its influence was negligible.

AFRIKANER NATIONALISM. From the time of the Great Trek (q.v.), whites who spoke Afrikaans (q.v.) as their mother tongue were deeply divided. It was not until the 1870s that a common consciousness began to develop among Afrikaners (q.v.) in the interior and at the Cape (q.v.), formed on the basis of the idea of a distinct culture and history and in opposition to British imperialism, at the time of the British annexation of the Transvaal (q.v.). A strong nationalist movement did not emerge until the early 20th century. This had the goal of winning political power in the Union (q.v.) inaugurated in 1910 and creating an Afrikaner republic (q.v.). *See also* BRITAIN IN SOUTH AFRICA.

In the process of welding different Afrikaner groups into an ethnic coalition large enough to win political power, important roles were played by the Afrikaner Broederbond (q.v.), the Nasionale Pers group of newspapers, and the financial institutions Santam and Sanlam. Afrikaner intellectuals dwelt on the second-class status of Afrikaans, and in the 1930s they took advantage of the economic crisis to mobilize poor Afrikaners with the message that their future was bound up with that of the *volk* (people) as a whole. Immense popular enthusiasm for the nationalist cause was whipped up in 1938 during the commemoration of the centenary of the Great Trek. Gustav Preller and other writers created a largely mythical history in which a united Afrikaner people, chosen by God, had been oppressed by Britain and the English in South Africa. Eventually, sufficient Afrikaner farmers and urban workers, though still a minority of the white (q.v.) electorate, were persuaded to vote for the National Party (NP) (q.v.) to enable it to form a government in 1948. It was another decade before Afrikaner nationalist control was firmly in place, and not until 1961 was the NP able to introduce the promised republic. Only in the early 1990s, when the prospect of losing political power loomed, did a significant section of Afrikaners seek a separate territory (a *volkstaat*) for themselves, though no realistic, specific proposal for such a territory was advanced. *See also* AFRIKANER VOLKSFRONT.

AFRIKANER PARTY (1941-51). After Jan Smuts (q.v.) had taken South Africa into World War II (q.v.), J. B. M. Hertzog (q.v.) and his followers joined D. F. Malan (q.v.) in a Herenigde (Afrikaans, "Reunited")

National Party. But old suspicions soon flared up, and by the end of 1940 the Hertzogites had broken with Malan; early in 1941 they formed the Afrikaner Party. After all its candidates had met defeat in the 1943 general election, its leader, N. C. Havenga (1881–1957), made overtures to the United Party (q.v.), but Smuts rejected them. In 1947, Malan and Havenga agreed that their parties would not compete against each other in the next election. The Afrikaner Party gained nine seats in 1948, a sufficient number to enable the National Party (NP) (q.v.) to form a government. After South West Africa (now Namibia [q.v.]) was given six seats in the House of Assembly in Cape Town (q.v.), and NP candidates had been returned for all of them, the Afrikaner Party was no longer needed for Malan's majority, and it was absorbed by the NP in 1951.

AFRIKANER REBELLION. In 1914, Afrikaners (q.v.) in the Orange Free State (q.v.) and the Transvaal (q.v.), many of them poor farmers or *bywoners* (q.v.), staged a rebellion to protest the government's decision, at the beginning of World War I (q.v.), to invade South West Africa (now Namibia [q.v.]) and seize it from the Germans. The rebels hoped to overthrow the government of Louis Botha (q.v.) and regain their lost republican independence. When government troops quickly put down the rebellion, the rebels were treated leniently, but the execution of Jopie Fourie turned him into a martyr, and some Afrikaners never forgave Botha and Jan Smuts (q.v.) for their role in suppressing the rebellion.

AFRIKANER RESISTANCE MOVEMENT / AFRIKANER WEER-STANDSBEWEGING (AWB). A neo-Nazi, protofascist political movement led by the charismatic Eugène Terre'Blanche, the AWB was established in 1973 to promote the interests of the Afrikaner (q.v.) *volk* (people), which its members claimed were being betrayed by the National Party (q.v.) and Afrikaner intellectuals. The movement first came to public prominence in 1979, when Terre'Blanche and others tarred and feathered the well-known historian Floors van Jaarsveld in Pretoria for challenging the orthodox notion of divine intervention at the Battle of Blood River (q.v.). When the government began to negotiate the establishment of a democratic order, the AWB threatened to prevent any such transition by force. On 25 June 1993 a group of AWB members stormed the World Trade Centre, where multiparty negotiations (q.v.) were taking place. Driving an armored vehicle through its plateglass doorway, they occupied and trashed the negotiating chamber before withdrawing. In March 1994, the AWB again overplayed its hand, when its armed wing, the Ystergarde, entered Bophuthatswana (q.v.) and then had to withdraw, but not before the murder of three AWB members was captured on television. Some of its members set off bombs as the democratic election began in April 1994, but the threat of serious resistance to majority rule did not materialize. Concern about the far right as a potentially destabilizing force nevertheless helped make the new ANC-led government move cautiously in its first years in power.

AFRIKANER VOLKSFRONT (AFRIKANER PEOPLE'S FRONT). General Constand Viljoen (q.v.) emerged from retirement in late 1993 to lead right-wing Afrikaners (q.v.) who believed the National Party (q.v.) had betrayed Afrikaner interests but rejected the extremism of the Afrikaner Resistance Movement (q.v.). The Volksfront that Viljoen helped establish wanted a territory (*volkstaat*) to be demarcated within which Afrikaners could enjoy self-determination. To that end, it sought for a time to forge an electoral alliance with the Inkatha (q.v.) Freedom Party and bantustan (q.v.) leaders. The Volksfront was divided about participation in the April 1994 election, however, and Viljoen went his own way, registering a Freedom Front (q.v.) party for the election. The fiasco of failed intervention to prop up the Mangope regime in Bophuthatswana (q.v.) in March 1994 gravely weakened the Volksfront movement, which thereafter bore little independent significance.

AFRIKANERS. Before the 20th century, *Afrikaner* often meant "native of Africa," a person who identified with, and was usually born in, South Africa rather than Europe; Afrikaners (or *Afrikanders*) could therefore be of diverse origins. In the 20th century the term became confined to whites (q.v.) whose home language (q.v.) was Afrikaans (q.v.). Always the majority of whites, and for most of the 20th century politically dominant, by the 1990s Afrikaners constituted less than 7 percent of the total population. At the beginning of the 20th century, most were rural people, but by the mid-1990s, when white Afrikaners numbered more than three million people, more than 80 percent lived in towns and cities.

Those whites who came to be known as Afrikaners were often called Boers or, in the Cape (q.v.), Cape Dutch. Descendants of immigrants of mainly Dutch, German, and French extraction, they had by 1800 established themselves as a distinct people who saw themselves as independent of Europe. Under British rule in the 19th century, some in the western Cape became anglicized, others sought to maintain a separate identity through the Dutch Reformed Church (q.v.) and the promotion of their language, while yet others sought to escape British rule in the Great Trek (q.v.). *See also* BRITAIN IN SOUTH AFRICA.

The South African War (q.v.) was the most significant attempt by Afrikaners in the two republics to maintain their independence from Britain. Their terrible experiences in that conflict left a legacy of great bitterness, which was channeled into an incipient Afrikaner nationalism (q.v.). The political party representing this nationalism, the National Party (q.v.), won exclusive political power in 1948. Afrikaner hegemony was strongest during the 1960s and early 1970s, after which deep divisions among Afrikaners over the best methods to preserve Afrikaner identity again became significant. In 1990, F. W. de Klerk (q.v.) seized what he saw as the best moment to end apartheid so as to preserve Afrikaner identity in the long term.

AGRICULTURE. Knowledge of farming is thought to have entered South Africa along with iron technology and the kind of pottery characteristic of the early Iron Age (q.v.). There is evidence of both cereal cultivation and livestock keeping in the Transvaal (q.v.) from the third century A.D., and it is often assumed—though it is impossible to prove—that these Iron Age farmers were Bantu speakers (q.v.). By early in the second millennium A.D. such farmers were engaging in more sophisticated farming and the exchange of agricultural produce. In African societies, the task of raising food was usually entrusted to women (q.v.); men cleared the ground, and the women sowed, weeded, gathered, and threshed the crop. The main grain crop was sorghum (often called kafir corn), gradually supplanted by maize (corn; mealies) from the 18th century. In the late 17th century white settlers in the southwestern Cape (q.v.) began the intensive production of both wheat (q.v.) and wine (q.v.), and in the 18th century wine became the staple export of the colony.

The British settlers of 1820 pioneered scientific farming in the Zuurveld (q.v.) or Albany district. With the introduction of merino sheep, wool (q.v.) became the major item of export from the eastern Cape in the 1830s. The introduction of the ox-drawn plough by missionaries (q.v.) in the 19th century encouraged Bantu-speaking Africans to give more attention to cultivation, increased areas open to such cultivation, and meant that men became more active in tillage. A relatively prosperous African peasantry emerged in response to new market opportunities.

The growth of population consequent on the discovery of first diamonds (q.v.) in the center of what is now South Africa, and then gold (q.v.) on the Witwatersrand (q.v.), created large internal markets for food. For a time African farmers in Basutoland (q.v.) and elsewhere supplied the new demand, but in the last years of the 19th century it was cheaper to import wheat from the United States than to obtain it locally. From about the time of the South African War (q.v.), at the turn of the century, white farming began to become much more commercialized and productive. The votes of white farmers counted for more than those of people living in urban areas, and they received massive state aid. Black farmers, by contrast, were not given such aid, and the competition from the independent African peasantry was eliminated. *See also* BUNDY THESIS.

Part of the revenue from the gold mines, which were relatively heavily taxed, was transferred to aid agriculture. A subsidy system introduced after 1924 ensured that farmers received higher than average world prices for their products. This process of subsidizing agriculture reached a high point in the Marketing Act of 1937, which provided for the establishment of central marketing boards. Railways (q.v.) subsidized the movement of agricultural products by reducing the rates for agricultural shipments, especially for export, and farmers were allowed special income-tax concessions. By the last quarter of the 20th century, South Africa was exporting 20 percent of its agricultural output. Maize, grown mainly in a triangle of land in the northern Orange Free State (q.v.) and southern Transvaal, was by far the largest crop, followed by sugar, grown mainly on Natal's (q.v.) north coast, and then fruit, most of which was produced in the southwestern Cape and exported through Cape Town (q.v.). The export of agricultural products was hard hit during the era of sanctions (q.v.) but revived quickly in the 1990s once sanctions were lifted. *See also* ECONOMIC CHANGE.

AIDS (ACQUIRED IMMUNE DEFICIENCY SYNDROME). The first documented cases of AIDS in South Africa were recorded in 1982, when two white males died after infection by the human immunodeficiency virus (HIV). The majority of initial infections in South Africa occurred among white homosexual and bisexual men, but by the early 1990s, as was the case in the rest of Africa, most people infected were black heterosexuals, with men and women affected in roughly equal proportions. By November 1991, there were 985 known cases of people afflicted with AIDS, of whom 385 had died; many thousands more had been exposed to HIV, but as AIDS was not a notifiable disease, accurate statistics of infections were difficult to obtain. By November 1996, official estimates by the Department of Health, based on the number of pregnant women entering prenatal clinics of the public health service, placed the number of people infected with HIV/AIDS at 2.5 million people, 6 percent of the total population, and it was estimated that new infections were occurring at the rate of approximately 1,500 people per day, mainly among the economically active sector of the population in the 15–29-year-old age group. This made the South African epidemic one of the fastest growing in the world. Although HIV/AIDS was well established throughout the country, the worst-affected region was KwaZulu-Natal (q.v.). The rapidity of its spread was attributed in part to the legacy of apartheid (q.v.), as migrancy (q.v.), the disruption of family life, illiteracy, poverty, malnutrition, and inadequate primary health-care facilities contributed to infection in rural areas and overcrowded urban settlements.

Government anti-AIDS programs were dogged by controversy: much money was wasted over the production of a play, *Sarafina 2*, and the government was criticized in 1997–98 for backing South African–based research into the drug Virodene before it had been properly tested.

ALL-AFRICAN CONVENTION. The All-African Convention was an umbrella African political movement established in 1935 to try to halt the passage of legislation removing Cape (q.v.) African voters from the common voters' roll. After that legislation was passed in 1936, the movement remained in existence and for a time existed alongside, and posed a challenge to, the African National Congress (ANC) (q.v.). But though the All-African Convention tried to enter alliances with Coloured (q.v.) and Indian (q.v.) organizations and gained considerable support in the Transkei (q.v.), it lacked cohesion and disintegrated as the ANC revived itself in the 1940s.

AMABUTHO. On reaching puberty, Zulu men and women were grouped into age or circumcision sets, known as *amabutho* (the plural form of the Zulu word, *ibutho,* meaning "those gathered together"). In the 18th century, in what became northern Natal (q.v.), *amabutho* had important nonmilitary functions: they colonized new land, hunted, and provided labor for their chiefs. The restrictions placed by the king on the marriage of members of *amabutho* (who were typically forbidden to marry for many years after recruitment) gave him control over their labor power for that period. The transition of male *amabutho* from traditional age sets into military units stationed at royal barracks has been seen as crucial to the process leading to the formation of the Zulu kingdom (q.v.) in the early 19th century. At a time of increasing competition for scarce resources and a share in the benefits of trade with Delagoa Bay (q.v.), extended military and nonmilitary service was required. The *amabutho* system remained fundamental to the organization of the Zulu kingdom throughout its independent existence.

AMAKHOLWA. The *amakholwa* (plural of *kholwa,* Zulu word for "believer") were Africans in Natal (q.v.) who were converted to Christianity (q.v.) during the 19th century and received some formal education (q.v.). By the end of the century, there were an estimated 40,000 African communicants and 100,000 church adherents in Natal. Although often as critical as whites of the primitive practices of unconverted Zulu (q.v.) people, they were not accorded equal status with the colonists, most of whom feared the challenge posed by the growth of the large *kholwa* community.

AMANDLA. The shouted slogan "*Amandla ngawethu*" (Zulu for "power is ours"), accompanied usually by a clenched-fist salute, was much used in the 1950s and again from the 1970s by African National Congress (q.v.), black consciousness (q.v.), and Inkatha (q.v.) supporters. It was sometimes accompanied by the call "*Mayibuye i Afrika*" (come back, Africa).

ANGLICAN CHURCH. After the second British occupation (q.v.) of the Cape (1806), Church of England ministers were appointed to serve the spiritual needs of colonial and military officials. With the arrival of the first bishop of Cape Town (q.v.), Robert Gray, the church began to expand. Gray organized five dioceses and created the autonomous Church of the Province of South Africa (CPSA) in 1870, but his episcopate was plagued by controversy. Above all, he clashed with the Bishop of Natal (q.v.), J. W. Colenso (q.v.), whom he accused of heresy. Colenso's supporters formed a splinter church, but the CPSA was recognized by the Anglican Church in England and remained by far the more important of the two institutions. The Anglican Church thereafter enjoyed slow but steady growth, nurturing mission (q.v.) activities and educational work, in particular. After 1948, some leading Anglicans became prominent in the struggle against apartheid (q.v.). The most notable of these was Desmond Tutu (q.v.), who became the first black Archbishop of Cape Town. In the 1990s more than two million South Africans owed allegiance to the CPSA.

ANGLO AMERICAN CORPORATION. (AAC). Realizing that only with new capital could he exploit the gold (q.v.) reserves on the East Rand, the area of the Witwatersrand (q.v.) to the east of Johannesburg (q.v.), Ernest Oppenheimer (q.v.) launched the AAC in 1917. The issued-share capital amounted to £1 million, of which half was subscribed in the United States, the remainder in Britain and South Africa. In 1957, Ernest Oppenheimer was succeeded as chairman by his son Harry, who retired in 1982. His son Nicholas was groomed as a possible successor as chairman, but, although the Oppenheimer family retained a large stake

in the AAC, the chairmanship passed from Harry Oppenheimer to Gavin
Relly and then, in 1992, to Julian Ogilvie Thompson.

The relationship between the diamond (q.v.) company De Beers (q.v.)
and the AAC was not straightforward. De Beers remained legally and
administratively independent but became part of the Anglo American empire, along with Central Mining, Rand Mines, and Johannesburg Consolidated Investments. The AAC had the capital to exploit the new Orange Free State (q.v.) gold fields, which it opened after World War II
(q.v.). In the 1980s and 1990s, the AAC was responsible for more than
one-third of South Africa's gold production.

In the 1950s, the AAC began to diversify into other minerals, including uranium and platinum, and other forms of industry. In 1960 its
nonmining industrial interests were worth £30 million; by 1969 they were
worth £143 million. It entered the property business in the 1970s, and
life insurance in 1982, and acquired extensive investments around the
world, in such companies as the Mineral and Resources Corporation
(Minorco), the Anglo American Corporation of Rhodesia, Zambia Copper Investments, the Anglo American Corporation of Canada, and Australian Anglo American. With these diversified interests, the AAC was
easily South Africa's largest company; it was listed on the Johannesburg
Stock Exchange, and its name became synonymous with wealth in the
country.

In the 1960s and 1970s, the AAC and its subsidiaries in Zambia and
other African countries backed the government's foreign relations (q.v.),
and in South Africa itself a number of its leading officials were linked
in various ways with the Progressive Party (q.v.). In September 1985,
Gavin Relly, the AAC's chairman, went to Zambia to meet Oliver Tambo
(q.v.) and other leaders in the African National Congress (q.v.), a move
that irked the National Party (q.v.) government but sent a powerful
signal.

The AAC prospered under the new democratic dispensation as it did
under apartheid (q.v.). By 1998, its market capitalization was some R45
billion, and the company had an operating profit of close to R10 billion.
In October 1998, the AAC announced far-reaching restructuring plans.
It would merge with its offshore arm, Minorco, thereby becoming one
of the world's three largest mining and natural resources companies and
some 50 percent larger than its current size. It would also relocate its head
office to London, where its primary listing would be on the London Stock
Exchange. The company intended to shed its noncore interests in South
Africa, concentrating on its key gold, platinum, and diamond business

as well as coal, base and ferrous metals, industrial minerals, and forest products.

ANGLO–BOER WAR. *See* ANGLO–TRANSVAAL WAR; SOUTH AFRI-CAN WAR.

ANGLO–TRANSVAAL WAR (1880–81). Sometimes known as the First Anglo–Boer War or the Transvaal War of Independence, the Anglo–Transvaal War was a short conflict in which Afrikaners (q.v.) in the Transvaal (q.v.) sought to recover the independence lost when the British annexed South Africa in April 1877. After the failure of protests and petitions, they took up arms in December 1880. Their strategy was to besiege British garrisons, particularly at Potchefstroom and Pretoria (q.v.), and prevent British reinforcements from entering the Transvaal from Natal (q.v.). The fiercest fighting took place in Natal, where the republican Afrikaners won a number of victories, most notably at Majuba (q.v.) in February 1881.

By the time that battle took place, Britain had decided to restore a large measure of self-rule to the Transvaal. The Convention of Pretoria of 1881 revoked Britain's annexation and provided for self-rule subject to the suzerainty of Queen Victoria. The Transvaal's foreign relations remained under British control, and the Transvaal was forbidden to alter its boundaries without British consent. A British veto over legislation dealing with Africans was, however, removed by the London Convention of 1884.

ANGLO–ZULU WAR (1879). The most important in a series of wars between white and black in southern Africa in the late 1870s, the Anglo–Zulu War broke out following the presentation of an ultimatum by the British high commissioner, Sir Henry Bartle Frere (q.v.), demanding that Cetshwayo (q.v.), the Zulu king, dismantle the Zulu military system—an order Frere knew was impossible for Cetshwayo to accept. Frere believed that he would have to deal with the Zulu threat if confederation (q.v.) in South Africa were to be achieved.

The advance of British and colonial forces into the Zulu kingdom (q.v.) was halted in January 1879 at Isandlwana (q.v.), where the British suffered a shocking defeat. The British soon recovered from this disaster and by July had triumphed: Ulundi, the Zulu capital, was occupied, and Cetshwayo was captured and sent into exile in Cape Town (q.v.). General Garnet Wolseley then imposed a settlement that divided the Zulu territory into 13 separate units, each under a ruler appointed by the British authorities. The aim was to balance mutually antagonistic forces (many of the new rulers were hostile to the Zulu royal establishment), but the result was a bitter civil war (1883–84), which was followed by the annexation of Zululand by the British in 1887.

ANGOLA. Under Portuguese rule, Angola was a buffer between South African–ruled Namibia (q.v.) and countries under African rule to the north. When the Portuguese withdrew from Angola in 1975, the South African Defence Force (SADF) (q.v.) moved across the Namibian border to protect the hydroelectric scheme, built jointly with the Portuguese, at Ruacana. In October of that year a relatively small force of South African soldiers moved north to the outskirts of Luanda, the capital, in an attempt to ensure that the Marxist MPLA (Movement of the People for the Liberation of Angola) did not become the new government, for it was known that the MPLA would give succor to the South West African People's Organization (SWAPO), against which the South Africans were fighting. When the South Africans confronted Cuban forces and the United States pulled out, the South Africans had to retreat early in 1976.

SWAPO then established bases in southern Angola, from which its guerrillas moved into northern Namibia. The SADF launched an airborne assault on what was said to be SWAPO's main military base at Cassinga in May 1978. Most people there were refugees; more than 600 civilians were killed. Numerous cross-border raids followed, and from 1981 the SADF was in permanent occupation of a strip of southern Angola north of the Namibian border. The SADF increasingly found itself fighting units of the Angolan army and lending support to UNITA (National Union for the Total Independence of Angola), the main opposition to the MPLA government. By early 1984, in part because of American pressure, the South African government was ready to sign an agreement with the Angolans that provided for the withdrawal of South African forces. But problems ensued in the implementation of the Lusaka Accord (February 1984), and in May 1985 a South African commando (q.v.) was captured in the northern Angolan enclave of Cabinda, where he was planning to blow up oil-storage tanks. South African aid for UNITA then escalated, and by early 1988, South African forces were engaged in a major battle outside the Angolan town of Cuito Cuanavale (q.v.). The stalemate in that battle helped lead to formal negotiations with the Angolans and Cubans and to an agreement providing for the withdrawal of all South African forces from Angola by September 1988 and the withdrawal of Cuban forces from Angola by 1991. The South African government did not pay Angola any reparations for the vast damage caused by the SADF in years of fighting in the country.

ANTHEM. The question of a national anthem became a heated one in white politics in 1938, when J. B. M. Hertzog (q.v.), the prime minister, claimed that South Africa had no anthem of its own, since God Save the King, which was sung on state occasions, was the British anthem. From that year, both God Save the King and Die Stem van Suid-Afrika, written in Afrikaans (q.v.) in 1918 and long an unofficial anthem, were played on state occasions. The National Party (q.v.) government decreed in May 1957 that Die Stem should be the only official anthem. English-speakers (q.v.) saw this as another sign of the Afrikanerization of the country; few of them bothered to learn the words of the English version (The Call of South Africa).

Nkosi Sikeleli i'Afrika (God Bless Africa), written in the late 1890s by Enoch Sontonga, was adopted as the anthem of the African National Congress (ANC) (q.v) and later chosen by neighboring African countries, as well as by the Transkei (q.v.), when it was given nominal "independence," as their anthem. Part of the compromise deal agreed to at the Multi-Party Negotiating Forum (q.v.) in 1993 was that the anthem of the new South Africa would include both Nkosi Sikeleli i'Afrika and Die Stem. In the years after 1994, Nelson Mandela (q.v.) often expressed his irritation when both parts of the new anthem were not sung. He recognized, however, that the anthem was too long, and a shortened version was substituted.

ANTI-COLONIAL REBELLIONS. Having been subjected to white control by a variety of means, including conquest in frontier wars (q.v.), blacks on a number of occasions rebelled in attempts to throw off that control. Similarly, groups of whites tried to throw off British control (*see also* AFRIKANER REBELLION; GREAT TREK).

Between 1799 and 1802, many Khoikhoi (q.v.) of the eastern Cape (q.v.) joined still-independent Xhosa (q.v.) in an abortive attempt to recover their lost freedom. Half the settlers of the Kat River Settlement (q.v.) rose in revolt against the colony during a Cape–Xhosa war in 1851. The rebellion by Langalibalele (q.v.) in 1873, petty episode though it was, shocked the Natal (q.v.) colonists, for it was the first rebellion of any significance in their colony. Yet another Cape–Xhosa war (1877–78) provided the context for revolts by portions of the Griqua (q.v.), both east and west of the Drakensberg (q.v.) and of the Tlhaping (q.v.) in 1878.

Less than three years after the last Cape–Xhosa war, much of the portion of the Transkei (q.v.) that had been brought under white rule without force rose in revolt. At the same time, the Sotho (q.v.) north of the Drakensberg went into rebellion against Cape rule (1880). The Cape was able to subdue the rebellion in the Transkei without calling on the aid of British troops, but north of the mountains it was unable to reassert its authority. In 1883, therefore, it decided to hand Basutoland (q.v.) back to Britain to rule. The last major revolt of this kind in the Cape took place among the Tswana of the Langeberg mountains in 1897, while the last in any part of South Africa occurred in Natal in 1906. Like all others except the one in Sotho, the Bambatha rebellion (q.v.) was soon suppressed, with much loss of life on the rebel side.

Thereafter, African resistance for long took nonviolent forms; even the Israelites of Bulhoek (q.v.) used violence only when surrounded. It was not until the 1960s that first sabotage and then other forms of armed struggle took resistance into a new phase (*see also* UMKHONTO WE SISWE).

ANTI-PASS CAMPAIGNS. For much of the first half of the 20th century, pass laws (q.v.) were the main target of African protest, and various campaigns were mounted against the *dompas* (*dom* meaning "stupid" in Afrikaans [q.v.]), which was seen as a humiliating badge of inferior status. In 1913, African women in the Orange Free State (q.v.) waged an extensive passive resistance campaign against a local requirement that they carry passes. Another such campaign by both men and women in the Transvaal (q.v.) in March 1919 achieved nothing, and the Natives (Urban Areas) Act of 1923 extended the pass system. The African National Congress (ANC) (q.v.) protested through petition, while the Communist Party (q.v.) organized occasional pass burnings. Another anti-pass campaign took place in 1944, after a brief period in which pass controls had been relaxed. The extension of passes to African women provoked widespread protests, culminating in a march of 20,000 women on the Union Buildings in Pretoria (q.v.) in August 1956, organized by the Federation of South African Women (q.v.). The anti-pass campaign of the Pan Africanist Congress (q.v.) in March 1960 ended tragically at Sharpeville (q.v.), in the aftermath of which Albert Luthuli (q.v.), leader of the ANC, and others burnt their passes in defiance of the law. For a few weeks the pass laws were suspended, but they were then reimposed and enforced with new vigor as government efforts to prevent more Africans settling in the urban areas intensified.

APARTHEID. This term, Afrikaans for "apartness," is often used loosely to include all forms of racial segregation. It was coined to refer to the policy adopted by the National Party (NP) (q.v.) in the early 1940s to extend existing segregation, make it more comprehensive, apply it more rigorously, and broaden its application. This policy was implemented after the NP won the election in 1948, reversing tentative proposals for lessening segregation put forward under the Smuts (q.v.) government.

To begin with, apartheid was applied by the NP in a rather ad hoc, pragmatic fashion. It chiefly involved extending various forms of segregation, which had formerly applied only to Africans, Indians (q.v.), and Coloureds (q.v.). In its most developed form in the 1960s, it meant, on the one hand, racial discrimination in almost all areas of life and, on the other, the grand apartheid of the bantustan policy (q.v.). Beyond this it continued to lack coherence.

An early Marxist interpretation of apartheid saw it as a rational response to the breakdown of the reserve economy, and a means of keeping labor costs low when the reserves (q.v.) could no longer bear the cost of reproducing the labor force. Most scholars have, however, viewed apartheid as primarily a political device to preserve racial identity and secure and bolster white supremacy and white privilege. In its early years it was also a means of consolidating the position of the Afrikaner nationalist (q.v.) movement. By the end of the 1950s, apartheid had become, in the guise of separate development, a policy to enable white supremacy to survive in the face of an emerging African nationalism, by dividing and repressing that nationalism and obscuring a naked white supremacist position (*see also* BAASSKAP).

It is impossible in a few words to express the extent of the hardships suffered by the victims of apartheid; it was enormously damaging psychologically, and it led to such atrocities as the forced removal of over three million people in an attempt to remove from white South Africa as many blacks as possible without endangering the labor supply.

Relatively minor aspects of apartheid began to be abandoned by the government in the 1970s. In stages, multiracial sport was allowed and certain color-bar restrictions were eased. From the late 1970s, apartheid began to be reformulated, partly as a result of strong resistance from within the country and from the international community, and in part because it was economically impractical and was creating ever more violent conflict within the country. A major step in this process was taken in 1983 when Coloureds and Indians were brought into parliament through the tricameral (q.v.) system. The pass laws (q.v.), a central feature of apartheid, were abolished in 1986. But the mid-1980s saw some of the harshest repression and the most violent actions in support of apartheid, including the killing of anti-apartheid activists by members of the security forces. It was not until the early 1990s that the remaining central pillars of the policy were abandoned. Apartheid in education (q.v.) remained for a time after the election of the first democratic government in 1994. The ruinous legacies of apartheid would bedevil the attempt to consolidate the new democracy and create a just and prosperous society.

APPRENTICESHIP. An *inboekeling* (from the Dutch, meaning "those booked in") system of labor, widely used in the interior of South Africa in the late 18th and early 19th centuries. Khoisan (q.v.) boys and girls seized in raids or military campaigns were apprenticed to trekboer (q.v.) farmers, in theory for a limited period but usually until well into adulthood. Their children were in turn bound to the masters of their parents. In 1812, a Cape (q.v.) proclamation sought to regularize indentured servitude by restricting the practice to persons from 8 to 18 years of age. In addition to food, clothing, and shelter, apprentices were supposed to be given some form of instruction by employers, but this was rarely done.

When slaves (q.v.) at the Cape were emancipated in 1834, they were apprenticed to their former masters for a further four years, but few received any education. Similarly, people freed from slave ships by the British navy after 1808 received little instruction; more than 4,000 of these "prize Negroes" were indentured for 14-year periods between 1808 and 1844. The practice of apprenticeship was extended into the interior by the Voortrekkers (q.v.) and their descendants after the late 1830s. African homesteads were raided regularly by Boers (q.v.) in search of "black ivory," and thousands of children were captured. This captive labor formed an important basis of the economies of the fledgling Boer states, enriching state officials in particular. Boer leaders agreed not to practice slavery when their independence was recognized by Britain in the early 1850s, but they regarded the apprenticeship system as qualitatively different: male apprentices worked until the age of 25, could not be sold for cash (though they could be bartered for goods), and were registered (or "booked in") by court officials to ensure regulation of the system.

ARMS EMBARGO. A nonmandatory embargo was imposed by the United Nations (UN) (q.v.) Security Council in 1963, in the aftermath of the Sharpeville massacre (q.v.). This became a mandatory embargo when on 4 November 1977, after the Soweto uprising (q.v.) and the murder of Steve Biko (q.v.), the Security Council passed a resolution declaring it illegal for any member of the UN to supply South Africa with arms. Some arms continued to flow in from Eastern Europe and Third World countries, with Israel and Taiwan acting as third-party agents. In the mid-

1980s, the United States, which had a more restrictive policy than the UN embargo required, threatened to cut off military aid to allies suspected of breaking the international arms embargo. This induced Israel to renounce new military contracts and cut back on scientific cooperation on arms-related items.

In response to the embargo, South Africa developed its own arms industry, which grew until it not only met most local requirements but was also able to export weapons to other countries. Armscor, a public armaments manufacturing corporation, was established in 1966 to promote self-sufficiency in arms, and by 1988 arms were the country's largest type of manufactured export. In 1988 a new armored vehicle, the Rooikat, was unveiled, and work was begun on an attack helicopter, the Rooivalk. The South African–developed G5 and G6 155 mm howitzers, seen in action in southern Angola (q.v.) in 1988, were later used in the Iran–Iraq War.

Despite the lifting of most sanctions (q.v.) in 1991, the arms embargo remained in place until after the installation of the first democratic government in May 1994. Even after it was lifted, Armscor had to deal with arms-smuggling charges, which had been brought against it, and associated companies in the United States, in November 1991. The new government argued that the charges should be dropped, because the smuggling had taken place under the former regime, but the United States administration would not lift sanctions against Armscor until it had appeared in court. After years of dispute, a settlement was reached in 1997: Armscor and the other companies were fined for violating U.S. arms export controls, and the arms embargo was finally lifted in February 1998. Under the democratic government, South Africa continued to sell considerable quantities of weapons, and much about the arms trade continues to be shrouded in secrecy.

ART. South Africa's earliest paintings date back more than 20,000 years to the rock art of the San (q.v.), who depicted their physical environment and spiritual experience through paintings and engravings. During the 18th and 19th centuries, European travelers and colonial officials began to sketch their surroundings and produced a significant amount of pictorial Africana. Thomas Baines (q.v.) was perhaps the leading figure in this genre of art. During the 20th century, South African–born professional painters began to establish their reputations locally and internationally. Landscapists such as J. E. A. Volschenk, Hugo Naudé, Frans Oerder, and Pieter Wenning contributed significantly to the development of South African art. Irma Stern and Maggie Laubser were important pioneers of expressionist innovation from the 1920s, and in the late 1930s the postimpressionist work of Walter Battiss and Alexis Preller, inspired by African symbols from the past, won considerable recognition. Gerard Sekoto and black artists from the townships represented a different tradition of humanistic figurative expressionism; Sydney Kumalo and Michael Zondi were among the country's most important sculptors.

ASIANS. *See* CHINESE; INDIANS.

AUTSHUMATO (d. 1663). Also known as Harry or Herry, Autshumato was an important intermediary between the first European settlers at the Cape (q.v.) and the indigenous people they found there. He led the Goringhaicona, a small, impoverished group of Khoikhoi (q.v.) outcasts who lived on the shores of Table Bay and were known to early European sailors and settlers as "Strandlopers" (literally, "beach walkers"). Autshumato learned to speak English when he was taken to Java by English sailors in about 1631. After the first Dutch settlement in 1652, he developed close ties with the settlers, who were heavily reliant on his knowledge of local conditions. He managed to build considerable prestige and wealth but fell victim to interclan Khoikhoi rivalry and was banished to Robben Island (q.v.) after losing the trust of the settlers.

AZANIA. The term *Azania,* a Greek form of the Persian word *zanj-bar* (Zanzibar) meaning "land of the blacks," has been used since the first century A.D. to denote the east African coast. In the 1970s it was taken over by some black (q.v.) South Africans, especially in the Pan Africanist Congress of Azania (q.v.) and black consciousness (q.v.) organizations, as an authentic "African" name for their country. After the banning (q.v.) of the black consciousness organizations in 1977, an Azanian People's Organization (q.v.) was founded with similar objectives, but these organizations remained peripheral, and the name "Azania" never acquired widespread acceptance.

AZANIAN PEOPLE'S LIBERATION ARMY. *See* PAN AFRICANIST CONGRESS.

AZANIAN PEOPLE'S ORGANIZATION. The Azanian People's Organization was a black consciousness (q.v.) organization founded in 1978 to work for a socialist state to be known as Azania (q.v.). Although its rhetoric was radical, its membership remained small. It rejected the compromises that the African National Congress (q.v.) made in the negotiations prior to the April 1994 election and refused to participate in that election. It then fell victim to internecine quarrels, which split the organization in two.

-B-

BAARTMAN, SAARTJE (d. 1815). A Khoisan (q.v.) woman, Saartje Baartman was transported from the Cape (q.v.) to England in 1810, at about the age of 20. Exhibited as a freak and perceived and portrayed as the Hottentot (q.v.) Venus, she was taken in 1814 to Paris, where an animal trainer paraded her daily in a shed until her death. Her body was then dissected, and her genitals and buttocks, seen as protuberant, excessive, and grotesque, were turned into scientific exhibits. She became an icon for alleged sexual and racial differences between whites (q.v.) and blacks (q.v.) in the development of 19th-century racial science. In 1996–97 a movement led by mostly Griqua (q.v.) people campaigned for the return of her remains from Paris as part of a way to claim back their past.

BAASSKAP. In the late 1950s, Prime Minister J. G. Strijdom (q.v.) described his government's policy as *baasskap* (Afrikaans for "boss-ship"; thus, grounded in blatant racial domination). H. F. Verwoerd (q.v.), who became his successor in 1958, realized that *baasskap* was morally indefensible and hoped to deflect international criticism by reformulating the policy as "separate development." *See also* APARTHEID; BANTUSTAN POLICY.

BADEN-POWELL, ROBERT (1857–1941). Robert Baden-Powell, a British soldier, became famous in the South African War (q.v.) for his leadership during the seven-month Boer siege of Mafeking in the western Transvaal (q.v.). Because of the siege, he was able to establish the Boy Scout movement, to which he devoted his energies after he resigned from the army.

BAILEY, ABE (1864–1940). Mine magnate and politician, Abe Bailey made a fortune on the Witwatersrand (q.v.) goldfields and from other investments. He worked to promote British interests in South Africa and became a leading philanthropist.

BAINES, THOMAS (1820–75). Prominent artist, traveler, and explorer, Thomas Baines left a priceless legacy in the thousands of paintings, drawings, and sketches he completed between his arrival in Cape Town (q.v.) in 1842 and his death in Durban (q.v.). His works mainly depict the landscapes and peoples of southern Africa and reveal keen powers of observation and great perception.

BAKER, HERBERT (1862–1946). The most significant figure in South African architecture, Herbert Baker sailed to South Africa from England in 1892, became a close friend of Cecil Rhodes (q.v.), and designed numerous buildings, from modest houses to the Union Buildings, in Pretoria (q.v.). He left South Africa in 1912.

BALLINGER, MARGARET (1894–1980). An immigrant to South Africa from Scotland in 1904, Margaret Hodgson was educated at Rhodes and Oxford universities and was from 1920 a lecturer in history at the University of the Witwatersrand. She was forced to give up that post when she married William Ballinger of the Industrial and Commercial Workers' Union of South Africa (q.v.) in 1934. Three years later she entered Parliament as native representative for the Cape Division, having been asked to stand by the African National Congress (q.v.). A forceful critic of government policy and a strong champion of African interests, she retained her seat until African representation was abolished in 1960. From 1948 to 1960 she was the leading critic of apartheid (q.v.) in Parliament. A founding member of the Liberal Party (q.v.), she was also its first leader, but she resigned in 1955 because she could no longer combine her duties as parliamentarian with the party post. She disliked the party's shift to the left from the late 1950s but in the mid-1960s returned to party activity. In retirement she wrote *From Union to Apartheid* (1969).

BAMBATHA REBELLION (1906–7). The main precipitant of the Bambatha Rebellion, the last armed revolt in South Africa organized by a traditional ruler, was the imposition of a poll tax on all adult African males in Natal (q.v.) at the end of 1905. In February 1906, two white police officers were killed by armed Africans in the Richmond district; martial law was proclaimed, and the militia mobilized. Bambatha (ca. 1865–1906), a Zulu subruler in the Umvoti district, became the focus of resistance. He and his followers retreated to the Nkandla forest, where they engaged in guerrilla struggle. In June 1906, this resistance was crushed at the Mome Gorge, and Bambatha was killed, but further resistance continued in northern Natal until 1907. Between 3,500 and 4,000 Africans were killed, and about two dozen whites. Whites mainly blamed Ethiopianism, but although some *amakholwa* (q.v.) participated in the rebellion, most remained neutral and were regarded by the rebels as traitors. The uprising led the British government and many in the Cape (q.v.) to believe that small vulnerable states such as Natal would inevitably be prone to panic and brutality in their treatment of Africans, and this idea helped promote the cause of unification in South Africa.

BANNING. Various persons, meetings, organizations, and publications were banned under South African law in the apartheid (q.v.) era (1948–90). There were precedents for this: in 1929 an amendment to the Riotous Assemblies Act gave the minister of justice the power to order any person to leave a magisterial district; this was used to restrict the movement of trade union leaders and political opponents. Significantly wider powers, given to the government by the Suppression of Communism Act of 1950, were used extensively thereafter. The typical banning order issued under this act, as amended, restricted an individual to a magisterial district, required the banned person to report regularly to the police, prevented anything said by the person from being quoted, excluded him or her from visiting such places as educational institutions, factories, and harbors, and prevented him or her from meeting socially with more than one person at a time. A banned person was usually the subject of constant police surveillance, and if the police suspected noncompliance, the person was brought to court. There was no appeal to the courts against a banning order, which was usually for five years and was often renewed thereafter. From 1962, banning orders sometimes meant total or partial house arrest, the banned person being prevented from leaving home.

Banning sometimes meant banishment: hundreds of Africans were forced to move to remote areas, where they were then restricted. (One of these was Winnie Madikizela-Mandela [q.v.].) Major political prisoners were usually banned or banished, or both, on completion of their prison sentences. The Suppression of Communism Act also outlawed the Communist Party of South Africa (q.v.) and provided for persons to be reported for promoting the aims of communism, which was defined extremely broadly. Such named persons were then listed and were forbidden to attend gatherings or belong to certain organizations; nothing they said could be quoted, nothing they wrote published. Under other legislation the African National Congress (q.v.) and Pan Africanist Congress of Azania (q.v.) were banned in April 1960, the Black People's Convention (a black consciousness [q.v.] organization) and the Christian Institute of Southern Africa (q.v.) in October 1977. The United Democratic Front (q.v.) was heavily restricted in February 1988. Various left-wing and African newspapers were forced to close down. Between 1950 and 1990, some 30,000 political publications were banned under various laws. After the unbanning of political organizations on 2 February 1990, the entire system fell away.

BANTU EDUCATION. The 1953 Bantu Education Act instituted an educational system for Africans designed to fit them for their role in apartheid (q.v.) society as H. F. Verwoerd (q.v.), architect of the act, conceived that role: "There is no place for [the African] in the European community above the level of certain forms of labour. . . . It is of no avail for him to receive a training which has as its aim absorption in the European community" (from a speech in Parliament on the bill in 1952). In 1953, 90 percent of African schools were state-aided mission schools; the act removed control of African education from the churches and provincial authorities and placed it under a separate central government department. Only the Roman Catholic Church (q.v.) attempted to keep its schools going without state aid. The 1953 act also separated the financing of education for Africans from general state expenditure and linked it to a direct tax paid by Africans themselves, which meant that far less was spent on African children than on white children.

Expenditure on Bantu education increased dramatically from the late 1960s because of a recognition of the need for a trained African labor force; this meant that more and more African children obtained some education. Although Bantu education was designed to isolate Africans and prevent them from being exposed to subversive ideas, indignation at being given such inferior education became a major focus for resistance, most notably in the Soweto uprising (q.v.). In the 1980s very little education at all took place in the Bantu education system, which was the target of almost continuous protest. The legacy of decades of inferior education would last far beyond the introduction of a single educational system in 1995. *See also* EDUCATION.

BANTU-SPEAKING PEOPLE. The Bantu language group includes hundreds of related languages (q.v.) spoken in most of sub-Saharan Africa. Precisely when and how these languages spread into southern Africa remains uncertain, but it is probable that the first mixed (both pastoral and agricultural) farmers and first users of iron technology, who settled south of the Limpopo River (q.v.) about 1,800 years ago, brought with them a Bantu language. Those who spoke such languages are thought to have spread slowly southward and westward. Whites (q.v.) first encountered Bantu speakers in the eastern Cape (q.v.) in the 16th century and in the central interior at the beginning of the 19th century. Linguists have divided Bantu speakers into four main categories: Nguni (q.v.) speakers settled in the eastern coastal region, between the Indian Ocean and the Drakensberg (q.v.) range, and practiced pastoralism, cultivation, and hunting. Settlements tended to be small, although toward the end of the 18th century the northern Nguni began a process of consolidation and state formation. The Sotho–Tswana (qq.v.) lived on the high veld (q.v.) in the interior in large settlements and engaged in mining, smelting, and extensive trade as well as herding, cultivation, and hunting. Venda and Thonga (qq.v.) speakers remained confined to the extreme northern and northeastern parts of the country, respectively.

When white settlement began in the mid-17th century, Bantu-speaking farmers, perhaps between one million and two million in all, occupied most of the well-watered areas of the country, apart from the extreme southwestern portion. Their polities, though still relatively small, were stronger and more complex than those of the Khoikhoi (q.v.) pastoralists, some of whom were absorbed into Bantu-speaking groups.

The term *Bantu* replaced *native* in official government usage during the 1960s and 1970s and was despised by Africans chiefly because of its association with apartheid (q.v.) and inferior treatment. The words *Bantu* and *Bantus* were grammatical absurdities. From 1977 *Bantu* was gradually replaced by *black* (q.v.). *See also* AFRICAN.

BANTUSTAN POLICY. H. F. Verwoerd (q.v.), minister of native affairs and then prime minister, and Dr. W. M. Eiselen, his secretary for native affairs, were the architects of the policy of transforming the African reserves (q.v.) into self-governing states, the bantustans. In 1951, Verwoerd ruled out the possibility of full independence for these states, but in 1959 this became the goal of policy. Formulated in part as a response to increasing international pressure on South Africa to give some political rights to Africans (q.v.) in an era of African decolonization and independence, the bantustan policy was designed to maintain and strengthen white supremacy in the greater part of the country.

There were three main phases in the evolution of the bantustan policy. The Bantu Authorities Act (1951) created a hierarchical system of authority in the reserves in which appointed chiefs and headmen played a key role. Territorial authorities were set up for each so-called ethnic group, except that the Xhosa (q.v.), for historical reasons, were given separate authorities on either side of the Kei River. Chiefs who did not cooperate in the new system were deposed and replaced, whereas those who cooperated became more clearly identified as instruments of the state. There was considerable resistance at the popular level to the implementation of the Bantu Authorities Act, especially in Pondoland (q.v.), in the Transkei (q.v.), in the Pedi bantustan (q.v.), and in the eastern Transvaal (q.v.). In the second phase, the Promotion of Bantu Self-Government Act (1959) recognized eight national units (also called homelands) on ethnic grounds and provided the machinery for these territories to be led to self-government. A ninth was later created in the Transvaal (q.v.) for the Ndzundza Ndebele (q.v.). The Transkei, which had the largest single block of land under African occupation, was the first to be given limited self-government in 1963.

The third phase took the bantustans from self-government to full independence. Again the Transkei led the way, being given its independence in October 1976, followed by Bophuthatswana (q.v.) in the western Transvaal, the Ciskei (q.v.) in the eastern Cape (q.v.), and Venda (q.v.) in the far northern Transvaal. Other bantustans, including KwaZulu (q.v.), obtained self-government but not nominal independence, for Mangosuthu Buthelezi (q.v.) of KwaZulu and Cedric Phatudi, chief minister of Lebowa in the Transvaal, refused to consider independence for their territories. Because the whole bantustan policy was an integral part of apartheid (q.v.), none of the independent bantustans received international recognition. Each was recognized only by South Africa and the other independent bantustans (though the Transkei did not recognize Ciskei, because it wanted one political unit for all Xhosa speakers).

For the new ruling elites, "independence" brought a certain power and status, considerable investment by Pretoria (q.v.), and the opportunity to rid their countries of the racial indignities of apartheid. The rulers were quick to use authoritarian methods against their opponents, and their regimes were soon notorious for corruption. The possession of a casino, forbidden in South Africa proper, was often the best-known token of independence. As bantustans became independent, large numbers of Africans, whether they lived in them or not, were deprived of their South African citizenship and made citizens of the new states. Government spokesmen expressed the hope that if all bantustans could be led to independence or absorbed by other states—KaNgwane (q.v.), for Swazis, by Swaziland (q.v.); QwaQwa (q.v.) by Lesotho (formerly Basutoland [q.v.])—no Africans would have South African citizenship or any claim to rights within South Africa.

In reality, the bantustans were rural slums, totally dependent on South Africa. Only the minute QwaQwa (q.v.), on the border of Lesotho, was a single block of land. The South African government spent vast sums buying land for homeland consolidation. In 1960 about one-third of the African (q.v.) population of South Africa lived within the borders of these territories; by 1980 more than 40 percent did, because of some adjustments of borders, a fierce influx control (q.v.) policy, and forced removals. In 1955, the Tomlinson Commission (q.v.) found that the maximum number of people these territories could support was 2.3 million, but by 1981 three times that number were living in them, and in that year they contributed only 3 percent to the country's total output. Well over half their economically active men were away working as migrants (q.v.) at any one time. Although Bophuthatswana was the best endowed, thanks to platinum and the Sun City hotel complex, all the bantustans could survive only on handouts from Pretoria. Superfluous bureaucracies were created, at great expense to the South African taxpayer. In Transkei, Ciskei, and Venda, military rulers took power and governed autocratically.

The reincorporation of the bantustans was a sine qua non for the African National Congress (ANC) (q.v.), and in the run-up to the April 1994 election, ANC leaders targeted bantustan governments hostile to them, in particular Ciskei, Bophuthatswana, and KwaZulu. An ANC-organized march across the Ciskei border to the capital, Bisho (q.v.), on 7 September 1992, was fired upon by Ciskeian troops. With the advent of a democratic order in April 1994, all the bantustans became part of the nine provinces of the new South Africa.

BARENDS, BAREND (ca. 1770–1839). Leader of a group of people of mixed descent in the Orange River (q.v.) area at the end of the 18th century, Barend Barends was persuaded by missionaries (q.v.) of the London Missionary Society (q.v.) to settle at Klaarwater (later Griquatown) in 1804. Within 10 years, his people had merged into those called Griqua (q.v.), a relatively stable and established community in the area that came to be called Griqualand West (q.v.).

BARNARD, LADY ANNE (1750–1825). Lady Anne Barnard was a writer and socialite who lived at the Cape (q.v.) between 1797 and 1802. Her journals and letters, which record her extensive travels at the Cape and her close contacts with British and Dutch leaders from all walks of life, provide a valuable source of information on the period of the first British occupation (q.v.) of the Cape.

BARNATO, BARNEY (1852–97). A prominent diamond magnate, Barney Barnato's career epitomized the dreams of thousands who sought their fortunes from the diamond (q.v.) mines of Kimberley (q.v.). Born Barnett Isaacs into a Jewish family from the Whitechapel district in London's East End, he arrived in Kimberley penniless in 1873 and managed to build his wealth through the Kimberley Central Company, which by 1888 had succeeded in taking over all the holdings at the Kimberley mine. Barnato's company was, in turn, taken over by the De Beers (q.v.) Company of Cecil Rhodes (q.v.), for a sum of more than £5 million. Barnato served as a member of the Cape Legislative Assembly. He died mysteriously at sea.

BARRY, JAMES (ca. 1795–1865). A prominent surgeon at the Cape (q.v.) and the personal physician to Lord Somerset (q.v.), who was the governor of the Cape from 1814 to 1826, Barry was later medical inspector for the Cape Colony (q.v.) and principal medical officer of the army at the Cape. She clashed regularly with the authorities over conditions in prisons and hospitals and gained posthumous notoriety when it was discovered, on her death, that she had spent her life disguised as a man, in order to pursue a medical career.

BARRY COMMISSION (1881–83). The Cape (q.v.) government Commission on Native Laws and Customs was known as the Barry Commission, after its chairman, J. D. Barry (1832–1905), a judge of the Cape's Eastern Districts Court. Appointed immediately after the Transkeian rebellion of 1880, the last armed African resistance to Cape rule, the commission recommended a system of law for the conquered societies east of the Kei River. It collected a mass of valuable evidence from Theophilus Shepstone (q.v.) and others, and its report helped reshape Cape African policy from "identity"—one law for all—toward differential administration for the large African (q.v.) population of the Transkei (q.v.).

BASTARDS. The term *bastard (bastaard, baster)* was used in the 18th century for the offspring of mixed unions of whites with people of color, most commonly Khoikhoi (q.v.) but also, less frequently, slaves (q.v.). The offspring of African-Khoikhoi or slave-Khoikhoi unions were sometimes known as Bastard-Hottentots. Children produced of extramarital liaisons between whites (q.v.) and people of color were not usually regarded as white, and Bastards were not usually accepted as free burghers (q.v.). Only in a few rare cases were children born out of wedlock of white fathers and Khoikhoi mothers baptized and accorded burgher status. Most offspring of white-Khoikhoi unions were regarded by whites as free persons of color—"free" because they were not slaves.

Rejected by white society, Bastards often formed separate communities on or beyond the Cape's (q.v.) northern frontier. There, many lived a precarious existence between the advancing trekboers (q.v.) and indigenous peoples. Most Bastards used the name with pride, viewing themselves as superior to Khoikhoi because of their white blood. The term was also extended to poor whites and dispossessed Khoikhoi who spoke some Dutch and owned firearms. One group of Bastards living north of the Orange River (q.v.) in the early 19th century was persuaded by a missionary of the London Missionary Society (q.v.) to change its name to Griqua (q.v.).

BASUTOLAND. The country of the BaSotho (southern Sotho [q.v.]), the state created by Moshoeshoe (q.v.), was annexed by the British high commissioner, Sir Philip Wodehouse, in 1868. Called Basutoland by whites (q.v.), it was taken over by the Cape (q.v.) in 1871. The magisterial system the Cape government then imposed provoked Sotho resistance; a small revolt in the southwest of the region in 1878 developed into more widespread rebellion in 1880, when the Cape attempted to disarm the people. After the Gun War (1880–81) ended in stalemate, the Cape, unable to assert its authority, asked Britain to assume direct responsibility for the territory; this occurred in 1884. During the 1870s, Basutoland supplied large quantities of grain to the diamond (q.v.) fields, but by the early 20th century it was importing food and exporting only migrant (q.v.) laborers. The segregationist policies of South African governments after creation of the Union (q.v.) precluded its incorporation into South Africa.

When it achieved its independence from Britain in 1966 under the name Lesotho, the country was already suffering extreme poverty and so was almost entirely dependent on South Africa. In the late 1960s, Chief Leabua Jonathan, though still advancing a claim to land in the eastern Orange Free State (q.v.), developed friendly relations with the B. J. Vorster (q.v.) government, but in the 1970s he switched support to the African National Congress (ANC) (q.v.). This, in turn, led the opposition Basutoland Congress Party to seek support from elements within South Africa favoring apartheid (q.v.). In the early 1980s, the South African Defence Force (q.v.) twice launched raids to kill ANC cadres living in Maseru, the capital. The imposition of a trade embargo by the South African authorities forced out the government, allowing pro–South African military men to take over. With the advent of a democratic regime in South Africa in 1994, relations between the two countries became more harmonious. A giant Highlands Water scheme, designed in the mid-1980s to provide water to the Witwatersrand (q.v.), was continued and helped bind the two countries even further together; the first water from the Lesotho dams built in the first phase of the scheme reached South Africa at the beginning of 1998. At the same time, tens of thousands of Sotho migrants lost jobs on South Africa's gold (q.v.) mines, intensifying poverty in the mountain kingdom.

BATAVIAN RULE OF THE CAPE (1803–6). Following the first British occupation (1795–1803) (q.v.), the Cape (q.v.) was ruled by the Batavian regime then in power in the Netherlands. The military governor, Jan Willem Janssens (1762–1838), assisted by an astute administrator, J. A. U. de Mist (1749–1823), implemented an extensive reform of the system of government, but financial constraints prevented them from dealing with frontier (q.v.) issues. At the Battle of Blaauwberg (q.v.), near Cape Town (q.v.), in January 1806, a British force under General David Baird defeated Janssens and inaugurated the second, and permanent, British occupation. Historians once judged the Batavian period an enlightened one but now stress how conservative and authoritarian it was.

BECHUANALAND. Believing that the Transvaal's (q.v.) westward expansion was threatening the strategically and economically important Road to the North (q.v.) and fearing that the Transvaal might eventually link up with German South West Africa (now Namibia [q.v.]) and cut the Road completely, Britain annexed Bechuanaland ("land of the Tswana" [q.v.]) in 1885. The region south of the Molopo River, the crown colony of British Bechuanaland, was incorporated into the Cape in 1895; much of it was to form part of the Bophuthatswana (q.v.) bantustan (q.v.) in the 1970s. The large area north of the Molopo, the Bechuanaland Protectorate, remained a High Commission territory (q.v.) until 1966, when it acquired independence as Botswana. After independence a major diamond (q.v.) industry was built up with De Beers (q.v.) expertise, though Debswana emerged as a separate company. Seretse Khama (1921–80), a Botswana chief whose marriage to a white English woman had greatly upset the apartheid (q.v.) government of D. F. Malan (q.v.), skillfully allowed people fleeing apartheid to transit through Botswana but would not give open support to the African National Congress (ANC) (q.v.). In June 1985 and May 1986, however, the South African Defence Force (q.v.) launched raids on ANC cadres living in Gaborone, the Botswana capital. After South Africa became a democratic country in 1994, the two countries worked together in the Southern African Development Community (q.v.).

BEIT, ALFRED (1853–1906). A prominent mining magnate and a close confidant of Cecil Rhodes (q.v.), Alfred Beit assisted Rhodes in the amalgamation of the diamond (q.v.) mines in Kimberley (q.v.), as well as with the foundation of De Beers (q.v.) Consolidated Mines in 1888 and the British South Africa Company (q.v.) in 1889. A pioneer in the gold-mining (q.v.) industry in Johannesburg (q.v.), he provided capital for the sinking of deep-level shafts on the Witwatersrand (q.v.).

BERLIN MISSIONARY SOCIETY. Formed in Berlin, Germany, in 1824, the Berlin Missionary Society began to work in southern Africa in 1834, when five missionaries of the society established a mission station called Bethany among the Korana (q.v.), on land granted by the Griqua (q.v.) leader Adam Kok III (q.v.), in what became the Orange River Sovereignty (q.v.). The society established missions across southern Africa and also worked among laborers in the gold (q.v.) mines. *See also* MISSIONARIES.

BIKO, STEPHEN BANTU (1946–77). Founder and martyr of the black consciousness (q.v.) movement, Steve Biko was born in King William's Town. He attended a Roman Catholic school in Natal (q.v.) and then the University of Natal Medical School. Under his inspiration, African students broke with the National Union of South African Students (q.v.) and established their separate South African Students' Organization (q.v.) in 1969. Dropping his medical studies, the charismatic Biko emerged as an outstanding organizer and theoretician, promoting black consciousness through his writing, speeches, and actions. From 1973 he endured banning (q.v.) and other forms of state harassment. In September 1977 he died after being assaulted while in police custody. The minister of justice suggested Biko had died as a result of a hunger strike and said his death left him cold. The subsequent inquest revealed that Biko had suffered brain damage and other injuries and then been kept naked and chained while transported overland from Port Elizabeth to Pretoria (qq.v.). The magistrate who presided at the inquest failed to find any person responsible for his death. Biko's family sued the state for damages and in 1979 settled for an out-of-court payment. The policemen responsible for his death applied for amnesty from the Truth and Reconciliation Commission (q.v.) in 1997.

Biko's murder provoked an outraged reaction both in South Africa and abroad. The government responded in October 1977 by banning various individuals and organizations, including the black consciousness bodies Biko had been involved with. The following month the United Nations (q.v.) Security Council agreed to a mandatory arms embargo (q.v.) against South Africa.

BISHO MASSACRE. On 7 September 1992, tens of thousands of African National Congress (ANC) (q.v.) supporters marched from King William's Town to Bisho, capital of the Ciskei (q.v.) bantustan (q.v.) to push for the removal of the Ciskei military leader, Brigadier Oupa Gqozo, from power. The march was part of an ANC campaign to unseat bantustan leaders who were seen to be allies of the apartheid (q.v.) government and were unwilling to allow free political activity in their territories. Some of the unarmed demonstrators left the agreed path of the march, and Ciskei soldiers opened fire on them, killing 28 and injuring 200. This shock to the ANC helped bring it back to the negotiating table and led directly to the Record of Understanding (q.v.) between the government and the ANC.

BLAAUWBERG, BATTLE OF (1806). The Battle of Blaauwberg was fought just north of Cape Town (q.v.) between the Dutch defenders of the Cape (q.v.) and the invading British forces. The victory of the latter meant the reestablishment of British rule, which then lasted into the 20th century. *See also* BRITISH OCCUPATION OF THE CAPE.

BLACK CIRCUIT. Circuit courts were introduced by the Cape (q.v.) governor Sir John Cradock in 1811 to extend government control and justice over the frontier (q.v.) districts; they were partly intended to control Khoikhoi (q.v.) vagrancy and regularize master-servant relations. In 1812, the black circuit court sat, at which a number of colonists were accused of ill-treating their Khoikhoi servants on the basis of evidence collected by the missionaries (q.v.) James Read and Johannes van der Kemp (q.v.). Eight farmers were convicted, causing great resentment among the frontier colonists.

BLACK CONSCIOUSNESS. In reaction to white racism (q.v.) and liberal paternalism, black intellectuals, led by Steve Biko (q.v.), decided in the late 1960s that blacks (defined as all who were discriminated against on grounds of race) must organize themselves to promote black assertiveness and self-esteem, as blacks in the United States were doing. Blacks were told to rid themselves of their slave (q.v.) mentality: "Black man, you are on your own," was the cry, and other slogans were freely borrowed from the American Black Power movement.

From the all-black South African Students' Organization (SASO) (q.v.) there emerged in 1972 a Black People's Convention (BPC), an umbrella political organization, to unite and solidify the black people of South Africa with a view to liberating and emancipating them from both psychological and physical oppression. Advocates of black consciousness viewed the struggle in color, not class, terms; its philosophy appealed to a small educated elite, at the black universities and church seminaries, and it never won mass worker support. African critics of black consciousness either argued that Coloureds (q.v.) and Indians (q.v.) had different interests or rejected the emphasis black consciousness placed on race.

Various black self-help, legal aid, and community programs were established, but from 1973 the government, which initially had tolerated the movement because it seemed to fit in with "separate development" ideology, began to clamp down on the black consciousness movement. Virtually the whole leadership of SASO and the BPC was banned (q.v.); in 1974 rallies in support of the Frelimo government taking power in Mozambique (q.v.) were broken up by the police; and in 1975 twelve BPC and SASO leaders were charged under the Terrorism Act, nine of whom were subsequently convicted. *See also* APARTHEID; BANTUSTAN POLICY.

The black consciousness movement contributed significantly to the ferment behind the Soweto uprising (q.v.), but in September 1977 Biko died in detention, and the following month the black consciousness organizations were banned. Black consciousness ideas lived on in the Azanian People's Organization (q.v.) and the banned Pan Africanist Congress (q.v.) in particular. However, many leading black consciousness members, especially those who were imprisoned on Robben Island (q.v.) or went into exile after the Soweto uprising, were persuaded of the merits of the African National Congress (q.v.).

BLACK SASH. The Women's Defence of the Constitution League, later known as the Black Sash, was founded in 1955 to propagate respect for the constitution at the time of the Coloured (q.v.) vote issue. Its members stood in silence in public places, carrying placards and wearing white dresses crossed by broad diagonal black sashes, a symbol of mourning for the government's treatment of the constitution. Although such picketing continued in subsequent decades, mainly on civil rights issues, the Black Sash's most significant work in the 1970s and 1980s was carried out in its advice offices in urban centers, which tried to help Africans with such problems as influx control (q.v.), unemployment, contracts, housing, and pensions.

BLACK SPOTS. When whites (q.v.) took over land from blacks (q.v.) in the 19th century, small areas in the midst of white-owned land were sometimes left in African hands. These became known as black spots by the apartheid (q.v.) regime, which took steps, especially in the 1960s and 1970s, to clear them and consolidate all such land in white hands. In the late 1980s and 1990s some of these areas were given back to their former occupants.

BLACKS. The black consciousness (q.v.) movement of the late 1960s and early 1970s defined as blacks all those who were discriminated against on the grounds of race. The older inclusive terms for Indians (q.v.), Coloureds (q.v.), and Africans (q.v.), *nonwhite* and *non-European,* were vehemently rejected as negative definitions, and *black* went with the new aggressive image sought by the leaders of the black consciousness movement. Nevertheless, the use of the term *black* to refer only to Africans remained widespread and was taken over by the government itself from 1977. Although the government accepted that *Bantu* was disliked by those of whom it had been used, *African* could not be translated into Afrikaans (q.v.), except as *Afrikaner* or *Afrikaan,* which would be confusing, and *black,* with its stress on color, fitted in with government policy.

Whether Indians or Coloureds called themselves blacks depended on whether or not they saw it to be in their interests to identify with Africans. Whether Africans spoke of blacks in the wider sense depended on their preparedness to work with these other groups. In this book, *black* is used in the more inclusive sense, to refer to Africans, Coloureds, and Indians. *See also* FREE BLACKS.

BLEEK, WILHELM HEINRICH IMMANUEL (1827–75). A German-born linguist, scholar, and librarian, W. H. I. Bleek's most important work was on the /Xam language of the southern San (q.v.). Together with his sister-in-law, Lucy Lloyd, who transcribed San myths and ritual accounts, he compiled more than 12,000 pages of /Xam texts with English translations—an unrivaled ethnographic collection. His work was continued by his daughter, Dorothea Bleek, who produced a Bushman dictionary based on his research. *See also* SAN.

BLOEMFONTEIN. Capital of the Free State (q.v.), one of South Africa's nine provinces, Bloemfontein was founded in 1846 by Major Douglas Warden as a fort. It became the center of the British-administered Orange River Sovereignty (1848–54) (q.v.) and of the independent Boer Republic of the Orange Free State (q.v.) (1854–1900). After the creation of the Union (q.v.) of South Africa in 1910, Bloemfontein became the judicial capital of South Africa, housing the appellate division of the Supreme Court. In the late 1990s it put itself forward as a possible seat for Parliament, were it to move from Cape Town (q.v.).

BLOEMFONTEIN CONVENTION. In a February 1854 treaty, the British recognized the independence of the Boers (q.v.) living between the Orange (q.v.) and Vaal Rivers. Known as the Bloemfontein Convention, it made possible the establishment of the Republic of the Orange Free State (q.v.).

BLOOD RIVER, BATTLE OF (1838). After considerable conflict between the Voortrekkers (q.v.) and the Zulu king Dingane (q.v.) in what is now KwaZulu-Natal (q.v.), a Voortrekker (q.v.) commando (q.v.) of 470 men under the leadership of Andries Pretorius (1798–1853) set out to encounter the forces of Dingane. On 16 December 1838, at Blood River, their *laager* (a circle of ox-drawn wagons bound together to keep enemies at bay) was attacked by an army of some 10,000 Zulu soldiers. More than 3,000 Zulu were killed, while only three men on the Voortrekker side were wounded. The disaster forced the Zulu to recognize Voortrekker claims to Natal (q.v.), and white settlement in the region was never again seriously threatened. *See also* ZULU KINGDOM.

Before the battle, the Voortrekkers had made a vow to commemorate the day of victory. In the 20th century, 16 December became a day of great emotional significance for Afrikaner nationalists (q.v.), who used it to stress their divine mission and proclaim their faith that God would stand with them against their enemies. The day was long known as Dingaan's Day, but it was renamed the Day of the Covenant in 1952 (and renamed again, in 1980, the Day of the Vow). It was the day chosen by Umkhonto weSizwe (q.v.) to launch its armed struggle in 1961 and so acquired new significance in resistance politics. Since 1995 it has been celebrated as the Day of Reconciliation.

BOER REPUBLICS. *See* ORANGE FREE STATE; SOUTH AFRICAN REPUBLIC.

BOERS. In the 18th century, the Afrikaans word, *Boers* (farmers), referred to white farmers, but in the 19th century it came to be used for Afrikaners (q.v.) in general, for the white inhabitants of the Voortrekker (q.v.) republics, or for those who fought on the republican side in the South African War (q.v.).

The term came to have derogatory connotations when used by non-Afrikaners. When used by English-speakers (q.v.), it suggested backwardness and lack of culture, and many blacks (q.v.) used it for any white person associated with racism and apartheid (q.v.).

BOER WAR. *See* SOUTH AFRICAN WAR.

BOESAK, ALLAN (1946–). Preacher and politician. Having grown up in poverty and suffered under the Group Areas Act (q.v.), he studied in the Netherlands in the 1970s for a doctorate in black power and black theology. As a minister in the Coloured section (Sendingkerk) of the Dutch Reformed Church (q.v.), he asked a meeting of the World Alliance of Reformed Churches in 1982 to declare apartheid (q.v.) a heresy, and was elected president of that organization. A founding member of the United Democratic Front (UDF) (q.v.) in August 1983, he led much UDF resistance in the mid-1980s, most notably a planned march on Pollsmoor prison in August 1985. He also founded and headed a Foundation for Peace and Justice, to channel foreign money to aid those who suffered under apartheid.

In 1990 his extramarital affair with a television producer was exposed, and he left the church. In 1994 he led the African National Congress's (q.v.) election campaign in the Western Cape, and after the election was named as ambassador-designate to the United Nations (q.v.) in Geneva. But then the leading donor supporting his foundation, DanChurch Aid of Denmark, questioned where some of its funds had gone to, and his ambassadorship was canceled. He left for the United States to teach and preach, but returned in March 1997 to face charges that he had misappropriated donor funds.

BOOMPLAATS, BATTLE OF (1848). Sir Harry Smith, governor of the Cape (q.v.) and high commissioner, led British forces to the north of the present Free State (q.v.) to defeat a Voortrekker (q.v.) commando under Andries Pretorius, who was seeking to reverse the British annexation of the land between the Orange (q.v.) and Vaal (q.v.) rivers. The British victory confirmed the establishment of British rule north of the Orange, and the Boers (q.v.) who had sought to resist it retreated north of the Vaal.

BOPHUTHATSWANA. Bantustan (q.v.) for the Tswana (q.v.) that the South African government led to nominal independence in 1977. It then comprised seven non-contiguous pieces of land in the central and western Transvaal (q.v.) and the north-western Cape (q.v.), as well as Thaba Nchu in the Orange Free State (q.v.). The most economically viable of all the bantustans, thanks to its platinum and chrome mines and the revenue it derived from the Sun City casino complex, it nevertheless obtained a quarter of its budget directly from Pretoria (q.v.) and another 30 percent from the South African customs union. Half its labor force worked outside its borders.

The autocratic Lucas Mangope (1923–), its first chief minister and then president, was ousted by a military coup in 1988 but then restored to power by the South African Defence Force (q.v.). A white Bophuthatswanan representative played an active role in the negotiations for a democratic South Africa in the early 1990s, but the end came quickly. In March 1994 civil servants went on strike; violence erupted in Mmabatho, the capital; and Mangope, in enlisting the support of General Viljoen (q.v.), opened the door to the arrival of members of the Afrikaner Resistance Movement (AWB) (q.v.), whose presence further inflamed the situation. Television cameras recorded a local soldier shooting two members of the AWB as they lay wounded besides their car. Representatives of the Transitional Executive Council (TEC) informed Mangope that he had to resign. Bophuthatswana was then administered by the TEC until formally reincorporated into South Africa in April 1994. A commission of inquiry in 1995 found that Mangope had been involved in massive corruption, and in 1997 a large number of charges were brought against him.

BOTHA, LOUIS (1862–1919). First prime minister of the Union (q.v.) of South Africa. The son of Voortrekker (q.v.) parents, he spent his early life in the north-eastern Orange Free State (q.v.). He aided Dinuzulu (q.v.) in the Zulu civil war of 1884 and settled in the New Republic, which was later incorporated into the Transvaal (q.v.). During the South African War (q.v.), in which he rose to the rank of general, he displayed outstanding tactical and leadership abilities. After the war, he forged ahead with a political career, becoming chairman of Het Volk (q.v.) in the Transvaal (1904), prime minister of the Transvaal (1907), and prime minister of the Union in 1910, a position he held until his death in 1919. He preached reconciliation between Afrikaners (q.v.) and English-speaking (q.v.) whites, and defended the preservation of South Africa's imperial connections with Britain. Many former Afrikaner allies were alienated by this stance, in particular by his forceful suppression of the Afrikaner Rebellion (q.v.) of 1914. The occupation of German South West Africa (*see* NAMIBIA) by South African forces in 1915 was regarded as one of his most significant triumphs. He attended the Paris Peace Conference in 1919 shortly before his death.

BOTHA, PIETER WILLEM (1916–). National Party (NP) (q.v.) prime minister and state president. A full-time NP organizer from 1936, he served in the South African parliament from 1948 to 1989. From 1966 he was minister of defence. His election as prime minister in September 1978 by the NP caucus (the parliamentary members meeting together) was a result of the Information Scandal, which divided the Transvaal (q.v.) members of the caucus and gave Botha, Cape (q.v.) leader of his party, the support of the Orange Free State (q.v.) bloc. Closely associated with the military, he supported the South African army's invasion of Angola (q.v.) in 1975 and the great increase in military spending thereafter. After his election as prime minister, government rhetoric became dominated by talk of total onslaught and a strategy to combat this onslaught. During his premiership vast destabilization took place of neighboring countries, the work of covert South African forces. Though he told his electorate soon after becoming prime minister that they must adapt or die, his reformist vision did not extend much beyond the establishment of a new tricameral (q.v.) constitution, which provided for a measure of Coloured (q.v.) and Indian (q.v.) participation in central government. This was enough to drive the far-right members to break from the NP in 1982 and establish the Conservative Party (q.v.).

Under the tricameral constitution, Botha became the country's first executive state president in 1984, with greatly increased powers. Always authoritarian in manner, his irascibility increased as resistance grew. His "Rubicon speech" of August 1985, which failed to deliver on expectations for change, was a disaster for the country, and in May 1986 he ended the attempt by the Commonwealth Eminent Persons Group to bring about negotiations between the government and the African National Congress (ANC) (q.v.). But he did abolish the pass laws (q.v.), permitted his officials to begin negotiations with the ANC in 1986, agreed in 1988 to allow Namibia (q.v.) to move to independence, and had a cordial meeting with Nelson Mandela (q.v.) in July 1989, the month before he was ousted as state president by his own cabinet. His cabinet claimed that the stroke he suffered in January that year had impaired his health, but he charged that this was merely an excuse to get rid of him. In retirement, he settled at the Wilderness, in the Cape, and made clear that he disliked the course F. W. de Klerk (q.v.) took as state president. In late 1997 he was subpoenaed by the Truth and Reconciliation Commission (q.v.) to give evidence in public, but he refused to attend and was tried, but got off on a legal technicality.

BOTHA, ROELOF (PIK) (1932–). Flamboyant and controversial National Party (NP) (q.v.) politician who became the longest-serving foreign minister in the world. A lawyer by training, he joined the Department of Foreign Affairs, and became a member of South Africa's legal team in the South West Africa case (*see* NAMIBIA) at the International

Court of Justice at The Hague, then served as ambassador to the United Nations (q.v.), from 1974, and thereafter to the United States, until in 1977 he became minister of foreign affairs, a post he retained until the new government took office in May 1994. A political survivor, he was almost dismissed by P. W. Botha (q.v.) in 1986 when he suggested that South Africa might one day have a black president.

A popular speaker at NP rallies, Botha was regarded as being on the left of the party. He lost out in elections to the leadership of the party in 1978 and 1989 but strongly backed F. W. de Klerk (q.v.) in his reform initiative, was active in the negotiations of the early 1990s, and was appointed to the government of National Unity (GNU) (q.v.) as minister of mineral and energy affairs in 1994. He left politics when the NP withdrew from the GNU in mid-1996.

BOTSWANA. *See* BECHUANALAND.

BOYCOTTS. From the 1940s boycotts of various kinds were a much-used form of protest against white domination at a time when few other legal forms of protest were tenable. Between 1940 and 1945 rises in bus fares on the Witwatersrand (q.v.) produced a spate of bus boycotts, and further boycotts of public transport took place in the townships of Evaton in 1950 and Alexandra in 1957. The latter lasted more than three months and involved more than 60,000 commuters; the outcome was that employers had to subsidize the transport costs of their African workers. In 1959, the African National Congress (q.v.) organized a three-month consumer boycott of potatoes in protest against the oppressive treatment by farmers of their laborers. Schools were boycotted in 1955, in response to the implementation of Bantu education (q.v.), and school boycotts became frequent in the late 1970s and 1980s. In the 1980s numerous rent and service boycotts were mounted by township inhabitants; by 1990, R1.15 million was owed to local authorities. Such boycotts continued and grew during the transition period. After the establishment of a democratic government in 1994, a Masakhane (let us build together) campaign was launched to persuade township residents to pay rents and service charges; after the local government elections of November 1995, this campaign began to achieve some success.

BRAND, JOHANNES HENRICUS (1823–88). In 1864, J. H. Brand, a Cape (q.v.) lawyer and parliamentarian, was summoned from Cape Town (q.v.) to become president of the Orange Free State (q.v.), an office he held until his death. Under his leadership, the Orange Free State seized the land west of the Caledon River from the Sotho (q.v.) and would have taken more had not Britain annexed Basutoland (q.v.) in 1868. Brand was then able to say that the Orange Free State had "solved" its "native [African] problem." Unable to obtain the diamond (q.v.) fields for the Orange Free State, he got £90,000 in compensation from the British in 1876. An able administrator—the Orange Free State became known as the "model republic"—Brand acted as conciliator between the Transvaal (q.v.) and Britain in the Anglo–Transvaal War (q.v.) in 1881. He continued to prefer closer cooperation with the Cape than with the Transvaal but became more favorably disposed toward the Transvaal in his later years.

BREYTENBACH, BREYTEN (b. 1940). Educated at the University of Cape Town, Breyten Breytenbach left South Africa in 1959 and lived as a painter and poet in Paris. He became known as an opponent of apartheid (q.v.) when the South African government refused his Vietnamese wife a visa to accompany him on a trip back to South Africa to receive a major literary prize. In 1972 he and his wife did return, a visit described in his *A Season in Paradise*, but in 1975 he came back alone, in disguise and traveling under an assumed identity. Arrested as he was leaving, he was tried and found guilty of being a member of a white wing of the African National Congress (ANC) (q.v.), called Okhela. Given a nine-year sentence, he was tried again in 1977 on new terrorism charges but was found guilty only of having smuggled letters and poems from jail. In the late 1970s, as his works were translated from Afrikaans (q.v.) into English (q.v.), his poetry began to acquire international recognition. After his release from jail, he settled again in Paris and was one of the organizers of the meeting in Dakar, Senegal, in 1987 between officials of the ANC and a party of Afrikaners (q.v.) from within South Africa.

BRITAIN IN SOUTH AFRICA. From the end of the 16th century, British ships engaged in trade with India and the East began calling at the Cape of Good Hope to allow their crews to rest. It was not until September 1795, however, that Britain occupied the Cape (q.v.), out of anxiety about the growth of French military power in Europe, which occurred partly at the expense of the Dutch, and fearing for the safety of its trading routes. Britain was concerned to prevent the French from capturing the Cape and sought to maintain the status quo at the Cape as far as possible, guaranteeing Dutch (q.v.) language (q.v.) rights, access to the legal system, and religious freedom. Under terms of the Treaty of Amiens between Britain and France, the Cape was handed back to the Dutch, now the Batavian (q.v.) authorities in the Netherlands, in 1803. The British reconquered the Cape in January 1806 after relations with France deteriorated. Again, Britain regarded its presence as temporary, emphasizing only the importance of protecting the sea route and doing little to disturb social structures in the colony. British troops were, however, used in the frontier (q.v.) war of 1811–12 to help expel the Xhosa (q.v.) from the disputed Zuurveld (q.v.). British rule became permanent under the terms of the London Convention of August 1814, when the Dutch formally ceded the Cape to Britain. Thereafter, the British swiftly established a stronger and more efficient colonial state and remained the dominant power in southern Africa for the remainder of the 19th century.

British troops continued to play an important role on the Cape's eastern frontier in a series of wars from 1819 to 1878. Britain was anxious that commercial expansion should occur at the Cape, so that it could be an effective part of its imperial system of free trade and private enterprise. To this end, economic reforms were sporadically implemented in the first decades of British control. Monopolies and trading restrictions were loosened, roads and communications were improved, the land-tenure system was reformed, and banks and insurance companies were founded. Wheat (q.v.) and wine (q.v.) production increased until the 1820s, after which eastern Cape wool (q.v.) began to take over as the colony's chief export. Economic imperatives also led to the ending of slavery (q.v.) in 1834. The British made far-reaching administrative, legal, and bureaucratic reforms, which culminated in a new constitution; this conferred representative government on the Cape in 1854 and in essence transferred political power from London to the Cape's white inhabitants, though the franchise (q.v.) was nonracial.

From the beginning of the century, but particularly from the 1830s, British traders, hunters, speculators, and missionaries (q.v.) moved beyond the borders of the Cape into the interior of the subcontinent. In Natal (q.v.), conflict between Voortrekkers (q.v.), English traders, and Africans (q.v.) led to British annexation in 1843. Thereafter, Natal became a second major territorial and political focus for the British in southern Africa. The constitution granted to Natal in 1856 allowed Britain to continue controlling executive appointments but permitted the white minority to elect a legislature.

Conflict between and within Boer (q.v.), Griqua (q.v.), Tswana (q.v.), and Sotho (q.v.) polities on the Cape northern frontier during the 1830s and 1840s increasingly occupied Britain's attention. The Orange River Sovereignty (q.v.) was annexed in 1848 in the hope of settling territorial disputes, but Britain's military reversal at the hands of Moshoeshoe (q.v.) in 1851 prompted it to withdraw, because military and administrative obligations were too expensive. Britain recognized the independence of the Transvaal (q.v.) in 1852 and the Orange Free State (q.v.) in 1854. Out of concern that ongoing disputes between the Orange Free State and Moshoeshoe would threaten its strategic interests and the stability of the Cape's frontiers, Britain again intervened in 1868 by annexing Basutoland (q.v.) as a British colony.

Britain's major motive for involvement in the interior was to ensure the security of its economic interests further south: the control of the Cape sea route and the monopoly of southern Africa's external trade. The discovery of diamonds (q.v.) at the end of the 1860s, however, gave Britain a new economic interest in the interior. In 1871, Britain annexed Griqualand West (q.v.), which was incorporated into the Cape in 1880; major industrialists and local diggers effectively controlled the area with the support of British officials. During the 1870s, the economic necessity of securing a stable labor supply to the diamond fields became a priority for the British, and political solutions were sought in the form of confederation (q.v.). Confederation schemes failed, but this did not eliminate the powerful interests who argued that the political fragmentation of southern Africa into British colonies, independent Boer republics (q.v.), and autonomous African societies was disadvantageous to Britain. Britain adopted a more forceful stance, annexing the Transvaal in 1877, defeating the Pedi (q.v.) in 1879, and provoking the Anglo–Zulu War (q.v.) in 1879. Britain thus achieved a decisive shift in the balance of power in southern Africa in favor of white colonists and imperial economic interests. During the 1880s, Britain extended its political and economic interests by annexing Bechuanaland (q.v.) in 1885 to prevent the Germans in South West Africa (now Namibia [q.v.]) from forming a common boundary with the Transvaal, while Rhodesia (now Zimbabwe [q.v.]) was brought under the British flag (q.v.) by Cecil Rhodes (q.v.) in 1890.

The discovery of gold (q.v.) in the Transvaal deepened Britain's commitments and economic interests significantly. The majority of the 44,000 Uitlanders (q.v.) on the Witwatersrand (q.v.) were British, and their grievances with the government of Paul Kruger (q.v.) gave impetus to a process of more aggressive British involvement. Under Joseph Chamberlain (q.v.), the colonial secretary, and Sir Alfred Milner (q.v.), the high commissioner, British policy led to increasing tension with the Transvaal, culminating in the outbreak of the South African War (q.v.) in 1899. The war proved unexpectedly difficult to win and enormously costly to

Britain, which had anticipated the rapid demise of republican power. Although it emerged victorious in 1902 and Milner valiantly attempted to cement British supremacy through autocratic government and anglicization policies in the immediate aftermath of the war, Britain began to reassess its approach to southern Africa. After the election of a Liberal government in Britain at the beginning of 1906, self-government was granted to the Transvaal and Orange River Colony, and negotiations for a unified South Africa began formally at the National Convention (q.v.) in 1908. The Union (q.v.) of South Africa was inaugurated in 1910. This suited Britain's interests: its military, financial, and political obligations were lessened, and as long as South Africa remained within the empire there was little threat to its economic and strategic concerns.

Although the British government was much less directly involved in South African affairs after 1910, strong links between the two countries were retained. South Africa actively fought in both world wars (q.v.) on Britain's side, despite the opposition of Afrikaner nationalists (q.v.) and a measure of discord between the two main white groups in the country. Britain remained South Africa's chief trading partner and largest source of foreign investment even after South Africa declared itself a republic (q.v.) and withdrew from the Commonwealth (q.v.) in 1961.

BRITISH KAFFRARIA. British Kaffraria, the region that lay between the Keiskamma and Kei Rivers, was annexed by Sir Harry Smith (1787–1860), Cape (q.v.) governor and high commissioner, in 1847 at the end of a frontier (q.v.) war, the War of the Axe. The land seized had long been inhabited by Xhosa (q.v.); as an African-inhabited territory, it was ruled directly by the high commissioner until 1860, when the legality of the annexation was confirmed by its being constituted a separate crown colony. By the mid-1860s the imperial government insisted that the Cape Colony (q.v.) assume responsibility for British Kaffraria, which from the first day of 1866 became an integral part of the Cape. After the cattle killing (q.v.), Cape governor Sir George Grey (q.v.) was able to settle white settlers, mostly Germans, in British Kaffraria. The result was a "white corridor," which into the late 20th century ran between the Ciskei (q.v.) and the Transkei (q.v.).

BRITISH OCCUPATION OF THE CAPE. The strategic value of the Cape of Good Hope on the sea route to India and a desire to prevent the capture of the Cape peninsula by France during the Napoleonic Wars persuaded the British to take over the Cape (q.v.) in September 1795. A large British garrison was stationed in Cape Town (q.v.), and the trading monopolies of the Dutch East India Company (q.v.) were loosened, but the British authorities otherwise did little to alter patterns of government and life in the Cape. They also failed to bring stability to the troubled eastern frontier.

One of the terms of the Treaty of Amiens between Britain and France provided for the handing back of the Cape to the Dutch, and in 1803 the new Batavian (q.v.) regime in the Netherlands assumed control. The resumption of the Napoleonic Wars, however, resulted in the reoccupation of the Cape by the British in January 1806. Again, Britain regarded its presence there as temporary and did little to disturb the status quo. In August 1814, at the end of the Napoleonic Wars in Europe, the Cape was formally ceded by the Dutch to Britain, which as a result became the dominant power in southern Africa for the remainder of the century.

BRITISH SOUTH AFRICA (BSA) COMPANY. Founded by Cecil Rhodes (q.v.) and granted a royal charter by Queen Victoria in October 1889 to operate in a large territory north of the Limpopo River (q.v.), the BSA Company played a role in the Jameson Raid (q.v.). This raid was launched from a strip of territory that Joseph Chamberlain (q.v.), the British colonial secretary, had given the BSA Company for a railway. Otherwise, the history of the company belongs to that of Zimbabwe (q.v.).

BROOM, ROBERT (1866–1951). The prominent palaeontologist Robert Broom worked at the Transvaal Museum and contributed important insights into the origins of mammals, based on his work on reptilian fossils found in the Karoo (q.v.). In 1947 he discovered an adult skull, which he named Mrs. Ples (q.v.), at Sterkfontein near Johannesburg (q.v.); his identification of the skull as belonging to the species *Australopithecus* verified the earlier studies of Raymond Dart on the Taung skull (q.v.).

BULHOEK MASSACRE (1921). When the Israelites, a religious sect led by Enoch Mgijima, refused to move from land near Queenstown in the eastern Cape (q.v.), the government of General Jan Smuts (q.v.) resorted to force, and 163 Israelites, armed only with ceremonial weapons, were killed. Bulhoek became a symbol of white savagery against Africans.

BUNDY THESIS. In a seminal article in *African Affairs* (1972) and then in *The Rise and Fall of the South African Peasantry* (1979), Colin Bundy, a South African historian educated at Oxford University, argued that African agriculturalists responded positively and successfully to new market opportunities in the 19th century. The growth of such a peasantry producing for the market was encouraged by both merchants and missionaries (q.v.) in the eastern Cape (q.v.) in the middle decades of the century. With the development of the diamond (q.v.) fields a vast new market for foodstuffs opened, and again Africans met many of the new demands. But after 1886, mining and farming interests sought to force Africans into wage labor. Pressures on land, the imposition of taxes, and competition from those white farmers who now began to commercialize helped force the African peasantry out of business. Rinderpest (in 1896–97) and then East Coast fever (in 1912–13) decimated the cattle herds of the Africans of the coastal belt and aided this process. But the decline of African agriculture (q.v.) was essentially brought about, Bundy argued, by an assault on the peasantry by the state. The poverty of African agriculture in the 20th century was not caused by any unresponsiveness to market opportunities, as had previously been suggested, but was rather a direct result of massive state intervention on behalf of white mining and commercial farming interests.

Critics charged that Bundy exaggerated both the "rise" and the "fall" of that group of farmers he called the peasantry. They produced evidence to show that production for the market had begun much earlier than Bundy suggested and that some of his evidence for massive increases in production was not typical. A significant peasantry, moreover, survived well after World War I (q.v.). Despite these qualifications, the overall thrust of Bundy's thesis found general acceptance among historians.

BURCHELL, WILLIAM JOHN (1781–1863). Botanist, artist, and author, William Burchell traveled extensively, building up valuable and extensively annotated botanical collections. His *Travels in the Interior of Southern Africa*, written in the early 1820s, is one of the most important accounts of the environment and peoples of early-19th-century southern Africa.

BUREAU OF STATE SECURITY (BOSS). Created by Prime Minister B. J. Vorster (q.v.) in 1969, the Bureau of State Security coordinated and evaluated intelligence and engaged in clandestine operations, both within South Africa and abroad, in support of apartheid (q.v.). It infiltrated agents into a number of anti-apartheid organizations and engaged in dirty-tricks campaigns. Under Vorster, it became the elite security apparatus of the state; its head, General Hendrik van den Bergh, was Vorster's close friend. After Vorster's fall, the discredited BOSS was restructured and renamed the Department of National Security, which became the National Intelligence Service and, after 1994, the National Intelligence Agency.

BURGERS, THOMAS FRANÇOIS (1834–81). The liberal, reformist Dutch Reformed Church (q.v.) theologian Thomas Burgers served as president of the South African Republic (q.v.) from 1871 to 1877. During his presidency, he initiated reforms in administration, the judiciary, and education and strongly supported the construction of a railway (q.v.) between the Transvaal (q.v.) and Delagoa Bay (q.v.) as a way to limit British influence in the interior of southern Africa. But he was disliked by many Transvaal Boers (q.v.), who refused to pay taxes and serve with commandos (q.v.), and his government was easily ousted by Theophilus Shepstone (q.v.) in April 1877.

BUSHMEN. *See* SAN.

BUSINESS CYCLES. The 18th-century Cape (q.v.) economy was lifted from its almost constant depression by booms caused by the Seven Years' War in the early 1760s and by the American Revolution (1776–83). The British occupation (q.v.) in 1795 meant a considerable increase in shipping and a revival of economic activity generally. A collapse in the wool (q.v.) trade helped bring on the depression of the mid-1860s, from which the Cape emerged only as a result of the opening up of the diamond (q.v.) mines at Kimberley (q.v.).

The most severe depression of the 19th century occurred between 1882 and 1886. There were various causes: an excessive speculation in diamond mining shares, a severe drought, and a depression in England and the United States. In the immediate aftermath of the South African War (q.v.) there was another boom, but it was followed by a recession that lasted until 1909, caused in part by the legacy of destruction in the interior left by the war. Another recession, following the post–World War I (q.v.) boom of 1918–19, lasted until about 1922.

The greatest depression of all hit the country in the early 1930s, closely linked to that in Europe and the United States. Had it not been for gold (q.v.), South Africa would probably have had to devalue before Britain. General J. B. M. Hertzog (q.v.), the prime minister, initially decided to remain on the gold standard after Britain had abandoned it, to demonstrate South Africa's independence. Once the South African pound lost its parity with gold (in December 1932), the consequent increased price of gold stimulated the economy and began the recovery. The depression had important political effects, being a major factor in producing the coalition between Jan Smuts (q.v.) and Hertzog, and it promoted urbanization, especially of Afrikaners (q.v.). *See also* FUSION.

A mild recession in 1952–53 was followed by a much more serious one in 1960–62, in the aftermath of the Sharpeville massacre (q.v.), which produced an international outcry and a crisis of confidence in the stability of the South African regime. The government's tough measures to meet the crisis helped produce another period of great economic growth, which ran to 1974. The recession that followed was partly a result of the world recession following the rise in oil prices but was greatly exacerbated by the crisis caused by the Soweto uprising (q.v.) of 1976 and the new situation in southern Africa after the advent of Marxist regimes in Mozambique and Angola (qq.v.). The crisis of confidence was greater than that following Sharpeville, but once again the crisis was followed by a spectacular boom, this time fueled by a dramatic rise in the gold price. In 1980, South Africa's growth rate of 8 percent was among the highest in the world. From late 1981, with a steeply falling gold price, the country once again, following the world trend, moved into recession, which the township revolt (q.v.) of the mid-1980s helped intensify, as did the country's increasing economic isolation, as sanctions (q.v.) began to bite and it seemed the country was moving toward civil war.

Even when F. W. de Klerk (q.v.) initiated his reform strategy, great instability prevailed. It was not until the new democratic government took power in 1994 that the country began to emerge again from negative growth rates. For a couple of years there was a period of considerable optimism, until in 1998 the Asian economic crisis affected South Africa, at a time when the initial "honeymoon" was fading and the reality of the problems facing South Africa was becoming clearer. The result was another financial crisis and the expectation that in 1998 there would be virtually no economic growth at all.

BUTHELEZI, MANGOSUTHU GATSHA (b. 1928). Buthelezi, a Zulu politician, was descended from both Cetshwayo (q.v.) and Cetshwayo's chief minister at the time of the Anglo–Zulu War (q.v.); he was also a nephew of Pixley Seme (q.v.). Expelled from Fort Hare (q.v.) in 1952 for African National Congress (ANC) (q.v.) activities, he became an adviser to the Zulu king. Having attempted unsuccessfully to resist the imposition of the bantustan (q.v.) system on his people, Buthelezi decided to work through it, becoming chief minister of KwaZulu (q.v.) in 1972. He emerged as the most outspoken bantustan leader, rejecting independence for his fragmented and impoverished territory. Accused of lending credibility to the bantustan policy, he argued that use should be made of any platform to fight apartheid (q.v.), even a platform created by apartheid. He supported federalism as a device that would allow for redistribution of wealth to Africans while allaying white fears, and he encouraged foreign investment in South Africa on the ground that it provided jobs for Africans (q.v.).

In the mid-1970s he revived Inkatha (q.v.) as a mass organization with the tacit support of the ANC. In the Soweto uprising (q.v.), he backed the Zulu hostel-dwellers against the youth. Black consciousness (q.v.) supporters condemned him as a sellout and threatened his life at the funeral of Robert Sobukwe (q.v.) in March 1978. He broke decisively with the ANC at a meeting with the exile leadership in London in 1979, refusing to adopt a different strategy and rejecting the armed struggle. Although he continued to work for the release of Nelson Mandela (q.v.) from jail, from the mid-1980s his party was involved in a virtual civil war with the United Democratic Front (q.v.) in the KwaZulu and Natal (q.v.) regions. In the early 1990s this became a conflict between Inkatha and the ANC itself, and in all perhaps 10,000 people lost their lives. Having rejected the interim constitution negotiated at the World Trade Centre in 1993 because of its failure to accept federalism, he held out against participation in the April 1994 election but was persuaded to join in at the very last minute, on 19 April. His party won more than 10 percent of the vote, as well as control of KwaZulu-Natal (q.v.).

After the 1994 election, he became minister of home affairs in the government of National Unity (q.v.). In 1997 there was speculation that he might be offered the post of deputy president.

BYWONER. There had been *bywoners* ("white tenant farmers"; from the Dutch, *bijwoner,* meaning "one who lives with another") at the Cape (q.v.) from the late 17th century, but they came to prominence as a group only toward the end of the 19th century, when land had become scarce and their numbers had increased in consequence. The Roman-Dutch system of partible inheritance led to the subdivision of land into small and uneconomic units, forcing increasing numbers of landless men to work for others. *Bywoners* were given the use of land in exchange for a share of their crop or herd and sometimes for seasonal labor service. Some were virtually independent farmers; others could be little distinguished from wage laborers. Pressures on *bywoners* became intense at the end of the 19th century: as land values rose and agriculture (q.v.) became more commercialized, *bywoners* were ejected from many farms. Some became transport riders, but the completion of the railways (q.v.) to the Witwatersrand (q.v.) in the 1890s put most transport riders out of business. Many *bywoners* were hard hit by the rinderpest epidemic among their cattle in 1896 and 1897, and the South African War (q.v.) escalated the process by which many were transformed into an impoverished urban proletariat. In the early 20th century, *bywoner* became virtually synonymous with the term *poor white.*

-C-

CALEDON CODE. A systematic collection of laws relating to the Khoikhoi (q.v.), the Caledon Code was issued in 1809 by the Earl of Caledon, governor of the Cape. It provided that there had to be a written contract between employer and employee and contained clauses designed to protect the Khoikhoi but also to encourage them to work: they were required to have a fixed place of abode and to carry a pass (q.v.) if they moved about. It was these restrictive clauses, along with others in the apprenticeship (q.v.) law of 1812 tying the Khoikhoi further to their white masters, that John Philip (q.v.) of the London Missionary Society (q.v.) campaigned against, and they were repealed in Ordinance 50 (q.v.) of 1828.

CAPE, BRITISH OCCUPATIONS OF. *See* BRITISH OCCUPATION OF THE CAPE.

CAPE COLONY (1652–1910). The name "the Cape" was first given to the southwestern tip of the African continent by the Portuguese, the first Europeans to see it. The colony was founded by Jan van Riebeeck (q.v.), an employee of the Dutch East India Company (VOC) (q.v.). When he landed on the shore of Table Bay in 1652, at the site of present-day Cape Town (q.v.), Van Riebeeck intended to establish not a colony of settlement but merely a refreshment station for Dutch ships trading between the Netherlands and the VOC's eastern possessions. The aim was to grow sufficient crops and to establish favorable trading relations with the indigenous Khoikhoi (q.v.). But in 1657, farms beyond the VOC's area of jurisdiction, behind Table Mountain, were allocated to nine free burghers (q.v.). The following year the first slaves (q.v.) were imported; from then on, the slave community remained an important component of the colonial population, and indeed for most of the 18th century exceeded in number the colonists. In 1659 the first conflict took place between the colonists and the Khoikhoi (q.v.) pastoralists, who found themselves excluded from the land on which the colonists had settled. Some Khoikhoi retreated into the interior, others became laborers for the whites.

By the beginning of the 18th century the colonists had settled almost all of the southwestern Cape, whose Mediterranean climate made possible the growing of wheat (q.v.) and the cultivation of wine (q.v.) grapes. From early in that century increasing numbers of colonists trekked north and east into the more barren interior, where they engaged in pastoralism on large tracts of land. This trekboer (q.v.) movement greatly enlarged the area of the colony, for in its wake the colonial boundary was moved progressively further into the interior. The trekboers demanded extensive tracts of land for their livestock and hunting activities, and the VOC loaned them farms, the boundaries of which the farmers were able to set themselves.

San (q.v.) hunter-gatherers and Khoikhoi offered sporadic but limited resistance to the white advance, and many of these indigenous people had no choice but to become serfs on white farms. By the end of the 1770s the colonial boundary in the east was fixed some six hundred miles from Cape Town, on the Fish River. To the west of this frontier (q.v.) the advancing trekboers had encountered their first serious obstacle, Bantu-speaking (q.v.) pastoral farmers, who effectively blocked significant further eastward expansion for a period of one hundred years, from the time of the first frontier war in 1779 until the ninth and last in 1878.

The British occupied the Cape in 1795, and although it reverted briefly to Batavian (q.v.) control between 1803 and 1806, the British consolidated their rule after 1806. During the 19th century, the Cape doubled in size. The northern boundary was extended to the Orange River (q.v.) in 1847, and separate crown colonies on the frontiers were incorporated during the latter part of the century: British Kaffraria (q.v.) in 1866, Griqualand West (q.v.) in 1880, and Bechuanaland (q.v.) in 1895. Basutoland (q.v.) was annexed in 1871 but reverted to British government control in 1884; the Transkeian (q.v.) territories were incorporated in stages between 1879 and 1894. *See also* BRITISH OCCUPATION OF THE CAPE.

Until the 1880s, the Cape was by far the most powerful state in southern Africa, but the political and economic balance then swung toward the gold-rich (q.v.) Transvaal (q.v.). Although the South African Republic (q.v.) was defeated during the South African War (q.v.), the Transvaal was quickly able to reassert its power thereafter, and its representatives dominated the crucial debates during the National Convention (q.v.), particularly on the franchise (q.v.) question. The convention refused to allow the extension of the Cape's nonracial franchise to the rest of what would become the Union (q.v.) of South Africa. Thus, although the Cape entered the Union of 1910 as the largest province by area, its political influence was secondary to that of the Transvaal, and it was the Witwatersrand (q.v.) that remained the economic powerhouse of the country.

CAPE TOWN. As the place of the first permanent European settlement in South Africa, Cape Town became known to many white South Africans as the mother city. The Table Bay area had been inhabited by San (q.v.) hunter-gatherers and Khoikhoi (q.v.) pastoralists for centuries before the Dutch East India Company (q.v.) established a small settlement in 1652. As the number of houses in the white town grew, from 155 in 1710 to about 550 in 1770 and 1,200 by the early 19th century, so "De Kaap" became "Kaapstad" and then "Cape Town." In 1806 the population (excluding government employees and the British garrison) was 16,500, of whom almost 10,000 were slaves (q.v.) and 800 free blacks (q.v.). The number of slaves declined after the end of the slave trade in 1808, and with growing British immigration whites became a majority of the town's population in about 1840.

Cape Town was the military headquarters of the expanding Cape Colony (q.v.), the administrative center of the hinterland, and the marketing center for the wine (q.v.) and wheat (q.v.) farmers of the southwestern Cape (q.v.), but until the mid-19th century it was chiefly dependent on its trade with passing ships and its position as port of entry to the interior. After the wool (q.v.) boom in the eastern Cape during the 1840s and 1850s, Cape Town lost its preeminent commercial position, although its merchants remained powerful, providing the capital for commercial expansion in the east. Only in 1860 was work begun on the harbor breakwater, to give protection from the gales in Table Bay. After the discovery of diamonds (q.v.) and gold (q.v.), Cape Town became one of the main ports of entry into the interior; with the increase in shipping, by the end of the 19th century the docks became the largest employer of labor in the city.

At the turn of the 20th century, the population of the city had reached 77,000. Africans (q.v.) began to move to Cape Town in significant numbers only during the last decade of the 19th century. No enforced residential segregation existed until 1901, when Africans were placed in a location at Ndabeni, outside the city, during a plague epidemic. Former slaves and their descendants lived on the fringes of the city, in the Malay Quarter, and in the area that became known as District Six. Cape Town enjoyed a reputation for racial tolerance and political liberalism, partly because of its nonracial municipal franchise (q.v.) based on property.

During the 20th century, Cape Town became an industrial city, and the textile industry in particular developed as a key economic enterprise. From 1910 the city was the seat of the Union (q.v.) Parliament. After 1945 the pace of urbanization increased. Afrikaner (q.v.) migrants tended to settle in the northern suburbs, and Africans were placed in the new locations of Nyanga and Guguletu. Residential apartheid (q.v.) was strictly enforced after 1966, when District Six was proclaimed a white area, and thousands of people were forced to move to the Cape Flats. This coercion attracted international attention, as did conflict during the 1980s within the squatter settlement of Crossroads, close to Cape Town's airport. Crossroads was one of several areas housing a large number of Africans attracted to Cape Town in the hope of finding employment, despite legislation designed to keep them away.

By the 1990s, Greater Cape Town had a population of almost three million people and a high rate of unemployment, particularly in some of the newer townships such as Mitchell's Plain and Khayelitsha, to which Coloureds (q.v.) and Africans, respectively, had been forced to move. In the Coloured areas in particular, a gang culture flourished, which led, in turn, to the formation of the antigang group People against Gangsterism and Drugs in 1995. It was from the balcony of Cape Town's City Hall that Nelson Mandela (q.v.) delivered his first speech after walking out of jail on 11 February 1990; he was made a freeman of the city in 1997. After the successful completion of the democratic transition, Parliament continued to meet in Cape Town, although there was much agitation for it to be moved to Gauteng (q.v.). Cape Town became the seat of the new provincial government of the Western Cape (q.v.). In 1997, Cape Town won a place on the shortlist of five cities bidding for the summer Olympic Games in 2004 but in September 1997 heard that its bid had not been successful.

CARNARVON, HENRY HOWARD MOLYNEUX HERBERT, FOURTH EARL OF (1831–90). Henry Carnarvon was secretary of state for the colonies from 1874 to 1878. Having confederated Canada, Carnarvon was keen to do the same in South Africa. He began by attempting to bring together the leaders of the various white-ruled states at a conference. When that failed, he appointed Sir Henry Bartle Frere (q.v.) as high commissioner to pursue the goal of confederation (q.v.) and steered enabling legislation through the British Parliament. But he left office before Frere led Britain into the Anglo–Zulu War (q.v.), after which confederation was abandoned as British policy. Although confederation was not achieved, in trying to confederate South Africa Carnarvon set in motion forces that were to transform the subcontinent.

CATTLE KILLING (1856–57). In 1856 a Xhosa (q.v.) girl by the name of Nongqawuse (q.v.) prophesied that if cattle were killed and no crops cultivated a new age would dawn for her people. The Xhosa paramount chief Sarili (q.v.) believed her, and a large number of his followers, devastated by recent intense frontier (q.v.) conflicts and an epidemic of lung-sickness among their cattle, did as she advised. On 16 February 1857, she claimed, the ancestors would arise and provide abundant cattle and food. When this did not happen, the unbelievers (who had refused to believe the prophecy) were blamed for the catastrophe by the desperate majority who had slaughtered their cattle. Well over 20,000 people starved to death, and many more were forced as refugees into the Cape Colony (q.v.) to seek work. The Cape's governor, Sir George Grey (q.v.), took advantage of the situation by driving Sarili from his land east of the Kei River and resettling whites and Mfengu (q.v.) in the cleared area. The ability of the Xhosa to resist colonial advance was destroyed for almost a generation.

Xhosa tradition ascribes the cattle killing to the manipulation of Grey, the missionaries (q.v.), and white traders, all of whom did indeed benefit from the subsequent events. At the time, Grey himself blamed Sarili and Moshoeshoe (q.v.) for plotting to instigate these events in order to force their people into the colony. The cattle killing is best understood as a millenarian response to the processes of colonization, which had been eating into the fabric of Xhosa society for decades.

CENSORSHIP. Censorship of the press (q.v.) began at the Cape (q.v.) as early as the 1820s. Political censorship took on new meanings in the apartheid (q.v.) era. The Suppression of Communism Act (1950 and later amendments) prevented banned (q.v.) and listed persons from being quoted and anything they wrote from being published. Radical newspapers were suppressed. Although such censorship fell under the Ministry of Justice, the Publications and Entertainments Act of 1963 created a government-nominated Publications Control Board under the Ministry of the Interior, which could ban publications for a number of reasons, one of which was harming relations between sections of the community. Few appeals against bans were attempted, because of the costs involved. New legislation in 1974 provided for decisions on banning to be made by local committees of censors, with appeals going to a Directorate of Publications. A new category, prohibited possession, was added to earlier bans on distributing material, so that mere possession became a crime, whether or not the publication had been acquired legally and in good faith and whether or not the owner knew of the findings of the censor board. In the early 1960s many of South Africa's black writers had their works proscribed, and by the late 1980s well over 30,000 works had been banned, the majority for endangering the state. Censorship helped prevent whites from realizing the nature of apartheid's crimes and understanding the opposition to apartheid. With the end of apartheid in the 1990s, political censorship disappeared.

CETSHWAYO (ca. 1826–84). The son of the Zulu (q.v.) king Mpande (q.v.), Cetshwayo showed considerable political and military skill in surviving intense power struggles with both his father and his brother in the 1850s and 1860s. On the death of Mpande in 1872, Cetshwayo inherited a united and loyal kingdom. He agreed to be crowned by Theophilus Shepstone (q.v.) but was determined to maintain the independence of his kingdom. Within a few years, however, the Natal (q.v.) settlers, Shepstone himself, and the high commissioner had all come to view Cetshwayo as a danger to imperial and settler interests. He was portrayed as a military dictator who posed a threat to white-ruled Natal and who prevented his people from leaving the kingdom to work for whites. In December 1878, Sir Henry Bartle Frere (q.v.) presented him with an ultimatum he could not accept, and in January 1879, British forces invaded his kingdom. Within months Cetshwayo's armies had been defeated, and he was arrested and sent to Cape Town (q.v.). After a visit to England to meet Queen Victoria, he was allowed to return to Zululand, now divided by internecine feuding, in 1883. He died shortly afterward under mysterious circumstances.

CHAMBER OF MINES. Formed in 1887, the Chamber of Mines was a coordinating body that represented the interests of the mining houses, particularly in seeking to formulate policy regarding labor recruitment and conditions of service for workers. Centralized organizations were established to handle labor recruitment from Mozambique (q.v.) in 1896 and within South Africa's borders and the High Commission territories (q.v.) in 1912. The Chamber of Mines largely succeeded in eliminating competition between its members and different mines for labor and remained a powerful voice within the country's most important wealth-generating industry for much of the 20th century.

CHAMBERLAIN, JOSEPH (1836–1914). Joseph Chamberlain was the British secretary of state for the colonies from before the Jameson Raid (q.v.) until after the South African War (q.v.). Coming into office in 1895, he helped Cecil Rhodes (q.v.) prepare for the coup he was planning against the Transvaal (q.v.). When the raid failed, Chamberlain denied knowledge of it and thereby survived politically. A staunch British supremacist, he was responsible for the appointment of Sir Alfred Milner (q.v.) as high commissioner and worked closely with him in formulating British policy toward the Transvaal. He was responsible in part for pushing South Africa toward war in 1899, believing, like Milner, that the war would be a short one and was necessary for the maintenance of British supremacy. *See also* BRITAIN IN SOUTH AFRICA.

CHASKALSON, ARTHUR (b. 1931). The first president of the 11-member Constitutional Court (q.v.), Arthur Chaskalson received a law degree from the University of the Witwatersrand and was admitted to the Johannesburg (q.v.) bar in 1956. He helped found the Legal Resources Centre, a public interest law firm, and headed it for 15 years, during which time it successfully argued cases that brought relief to large numbers of Africans. In 1985 he was elected an honorary member of the Bar Association of New York, but he was not given a judicial appointment by the apartheid (q.v.) government. In 1989–90 he was a consultant to the Constituent Assembly in Namibia (q.v.) and helped draft the Namibian constitution. Then in the negotiations in 1993 he served, as a member of the African National Congress's (q.v.) constitutional committee, on the technical committee that drafted the interim constitution. From 1995 he played a major role in developing the jurisprudence of the Constitutional Court (q.v.).

CHINESE. Although Chinese laborers were brought to the Cape (q.v.) in the 18th century, the present-day Chinese community in South Africa is descended from 19th-century traders and merchants. Like Indians (q.v.), early immigrants suffered from trading and immigration restrictions. Many were imprisoned at the beginning of the 20th century for resisting registration laws.

After the South African War (q.v.), the gold (q.v.) mines on the Witwatersrand (q.v.) faced a critical labor shortage: the need to bring them back to full production as rapidly as possible, and the shortage of African labor, prompted Sir Alfred Milner (q.v.), the high commissioner, to recruit labor from North China. The first 10,000 workers arrived in South Africa in May 1904. Over the next four years, 63,296 Chinese indentured workers were sent to the Witwatersrand on three-year contracts. They were housed in compounds (q.v.), prevented from holding skilled positions, and barred from trading and from owning land. Whites, who feared competition, strongly opposed their presence, and by 1910 all the Chinese laborers introduced under this scheme had been repatriated. They played an important role in the rehabilitation of the mines, and their acceptance of low wages undercut the bargaining power of African miners, who after 1906 began to seek work in the mines again in significant numbers.

During the apartheid (q.v.) era, the small Chinese community—estimated to be less than 9,000 in 1980—experienced some statutory discrimination, but it was not as far-reaching as that experienced by other ethnic groups. They were classified as Coloured (q.v.) under the Population Registration Act of 1950, and the Group Areas Act (q.v.) of the same year made provision for separate residential areas for Chinese people, but few such areas were in fact proclaimed. Most Chinese benefited from their honorary white (q.v.) status: they were allowed to live and trade in white areas, send their children to white schools, and attend recreational venues in white neighborhoods. Few participated actively in politics, either in support of or against the apartheid political order.

CHRISTIAN INSTITUTE OF SOUTHERN AFRICA. An independent ecumenical organization for promoting dialogue and witnessing to reconciliation, the Christian Institute of Southern Africa was founded in 1963 by Beyers Naudé, a former moderator of the Dutch Reformed Church (q.v.). As it became more involved in work with Africans, the institute grew more radical. It promoted the study of the role of Christianity (q.v.) in apartheid (q.v.) society and reacted sympathetically to the development of black theology, which was ideologically tied to the black consciousness (q.v.) movement. In 1975 the Christian Institute was declared an affected organization, which meant it could no longer receive financial aid from outside the country, and in October 1977 it was banned (q.v.), along with its journal, *Pro Veritate*, Beyers Naudé, and other officials.

CHRISTIANITY. Bartolomeu Dias (q.v.) erected a limestone pillar capped by a Christian cross at Kwaaihoek, near the mouth of Bushman's River on the southern Cape (q.v.) coast, on 12 March 1488. A permanent Christian presence in southern Africa began with the founding of the refreshment station at Table Bay by the Dutch East India Company (q.v.) in 1652. The company established the Dutch Reformed Church (q.v.) as the only lawful religious organization at the Cape. No other religious body could function in public until 1778, when Lutherans were permitted public worship. Despite formal commitment to the spread of Christianity, little missionary (q.v.) activity occurred during the 18th century. Because whites appear to have regarded their Christian identity as a key characteristic distinguishing them from other groups, they did not consider religious conversions to be a priority.

By contrast, the 19th century, the period of British colonial and commercial conquest (*see* BRITAIN IN SOUTH AFRICA), saw determined work by Christian missionaries. Evangelical concerns were conspicuous ingredients of the message of the missionaries, but these were closely linked to the advance of European notions of civilization and education (q.v.), the promotion of trade and commerce, and the expansion of British political and military hegemony. The influence of missionaries varied from region to region, as did the responses of Africans to Christianity. Many African societies rejected the Christian gospel, while using missionaries for their own purposes, particularly the exploitation of material and technological benefits such as firearms and ammunition, irrigation, and the plough. Missionaries and Africans frequently found themselves in deep confrontation on the material as well as spiritual and cultural levels. Only after the weakening of African societies during the latter half of the 19th century did missionaries achieve a significant number of conversions.

Also during the 19th century, various denominations founded institutional structures and congregations. The majority of these were Protestant and, despite different historical and cultural origins, often shared similar values. The Dutch Reformed Church (q.v.), divided into three separate churches, established itself among the Dutch-speaking white population and set up racially separate congregations for Coloureds (q.v.) and Africans. Among the English-speaking (q.v.) population, Anglicans (q.v.), Methodists, Presbyterians, Congregationalists, and Baptists were the prominent denominations. Roman Catholicism (q.v.) grew steadily after the arrival of the first bishop in 1838.

The 20th century saw the most rapid growth of Christianity, which developed from a mainly white, minority, and imported faith to one embraced by a majority of South Africans and expressed in a wide variety of ways. Christianity was used during the 20th century to justify apartheid (q.v.) and Afrikaner nationalism (q.v.), but many of the mainline churches, whose membership crossed social and racial divides, opposed apartheid, often in pronouncements issued by church leaders.

By the 1990s, some 80 percent of the population claimed some form of Christian allegiance. Whites had become a numerical minority within most denominations; there were also 5,000 African independent churches (q.v.) with a following of over eight million people, encompassing a wide range of religious, ritual, faith-healing, and prophetic expressions.

CHURCH OF THE PROVINCE. *See* ANGLICAN CHURCH.

CISKEI. Word meaning "land this side (west) of the Kei River." The Ciskei, home of the Xhosa (q.v.), was annexed as Queen Adelaide Province by

Governor Benjamin D'Urban in 1835, but the authorities in London insisted it be given up the following year. It was not until 1847, at the end of the War of the Axe, that it once again became British territory, this time permanently. The Xhosa who lived there tried to maintain their independence, but were defeated in the War of Mlanjeni (1850–1853) and then suffered the disaster of the cattle-killing (q.v.). They nevertheless rebelled for a final time in 1878. By then numerous whites had been given land in parts of the Ciskei, which became a checkerboard of black and white areas of settlement.

The African areas were brought together under a separate administration. When the bantustan (q.v.) of Ciskei was granted nominal independence in December 1981, it had a de facto population of 650,000, almost all Xhosa-speakers, but its independence meant the loss of South African citizenship for some 1.5 million others who were classified as Ciskeian but who did not live in the territory. In the 1970s, the Ciskei served as the dumping ground for at least 150,000 people who were forcibly moved there, and an additional 250,000 Africans were moved from the port city of East London and settled within the Ciskei at Mdantsane, which was by 1980 the second largest dormitory town for Africans in the country after Soweto (q.v.). By independence half the Ciskeian population lived below the poverty line, and well over half of all earnings came from migrant labor outside the bantustan. Malnutrition was rife and it was estimated that half of all children died before the age of five.

Once independent, the Ciskei, with its capital at Bisho, was run by an authoritarian oligarchy headed by Lennox Sebe, whose Ciskei National Independence Party had won every seat in the rigged 1978 election and who accepted independence against the advice of a commission he himself had appointed. In a referendum on the issue in 1980, although almost everyone supported independence, only 60 percent of the population voted and widespread intimidation was alleged. Sebe, who made himself "president for life," was eventually ousted by Brigadier Oupa Gqozo, whose troops fired on African National Congress (q.v.) demonstrators in the Bisho massacre (q.v.) of September 1992 and who left office in March 1994 after Lucas Mangope had been forced from power in Bophuthatswana (q.v.). From April that year the Ciskei was reincorporated into South Africa as part of the new Eastern Cape province (q.v.).

CIVIC ORGANIZATIONS. Community-based organizations became important in black townships beginning in the late 1970s. The Soweto uprising (q.v.) led to the creation of the Committee of Ten in Soweto (q.v.), from which emerged the Soweto Civic Association, headed by Dr.

Nthato Motlana. Other prominent civics included the Port Elizabeth Community Organization (PEBCO), in which Thozamile Botha was the leading figure, and the Alexandra civic, led by Moses Mayekiso, a union organizer. Many civic organizations affiliated themselves with the United Democratic Front (UDF) (q.v.) in 1983 and played an important mobilizing role in the township revolt of 1984–1986. They participated in rent and consumer boycotts, and in some areas became de facto local administrations. In the new era after 1990, in which they could openly support the African National Congress (q.v.), their importance declined. The South African National Civic Organization (SANCO), launched in March 1992 under Moses Mayekiso, failed to strengthen the civic movement on the ground, and a number of its leading figures soon moved into government. SANCO declined further when it engaged unsuccessfully in business-type operations after the 1994 election; by early 1998 it was reputedly bankrupt.

CIVIL COOPERATION BUREAU (CCB). In 1986 approval was given (at what level remains unclear) for the establishment of a covert organization operating under the Special Forces of the South African Defence Force (q.v.) and linked to military intelligence. Its main objective was maximum disruption of South Africa's enemies, perceived to be the African National Congress (ANC) (q.v.) and its allies. It was not until 1990 that news of some of its projects began to be leaked to the media. They included attempts at intimidation, arson, bombing, and the assassination of left-wing activists, such as the University of the Witwatersrand activist-anthropologist Dr. David Webster, in May 1989, and the Namibian lawyer Anton Lubowski, shot in Windhoek in September 1989.

In August 1990 the National Party (q.v.) government announced that the CCB would be disbanded, but over two years later some of its projects had not yet been wound up. Some commentators saw the CCB as a product of the P. W. Botha (q.v.) regime and believed that F. W. de Klerk (q.v.) had acted to the best of his abilities to end covert operations against his main negotiating partner; others believed that such operations had been allowed to continue because weakening the ANC served the interests of the government.

CIVILIZED LABOR. The name for the labor policy of the Pact (q.v.) government, which came into office in 1924. It purported to be based on providing jobs to civilized people, but "civilized" meant "white" in practice, and extended the pre-Union (q.v.) policy of securing jobs for whites only. Whites were given employment in semi-skilled jobs, mostly in the public sector—the post office and the railways (q.v.) in particular—at protected rates of pay, so the lowest-paid white workers were paid considerably more than the highest-paid African workers. This helped deal with 'poor whiteism' (q.v.) and divided the working class on racial lines, removing the white worker from the mass of the working class. (*See also* COLOR BAR; MANUFACTURING.)

COLENSO, JOHN WILLIAM (1814–1883). Controversial bishop of Natal (q.v.), who took up his post in 1853. His theological ideas split the Anglican Church (q.v.) during the 1860s, and his support for the Zulu (q.v.), particularly at the time of the Langalibalele (q.v.) affair in the 1870s, earned him the censure of the majority of white settlers in Natal. The Zulu knew him as "Sobantu, father of the people."

COLOR BAR. The color bar has been a key element in South African policies of racial segregation (q.v.) and apartheid (q.v.). The term *color bar* has often been used to mean the job color bar (q.v.) only, that is, racial discrimination in access to employment. But in *Class, Race, and Gold* (1976), F. R. Johnstone broadened the usage and spoke of "exploitation colour bars," including the pass laws (q.v.), the compound (q.v.) system, and other means of keeping African wages low. Johnstone argued that these exploitation color bars were more significant than the job color bar, for they were the chief guarantor to capital of cheap labor.

COLOURED LABOUR PREFERENCE POLICY (CLPP). The origins of the CLPP lie in the 1920s, with attempts by the City Council of Cape Town (q.v.) to ensure that jobs went to Coloureds (q.v.) rather than Africans (q.v.). It became official policy of the apartheid (q.v.) government in 1954, the aim being to reduce the number of African workers in the western Cape (q.v.). It fell away in the late 1980s, by which time the number of Africans in the western Cape had increased greatly despite the CLPP.

COLOURED PERSONS' REPRESENTATIVE COUNCIL (CRC). The apartheid (q.v.) government established the CRC in 1968 as an attempt to delegate certain powers to Coloured (q.v.) people, but the majority of Coloureds boycotted elections for the council. When the (Coloured) Labour Party (q.v.) gained control of the CRC in 1975, it set out to make it unworkable, and the CRC was disbanded in 1981.

COLOUREDS. In the early 19th century, white colonists at the Cape (q.v.) distinguished themselves from "people of color," a category that included Khoikhoi (q.v.), free blacks (q.v.), and people of mixed descent. Slaves (q.v.) formed a separate legal category. During the 19th century, and particularly in the decades after the emancipation of slaves in 1838, a nascent shared identity developed among these diverse components of the laboring class in the western Cape. As the social changes brought about by industrialization and the mineral revolution began to take hold at the end of the 19th and beginning of the 20th centuries, a more distinct "Coloured" identity emerged. The arrival of significant numbers of Africans (q.v.) in the western Cape led Coloureds to assert their difference, on the basis of partial descent from European settlers and generations of incorporation into colonial society, but the category was an extremely fluid and ill-defined one.

Although Coloureds had long had close contact with whites and spoke the same language (Afrikaans [q.v.], rather than English [q.v.]), they were not accepted into white society, and they came to occupy an intermediate position in South Africa's racial hierarchy. Light-skinned Coloureds were able to "pass" into white society, and the Cape Supreme Court found in 1911 that there was no clear way in which such people could be distinguished from whites. Coloureds were not subject to the same discrimination as Africans: for example, they did not have to carry passes (q.v.) and could enter cities as they wished. Segregationist measures and treatment were nonetheless applied, although white supremacists remained divided on whether Coloureds belonged on the white or African side of the racial divide. The Cape School Board Act of 1905, for example, excluded most Coloureds from the new system of general public education (q.v.). Franchise (q.v.) privileges were not extended to Coloureds in the northern provinces at the time of the creation of the Union (q.v.) of South Africa. The economic position of Coloureds, particularly the educated elite, was undermined during the 1920s and 1930s by government policies designed to favor whites (q.v.) over blacks (q.v.) in the competition for jobs. When the franchise was extended to white women, as well as to all white males over the age of 18, at the beginning of the 1930s, only Coloured males over the age of 21 who met the predetermined economic and literacy criteria retained the right to vote.

During the apartheid (q.v.) era, Coloureds endured far more severe restrictions. The Population Registration Act of 1950 emphasized association and ancestry rather than color to establish who was Coloured; Griquas (q.v.) and Malays were treated as specified subgroups. Mixed marriages were outlawed, public facilities segregated, and remaining franchise rights lost when Coloureds in the Cape were removed from the common voters' roll in 1956. During the 1960s, tens of thousands of

Coloureds were forcibly relocated to live in their own "group areas," under the terms of the 1950 Group Areas Act (q.v.); white extremists even toyed with the idea of establishing a Coloured homeland.

Considerable division existed among Coloureds about the wisdom of forming separate political parties. This reflected the ambivalent position of Coloureds within the wider society. The need to oppose the spread of racial segregation (q.v.), however, led to the founding of the first major political body for Coloureds, the African Political Organization (APO), later renamed the African People's Organization (q.v.) in Cape Town (q.v.) in 1902. Under its president for 35 years, Abdullah Abdurahman (q.v.), the APO was moderate in its approach to white racism (q.v.) and exclusivity and advocated assimilation and cooperation with whites as far as possible. More radical groups, which rejected the APO's restrained strategies, established themselves during the 1930s and 1940s. The most prominent of these were the National Liberation League (founded 1935) and the Anti-CAD (Anti–Coloured Affairs Department) movement, affiliated with the Non-European Unity Movement (NEUM) (q.v.), founded in 1943. After the Coloureds were removed from the voters' roll in 1956, they were given the right to elect four white members to Parliament on a separate roll. The Anti-CAD movement organized a successful boycott of these elections. In 1959, a Coloured Affairs Department was established, with its own minister of Coloured affairs. In 1968, the system of representation of Coloureds in Parliament by whites was abolished and replaced by a Coloured Persons' Representative Council (CRC), which was empowered to administer "Coloured affairs" in areas such as local government, finance, education, welfare, and pensions. A boycott of elections to this council was again advocated, but the Coloured Labour Party (q.v.) decided to contest the elections, although it rejected the body as an apartheid creation. After the CRC was closed in 1975, the authorities sought new ways of incorporating Coloureds into the political process.

With the inauguration of the tricameral parliamentary (q.v.) system in 1983, a separate House of Representatives was created with powers granted to Coloureds to administer their "own affairs." Coloured people again split over the desirability of participation in these structures, and many Coloureds became involved in various extraparliamentary movements, led by the broadly based United Democratic Front (q.v.). In these movements the label "Coloured" was rejected as an artificial category imposed by an authoritarian and racist state. The idea that Coloureds had specific group interests was rejected, and people identified themselves as "blacks" or as belonging to "the oppressed." But a Coloured identity, distinct from that of the white minority or the black majority, proved enduring. In the democratic election of 1994, both the National Party (q.v.) and the African National Congress (q.v.) appealed to some extent to Coloured identity; one key factor in the National Party's victory in the provincial election in the Western Cape (q.v.) was its successful play on Coloured fears about the security of their homes and employment under a black majority government.

In the 1990s the approximately three million Coloureds in South Africa constituted some 8 percent of the country's population. More than two-thirds of them lived in the Western Cape, although there are sizable Coloured communities in the Eastern Cape (q.v.), the Northern Cape (q.v.), and Gauteng (q.v.).

COMMANDOS. As white settlement began to expand from the southwestern Cape (q.v.) in the 17th century, free burghers (q.v.) began to organize their own militia units, which were officially sanctioned by the Dutch East India Company (q.v.) in 1715. The commandos, usually mounted, were largely independent of company control; the company supplied them with ammunition but allowed them to operate independently under the command of their elected leaders. During the 18th century, commandos undertook frequent punitive expeditions against the Khoisan (q.v.) and the Xhosa (q.v.). The San (q.v.) were hunted like vermin; thousands were killed, and many children captured and forced into labor on white farms. Commandos were unable to dislodge the Khoisan from the Sneeuberge or the Nuweveldberge in the last quarter of the 18th century and were similarly blocked in the Zuurveld (q.v.) by the Xhosa; in both cases, British aid in the early 19th century was required to establish white supremacy. In the late 1830s, the Voortrekkers (q.v.) took the commando system into the interior, where it was used extensively against Africans. Commando service was compulsory for males in the two Boer republics (namely, the Orange Free State and the South African Republic [qq.v.]), and commandos fought the British in the Anglo–Transvaal War and the South African War (qq.v.) with considerable success.

During the Rand Revolt (q.v.) of 1922, striking white miners organized themselves into paramilitary units known as commandos to enforce the strike. In the early 1950s, the Torch Commando (q.v.)—an organization of World War II (q.v.) veterans—staged large marches to protest against the bill proposing the removal of Coloured voters from the common voters' roll. Local citizen units consisting of part-time soldiers in the South African Defence Force (q.v.) were also known as commandos.

COMMONWEALTH. South Africa played an important role in the evolution of the British Empire into the Commonwealth. Largely in response to pressure from J. B. M. Hertzog (q.v.), the Imperial Conference of 1926 declared that Britain and the dominions, including South Africa, were autonomous communities within the British Empire, equal in status, in no way subordinate the one to the other in any aspect of their internal or external affairs. South Africa then adopted its own flag (q.v.). Although Hertzog favored the establishment of a republic (q.v.) in South Africa, he did not consider that practical politics. When South Africa took full power to alter or amend any legislation by the Status of the Union Act (1934), he accepted the new relationship with Britain and on that basis entered fusion (q.v.) with Jan Smuts (q.v.). In 1939 he split with Smuts over South Africa's entry into World War II (q.v.).

The republican movement gathered pace in the 1950s, and after a referendum among whites had endorsed the idea, H. F. Verwoerd (q.v.) attended a Commonwealth prime ministers' conference in London, in March 1961, to ask that South Africa remain a member of the Commonwealth after the change in status. But when it became clear that South Africa's continued membership was contentious and would result in others leaving the Commonwealth, he formally withdrew South Africa's application. On 31 May 1961, when it became a republic, South Africa ceased to be a member of the Commonwealth. This helped increase the country's international isolation, and South Africa lost its privileged access to markets in Britain. The South African issue both helped hold the Commonwealth together in the 1970s and 1980s and proved divisive at meetings of heads of government when British prime minister Margaret Thatcher refused to support sanctions (q.v.) against the country. The African National Congress (q.v.), meanwhile, made it clear that when it came to power it would ask that South Africa be readmitted to the Commonwealth; this happened in July 1994.

COMMUNIST PARTY OF SOUTH AFRICA. The Communist Party of South Africa was founded in July 1921 as a result of the amalgamation of the International Socialist League, which had been formed by those who broke with the (white) Labour Party in 1915 over its support for the war effort, and other left groups. A section of the Communist International, the party from the beginning maintained relatively close links with Moscow. During the Rand Revolt (q.v.) some of its members attempted to combine radicalism and racialism, their slogan in support of the strikers being, "Workers of the world, unite and fight for a white South Africa." Three communists on the executive of the Industrial and Commercial Workers' Union (q.v.) were expelled in 1926, but the communists won recruits in the African National Congress (ANC) (q.v.) in the late 1920s before the ANC too swung to the right. The party had only 200 African members in 1927, and 1,600 in 1928 out of a total membership of 1,750. Orders then came from Moscow that it should work for a native republic (q.v.) in South Africa. S. P. Bunting, the party general secretary, and other leading white members opposed the new policy, because they still hoped to radicalize the white working class and make it the vanguard of a class-conscious proletariat. The expulsion of Bunting's group from the party as deviationists in 1931 decimated the party, which by the mid-1930s had very few members but was nevertheless the only nonracial party in the country.

In the 1930s, the Communist Party of South Africa did pioneering work in organizing African (q.v.) workers. Some of its African members served on the executive of the ANC, and the Africans of the western Cape (q.v.) elected three white communists to Parliament as native representatives, two of whom were prevented from taking their seats. In 1950, under the threat of the apartheid (q.v.) government's Suppression of Communism Act, the party dissolved itself, but in 1953 it formed itself into the underground South African Communist Party (q.v.).

COMPOUNDS. The compound system introduced on the Kimberley (q.v.) diamond (q.v.) fields in 1885 was an extended variant on the use of prison labor from the Kimberley convict station and was designed to accommodate black migrant (q.v.) workers during their period of employment in the mines. Between 1885 and 1889 the bulk of the African labor force of 10,000 men were placed in 12 large closed compounds. Mine owners justified the system as a measure to prevent the theft of diamonds and also argued that it would cost the workers less, allowing them to return to their homes with a greater proportion of their earnings. The compound system, however, was devised to keep labor as cheap as possible. It served primarily as a means of control, preventing workers from breaking their contracts, reducing their freedom of movement, and even enabling management to force workers underground, which many tried to resist.

The term *compound* was also used more loosely from the late 19th century to include any living quarters for a number of African workers, whether or not they were subject to controls. In Cape Town (q.v.), for example, there was a large harbor compound, as well as smaller compounds housing African workers for private concerns. The compound system at the Witwatersrand (q.v.) gold (q.v.) mines was similar to that of Kimberley, although these compounds were not as totally closed as in Kimberley. Both Chinese (q.v.) and African workers were required to live in barracklike, single-sex hostels for the duration of their contracts. Conditions were harsh, with workers sleeping on bunklike concrete slabs in very overcrowded circumstances. The compounds limited the independence of workers and isolated them from society at large and from other workers in particular. During strikes (q.v.), such as those of 1920 and 1946, compounds were surrounded and became virtual prisons, allowing the strikes to be broken. Compounds, and the hostels that took their place, remained crowded and unsanitary places until the 1990s. They were political flash points on the Witwatersrand during township conflict in the early 1990s, sometimes serving as bases for armed groups to attack surrounding township residents. Demands for their dismantling became a complex political issue during negotiations between the National Party (q.v.) government, the African National Congress (q.v.), and the Inkatha (q.v.) Freedom Party during this period.

CONCENTRATION CAMPS. During the last quarter of 1900, in an attempt to prevent Boer (q.v.) guerrillas from receiving assistance from civilians in the South African War (q.v.), the British military authorities established concentration camps for Boer women and children, families of Boers who had surrendered, and Africans (q.v.) who had the potential to supply provisions to Boer commandos (q.v.). In all, 44 camps, largely ill equipped and disease ridden, were established in the Transvaal (q.v.) and Orange River Colony for the Boers; almost 28,000 people died in these camps, the majority of them children under the age of 16. The loss of life helped to force the Boers to negotiate peace with the British in 1902 but also left deep and indelible scars on the Afrikaner (q.v.) consciousness. The concentration camps for Africans were similarly unsanitary and overcrowded; more than 100,000 people were interned in some 66 camps, and more than 14,000 deaths were recorded. It is likely that almost as many Africans died in such camps as Boers.

CONFEDERATION. In the late 1850s, Sir George Grey (q.v.), the Cape governor, proposed a federal union of southern Africa's white-ruled states, but the idea was not developed. In 1867 the British colonial secretary, Lord Carnarvon (q.v.), steered the British North America Act through the British Parliament and hoped to accomplish a similar arrangement in South Africa during his second term as colonial secretary, between 1874 and 1878. Carnarvon and his advisers were keen to secure British strategic and economic interests in South Africa, particularly after the discovery of diamonds (q.v.) and with the need to secure a regular flow of migrant (q.v.) labor. *See also* BRITAIN IN SOUTH AFRICA.

Carnarvon initially attempted to arrange a conference at which representatives of the various states would meet to discuss political unity. This proved a failure; he subsequently authorized Theophilus Shepstone (q.v.) to annex the Transvaal (q.v.), sent out Sir Henry Bartle Frere (q.v.) as high commissioner with instructions to bring about confederation, and carried legislation permitting such a confederation through the British Parliament in 1877. Although Carnarvon resigned as colonial secretary in 1878, the quest for confederation continued. The British army's defeat at Isandlwana (q.v.) in January 1879 proved a major setback, as did the Cape Parliament's rejection of the idea in June 1880; Frere was subsequently recalled. After the Transvaal revolt against British rule later in 1880, plans for confederation were finally shelved. Although the scheme failed, attempts to achieve it did much to transform southern Africa. *See also* ANGLO–TRANSVAAL WAR.

CONGRESS ALLIANCE. The Congress Alliance was a joint anti-apartheid front established in the mid-1950s, in which the African National Congress (q.v.) was the leading member. Other members included the South African Indian Congress and the Congress of Democrats. The high point of the alliance was the Congress of the People, held at Kliptown in Soweto (q.v.), outside Johannesburg (q.v.), in June 1955, at which the Freedom Charter was approved. Many of the leading individuals involved in the alliance were arrested and charged with high treason (q.v.) in 1956.

CONGRESS OF SOUTH AFRICAN TRADE UNIONS (COSATU). Formed in 1985, when it claimed 450,000 members, the Congress of South African Trade Unions (COSATU) had by 1994 more than 1.3 million members and was by far the largest trade union federation in the country. Its three largest affiliates were the National Union of Mineworkers, the National Union of Metalworkers of South Africa, and the Transport and General Workers' Union. In the debate in the 1980s over the political role the trade unions (q.v.) should play, the populists, who favored a direct role, won out over the workerists, and COSATU aligned itself first with the United Democratic Front (q.v.) and then with the African National Congress (ANC) (q.v.). Among its leading figures were Jay Naidoo, its general secretary, and Alec Erwin, both of whom became cabinet ministers in the government of National Unity (q.v.) in 1994. COSATU played a leading role in formulating the Reconstruction and Development Programme (q.v.), but once the ANC was in power, it found itself sidelined, though it remained part of what was loosely termed the Triple Alliance, the third member of which was the South African Communist Party (q.v.).

CONSERVATIVE PARTY. The right-wing white party founded by Andries Treurnicht and 22 other members of Parliament in 1982, after they had broken from the National Party (q.v.), the Conservative Party became the official opposition in 1987 and in the September 1989 election won 31 percent of the white vote. Most of its support was from the rural areas and from lower-middle-class whites. After the decision by F. W. de Klerk (q.v.) to negotiate with the African National Congress (q.v.), the party was sidelined. It refused to participate in most of the negotiations, and it boycotted the 1994 democratic election and associated itself with other Afrikaner (q.v.) parties calling for self-determination.

CONSTITUTIONAL ASSEMBLY (CA) (1994–96). When negotiations began at the Convention for a Democratic South Africa (q.v.) in 1991, the African National Congress (q.v.) followed the Pan Africanist Congress of Azania (q.v.) in demanding an elected Constitutional Assembly, but the National Party (q.v.) opposed the idea. The compromise reached in 1993, and embodied in the interim constitution, was that the first election of April 1994 would establish a CA but that it would be bound by constitutional principles (q.v.) agreed to at the Multi-Party Negotiating Forum (q.v.). The CA comprised the members of the House of Assembly and the Senate sitting together, and it began its work soon after the new Parliament assembled in May 1994. It had two years in which to draw up a final constitution. It completed its task in May 1996, just within the two-year deadline. When the Constitutional Court (q.v.) rejected the initial draft, the CA met again later in 1996 and prepared a new draft, which the court then approved. The final task of the CA was to popularize the new constitution, millions of copies of which were distributed in early 1997.

CONSTITUTIONAL COURT. This 11-member body was created in 1994 to adjudicate on issues relating to the constitution and to certify that the new constitution adhered to the 34 constitutional principles laid down during the negotiations. It was headed by Arthur Chaskalson (q.v.), who had been the African National Congress's (q.v.) chief legal adviser during the negotiations, and initially comprised nine men and two women, seven whites and four blacks. Its first contentious ruling was that the death penalty was unconstitutional. Critics who did not understand the concept of the rule of law maintained that the court was undemocratic in its ruling, given that there was widespread popular support for the death penalty. In 1997 the Constitutional Court approved the constitution drawn up by the Western Cape (q.v.) legislature.

CONSTITUTIONAL PRINCIPLES. Some 34 principles were included in the interim constitution adopted at the Multi-Party Negotiating Forum (q.v.) in 1993, approved by Parliament in December of that year, and amended early in 1994. They were meant to provide a framework for the final constitution, to be drawn up by the Constitutional Assembly (CA) (q.v.), and were binding on that body. They provided that South Africa must be a multiparty democracy, with a justiciable Bill of Rights. The last principle to be added provided for the possible right to self-determination of a community sharing a common cultural and language (q.v.) tradition (to allow for a *volkstaat* [Afrikaner people's republic] and a Zulu kingdom [q.v.]). When the Constitutional Court (q.v.) reviewed the first draft of the new constitution for the country, it sent it back to the CA, largely because it did not adequately represent the principle that the powers and functions of the provinces would not be less than those embodied in the interim constitution. The amended draft was later approved.

CONVENTION FOR A DEMOCRATIC SOUTH AFRICA (CODESA). A negotiating body, CODESA convened on 20 December 1991 at the World Trade Centre near Johannesburg's (q.v.) airport to draw up a new constitution. The 19 delegations included eight main parties and various bantustan (q.v.) governments. When F. W. de Klerk (q.v.) berated the African National Congress (ANC) (q.v.) for not having disbanded Umkhonto weSizwe (q.v.), a furious Nelson Mandela (q.v.) insisted on the right to reply and accused De Klerk of pursuing a double agenda, negotiating in public while encouraging units in the security forces to destabilize the ANC. A Declaration of Intent was adopted, and five working groups were appointed to prepare the way for a nonracial democratic government. The groups reached agreement, except that Working Group 2 deadlocked on the number of votes needed for the adoption of the constitution (the National Party [q.v.] wanted three-quarters, and the ANC would not go higher than 70 percent). A second CODESA was held in May 1992 to try to resolve the issue, but when the ANC suggested the deadlock should be broken by a referendum after six months in which a simple majority would decide the issue, the meeting broke up in disarray. When a similar negotiating body was constituted in 1993, it was called the Multi-Party Negotiating Forum (q.v.) and not CODESA 3, because CODESA seemed a failure.

CORY, GEORGE EDWARD (1862–1935). Educated at Cambridge, the historian George Cory went to South Africa in 1891 as vice principal of the Grahamstown (q.v.) Public School and was professor of chemistry at Rhodes University College from 1904 until his retirement in 1925. But he devoted much of his time to collecting historical materials and writing history, and after the death of George Theal (q.v.) he became the country's best-known historian. His multivolume history of the British settlers in the eastern Cape was rather misleadingly entitled *The Rise of South Africa*. Volume 6 of this work was published posthumously. In general, Cory took a prosettler view, but he was a pioneer in the collection of oral tradition and made numerous field trips to collect materials for his histories.

CRESWELL, FREDRIC HUGH PAGE (1866–1948). Trained as a mining engineer in England, the labor leader Frederic Creswell arrived in South Africa in 1893 and became a mine manager. After the South African War (q.v.), he was the main champion of a white labor policy in the gold (q.v.) mines, attempting unsuccessfully to put this into practice at the Village Main Reef mine. Elected to the first Union (q.v.) of South Africa Parliament, he became leader of the newly established white Labour Party. In World War I (q.v.) he gave full support to the war effort and saw Labour split. He then grew increasingly friendly with J. B. M. Hertzog (q.v.), and in 1922 they agreed to form a joint opposition against Jan Smuts (q.v.). In 1923, a pact (q.v.) was announced, and when it came to power in 1924, Creswell became minister of labor and of defense. When he opposed the right of the National Congress of his party to dictate policy to members of Parliament, he was ousted as its leader, but Hertzog kept him in his cabinet until 1933.

CROSSROADS. *See* CAPE TOWN.

CUITO CUANAVALE, BATTLE OF (1987–88). In a large, conventional battle around the town of Cuito Cuanavale in southern Angola (q.v.), South African Defence Force (q.v.) troops and their UNITA (National Union for the Total Independence of Angola) allies faced the forces of the Angolan army, crack Cuban troops, and members of the armed wing of the South West African People's Organization (SWAPO), the People's Liberation Army of Namibia (q.v.). The result was a stalemate, rather than the defeat for South African forces that the Cubans claimed it to be, but the stalemate was an important factor promoting negotiations in 1988: these led to the decision to implement United Nations (q.v.) Resolution 435, providing for the independence of Namibia. The huge cost of the battle for South Africa (the shells fired from the G5 and G6 guns alone cost more than R200 million) put strong pressure on the South African government to negotiate independence for Namibia, as did the need to extricate the South African troops from Cuito Cuanavale once the Cubans had moved close to the Namibian border.

CURRENCY. As part of the apartheid (q.v.) government's policy of severing links with Britain, pounds, shillings, and pence were replaced by rands and cents after the declaration of the Republic (q.v.) of South Africa in 1961. The rand, issued by the South African Reserve Bank, was briefly linked to the British pound, but from October 1972 the rand–U.S. dollar rate became the only fixed one. In September 1975, the rand was devalued from $1.40 to $1.15. From January 1979, the rand's value against the dollar was permitted to float. The currency depreciated sharply against the dollar after the political situation deteriorated from mid-1984; the rand fell from $0.80 in January 1984 to $0.42 in January 1985 and to $0.35 by August 1985. A two-tier system of a commercial and a financial rand was then introduced to protect the currency; this lasted until March 1995, when the financial rand was phased out. Owing to currency speculation in early 1996, the rand lost 18 percent of its value against the U.S. dollar and several other currencies, and its value stood at $0.23 in June 1996. South Africa's inflation continued to be considerably higher than that of the countries with which it conducted the bulk of its trade, and in April 1998 the rand was worth $0.20. The worsening Asian financial crisis adversely affected South Africa's currency, and by July 1998 the rand had declined further to less than $0.16.

-D-

DA GAMA, VASCO (ca. 1460–1524). Commander in chief of the first Portuguese expedition to sail around the entire South African coast en route to India, Vasco da Gama and his men encountered Khoikhoi (q.v.) pastoralists in November 1497 at St. Helena Bay and then at Mossel Bay, the furthest point reached by Bartolomeu Dias (q.v.). In December 1497, da Gama gave the name "Natal" (q.v.) to the Pondoland coast, which his ships were passing at Christmas time.

DADOO, YUSUF (1909–83). Yusuf Dadoo was a leading member of the Communist Party of South Africa (q.v.) and the South African Indian Congress (SAIC). In 1946, as head of the SAIC, he led a passive resistance campaign against anti-Indian legislation. He then took the SAIC into an alliance with the African National Congress (q.v.). A key figure in the Congress Alliance (q.v.) in the 1950s, he went into exile in 1961 and remained active in anti-apartheid work until his death.

DE BEERS. The Kimberley (q.v.) and De Beers diamond (q.v.) mines were discovered on land owned by Nicholas de Beer (1830–before 1894). The land was bought by a syndicate of merchants and members of the Cape Parliament and later taken over by the government of Griqualand West (q.v.). The De Beers Company was formed by Cecil Rhodes (q.v.) in 1880, with an issued capital of £200,000. By 1885 it had capital of almost £850,000 through consolidation of claims in the De Beers mine. With a loan of £1 million from the Rothschilds, Rhodes bought a large holding in the Kimberley mine. De Beers Consolidated was formed in 1888 and by 1891 had effective control of the industry. De Beers then made an agreement with a powerful group of dealers, the Diamond Syndicate, who bought the entire output. From 1902 profits from sales were divided between De Beers and the syndicate.

Having a monopoly on production, De Beers could control the output to avoid overproduction and so could realize high prices. The company bought up land it thought might contain diamonds, fearing the emergence of a major new source of supply it could not control. Competition from the Premier Diamond Mine, founded in 1902 to exploit the rich Cullinan deposits near Pretoria (q.v.), hurt De Beers, especially in the recession of 1907–8. Rich alluvial discoveries in German South West Africa (now Namibia [q.v.]) also undermined its monopoly for a time. But by the end of World War I (q.v.), De Beers had acquired a controlling holding in the Premier Diamond Mine, and by the early 1920s Ernest Oppenheimer (q.v.), chairman of the holding company Anglo American (q.v.), gained control of the South West African mines. After the major find of diamonds in Botswana (formerly Bechuanaland [q.v.]) in the late 1960s and following the independence of Namibia, arrangements were made in which the governments of those countries acquired equal shares with De Beers in new diamond companies, Debswana and Namdeb, under the De Beers umbrella.

In the 1930s the producers themselves took over the distribution and marketing of diamonds through the London-based Central Selling Organisation. That arrangement has continued to the present, with De Beers trying, sometimes unsuccessfully, to control others from exploiting diamonds—whether the Argyle mine in Australia or individual prospectors in Angola (q.v.). Agreements were reached in Russia, both before and after the fall of communism, for De Beers to market Russian diamonds. Until the Asian crisis of 1998, Japan and other countries in the Far East were among the main customers for De Beers's diamonds.

DE KIEWIET, CORNELIS WILLEM (1903–86). Cornelis de Kiewiet, one of the greatest historians of South Africa, was taken to South Africa from Holland when young. He studied at the University of the Witwatersrand in the early 1920s, where he fell under the influence of W. M. Macmillan (q.v.), the professor of history. After working for Macmillan on the papers of John Philip (q.v.), he went to the University of London for his doctorate, which was subsequently published as *British Colonial Policy and the South African Republics* (1929). That volume was followed by *The Imperial Factor in South Africa* (1937), which took the story of British policy from the early 1870s to the mid-1880s. De Kiewiet settled in the United States, teaching in Iowa and then at Cornell. Although cut off from South African materials, he wrote a masterly *History of South Africa Social and Economic*, published in 1941, which made him even more influential than Macmillan. It long remained the best single-volume history of South Africa. A greater stylist than Macmillan, the two historians together did much to overturn the prosettler view of South African history advanced by George Theal (q.v.) and George Cory (q.v.). De Kiewiet argued that blacks had played as significant a role in South African history as whites and that relations between white and black were the key to that history. More than anyone else in his time, he explored central themes in the social and economic history of the country. In later life he was a university administrator in the United States. He continued to take a keen interest in South Africa but never returned to live in the country to which he devoted so much of his work.

DE KLERK, FREDERIK WILLEM (b. 1936). F. W. de Klerk, state president from 1989 to 1994 and one of the architects of the negotiated settlement of 1990–94, was born into a political family in the Transvaal (q.v.). He received an early training in politics through his membership of the Jeugbond, the youth section of the National Party (NP) (q.v.). He graduated from Potchefstroom (q.v.) University, practiced as an attorney, and then entered Parliament in 1972, becoming a cabinet minister in 1978 and leader of the Transvaal NP in 1982. When elected leader of the NP in early 1989, he had the reputation of being on the conservative wing of the party. He became acting state president in August of that year, after the resignation of P. W. Botha (q.v.), and state president the following month. On becoming president he quickly revealed himself to be a pragmatist. Realizing that he had to make drastic changes and that the collapse of communism in Eastern Europe presented new opportunities for decisive action, he chose the opening of Parliament on 2 February 1990 to announce the unbanning of the liberation movements and the unconditional release of Nelson Mandela (q.v.).

De Klerk played a leading role in the negotiation process that followed, holding face-to-face meetings with Mandela when the negotiations themselves were deadlocked. Mandela had called him a man of integrity in early 1990, but relations between the two men became very strained as Mandela accused him of not doing enough to bring the political violence in the country to an end. Throughout the shift in policy, de Klerk carried his cabinet and party with him, and the NP evolved from a racially based party to a nonracial one. He won a clear victory in an early-1992 referendum testing his support among whites. In 1993, with Mandela, he was awarded the Nobel Peace Prize. In early May 1994 he accepted defeat gracefully and became a deputy president in the new government of National Unity (GNU) (q.v.). Once the final constitution had been agreed to, he took his party out of the GNU, and from June 1996 he was leader of the opposition. In early 1997 he came under fire from commentators who claimed that he had proved himself a poor negotiator, inasmuch as he had failed to secure the guarantees for his Afrikaner (q.v.) constituency that he had promised. He was also criticized for failing to provide an adequate apology before the Truth and Reconciliation Commission (q.v.). In August 1997 he suddenly announced his resignation as leader of the NP and from Parliament, after which he spent some time on the North American lecture circuit and devoted himself to the writing of his memoirs. An extramarital affair he had been carrying on for some years became public knowledge in early 1998.

DE LA REY, JACOBUS HERCULES (1847–1914). The Boer (q.v.) general and politician, J. H. de la Rey, who opposed South African involvement in World War I (q.v.), planned a rebellion in an attempt to restore the independence of the Boer republics. Shot dead by a police patrol while en route to Potchefstroom (q.v.) to begin the military uprising, he became a martyr for Afrikaner nationalists (q.v.). *See also* AFRIKANER REBELLION; ORANGE FREE STATE; SOUTH AFRICAN REPUBLIC.

DEBT. Until the 1980s, South Africa's national debt was relatively small, but it began to increase rapidly from the early 1980s because of the need to pay for the huge cost of the war in Angola (q.v.) and numerous expensive apartheid (q.v.) projects, such as the Mossgas offshore gas development and the production of long-range missiles capable of carrying the nuclear warheads being built. The transition after 1990 from apartheid to democracy was also very expensive, with vast amounts paid for the negotiations themselves, integrating the armed forces, and running the April 1994 election. By the end of 1994, South Africa's total public-sector debt stood at R215.1 billion, of which only R1.64 billion (or 0.7 percent) was said to consist of foreign debt. The 1996–97 budget made provision for the borrowing of R2.5 billion from foreign funders. By the end of 1997 the national debt had soared to more than R325 billion, and more than 20 percent of the annual budget was going to service the debt itself. There were calls for the debt incurred in the apartheid era to be written off; South Africa's agreement after 1994 to take over Namibia's (q.v.) debt, incurred during the years of South African occupation, was cited as a precedent.

DEFENCE FORCE. *See* SOUTH AFRICAN DEFENCE FORCE.

DEFIANCE CAMPAIGN (1952). A civil disobedience campaign, known as the Defiance Campaign, was launched by the African National Congress (ANC) (q.v.) and the South African Indian Congress in June 1952 to bring about changes in government policy relating to pass laws (q.v.), livestock limitation, Bantu authorities, group areas (q.v.), separate representation of voters, and the suppression of communism. Large numbers of volunteers, most of them in the Transvaal (q.v.) and the Cape (q.v.), deliberately courted arrest by disobeying minor regulations, hoping this would disorganize authority by filling the prisons and courts to capacity. By the time the campaign ground to a halt in November 1952, 8,326 people had been arrested and, in nearly all cases, convicted of an offense. Police countermeasures, aided by the new Public Safety and Criminal Law Amendment Acts, brought an end to the campaign, whose main achievement lay in gaining widespread popular support for the ANC. The ANC's membership rose to 100,000 as a direct consequence of the Defiance Campaign.

DELAGOA BAY. The Portuguese began trading from Delagoa Bay—the finest harbor in southeast Africa, on which Maputo, capital of present-day Mozambique (q.v.), is situated—in the 1540s, and trade routes ran from the port to the mining areas of the eastern Transvaal (q.v.) and to the elephant hunting lands of Natal (q.v.). During the 18th century, the port became an important base for both slave (q.v.) and ivory traders. Some historians argue that this trade was a central factor in explaining the process of political centralization, which led to the emergence of the Zulu kingdom (q.v.) early in the 19th century.

Ownership of Delagoa Bay was claimed by the British, Dutch, and Portuguese, as well as by the Transvaal, in the 19th century. A French arbitrator awarded the port to Portugal in 1875. After the discovery of gold (q.v.) on the Witwatersrand (q.v.), the Transvaal built a railway (q.v.) line to Delagoa Bay in order to avoid Cape (q.v.) and Natal ports. Completed in 1895, the line continued to serve as an important link during the 20th century. Much of the Witwatersrand's exports left southern Africa through Delagoa Bay, and thousands of migrant (q.v.) laborers from Mozambique were transported along the line to the mines. After 1975, when Mozambique achieved its independence from Portugal, links between South Africa and Mozambique were largely severed, but in the 1990s the railway again transported goods between the two countries, and an ambitious plan was unveiled for a Maputo corridor linking the Witwatersrand with the port.

DEMOCRATIC PARTY (DP). To form a unified parliamentary party to the left of the government, the Progressive Federal Party (PFP) (originally the Progressive Party [q.v.]), the National Democratic Movement (NDM), and the Independent Party (IP) decided to merge, and the DP was launched in April 1989. Initially, its joint leaders were Denis Worrall, who had resigned as ambassador in London to oppose his erstwhile National Party (NP) (q.v.) colleagues as leader of the IP; Wynand Malan, who had left the NP caucus on the issue of reform and established the NDM; and Zach de Beer, leader of the PFP and subsequently sole DP leader. In the 1989 general election the DP increased the number of its parliamentary seats from 20 to 33. Democratic Party representatives played important roles in the negotiations that followed, and though the DP fared badly in the 1994 election, its handful of members of Parliament performed capably as a critical opposition in the new Parliament, advocating the principles of liberal democracy. The party remained a mostly white body, strongly committed to free-market principles. It rejected an offer by Nelson Mandela (q.v.) to join the government of National Unity (q.v.) in early 1997, but at the end of that year agreed to join the National Party–led government in the Western Cape (q.v.).

DESTABILIZATION. As part of the total strategy of P. W. Botha (q.v.), South African security forces acted in a variety of ways to try to prevent neighboring states from assisting the African National Congress (ANC) (q.v.). Massive military incursions into Angola (q.v.) became routine, while dirty tricks of various kinds were used, along with support for opposition movements and covert interference with cross-border trade. In the late 1980s, with the move toward independence for Namibia (q.v.) and the beginnings of the transition to democracy in South Africa, the policy was abandoned in relation to South Africa's neighbors, but new forms of internal destabilization, aimed at destroying the negotiations and preventing the ANC from coming to power, were undertaken by elements in the security forces.

DIAMONDS. Alluvial diamonds were found along the Orange River (q.v.) in 1867, but only after further discoveries in 1870 did digging begin in earnest in the pipes of blue ground at the so-called dry diggings, where Kimberley (q.v.) developed. Work at the Kimberley mine itself, which was to become the richest diamond mine in the world, began in 1871. By 1872, over 50,000 people had converged on the area; some 3,000 individual diggers acquired small claims and worked them with the assistance of laborers, using picks, shovels, and buckets. By the mid-1870s, amalgamation of these claims began to take place on a large scale, because of the collapse of the reef, the accumulation of water in the diggings, and the need for expensive steam machinery to facilitate more extensive underground digging. Overproduction of diamonds by the beginning of the 1880s intensified competition between the larger organizations, leading to further amalgamation and the emergence in 1888 of De Beers Consolidated Mines, owned by Cecil Rhodes (q.v.), with a monopoly of mining operations in Kimberley. De Beers eventually won control of other diamond deposits discovered later, in the Transvaal (q.v.) and in South West Africa (*see* NAMIBIA).

Ownership of the diamond fields was much disputed, and conflicting land claims by the Orange Free State (q.v.), the Transvaal (q.v.), and the Griqua (q.v.) state under Nicholaas Waterboer were resolved in 1871, when Waterboer's claims to the fields were recognized by the British High Commissioner, who extended British protection to the Griqua and annexed the area as the Crown Colony of Griqualand West (q.v.). A cash payment of £90,000 was given to the Orange Free State in 1876 in compensation, and in 1880 the Cape (q.v.) was finally persuaded to incorporate Griqualand West.

By 1872, Kimberley was a town second only to Cape Town (q.v.) in size on the subcontinent. As southern Africa's first industrial community, it created a new market for farmers. It also brought new prosperity to the ports of Cape Town and Port Elizabeth (q.v.), and railways (q.v.) linking Kimberley to the coast were constructed. Capital accumulation on the diamond fields made possible the rapid exploitation of gold (q.v.) on the Witwatersrand (q.v.) from the late 1880s. Patterns of labor that became conventional elsewhere in the country were also first established in Kimberley. Migrant laborers (q.v.) from as far as the Delagoa Bay (q.v.) hinterland and the northeastern Transvaal journeyed to the diamond fields, and were often paid in kind rather than in wages. The small number of black diggers were put out of business by the mid-1870s, pass laws (q.v.) were introduced to control the labor force in 1872, and a much tighter system of control was instituted through the closed compound system (q.v.) begun in 1885.

DIAS, BARTOLOMEU DE NOVAES (ca. 1450–1500). Commander of the first European ship to round the southern tip of Africa, in January 1488. He dropped anchor in Mossel Bay at the beginning of February 1488. Two caravels under his command sailed further east to Algoa Bay before the crews demanded that they return to Portugal. His voyage opened the way for Vasco da Gama (q.v.) to sail on to India.

DINGANE (ca. 1795–1840). Zulu (q.v.) king who assumed power after participating in the assassination of his half-brother Shaka (q.v.) in 1828. Determined to maintain Zulu domination, he sent a large force onto the high veld to attack the Ndebele (q.v.) under Mzilikazi (q.v.), who had fled from Shaka in the early 1820s. Though the Ndebele defeated Dingane's army in 1832, he retained his control in Natal (q.v.), where he was obliged to deal with Voortrekker (q.v.) incursions under the leadership of Piet Retief (q.v.) in 1838. After initially concluding an agreement with the Voortrekkers, Dingane had Retief murdered in February that year, and then attempted to drive the Voortrekkers out of Natal. The Zulu army was overcome at Blood River (q.v.) by a Voortrekker commando under Andries Pretorius in December 1838, and Dingane's authority was much weakened. Ousted by his half-brother Mpande (q.v.) in 1840, he escaped to Swaziland (q.v.), where he was murdered.

DINGISWAYO (ca. 1770–1818). Chief of the Mthethwa chiefdom. Though he seized power in a violent manner in 1809, he displayed considerable skill in winning loyal followers and extending the influence of his chiefdom. He played a leading role in developing the fighting methods of the Mthethwa army, and won control of the lucrative trade routes to Delagoa Bay (q.v.), which made him the most influential figure in southeast Africa until his murder by the chief Zwide (q.v.) of the Ndwandwe, ca. 1818. Dingiswayo's death paved the way for the rise to power of Shaka (q.v.) of the Zulu (q.v.), to whom he had given refuge.

DINUZULU (ca. 1870–1913). The son of the Zulu (q.v.) king Cetshwayo (q.v.), he was caught in a bitter struggle for succession with Zibhebhu, a relative and a powerful chief, after the death of his father in 1884. He defeated Zibhebhu with the support of Transvaal (q.v.) Boers (q.v.), to whom he ceded land in return for military assistance. After the British annexed Zululand in 1887, Dinuzulu was exiled to St. Helena for 10 years on charges of rebellion. On his return in 1898, he enjoyed the status of only a minor chief. He was again put on trial for treason, public violence, and sedition after being implicated in the Bambatha Rebellion (q.v.) of 1906, and was sentenced to four years of imprisonment. He was released in 1910, and spent the remainder of his life in exile on a farm in the Transvaal.

DITHAKONG, BATTLE OF. Dithakong, the Tlhaping (q.v.) capital northeast of Kuruman, was defended successfully by the Tlhaping, with the assistance of Griqua (q.v.) troops who had horses and firearms, from attack by thousands of invaders in June 1823 at the time of the Mfecane (q.v.). This prevented disruption from spreading further west in the southern African interior.

DOMINION PARTY. Founded in 1934 by Colonel C. F. Stallard (1871–1971). Most members were English-speakers (q.v.) from Natal (q.v.) who would not follow Jan Smuts (q.v.) into fusion (q.v.) with J. B. M. Hertzog's (q.v.) National Party (q.v.). They distrusted Hertzog and feared that fusion would endanger the Imperial connection. They voted against Hertzog's legislation on land and franchise passed in 1936, and supported Smuts in 1939 over entering World War II (q.v.). When Smuts broke with Hertzog, the rationale for a separate party faded away, and most members soon cast in their lot with Smuts's United Party (q.v.).

DRAKENSBERG. Afrikaans for "dragon mountain," this mountain range runs for 650 miles with major peaks over 11,000 feet, separating the coastal corridor from the interior plateau (the high veld) of South Africa. To Nguni-speakers (q.v.), the central portion of the range, a formidable barrier, was known as Qathlamba, meaning "mountain of spears." The southern and northern sections were relatively easy to cross, for example, by those uprooted from Natal (q.v.) by the Mfecane (q.v.) in the early 1820s and by Voortrekkers (q.v.) moving in the opposite direction in 1837. The Drakensberg also offered a relatively secure refuge to the San (q.v.) in the 19th century. Langalibalele (q.v.) fled into the Drakensberg in 1873, and the mountains saw fighting during the Anglo–Transvaal War (q.v.) and the South African War (q.v.). In the 20th century, the mountains became a major tourist attraction.

DRUM. A popular magazine, first published in 1951, which appeared monthly for the next 12 years. It was a unique product and record of the 1950s. *Drum* played a fundamental role in recording the formation of an emerging black urban culture, focused particularly but not exclusively in Johannesburg (q.v.). It also provided almost the sole platform for aspiring black writers, such as Ezekiel Mphahlele and Alex la Guma, as well as Can Themba, Casey Motsisi, Bloke Modisane, and Lewis Nkosi. Coloured (q.v.) writers such as James Matthews, Peter Clarke, and Richard Rive also published in *Drum*. The work of the period—documentary reportage, creative literature, and protest writing—was closely intertwined, and *Drum* afforded many black journalists and creative writers the opportunity to begin, shape, and advance their careers. As such, it occupies a crucial and distinctive position in the emergence of black literature in South Africa.

DUBE, JOHN LANGALIBALELE (1871–1946). The educator, journalist, and politician John Dube, educated in Natal (q.v.) and the United States, founded the Ohlange Institute outside Durban (q.v.) in 1901 as an educational center. He established Natal's first black newspaper, *Ilanga lase Natal*, in 1903 and edited it until 1915. He was the first president-general of the South African Native National Congress, later the African National Congress (q.v.), serving from 1912 until 1917. Thereafter, he ceased to play a role in national politics but continued to be active in political and educational work in Natal.

DUNCAN, SIR PATRICK (1870–1943). One of the Milner Kindergarten (q.v.), Duncan was colonial secretary for the Transvaal (q.v.) from 1903 to 1907, a member of Parliament, cabinet minister under Jan Smuts (q.v.), legal adviser on Bechuanaland (q.v.) to the British high commissioner, and then governor-general of South Africa from 1936. He supported the Unionist Party (q.v.), was later a leading member of the South African Party (q.v.), and was a founding member of the United Party (q.v.). Keen to reconcile English speakers (q.v.) and Afrikaners (q.v.), Duncan worked with Smuts, J. B. M. Hertzog (q.v.), and J. C. Havenga to form a coalition in 1933 and fusion (q.v.) in 1934. In 1939, as governor-general he played an important role in the decision that South Africa should participate in World War II (q.v.). He died in office in 1943.

DURBAN. White settlement began in 1824, when a small party of traders from the eastern Cape (q.v.) was granted a cession of land from the Zulu (q.v.) ruler Shaka (q.v.) at a natural harbor, which they named Port Natal. In 1835, its name was changed to honor Sir Benjamin D'Urban, Cape governor at the time. After Britain annexed Natal (q.v.) in 1843, greater numbers of British immigrants arrived; by 1854, when Durban received a municipal charter, it had a population of 1,200 whites and a smaller number of Africans. The development of the harbor mouth, which chiefly required the elimination of a sandbar to enable large ships to enter the harbor, was completed in 1904; by then it was connected by rail to the Transvaal (q.v.), and in the 20th century the port handled more cargo than any other in the country.

By 1950, Durban was the country's third-largest city, and its population comprised Africans, Indians (q.v.), and whites in almost equal numbers. A manufacturing center and the headquarters of the country's sugar industry, it was a popular tourist destination. By the end of the 1980s, when it was reputed to be Africa's fastest-growing city and its port the busiest in Africa, Durban's population exceeded three million people, the large majority of whom were Africans. By the mid-1990s large numbers of foreign tourists were visiting the city, attracted in part by its cosmopolitanism.

DUTCH. Under the rule of the Dutch East India Company (q.v.) and the British, Dutch was the official language (q.v.) of the Cape (q.v.) until 1822, when English (q.v.) was proclaimed the language of government and justice; English also increasingly became the language used in Cape schools. In the Boer republics established after the Great Trek (q.v.), Dutch was the language of government, law, the church, and the schools. In the Cape, meanwhile, campaigns on behalf of the Dutch language undertaken by J. H. Hofmeyr ("Onze Jan") (q.v.), editor of *De Suid-Afrikaan,* during the 1870s began to bear fruit: in 1882, Dutch was recognized as an official language of the Cape Parliament, and it gradually gained equal recognition with English as an official language in the colony. The South Africa Act of 1909, which created the Union (q.v.) of South Africa, provided that Dutch and English should both be official languages and should be treated equally. In 1925, the Union Parliament passed legislation declaring that Dutch was to be understood as including Afrikaans (q.v.); Afrikaans in effect became an official language of the country from that date. *See also* BRITAIN IN SOUTH AFRICA; ORANGE FREE STATE; SOUTH AFRICAN REPUBLIC.

DUTCH EAST INDIA COMPANY / VERENIGDE OOST-INDISCHE COMPAGNIE (VOC). A private commercial trading company, the Dutch East India Company was founded in 1602 to coordinate Dutch trading expeditions to the East Indies. Under its charter from the States General (the government of the Netherlands), it enjoyed a monopoly of all Dutch trade east of the Cape of Good Hope, a position that enabled it to build enormous commercial and political power and to become the largest company in the world by the end of the 17th century. In 1652, the VOC established a base at the Cape of Good Hope to service and supply its ships on the sea route between the Netherlands and the East. This refreshment station was intended to be a contained supply post, and it was never envisaged that a colony of settlement would develop at the Cape (q.v.). The growth of the station into a large colony occurred under the supervision of the VOC, whose officials ruled the Cape until 1795.

The Dutch East India Company's rule at the Cape was directed toward narrow company goals: the maximization of profit at minimal expense. For most of the period to 1795, the VOC rule at the Cape was characterized by corruption and inefficiency. The governor and the seven-member Council of Policy at the Cape were all VOC officials; although technically responsible to the VOC's board of 17 directors in the Netherlands, they had extensive local power. They presided over a colony characterized by extreme inequality, though it never experienced any serious rebellion: a combination of repressive government, brutal punishment, bribery, and close networks of officials kept VOC power intact. By the 1780s, however, the VOC was in terminal decline as a result of competition from English and French traders and domestic events in the Netherlands. Its survival became dependent on loans from the States General after 1783, and in 1794 the company was declared bankrupt. At that stage, a commission of inquiry was compiling a large volume of evidence of VOC corruption and misgovernance at the Cape and elsewhere. In 1795, the British conquest of the Cape brought to an end VOC control of the Cape; the company was taken over in 1796 by the new Dutch government, the Batavian (q.v.) Republic, which terminated the company's operations shortly thereafter.

DUTCH REFORMED CHURCHES. The Reformed Church was the official church in the Cape Colony (q.v.) during the Dutch East India Company (q.v.) period. Its activities and ministers were controlled by the company and by the mother church in Holland, but these links were severed after the British occupation (q.v.) of the Cape. Its life was invigorated by a number of Scottish Presbyterian ministers who joined it from the 1820s. One result of this was the beginnings of missionary (q.v.) work on a large scale, something that had not been deemed necessary during the 18th century. In 1843, the church was given virtual self-government by the state and adopted the name Nederduits Gereformeerde Kerk (NGK). The NGK began work among the Voortrekkers (q.v.) during the 1840s, though the Cape-based church was initially reluctant to support the trekkers. In the early 1850s the trekkers at Potchefstroom (q.v.) decided to sever links with the church, associated as it was with the British-ruled Cape, and formed the Nederduitsch Hervormde Kerk, which was given official recognition in the republican constitution of 1856. Further religious dissension occurred when those who objected to the singing of hymns in public worship formed a separate Gereformeerde Kerk in Rustenburg in the Transvaal (q.v.) in 1859. A strict Calvinist church, its members developed close bonds with neo-Calvinists in Holland and became known as "Doppers." Although only a minority of Afrikaners (q.v.) supported it, the Gereformeerde Kerk nevertheless experienced strong growth and developed the Potchefstroom University for Christian Higher Education in the 20th century.

The Cape synod of the NGK decided in 1857 that separate services could be held for whites and blacks because of the "weakness" of the former; this was understood to be a practical solution to cultural differences rather than desirable on scriptural or doctrinal grounds. Separate congregations became the norm and led to the establishment of "daughter" mission churches defined on racial grounds: the Sendingkerk for Coloureds (q.v.) (founded in 1881), the Nederduits Gereformeerde Kerk in Africa for Africans (q.v.), and the Indian Reformed Church. During the early 1930s, this arrangement of "convenience" underwent profound reorientation as white church leaders developed theological and biblical justifications for the racial separation of the churches. In 1948, a report entitled "Racial and National Apartheid in the Bible" was accepted as official policy and became a foundation of the theological defense of apartheid (q.v.).

By the end of the 1940s, the NGK was largely isolated from mainstream ecumenical life and theological trends in the wider Reformed Church and devoted its attention to the creation of a federal structure for the four provincial churches. This was achieved in 1962. Widely perceived to be the National Party (q.v.) at prayer, the NGK was by far the largest of the three Dutch Reformed churches: in 1980, it had 1.7 million white members, as opposed to the 258,000 of the Nederduitsch Hervormde Kerk and the 127,000 of the Gereformeerde Kerk. The NGK's "daughter" churches were similarly strong, with a combined total of 1.8 million adherents. During the 1980s, the NGK was riven by failed attempts to unite the mission churches with the main church, as well as by its official stance over apartheid. Its pronouncements on church and society were largely uncertain and ambiguous, and the church experienced a decline in membership of close to 20 percent. In 1997 it formally apologized before the Truth and Reconciliation Commission (q.v.) for its role in apartheid. In October 1998, the Dutch Reformed Church finally declared that it fundamentally rejected apartheid and that it disowned the former government's policy on theological grounds. This opened the door to its being readmitted to the World Alliance of Reformed Churches.

DUTCH–KHOIKHOI WARS (1659–60; 1673–77). The first of the wars fought between newly arrived Dutch settlers and Khoikhoi (q.v.) hunterpastoralists in the southwestern Cape (q.v.) was confined to the peninsula, near the fledgling white settlement, where the first white farms encroached on Khoikhoi grazing land; it ended in stalemate after a year of inconclusive fighting, with the Khoikhoi having failed to expel whites from the peninsula. In the second war, the Dutch, having expanded gradually beyond the peninsula, attempted to defeat Gonnema, leader of the Cochoqua. He was subjugated in 1677, after the Dutch obtained the assistance of other Khoikhoi, and he agreed to pay an annual tribute to the Dutch governor. His defeat marked the end of serious Khoikhoi resistance to Dutch expansion in the southwestern Cape.

DU TOIT, STEPHANUS JACOBUS (1847–1911). Writer, educator, and cultural leader, S. J. du Toit is remembered most for his early campaigns on behalf of the Afrikaans (q.v.) language. He founded a cultural organization, Die Genootskap van Regte Afrikaners (1875), and the first Afrikaans newspaper, *Die Afrikaanse Patriot* (1876), and he produced the first Afrikaans grammar book (1876) and history (1877). He also founded the Afrikaner Bond (q.v.), the first organized party in the Cape (q.v.) Parliament.

-E-

EASTERN CAPE. The Eastern Cape Province was created in April 1994 from the Transkei (q.v.) and Ciskei (q.v.) bantustans (q.v.) and the former eastern part of the Cape Province, including the Port Elizabeth–Uitenhage industrial complex and much of the scenic Garden Route. Bisho (q.v.), the former capital of Ciskei, adjacent to King William's Town, became the capital of the new province. The African National Congress (q.v.) won a large majority in the Provincial Assembly in the 1994 election, with almost 85 percent of the vote, and Raymond Mhlaba, who had been imprisoned on Robben Island (q.v.) with Nelson Mandela (q.v.), became the first provincial premier. He proved unable to deal with the administrative problems caused by integrating two former bantustans with a portion of the former Cape Province, and in early 1997 he was succeeded by Arnold Stofile.

EASTERN CAPE SEPARATISM. In 1823 colonists in the eastern Cape called for separation from the government in Cape Town (q.v.), which they perceived to be antagonistic to their interests. For some, separatism meant the development of a loose federalism in the Cape Colony (q.v.). Others wanted the seat of government to be transferred from Cape Town to the eastern districts, a move they believed would dispose parliamentarians more favorably toward eastern problems. Yet others desired complete independence from the Cape Colony. Separatist issues were articulated most vociferously in the *Grahams Town Journal*, under the editorship of Robert Godlonton (1794–1884), a leading spokesman for the settlers. Farming, commercial, and urban groups in the eastern districts never achieved more than transient unity, however. In 1860, the Separatist League was established, led by wool (q.v.) producers fighting the imposition of a tax on wool, and in the early 1860s separatism appeared to be a serious force. The Cape (q.v.) Parliament met in Grahamstown (q.v.) in 1864, in part to assuage separatist feeling. Tensions between competing interests within the eastern Cape were never far from the surface, however, and after the discovery of diamonds (q.v.) rivalry between towns and interest groups intensified, weakening irrevocably any chance of a unified separatist movement. Separatist ideas surfaced from time to time in Grahamstown in the late 19th century, particularly in the late 1870s at the time of the confederation (q.v.) schemes, but never again carried significant weight.

ECONOMIC CHANGE. Some 2,000 years ago, Khoikhoi (q.v.) pastoralists practicing a nomadic lifestyle settled alongside the hunter-gatherers who had long inhabited the region. About two centuries later, Bantu-speaking (q.v.) agriculturists and pastoralists settled south of the Limpopo River (q.v.), bringing further economic diversification. They introduced mining, particularly for iron and copper. Both the Khoikhoi and the Bantu speakers engaged in considerable trade (mainly in livestock and manufactured goods such as iron objects, leather and wood crafts, and beads) over long distances, and ties were forged with traders beyond what is now South Africa.

With the establishment of the white settlement by the Dutch East India Company (q.v.) in 1652, trade increased as Khoikhoi bartered increasing numbers of livestock and hunting products for beads and manufactured European goods. Fruit and vegetables were supplied to passing ships, and the production of wheat (q.v.) and wine (q.v.) in the southwestern Cape (q.v.) slowly expanded during the 17th and 18th centuries, until viticulture became the main industry of the area by the beginning of the 19th century.

After the second British occupation (q.v.) in 1806, the Cape Colony (q.v.) was drawn into the British imperial economy. The tight trading and monopolistic restrictions of the Dutch East India Company were lifted, exports were encouraged by a lowering of tariffs, immigration was promoted, and agriculture (q.v.), commerce, banking, and transport all developed markedly during the first half of the 19th century. Merino sheep farming was introduced into the eastern Cape in 1827, and in the 1830s wool (q.v.) began to overtake wine as the Cape's major export. Production rose dramatically: 144,000 pounds weight in 1834, 1 million pounds in 1841, 5 million pounds in 1851, and 25 million pounds in 1862. Although the drought of the 1860s and the slump in world prices after the American Civil War greatly reduced production, wool remained the country's most important agricultural export. In Natal (q.v.) after 1860, but particularly from the 1870s, sugarcane became a valuable cash crop for white farmers, and black peasants supplied a large proportion of the grain market. The two Boer republics (the Orange Free State and the South African Republic [qq.v.]) practiced semisubsistence agriculture.

The discovery of diamonds (q.v.) in 1867 and then gold (q.v.) in the early 1870s set in motion changes that transformed much of the country's economy. The economic center of the country shifted from the eastern Cape to the Kimberley–Cape Town (qq.v.) axis and then firmly to the high veld (q.v.). Foreign capital poured into the country; profits from the diamond mines financed the country's first important railways (q.v.) as well as the initial development of the gold-mining industry; and coal mining also grew dramatically from the end of the 19th century. The new urban centers in the interior opened up an enormous new market for agricultural produce. White farmers began to commercialize, aided by the transfer of revenues obtained from mining, and competition from African peasant farmers was eliminated.

The creation of the Union (q.v.) of South Africa in 1910 underpinned further economic growth during the 20th century, although expansion was unevenly spread. Agriculture experienced severe difficulties during the 1920s and 1930s, as problems arising from soil erosion, drought, population pressure, and economic depression battered farmers. After the 1950s, agriculture was transformed by increasing specialization, technological improvements, and capital-intensive farming. Agriculture's position in the economy declined, however, during the second half of the century. New mines were opened during the interwar years, and gold, in particular, boomed during the 1930s.

In the 20th century, the most important structural change in South Africa's economy was the expansion of manufacturing (q.v.), at the expense of mining and agriculture, in the contribution to national income. In 1911–12, mining contributed 27.1 percent of net domestic product, agriculture 17.4 percent, and manufacturing 6.7 percent. During World War II (q.v.), manufacturing overtook mining as the leading sector. In 1995, manufacturing contributed 23.5 percent of gross domestic product (GDP), mining and quarrying 8.7 percent, and agriculture 4.7 percent. Although mining remained important and coal exports increased dramatically, the value of mining exports as a proportion of overall exports declined as the manufacturing sector grew. During the first half of the century, significant developments occurred in the textile, food-processing, engineering, and iron and steel industries. After World War II, the industrial base of the country broadened and diversified further. By the late 1980s, however, the economy was suffering severely from sanctions (q.v.), and only arms production boomed.

The average growth of the economy in the five decades between 1911–12 and 1961–62 was 1.8 percent per annum; allowing for price increases and population growth, real income per capita more than doubled during this period. During the 1960s, growth was exceptionally high, and GDP grew at an average rate of 5.9 percent per annum. This fell sharply during the decade of the 1970s, when GDP grew at an average of 3.3 percent. Further declines were recorded in the 1980s, when an average growth of only 1.4 percent in GDP was recorded (negative real growth rates occurred in 1982, 1983, 1985, and 1990); with the population increase of 2.6 percent per annum in this decade, per capita income was in decline. A similar situation occurred in the decade preceding 1995, when GDP grew at an average of just under 2.5 percent.

South Africa remained heavily dependent on international trade during the 20th century. At the same time the composition of imports changed markedly during the century. Imports as a proportion of national income did not change much from their average level of 24 percent in the 1930s, but in 1910 food, drink, clothing, and textiles constituted 46 percent of total imports, whereas these consumer goods constituted only 11.7 percent in 1994, when intermediate and capital goods made up the bulk of imports. In 1968, 92 percent of imports were manufactured, whereas only 38 percent of exports were classified as manufactured goods (and a large proportion of these were only lightly manufactured agricultural and mineral products). South Africa remains heavily dependent on mining and agriculture to pay for imported products.

The total value of South Africa's exports in 1994 was R87.5 billion, equivalent to 20.9 percent of gross national product (GNP). By 1994, the United Kingdom, traditionally South Africa's main trading partner, had slipped to third position. In that year, the main suppliers of imported goods were Germany (at 16.4 percent), the United States (15.7 percent), the United Kingdom (11.3 percent), and Japan (9.9 percent). South Africa's exports in 1994 went mainly to Switzerland (6.7 percent), the United Kingdom (6.6 percent), the United States (4.8 percent), and Japan (4.6 percent). Exports to all African countries totaled 9.6 percent, whereas imports from Africa constituted only 3 percent of all imported goods. The chief African markets for exports were Zimbabwe (q.v.), Zambia, and Mozambique (q.v.), whereas the only substantial supplier of imports was Zimbabwe. South Africa joined the Southern African Development Community (q.v.) in August 1994.

After the 1960s, when the country achieved remarkable economic development (although the results of this were unevenly distributed), the South African economy performed much less well. Although the instability of the world economy was sometimes to blame, domestic political upheaval, a weakening in the gold price, foreign sanctions, and periodic drought were more important in restricting economic growth. The country experienced its longest recession of the 20th century between 1989 and 1993, when real GDP fell by 4 percent and employment fell by 8 percent. In 1993, gross domestic investment was R59.9 billion, equivalent to 15.6 percent of GDP. This was financed by gross domestic savings of R65.9 million (17.2 percent of GDP), allowing for net capital outflows to the rest of the world of R8.8 billion, and a decrease in gold and other reserves of R2.9 billion.

Low levels of investment limited the ability of the economy to generate growth and create employment. More than 100,000 jobs in mining and 60,000 in manufacturing were lost during the first half of the 1990s. Employment levels had been poor, however, since the end of the 1960s. During the 1970s the number of those employed rose only by 2.7 percent per annum, barely in excess of the population growth, and during the 1980s employment among Africans (q.v.) grew at only 1.4 percent per annum, well under the population increase. Accurate statistics of unemployment are difficult to obtain, as official statistics cover only the limited number of registered unemployed people. A large migration to towns occurred in the country after the abolition of influx control (q.v.) in 1986, and disguised unemployment in the rural areas was increasingly registered as overt unemployment in the urban areas. An official survey in October 1994 placed the number of unemployed at 32 percent of the labor force (about 4.6 million people). The informal sector of the economy has absorbed some of these people, but unemployment has remained one of the most serious challenges for the new democratic government.

Although South Africa could thus boast a modern economy, its economic performance was hampered by the constraints of population increase exceeding economic growth, and large areas of the country remained underdeveloped. The economy was heavily dependent on the export of primary products, the prices of which had been falling since the early 1960s. After 1994 especially, as sanctions fell away and South Africa entered the global economy more fully, it was forced increasingly to compete on the world market. Basic needs of the entire population had to be addressed, while at the same time the country had to try to be competitive internationally.

EDUCATION. Before white settlement began, children were educated by their families and communities in different ways, from the transmission of oral traditions and rituals between generations and the instruction of children at puberty through initiation ceremonies to the communication of economic skills essential to the continuing survival of communities. Formal schooling began with a school established in 1658 by officials of the Dutch East India Company (VOC) (q.v.) at the Cape (q.v.) for slave (q.v.) children. This was meant to increase the usefulness of slaves to the colonists. The children of white colonists began to receive formal education from 1663, in a small school run by an official of the Dutch Reformed Church (q.v.). This inaugurated a segregated educational system that dominated education for the entire VOC period.

The history and development of formal schooling in South Africa is closely intertwined with the history of the Christian (q.v.) church and missionary (q.v.) activities. The educational responsibilities of the Dutch Reformed Church were widely accepted in the colony, and proposals by the commissioner-general of the Batavian (q.v.) Republic, J. A. U. de Mist, to secularize education under state control were met with considerable suspicion. After the British occupation (q.v.) of the Cape, an anglicization process was begun, and teachers were recruited from England and Scotland. In 1839, the Department of Education was established under a superintendent-general. The first holder of the office, James Rose Innes, initiated a two-tier system of state-maintained schools: first-class schools in large towns and second-class schools, providing only primary education, in small centers. Mission schools, as well as smaller farm and community schools, were entitled to state subsidies under certain conditions. Many state-aided schools were formed by local initiative in subsequent years, until the arrangement was formalized in the Cape by the Education Act of 1865. This pattern of state nondenominational schools and state-aided mission and church schools was extended to Natal (q.v.) and the Orange Free State (q.v.), although private schools, often founded on religious principles, were also permitted to function. In the Transvaal (q.v.), this British pattern was rejected in favor of a Dutch model, with teachers recruited from Holland. From the 1880s, a pattern of Christian national education (CNE) began to develop, based on Calvinism and nascent Afrikaner nationalism (q.v.); after the South African War (q.v.), CNE schools were strongly promoted in the Transvaal and Orange Free State, with the backing of the Dutch Reformed Church, in opposition to anglicization and other state initiatives.

After the establishment of the Union (q.v.) of South Africa in 1910, provincial control was maintained over white schools, while the great majority of blacks who received an education did so in schools that had been founded by missionary societies in the 19th century and were continued, often with grants from the state, either by those societies or by different churches. Much mission education was limited to vocational and manual training, although this slowly began to change during the early decades of the 20th century. After the election of the National Party (q.v.) to government in 1948, educational policy was reformulated along apartheid (q.v.) lines. A commission under W. M. Eiselen recommended in 1951 that control of education be removed from the churches and missions and, while white education would continue to be run by the provinces, that a separate central government department should henceforth supervise what was called Bantu education (q.v.). These proposals were taken up in the Bantu Education Act of 1953, which initiated separate and inferior state-controlled education for blacks, provoking considerable upheaval during the 1950s as churches were largely obliged to sever their links with education.

The Soweto uprising (q.v.) of 1976 marked the beginnings of overt black rejection of apartheid education and forced the state to begin planning for educational reform. Changes were very slow in implementation. Although the De Lange Commission of 1981 recommended the abolition of racially based education, the tricameral (q.v.) constitution of 1983 continued to categorize education along racial lines. After 1983, no fewer than 14 different official departments, together with various bantustan (q.v.) authorities, were responsible for education in various areas of the country and for separate sections of society. Private schools began to implement nonracial education during the 1980s, but it was only in the 1990s that state schools began to admit pupils from all backgrounds.

The challenges of education posed formidable challenges to the post-1994 government as it grappled with the legacy of apartheid and the enormous disparities in the quality and funding of education. Although considerable progress was made in rationalizing various educational authorities and examining bodies, the allocation of resources and funding remained contentious issues, as did syllabus changes. In 1997 a major new outcomes-based approach to learning, called Curriculum 2005 after the expected date of final implementation, was launched by the Ministry of National Education, to be phased in beginning in 1998.

ENGLISH. English-speaking settlers and their descendants have lived in close proximity to speakers of other languages (q.v.) for two centuries, and a form of English easily recognized as South African has emerged. Many words from Afrikaans, Khoisan, and Bantu (qq.v) languages have been adopted, and South African English has many distinctive pronunciations, adaptations, and constructions. A rich literature developed; some South Africans writing in English won international acclaim, such as Alan Paton for *Cry, the Beloved Country*, and Nadine Gordimer, who was awarded the Nobel Prize for literature in 1991.

In the 1990s, English was the first language of more than three million South Africans, or 8 percent of the population: about 39 percent of whites (q.v.), 15 percent of Coloureds (q.v.), and 95 percent of Indians (q.v.) spoke English as their first language. Its influence as a medium of communication between people of different backgrounds, and as the major language of public life, was vastly more important than was suggested by its status as merely one of eleven official languages. *See also* ENGLISH-SPEAKING WHITES.

ENGLISH-SPEAKING WHITES. When the British first occupied (q.v.) the Cape (q.v.) in 1795, there were few English-speaking people anywhere in southern Africa. After the second British occupation in 1806, their numbers grew steadily, reaching 4,000 by 1820. In that year, a further 5,000 settlers were recruited from England and were located by the Cape authorities in the Albany district (formerly the Zuurveld [q.v.]) on the eastern frontier (q.v.) of the colony. Although English (q.v.) speakers remained a distinct minority of the white population despite this influx of immigrants (there were some 43,000 Dutch speakers), they soon exercised a predominant influence in the colony.

The settlers of 1820 were socially and politically diverse. The majority of males were artisans and tradesmen, but they also included farmers, soldiers, teachers, and a handful of professionals; few had any substantial financial resources. They were ill equipped for conditions in the eastern Cape, where the colonial authorities wished to use them as small-scale agriculturists to secure the defense of the frontier against the Xhosa (q.v.). By 1824, almost two-thirds had abandoned their farms and moved to Grahamstown (q.v.) and other emerging small towns in the eastern Cape. Most of them quickly established themselves in a range of commercial pursuits, and legal and illicit trade across the frontier enriched many. Merchants and shopkeepers also moved into the interior, and small towns founded in the Orange Free State (q.v.) and the Transvaal (q.v.) often had a strong English-speaking presence. Those who stayed on farms began to prosper on larger holdings of land, particularly after the introduction of merino sheep farming. By the end of the 1830s, wool (q.v.) had become the principal export of the Cape.

The colonial authorities in Cape Town (q.v.) actively consolidated English influence in the Cape. During the 1820s, the autocratic governor, Lord Somerset (q.v.), sought to replace the use of Dutch (q.v.) in public life by English through his anglicization policies. English became the sole language (q.v.) of government from 1825 and of the courts from 1827. Anglicization was pursued less aggressively after 1827, but English enjoyed preferential treatment in schools, churches, and public life. English speakers dominated Cape politics for most of the century, though the Afrikaner Bond (q.v.) challenged their position from the 1880s.

In contrast with the Cape, the majority of white colonists in British-ruled Natal (q.v.) were English speaking. The earliest permanent white settlers there in 1824 were English speaking, and after annexation in 1843, English-speaking immigrants arrived in considerable numbers, particularly between 1849 and 1852, when just under 5,000 English and Scottish people arrived in Durban (q.v.) with government assistance. Many settled in Durban, Pietermaritzburg (q.v.), and other towns, and others prospered from growing sugar and fruit crops, from indigenous timber and wattle cultivation, and from cattle and sheep farming. Large numbers of English speakers, particularly artisans and skilled workers, were attracted to South Africa after the discovery of diamonds (q.v.) and gold (q.v.) in the interior. Their presence in the Transvaal provoked considerable tension between them and the government, especially after the Jameson Raid (q.v.). The South African War (q.v.) and Lord Milner's (q.v.) postwar attempts at anglicization deepened divisions between English speakers and Afrikaners (q.v.). A measure of reconciliation was achieved between these two groups after creation of the Union (q.v.) of South Africa in 1910, and the status of English was enshrined alongside Dutch (later, Afrikaans [q.v.]) in the constitution. English speakers were outnumbered by Afrikaners in the Union, despite ongoing immigration from Britain until 1948; this restricted their political influence. Between

1910 and 1948, most English speakers offered their political allegiance to the South African Party (q.v.), which was committed to reconciling Afrikaners and English-speaking whites, and then to the United Party (q.v.). The more chauvinistic Unionist and Dominion Parties (qq.v.), which relied exclusively on English-speaking support, never became significant political forces.

Despite their political weakness, English-speaking whites dominated commerce, industry, business, and banking. English was the principal language of South African urban life, even in places such as Pretoria and Bloemfontein (qq.v.), until the urbanization of Afrikaners during the interwar years. Considerable economic inequality between English- and Afrikaans-speaking whites persisted in towns until the 1960s. English-speaking immigration to South Africa, which stopped when the National Party (NP) (q.v.) came to power, began to increase again during the 1960s, and by the late 1970s as many as 20,000 English-speaking immigrants entered the country each year. Most immigrants from Europe, and from former European colonies in Africa, were absorbed into the English-speaking community, although few took out citizenship: in the 1980s at least one-fifth of English-speaking whites were not citizens.

The political influence of English-speaking whites declined markedly after 1948. Most gave their allegiance to the white-supremacist United Party, which slowly declined until its demise in 1977. After the NP achieved its goal of a republic (q.v.) in 1961 and toned down its aggressive Afrikaner nationalist (q.v.) rhetoric, it began to win English-speaking support and by the end of the 1970s had gained a significant number of votes from English speakers. More liberal English-speaking whites found a political home in the Progressive Party (q.v.) (the Progressive Federal Party after 1977), whose support base lay largely in more-affluent constituencies in the major cities. Among whites, most of the strongest critics of apartheid (q.v.) were English speakers: people such as Helen Suzman (q.v.), the Progressive Party MP; Alan Paton (q.v.), who was active in the Liberal Party (q.v.); and Helen Joseph, who worked closely with the African National Congress (q.v.). Several English-language newspapers won international prominence for their anti-apartheid campaigns.

ESAU, ABRAHAM (ca. 1856–1901). A martyr from Calvinia in the northwestern Cape (q.v.), Abraham Esau's support for the British during the South African War (q.v.) earned him the hostility of invading Boer (q.v.) commandos (q.v.) and Cape rebels. Because he had raised a force of Coloureds (q.v.) to fight on the British side, the Boers murdered him when they occupied Calvinia in 1901.

-F-

FAGAN COMMISSION (1946–48). The Native Laws Commission, appointed by the United Party (UP) (q.v.) government of Jan Smuts (q.v.) under the chairmanship of Henry Fagan (1889–1963), a former minister of native affairs, was expected to investigate the position of urban Africans (q.v.) and to make recommendations for possible legal and constitutional reform. Its response to the influx of Africans into the cities during World War II (q.v.) was to assert that the permanence of a settled African labor force in the towns must be accepted. Fagan did not believe that migrant (q.v.) labor could be stopped by legislation or by administrative decree; rather, African labor should be stabilized by encouraging male workers to bring their families with them. Urban Africans should be permitted to administer their own affairs, but the pass laws (q.v.) should remain in place, though not as harshly enforced. The Fagan Report, released in February 1948, was thus cautiously reformist, albeit equivocal. The Fagan recommendations were never implemented; the National Party (q.v.) exploited them as evidence of the dangers posed to whites should the Smuts government be returned to office in the election of May 1948, and it used its new doctrine of apartheid (q.v.) to rally white support against the supposedly liberal aspirations of the UP.

FAIRBAIRN, JOHN (1794–1864). The journalist and politician John Fairbairn edited the *South African Commercial Advertiser* in Cape Town (q.v.) from 1824 until 1859 and was widely known for his unyielding commitment to the freedom of the press (q.v.), his campaigns against slavery (q.v.), his leadership of the anticonvict movement of 1849, and his support for representative government at the Cape Colony (q.v.). He served as member of the Legislative Assembly from 1854 until 1864 and was prominent in promoting commercial activity at the Cape (q.v.).

FAKU (1780–1867). Through his links with Wesleyan missionaries (q.v.) as well as the Cape Colony (q.v.) and British authorities, Faku, the paramount chief of the Mpondo from 1820 until his death, successfully consolidated a large measure of Mpondo autonomy after the Mfecane (q.v.). During the 1850s, however, he was increasingly drawn into confrontation with the British over conflicting land claims, and his power base eroded markedly after the Xhosa (q.v.) cattle killing (q.v.) of 1857.

FEDERATION OF SOUTH AFRICAN WOMEN. Within a few months of its formation in 1954, the Federation of South African Women, a nonracial women's organization founded by Lilian Ngoyi, Ray Alexander, Florence Mkhize, Helen Joseph (q.v.), and others, claimed 10,000 members, mostly African (q.v.) urban (q.v.) women (q.v.), through affiliated organizations, and it became part of the Congress Alliance (q.v.) in 1955. It aimed to draw women's organizations together around issues of women's rights and to persuade more women to become involved in the wider political struggle of blacks (q.v.) against the apartheid (q.v.) government. It proved to be most successful in mobilizing mass demonstrations, particularly the march of 20,000 women to the Union Buildings in Pretoria (q.v.) on 9 August 1956 to protest the extension of pass laws (q.v.) to African women. It was severely affected by official repression at the end of 1956, when its main leaders were arrested and charged with treason (q.v.) alongside other activists of the Congress Alliance. Further state repression in the 1960s effectively prevented it from operating. After the democratic election in 1994, the African National Congress–led (q.v.) government introduced a new annual public holiday, Women's Day, to be commemorated on 9 August in remembrance of the 1956 march to Pretoria.

FIRST, RUTH (1925–83). Ruth First, a radical political activist, scholar, and journalist and an active communist, was detained and forced into exile in 1963. Her account of her detention provided a key exposure of security police (q.v.) methods. She was assassinated by a parcel bomb sent her by South African agents when she was working in Mozambique (q.v.); she was probably a target because of the role her husband, Joe Slovo (q.v.), played in Umkhonto weSizwe (q.v.).

FISCHER, ABRAM (BRAM) (1908–75). Grandson of a prime minister of the Orange River Colony and son of a judge-president of the Orange Free State (q.v.), Bram Fischer, an anti-apartheid activist lawyer, studied law at Oxford, and while a student traveled to the Soviet Union. From 1935 he was a member of the Johannesburg Bar and was active in the Communist Party (q.v.). He defended the accused in the treason trial (q.v.) in the 1950s and early 1960s and, in 1963–64, Nelson Mandela (q.v.) and the members of Umkhonto weSizwe (q.v.) arrested at Rivonia (q.v.). He was then himself arrested and charged with being an officeholder in an unlawful organization, the South African Communist Party (q.v.), and with acting to further the aims of that organization. He jumped bail and went underground to continue this work. Arrested after 10 months underground, he was sentenced to life imprisonment in 1966 and was released only when thought to be on the point of death. From 1990 he was often held up by the African National Congress (q.v.) as a model Afrikaner (q.v.), who courageously worked against an Afrikaner government committed to evil apartheid (q.v.) policies and who suffered for the cause of freedom.

FITZPATRICK, SIR JAMES PERCY (1862–1931). Politician, capitalist, author, and a prominent leader of the Uitlanders (q.v.) in Johannesburg (q.v.) during the 1890s, Sir James FitzPatrick enjoyed close ties with many of the leading mining magnates and was imprisoned for his part in the Jameson Raid (q.v.). He played an active role in politics after the South African War (q.v.), as a member of the Unionist Party (q.v.). He is best remembered as the author of the novel, *Jock of the Bushveld*, first published in 1907, which portrayed his life on the goldfields of Barberton.

FLAG QUESTION. A fierce controversy erupted among whites in 1926–27 over a new national flag for South Africa. In 1925, D. F. Malan (q.v.), then a minister in the Pact government (q.v.), proposed that a new flag should be designed to replace the Union Jack, which had become South Africa's flag in 1910 and which for many Afrikaners (q.v.) represented former injustice. After much contentious debate, it was agreed that the flags of the former republics as well as the Union Jack should be included in the center of the new flag, which was flown officially for the first time on 31 May 1928. The controversy damaged the (white) Labour Party (q.v.), many of whose supporters believed their leaders should be concerned with more important issues than a new flag. No attempt was made to consult black opinion on the new flag.

After the establishment of the Republic (q.v.) of South Africa in 1961 there was periodic talk about the need for another flag, but nothing was done, in part because of the memory of the bitterness the question had provoked in the 1920s. But in the early 1990s there was consensus that a new flag was required to symbolize the new South Africa. A state official proposed a colorful flag, in red, green, blue, white, black and gold, with a design that symbolized the convergence of diversity in the country's population, and this design was adopted in 1993 by the Multi-Party Negotiating Forum (q.v.) as an interim measure. It was flown from 27 April 1994 and soon proved so popular that the Constitutional Assembly (q.v.) in 1996, without controversy, agreed that it should become the permanent flag of democratic South Africa. The motto on the national coat of arms remained *Ex Unitate Vires*, "From Unity, Strength."

FOREIGN INVESTMENT. Foreign investment has played a vital role in the development of South Africa's economy, particularly the mining industry. By 1936, almost half of total foreign investment in Africa was in South Africa. Further foreign investment arrived after World War II (q.v.), mainly drawn to the gold (q.v.) mines of the Orange Free State (q.v.). There was an outflow of foreign capital between 1960 and 1964, following the Sharpeville massacre (q.v.), the consequent state of emergency, and the banning (q.v.) of African political organizations, but from 1965 to 1976 capital inflows into the country were again positive, except in 1973.

A sharp decline in investment from abroad occurred in the years 1977–80, when negative outflows of both long-term and short-term capital took place after the Soweto uprising (q.v.). From 1981 to 1983, foreign investment was again positive, but it turned sharply negative again from 1984, following the inauguration of the tricameral (q.v.) constitution and the state of emergency declared in mid-1985. With deepening recession and serious political disturbances, negative short-term capital movements reached record levels. A two-tier system of exchange rates for foreign investments (financial rand and commercial rand) was introduced in September 1985 to protect the currency (q.v.) and prevent further deterioration, and the government was obliged to declare a moratorium on the repayment of foreign debt (q.v.), as well as to reschedule the repayment of loans. Negative outflows of capital occurred until 1993, although international sanctions (q.v.) on trade and investment were widely abandoned in 1991; only after 1994, as the lengthy negotiations toward resolving the country's political turmoil were completed and a democratic government came to office, did foreign investment in the country begin to turn around from the negative period of the 1980s. Major investment then came from Malaysia, Britain, Germany, and the United States.

FOREIGN RELATIONS. Within the British Empire or Commonwealth (q.v.), South Africa began to develop its own foreign policy from the time of the Balfour Declaration of 1926. It became a member of first the League of Nations and then the United Nations (q.v.). Jan Smuts's (q.v.) reputation as an international statesman brought considerable international credit to his country. But under the National Party (q.v.) government after 1948, with the implementation of apartheid (q.v.), South Africa gradually moved into increasing isolation. This grew markedly after the Sharpeville (q.v.) crisis and with South Africa's departure from the Commonwealth in 1961. It was even more marked after the Soweto uprising (q.v.) of 1976.

In the mid-1980s various kinds of sanctions (q.v.) were imposed on the apartheid regime, which developed ties with other pariahs such as

Paraguay. After 1990, the country's international position was dramatically transformed. Not only were links with Britain, Germany, and France much strengthened—links that had never been severed during the sanctions period—but ties were again established with the likes of Russia, the Netherlands, and the Scandinavian countries, which had given massive support to the African National Congress (ANC) (q.v.). After the April 1994 election, South Africa rejoined the Commonwealth in July, became a member of the Non-Aligned Movement in May and the Organization of African Unity in June, and joined the Southern African Development Community (SADC) (q.v.) in August. Nelson Mandela's (q.v.) moral standing in the world brought his country great credit, and after he became chair of the SADC, he began to play a more active role in trying to bring about peace on the African continent, mediating in May 1997 in the Zairean crisis on board a South African ship off the Central African coast. He continued to regard Cuba, Syria, and Libya as friendly nations, because of their support for the ANC in its years of exile, despite strong international pressure to distance himself from them. From the beginning of 1998, South Africa switched recognition from Taiwan to China, a move designed in part to help South Africa win a permanent seat on an enlarged United Nations Security Council.

FORT HARE. J. T. Jabavu (q.v.) and others campaigned for the establishment of a college for Africans (q.v.) early in the 20th century. It opened as the South African Native College in 1916 on land given by the Church of Scotland adjacent to Lovedale, the leading mission high school for Africans, at Alice in the eastern Cape. Those who attended Fort Hare included Nelson Mandela (q.v.), Mangosuthu Buthelezi (q.v.), Kaiser Matanzima (q.v.), and Robert Mugabe of Zimbabwe (q.v.). Affiliated with Rhodes University in 1949, Fort Hare was, after 1959, taken over by the government and reconstituted as an ethnic college for Xhosa-speaking students. In the late 1960s it emerged as one of the leading centers of black consciousness (q.v.).

FRANCHISE. The constitution granted to the Cape Colony (q.v.) in 1853 gave the colony a nonracial franchise with a low qualification: every male citizen over 21 years of age who owned property valued at £25, received a salary of £50 per annum, or received a salary of £25 per annum plus free board and lodging was entitled to vote. By the 1880s, African and Coloured (qq.v.) voters were acquiring the vote in significant numbers, particularly in the eastern Cape (q.v.), as the Transkeian (q.v.) territories were progressively incorporated into the colony. Legislation was passed to limit the number of African voters: in 1887 land held on communal tenure was deemed unacceptable as a qualification for the franchise, and in 1892 the property qualification was raised from £25 to £75, the wage qualification was eliminated, and voters were required to sign their name when registering. By 1909, about 10 percent of voters at the Cape were Coloured, and 5 percent were African.

In Natal (q.v.), the franchise was theoretically color-blind, but in practice blacks (q.v.) were ineligible under the terms of legislation of 1865, which disqualified all Africans who had not been exempted from customary law. Indians (q.v.) were barred from the vote in 1896. In the Transvaal (q.v.) and the Orange Free State (q.v.) the franchise was limited to white males. Article 8 of the Treaty of Vereeniging (q.v.) of 1902, which concluded the South African War (q.v.), provided that there would be no change in the franchise before the restoration of self-government, after which the two former republics could decide the issue themselves. This meant there was no chance that the franchise would be extended to blacks in territories implacably opposed to a nonracial franchise.

The National Convention (q.v.) of 1908–9 decided that each of the four provinces of the Union (q.v.) would retain their own franchise arrangements. Only whites could stand for election to the House of Assembly or the Senate. Cape delegates hoped that in time the nonracial franchise would be extended to the northern provinces, but the Cape franchise instead came to be seen as anomalous. In 1930 the franchise was extended to white women, and in 1931 property and educational requirements for all whites were removed. The effect of these two measures was to reduce drastically the proportion of blacks in the Cape who were eligible to vote, from 20 percent in 1929 to 8.5 percent in 1935. In 1936, African voters (who numbered only 10,000, a mere 1.4 percent of the total number) were removed from the common voters' roll: the privilege of the franchise meant that they could not be subject to coercive and racially discriminatory measures. Cape Africans were then placed on a separate voters' roll and were entitled to vote for three native representatives to Parliament, who had to be white. This system was abolished in 1960.

When the National Party (NP) (q.v.) came to power in 1948, it was determined to remove Coloureds from the common voters' roll in the Cape, where Coloured voters held considerable influence in several constituencies. This provoked a prolonged and bitter constitutional crisis, but the NP achieved its goal in 1956. Coloureds were thereafter entitled to vote for white representatives to Parliament, a system that was abolished in 1968, when a Coloured Persons' Representative Council (q.v.) was established with limited powers to administer local government, education, welfare, and pensions for Coloured people. Africans, meanwhile, were expected to exercise political rights in their homeland (i.e., bantustan [q.v.]) of origin; in 1963 the first election of a bantustan government took place in the Transkei (q.v.).

In 1983, the constitution was altered to provide for a racially based tricameral parliament (q.v.). Separate legislative chambers for whites, Coloureds, and Indians were established, for which elections on separate voters' rolls took place. The white chamber was larger than the other two combined. Africans were excluded from the system, which never won acceptance among the majority of Coloured or Indian people. Fierce opposition to the tricameral constitution gave birth to the broad-based United Democratic Front (q.v.), which channeled most anti-apartheid activity within the country during the 1980s. Under the terms of the 1993 interim constitution, the franchise was extended to all South African adults over the age of 18 years, and in the April 1994 election Nelson Mandela (q.v.) and other black leaders and their black followers cast their votes for the first time.

FREE BLACKS. The term *free blacks* was used to denote blacks at the Cape (q.v.) who were neither slaves (q.v.) nor of Khoikhoi (q.v.), Bastard (q.v.), or Bantu-speaking (q.v.) descent. Free blacks were of Asian and African origin, and most had been slaves; a few entered the Cape as free persons. They were always a small minority of the Cape's population: in 1670 they constituted 7.4 percent of the total free population, and in 1770, when they numbered just over 1,000 people, only 4.4 percent. In the 18th century, most free blacks lived in Cape Town (q.v.) in conditions of poverty, and though they were in charge of the town's fire brigade, they suffered statutory discrimination: the curfew, for example, applied to both slaves and people of color, and so also to free blacks. Ordinance 50 (q.v.) of 1828 removed such legal disabilities, and thereafter the free blacks were gradually absorbed into the Coloured (q.v.) population.

FREE BURGHERS. Initially, free burghers were the former officials of the Dutch East India Company (VOC) (q.v.) who were given land to farm, but the term came to be used for all whites who were not company officials. In 1657, hoping to reduce expenditure, the VOC released nine employees from their contracts of service and gave them smallholdings of land in the Liesbeek River valley, east of Table Mountain. These first farmers bound themselves to supply produce at fixed prices. By the end of the 17th century, there were 1,334 free burghers, their numbers having increased partly due to immigration (for example, 180 Huguenot refugees from France arrived in 1688). Little immigration occurred during the 18th century, however, and mainly through natural increase the number of free burghers rose to 15,000 by 1795. Relations between the free burghers, particularly the wealthier farmers, and the VOC were frequently tense. The grievances of free burghers focused mainly on economic restrictions imposed by the VOC, though frustrations were also expressed over the denial of political rights and the corruption and incompetence of officials.

FREE STATE. The former Orange Free State (q.v.) was renamed the Free State and became one of South Africa's nine provinces in April 1994, with the provincial capital at Bloemfontein (q.v.). The province comprised just over 10 percent of the country's area. A strong African National Congress (ANC) (q.v.) provincial government under Patrick Lekota (q.v.) assumed control of the territory, after the party won 77 percent of the vote in the region. Despite this, the provincial ANC was riven by internal discord and personality clashes, which eventually led to Lekota's replacement as premier by Ivy Matsepe-Casaburri, a former head of the South African Broadcasting Association, in 1996. Mining (at 27 percent) and agriculture (q.v.) (at 17 percent) were the most significant contributors to the province's gross geographic product.

FREEDOM CHARTER. *See* AFRICAN NATIONAL CONGRESS; CONGRESS ALLIANCE.

FREEDOM FRONT. A white Afrikaner political party born in early 1994 under the leadership of General Constand Viljoen (q.v.), the Freedom Front campaigned for self-determination for white Afrikaners (q.v.) and for the establishment of an Afrikaner *volkstaat* (people's state) in a part of South Africa. In the April 1994 election, the Freedom Front won 640,000 votes. Its acceptance of negotiation rather than confrontation helped avert a civil war in early 1994, and in return the African National Congress (q.v.) agreed to set up a Volkstaat Council—a talking shop, as there was no question of allowing self-determination—and to the provision in the 1996 constitution for a commission dedicated to the promotion of rights of cultural, linguistic, and religious communities.

FRERE, SIR HENRY BARTLE (1815–84). After a distinguished career in India, Sir Henry Bartle Frere was offered the post of governor of the Cape (q.v.) and high commissioner in 1877 as the best person to bring about confederation (q.v.). Frere came to South Africa determined to achieve that goal and expected to become first governor-general of a new British dominion. But at the Cape he found himself first involved in another war with the Xhosa (q.v.) and then dealing with the Zulu kingdom (q.v.), for he believed that before a self-governing white-ruled dominion could be left to defend itself, white supremacy had to be established throughout South Africa. He therefore took actions that brought on the Anglo–Zulu War (q.v.) in January 1879. The war opened with the British defeat at Isandlwana (q.v.), and as a result of this disaster, the High Commission (q.v.) was divided and Frere was kept in South Africa only as long as some possibility of a confederation remained. The annexation of the Transvaal (q.v.), however, roused its white inhabitants against the British, and the Cape Parliament opposed confederation. Frere was recalled in 1880, his hopes shattered.

FRONTIERS. The term *frontier* is most often associated with the eastern Cape (q.v.) region, where conflict between Xhosa (q.v.) and whites occurred over the period of about 100 years (from the mid-1770s until the last frontier war of 1878–79). There were, however, numerous other frontiers, where different societies encountered one another and attempted to resolve their conflicting interests. As white trekboers (q.v.) began to move inland from the Cape at the beginning of the 18th century, for example, frontiers opened in which many different forms of conflict and cooperation existed. Another frontier situation occurred between the mid-18th and mid-19th centuries in the Orange River (q.v.) area, where numerous communities experienced profound transformation through their dealings with one another; new societies emerged, and cooperation for mutual economic benefit frequently occurred across cleavages of race or status. Further frontier situations manifested themselves in the southern African interior during the 19th century, as white conquest shifted its efforts to the areas that became Natal (q.v.), the Orange Free State (q.v.), and the Transvaal (q.v.).

Historians have long debated the best ways of conceiving the South African frontiers and their significance. Procolonist historians of the early 20th century, as well as Afrikaner nationalist (q.v.) historians, viewed the frontier as a clash between heroic Christian whites and hostile, barbaric blacks to whom they were attempting to bring order and civilization. A different view emerged in the 1930s, articulated by liberal historians, most notably Eric Walker, who argued that white frontiersmen, through their disregard for black society and land on the frontiers, developed racist attitudes, which took root during the 19th century, particularly in the Boer (q.v.) republics (Orange Free State and South African Republic [q.v.]), and were carried into the 20th century, when segregationist and apartheid (q.v.) policies developed. The psychologist I. D. MacCrone extended Walker's arguments in his *Race Attitudes in South Africa* (1937) by providing detailed evidence about the isolation of frontier life; in his view, early white frontier settlers lost touch with civilization and thus evolved racist attitudes that their society carried forward into the 19th and 20th centuries.

More recently, scholars have challenged the notion of conflict and racism (q.v.) as essential features of southern African frontier communities. Liberal Africanist work, notably Wilson and Thompson's *The Oxford History of South Africa* (1969 and 1971), stressed cooperative forms of interaction as well as conflict. The revisionist historian Martin Legassick, in a powerful critique of the liberal frontier tradition (1970), argued that some of the least color- and race-conscious interaction between different societies occurred on the frontier, and the origins of white racism should be sought elsewhere. Together with other revisionists, he maintained that 18th-century racism was quite different from the systematic and overt racism of the late 19th and 20th centuries, which was the product rather of the industrial and mineral revolutions. South African frontiers can thus no longer be viewed in terms of two or more sharply divergent societies coming into conflict with one another. Internal cleavages, changing alliances, peaceful interchanges, and complex forms of interaction all occurred in addition to, and parallel with, conflict and warfare. Although in some ways frontier life undoubtedly strengthened white racist attitudes, the precise influence of frontiers in shaping white racism remains elusive.

FUGARD, ATHOL HAROLD LANNIGAN (b. 1932). South Africa's most influential dramatist and playwright, Athol Fugard was born in the Karoo (q.v.) and spent a significant portion of his life in Port Elizabeth (q.v.). From the early beginnings of his career, he was a prominent opponent of apartheid (q.v.), rejecting racially segregated (q.v.) theater, casts, and audiences, and writing powerfully against the prevailing racial order. His first major play was *The Blood Knot* (1961), which was followed by *Hello and Goodbye* (1966), *People Are Living There* (1969), and *Boesman and Lena* (1969). These plays centered on family relationships within intimate settings in lower-class social circumstances. *Sizwe Bansi Is Dead* (1972) saw him collaborating with two prominent black actors, John Kani and Winston Ntshona, in a play that won international acclaim for its exploration of identity and personal freedom in a society seeking to regiment every aspect of black peoples' existence. Important later works include *A Lesson from Aloes* (1978), *Master Harold and the Boys* (1983), and *The Road to Mecca* (1984). Fugard's major achievement was to show the possibilities of South African theater, in contrast with the imported drama that dominated the local stage before the 1960s; he won local and international recognition for his stance against racism (q.v.) and political intolerance, as well as his nurturing of the roots of black theater in the country.

FUSION (1934). In 1933, the economic depression of the early 1930s and a commitment to white cooperation persuaded the National Party (q.v.) of J. B. M. Hertzog (q.v.) and the South African Party (q.v.) of Jan Smuts (q.v.) to form a coalition government; this was followed by fusion in 1934, when the two parties merged to form the United Party (q.v.). Hertzog believed that South Africa's independence from Britain had been secured by the Statute of Westminster (1931) and the Status Act (1934) and that white unity was now possible on the basis of "South Africa first" and full equality between the two white language (q.v.) groups. Fusion precipitated the formation of the Purified National Party of D. F. Malan (q.v.), who rejected the notion that Afrikaner (q.v.) security had been achieved. Fusion ended in 1939, when Smuts parted with Hertzog over South Africa's entry into World War II (q.v.).

-G-

GANDHI, MOHANDAS KARAMCHAND (1869–1948). The central figure in South African Indian (q.v.) politics between 1893 and 1914, Mohandas Gandhi—often known by the title *Mahatma,* or "great soul"—settled in Natal (q.v.) in 1893 after obtaining legal training in England. Almost immediately, he became involved in campaigns to ensure that Indians be accorded treatment equal to that of whites (q.v.). He founded the Natal Indian Congress in 1894 and served as its first secretary. In 1895 he led an unsuccessful campaign against legislation that denied Indians the vote in Natal. During the South African War (q.v.), he organized an Indian ambulance corps, and in 1903 he founded the influential weekly newspaper, *Indian Opinion.*

After the war, Gandhi tackled discrimination against Indians in the Transvaal (q.v.). He developed his famous philosophy of *satyagraha* ("keep to the truth") and launched a nonviolent resistance campaign based on its principles, in September 1906, to persuade the postwar British administration to lift restrictions on the number of Indians entering the Transvaal. An agreement was reached, stipulating that the registration of Indians would be voluntary rather than compulsory. Later campaigns focused on the poll tax paid by Indians and the nonrecognition of marriages solemnized under Indian rites; after Gandhi was himself imprisoned, concessions on these issues were granted by the authorities. He also organized strikes on the Natal coalfields and sugar plantations and in 1913 led a march of Indians from Natal to the Transvaal, which temporarily bridged class divisions within the Indian community. In July 1914, Gandhi left South Africa for India, where he led the struggle for Indian independence from Britain.

GAUTENG. South Africa's richest province, Gauteng (Sotho for "place of gold"), included not only Johannesburg (q.v.), the largest city, but also Pretoria (q.v.), the administrative capital, and Johannesburg International Airport, the main point of entry for visitors to South Africa. Part of the former Transvaal (q.v.) Province, Gauteng came into being in April 1994, with the transition to democracy and the coming into force of the interim constitution, and Johannesburg was chosen as its capital. Gauteng was the country's smallest province, comprising only 1.6 percent of the country's area, and the most densely populated. Initially called PWV (Pretoria–Witwatersrand–Vereeniging), its name was changed to Gauteng in 1995. Gabriel Tokyo Sexwale of the African National Congress (ANC) (q.v.), a former prisoner on Robben Island (q.v.), became its first premier, after the ANC won 59 percent of the provincial vote in the election of April 1994. Manufacturing (at 30 percent), finance (at 21 percent), and trade (at 13 percent) were the most significant contributors to Gauteng's gross geographic product. In January 1998, Sexwale left office to pursue a business career and was succeeded as premier by Mathole Motshekga. One of the major issues he had to deal with was crime, for Johannesburg was the crime center of the country.

GENADENDAL. The oldest mission station in South Africa, founded in 1737 by George Schmidt of the Moravian Missionary Society, Genadendal served Khoikhoi (q.v.) in the district of Swellendam. Originally called Baviaanskloof, the mission was closed after six years because of hostility from the Dutch Reformed Church (q.v.) and white colonists. Reopened in 1792, it prospered. Many of the early missionaries (q.v.) to southern Africa, from a range of missionary societies, visited Genadendal and organized their missions along lines similar to the Genadendal pattern of closed settlement around the mission church.

GERMAN IMMIGRANTS. More German than Dutch immigrants entered the Cape under Dutch East India Company (q.v.) patronage during the 18th century, but the Germans, mainly single men, were absorbed into the local Dutch (q.v.) population. During the 19th century, colonial authorities in the Cape Colony (q.v.) and Natal (q.v.) sponsored immigration from Germany on a larger scale, and immigrants entered southern Africa with their families or in large parties. In Natal, a group of immigrants settled at New Germany outside Durban (q.v.) in 1848, and in 1857 soldiers of the disbanded Anglo–German Legion from the Crimean War were settled with their families in British Kaffraria (q.v.). They were followed shortly afterward by some 4,000 peasants from north Germany, who founded communities such as those of Stutterheim, Berlin, and Hanover.

During the 20th century, immigrants from Germany continued to enter the country, though not as part of large state-sponsored programs. The National Party (q.v.) government after 1948 encouraged immigration from Germany more actively and implemented a scheme to settle German children orphaned by World War II (q.v.) with Afrikaner (q.v.) families. By 1991 there were approximately 33,000 German-speaking whites in South Africa.

GLEN GREY ACT (1894). Introduced into the Cape (q.v.) Parliament by Cecil Rhodes (q.v.), the Glen Grey Act was initially designed for the Glen Grey district of the eastern Cape but was extended to the whole of Transkei (q.v.) in 1898. Rhodes hoped it would become a blueprint for southern Africa and spoke of it as a "Bill for Africa."

The act had three main elements. First, it altered the system of land tenure, replacing communal tenure with small individual lots; land held under the new system, however, did not count toward the qualifications for the Cape franchise (q.v.). As there were not enough individual lots, some Africans found themselves permanently landless. Second, in order to force Africans into migrant (q.v.) labor, a tax was imposed on all men who could not prove they had been in bona fide wage employment for any three months in any single year. The tax, to which there was much hostility and which proved unworkable, was withdrawn in 1905. Third, a system of district councils was introduced to provide for African participation in local government on an advisory basis.

GOLD. Africans mined gold at several places in the Transvaal (q.v.)—those later known as Lydenburg, Pilgrim's Rest, the Soutpansberg, and the Limpopo River (q.v.) valley—during the precolonial period, but gold was used only for ornamentation or trade and was mined on a fairly small scale. In the early 1870s, considerable deposits of alluvial gold were worked by white prospectors in the eastern Transvaal. Small amounts were also found at Rustenburg and on the Witwatersrand (q.v.) before the discovery of the Witwatersrand main reef in 1886. The potential of the goldfields was not fully appreciated until the early 1890s, when the invention of the cyanide process revealed the extent of the deep-level ores and made their exploitation possible. In 1930, new prospecting methods exposed vast new reefs to the southwest of the Witwatersrand, and after World War II (q.v.) a number of new mines were opened up in the northern Orange Free State (q.v.).

Although the Witwatersrand gold deposits were the largest and richest in the world, the average gold content per ton of rock was very low. The gold-bearing reef, hundreds of meters underground, required deep-level mining. which meant large-scale operations and huge amounts of capital. The few mining houses that could function in such an environment drew on capital from the Kimberley (q.v.) diamond (q.v.) fields or from abroad. Of the £200 million invested between 1887 and 1934, 60 percent came from foreign sources. With the price of gold fixed and high development costs inevitable, attempts were made to keep labor costs as low as possible. Skilled jobs went to whites, mostly immigrants from Europe, who were able to command high wages; remuneration for the large numbers of African migrant (q.v.) workers was pushed down to the minimum.

Within a few years the discovery of gold turned the Transvaal from the poorest state in southern Africa into the wealthiest. By 1896, gold accounted for 96 percent of its exports. Gold played a major part in bringing about both the South African War (q.v.) and the Union (q.v.) of South Africa in 1910. It remained the backbone of the South African economy, contributing massively to state revenue and earning large quantities of foreign exchange.

The international price of gold played a significant part in South Africa's prosperity during the 20th century. South Africa's departure from the gold standard in 1933 increased the price of the commodity by 65 percent, boosting domestic economic activity and making possible the opening of new mines. Until 1970, the price was fixed at $35 a fine ounce, but the introduction of a second-tier free market in gold resulted in a greatly increased gold price, heralding a decade of enormous profit for the gold industry. By 1978, 36 active mines produced almost 700 tons a year, roughly half the world's total production. An average price of $613 per fine ounce in 1980 created a record year of growth for the South African economy.

For most of the 1980s and early 1990s, however, the gold price averaged between $300 and $400 an ounce, placing increasing pressure on the gold-mining industry, and the amount mined per year went down steadily. In 1996 less than 500 tons was produced. Growing competition from mines abroad, ongoing enormous capital expenditure, and organized and militant labor activity combined to reduce profits and yields. Marginal mines found it increasingly difficult to operate, and some were forced to close. Although gold remained significant in the South African economy, it was by the 1990s much less important than it had been. In late 1997 the price collapsed to less than $300 dollars an ounce, once again threatening many shafts, though the development of gold futures, productivity agreements with workers, and a restructuring of the industry all helped mitigate the effects of the falling price.

GOLDSTONE COMMISSION. The Prevention of Public Violence and Intimidation Act of 1991 established a standing commission to investigate such violence and make recommendations for its prevention. Chaired by Judge Richard Goldstone, the commission acquired further powers in 1992, and in November of that year it announced that some of its investigators had uncovered a secret military intelligence operation designed to carry out dirty tricks against opponents of the government. Further revelations followed prior to the April 1994 election, after which the commission ceased operating.

GORDIMER, NADINE (b. 1923). Since the 1950s, Nadine Gordimer, who was born in the town of Springs, east of Johannesburg (q.v.), the city in which she has spent most of her life, has established herself as one of South Africa's most distinguished novelists and writers of short stories. She was an outspoken opponent of racism (q.v.) and apartheid (q.v.), which, coupled with her forthright opinions and writings on subjects such as sexuality and censorship, meant that some of her work was banned (q.v.) by the National Party (NP) (q.v.) government; unlike many other writers, however, she did not go into exile. From her first novel, *The Lying Days* (1953), which was set in the early days of NP rule, her writing closely reflected the changing political moods of the country. Her many accomplished novels included *A World of Strangers* (1958), *The Late Bourgeois World* (1966), *Burger's Daughter* (1969), *A Guest of Honour* (1971), *The Conservationist* (1974), and *July's People* (1981). Gordimer's writing was often characterized by brilliant intellect, penetrating search for truth, and vivid evocation of detail. Some regard her numerous collections of short stories as an even greater accomplishment than her novels. Gordimer devoted much energy to the nurturing of black writing within the country, particularly through the Congress of South African Writers. She has won several major international awards, including the James Tait Black Memorial Prize (1972), the Booker Prize (1974), and the Nobel Prize for Literature (1991).

GOVERNMENT OF NATIONAL UNITY (GNU). The GNU came into being, under the terms of the interim constitution of 1993, in May 1994. The idea of a coalition government for a limited period of five years was advocated by Joe Slovo (q.v.) in the negotiations in 1992 as a compromise, to meet the National Party's (NP) (q.v.) concern for power sharing, to allay white fears, and as a device for constitutional continuity in a period when threats from the far right seemed serious. An African National Congress (ANC) (q.v.) document, entitled "Negotiations: A Strategic Perspective," supported the idea. Nelson Mandela (q.v.) later said the coalition government was essential for national reconciliation.

The interim constitution provided that the GNU was to last for five years. Any party that received more than 20 percent of the vote was entitled to a deputy president, and parties that received more than 10 percent of the vote were to be represented in the cabinet in proportion to the number of seats they held. In the election, the ANC won 252 seats, the NP 82, and the Inkatha (q.v.) Freedom Party 43. This enabled the ANC to nominate Thabo Mbeki (q.v.), and the National Party, F. W. de Klerk (q.v.), as the two vice presidents, and the three parties together formed the GNU. The NP was frustrated in the coalition, however, and once the new constitution was drawn up in May 1996, the NP announced that it would withdraw from the government at the end of June of that year, leaving Inkatha and the ANC the only other remaining members.

GRAHAMSTOWN. Grahamstown, in the eastern Cape Colony (q.v.), was founded as a military post by Colonel John Graham in 1812 to prevent the Xhosa (q.v.) from reentering the Zuurveld (q.v.). Many British immigrants who settled as farmers in the Zuurveld after 1820 moved to Grahamstown, which grew to become the most important trading and administrative center in the eastern Cape and, by the middle of the 19th century, was second in size only to Cape Town (q.v.). The Cape Parliament met in Grahamstown in 1864, when the town was a political focus of the eastern Cape separatist movement. Its economic decline began in the 1870s, when railway (q.v.) development between the coastal ports of East London and Port Elizabeth (q.v.) and the interior bypassed the town. During the 20th century, Grahamstown was known chiefly for its educational institutions, which included Rhodes University and a number of leading schools. In the 1980s and 1990s it was home to the National Festival of the Arts, South Africa's most important arts festival.

GREAT TREK. In the late 1830s, a group of Afrikaner (q.v.) farmers from the Cape (q.v.) moved into the interior of South Africa, in a migration known as the Great Trek. Small exploratory parties had surveyed conditions in Natal (q.v.) and on the high veld (q.v.) in 1834 and 1835 and reported the existence of fertile and apparently unpopulated land. In 1836 the first of several large organized groups of Voortrekkers (q.v.) left the eastern Cape. By 1840, leaders such as Piet Retief (q.v.), Andries Pretorius, Louis Trichardt, and others guided some 14,000 people out of the Cape, about one-tenth of the Cape Afrikaner population.

Most of the trekkers were pastoral farmers from the eastern Cape, who were responding to a shortage of land and fears of a scarcity of labor. But they were also rebelling against the British government at the Cape, whose interference in their lives they found intolerable. Ordinance 50 (q.v.) of 1828 and the emancipation of Cape slaves (q.v.) unsettled the eastern Cape Afrikaners. By outflanking the Xhosa (q.v.) and moving into the interior, the trekkers hoped to rule themselves and their laborers as they wished, recreating as far as possible the conditions of the trekboers (q.v.) of the 18th century.

But the land of the interior proved far from empty, and the trekkers clashed with both the Ndebele (q.v.) and the Zulu (q.v.) during the late 1830s. Most of the trekkers who went to Natal returned to the high veld after 1843, when the British annexed Natal; those who had settled on the high veld had by then successfully acquired sufficient land for their needs. In 1852, the independence of the trekkers north of the Vaal River was recognized, and they formed the South African Republic (q.v.), or Transvaal (q.v.); the independence of those between the Orange (q.v.) and Vaal Rivers was recognized in 1854.

For much of the 20th century, the Great Trek occupied a major place in the mythology of Afrikaner nationalism (q.v.). Afrikaner historians, particularly Gustav Preller (1875–1943), regarded the trek as a central event in Afrikaner history, and portrayed it as the formative moment in the assertion of Afrikaner identity. The Great Trek echoed the movement of Israelites from captivity in Egypt into the Promised Land; it was presented as a heroic tale of small numbers of self-reliant people escaping oppressive British dominance and conquering hostile African forces with the assistance of God. Such ideas were popularized in the decades after the South African War (q.v.), most particularly at the centenary celebrations of the trek held across the country in 1938, which the National Party (q.v.) successfully used to mobilize political support and consolidate its following. The foundation stone of the Voortrekker Monument outside Pretoria (q.v.) was laid in that year, and the building was completed in 1949, a year after the party came to power and began to implement its apartheid (q.v.) policies. The day on which the trekkers in Natal defeated the Zulu army in 1838, 16 December, was celebrated by Afrikaners as a sacred day throughout the apartheid era. During the 1980s, however, the resonance of the Great Trek waned, and only Afrikaners of the far right continued to view it in the terms in which it was formerly regarded.

GREY, SIR GEORGE (1812–98). Governor of the Cape Colony (q.v.) and high commissioner from 1854 until 1861, Sir George Grey disapproved of the treaties recognizing the independence of the Transvaal (q.v.) and the Orange Free State (q.v.) and was the first British administrator to regard South Africa as a potential federation. One of Grey's main motives for suggesting a federation was the formulation of a common "native policy" in the region. He believed blacks should be civilized by being gradually assimilated into white society. He pursued this goal with vigor among the Xhosa (q.v.) on the Cape's eastern frontier (q.v.), encouraging their participation in the money economy, reducing the power of chiefs in British Kaffraria (q.v.), and building schools for their education (q.v.). Grey exploited the cattle killing (q.v.) of 1856–57, in particular, to further these ends.

GRIQUA. Pastoralists of Khoikhoi (q.v.) and mixed descent, initially known as Bastards (q.v.), or Basters, the Griqua left the Cape (q.v.) in the late 18th century under their first leader, Adam Kok I (ca. 1710–ca. 1795). They moved north through Namaqualand, and their horses and guns enabled them to gain dominance in the middle Orange River (q.v.) region at the beginning of the 19th century. With the encouragement of the London Missionary Society (LMS) (q.v.), they settled at Klaarwater, later called Griquatown, in 1804. Here missionaries (q.v.) sought to create an ordered settlement based on agriculture (q.v.) and provided the Griqua with a constitution; many, however, were reluctant to abandon their nomadic pastoralist, hunting, and trading economic activities. Griqua raiding bands were active in the interior in the 1820s and played an important role at the Battle of Dithakong (q.v.) in 1823. One seminomadic group, mostly Bergenaars ("mountain people"), settled at Philippolis, an LMS mission in southern Transorangia (q.v.), in 1825 under the leadership of Adam Kok II (ca. 1790–1835). Many Griqua at Philippolis became successful commercial farmers, particularly in response to the economic opportunities in the wool industry (q.v.) offered by the introduction of merino sheep farming.

Toward the end of the 1830s, the Griqua at Philippolis began to suffer white encroachment on their lands. In 1843, Adam Kok III (q.v.) entered an agreement with the Cape government, promising to keep order along the frontier (q.v.). A further treaty in 1846 divided Griqua lands into a leasable portion, in which Griqua could lease their farms, and an unleasable reserve (q.v.), in which no whites were to have access to land. After the proclamation of the Orange River Sovereignty (q.v.) in 1848, however, Kok was stripped of jurisdiction outside the reserve and lost the leasable land, and whites steadily encroached on the reserve itself. In 1861, the Griqua decided to sell their remaining farms to the Orange Free State (q.v.), and some 2,000 people moved across the Drakensberg (q.v.), suffering considerable privations en route to Nomansland on the eastern side of the mountain range, which became known as Griqualand East (q.v.). Kokstad was founded as the main settlement, but in the early 1870s the east Griqua began to lose their farms to whites, a process that accelerated after Cape officials arrived in Kokstad in 1874 and after Kok's death in 1875. A rebellion in 1878 against the Cape administration was quickly suppressed, and the territory was formally incorporated into the Cape the following year. The demoralized and impoverished Griqua of Griqualand East never recovered their cohesion as a community or their independence.

Meanwhile, the inhabitants of Griquatown and the surrounding country experienced considerable economic hardship as a result of cattle disease, declining resources of game, and drought during the 1840s and 1850s. Their land rights, however, were not seriously challenged until the rich diamond (q.v.) reserves of the region were discovered toward the end of the 1860s. The Griqua claim to the land was asserted by David Arnot, who was of Scottish-Griqua descent, and their leader, Nicholaas Waterboer (q.v.). When Britain sought to take over the diamond fields, it accepted the Griqua claim, granted them British protection, and annexed Griqualand West (q.v.) in 1871. Thereafter, the Griqua were given individual tenure, but many sold their farms to whites, and others lost their land when they went into rebellion in 1878. By the end of the century, only a few Griqua retained any claim to land; the great majority were landless and impoverished. In the 1990s some of their descendants talked of claiming compensation from the British government for being robbed of their land.

GRIQUALAND EAST. In 1861–62, Griqua (q.v.) refugees settled on the eastern slopes of the Drakensberg (q.v.), south of Natal (q.v.). The territory, known as Griqualand East, was formally annexed to the Cape Colony (q.v.) in 1879. A century later, Griqualand East was transferred from the provincial administration of the Cape (q.v.) to that of Natal.

GRIQUALAND WEST. The territory north of the Gariep, or Orange (q.v.), River was settled by Griqua (q.v.) pastoralists from the Cape (q.v.) at the beginning of the 19th century. It was named Griqualand West when it was annexed by the British in 1871, four years after the discovery of diamonds (q.v.) in the area. Although the legitimacy of the Griqua title was recognized, British annexation led to the rapid alienation of the Griqua people from the land. Griqualand West was incorporated into the Cape in 1880.

GROOTE SCHUUR MINUTE. The Groote Schuur Minute was a document agreed to at a May 1990 meeting between the newly unbanned African National Congress (ANC) (q.v.) and the National Party (q.v.) government at Groote Schuur, the presidential residence in Cape Town (q.v.). The minute sought to clear obstacles that stood in the way of negotiations—in particular, those relating to the release of political prisoners. It was followed by the Pretoria Minute (q.v.) of August 1990, which continued the process and provided for the suspension of the ANC's armed struggle.

GROUP AREAS ACT (1950). A central pillar of apartheid (q.v.), the Group Areas Act provided for residential segregation on the basis of race in urban areas. Under the terms of the act, mainly Coloured (q.v.) and Indian (q.v.) people were removed and relocated, usually far from their places of work. (Africans (q.v.) were removed to separate areas under different legislation.) One of the most notorious proclamations under the Group Areas Act provided that Cape Town's (q.v.) District Six, inhabited at the time primarily by Coloured people, would be reserved for whites only. The buildings of District Six were demolished, and the people who had lived there were forcibly removed, mostly to new accommodations on the Cape Flats, away from the city center. Immense bitterness was caused by the Group Areas Act before it was repealed in 1991. By then it had shaped the social geography of most South African cities and towns in ways that were likely to last a very long time.

GROWTH, EMPLOYMENT, AND REDISTRIBUTION STRATEGY (GEAR). In June 1996, Trevor Manuel, the minister of finance, announced that the government had adopted a new macroeconomic growth, employment, and redistribution strategy. GEAR was immediately attacked, in particular by the Congress of South African Trade Unions (COSATU) (q.v.) and the South African Communist Party (q.v.), for being a neoliberal policy with more emphasis on growth than on reconstruction and development. Among the key aspects of GEAR were privatization and the relaxation of exchange controls. The policy as a whole was designed to be investor friendly and to encourage investment as a basis for economic growth. The policy anticipated economic growth of 6 percent within a few years and the creation of hundreds of thousands of new jobs.

The government may have adopted it without wide public debate because it anticipated the opposition that followed. It soon became clear that the GEAR targets were not being met: instead of new employment opportunities, hundreds of thousands of jobs were lost in the formal sector of the economy in 1996 and 1997. Exchange controls were relaxed in June 1997, but privatization proceeded very slowly: by mid-1998 only six state concerns had been wholly or partially privatized. Some said that although the government proclaimed GEAR as its policy, its actions were often, under the influence of COSATU and the Communist Party, contrary to that policy: the Basic Conditions of Employment and Employment Equity Acts, for example, did not liberalize the labor market but, rather, made it more difficult for employers to hire the labor they wanted.

In October 1998, the government, which had maintained its position that GEAR was nonnegotiable despite growing criticism from the labor movement, announced that GEAR policy would not meet its targets and that some adjustments to the policy would have to be undertaken. The global financial crisis sparked by Asian markets in 1997 had undermined South Africa's economy, causing capital flight; speculative attacks on the rand had resulted in high interest rates, putting further pressure on growth and undermining GEAR's ability to create jobs. According to the Reserve Bank, the economy had shed some 500,000 jobs in the previous four years, and official unemployment stood at almost 23 percent.

-H-

HANI, MARTIN THEMBISILE (CHRIS) (1942–93). A devout Christian in his youth, Martin "Chris" Hani joined the African National Congress (ANC) (q.v.) in 1957 while at school in the eastern Cape (q.v.). At the University of Fort Hare (q.v.) he was influenced by Marxist ideas and became a lover of Latin and literature. He left South Africa in 1963 to undergo military training and fought in Rhodesia (now Zimbabwe [q.v.]). From 1974, based in Lesotho (formerly Basutoland [q.v.]), he worked to create a political structure for the ANC in the eastern Cape. He rose through the ranks of Umkhonto weSizwe (q.v.) to become chief of staff in 1987. After the ANC and the South African Communist Party (SACP) (q.v.) were unbanned, he returned to South Africa and soon became a popular speaker in the townships. Long an active member of the SACP, Hani was elected its general secretary in 1991. In the last year of his life he repeatedly urged militant youth to work for peace. His assassination in April 1993 sent shock waves through South Africa. A massive funeral was held; and in the aftermath of the assassination, violence increased markedly and racial tensions grew. On the other hand, his assassination helped persuade the negotiators in the Multi-Party Negotiating Forum (q.v.) to agree to a date for South Africa's first democratic election.

HEAD, BESSIE (1937–86). One of the country's most accomplished African writers, Bessie Head, though she grew up in Natal (q.v.) and worked in Johannesburg (q.v.), left the country in 1963 and settled in Botswana (formerly Bechuanaland [q.v.]). Her novels, *When Rain Clouds Gather* (1969), *Maru* (1971), and *A Question of Power* (1973), were intensely personal, focusing on exile, loneliness, mental conflict, and private identity. She worked as a teacher and also published short stories and histories of Botswana, based in part on interviews with village communities.

HERSTIGTE NASIONALE PARTY (HNP). In September 1969, a small group of dissident members of the National Party (NP) (q.v.) under the leadership of Dr. Albert Hertzog, son of J. B. M. Hertzog (q.v.), broke away and established the Herstigte Nasionale Party (Afrikaans for the "Reestablished National Party"). As the name of the party implied, the HNP felt that the NP under B. J. Vorster (q.v.) had betrayed the earlier tradition of the party from D. F. Malan (q.v.) to H. F. Verwoerd (q.v.). They objected to Vorster's foreign policy, and particularly his accepting a black ambassador from Malawi, as well as his permitting a New

Zealand rugby team with a few Maori players to tour the country; they also objected to Vorster's attempts to woo the English vote.

The HNP sufficiently concerned Vorster that he advanced the scheduled election by a year; the HNP was eliminated from Parliament in the white election of 1970, before it had time to organize. Thereafter, its sole parliamentary success was a solitary by-election victory at the end of the 1970s, but it continued to contest stridently government policies through the 1970s and 1980s, attracting some 30 percent of the Afrikaner (q.v.) vote, mainly poorer whites, at the peak of its support in the 1981 election. After 1982, it was speculated that the HNP might merge with the newly formed Conservative Party (q.v.), but this did not occur. Most of its supporters switched their loyalty to the Conservative Party, and the two parties remained rivals for the right-wing Afrikaner vote, cooperating only briefly during the referendum of March 1992. The HNP's passionate defense of Verwoerdian apartheid (q.v.) in an undiluted form, its belief in Afrikaner hegemony over English speakers, and bitter personal rivalries relegated it to the extreme far-right fringe of white Afrikaner politics.

HERTZOG, JAMES BARRY MUNNIK (1866–1942). J. B. M. Hertzog was prime minister of the Union (q.v.) of South Africa from 1924 to 1939. Born near Wellington in the Cape Colony (q.v.), Hertzog moved with his family to the diamond (q.v.) fields at Kimberley (q.v.) in 1872 and then to the Orange Free State (q.v.). Educated at Stellenbosch and in Amsterdam, he worked as a lawyer, first in the South African Republic (q.v.) and then in the Orange Free State. He gained fame as a guerrilla general in the South African War (q.v.), leading a daring raid into the Cape Colony in 1900–01. He then played an important role at the peace talks at Vereeniging (q.v.) in 1902, after which he challenged the policy of anglicization that Lord Milner (q.v.) sought to impose on the former republics. Hertzog was a cofounder of the Orangia Unie party in the Orange River Colony in 1906 and served in the government of that colony from 1907 until the advent of Union. In the National Convention (q.v.) in 1908–9, he argued strongly for the equality of Dutch (q.v.) and English (q.v.) as the two official languages (q.v.) of the new united country. He was appointed a minister in the first cabinet of Louis Botha (q.v.) but opposed Botha's policy of "conciliation," insisting instead that Dutch- and English-speaking people were not equal and that only those who put "South Africa first" were true citizens. When Botha was unable to persuade him to resign, Hertzog was forced out of the government in 1912.

Hertzog then formed his own party, the National Party (NP) (q.v.). When World War I (q.v) broke out, he opposed the invasion of South West Africa (now Namibia [q.v.]) but was too wise to come out in support of the Afrikaner Rebellion (q.v.). Hertzog played a key role in building up the NP, criticizing the conciliation policy of Jan Smuts (q.v.) and Botha as not being in Afrikaner (q.v.) interests and claiming that Smuts was too subservient to the gold-mining magnates and to Britain. In the aftermath of the Rand Revolt (q.v.), Hertzog made an election pact with the (white) Labour Party (q.v.) of Colonel Frederic Creswell (q.v.). When the Pact coalition won the general election of 1924, he became prime minister.

At an imperial conference in 1926, Hertzog was instrumental in helping to word the Balfour Declaration, which spoke of "sovereign independence" for the dominions. He came to accept South Africa's status as an independent state within the British Empire. Accusing Smuts of working for an African-ruled state in which white "civilization" would be "swamped," he won an absolute majority in the House of Assembly in the 1929 general election. But then came the depression and economic crisis, in which he was forced to abandon the gold (q.v.) standard. By 1933, Hertzog was prepared to enter a coalition with the South African Party (q.v.) of his rival, Smuts. He remained prime minister when coalition became fusion (q.v.), and the new United Party (q.v.) was formed in 1934.

The so-called Hertzog bills, first proposed in 1926, provided for political segregation and a new land deal for Africans (q.v.). After much opposition and controversy, the legislation was eventually passed in 1936–37. Abolition of the African franchise (q.v.) at the Cape required a two-thirds majority in Parliament, and this was not achieved until early 1936. As a quid pro quo for losing their vote on the common voters' roll, Africans were given indirect communal representation in Parliament, and an advisory Natives' Representative Council (q.v.) was established.

Hertzog lost office when he opposed South Africa's entry into World War II (q.v.). He then joined the Purified National Party (q.v.) of D. F. Malan (q.v.) but was unhappy with Malan's rejection of cooperation with English speakers (q.v.), whom he now accepted as true South Africans, so he retired from politics in 1940. His main legacy was to have done much to advance racial segregation (q.v.).

HET VOLK. A political movement founded by Louis Botha (q.v.) in January 1905, the Het Volk demanded full self-government for the Transvaal (q.v.) and the Orange River Colony. Other key demands were the immediate termination of the importation of Chinese (q.v.) labor, the end of restrictions on the public use of Dutch (q.v.), and economic relief for impoverished Afrikaners (q.v.). The movement was initially built up among farmers' associations and rapidly gained support among Transvaal Afrikaners. Botha and Jan Smuts (q.v.) also began to woo English-speaking (q.v.) artisans by deriving political advantage from the tensions between capital and labor in Johannesburg (q.v.). In the first general election held in the Transvaal in February 1907 under the new self-government constitution, Het Volk won a comfortable majority, securing 37 of the 69 Legislative Assembly seats. Het Volk thereafter intensified its program of "conciliation," or cooperation with English speakers, which eased the path toward creation of the Union (q.v.) of South Africa in 1910. After 1910, Het Volk was absorbed into the new South African Party (q.v.).

HIGH COMMISSION. The first High Commission was added to the Cape (q.v.) governor's charge in 1846. It was devised to assist the governor in settling the colony's eastern frontier (q.v.), giving him vague powers to act beyond it. Successive holders of the office used it as an informal means of extending British sovereignty. British Kaffraria (q.v.) was established under the High Commission in 1847, and the Orange River Sovereignty (q.v.) in 1848. Although it doubted the High Commission's legal power to act in this way, the Colonial Office in London accepted both cases as faits accomplis. In 1868, Basutoland (q.v.) was similarly annexed under the terms of the High Commission, as was Griqualand West (q.v.) in 1871. In 1877, the High Commission was enlarged, and the new holder of the office, Sir Henry Bartle Frere (q.v.), arrived as Cape governor and high commissioner for all southern Africa, to work for confederation (q.v.). After the defeat of the British forces at the beginning of the Anglo–Zulu War (q.v.) in 1879, a separate high commissioner for southeast Africa was appointed. The unity of the office was restored in 1881, and in 1884 the first official High Commission territory (q.v.) came into being, when Basutoland was taken back from Cape rule.

Lord Milner (q.v.) actively used the High Commission in the buildup to the South African War (q.v.), and after the war he was the first high commissioner to attempt to reshape all of South Africa. His successor, Lord Selborne (1859–1942), gave public backing to closer union (q.v.). From 1910, the high commissioner retained responsibility for the High Commission territories (q.v.) and, until 1930, was also governor-general of the Union of South Africa, representing the Crown in South Africa.

After the declaration of the Republic (q.v.) of South Africa in 1961, and with the impending independence of the High Commission territories (q.v.), the High Commission was abolished in 1964.

After 1994, when South Africa rejoined the Commonwealth (q.v.), the British ambassador to South Africa became known as the high commissioner, but that title did not confer the responsibilities of previous high commissioners.

HIGH COMMISSION TERRITORIES. The High Commission territories were the three British territories of Basutoland (q.v.), Bechuanaland (q.v.), and Swaziland (q.v.), ruled under the terms of the High Commission (q.v.). They were sometimes referred to, less accurately, as the protectorates. Although the South Africa Act of 1909 envisaged their transfer to the Union (q.v.) of South Africa, they were excluded from the Union in 1910 because of Britain's special relationship with them and the concern that South Africa would not safeguard the interests of their African (q.v.) inhabitants. Every Union prime minister sought their transfer, J. B. M. Hertzog (q.v.) most vociferously, for he disliked the constant reminder of Britain's continued direct involvement in southern African affairs; the inhabitants of the territories, however, opposed any transfer.

After the election of the National Party (NP) (q.v.) to power in 1948, transfer of the territories to South Africa became highly unlikely; after the declaration of the Republic of South Africa (q.v.) in 1961, it was out of the question. In 1963, H. F. Verwoerd (q.v.) made a final appeal to Britain to allow South Africa to lead them to independence. When it became clear that Britain would not do that, he became the first prime minister to accept that they would not be incorporated and spoke, instead, of a friendly neighbor policy toward them.

When referring to land in African hands, the NP sometimes added the three territories to the South African reserves (q.v.) to obtain a more impressive, but misleading, figure. The territories were, however, locked into the migrant (q.v.) labor system and so were heavily dependent on the South African economy, to the extent that some described them as "South Africa's hostages."

HINTSA (ca. 1790–1835). The British believed Hintsa—chief of the Gcaleka people and paramount chief of the Xhosa (q.v.) from 1804—to have been the prime mover behind the Xhosa invasion of the Cape Colony (q.v.) in 1834. In 1835, while being held hostage by Sir Henry Smith (q.v.), he was shot when allegedly trying to escape. His body was then mutilated, and it was later rumored that his skull had been taken back to Britain. His brutal death under mysterious circumstances made him a national martyr among the Xhosa.

HISTORIOGRAPHY. A number of travelers and missionaries in the late-18th- and early-19th-century Cape (q.v.) wrote books in which there were historical sections. The fullest such survey of the previous history of the Cape was contained in the two volumes of *Researches in South Africa,* which the missionary John Philip (q.v.) published in 1828. An attempt was made to rebut what was seen to be a pro-Khoikhoi (q.v.) and antisettler view in *The Record*, a collection of documents compiled by Donald Moodie, originally published beginning in 1838. Then, in the mid-19th century, English-speaking (q.v.) white settlers began producing accounts that set out to be histories of the founding and development of the Cape and Natal (q.v.). Mainly narrative in form, these histories were mostly written from a British imperial perspective. An anti-imperial historiography began with a popular history in Afrikaans (q.v.) by S. J. du Toit (q.v.) (1847–1911), published in 1877, and was seen in most striking form in the polemic penned by Jan Smuts (q.v.) (though issued under the name of F. W. Reitz, in 1899), *A Century of Wrong,* which chronicled the wrongs done by Britain in the 19th century to the Afrikaner (q.v.) people.

By that time, a local settler tradition had emerged that sought to be even handed in its treatment of both British settlers and Afrikaner Voortrekkers (q.v.). The key figure, and the most prolific historian South Africa has ever produced, was George McCall Theal (q.v.), the first historian to spend long hours in the archives and the first to attempt a detailed general history of South Africa. In his multivolume *History of South Africa*, Theal was sympathetic both to those who had gone on the Great Trek (q.v.) and to those colonists who had remained in the Cape Colony (q.v.), but he was critical of the missionaries (q.v.) and of the British government in London, both of whom he believed had interfered unwisely in South African affairs. Although he had earlier been interested in the history of Africans (q.v.), Theal became increasingly racist in his writing, and much of his *History* was designed to justify white conquest of the bulk of the land.

In the early 20th century, posts in history began to be established at the South African universities, and a new professionalism entered history writing. Afrikaner historians tended to focus their attention on the heroic history of the Great Trek and the later history of Afrikaners, and their histories were often highly descriptive and unimaginative, but P. J.

van der Merwe (1912–79) wrote with great insight on the history of the trekboers (q.v.) and was a pioneer in considering social and economic aspects. Eric Walker, professor of history at the University of Cape Town, was the first professional historian to attempt a general survey of South African history (1928) and wrote prolifically on numerous aspects of that history. But it was William Miller Macmillan (q.v.), professor of history at the University of the Witwatersrand, who in the 1920s pioneered what became known as the "liberal" approach, which recognized relations between white and black to be the central theme of South African history and attempted to understand black history as well as white. Of those who followed in the Macmillan tradition, the most brilliant was his student C. W. de Kiewiet (q.v.), who settled in the United States and did not return to South Africa to live.

In the 1960s there emerged a new generation of liberal historians, aware of the historiographical revolution that had transformed the writing of the history of tropical Africa and anxious to use anthropology and other disciplines to understand African societies. The doyen of these "liberal Africanists" was Leonard Thompson, who with the anthropologist Monica Wilson edited the two-volume *The Oxford History of South Africa* (1969, 1971). In an influential collection of essays published in 1969, Thompson argued that the history of African societies was the "forgotten factor" in South African history.

It was in large part through their critical reviews of the *Oxford History* that a new school of "radicals" or "revisionists" began to take center stage in the early 1970s. Mostly younger scholars, many of them political exiles from South Africa and all influenced by Marxist historiography, they developed a critique of the liberal tradition from a materialist perspective. They pointed out that liberals had played down or ignored material factors, and they suggested that liberal historians believed that had ideological factors like racism (q.v.) and Afrikaner nationalism (q.v.) not intervened, the capitalist marketplace would have produced a nonracial society. The revisionists showed that racial oppression and capitalist exploitation had gone hand in hand and that the relationship between capitalist industrialization and racial segregation (q.v.) had been an essentially complementary one. Instead of imposing constraints on profit maximization, apartheid (q.v.) policies had aided it. Segregation, they argued, was in essence a response to capitalist demands for cheap labor.

By the 1980s the revisionists had divided into structuralists, who laid little emphasis on human agency, and social historians, who increasingly became empiricist in their work. The leading social historian was Charles van Onselen of the University of the Witwatersrand, who wrote about the social and economic history of the Witwatersrand (q.v.) and then devoted 15 years to writing the biography of a previously unknown share-cropper, Kas Maine. The social history tradition was particularly concerned with the history of the previously marginalized or forgotten, and many new areas of history were explored for the first time. In the early 1990s some of these historians, influenced by postmodernist trends in international scholarship, turned their attention to representation and put new emphasis on the importance of the fact that what we know about the past has been shaped by how it has been produced. Old-style political and economic history had long since fallen into virtual disrepute, but by the late 1990s there were signs that it might be beginning to make a comeback, at a time when the historical profession was under threat from falling student numbers at universities and a culture that placed little value on the study of the past.

HOBHOUSE, EMILY (1860–1925). Emily Hobhouse, a British philanthropist, exposed conditions in Boer (q.v.) concentration camps (q.v.) during the South African War (q.v.), so bringing the conduct of British policy into question in Britain. She also assisted impoverished Boer women to establish self-help schemes after the war.

HOFMEYR, JAN HENDRIK (1845–1909). A Cape (q.v.) political leader and champion of the Dutch (q.v.) language, Jan Hofmeyr, called "Onze Jan," led the Afrikaner Bond (q.v.), representing Afrikaner (q.v.) agrarian interests, in the Cape Parliament during the 1880s and 1890s and used this base to make and break several prime ministers. His alliance with Cecil Rhodes (q.v.) between 1890 and 1895 was to their mutual advantage, but he broke with Rhodes after the Jameson Raid (q.v.), of which he strongly disapproved. He actively promoted reconciliation between white (English and Dutch) South Africans before and after the South African War (q.v.).

HOLOMISA, BANTUBONKE (b. 1955). While a soldier in the Transkei (q.v.) Defence Force, Bantubonke "Bantu" Holomisa accused the bantustan (q.v.) government of corruption; he was detained, and then released, in April 1987, and later that year seized power from Stella Sigcau's government in a bloodless coup. As head of the Transkei Military Council, he allowed both the African National Congress (ANC) (q.v.) and the Pan Africanist Congress (q.v.) to operate in the Transkeian (q.v.)

bantustan and unbanned both organizations before the South African government did so in February 1990. He survived a coup, allegedly arranged from Pretoria (q.v.), in November 1990 and later embarrassed the South African government by releasing a Military Intelligence order authorizing the murder of the eastern Cape (q.v.) activist Matthew Goniwe in 1985. He became a popular ANC leader, especially among younger members. Shortly before the Transkei was reincorporated into South Africa, he gave Transkeian soldiers and public servants rapid promotions. Blunt and outspoken, he was made deputy minister for environment affairs in the government of National Unity (q.v.) but was expelled from the party when he accused some of the leadership in the ANC of corruption. In 1997 he founded the United Democratic Movement (q.v.) with Roelf Meyer (q.v.) and in 1998 emerged as the sole leader of the new political party.

HOTTENTOTS. Derived from what seemed, to the Dutch, their unintelligible speech, *Hottentot* was the name given to Khoikhoi (q.v.) in the 17th and 18th centuries. By the 19th century, it had become a general term for all Khoisan (q.v.) people and their descendants at the Cape (q.v.). The terms *Hottentot* and *Hotnot* gradually acquired a strongly pejorative connotation.

HUDDLESTON, TREVOR (1913–98). An Anglican (q.v.) priest and member of the Community of the Resurrection, Trevor Huddleston lived in Johannesburg (q.v.) from 1943 until 1956. His work in Sophiatown and the forced removal of people from the suburb in 1955 by the government under the terms of the Group Areas Act (q.v.) prompted him to write a damning account of apartheid (q.v.), entitled *Naught for Your Comfort* (1956). Banned (q.v.) from South Africa, he served as president of the British anti-apartheid movement and in October 1987 convened the Harare Conference, which brought together a range of resistance groups from within and outside the country.

HUGUENOTS. The Huguenots, French Protestant refugees, about 200 of whom were settled at the Cape (q.v.) by the Dutch East India Company (q.v.) between 1688 and 1700, established themselves mainly in the Stellenbosch district, at present-day Franschhoek, where many became involved in the fledgling Cape wine industry (q.v.). By the mid-18th century, they had become absorbed into the Dutch population.

HUNTER-GATHERERS. *See* SAN.

-I-

IMVO ZABANTSUNDU. An influential weekly Xhosa (q.v.) newspaper founded in 1884 by J. T. Jabavu (q.v.) in King William's Town in the eastern Cape (q.v.), *Imvo Zabantsundu* ("Opinions of the People") was published in English (q.v.) and Xhosa. *Imvo* was the leading voice of Xhosa opinion for more than a decade. From 1898, however, it was challenged by *Izwi Labantu* ("Voice of the People"), edited from East London. *Imvo* was closed in August 1901 by government order for being critical of the South African War (q.v.) and did not resume publication until October 1902. Although it has continued to appear until the present, it has never again been as influential as when Jabavu was its editor.

INDEPENDENT CHURCHES. African independent churches began to be formed in the late 19th century, when a number of individuals and congregations broke away from mission churches, frustrated with paternalistic missionaries (q.v.), the rejection of African (q.v.) tradition and culture, and the denial of African leadership. In 1884, Nehemiah Tile (ca. 1850–91), a Methodist preacher, established the Thembu Church in the Transkei (q.v.); in 1892, Mangena Mokone, a Methodist minister, founded the Ethiopian Church in Pretoria (q.v.), taking the name from Psalm 68:31 ("Ethiopia shall stretch out her hands unto God"). Mokone was joined in the enterprise in 1896 by James Dwane (1848–1916), another minister disillusioned with Methodism, who went to the United States that year and established a link between the Ethiopian Church and the American-based African Methodist Episcopal Church (AMEC) (q.v.), a black church that had been founded in Philadelphia in 1816. The AMEC made him its general superintendent in South Africa. Dwane was consecrated vicar-bishop of the AMEC two years later, by which time the church in South Africa had more than 10,000 adherents. In 1900, Dwane led a large body of followers into the Anglican Church (q.v.), in which he established a separate Order of Ethiopia, with a measure of autonomy. By the turn of the century, other churches had also been established: the Bantu Presbyterian Church, the Zulu Congregational Church, and the Lutheran Bapedi Church were among the most prominent to secede from their white "parent" churches.

The word *Ethiopianism* was frequently used when whites in the early 20th century accused independent churches of being a sinister cover for political opposition to white authority. In his classic work, *Bantu Prophets in South Africa* (1948), Bengt Sundkler, a Lutheran missionary in

Zululand, employed the term *Ethiopianism* for those independent churches that retained the outward form, structure, and much of the theology of their parent churches, and he labeled as *Zionist* those that were also an expression of African independence but blended African tradition with Christian beliefs, laying more emphasis on prophecy, healing, and purification rituals. Independent churches varied enormously from one another, making such classification difficult. Some, such as the Israelite sect founded by Enoch Mgijima at Bulhoek (q.v.) in 1918, were millenarian in character. They also represented a wide range of political opinion. Although a few ministers from independent churches were active in the African National Congress (q.v.), many of them shunned political involvement altogether.

The potential power of the independent churches was weakened by constant fission; by the 1970s, there were more than 3,000 of them, and by the 1990s more than 5,000. Many of these were made up of a single congregation with fewer than 200 followers. The combined membership of the independent churches was almost six million by 1991, representing more than 30 percent of all practicing Christians in the country. The largest church was the politically conservative Zion Christian Church, based at Moria in the Northern Province (q.v.), which claimed a membership of between two million and three million people.

INDIANS. Some Cape slaves (q.v.) were of Indian origin, but South Africa's Indian community traces its origins to two groups of migrants who settled in the country in the latter part of the 19th century. Between 1860 and 1911, just over 152,000 people from south and northeastern India arrived in Natal (q.v.) as indentured laborers. The majority of them worked on sugar plantations, but others were employed on the railways (q.v.), in the coal mines, and on wattle plantations. At the end of their five-year contracts, workers could enter a further five-year term, after which they were entitled to a free trip back to India or could remain in Natal as free Indians. Most elected to stay in Natal and became itinerant hawkers, shopkeepers, market gardeners, and artisans. Some made their way to the diamond (q.v.) fields at Kimberley (q.v.) or to the Transvaal (q.v.).

The other group of migrants were known as "passenger Indians," because they paid their own passage to Natal. They were traders and merchants, mainly Gujarati-speaking Muslims from the west coast of India, though some were Hindu and some came from Mauritius; a few passenger Indians were Christian teachers and priests. Most remained in Natal, though some proceeded to the Transvaal and the Cape (q.v.). Because of their economic and social position, passenger Indians provided leadership to the Indian communities all over Natal.

In 1911 the Indian community numbered 150,000, 89 percent of whom lived in Natal. By this time, Indians had encountered official restrictions from various authorities. Natal imposed a £3 tax to encourage them to return to India; they were barred from the vote (1896); trading restrictions were enacted (1897); and new immigrants were required to know a European language (1897), a measure that succeeded in reducing the flow of immigration. In the Transvaal, Indians were denied citizenship rights and could own property only in certain designated areas (1885); they were obliged to carry registration certificates (1907); and immigrants were required to pass a test in a European language (1908). In the Orange Free State (q.v.), they were unable to own or rent property (1885), nor could they pursue business without government approval (1890). Resistance to such measures, led by the Natal Indian Congress (NIC), founded in 1894, and particularly by Mohandas Gandhi (q.v.), was largely unsuccessful, though Gandhi's *satyagraha* campaign, which culminated in 1913, did succeed in having the £3 tax abolished in Natal and in securing recognition for Indian marriages.

The new Union (q.v.) of South Africa government prohibited all further immigration of Indians in 1913, with the exception of the wives and children of Indians already settled in South Africa. For several decades after creation of the Union, successive governments regarded the Indian community as only temporarily resident in South Africa. The Cape Town (q.v.) agreement (1927) between the governments of South Africa and India provided for voluntary state-aided repatriation of Indians, but only a minority availed themselves of the opportunity; many passenger Indians in particular had prospered economically.

The wartime government of Jan Smuts (q.v.) appointed commissions in 1941 and 1943 to investigate Indian "penetration" of white areas; this resulted in the Pegging Act of 1943, preventing the purchase of property by Indians from whites in Durban (q.v.). In 1946, a more far-reaching Asiatic Land Tenure and Indian Representation Act divided Natal into exempted and unexempted areas: in the latter, Indians were not permitted to own or occupy property without permission of the government. Under the influence of a younger, more radical leadership, the NIC launched another passive resistance campaign, while the government of India withdrew its high commissioner, broke off trade relations, and raised the issue in the United Nations (q.v.). Tougher legislation ensued, however: the Group Areas Act (q.v.) of 1950 heralded the effective segregation of Indians, large numbers of whom were forced from their homes and businesses in the cities and resettled in small, overcrowded suburbs, where they often had to pay inflated prices for accommodation. The NIC meanwhile forged closer links with the African National Congress (q.v.), and Indian leaders played an important role in the Defiance Campaign (q.v.); many, however, suffered banning (q.v.), which significantly weakened the NIC and prevented coordinated opposition to removals under the Group Areas Act.

In 1961 the Indian community was finally accepted as a permanent part of the South African population by the National Party (q.v.) government. A nominated National Indian Council was established in 1964, which became the South African Indian Council in 1968. Provision was made at the end of the 1970s for 40 of its 45 members to be elected, but because of opposition to the council within the Indian community elections were held only in November 1981, and a mere 6 percent of voters turned out. The tricameral (q.v.) constitution of 1983 created the House of Delegates for Indian representation in Parliament, giving Indians control of their "own affairs" in matters such as health, housing, and education. Less than 20 percent of the electorate voted for members of Parliament in the election of 1984.

In 1991, the Indian population numbered 864,000, just under 3 percent of the total population. More than 80 percent of Indians lived in Natal. Significant religious, linguistic, class, and political cleavages existed within the community: for example, some 57 percent were Hindu, 24 percent Muslim, and 18 percent Christian, and although some Indians participated willingly in the 1980s in government-created structures, others joined a range of opposition movements. Tensions between Indians and Africans also occasionally manifested themselves violently, as in Natal in 1985, when Gandhi's Phoenix settlement was burned down.

INDUSTRIAL AND COMMERCIAL WORKERS' UNION OF SOUTH AFRICA (ICU). The ICU was formed by Clements Kadalie, a mission-educated Malawian, in 1919 in the Cape Town (q.v.) docks. In the 1920s, as national secretary, he built up the trade union into a massive movement, which expanded especially in the rural areas of Natal (q.v.), the Transvaal (q.v.), and the Orange Free State (q.v.). In 1927 it claimed a membership of 100,000, the majority being rural Africans (q.v.). It voiced a broad range of popular grievances. In the towns, its main success was in organizing workers in the docks, railways (q.v.), and municipal services. In the countryside, it concentrated on issues relating to land, wages, and the pass laws (q.v.). Kadalie consistently sought to win recognition for the ICU as a legitimate trade union (q.v.) and a voice for black workers. Failing to secure acceptance by white-led unions in South Africa, he went abroad in 1926 in a bid to secure international recognition for the ICU. William Ballinger, an adviser sent out by the British labor movement in 1928, found the affairs of the ICU in chaos, and Kadalie fell out with both Ballinger and A. W. G. Champion, leader of the Natal ICU, who broke away in 1928 and established a rival ICU. The ICU was destroyed in part by mismanagement and internal conflict but also by action taken against it by the government and employers. By 1929 it was in decline, and by 1933 it had virtually disappeared, though Kadalie established an independent ICU, which for a time had an organized following in East London. The ICU was remembered for having given many a brief taste of freedom.

INFLUENZA EPIDEMIC. Spanish influenza, estimated to have killed 20 million people worldwide in 1918–19, arrived in South Africa in September 1918. Its impact was uneven: urban centers tended to be severely affected, particularly places such as the African compound (q.v.) in Kimberley (q.v.), and parts of the Transkei (q.v.) and Ciskei (q.v.). Natal (q.v.) was relatively unscathed. The official death toll was 139,471 people, of whom 11,726 were whites, but more recent research suggests that this was an underestimate, and it is likely that some 250,000 Africans died.

The influenza epidemic was the worst natural disaster in South Africa's history, and the country experienced one of the highest per capita death rates in the world. The epidemic drew attention to the poor living conditions of urban Africans, but little was done to improve their situation in the aftermath.

INFLUX CONTROL. Jan Smuts's (q.v.) Natives (Urban Areas) Act of 1923 imposed a system of segregation and influx control on Africans (q.v.), who were to be allowed into the towns only to serve white labor needs and in strict proportion to the availability of work. All Africans except domestic workers would be housed in locations outside the towns, thus keeping the towns themselves white. In 1937, male Africans were given 14 days in which to find work in the towns or return to the reserves (q.v.), and from 1938 influx control regulations were applied systematically. In 1952 the notorious Section 10 legislation was enacted, which denied the right to live in an urban area to any African, male or female, who was not born there, unless he or she had lived there continuously for 15 years or had served under the same employer for 10 years. It also reduced to 72 hours the time allowed blacks for finding employment in an urban area. Despite all such measures, the number of Africans in the towns grew. Influx control caused immense social distress—husbands and wives were separated, homes were broken up—and the administration of the system led to the growth of a vast and corrupt bureaucracy. In 1986 the pass (q.v.) system, which underpinned influx control, was abolished by the P. W. Botha (q.v.) government.

INFORMATION SCANDAL. Dubbed "Muldergate" by the press (q.v.), this scandal in the Department of Information in the 1970s in some ways resembled the Watergate scandal in the United States. The prime minister, John Vorster (q.v.), was persuaded by the secretary for information, Eschel Rhoodie, and the minister, Connie Mulder, to bankroll various schemes for putting South Africa's case in influential newspapers and journals. The single largest sum went to establish an English-language, progovernment newspaper in Johannesburg (q.v.), the *Citizen*. When news of this arrangement began to emerge, those involved sought to cover up their deeds, and Mulder denied to Parliament that any government money had gone to finance the *Citizen*. This may have cost him the premiership, which went to P. W. Botha (q.v.) instead. Vorster was forced to resign, first as prime minister and then as state president. Of those directly involved, only Rhoodie was prosecuted, and he was acquitted on appeal.

INKATHA. First established as a cultural organization in 1922–23, Inkatha was revived by Mangosuthu Buthelezi (q.v.) in March 1975 and took over the symbols and anthem used by the African National Congress (ANC) (q.v.). By 1985 Inkatha claimed to have more than 1 million members, and at the end of the 1980s, 1.5 million members, with a youth brigade of 60,000 and a women's brigade of 500,000. Buthelezi's gradualist approach, working within the bantustan policy (q.v.) while rejecting independence, was condemned as collaborationist by radical black urban youth. After Buthelezi broke with the ANC in 1979, refusing to accept the authority of the exile leadership, Inkatha appeared as a rival to the ANC and the United Democratic Front (UDF) (q.v.), and conflict increased. Inkatha *impis* (armed groups) fought University of Zululand students in 1983. From August 1985 bitter fighting with the UDF also took place in the Pietermaritzburg (q.v.) area as the two organizations struggled for turf. By 1989 they were locked in a low-intensity civil war, with Inkatha warlords sending out their men to burn down the homes of "comrades" in cycles of revenge. Soon after it was announced in July– August 1990 that Inkatha would become a political party—the Inkatha

Freedom Party (IFP), open to all—the Witwatersrand exploded in a new burst of conflict between Inkatha and the "comrades" (*amaqabane*).

The IFP stood for multiparty, nonracial democracy supported by a free-market system. Its funding came at this time in part from conservative sources in Germany and from the South African government, as was revealed in the Inkathagate (q.v.) scandal of July 1991, which severely weakened Buthelezi's credibility. Buthelezi signed the National Peace Accord in September 1991, but relations with F. W. de Klerk (q.v.) were ruptured a year later when the government signed the Record of Understanding (q.v.) with the ANC, one of the clauses of which prevented IFP members from carrying their "traditional weapons" in public. Another clause provided for the fencing of the hostels of migrant workers, most of which were Inkatha strongholds. In direct response to the Record of Understanding, in October 1992 an angry Buthelezi took the IFP into a right-wing Concerned South Africans' Group (COSAG), alongside such reactionary parties as the ultraright, white Conservative Party (q.v.). In mid-1993, the IFP refused to continue participation in the constitutional talks at Kempton Park because the talks did not provide for the federal system the IFP wanted and because Buthelezi rejected the principle of "sufficient consensus" in the negotiations. *See also* MULTI-PARTY NEGOTIATING FORUM.

On 19 April 1994, at the very last minute, Buthelezi was persuaded by a friend, Professor Washington Okumu of Kenya, to join the election battle; he feared that if he did not do so, he and the IFP would become politically irrelevant in the new order. Special stickers were hastily printed and stuck onto the ballot papers. In the election, the IFP won more than 10 percent of the vote and, as the result of some bargaining, a majority in the KwaZulu-Natal (q.v.) legislature. Buthelezi then became minister of home affairs, with a seat in the government of National Unity (q.v.), and talk that the IFP might consider a secession option disappeared. The IFP claimed it had been promised international mediation on certain disputed constitutional issues; because this did not materialize, the IFP again refused to join in the discussions on the final constitution, walking out of the Constitutional Assembly (q.v.) in both 1995 and 1996. The KwaZulu Legislative Assembly, dominated by the IFP, went ahead and drew up its own constitution, but this was rejected by the Constitutional Court (q.v.). Buthelezi nevertheless remained in the GNU, even after the National Party (q.v.) left it.

The first local government election in KwaZulu-Natal in 1996 revealed that the IFP had retained its rural support in KwaZulu but was losing support in the urban areas. By this time, its support was almost entirely limited to that province. In late 1997 there was talk of a merger between the IFP and the ANC before the 1999 election, but Buthelezi himself rejected the idea.

INKATHAGATE. The Inkathagate scandal broke in July 1991, when it was revealed that the National Party (NP) (q.v.) government had secretly funded Inkatha (q.v.) and its associated trade union, allegedly for antisanctions activities. The government had long aided Inkatha and had helped arrange secret military training for IFP recruits in northern Zululand (q.v.) and in the Caprivi strip area of Namibia (q.v.). As a result of the revelations, the personal reputation of F. W. de Klerk (q.v.) as a man of integrity suffered a major blow, and Inkatha's claim to be an independent player in the negotiations was compromised. Ties between Buthelezi and the NP were loosened, though they were to be severed only as a result of the Record of Understanding (q.v.) in 1992.

IRON AGE. For much of the 20th century, it was commonly believed that southern Africa was populated from the north during the 15th and 16th centuries, at roughly the same time that white colonization began from the south. Incontrovertible archaeological evidence collected since the 1960s shatters this myth. In about A.D. 200, new groups of farming communities moved south across the Limpopo River (q.v.) and settled in parts of present-day South Africa. Because they smelted and processed ore to make iron tools, they have been defined as belonging to the "Iron Age."

These Iron Age people were also the first to practice agriculture (q.v.), growing crops such as sorghum and millet; they kept livestock and lived in houses constructed from wood and reeds in small permanent villages. Their settlements were located in low-lying regions near the coast or in river valleys where fertile soil and good summer rainfalls ensured reliable harvests. The remains of pottery and other material such as burnt wood reveal that by A.D. 800 they were well established in the present-day Northern Province (q.v.), Mpumalanga (q.v.), KwaZulu-Natal (q.v.), and the Eastern Cape (q.v.). Patterns of settlement began to change around A.D. 800–1000, probably as a result of the increasing importance of cattle. Farming continued in the river valleys, but people also moved onto the grasslands of the interior, and by A.D. 1200 almost the entire high veld (q.v.) was inhabited by Iron Age people. Settlement patterns from this period differed: villages were much larger, accommodating hundreds of people, and stone building was extensive, both for houses and for livestock enclosures and walls around settlements. Limited timber resources also meant that opportunities for iron smelting were restricted; trade networks consequently developed with the communities in the eastern part of the region. In the main, cattle was exchanged for iron, but long-distance trade also occurred, conducted by Arab traders who established trading posts on the Mozambique (q.v.) coast; their commodities, such as glass beads, were prized in southern Africa.

Perhaps the most important result of trade and control of trading networks was the concentration of wealth in the hands of some Iron Age communities. Between A.D. 1200 and 1500, powerful centers emerged, the most significant of which were Mapungubwe (q.v.) and Great Zimbabwe (q.v.). Mapungubwe (q.v.), situated south of the Limpopo, developed into the dominant power of the region during the 13th century and was home to more than 10,000 people at the peak of its power. Wealthy inhabitants lived on the defensible hilltop, which overlooked the valley where poorer people were located. The ruling classes presided over a diversified economy: pastoralism, agriculture, a significant manufacturing sector (in iron, gold, pottery, and weaving), and extensive trade. By the end of the 13th century, Mapungubwe's power was waning, as Great Zimbabwe further north rose to prominence.

By the 15th and 16th centuries, the entire interior of South Africa, with the exception of the Karoo (q.v.) semidesert (which prevented further southern expansion), was settled by Iron Age people who practiced mixed agriculture and pastoralism and engaged in extensive trade. The majority lived in small villages, although some in the interior occupied larger, more concentrated settlements. By the time they came into contact with white settlers toward the end of the 18th century, they could trace a history of settlement of more than 1,500 years.

ISANDLWANA. The first major battle of the Anglo–Zulu War began on 22 January 1879, when the invading British troops stumbled unexpectedly across a Zulu (q.v.) army numbering 20,000 men. The British force of some 1,250 men, which had been left to guard the encampment at Isandlwana, was completely overwhelmed, and few escaped with their lives. The battle represented a crushing defeat for the British and their plans for confederation (q.v.) in southern Africa. Although it was a Zulu victory, losses among the Zulu were high, and the war ended with their defeat a few months later.

ISLAM. The first Muslims at the Cape (q.v.) were political exiles, convicts banished from the possessions of the Dutch East India Company (q.v.) in the East, or slaves (q.v.). Most of the slaves came from Bengal, the west coast of India, and the Indonesian islands. Slaves of Indonesian origin formed about half of Cape Town's (q.v.) slave population, and many Indonesian customs, relating to clothing, food, and ritual, were brought to the Cape.

Toward the end of the 18th century, a remarkable growth of Islam occurred among Cape slaves. The religion appealed to them because the *imams* identified with their needs, performing marriages and funerals denied by Christian (q.v.) churches, and because it was color-blind. Slave owners welcomed the conversion of their slaves to Islam because of official restrictions on the buying and selling of Christian slaves and because of the Muslim prohibition on alcohol. Many free blacks (q.v.) were also attracted to Islam. During the first British occupation (q.v.) of the Cape, Muslims in Cape Town were able to persuade the authorities to allow them to practice their religion freely, and the first mosque opened in 1804.

The majority of Cape Muslims followed the Shafi school, though a minority were persuaded by Abu Bakr Effendi (1835–80), sent to Cape Town by the sultan of Constantinople in 1862, to adopt Hanafi beliefs. After 1860, Indian (q.v.) indentured laborers arrived in South Africa to work on the Natal (q.v.) sugar plantations; of the initial groups, which came mainly from Madras, about 12 percent were Muslim. From the late 1870s, a new class of passenger Indians, mostly Gujarati-speaking Muslims, settled in Natal. By the 1990s, about half of the country's 350,000 Muslims were descended from those in the 19th-century Cape; the other half traced their roots to the Indian settlers in Natal.

Apartheid (q.v.) radicalized some Muslims, and Muslim youth movements challenged the conservative Muslim Judicial Council. Imam Haron, who died in police custody in 1969, became a martyr, and many Cape Town Muslims joined the militant People against Gangsters and Drugs in the mid-1990s. Pan-Islamic contacts grew, and by the mid-1990s South Africa's Muslims had one of the highest rates of *hajj* (the pilgrimage to Mecca) outside the Middle East.

-J-

JABAVU, JOHN TENGU (1859–1921). Journalist, educator, and political leader, John Tengu Jabavu qualified as a teacher at Healdtown Missionary Institution in the eastern Cape (q.v.) but became prominent through his editorship of *Imvo Zabantsundu* (q.v.), which he founded with white Cape liberal support in 1884. Until the end of the century, he was the most powerful African spokesman in the Cape Colony (q.v.). He lost political credibility in the early 20th century, when he was accused of personal ambition and overly intimate ties with the white establishment. He refused to champion the South African Native National Congress (later the African National Congress [q.v.]), he supported the Natives Land Act (q.v.) of 1913, and he split the Cape African vote in standing for election to the Cape Provincial Council in 1914. Jabavu did much to promote the founding of a university college for Africans (q.v.); the establishment in 1916 of the South African Native College, later Fort Hare (q.v.) University, owed much to his efforts. His son D. D. T. Jabavu taught there.

JAMESON RAID. In December 1895, Leander Starr Jameson, one of Cecil Rhodes's (q.v.) closest friends, led an abortive attempt to overthrow the government of the South African Republic (q.v.). An administrator in the British South Africa Company (q.v.) in Matabeleland, Jameson was commissioned by Rhodes, prime minister of the Cape Colony (q.v.), to head a force of mounted men to invade the Transvaal (q.v.) from Bechuanaland (q.v.) and link up with an expected Uitlander (q.v.) uprising. The attempt failed, and Jameson and his 500 men surrendered to Transvaal troops on 2 January 1896. The Uitlander leaders in the conspiracy were sentenced to death for their part in it but had their sentences commuted to heavy fines; Jameson served only four months of a 15-month sentence. The raid had far-reaching political repercussions: Rhodes was forced to resign as prime minister, his alliance with J. H. Hofmeyr (q.v.) of the Afrikaner Bond (q.v.) was destroyed, and the Transvaal, more convinced than ever of British bad faith and duplicity, forged a close alliance with the Orange Free State (q.v.).

In 1965 the Australian historian Geoffrey Blainey suggested that owners of deep-level gold (q.v.) mines had supported the raid, seeking to replace the government of Paul Kruger (q.v.) with one more amenable to their interests, whereas the owners of outcrop mines, which required less capital, did not. Later research showed this to be too simple but suggested that those implicated in the raid had longer-term commitments to the industry and were more development-oriented than those who were not involved.

JEWISH COMMUNITY. Only after the British occupation (q.v.) of the Cape did Jews arrive in any numbers. Some became merchants in Cape Town (q.v.), where the first permanent Hebrew congregation was formed in 1841; others traded in the interior, where they formed an accepted constituent of the white rural population. In 1880, there were about 4,000 Jews in southern Africa.

During the 1880s and 1890s, a large number of Jews from eastern Europe, particularly Lithuania, settled in South Africa. A literacy test, introduced by the Cape (q.v.) in 1902 to restrict Indian (q.v.) immigration, threatened to cut off this flow, but in 1906, Yiddish was recognized as a European language, and by 1914 more than 40,000 Lithuanian Jews had entered the country. The Immigration Quota Act of 1930 reduced the flow of immigrants from eastern Europe to a trickle. Some 7,000 refugees from Nazi Germany settled in South Africa before the Aliens Act of 1937 closed the door to further immigration.

Anti-Semitism displayed itself in various guises during the early 20th century, most explicitly in Afrikaner (q.v.) circles during the 1930s, particularly among extremists who viewed Hitler as a hero. After World War II (q.v.), however, both Jan Smuts (q.v.) and D. F. Malan (q.v.) supported the Zionist cause, with which South African Jews closely identified themselves, and the overt hostility of the prewar years subsided to some extent. Although there were sometimes tensions between the Jewish community and the political establishment during the apartheid (q.v.) period, Jewish people generally prospered and made notable contributions in commerce, industry, politics, and the professions.

Jews constituted about 4 percent of the white population in 1936, but their numbers declined proportionately thereafter, mainly because of restricted immigration and low birthrates. In 1991, the Jewish community numbered almost 120,000 people, about 0.3 percent of the country's population.

JOB COLOR BAR. In the era of racial segregation (q.v.) and apartheid (q.v.), certain jobs were reserved for whites. Liberal analysts argued that the job color bar impeded economic growth, and revisionist scholars believed that economic growth was underpinned by cheap African labor and that, by dividing the working class along racial lines, the job color bar helped to keep African wages low.

Most firmly entrenched in the mining (q.v.) industry, the job color bar spread from there to other fields of employment. Under the terms of a mining act passed by the Cape (q.v.) Parliament in 1883, regulations were promulgated in 1885 providing that Africans (q.v.) should not be allowed to undertake blasting. A Transvaal (q.v.) law of 1893 prohibited Africans, Indians (q.v.), and Coloureds (q.v.) from preparing charges, loading drills, or lighting fuses. From 1896, skilled gold (q.v.) miners were required to have blasting certificates; it was understood that only whites would be able to obtain such a certificate. The Transvaal Boilers and Machinery Act of 1898 provided that no person of color could be an engine driver. These color-bar provisions remained in force under the British administration after the South African War (q.v.). When the importation of Chinese (q.v.) labor was authorized, the Transvaal Labour Importation Ordinance (1904) reserved more than 50 specific occupations and trades for whites. After creation of the Union (q.v.) of South Africa, the Mines and Works Act (1911) empowered the government to make regulations to control the grant of certificates of competence needed for skilled and semiskilled jobs. In the regulations made under the act, 51 occupations were reserved for white workers by 1920.

An attempt by mine management to adjust the job color bar and employ Africans in semiskilled jobs previously reserved for whites led to the Rand Revolt (q.v.) of 1922. With the revolt suppressed, the Chamber of Mines (q.v.) instigated a test case before the Transvaal Supreme Court, which found that the Mines and Works Act did not expressly sanction racial discrimination, and therefore regulations discriminating on that basis were *ultra vires*. When the Pact government (q.v.) came to power in 1924, the act was amended to provide expressly for racial discrimination in the issue of certificates of competence. The amended act (1926) was often referred to as the Color Bar Act.

After the National Party (NP) (q.v.) was returned to power in 1948, it took further steps to secure the position of white workers. An act of 1951 prevented skilled African building workers from working in "white" urban areas. The Industrial Conciliation Act was amended in 1956 to empower the minister of labor to reserve any work for people of a particular racial group. Not more than 2 percent of jobs, however, were ever reserved in terms of determinations under this act. Most job reservation was implemented through state-enforced industrial council agreements between employers and white craft unions operating a closed shop. Besides the apprenticeship (q.v.) system, such measures as the Group Areas Act (q.v.), influx control (q.v.), and the Coloured Labour Preference (q.v.) policy in the western Cape (q.v.) all served to restrict job opportunities on a racial basis.

International pressure and the growing shortage of skilled and semiskilled labor worked to undermine statutory job reservation in the late 1970s. In 1979 the government accepted a recommendation from the Wiehahn Commission (q.v.) that it reject the principle of job reservation. Existing work reservation determinations were to remain in force, however, until they could be phased out with the consent of the relevant white union. In February 1982, resistance by a white union to the ending of job reservation in Cape Town's (q.v.) municipal services was finally overcome, and these jobs were opened to people of all races. The powerful white Mine Workers' Union continued to oppose the scrapping of job reservation in the mines, the last area where determinations remained in force, until the mid-1980s. *See also* CIVILIZED LABOUR POLICY; COLOR BAR.

JOHANNESBURG. The largest city in South Africa, center of the country's gold-mining industry, manufacturing (q.v.), and commerce, Johannesburg emerged as a direct result of the discovery of gold (q.v.) on the Witwatersrand (q.v.) in 1886. It mushroomed out onto the farms above the gold-bearing reef: in 1887, the diggers' camp housed 3,000 people; by 1899, the population of Egoli, as it became known to Africans, was 120,000; and by 1914 it had grown to 250,000, a figure that excluded Africans (q.v.) living illegally on the outskirts of the town.

By the first two decades of the 20th century, Johannesburg had become a city of immense inequalities of wealth, ranging from randlords (q.v.) who lived in great opulence in the northern suburbs to numerous impoverished migrant (q.v.) workers and unemployed people eking out an existence around the mines and factories of the city. By mid-century, Johannesburg was the heart of the country's business activity and was by far its largest commercial and industrial center. From the 1960s, as air travel replaced sea travel, it became the main gateway to South Africa. By the beginning of the 1990s, greater Johannesburg had a population of between four million and five million people and was attracting new inhabitants from all over South Africa as well as beyond the country's borders. It became the capital of the newly formed Gauteng (q.v.) Province in 1994.

JOSEPH, HELEN BEATRICE MAY (1905–92). Born and educated in England, Helen Joseph taught in India before settling in South Africa in 1931. She served as a welfare and information officer in the South African Air Force during World War II (q.v.) and, in 1951, became secretary of the medical aid fund of the Garment Workers' Union, after which she became deeply involved in extraparliamentary opposition politics during the 1950s. In 1954, she helped to found the Federation of South African Women (q.v.) and became its national secretary in 1956, playing a leading role in the antipass (q.v.) demonstrations in Pretoria (q.v.). She was arrested in the same year as one of the 156 treason trialists (q.v.).

Thereafter, Joseph was constantly persecuted by apartheid (q.v.) security police (q.v.) over a period of more than 30 years: she was banned (q.v.) in 1957 for the first time and imprisoned in solitary confinement in 1960 after the Sharpeville massacre (q.v.), and she was the first person in the country to be placed under house arrest in 1962. That same year, she also became a "listed" person, which prevented her from belonging to any organization opposed to the government. During periods when her house arrest was lifted, she was again active in extra-parliamentary opposition politics and was a popular and widely respected symbol of defiance for many people. A patron of the United Democratic Front (q.v.) from 1983, her listing was finally lifted in 1990, when she was 85. She published three books, *If This Be Treason* (1963), *Tomorrow's Sun* (1966), and her autobiography, *Side by Side* (1986).

-K-

KANGWANE. A small bantustan (q.v.), KaNgwane ("land of the Ngwane") was created for the Swazi within South Africa. When it was given a legislative assembly in 1978, only 100,000 of the estimated 600,000 Swazis in South Africa lived in the territory, which was divided into a portion adjoining the northern Swaziland (q.v.) border and another bordering the Kruger National Park (q.v.). In the 1970s the South African and Swaziland governments entered into secret negotiations on the transfer of the territory to Swaziland, and in June 1982 the South African government announced that KaNgwane was to be incorporated in Swaziland, along with a portion of KwaZulu (q.v.). The KaNgwane Legislative Assembly, which was known to oppose incorporation, was dissolved. But transfer never happened, and in 1994, like all other former bantustans, KaNgwane was reincorporated into South Africa.

KAROO. Derived from a Khoikhoi (q.v.) word meaning "dry country," the name *Karoo* refers to the semidesert region covering a third of the area of South Africa. It stretches from the Langeberg range in the south to the southern Orange Free State (q.v.) and is characterized by flat-topped hills and open treeless plains. Khoisan (q.v.) hunters and herders once occupied the area, but Bantu-speaking (q.v.) farmers did not settle there because of its aridity. White trekboers (q.v.) moved across the Karoo from the 1740s, encountering considerable opposition from the San (q.v.). During the 19th century, sheep farming became the dominant economic activity, but wasteful farming practices over the past century have caused environmental degradation, resulting in an enlargement of the Karoo. The Karoo has been evoked powerfully by several South African writers, particularly Olive Schreiner (q.v.) in *The Story of an African Farm* (1883), Pauline Smith in *The Little Karoo* (1925), and Guy Butler in *Karoo Morning* (1977). *See also* WOOL INDUSTRY.

KAT RIVER SETTLEMENT. The right of the Khoikhoi (q.v.) and other free persons of color to own land was recognized in Ordinance 50 (q.v.) of 1828, but they had no access to land outside the mission (q.v.) stations. The Kat River Settlement was the sole experiment in the granting of land to such people: in 1829, the Cape (q.v.) government made available to some 250 families land in a relatively fertile valley in the eastern Cape (q.v.), from which the Xhosa (q.v.) chief Maqoma (q.v.) had recently been ejected. The government intended the settlement to act as a buffer between the colony and the Xhosa. The inhabitants fought on the side of the colony in the wars of 1834–35 and 1846–47, in the second of which the settlement suffered severely.

White colonists increasingly coveted the land of the Kat River valley, particularly when some members of the settlement became successful peasant farmers. Some whites wished to use the settlement as a labor resource; others desired the land for sheep farming. Driven to rebellion, about half the settlers took up arms in 1851 against the colonial authorities, when the Cape was involved in another war with the Xhosa. Andries Botha, a leading rebel, was convicted of high treason, and the land of the rebels was confiscated and given to whites. Loyalists remained in the settlement, and some retained their title to the land. A number of their descendants were finally driven from the area when the Kat River valley was incorporated into the Ciskei (q.v.) bantustan (q.v.) in 1981.

KHOIKHOI. Those Khoikhoi ("men of men") who lived in the southwestern Cape (q.v.) during the late 15th century were the first southern Africans encountered by Portuguese explorers. The Dutch who settled at the Cape in the 17th century called these pastoralists "Hottentots" (q.v.), an insulting imitation of their staccato speech.

Although the origins of the Khoikhoi are not entirely clear, it is generally accepted that they first appeared some 2,000 years ago among Khoi-speaking hunting groups in the northern parts of present-day Botswana (formerly Bechuanaland [q.v.]) and Namibia (q.v.). Precisely how these hunters acquired livestock is uncertain, but it most likely occurred through contact with early Iron Age (q.v.) peoples moving south.

The Khoikhoi themselves then moved farther south, probably because of the need for additional grazing land as well as population pressure. Some evidence suggests that they migrated south along the coast from northern Namibia until they reached the Cape peninsula, whereupon they turned east until they reached the present-day eastern Cape. Another theory is that some (the ancestors of the Nama) moved west along the Orange River (q.v.), and others (the ancestors of the Cape Khoikhoi) migrated southward into the eastern Cape and then west along the coast until they reached the Cape peninsula. By A.D. 500, Khoikhoi groups were settled along the western, southern, and eastern Cape coasts as well as along the Orange River and in much of Namibia; there was a less dense population in the Cape interior and on the high veld (q.v.).

Initially the Khoikhoi possessed only sheep, but they later acquired cattle through contact with farmers in the eastern Cape. They practiced a seminomadic lifestyle, the needs of their livestock—their major source of wealth—taking precedence. They followed regular transhumant patterns, shifting between different vegetation zones from winter to summer. Societal structures were flexible, clans consisting of related families and their clients; clans, in turn, were often grouped together under the loose control of chiefs, who lacked the power to prevent regular fission of communities. Raiding occurred frequently between groups for cattle and for control of water and pasture. The shelters of Khoikhoi consisted of wooden structures and reed mats, which could be easily dismantled and transported on the backs of oxen; their equipment was similarly designed for mobility. Their relationship with hunter-gatherers was complex: the latter sometimes raided their livestock but also acted as their clients. They had close ties as well with various Bantu-speaking groups, intermarrying in particular with the Tlhaping (q.v.) north of the Orange River and with the Xhosa (q.v.) in the eastern Cape.

After the Dutch settled in the southwestern Cape in the 1650s, pressures on Khoikhoi land and livestock resources began to increase. Some of the Dutch wished to enslave the Khoikhoi, but others recognized the need to acknowledge their independence so as to sustain a reliable trade with them. Two wars were fought between the Khoikhoi and the Dutch, in 1659–60 and in 1673–77, the second of which saw the Dutch firmly established in the southwestern Cape at the expense of continued Khoikhoi autonomy there. Groups were forced to retreat from the region or to take work on white farms, where they became herdsmen, ox trainers, and wagon drivers. Their numbers were further weakened by serious outbreaks of smallpox (q.v.) between 1713 and 1720 and then in 1735 and 1767. It is estimated by some that Khoikhoi numbers south of the Orange declined from approximately 200,000 in the mid-17th century to about 20,000 at the end of the 18th century. *See also* DUTCH–KHOIKHOI WARS.

Khoikhoi resistance to white expansion should not be underestimated: during the 18th century, many joined bands of San (q.v.) raiders and seriously hindered white advance into the interior. Khoikhoi who had been reduced to a landless proletariat in the eastern Cape took up arms in 1799 and joined Xhosa resistance to the colonists; it took the British more than two years to suppress this rebellion. Some succeeded in escaping to the middle Orange area, where they became known as the Korana (q.v.) during the 19th century, and others formed the nucleus of Griqua (q.v.) groups. Most independent Khoikhoi communities were unable to cope with the commercial pressures of white colonization. Those who survived within the colony remained legally free, but in practice their position was not much different from that of the Cape slaves (q.v.). The pass laws (q.v.) to which they were subject were removed by Ordinance 50 (q.v.) of 1828, and gradually Khoikhoi people were absorbed into the emerging community of those called Coloureds (q.v.). Some Khoikhoi managed to survive at the mission stations of Namaqualand, which were designated as reserves (q.v.) for Coloureds in 1909 by the Cape government.

KHOISAN. The anthropologist Isaac Schapera, in his book *The Khoisan Peoples of South Africa* (1930), and later scholars used the term *Khoisan* for the Khoikhoi (q.v.) and the San (q.v.) together. Although the Khoikhoi language was distinct from San, historical evidence frequently fails to distinguish adequately between them, nor does it tell us whether the people being described were hunters or herders. *Khoisan* is thus a convenient composite term.

KIMBERLEY. The foremost diamond (q.v.) center of South Africa, the Kimberley settlement expanded out of the mining camp that developed after the discovery of diamonds in the area in 1869 and 1870. Named after the British colonial secretary, the Earl of Kimberley (1826–1902), when the diamond fields were annexed in 1871, within two years the town grew to become the second-largest settlement in southern Africa after Cape Town (q.v.), with a population of more than 50,000. Kimberley was incorporated into the Cape Colony (q.v.) in 1880, by which time it was also the center of a thriving gun trade. Kimberley was besieged for four months during the South African War (q.v.). It remained the headquarters of De Beers (q.v.) Consolidated Mines, the world's largest diamond company, until the early 1990s. In 1994 it became the capital of the new Northern Cape (q.v.) Province.

KINDERGARTEN. A group of brilliant young men from Oxford, known collectively as the Kindergarten, attracted by the reputation of Lord Milner (q.v.), came to South Africa to assist him in his administration of the Transvaal (q.v.) and Orange River (q.v.) Colony after the South African War (q.v.). Their chief importance was probably as extremely able administrators, but they are remembered more for having, after Milner's departure, promoted the cause of the unification of South Africa. Lionel Curtis drafted the Selborne Memorandum advocating union (q.v.), and he and others founded an influential periodical, *The State*. Most of the Kindergarten went on to distinguished careers elsewhere, but Patrick Duncan (q.v.) remained and became governor-general of the Union of South Africa.

KITCHENER, HORATIO HERBERT (1850–1916). Chief of staff to Lord Roberts during 1900 and commander in chief of the British forces in South Africa from November 1900 until the end of the South African War (q.v.) in May 1902, Horatio Kitchener was responsible for wearing down Boer (q.v.) guerrilla opposition to the British by three deeply unpopular and controversial means: the scorched-earth policy, a system of blockhouses, and the establishment of concentration camps (q.v.).

KOK, ADAM III (1811–75). White pressure forced Adam Kok III, chief of the Griqua (q.v.) at Philippolis from 1837, to sell the remaining Griqua land to the Orange Free State (q.v.) government in 1861, and he led 2,000 of his followers on a long, arduous journey across the Drakensberg (q.v.) to the area that was renamed Griqualand East (q.v.). He considered himself an independent ally of the British, but his position was undermined by the Cape Colony (q.v.) in the 1870s.

KORANA. Khoikhoi (q.v.) pastoralists who settled north and south of the middle Orange River (q.v.) toward the end of the 18th century, the Korana were distinguished from other Khoikhoi groups by their language, Korana. Through their contact with trading networks from the Cape (q.v.), they obtained guns and horses, which enabled them to control the entire middle Orange region by the mid-19th century. White pastoral encroachment on Korana lands resulted in a number of clashes in the area during the 1850s and 1860s. Two wars were fought between the Cape government and the Korana (in 1868–69 and 1878–79), which resulted in most Korana being sent into the Cape as laborers, and their chiefs were imprisoned on Robben Island (q.v.). The middle Orange region was thereafter named Gordonia.

KROTOA (ca. 1642–74). Known to the Dutch settlers as Eva, Krotoa played an important role in facilitating trade between the Khoikhoi (q.v.) and the Dutch in the early days of the Dutch settlement at the Cape (q.v.). Through her personal ties she had privileged access to the Khoikhoi, and she succeeded her uncle Autshumato (q.v.) as the main interpreter for the Dutch. A servant in Jan van Riebeeck's (q.v.) household, she was probably the first Christian (q.v.) convert in South Africa. She married the Dutch soldier and surgeon Pieter van Meerhoff, but her influence declined in the 1660s, and her husband's death in 1667 marked the end of her links with the Dutch. She was arrested the following year for drunkenness and prostitution and banished to Robben Island (q.v.), where she died.

KRUGER, STEPHANUS JOHANNES PAULUS (1825–1904). President of the South African Republic (q.v.) from 1883 until 1900, Paul Kruger, the son of Voortrekker (q.v.) parents, became commandant-general (military leader) of the Transvaal (q.v.) in 1863. After the British annexation of the Transvaal in 1877, he headed negotiations for the restoration of independence and led the subsequent armed revolt in 1880, which brought about the return of self-rule. Elected president in 1883, he won three further terms of office. Although respected for his military capabilities, he was not universally popular among the somewhat fractious white electorate, many of whom resented his autocratic style. His last election victory in 1898, however, was a landslide, the Afrikaner (q.v.) electorate unifying in the aftermath of the Jameson Raid (q.v.) and in the context of increasing British pressure on the Transvaal's continued independence. *See also* ANGLO–TRANSVAAL WAR.

After negotiations with Lord Milner (q.v.) on the position of the Uitlanders (q.v.) failed in 1898–99, Kruger took the initiative and, with the support of the Orange Free State (q.v.), sent the British an ultimatum, which led to the outbreak of the South African War (q.v.). Forced to flee the Transvaal in 1900, he went abroad to seek foreign support. He died in Switzerland in 1904. Portrayed by the British as a dour and inflexible reactionary, he was regarded by Afrikaners (q.v.) in the 20th century as among the greatest of leaders, and his career served as a source of inspiration for resurgent Afrikaner nationalism (q.v.) from the 1930s.

KRUGER NATIONAL PARK. South Africa's largest and most famous national park, Kruger National Park, which comprises an area of some

19,000 square kilometers, stretches 322 km along the Mozambique (q.v.) border from the Limpopo River (q.v.) in the north to the Crocodile River in the south. Its wide diversity of vegetation and flora provides a natural habitat for many animals, reptiles, and birds, including the "big five"—lion, leopard, elephant, buffalo, and rhinoceros. The park has for some decades been one of South Africa's major tourist attractions; it has been marketed abroad as a showcase for southern African wildlife and also used to project a positive image of the country internationally.

The Sabi Game Reserve was established in March 1898 and enlarged in 1903 with the addition of areas to the north. James Stevenson-Hamilton was the first warden of the area, and, during his term of office, Parliament passed the National Parks Act of 1926, the statute that founded and renamed the area as the Kruger National Park, after Paul Kruger (q.v.). Kruger was popularly regarded as a passionate conservationist of wildlife; recent research has shown this to be a myth. The park's history was closely allied to the growth of Afrikaner nationalism (q.v.), for which Kruger provided a powerful symbol. During the apartheid (q.v.) era, the park's aesthetic and conservationist appeal held little relevance for black South Africans, excluded as they were from its recreational and educational benefits. Parts of the park's southern and western borders were surrounded by bantustans (q.v.), whose conditions of worsening poverty and overcrowding contrasted sharply with those in the park. Periodic calls for the abolition of the park and for the allocation of its land to neighboring communities for agricultural and pastoral purposes thus occurred.

Since 1994, the park management has been far more sensitive to the needs of people surrounding the park. With the celebration of its centenary in March 1998—commemorating the founding of the Sabi Reserve—the park's future as a conservation area seemed secure; indeed, plans for further expansion by linking the park with protected areas in Mozambique (q.v.) and South Africa have reached an advanced stage of discussion. A more consultative and participative style of management, in which park authorities and neighboring communities share decision making, is gaining momentum.

KWANDEBELE. *See* NDZUNDZA NDEBELE.

KWAZULU. The largest and most populous of the bantustans (q.v.), KwaZulu, which consisted of large and small fragments of land across Natal (q.v.) and Zululand, became self-governing in 1977. Its chief minister, Mangosuthu Buthelezi (q.v.), who controlled the legislature, refused to consider accepting independence, as had other bantustan leaders, which alienated the National Party (q.v.) apartheid (q.v.) planners. Buthelezi worked instead to explore the potential of political unification of Natal and Kwazulu, but his initiatives, which enjoyed some support in the area, were rejected by the government.

KwaZulu was an impoverished bantustan, and almost three-quarters of its income was derived from migrant (q.v.) and commuter workers employed outside its borders. In the early 1990s, before it was incorporated into the province of KwaZulu-Natal (q.v.), KwaZulu accounted for 66 percent of the population of the KwaZulu-Natal region but only 6 percent of the area's gross domestic product.

KWAZULU-NATAL. In April 1994, Natal (q.v.) and the former KwaZulu (q.v.) bantustan (q.v.) were joined in the new province of KwaZulu-Natal. In the election held that month, the Inkatha (q.v.) Freedom Party (IFP) won 48 percent of the votes as opposed to the 32 percent gleaned by the African National Congress (ANC) (q.v.). The IFP formed a provincial government, which included some ANC members, under the leadership of Dr. Frank Mdladlose. Mdladlose was replaced in 1997 by Dr. Ben Ngubane. There was much disagreement over whether the provincial capital should be at Ulundi, the former bantustan capital, or Pietermaritzburg (q.v.). By 1996, negotiations between the local IFP leadership and Jacob Zuma and Thabo Mbeki (q.v.) of the ANC began to have some effect on reducing the war between the IFP and its opponents, which had continued sporadically from the early 1980s and had resulted in the deaths of perhaps 12,000 people. A provincial constitution was drawn up but was rejected by the Constitutional Court (q.v.) in 1997. KwaZulu-Natal comprises 8 percent of the country's area and is the most populous of the nine provinces.

-L-

LABOUR PARTY. The South African Labour Party was launched at a series of meetings held soon after creation of the Union (q.v.) of South Africa, to promote the interests of white labor. The leading figures were skilled artisans who had come from Britain or Australia. The industrial militancy before World War I (q.v.) and the political disarray after General J. B. M. Hertzog (q.v.) broke with Louis Botha (q.v.) and the South African Party (q.v.) boosted support for Labour, which in 1914 won control of the Transvaal Provincial Council. But although the right wing of the party, led by F. H. P. Creswell (q.v.), supported the war effort, a smaller pacifist section under William (Bill) Andrews (1870–1950) broke with the party to form the International Socialist League, a forerunner of the Communist Party of South Africa (q.v.). As a result of this split, Labour did poorly in the 1915 election. It had been the first political party to campaign for a full-blown policy of racial segregation (q.v.); with the loss of its left wing, it more than ever pandered to white racism (q.v.). *See also* STRIKES.

After being joined by the Unionists (q.v.), the South African Party (q.v.) took a number of seats from Labour in the 1921 election, reducing Labour's strength to nine. But Creswell then entered into a Pact (q.v.) coalition with Hertzog, and in the 1924 election Labour won 18 seats and a place in government. Labour then began to die a slow death. Overwhelmingly English in its ethos, it never attracted Afrikaner (q.v.) workers in any numbers, and those who had previously voted for it now switched to the National Party (q.v.). Many of its English supporters were critical of its leaders for spending so much time on the flag question (q.v.). Its main achievement in office was the Mines and Works Amendment Act, which protected skilled white artisans in their jobs. When one of Labour's leaders developed close ties with Clements Kadalie of the Industrial and Commercial Workers' Union (q.v.), he was dismissed from Hertzog's cabinet in 1928. This further divided the party, which lost 10 seats in the 1929 election. With the outbreak of World War II (q.v.), Labour backed Jan Smuts (q.v.) and the war effort, and a Labour member was included in Smuts's coalition ministry. With United Party (q.v.) help, Labour maintained a toehold in Parliament until 1958. That the party never sought to win support by working through a strong trade union (q.v.) base was not the least of the reasons for its decline into insignificance. *See also* JOB COLOR BAR.

LABOUR PARTY (1965–94). The Labour Party, a Coloured (q.v.) political party, was formed in 1965 in anticipation of the establishment of the Coloured Persons' Representative Council (CRC) (q.v.), with the aim of using this body to help overthrow apartheid (q.v.). In the CRC elections in 1969, the Labour Party won the most seats (23), but the government rigged a majority in its own favor. In 1975, the Labour Party, having won 34 seats, took over the executive branch and worked to destroy the CRC from within. This led to the disbandment of the CRC in 1981. At a conference at Howick in Natal (q.v.) in 1983, the party nevertheless agreed to participate in the tricameral Parliament (q.v.), giving that body significant legitimacy, even though many Coloureds made clear their rejection of it. The Labour Party explained that it would work within the new system for the socioeconomic advancement of the Coloured community and against apartheid. The party became the governing party in the House of Representatives from 1984, and its leader, the Reverend Allan Hendrickse, was for a time a cabinet minister in P. W. Botha's (q.v.) government. The Labour Party claimed credit for some apartheid reforms, but Hendrickse was humiliated by Botha when he challenged beach apartheid. *See also* UNITED DEMOCRATIC FRONT.

In the new order inaugurated by F. W. de Klerk (q.v.) in February 1990, the Labour Party had difficulty in defining its role. After it was replaced by the National Party (q.v.) as the majority party in the House of Representatives in February 1992, it developed increasingly close ties with the African National Congress (ANC) (q.v.) and in 1994 supported the ANC in the first democratic elections.

LAGDEN COMMISSION (1903–5). The South African Native Affairs Commission was appointed by Sir Alfred Milner (q.v.), British administrator of the former Boer republics (the Orange Free State and the South African Republic [qq.v.]) and high commissioner after the South African War (q.v.). Under the chairmanship of Sir Godfrey Lagden (1851–1934), who had been in charge of African administration in the Transvaal (q.v.), the commission set out to provide guidelines for a uniform African policy in the various British colonies. After collecting voluminous, valuable evidence, it issued a report in 1905, which came out in favor of an essentially segregationist set of policies: the Cape (q.v.) system of clearly demarcated reserves (q.v.) and provision for Africans to vote on a separate roll for a fixed number of white members of Parliament. It recommended that squatting (q.v.) on white farms be checked, that Africans be able to acquire freehold title in urban locations, and that a college be established for the higher education of Africans (q.v.). Many of its recommendations were implemented after union (q.v), though not that concerning freehold title. *See also* FORT HARE.

LAND REFORM AND RESTITUTION. Beginning in the 1650s, indigenous people began to lose their land as a result of white settlement and conquest. A long history of legislation to restrict African rights to land followed. In that history, the Natives Land Act (q.v.) of 1913 occupies a central place. Millions were dispossessed of land or forcibly removed from it, for segregationist reasons, after 1913. The body of discriminatory legislation that had permitted this began to be repealed by the F. W.

de Klerk (q.v.) government, most notably in the Abolition of Racially Based Land Measures Act (1991) and the amending legislation of 1993, but such measures did not provide redress, except where the state had itself taken over private or communal land and was willing to hand it back.

The democratic government elected in 1994 had to find a way to give redress without driving those in possession, most of whom were whites, into open defiance. The Restitution of Land Rights Act, steered through Parliament by the minister of land affairs, Derek Hanekom, an Afrikaner (q.v.) farmer who had been imprisoned for working for the African National Congress (ANC) (q.v.), established a land rights commission to deal with claims to land held in private as well as public hands and provided for referral to a land claims court if consensus could not be reached. The year 1913 was the cutoff date for such claims. Expropriated land was to be returned, or alternative land provided, or compensation paid to those whose claims were valid. The process proved slow and cumbersome, and the issue of land reform itself still remained to be tackled. The Pan Africanist Congress (q.v.) and the Azanian People's Organization (q.v.) demanded the return of all land seized by white settlers.

LANGA MARCH. On 30 March 1960, some 30,000 Africans marched from Langa township into the center of Cape Town (q.v.) to protest police (q.v.) activity in the aftermath of the events of 21 March at Sharpeville (q.v.) and Langa itself. But the march was not a prelude to insurrection. The large and peaceful crowd was persuaded by Philip Kgosana, the young Pan Africanist Congress (PAC) (q.v.) organizer who became its leader, to return to Langa. The police promised him a meeting, which never took place. Kgosana and others were arrested under the state of emergency regulations promulgated that day. Kgosana later left the country and lived in exile until the mid-1990s, when he returned to take up a leadership position in the PAC.

LANGALIBALELE (1818–89). Langalibalele was ruler of the Hlubi people, who lived in the foothills of the Drakensberg (q.v.) in northwestern Natal (q.v.) in the 19th century. Their independence and growing prosperity caused increasing concern to nearby white farmers and to the colonial authorities in Natal. In 1873, Langalibalele refused to comply with a law to register rifles acquired by his men on the diamond (q.v.) fields and ignored summonses to explain his conduct. An armed force was sent to arrest him; as he fled, a skirmish occurred, in which three whites and two loyal blacks were killed. This rebellion shocked white

Natalians; Langalibalele was deposed by Theophilus Shepstone (q.v.), captured, given a mockery of a trial, and banished for life to Robben Island (q.v.). Thousands of his Hlubi people and their neighbors were dispossessed of their land and cattle.

The panic reaction of the Natal colonists to this petty episode displayed their insecurity. Lord Carnarvon (q.v.) took advantage of the emotional situation to push Natal into support for his plans for confederation (q.v.). Natal's lieutenant-governor was recalled, and Carnarvon refused to allow Langalibalele to remain on Robben Island. He was imprisoned on the Cape Flats near Cape Town (q.v.) until 1887, when he was allowed to return to Natal.

LANGENHOVEN, CORNELIS JACOB (1873–1932). Writer, journalist, and politician, Cornelis Langenhoven campaigned for Afrikaans (q.v.) to be recognized as an official language (q.v.) and to be used as a medium of instruction in schools. He wrote "Die Stem van Suid-Afrika" ("The Call of South Africa"), which was sung alongside "God Save the King" as South Africa's national anthem (q.v.) from 1938 until 1957, when it became the sole national anthem until the first democratic election of 1994, after which it formed part of the new anthem.

LANGUAGES. Part of the compromise of union (q.v.) in 1910 was that there should be two official languages, Dutch (q.v.) and English (q.v.). Afrikaans (q.v.) replaced Dutch as an official language in 1925 and became the dominant language of government under the National Party (q.v.) after 1948. African (q.v.) languages received no official recognition until the constitutions of 1993 and 1996 provided for the recognition of 11 official languages: Sepedi, Sesotho, Setswana, siSwati, Tshivenda, Xitonga, Afrikaans, English, isiNdebele, isiXhosa and isiZulu. Until 1998, official documents continued to be published in Afrikaans as well as English, but English, which had always been the main language of business, became the de facto official language of government.

LE FLEUR, ANDREW ABRAHAM STOCKENSTRÖM (1867–1941). The Griqua (q.v.) leader Andrew Le Fleur, who over several decades fought for land for Griqua and Coloured (q.v.) people, was imprisoned for sedition between 1898 and 1903 and barred from returning to Griqualand East (q.v.). He settled in Cape Town (q.v.), where he tried to establish various self-help schemes. In 1917, he organized a trek of landless Griqua from Griqualand East to Touws River in the western Cape (q.v.), where he hoped to establish a farming settlement. The venture failed, as did similar settlements on the Olifants River (in 1922) and at

Victoria West (in 1926) for Coloureds from the mission reserves (q.v.) in Namaqualand. Only one such settlement scheme was successful: a community of landless people trekked from the Cookhouse-Bedford district to the Plettenberg Bay area in the southern Cape, finally settling at Krantzhoek. That settlement became a symbol of Griqua hopes and endeavors and remains today the main Griqua establishment in the country.

LEAGUE OF NATIONS MANDATE (1920). Under the terms of the Charter of the League of Nations, South Africa was provided with a C-class mandate to rule South West Africa (now Namibia [q.v.]). This enabled South Africa to administer the territory as if it were an integral part of South Africa itself. South Africa was supposed to concern itself with the well-being of the indigenous inhabitants, but did not. When the League of Nations collapsed, the newly established United Nations (UN) (q.v.) claimed its authority, and in 1966 the UN General Assembly unilaterally terminated the mandate. South Africa never recognized the UN as successor to the League of Nations in this respect.

LEIPOLDT, CHRISTIAAN FREDERIK LOUIS (1880–1947). Medical doctor, journalist, poet, dramatist, and teacher, Christiaan Leipoldt was versatile in English (q.v.) and Dutch (q.v.) as well as Afrikaans (q.v.). He published prolifically in various genres, including poetry, short stories, novels, drama, travelogues, and popular and scientific papers. His most important contribution was in the development of Afrikaans as a written language. He is best remembered for several volumes of poetry, the most significant of which was *Oom Gert Vertel en Ander Gedigte* (1911), and for his greatest drama, *Die Heks* (1923), a pathbreaking dramatic work.

LEKOTA, PATRICK (b. 1948). Patrick Lekota grew up in Kroonstad in the Orange Free State (q.v.) and was educated at the University of the North but was expelled in a student protest and became a permanent organizer for the South African Students' Organisation (q.v.), the first major black consciousness (q.v.) organization. With other black consciousness leaders, he was charged under the Terrorism Act and found guilty of conspiring to commit acts that might endanger the maintenance of law and order. Imprisoned for six years on Robben Island (q.v.), he became a staunch supporter of the African National Congress (q.v.) under the influence of Nelson Mandela (q.v.) and others. Released in 1982, he became publicity secretary for the United Democratic Front (q.v.) the following year. He was detained, then charged with high treason relating to the revolt in the Vaal Triangle. Convicted with others in 1988, he received a 12-year sentence, which was overturned on appeal. He worked for the ANC from 1990, then in 1994 became premier of the Free State (q.v.). He won wide support for his bluff and positive approach, but he clashed with his colleagues and was eventually replaced as premier. He was subsequently given the post of chairperson of the National Council of Provinces, the new upper house in the central legislature, which in the final constitution of 1996 replaced the Senate.

LEMBEDE, ANTON MUZIWAKHE (1914–47). One of the founders of the African National Congress Youth League (q.v.) and its first president, Anton Lembede, the son of a Zulu farm laborer, was educated at Adams College and the University of South Africa. A Roman Catholic (q.v.) and strong anticommunist, he urged Africans to work together to throw off their oppressors and was the first South African to articulate a philosophy of African nationalism. His premature death was widely regarded as a great setback to the cause of African liberation.

LESOTHO. *See* BASUTOLAND.

LIBERAL PARTY (LP) (1953–68). A nonracial political party, the Liberal Party was founded by whites who rejected both the feeble opposition the United Party (q.v.) offered to apartheid (q.v.) and the procommunist leanings of the Congress of Democrats. Its members included such people as Margaret Ballinger (q.v.), native representative (q.v.) in Parliament, and Alan Paton (q.v.), author of *Cry, the Beloved Country*, who became its leader. Although the Liberal Party began by adopting a policy of a qualified franchise (q.v.), it accepted universal suffrage in 1960, and the number of its African members began to increase considerably. When its attempts to win white votes in parliamentary elections proved futile, some of its members turned away from nonviolence after the Sharpeville massacre (q.v.) and joined nonliberals in the African Resistance Movement, which organized acts of sabotage to bring home to whites the evils of the apartheid system. This activity gave the National Party (q.v.) government justification for continued and increased harassment of members of the LP. Many were banned (q.v.). The party was dying even before the government introduced legislation making multiracial parties illegal. Faced with this legislation, the Liberal Party took a principled stand and dissolved itself. Many of the ideas and ideals for which it had fought were realized in the constitutions of 1993 and 1996. *See also* CONGRESS ALLIANCE.

LIBERALISM. In the South African context, *liberalism* long meant not merely adherence to liberal values, such as the rule of law and freedom of speech, but also involved what was called in the 19th century being "a friend of the native" and believing in the possibility of evolutionary change toward a more equitable and just society. Liberals were long the target of suspicion and abuse, and liberalism was more often defined by its enemies than by those who adhered to it. Although all liberals believed in a pluralistic society with relative autonomy for such institutions as the press (q.v.), business, the judiciary, and the universities (q.v.), in recent years, some liberals came to see liberalism as meaning, above all, commitment to free enterprise and a rejection of state intervention. In the post-apartheid era some liberals accepted affirmative action as necessary to compensate for past discrimination; others disliked it because it meant a return to racial classification and was a restriction on freedom.

Liberal ideas entered the Cape (q.v.), in the late 18th century, from the Europe of the French Revolution and, after 1806, through the imperial connection. It was above all the missionaries (q.v.) who in the early 19th century introduced liberal ideas, which included a rejection of distinctions based on race and a concern that people of color, whether Khoisan (q.v.), slave (q.v.), or Bantu speaking (q.v.), should be treated with justice. When representative government was granted to the colony in 1853, Britain insisted that the franchise (q.v.) be color-blind. But Cape liberalism was not merely an imperial imposition; it took root in the colony and became the ideology of local interest groups. Mercantile interests, in particular, favored the growth of a prosperous black peasantry and a black elite incorporated politically through the nonracial qualified franchise, which was seen as a safety valve likely to prevent an eventual explosion of protest by those denied the vote. There were, of course, strict limits to the enlightened paternalism found in Cape Town (q.v.), a long way from a large African population, and in the Eastern Cape: nonracialism was not extended to social relations, nor was it part of the culture of the political parties that began to emerge in the late 19th century. For all its shortcomings, however, there was a real difference between the Cape tradition, summed up by Cecil Rhodes (q.v.) in the dictum, "Equal rights for every civilized man," and the "No equality in church or state" of the Transvaal (q.v.) and Orange Free State (q.v.). Natal (q.v.) had a nominally nonracial constitution but in practice was as racist as the republics of the interior.

With the advent of the mineral revolution, mining interests sought labor from the African reserves, and the black peasantry was undermined in ways that the historian Colin Bundy (q.v.) was the first to document. Liberal values survived, however, both in a segment of the white community and among the black elite, who looked to Britain for help in extending their access to rights in South Africa. After union (q.v.) in 1910, liberalism was sustained not only in the churches, the English-speaking (q.v.) universities, and white-dominated institutions, such as the Joint Councils of Europeans and Natives, that had their heyday in the 1920s, but also in the South African Institute of Race Relations, founded in 1929, and in the African National Congress (ANC) (q.v.) itself. Such leading ANC figures as Z. K. Matthews (q.v.) and Albert Luthuli (q.v.) were men of liberal views.

A century after the grant of a nonracial constitution to the Cape, the Liberal Party (q.v.) was founded in 1953 and until it dissolved itself in 1968 was the main organization embodying liberal values. But other liberals worked in such organizations as the Black Sash (q.v.) or joined the Progressive Party (q.v.), founded in 1959, the most prominent member of which was Helen Suzman (q.v.). From 1968 that party was, by state policy, open to whites only.

Liberals were to be found in the churches, the universities, the press, and the legal profession in the apartheid years. Although the ANC moved away from liberalism in its exile years, a handful of lawyers within it promoted the ideas of a liberal constitution, and from 1987 those ideas were taken up in formal constitutional proposals. For its own reasons, the National Party (q.v.) in the early 1990s also favored a liberal democratic constitution, and such a constitution was put in place by mutual agreement in 1994. Ironically, at a time when liberals were at last able to celebrate the triumph of the ideas for which they had stood, they were without any political organization to represent them, and there were few prominent liberals in public life.

LIMPOPO RIVER. Second largest of the African rivers that enter the Indian Ocean, the Limpopo, unlike the larger Zambezi, often carries little water, and it has never been a barrier to human movement. For many centuries before it became the northern and northwestern boundary of the Transvaal (q.v.), it was an important trade route between the interior and Delagoa Bay (q.v.). A road to Zimbabwe (q.v.) over Beit Bridge opened in 1929; a rail link across the river at the same place began operating in 1974. The name *Limpopo* may come from a Sotho word meaning "river of the waterfall."

LITERATURE IN ENGLISH. Any attempt to define a national literature in a multilingual country with as turbulent a history as South Africa's is extremely problematic. Literature has generally been demarcated according to linguistic units rather than as national literature: thus, South African literature in English (q.v.), Xhosa (q.v.) literature, Zulu (q.v.) literature, Afrikaans (q.v.) literature, and so on, each with its own conventions and traditions, have tended to be described in discrete categories. These divisions were intensified and entrenched by apartheid (q.v.). During the 1990s, literary scholars engaged in intense debates as they grappled with various conflicting concerns. Some demanded a redefinition of a national "canon" to fit the requirements of the post-apartheid nation; others challenged the necessity and the desirability of such an approach, questioning the very concept of "nation" in the southern African context. Critics have also stressed the difficulties in accommodating the enormous diversity of oral and written texts in a range of languages (q.v.) and traditions. This absence of a common linguistic, cultural, and historical heritage has led many to explore so-called cross-cultural fertilization and transcultural intertextuality, in an attempt to break down ethnic and linguistic categories by exploring common themes and subject matters such as travel writing, rural and pastoral motifs, and urbanization.

Until the beginning of the 20th century, literature in English was characterized by a tradition of fictional realism; for the remainder of the 20th century, the social and political realities of the country were the single most important influences shaping writers of novels, poetry, and drama. The largely nonfictional writing of the first half of the 19th century, such as traveler and missionary accounts, hunting stories, diaries, and journalism, foreshadowed these trends. Imperialist romances such as Henry Rider Haggard's *Allan Quartermain* (1887) enjoyed some popular success among the settler population, but more enduring was Olive Schreiner's (q.v.) realist novel in a pastoral setting, *The Story of an African Farm* (1881). Early writing in English by blacks was largely limited to journalism, and it was only after World War I (q.v.) that the first significant novels were published: R. R. R. Dhlomo's *An African Tragedy* (1928) and Sol Plaatje's (q.v.) *Mhudi* (1930). These appeared at the same time as William Plomer's *Turbott Wolfe* (1929), the first novel by a white English speaker (q.v.) that explicitly challenged racism (q.v.) through its treatment of miscegenation. Other whites, meanwhile, were concerned with images and notions of Africa; the preeminent poet of the period, Roy Campbell, explored intersections between Europe and Africa in *The Flaming Terrapin* (1924) and *Adamastor* (1930).

After World War II (q.v.) and the election of the National Party (q.v.) government in 1948, white and black writers increasingly wrote politically committed material that challenged the social injustices of ingrained racism. Much of this writing was also concerned with social transformation, urbanization, and the demands of the mineral revolution and industrialization. An early example was Peter Abrahams' *Mine Boy* (1946); Alan Paton's (q.v.) *Cry the Beloved Country* (1947), which explores racial tensions within rural and urban landscapes, won international acclaim. During the 1950s, fictional writing by blacks flourished, nurtured particularly by the Johannesburg-based magazine *Drum*. Writers such as Ezekiel Mphahlele, Nat Nakasa, Lewis Nkosi, and Can Themba had a large popular following among urban blacks in the townships. Mphahlele's autobiographical *Down Second Avenue* (1959) was arguably the most important book of that decade. From the end of the 1950s, however, many black writers were forced into exile; prominent among them were Alex la Guma, Mongane Wally Serote, Dennis Brutus, and Mazizi Kunene. Much of their writing took the form of protest literature, particularly poetry. Serote's *Yakhal'inkomo* (1972) helped to shape a new poetic idiom, which was closely linked to the black consciousness (q.v.) movement and which flowered after the Soweto uprising (q.v.). The language of resistance dominated poetic writing throughout the 1980s; more recently, African oral traditions have been incorporated into such poetry, notably in the work of Mzwakhe Mbuli, dubbed the "people's poet."

South Africa's major novelist from the 1950s to the 1980s was Nadine Gordimer (q.v.), whose short stories and novels, from *The Lying Days* (1953) and *A World of Strangers* (1958) through to *Burger's Daughter* (1979) and *My Son's Story* (1990), were all set in mainly urban situations during the apartheid years and powerfully challenged white superiority and power. During the 1960s and 1970s, Athol Fugard's (q.v.) writing for the stage provided a similar critique of racism; his drama was the forerunner of an era of community theater during the 1980s, which was written by both blacks and whites and which provided a focus for anti-apartheid protest. From the 1980s, South African writers began to experiment with postmodern discourse, chiefly in the field of fiction. J. M. Coetzee's harsh and compelling writing, in such novels as *Waiting for the Barbarians* (1980), *The Life and Times of Michael K* (1983), and *Foe* (1986), as well as his autobiographical *Boyhood: Scenes from Provincial Life* (1997), won international praise. *See also* AFRIKAANS.

LOBOLA. *Lobola* (singular of *ukulobola,* often referred to as "bride wealth") was an agreement common among Bantu-speaking (q.v.) peoples to exchange gifts and cattle between the bride and groom's families as a way of binding the families together socially and economically. For many of the coastal Natal (q.v.) peoples, including the Zulu (q.v.), it seems to have been an ongoing arrangement, one that did not imply "ownership" of the woman. Missionaries (q.v.) misunderstood it to mean that women were bought, and they often condemned the custom. With the penetration of capitalism into the rural areas, the practice was transformed over time, with cash, farming implements such as hoes, and other commodities being substituted for cattle. Traditionally minded people, however, tried to continue the use of cattle. The appropriate rate and the question of whether cash could be substituted was often contested: women, fathers, and chiefs usually tried to keep the rate high; working men tried to reduce it.

LONDON MISSIONARY SOCIETY (LMS). The most active Protestant missionary (q.v.) society in southern Africa during the first half of the 19th century, the LMS, founded in 1795 as an interdenominational organization, was active in a variety of locations at the Cape (q.v.), and many LMS missionaries clashed with the Cape authorities over policy toward slaves (q.v.) and indigenous peoples. The most prominent LMS missionaries included Johannes van der Kemp (q.v.), founder of the Bethelsdorp mission outside what became Port Elizabeth (q.v.); John Philip (q.v.), superintendent of the LMS in South Africa from 1819 to 1849; Robert Moffat (q.v.), who worked at Kuruman; the explorer and missionary David Livingstone; and van der Kemp's colleague James Read, whose latter years were spent as LMS missionary in the Kat River Settlement (q.v.). In the later 19th century the LMS mission stations were gradually incorporated within the Congregational Church.

LUTHULI, ALBERT JOHN (ca. 1898–1967). Chief, teacher, and politician, Albert Luthuli gave up his traditional leadership position at Groutville in Natal (q.v.) to become president-general of the African National Congress (q.v.), an office he held from 1952 until his death. In his 1960 speech accepting the Nobel Peace Prize, Luthuli, a man of great charm and moderation, observed that the African people of South Africa had long knocked at the door and found it locked against them. He died while out walking, being hit by a train under circumstances some found mysterious.

LYDENBURG HEADS. Terra-cotta representations of human heads, the Lydenburg heads were found in the eastern Transvaal (q.v.), now Mpumalanga (q.v.), in the 1950s. They are thought to date from ca. A.D. 500 and to have been the work of Iron Age (q.v.) Bantu-speaking (q.v.) people.

-M-

MACKENZIE, JOHN (1835–99). London Missionary Society (q.v.) missionary, author, and advocate of British rule in Bechuanaland (q.v.), John Mackenzie arrived in South Africa in 1858 and worked first at the missionary center of Kuruman on the "missionaries' road" and thereafter in what is now Botswana. He believed in the extension of British rule to protect African peoples from settler encroachment. Fearing the Tswana (q.v.) would fall under Transvaal (q.v.) Boer (q.v.) rule, he campaigned in England in 1882 for British rule to be extended and in 1884 briefly worked as British commissioner in Bechuanaland, the year before Sir Charles Warren proclaimed the establishment of a British protectorate over the country.

MACMILLAN, WILLIAM MILLER (1885–1974). Taken to South Africa as a child, William Macmillan returned to Britain to study at Oxford. In 1910 he accepted an appointment to the Department of History and Economics at Rhodes University College in Grahamstown (q.v.). He moved from there to the School of Mines in Johannesburg (q.v.), soon to be renamed the University of the Witwatersrand, in 1917. He remained at "Wits" until the early 1930s, when he resigned, in large part because of his dislike of the racial policies of the J. B. M. Hertzog (q.v.) government and the failure of the university, as he saw it, to support him in his criticisms. He also wished to spend time exploring the British colonies in the tropics and returned to South Africa only for short visits thereafter.

Macmillan pioneered the writing of social and economic history in South Africa and was the founder of what became known as the "liberal" school of South African historiography (q.v.) (though he was a Fabian socialist in Britain and would probably have identified himself as a radical rather than a liberal historian). His first published pamphlets concerned social conditions in Grahamstown. In 1919 a set of his lectures appeared, entitled *The South African Agrarian Problem and Its Historical Development*. In 1920 he received the first batch of the papers of John Philip (q.v.) of the London Missionary Society (q.v.). Through Philip's eyes he became deeply interested in policies toward Khoikhoi (q.v.) and Africans (q.v.) in the early-19th-century Cape (q.v.). On the Philip papers he based his two seminal works, *The Cape Coloured Question* (1927) and *Bantu, Boer, and Briton* (1929), as well as his chapters in *The Cambridge History of the British Empire* (1936). From studying poor whites (q.v.) in Grahamstown, he turned to the story of poor blacks (q.v.) in the Herschel district of the Cape and produced *Complex South Africa* in 1930. His most able student was the historian C. W. de Kiewiet (q.v.), who took further Macmillan's work.

MADIKIZELA-MANDELA, WINNIE (b. 1934). Born in the Transkei (q.v.), Winnie Madikizela became involved with the African National Congress (ANC) (q.v.) after moving to Johannesburg (q.v.), where in 1958 she became Nelson Mandela's (q.v.) second wife. In 1962 he was arrested and she was banned (q.v.) for the first time. In 1969 she was detained under the Suppression of Communism Act and spent a long period in solitary confinement; jailed again in 1974 and 1976, she was then banished in 1977 to the small Orange Free State (q.v.) town of Brandfort. After eight years there, she returned to Soweto (q.v.), where she organized a Mandela United Football Club of youths to protect her. By early 1989 leading members of the United Democratic Front (UDF) (q.v.) were forced to issue a statement distancing the UDF from her, because of the actions of the football club and its members.

After her husband's release, Winnie Madikizela-Mandela was charged with kidnapping and with protecting the assailants of youths who had been taken to her home in December 1988 and beaten. One of them, a young activist by the name of Stompie Seipei, died. She was convicted on the kidnapping charge, but on appeal she was exonerated of the more serious ones. In 1992 her husband announced that they were separating. She became a deputy minister in the government of National Unity (q.v.) in 1994 but increasingly fell out with her former husband, who began divorce proceedings against her after she was dropped as deputy minister. Despite her record, she retained popular support in the ANC and headed its Women's League; in 1997 she was reelected leader of the latter organization. She then asked for a public hearing before the Truth and Reconciliation Commission (q.v.), at which much testimony pointed to her involvement in a series of murders in the late 1980s. Although she denied all, her position was much weakened, and she failed in her candidacy for the deputy presidency of the ANC at the Mafikeng (formerly Mafeking [q.v.]) conference in December 1997.

MAFEKING. The most northerly town in the Cape Colony (q.v.) and the administrative capital of the Bechuanaland (q.v.) Protectorate from 1885, Mafeking became famous when besieged by the Boers (q.v.) between October 1899 and May 1900 during the South African War (q.v.); in many ways, the ending of the siege served as a symbol of the resurgence of British pride after the initial setbacks of the war. In 1980 the town was transferred to Bophuthatswana (q.v.) and its name was changed to Mafikeng (Tswana, meaning "place of stones"). Today it is the capital of North-West Province (q.v.).

MAJUBA. When British and Boer (q.v.) forces clashed on Majuba Hill in February 1881 in the Anglo–Transvaal War (q.v.), the British troops were soundly defeated by Boer volunteers determined to restore the independence of the Transvaal (q.v.). By then the British government had already decided to restore self-government to the Transvaal (q.v.), and an armistice was signed between the two sides in March 1881, but the cry, "Avenge Majuba," did not help the cause of British-Transvaal reconciliation.

MAKEBA, MIRIAM (b. 1935). Miriam Makeba's career began during the 1940s in schools and churches near Pretoria (q.v.). She worked with various township jazz groups before going into exile and settling in the United States. She was active in civil rights, anti-apartheid, and Africanist campaigns during the 1960s and beyond, while achieving an international reputation as a singer and musician.

MALAN, DANIEL FRANÇOIS (1874–1959). D. F. Malan, a dour, unsmiling man, was South Africa's prime minister from 1948 to 1954. Malan grew up north of Cape Town (q.v.) and knew Jan Smuts (q.v.) as a child. He left his Dutch Reformed Church (q.v.) ministry to edit the National Party (NP) (q.v.) newspaper, *De Burger* (later, *Die Burger*). When J. B. M. Hertzog (q.v.), leader of the NP, came to power in 1924, Malan joined his government, but he broke with Hertzog when the latter moved toward Smuts. He formed a new Purified National Party, which he held together in opposition until it took power in May 1948 and began to put its policy of apartheid (q.v.) into practice.

MALAYS. *See* ISLAM.

MANDELA, NELSON ROLIHLAHLA (b. 1918). Born into the Madiba clan of the Thembu in the Transkei (q.v.), Nelson Mandela was the son of the chief councillor to the paramount chief, and the acting paramount chief became his guardian. He attended the Methodist college of Healdtown, then Fort Hare (q.v.) University, which he left on a matter of principle. He went to Johannesburg (q.v.), where he worked as a clerk in a law firm while completing his first degree through the University of South Africa. During his law studies at the University of the Witwatersrand he was active as a founding member of the African

National Congress Youth League (q.v.). From 1947 he was a member of the executive of the Transvaal (q.v.) African National Congress (ANC) (q.v.). In 1951 he opened a law office, but his political work dominated; he was first banned (q.v.) and then arrested in December 1956 and charged with treason. After the long drawn-out treason trial (q.v.) ended in 1961, he went underground to establish and organize the armed wing of the ANC, Umkhonto weSizwe (MK) (q.v.). Known as the Black Pimpernel, he traveled abroad; but in August 1962 he was arrested in Natal (q.v.) and then joined in the dock the other MK leaders arrested at Rivonia (q.v.). He was sentenced to life imprisonment and sent to Robben Island (q.v.). There his moral authority and leadership did much to improve conditions for the prisoners.

In 1976, Mandela rejected an offer by Jimmy Kruger, minister of police (q.v.), that he settle in, and recognize, the Transkei bantustan (q.v.). Instead, he became the main international symbol of apartheid (q.v.) repression. Probably because of the campaign for his release, he was moved to Pollsmoor prison on the mainland outside Cape Town (q.v.) in 1982. In 1985 he rejected state president P. W. Botha's (q.v.) offer of freedom in return for renouncing violence. When he went into the hospital for prostate treatment in November of that year, the minister of justice, Kobie Coetsee, went to see him, and from May 1988 he was engaged in regular talks with senior government officials. In December 1988, after treatment for tuberculosis, he was transferred to a house at Victor Verster prison near Paarl; from there he was taken to have tea with P. W. Botha in July 1989. In December of that year, he met Botha's successor, F. W. de Klerk (q.v.). On 11 February 1990, Mandela walked to freedom, after 10,000 days of imprisonment, at the age of 71, without any bitterness for his lost years. The ANC elected him its deputy president and then, in July 1991, president.

At a number of points in the negotiations that followed, Mandela's leadership was decisive in moving the process forward. In 1993 he and de Klerk were jointly awarded the Nobel Peace Prize. He was the ANC's main drawcard in the 1994 election, the first election in which he was able to cast a vote. On 10 May 1994 he was sworn in as the country's first democratically elected president at the Union Buildings, Pretoria (q.v.). Later that year, he told his life story in his autobiography, *Long Walk to Freedom.* As president, he worked for national reconciliation and to promote South Africa abroad. Handing over the leadership of the ANC to Thabo Mbeki (q.v.) in December 1997, he made clear that he would stand down as president in the elections in 1999.

In April 1992, Mandela separated from his wife, Winnie Madikizela-Mandela (q.v.), and in 1996 announced a relationship with Graca Machel, widow of the former president of Mozambique (q.v.), Samora Machel. They were married in July 1998, on the day of his 80th birthday.

MANDELA, WINNIE. *See* MADIKIZELA-MANDELA, WINNIE.

MANTATEES. The name *Mantatee,* given to Sotho (q.v.) people at the time of the Mfecane (q.v.), was derived from Mnanthatisi (ca. 1780–after 1835), the female regent of the Tlokoa, a Sotho group that moved across what became the Orange Free State (q.v.) in about 1822, perhaps in response to the arrival of the Hlubi in the Caledon River valley. The fearsome reputation of Mnanthatisi spread far and wide, and many people, most notably those who attacked the town of Dithakong (q.v.), near Kuruman, in 1823, were called by whites "Mantatees," whether or not Mnanthatisi's people were among them. The tens of thousands of Sotho refugees who moved south to escape the upheavals in the interior were also known as Mantatees when they arrived in the Cape Colony (q.v.).

MANUFACTURING. Before the mineral discoveries of the 1870s, there were some 70 small-scale manufacturing concerns in the Cape Colony (q.v.), with Cape Town (q.v.) the main center. These factories processed agricultural products, built wagons, and made bricks. The development of the diamond (q.v.) and gold (q.v.) mines provided the first large-scale market for manufactured products, and soon factories were built to produce dynamite, mining equipment, miners' boots, and associated needs. The growth of the manufacturing industry was slow before World War I (q.v.) because the mines drew off skilled labor and capital, and the large earnings of foreign exchange from the export of diamonds and gold enabled the country to pay for industrial imports. Output of the manufacturing sector was valued at less than £20 million in 1904 and at £35 million by 1915.

During World War I, imports were difficult to obtain, which did much to boost local manufacture, the output of which had risen by 1920 to £75 million. The Federated Chamber of Industries was founded in 1917. After 1924, when the National Party (q.v.) government under J. B. M. Hertzog (q.v.) introduced tariff protection through the Tariff Act of 1925, industrial output grew further. At the same time, whites were given preferential treatment in the provision of jobs in the manufacturing industry. As a result of the government's Civilized Labour policy (q.v.), the proportion of whites in the manufacturing industry, which had been 37.5 percent in 1919, rose to 40.6 percent by 1936.

When the postwar depression arrived, the (white) Labour Party (q.v.) pressed for protection to provide employment for whites in local industry. Mine owners, on the other hand, opposed protection because tariffs would increase their costs. The decision to abandon the gold standard in 1932 sent the price of gold soaring, and a large part of the increased profits went to stimulate the manufacturing industry further. This occurred through direct investment, state subsidization, and expanded consumer spending. In 1943 the value of output from manufacturing overtook that of the mining sector. World War II (q.v.) provided extra protection from foreign competition and further stimulated production. Clothing and textiles, metals and engineering, and commodities for construction more than doubled in output. The number of manufacturing establishments, which had risen from 6,543 in 1933 to 8,505 in 1939, increased to 9,999 by 1946, and output, which had increased by 140 percent between 1933 and 1939, rose another 141 percent during the war.

Well over three-quarters of the country's factories were located in the four main metropolitan regions, three of which were on the coast: the southwestern Cape (q.v.), Port Elizabeth–Uitenhage, and Durban–Pinetown. The most important center was inland: the Pretoria–Witwatersrand–Vereeniging (PWV) triangle, with its mines and heavy industry as well as light secondary industry. During the 1960s there was a large flow of foreign capital into the manufacturing industry; by 1965 the contribution of manufacturing to gross domestic product (GDP) exceeded that of mining and farming together, and by 1973, 40 percent of all foreign capital was invested in the manufacturing sector. By then, along with food, clothing, textiles, and wood and paper products, much machinery, chemical and metal products, and electronic equipment was being produced, some for defense requirements. The arms industry grew until it was the eighth largest in the world. *See also* ARMS EMBARGO.

There was a considerable export sector. The proportion of whites employed in the labor force in the manufacturing sector, which fell to 21 percent in 1976, continued to fall thereafter. In the 1980s, sanctions (q.v.) began to impact severely on this sector, which revived somewhat after they were lifted in the early 1990s. By 1990 manufacturing was responsible for 23 percent of GDP, the largest single share, and employed 1.5 million people, about 13.2 percent of the economically active population. As South Africa became ever more integrated into a global economy, competitiveness increased, and low productivity in South African industry, coupled with a relatively high wage structure, counted against significant growth in manufacturing output, though the decline in the value of the rand helped exports.

MAPUNGUBWE. The capital of one of the largest precolonial Iron Age (q.v.) states known to have existed in what is now South Africa, Mapungubwe is thought to have been at its peak in the 13th century A.D. Today all that remains is some ruins close to the Limpopo River (q.v.) in the Northern Province (q.v.).

MAQOMA (1798–1873). A Xhosa (q.v.) chief, half brother of Sandile (q.v.) and heir to the Rharhabe (q.v.) paramountcy, Maqoma was expelled from the fertile Kat River valley, the site of the later Kat River Settlement (q.v.), in 1828 and subsequently played a leading role in opposing colonial expansion into Xhosa land during the frontier wars of 1834–35 and 1850–53. After the cattle killing (q.v.), he was exiled on Robben Island (q.v.), where he died.

MARABI. *Marabi*—highly rhythmic, cyclical, and repetitive dance tunes and melodies developed by urban Africans (q.v.) after World War I—was the music of various secular social occasions in the townships and compounds (q.v.) of the country, and both dancing and the consumption of alcohol were features of these gatherings. The most famous of its venues was the *shebeen,* an illegal backroom or backyard liquor den, and it became known as the music of the township ghettos. *Marabi* was associated with illegality and a hedonistic subculture among the impoverished working class and was stigmatized as evil and corrupting by many blacks who espoused Christian (q.v.) middle-class values. Early *marabi* musicians were never recorded, but by the early 1930s, black dance bands began to appear, inspired partially by American influences but also by *marabi*-based swing-style music, a genre that came to be known as African jazz, or *mbaqanga*. By the 1940s, the best of these groups—the Jazz Maniacs, the Merry Blackbirds, the Rhythm Kings, the Jazz Revellers, and the Harlem Swingsters—achieved countrywide fame and played to capacity crowds in the townships. Another innovation of the 1940s and 1950s was the *marabi*-derived pennywhistle music of the streets, called *kwela*, often produced by children in the township slums. Vocal groups of this period, such as the Manhattan Brothers and the African Inkspots, also produced compositions based on *marabi*, though they were partially inspired by American groups. Prominent exiled South African musicians, such as Abdullah Ibrahim (Dollar Brand), Hugh Masekela, and Jonas Gwangwa, were nurtured in their early years by this union of American and *marabi* influences.

MARKS, SAMUEL (1843–1920). A wealthy and influential Transvaal (q.v.) industrialist, Samuel Marks arrived in South Africa in 1868 and, with his cousin and business partner, Isaac Lewis, earned his first fortune on the diamond (q.v.) fields. They launched a major business enterprise, called Lewis and Marks, during the gold (q.v.) rush in Barberton in 1885. Marks then moved to Pretoria (q.v.), where he built a splendid house to the east of the city at Zwartkoppies. He formed close ties with the government of Paul Kruger (q.v.) and founded numerous industries on the Witwatersrand (q.v.). His financial and industrial interests included coal, forestry, land, liquor, glassworks, food processing, brickworks, and tanning.

MASS DEMOCRATIC MOVEMENT (MDM). After the apartheid (q.v.) government restricted the United Democratic Front (UDF) (q.v.) and other organizations in 1988, the MDM emerged as an even broader, but also looser, resistance front to apartheid, made up of UDF and African National Congress (q.v.) supporters and with close links to the Congress of South African Trade Unions (q.v.). It had no permanent structure, which prevented the government from banning (q.v.) it.

MASS REMOVALS. By 1950 there was a long history of the forced relocation of people, such as Africans (q.v.) from Cape Town (q.v.) in 1901, but the apartheid (q.v.) state from 1950 began to move people on an entirely new scale. Between 1950 and 1980 more than two million people, almost all blacks (q.v.), were forced to move, for ideological and economic reasons. Forced removals of non-Africans within urban areas largely took place under the Group Areas Act (q.v.); Africans were removed under other legislation. Sophiatown, for example, a vibrant community of more than 60,000 some five miles from downtown Johannesburg (q.v.), was destroyed, and the white suburb of Triomf (Afrikaans, "triumph") created in its place. African residents of Sophiatown, some with freehold title, were forced to move to Soweto (q.v.) township, where no freehold was allowed. In Alexandra township, on Johannesburg's northeastern boundary, Africans and Coloureds (q.v.) had been able to acquire freehold titles from 1912. Well over half its population was ejected in the 1960s and 1970s before the government announced in 1979 that the remaining families might stay. In other urban centers Africans were moved out to "dormitory towns," devoid of any industry or service facilities, in adjacent bantustans (q.v.). The people of Duncan Village, for example, in the port city of East London, were relocated to Mdantsane in the Ciskei (q.v.), more than 20 miles away, from where they had to commute to work in East London.

There were many other types of forced mass removal. Africans who held freehold land in rural so-called black spots (q.v.), surrounded by white-owned farmland, or who farmed mission-owned land were forced off their land. Residents of more than 200 such communities were forced off their land in Natal (q.v.) between 1950 and 1980, for example, and the process continued to the late 1980s. In excess of 150,000 Africans were forced out of the Western Cape (q.v.) under the Coloured Labour Preference policy (q.v.). Larger numbers were relocated because of the ending of squatting (q.v.) on white-owned farms or under influx control (q.v.) measures controlling entry into, and residence in, metropolitan areas. Those considered surplus to production requirements—the unemployed, the old, the very young, and women—were dumped in the bantustans. In remote rural areas, already overpopulated and overgrazed and lacking any employment opportunities, they were given temporary accommodation in tents or bare corrugated-iron rooms or sometimes nothing at all. From time to time the shocking conditions in resettlement camps were publicized, and some improvements were made, as at Dimbaza in the Ciskei after the release of the film "Last Grave at Dimbaza," but the process of relocation continued into the 1980s. In 1983, Surplus People Project, a nongovernmental organization, published a detailed set of volumes entitled *Forced Removals in South Africa*, which gave greater publicity than ever before to what was happening, and this and other documentation collected by groups concerned with land and human rights issues helped to produce a slackening of forced removals by the late 1980s. In the 1990s a number of groups ejected from land in the apartheid era were able to regain their land under the terms of the land restitution policy of the first democratic government. *See also* LAND REFORM AND RESTITUTION.

MATANZIMA, KAISER (b. 1915). The bantustan (q.v.) leader Kaiser Matanzima studied at Fort Hare (q.v.) University with Nelson Mandela (q.v.). He became a chief in the St. Mark's district of Transkei (q.v.). He was appointed by the government as paramount chief of Emigrant Thembuland, with a status equal to that of King Sabata Dalindyebo of Thembuland. Believing that H. F. Verwoerd's (q.v.) policy of separate development was in the best interests of his people, he became head of the Transkei government in 1963 and led this region to "independence" in 1976. He later became Transkei president. Authoritarian in manner, he was despised by many blacks as a collaborator. *See also* APARTHEID; BANTUSTAN POLICY.

MATTHEWS, ZACHARIAH KEODIRELANG (1901–68). Educator, academic, and political leader, Zachariah Matthews was the first African to obtain a bachelor's degree (from the University of South Africa).

He became the first African principal of Adams College in Natal (q.v.), in 1925, and then a lecturer in social anthropology at the South African Native College at Fort Hare (q.v.) in 1936. Appointed professor and head of African Studies there in 1945, he was thereafter increasingly drawn into political activity on the Natives Representative Council (NRC) (q.v.) and in the African National Congress (ANC) (q.v.). He resigned from the NRC in 1950 in protest against government apartheid (q.v.) policy and was involved in preparations for the Defiance Campaign (q.v.) and the drafting of the Freedom Charter. After he was acquitted in the treason trial (q.v.) in April 1959, he left the country and spent his remaining years in Botswana (formerly Bechuanaland [q.v.]), Switzerland, and the United States. His autobiography, *Freedom for My People*, won international acclaim.

MAXEKE, CHARLOTTE MAKGOMO MANYE (1874–1939). Born in the eastern Cape (q.v.), Charlotte Makgomo was a member of an African choir that toured England and then went on to the United States. She remained behind in the United States and attended Wilberforce University, in Ohio, becoming the first African (q.v.) woman from South Africa to obtain a degree in 1905. At Wilberforce, which was run by the African Methodist Episcopal Church (q.v.), she met and married a fellow South African, Maxwell Maxeke. After returning to South Africa, the couple founded Wilberforce Institute, a secondary school in the Transvaal (q.v.).

The founder and the first president of the Women's League, an affiliate of the African National Congress (q.v.), and prominent in protests against pass laws (q.v.), she also worked as a social worker, ran an employment bureau, and was active in the Joint Council movement in the 1920s, often speaking at white women's clubs. In the 1930s, however, she fell on hard times and lived in poverty. She was nevertheless elected first president of the National Council of African Women, an affiliate of the All-African Convention (q.v.) in 1937. She was remembered as a role model and inspiration for later politically active women (q.v.).

MBEKI, GOVAN ARCHIBALD (b. 1910). The activist and intellectual Govan Mbeki was born in the Transkei (q.v.) and attended mission schools there before graduating from the University of Fort Hare (q.v.) in 1937. After being dismissed as a teacher because of his political activities, he ran a Transkeian trading store and edited the *Territorial Magazine*. He returned to teaching in the 1950s but was again dismissed. He then edited *New Age* in Port Elizabeth (q.v.). As leader of the African

National Congress (q.v.) in the eastern Cape, he helped build up the organization there. Secretary of the High Command of Umkhonto weSizwe (q.v.), Mbeki was arrested at Lilliesleaf farm, Rivonia (q.v.), and sentenced to life imprisonment. He was released in November 1987. With the establishment of the new order in 1994, he became deputy speaker of the Senate, retiring in 1997.

MBEKI, THABO (b. 1942). Born in the Transkei (q.v.), son of veteran activist Govan Mbeki (q.v.), Thabo Mbeki joined the African National Congress Youth League (q.v.) in 1956; after being detained in 1962 he left the country. He studied economics at the University of Sussex and then worked in the African National Congress (ANC) office in London, undergoing a brief period of military training in the Soviet Union. In 1984, he became the ANC's director of information and publicity and, in 1989, head of the ANC's department of international affairs. He was the leading member of the ANC team that held a series of meetings with a group of South Africans in England in 1988; he also met with South African intelligence officers in Switzerland in September 1989.

After his return to South Africa, Mbeki rose through the ANC ranks and was made deputy president in the government of National Unity (q.v.); with the sidelining of Cyril Ramaphosa (q.v.), he emerged as the only successor to Nelson Mandela (q.v.). Charming in public, he gained a reputation for being ruthless and tough in behind-the-scenes negotiations. By 1997 he was effectively ruling the country, and in December of that year he took over from Mandela as president of the ANC at the Mafikeng (formerly Mafeking [q.v.]) conference.

MBOWENI, TITO (b. 1959). The son of a hotel chef, Tito Mboweni went into exile and joined the African National Congress (ANC) (q.v.) in 1980. He obtained degrees in economics and political science at the National University of Lesotho and the University of East Anglia in England during the 1980s, while working to isolate the apartheid (q.v.) government by persistent campaigning for sanctions (q.v.). On his return to South Africa in 1990, he played a leading role in the ANC's economic planning department and national executive committee. He was appointed minister of labor in the government of National Unity (q.v.) after the democratic election of 1994 and gained a reputation as a competent and principled administrator. His controversial and much-debated Labour Relations Act of 1997, which aimed to alter relationships between employers and workers into a more cooperative system, was one of the most far-reaching legislative changes of the new government.

In July 1998, Mboweni was appointed governor-designate of the Reserve Bank and succeeded the long-serving governor Dr. Chris Stals in mid-1999. The appointment initially aggravated the country's deepening economic crisis, as the stock market and some economists questioned his financial expertise and political independence. Mboweni's firm assurances that he would safeguard the autonomy of the Reserve Bank helped to stabilize the currency (q.v.), and his appointment was then widely, though cautiously, accepted.

MERRIMAN, JOHN XAVIER (1841–1926). John Merriman, a Cape politician, served in the first cabinet of the self-governing Cape (q.v.) under John Charles Molteno and then under Cecil Rhodes (q.v.) from 1890 to 1893. He became prime minister of the Cape from 1908 to 1910. As a Cape liberal, he stood against the polarization of southern African politics and condemned the Jameson Raid (q.v.) and the South African War (q.v.). He worked toward the rapid restoration of self-government in the defeated republics and played a prominent role in the National Convention (q.v.) of 1908–9. Believed by some to be an ideal first prime minister of the new Union (q.v.) of South Africa, he was passed over because of his Cape background and in retirement became an elder statesman.

MEYER, ROELF (b. 1947). Roelf Meyer rose from a humble background to become chair of the Afrikaanse Studentebond and the Ruiterwag (a junior version of the Afrikaner Broederbond [q.v.]), a National Party (NP) (q.v.) member of Parliament, and a member of P. W. Botha's (q.v.) cabinet. In the late 1980s he came to see the need for fundamental reform and backed F. W. de Klerk (q.v.) when he decided to negotiate with the African National Congress (q.v.). From 1992 he played a key role as the chief government negotiator, and his special relationship with Cyril Ramaphosa (q.v.) helped prevent the negotiations from breaking down completely at a number of points. He was accused by others in the NP of selling out the interests of the Afrikaners (q.v.), but he believed that majority rule was inevitable and that it was in the interests of the governing party to work for that end, not oppose it.

MFECANE. From the 1920s, the word *mfecane* (Zulu [q.v.] term meaning "the crushing"; the Sotho [q.v.] used the terms *difaqane,* meaning "hammering," and *lifaqane,* meaning "forced migration") has been used by historians to describe the period of crisis and revolutionary change among African peoples in the Natal (q.v.) and Zulu (q.v.) regions and on the high veld (q.v.) interior during the second and third decades of the 19th century.

Many historical works have portrayed the period as one of enormous destruction and violent upheaval, caused by the rise of the Zulu kingdom under Shaka (q.v.), which set in motion a chain of warfare and raiding across the entire southern African interior. Fierce competition between northern Nguni (q.v.) societies resulted in the flight of defeated groups out of Natal and Zululand west across the Drakensberg (q.v.) and south into the Transkei (q.v.). This disrupted long-established settlement patterns in these regions, provoking intense conflict for a number of years. Some parts of the country were depopulated; others saw the emergence of new states, such as those of the Ndebele (q.v.), under Mzilikazi (q.v.), and of the southern Sotho, under Moshoeshoe (q.v.). The apparent depopulation of the interior made it easier for the migrant white farmers of the Great Trek (q.v.) to move into the areas that became the Transvaal (q.v.) and the Orange Free State (q.v.) during the 1830s.

In the 1960s the historian John Omer-Cooper attempted to emphasize the Mfecane period as one of positive state building rather than gratuitous destruction. During the late 1980s, Julian Cobbing, a lecturer in history at Rhodes University, questioned the entire notion of the Mfecane. He argued that historians, in their desire to legitimate white conquest of the interior, had deliberately exaggerated the ferocity and devastation of the period; that where disruption had occurred, particular causes should be found rather than a general apportioning of blame to the Shakan state; and that in any case Shaka's kingdom could not singlehandedly have been responsible for the events attributed to it, especially as it was neither as large nor as dominant as it was commonly made out to be. Cobbing argued that the Zulu state and others in the interior were defensive formations, constituted as protection against the influence of commercial capitalists who were encircling the region. Slave trading from Delagoa Bay (q.v.) and from the Cape frontier (q.v.) regions was far more pervasive than has commonly been accepted; white traders and their agents, such as Griqua (q.v.) raiders, were responsible for disrupting settlements in the interior in their desire to capture labor for the Cape. The cause of the disruption is thus to be found within white colonial society and its need for labor to ensure its continued commercial success.

Cobbing's theories have come under considerable scrutiny: the accuracy of his reading of many of the sources, particularly missionary (q.v.) accounts, has been challenged, and numerous questions of detail have been raised by those skeptical of his arguments. Answers remain elusive on many points because of the inconclusive nature of the evidence.

MFENGU. Some dispute surrounds the origins of the Mfengu (Fingo) people in the eastern Cape Colony (q.v.) during the 1820s. It is usually accepted that they comprised the impoverished and scattered remnants of various Nguni (q.v.) groups (including the Hlubi, Zizi, Bhaca, and Bhele) fleeing the disruption of the Mfecane (q.v.) further north. They apparently repeated the simple request, "Siyamfenguze" ("We seek work"), and formed a client relationship with the Gcaleka Xhosa (q.v.), who employed them to look after herds of cattle, from about 1823. They also proved to be successful traders. The pioneering Wesleyan missionary (q.v.) John Ayliff (1797–1862) saw the Mfengu as potential converts, speaking of their slave status among the Xhosa. During the frontier (q.v.) war of 1834–35 he persuaded them to seek the protection of the colonial authorities. After the war, some 16,000 Mfengu were placed on former Xhosa land east of the Fish River as a buffer between the Xhosa and the colonists; their acceptance of this land was regarded by the Xhosa as an act of ingratitude and treachery.

The Mfengu became successful agriculturists (q.v.); many were prosperous independent peasant farmers, and others were sought after by colonists because of their reputation as loyal servants. Many were quick to accept Christianity (q.v.) and Western education (q.v.). They fought on the side of the colonists during the frontier wars of 1846–47, 1850–53, and 1877–78 and received further grants of land seized from the defeated Xhosa. After the cattle killing (q.v.), from which many Mfengu prospered, the portion of Xhosa territory allocated to them became known as Fingoland, which itself became a springboard for further migration into the Transkei (q.v.) and East Griqualand (q.v.) in the 1870s and 1880s.

MIGRANCY. The movement of Africans (q.v.) to work for temporary periods became systematic state policy as the mining economy required large numbers of workers. Africans often did not wish to leave their homes in the rural areas permanently, and white governments did not want them settling permanently in so-called white areas. As time passed, however, the economy, especially manufacturing industry, required more settled labor, and urbanization increased, but migrant labor continued to be very important into the late 1990s.

MILNER, ALFRED (1854–1925). Governor of the Cape Colony (q.v.) and high commissioner of South Africa from 1897 to 1905, Sir Alfred Milner was an ardent imperialist and doctrinaire social engineer. He aimed to create a self-governing white dominion in which a well-controlled African labor force would ensure the efficient functioning of the country's mines. He viewed the Transvaal (q.v.) as an obstacle to the attainment of his objectives and used Uitlander (q.v.) grievances against the Paul Kruger (q.v.) government, forcing matters until the South African War (q.v.) broke out.

After the war, Milner administered the conquered republics, with the aid of a group of young men known as the Kindergarten (q.v.), and attempted to promote rapid economic growth, particularly the expansion of mining production, and to encourage large-scale British immigration so as to weaken Afrikaner (q.v.) power. He was not successful in either enterprise; the mining industry took some years to recover, immigration from Britain was not large enough to achieve his goals, and he alienated Afrikaners through his anglicization endeavors.

MINING. Mining was the major force leading to the growth of the South African economy from the discovery of diamonds (q.v.) at Kimberley (q.v.) in the late 1860s, although mining had been a feature of the economies of the Bantu-speaking (q.v.) peoples of the region for some 1,500 years before diamonds were mined on a large scale. The working of iron and the mining of copper were highly valued in these communities.

Modern mining began with the exploitation of copper in the northern Cape (q.v.) and Namaqualand in the 1850s. Copper mining was abandoned during the depression of the 1930s but was resumed during World War II (q.v.). It has remained a profitable industry, though it has never been a major factor in the country's economic growth. In this regard, the role of diamonds and gold (q.v.) can scarcely be exaggerated, as these minerals created large-scale wealth, as well as being responsible for technological development, the growth of cities, the building of railways (q.v.), the rapid expansion of trade, and the shaping of modern South Africa. *See also* ANGLO AMERICAN CORPORATION; DE BEERS; ECONOMIC CHANGE.

The most recent mining boom was that associated with coal after the 1960s. Although coal production had occurred from the turn of the century and was important in underpinning the growth of railways and the generation of electricity, technological developments made South African coal internationally competitive after the 1960s. Between 1960 and 1985, coal output trebled, and more than 29 million tons were exported annually by the beginning of the 1980s. By the end of the decade, coal was second only to gold as an earner of foreign exchange. A new deepwater harbor was built at Richard's Bay on the north coast of KwaZulu-Natal (q.v.) and linked by rail to the eastern Transvaal (q.v.), the major coal-producing region.

Another deep-water harbor was constructed at Saldanha Bay, on the west coast north of Cape Town (q.v.), for the bulk export of iron ore from the Sishen open-cast mine in the northwestern Cape. Of those minerals of special strategic significance, chrome and manganese were probably the most important; the bulk of the world's known reserves of both lay within South Africa. Uranium was important for South Africa's nuclear (q.v.) program, and platinum mined in the Rustenburg area northwest of Johannesburg grew in importance from the 1970s.

MISSIONARIES. The first European missionary sent to work among the indigenous people of the Cape (q.v.) was the Moravian evangelist George Schmidt (1709–85), who founded the Genadendal (q.v.) mission in 1737. He returned to Europe in 1744, and it was not until the 1790s that mission work was resumed, at Genadendal and elsewhere. The late-18th-century evangelical revival in Europe saw the founding of a number of mission societies, and the 19th century was the primary period of mission activity in southern Africa.

In the first half of the 19th century, the London Missionary Society (LMS) (q.v.) had more missionaries in the field, over a wider area, than any other missionary group. The LMS did little work among the settler population, preferring to concentrate its energies on the frontier (q.v.) areas and beyond them. In the east, the Bethelsdorp mission of Johannes van der Kemp (q.v.) was regarded with considerable hostility by white farmers, who feared the loss of Khoikhoi (q.v.) labor, and in the north the Kuruman mission of Robert Moffat (q.v.) became the center of enormous missionary work. As superintendent of the LMS between the 1820s and 1840s, John Philip (q.v.) played a central role in colonial developments. Most LMS stations in the colony were gradually incorporated into the Congregational Church.

The other major Protestant missionary society active in South Africa in the early 19th century was the Wesleyan Methodist Missionary Society. William Shaw (1798–1872) established a chain of six missions stretching from the colonial eastern frontier to the port of Natal (q.v.). The Wesleyans also did pioneering work among the Sotho (q.v.). Other missionary bodies active in South Africa included the Glasgow Society, which in 1824 founded Lovedale, the leading missionary educational institution in the Cape; the Berlin Missionary Society, which worked in the eastern Cape before turning its attention to Natal and the Transvaal (q.v.); the Rhenish Missionary Society, which operated missions in the western Cape and Namaqualand; and the Paris Evangelical Missionary Society, with eleven missions in Basutoland (q.v.) by 1850. In Natal, the most successful of the missions were those of the American Board, which experienced considerable growth among the Zulu (q.v.) and which founded Adams College in 1853; here, numbers of Natal's African elite were educated until its closure by the National Party (q.v.) government in 1956.

The major churches became involved in mission work only in the latter half of the 19th century. Anglicans (q.v.) began mission work in the eastern Cape during the 1850s; the Dutch Reformed Churches (q.v.) started in the 1860s; and the Roman Catholic Church's (q.v.) mission activities gained momentum only at the beginning of the 20th century.

Missionaries occupy a controversial place in South African history. Many of them were viewed by colonists as enemies of the colonial order, intruders who were too sympathetic toward people of color, a view that long lingered. They have also been portrayed as agents of colonial expansion who undermined African societies, convinced as most were of their superior culture and the benefits of colonial rule. Many, particularly those on the frontier, acted as intermediaries between African chiefs and the colonial government. Some African societies viewed them as agents of disruption, disease, and drought, and missionary intolerance of African customs aroused much hostility to their work. Mission success before 1850 was fairly limited, confined mainly to uprooted and severely unsettled communities; only in the second half of the century did they make significant numbers of conversions. Missionaries were not always able to dictate events; and they were frequently used by African leaders to their own advantage. Although some missionaries did attempt to limit the excesses of settler expansion, others advocated the conquest of African societies in the interests of the extension of Christianity (q.v.).

MOFFAT, ROBERT (1795–1883). A missionary of the London Missionary Society (LMS) (q.v.) whose work among the Tlhaping (q.v.) people at the Kuruman mission between 1824 and 1870 brought him considerable renown, Robert Moffat, an able linguist, was responsible for Tswana (q.v.) becoming the first written African language (q.v.) in South Africa and also for translating the Bible into Setswana. Kuruman, perhaps the most successful of all the LMS missions, became an important base for further mission work and exploration deeper into the interior, some of which was undertaken by Moffat's son-in-law, David Livingstone.

MOROKA II (ca. 1795–1880). From 1830 until 1880, Moroka II was a chief of the Rolong, a Sotho-speaking (q.v.) community. The Rolong established their capital at Thaba Nchu, in what is now the Free State (q.v.), in 1833, after moving from the western Transvaal (q.v.), where they were threatened by the westward expansion of the Ndebele (q.v.). Moroka assisted the Voortrekkers (q.v.) against the Ndebele and subsequently aided the British against the southern Sotho.

MOSHOESHOE (ca. 1786–1870). Leader of the main group of southern Sotho (q.v.), Moshoeshoe, the son of a minor Sotho ruler in the upper Caledon River valley, based himself at an impregnable mountain fortress, Thaba Bosiu ("the mountain of the night"), in 1824 and from there launched cattle raids, particularly on the Thembu south of the Drakensberg (q.v.). He recruited followers by loaning cattle, won a reputation for tolerance and magnanimity toward his enemies, and succeeded in uniting disparate Sotho groups into a federal state under his authority. *See also* XHOSA.

After 1848, Moshoeshoe had to preserve his state in the face of new pressures. In 1843, the British had recognized that his territory extended well to the west of the Caledon River; but their attempts to restrict his lands after the proclamation of the Orange River Sovereignty (q.v.) in 1848 caused him to lose faith in British promises. During the 1850s, the Boers (q.v.) of the Orange Free State (q.v.) began to encroach on his land, and an inconclusive war was fought between the two sides in 1858. A further conflict with the Boers in 1865–66 left the Sotho in a serious plight and forced Moshoeshoe to seek British protection. In March 1868, Basutoland (q.v.) was annexed as a British colony, but Moshoeshoe lost the fertile lands west of the Caledon in the following year, when the boundary was demarcated by the British high commissioner and the government of the Orange Free State.

MOZAMBIQUE. Slaves (q.v.) captured from Mozambique were taken to Cape Town (q.v.) in the early 19th century and released there. Mozambicans began to work on the Natal (q.v.) sugar fields in the 1860s and went to the diamond (q.v.) fields in the 1870s. In 1875 the port of Delagoa Bay (q.v.) (now Maputo) was awarded to the Portuguese. When gold (q.v.) was discovered on the Witwatersrand (q.v.), large numbers of men from what became Portuguese territory began going to the mines. For more than 80 years Mozambique remained the most important foreign source of migrant labor for the mines. "East coast natives," as the Mozambican miners were called, were contracted for longer periods than Africans within South Africa, and their employment pushed down wage rates. In the 1890s, over half the labor force on the Rand mines came from Mozambique; an average of 100,000 men a year worked on the mines from Mozambique during the 30 years after World War II (q.v.).

With the independence of Mozambique in 1975, the supply of mine labor began to dry up, and was soon only a fraction of what it had been. Large numbers of white South Africans had visited Delagoa Bay as tourists, but that ceased, and relations were soured when Mozambique, despite its poverty, allowed the African National Congress (ANC) (q.v.) to operate from its soil. ANC facilities in a suburb of Maputo were attacked in January 1981 by the South African Defence Force (q.v.). But then in March 1984, the two governments unexpectedly announced that they were to sign a formal nonaggression treaty, the Nkomati Accord (q.v.). Though the ANC had to close down its military operations in Mozambique, elements in the South African government continued to supply arms and ammunition to the Mozambican Resistance Movement (RENAMO).

The death of Mozambique's president, Samora Machel, in a plane crash just within South African territory on 19 October 1986 further damaged relations between the two countries, for there were allegations, never substantiated, of a South African plot to assassinate him. Large numbers of Mozambicans fled into the eastern Transvaal (q.v.) as refugees from the civil war in their country. After 1990, relations improved. In July 1998, Nelson Mandela married Graca Machel, former wife of Samora Machel. An ambitious Maputo Corridor project was initiated to develop infrastructural links between the Rand and Maputo, and South African tourists began to return to the beaches on the Mozambican coast.

MPANDE (1798–1872). Zulu (q.v.) king from 1840, Mpande was the half-brother of Dingane (q.v.) and the father of Cetshwayo (q.v.), who was the de facto ruler long before his formal succession. Mpande forged an alliance with the Voortrekkers (q.v.) at the end of the 1830s and defeated Dingane in 1840. He succeeded in maintaining Zulu independence until his death, avoiding direct confrontation with the growing colony of Natal (q.v.) south of the Zulu kingdom, and alternately dealing with the British and the Boers (q.v.) to prevent any erosion of his authority.

MPUMALANGA. Province created in April 1994, from the eastern part of the former Transvaal (q.v.) and incorporating the bantustan (q.v.) of KaNgwane (q.v.). The provincial capital was Nelspruit. Initially called Eastern Transvaal, the province, which comprised 6.4 per cent of the country's area, was renamed Mpumalanga ("where the sun rises") in

1995. The African National Congress swept to victory in the election of 1994, winning almost 82 percent of the vote. The first premier was Mathews Phosa, whose government was beset by a series of serious corruption and mismanagement scandals in its early years. Mining (34 percent), electricity generation (22 percent), and manufacturing (13 percent) were the most significant contributors to the province's gross geographic product, and its tourism potential was expected to further boost its economy. Mpumalanga hoped to profit greatly by the development of the Maputo corridor, a £1 billion project to open a new road link from the Witwatersrand (q.v.) to the harbor of Maputo in Mozambique (q.v.).

MRS. PLES. Name given to the cranium of a female of the species *Plesianthropus transvaalensis* (later classified as *Australopithecus africanus*), discovered by Robert Broom (q.v.) and J. T. Robinson at Sterkfontein near Johannesburg (q.v.) in 1947. Mrs. Ples was related to the Taung child (q.v.), though of a different subspecies, and was dated to 2.5 million years before the present. The discovery provided further evidence that the earliest hominids lived in southern Africa.

MUJAJI (ca. 1800–1895). Ruler of the Lovedu people in the northeastern Transvaal (q.v.), popularly known as the Rain Queen. She claimed tribute from many peoples surrounding her chiefdom during the latter part of the 19th century because of her position in the rain cult and her powers over rainfall. Since her reign, the Lovedu have always had a female ruler.

MULTI-PARTY NEGOTIATING FORUM. A continuation, in effect, of the Convention for a Democratic South Africa (q.v.), it drew up the interim constitution of 1993 and provisions for the transition to the new order. Meeting at the World Trade Centre at Kempton Park, outside Johannesburg (q.v.), from April 1993, it completed the draft of the interim constitution in November. The National Party (NP) (q.v.) negotiating team under Roelf Meyer (q.v.) agreed to the establishment of a five-year term for a Government of National Unity (q.v.), in which the NP had no veto over decisions. The NP also backed down over federalism and agreed to a two-thirds majority requirement for the passage of the final constitution by the Constitutional Assembly (q.v.) and a 60-percent majority in a referendum if deadlock was reached in the Assembly. The African National Congress (q.v.) negotiating team was ably led by Cyril Ramaphosa (q.v.).

MUSLIMS. *See* ISLAM.

MZILIKAZI (ca. 1795–1868). Leader of the Ndebele (q.v.) state from its inception in the 1820s. The son of the chief of the Khumalo chiefdom among the northern Nguni (q.v.), Mzilikazi rose to prominence during the conflict between the Zulu (q.v.) and the Ndwandwe. A most effective military commander, he switched allegiance from the Ndwandwe ruler Zwide (q.v.) to the Zulu leader Shaka (q.v.) in about 1819. He alienated Shaka by refusing to surrender captured cattle in 1821, and fled north the following year with about 300 followers. With this nucleus, he created a new state north of the Vaal River (q.v.) in the 1820s, which he moved progressively further west in order to escape possible Zulu retaliation. This state grew into a large polity, which by the mid-1830s embraced much of what became the southern and western Transvaal (q.v.). The Voortrekkers (q.v.) posed a new threat from the south from 1836, and after the defeat they inflicted on his army at Vegkop (q.v.), he withdrew northwards and reestablished his kingdom north of the Limpopo River (q.v.) in what became known as Matabeleland (*see* ZIMBABWE). He remained ruler there until his death in 1868, when power passed to his son Lobengula.

-N-

NAMIBIA. South Africa conquered German South West Africa (SWA) during World War I (q.v.), and the territory was granted to it as a C-class mandate by the League of Nations (q.v.) in 1920. South Africa extended the system of reserves introduced by the Germans, and permitted whites from the Union (q.v.) to settle there. Jan Smuts (q.v.) ordered that the resistance by the Bondelswartz people in 1922 be suppressed harshly. When the League dissolved during World War II (q.v.), Smuts hoped to be able to annex the territory, and formally applied to the newly established United Nations (UN) (q.v.) in 1946 to do so, but his request was refused, largely on the grounds that the indigenous people had not been adequately consulted. The UN instead asked South Africa to place the territory under the UN's trusteeship system, which provided for eventual independence for such territories. When South Africa refused, a long drawn-out legal battle began, in the course of which the International Court of Justice at the Hague handed down a series of judgments on the status of South West Africa. In 1966, the court decided that it had no legal standing in a case that hinged on whether South Africa was governing the territory in the spirit of its mandate. This led directly to the beginning of armed conflict in northern South West Africa, in which at first the South African Police sought to combat guerrilla insurgents of the South West African People's Organization (SWAPO). In October 1966, the UN General Assembly unilaterally terminated the mandate, a decision that was, a few years later, ratified by the Security Council. In 1971, the ratification was in turn given legal validity by the International Court. In the same year, a general strike of Namibian workers posed a new threat to South African rule in the territory.

In the face of these developments, the South African government decided to abandon its policy of seeking to incorporate the territory to a greater extent into its own administration, as a de facto fifth province. Instead, it determined that the territory should remain as one entity, despite the fact that it had begun to apply in Namibia a bantustan policy (q.v.) on the South African model, and that it should be drawn toward self-government and independence under a black-led government that would be friendly to South Africa. An ethnically based advisory council was established, and in 1975 a conference of ethnic representatives was brought together in the Turnhalle building in Windhoek. By that time the South African government feared that once Angola (q.v.) was independent, the People's Liberation Army of Namibia (PLAN), SWAPO's armed wing, would be able to operate from southern Angola and so pose a much greater threat to the South African army defending northern Namibia. A small South African expeditionary force moved toward the Angolan capital in October 1975 to try to prevent the pro-SWAPO MPLA from taking power in Luanda, but in the face of the arrival of Cuban troops and the failure of support from the West, the South African force had to withdraw, and SWAPO was able to establish itself in part of southern Angola.

In 1977, when it seemed that the Turnhalle discussions might produce an internal settlement, under the terms of which the South African government would give independence to a local client group, a so-called Western Contact Group was established, consisting of the five Western countries then members of the UN Security Council, to press for a form of independence that would mesh with the UN demand for a transfer of power to the people of the territory (UN Security Council Resolution 385 of 1976). By April 1978 a formula had been worked out providing for joint UN–South African administration during a transition period in which the UN would provide a monitoring team and a force to keep the peace. The South African government accepted this plan in April 1978, probably without any serious intention of ever implementing it.

Numerous reasons were later advanced by South African government spokespersons as to why the plan (embodied in UN Security Council Resolution 435) could not be implemented: the alleged partiality of the UN; the composition of the UN Transition Assistance Group force that would enter the territory during the transitional phase; the monitoring and location of SWAPO's military bases; and, from 1981, the presence of Cuban forces in Angola. From northern Namibia the South African forces—together, from 1980, with South West African forces under South African command—launched raids against SWAPO bases in southern Angola. Brutal repression was used in northern Namibia to try to destroy SWAPO, while at the same time the Democratic Turnhalle Alliance and other groupings were built up in an attempt to form an anti-SWAPO front.

It was events in southern Angola that did most to force the South African government to implement Resolution 435. By early 1988, the South African forces had had to intervene twice to save South Africa's ally, UNITA (National Union for the Total Independence of Angola), from annihilation by the Angolan army. After the second of these, the South African–led forces moved close to Cuito Cuanavale (q.v.), and there a military stalemate ensued, owing to the arrival of large numbers of Cuban troops to aid the Angolan army. By May 1988, the Cubans had also moved closer to the Namibian border, and the threat of a major war with Cuba loomed. A negotiated settlement was the only way out, and this meant the implementation of Resolution 435.

As a result of an agreement signed in December 1988 between South Africa, Angola, and Cuba, the date for implementation was fixed for 1 April 1989. After an initial crisis caused by a SWAPO armed incursion into the north of the territory, the plan was carried out as envisaged in 1978, and in November 1989 the electorate of Namibia chose a Constituent Assembly in which SWAPO won 41 of the 72 seats. SWAPO then agreed to abide by the constitutional principles (q.v.) it had agreed to in 1982, a liberal constitution was approved unanimously in a remarkably short time, and on 21 March 1990, in a moving ceremony attended by F. W. de Klerk (q.v.) and the recently released Nelson Mandela (q.v.), the South African administration came to an end and the territory finally became independent.

The Western Contact Group had accepted that Walvis Bay (q.v.), Namibia's main port, would not be included in the negotiations and that its status would be decided after Namibian independence. As long as South Africa controlled the port, it dominated the new nation economically. After discussions between the two governments, a joint administration was set up over the Walvis Bay enclave, and it was formally incorporated into Namibia at the end of February 1994. After Mandela took office as South African president he announced that Namibia's debt (q.v.) to South Africa would be canceled; after lengthy negotiations this debt, amounting to more than R1 billion, was written off in 1997.

NATAL. Comprising the territory lying between the Drakensberg (q.v.) and the Indian Ocean, Natal was given its name by the first European to pass by its shores, the Portuguese explorer Vasco da Gama (q.v.), at the end of the 15th century. By that time, it had been inhabited for centuries by San (q.v.) hunter-gatherers and by Nguni-speaking (q.v.) farmers. Toward the end of the 18th century, conflicts increased among various chiefdoms north of the Thukela River and resulted in the emergence of the Zulu kingdom (q.v.) under Shaka (q.v.) at the beginning of the 19th century.

The first white settlers established a trading post at Port Natal (later Durban [q.v.]), in 1824, but the first large group of whites (q.v.) to enter Natal were Voortrekkers (q.v.), who crossed the Drakensberg in 1837. By 1839, some 6,000 trekkers were living in the Republic of Natalia, situated south of the Thukela River. In 1843, Britain annexed the area, largely for strategic reasons, to prevent any hostile power from gaining a foothold on the southern African coast. Most of the trekkers left for the high veld (q.v.) and were replaced by immigrants from Britain, the first large group of 5,000 arriving between 1849 and 1852. By the mid-1850s, there were still fewer than 10,000 whites; these were greatly outnumbered by more than 100,000 Africans (q.v.), who were placed in reserves (q.v.) administered by Theophilus Shepstone (q.v.) through a system of paternalism and indirect rule.

Natal was an autonomous district of the Cape Colony (q.v.) until 1856, when it was given its own legislative council. Although Natal's franchise (q.v.) was theoretically nonracial, like that of the Cape (q.v.), in practice it was closer to that of the trekker republics: the Exemption and Native Franchise Laws of 1865 required Africans to obtain exemption from customary law before qualifying for the vote, an exemption that was extremely difficult to obtain. After the Langalibalele (q.v.) Rebellion in 1873, an attempt was made to reduce Natal to crown colony status, in part so that Natal could lend its support to the confederation (q.v.) scheme of Lord Henry Carnarvon (q.v.). In reaction, a movement grew for responsible government, which was finally achieved in 1893. In 1897, Zululand was incorporated into Natal (the Zulu kingdom having been annexed by the British in 1887 after the Anglo–Zulu War [q.v.] of 1879 and the subsequent civil war).

By the end of the 19th century, Natal's economy and political order were firmly in white hands. From 1860, indentured Indian (q.v.) laborers arrived in Natal, and the sugar plantations on which they worked became the mainstay of the economy. Other significant economic activities were agriculture (q.v.), pastoral farming, timber plantations, and coal mining. White dominance, though established, was insecure, as evidenced by the poor handling by the authorities of the Bambatha Rebellion (q.v.) of 1906, which helped to propel Natal into the Union (q.v.) of South Africa in 1910. Within the Union, Natal's English-speaking (q.v.) whites feared Afrikaner (q.v.) domination and occasionally spoke of secession. During the 20th century, Natal's white politicians were frequently preoccupied with attempts to secure further provincial rights rather than with broader issues.

During the 1970s, more than 40 separate pieces of land were excised from the province to constitute the bantustan (q.v.) of KwaZulu (q.v.). Many thousands of people living on white farms were forced to move into KwaZulu, which included the major black townships on the outskirts of Durban (q.v.), where most of the inhabitants worked. KwaZulu politics was dominated by Mangosuthu Buthelezi (q.v.), its chief minister from 1977. He rejected full independence for KwaZulu, to the annoyance of the National Party (q.v.) government, although his relations with the NP warmed during the 1980s as he became involved in a struggle against the United Democratic Front (q.v.) and rejected economic sanctions against South Africa.

Buthelezi tended to view the regional economy of the KwaZulu-Natal (q.v.) area as inextricably linked, arguing that it should be governed as such. During the 1990s, secessionist talk was again aired as a viable option for the region, as Buthelezi and his supporters adopted increasingly strident positions against the major thrust of South African politics and against the negotiations for a new national constitution and democratic elections. A low-key and violent civil war, which began in about 1986 and grew in intensity during the early 1990s, polarized the region: many commentators saw it as the product of the competition between Buthelezi's Inkatha (q.v.) Freedom Party and the African National Congress (q.v.) for political dominance. In 1994, the region was again united as the province of KwaZulu-Natal, one of the nine provinces of the country.

NATIONAL CAPITAL. South Africa is one of the few countries in the world to have a divided capital. The issue of which city would be its capital was resolved by a compromise in the National Convention (q.v.)

of 1908–9. Pretoria (q.v.), now in the province of Gauteng (q.v.), was to be the country's administrative capital, and splendid administrative headquarters, the Union Buildings, designed by Herbert Baker (q.v.), were erected there on a hill overlooking the city in 1914. Cape Town (q.v.), the "mother city," was chosen to be the Union's legislative capital, and Bloemfontein (q.v.) was to serve as the judicial capital, the seat of the country's highest court, the Appellate Division of the Supreme (now High) Court. The division between legislative and administrative capitals meant that every year the higher echelons of the central administration moved from Pretoria to Cape Town in January and then returned to Pretoria in mid-year. Foreign countries found they had to duplicate embassies.

The issue of the capital came up again in the discussions on a new constitution in 1993 and 1995–96. The government of National Unity (q.v.) was adamant that the division between administrative and legislative capitals could not continue, because it was expensive and inefficient. Parliament was now to sit for most of the year, and many African National Congress (q.v.) members of Parliament did not feel at home in the Cape (q.v.). Some argued that Parliament should be in Gauteng because a quarter of the country's population lived there and it generated 40 percent of the country's gross domestic product. Others thought that it would be wrong to centralize the country's power and wealth in the north. Although most Capetonians wanted Parliament to remain in Cape Town, where there were suitable buildings for it, Pretoria and Bloemfontein both proposed that Parliament be moved to their cities. It was also suggested that a new administrative and legislative capital should be built at Midrand, between Johannesburg and Pretoria. After a cabinet committee had considered the possible relocation of Parliament, the government announced that Parliament would decide the matter in 1997, but because it was such a controversial matter, the decision was postponed until after the 1999 general election. Parliament therefore continued to sit in Cape Town.

NATIONAL CONVENTION. The National Convention assembled in Durban (q.v.) on 12 October 1908, precisely nine years after the outbreak of the South African War (q.v.), to draft the constitution of the Union (q.v.) of South Africa. Thirty white delegates from the four colonies participated, the numbers being roughly proportionate to the white populations: 12 from the Cape (q.v.), eight from the Transvaal (q.v.), and five each from Natal (q.v.) and the Orange River Colony. The National Convention convened in Cape Town (q.v.) in February 1909 and finalized its business in Bloemfontein (q.v.) in May 1909. Its decisions were enshrined in the South Africa Bill, which was passed by both houses of the British Parliament. As the South Africa Act, it received royal assent on 20 September 1909. The most contentious issues confronting the National Convention were the franchise (q.v.) and the location of the national capital (q.v.). Compromise was reached on both. Existing franchise arrangements in each colony were to continue, but only whites (q.v.) were entitled to serve in the new Union Parliament. Cape Town was to be the seat of Parliament, Pretoria (q.v.) the administrative capital, and Bloemfontein the seat of the Appellate Division of the Supreme Court.

A South African Native Convention (SANC) also met in 1908–9 in response to the drive by whites to unify South Africa. The SANC was unable to prevent the inauguration of the Union on 31 May 1910, but was a forerunner of the South African Native National Congress of 1912, later the African National Congress (q.v.).

NATIONAL PARTY (NP). The National Party was founded in 1914 by General J. B. M. Hertzog (q.v.) to further Afrikaner (q.v.) interests, after he had broken with Louis Botha (q.v.) and Jan Smuts (q.v.) on their policy of reconciling English speakers (q.v.) and Afrikaners, and because he thought they were too pro-British. For a long time the NP's main support came from Afrikaner rural voters. The party came to power in 1924 with the aid of the white Labour Party (q.v.). When it merged with Smuts's South African Party (q.v.) in 1934, D. F. Malan (q.v.) broke with Hertzog and kept alive a separate Purified National Party as the party of Afrikaner nationalism (q.v.). After fighting off a challenge by the Ossewa Brandwag (q.v.) during World War II (q.v.), Malan led his party to victory in the 1948 election. From then on, successive NP governments implemented apartheid (q.v.) measures with zeal.

After F. W. de Klerk (q.v.) began his reform initiative in 1990, the NP soon decided to accept nonwhite members and to distance itself from apartheid. It was particularly successful in winning new support among the Coloured (q.v.) community in the Cape (q.v.), which sought to distance itself from an African-dominated African National Congress (q.v.) and surprisingly seemed able to forgive the way NP governments had treated it in the past. After winning 20 percent of the vote in the general election of 1994, the NP entered into the government of National Unity (GNU) (q.v.), and de Klerk became one of the two deputy presidents. But it found its marginal position in the government increasingly uncomfortable and withdrew from the GNU as soon as the final constitution had been agreed upon, which meant that de Klerk had to give up his deputy presidentship. In 1997, de Klerk suddenly resigned as leader of the party, and from Parliament, and it was later announced that he had been having an affair with a married woman. His successor, Marthinus van Schalkwyk, was a lightweight politician, and support for the NP at the national level plummeted. Estimates in mid-1998 suggested that the party's support had halved since the 1994 general election.

The NP's main area of support remained the Western Cape, the only province it controlled, and there the old-guard leader Hernus Kriel handed over the reins of power to a Coloured leader, Gerald Morkel, in early 1998. Many expected that the NP's continued support among the Coloured community in the Western Cape would enable the party to hold on to power there in the 1999 election, albeit very narrowly.

NATIONAL PEACE ACCORD. The 29 signatories of the National Peace Accord, which was signed in Johannesburg on 14 September 1991, included the National Party (q.v.) government, the African National Congress (q.v.), the Inkatha (q.v.) Freedom Party, and trade unions (q.v.). It was drawn up to combat the escalating level of political violence (q.v.) in the country and to create a suitable climate for negotiation. It laid down codes of conduct, provided for the establishment of local committees to resolve political disputes, and obliged all parties to refrain from violence for political ends. Its provisions were often blatantly ignored, and violence continued at a high level, but many of its local dispute-resolution committees were effective, and its monitors facilitated the work of peace monitors from the United Nations (q.v.), the European Community, and the Commonwealth (q.v.).

NATIONAL SECURITY MANAGEMENT SYSTEM. *See* STATE SECURITY COUNCIL.

NATIONAL UNION OF SOUTH AFRICAN STUDENTS (NUSAS) (1924–91). Formed initially to represent students from English (q.v.) and Afrikaans (q.v.) universities (q.v.), NUSAS shifted in its politics to the left after World War II (q.v.) and in the late 1950s strongly opposed the National Party (q.v.) government's policy of segregating tertiary education. From 1959, when the universities were segregated, NUSAS opposed apartheid (q.v.) in general. Some leading figures in NUSAS who were involved in the African Resistance Movement were arrested in 1964. B. J. Vorster (q.v.), minister of justice, had by then come to regard NUSAS as dangerously subversive. Although infiltrated by police (q.v.) spies, it nevertheless carried on its opposition to apartheid and helped radicalize thousands of students on those English-medium campuses on which it was able to operate. State harassment continued: after the Schlebusch Commission of 1972 investigated its activities, eight of its leaders were banned (q.v.) for five years.

By then, most of its black members had left to join the South African Students' Organization (q.v.), founded by Steve Biko (q.v.), but NUSAS continued to work closely with black students in anti-apartheid work in the 1980s. In 1989 it decided to link up with the black-dominated South African National Students' Congress, formed from the Azanian Students' Organization. The two bodies merged in 1991: NUSAS dissolved itself and a new student body, the South African Students' Congress Organization, was launched.

NATIVES LAND ACT (1913). One of the most crucial laws of 20th-century South Africa, the Natives Land Act imposed territorial segregation in an attempt to obtain uniformity in land policy after the creation of the Union (q.v.) of South Africa. In the Cape (q.v.) and Natal (q.v.) before union, there were no restrictions on Africans (q.v.) buying or leasing land outside the reserves (q.v.). In the Transvaal (q.v.), land owned by Africans had to be registered in the name of the chief African administrator, and in the Orange Free State (q.v.), Africans were forbidden by law to purchase or lease land. A Supreme Court case in the Transvaal in 1905 found that Africans could hold land in their own right outside the reserves. As African land purchase, often through syndicates, increased— 78 farms or portions of farms were acquired from 1910 to 1912—alarm among whites grew.

The 1913 act froze the existing racial distribution of land: Africans could no longer buy or obtain title to land outside the reserves (the "scheduled areas"), which constituted just 7 percent of South Africa's area. Whites in turn were not entitled to acquire title to land within the reserves. The act also envisaged more land being added to the reserves, especially in the Transvaal and the Orange Free State, where there was little reserve land.

A commission was established, under Sir William Beaumont (1851–1930), a retired Natal judge, to assess African needs for additional land and to recommend where such land could be found. Its 1916 report was, in turn, referred to local committees, the findings of which were accepted by the government of Jan Smuts (q.v.) in 1921. The additional land was not provided for until the Native Trust and Land Act of 1936, and then the land released (15.3 million acres) was much less than that allocated by the Beaumont Commission. After the release of additional land in 1936, the reserves constituted just over 13 percent of the total area of the country. Even by the end of the 1970s, however, not all this additional land had been acquired and added to the reserves, by now called bantustans (q.v.) or "national states."

The Natives Land Act did not only provide for a grossly inequitable division of land between Africans and non-Africans. It was also concerned with the eviction of African squatters (q.v.). With the increasing commercialization of farming, white farmers wished to eliminate competition from black peasant farmers and squatters while ensuring a plentiful supply of cheap labor. White farmers wanted labor tenants—working a set number of days (perhaps 90) in the year, in return for access to the land—or wage laborers. Eviction from land in the Transvaal and Natal could not occur until Parliament had "made other provision," but in the Orange Free State, previous antisquatting provisions were confirmed, and sharecroppers were forced from the land. These removals were vividly described by Solomon Plaatje (q.v.) in his classic *Native Life in South Africa* (1916).

The Natives Land Act could not apply to the Cape, for interference with the land rights of Africans represented interference with their access to the qualified franchise. Uniformity of policy thus had to wait until 1936, when Cape Africans were removed from the common voters' roll.

NATIVES' REPRESENTATIVE COUNCIL (NRC). An advisory body was established in 1936 under the terms of J. B. M. Hertzog's (q.v.) Representation of Natives Act of 1936. The African National Congress (q.v.) and the All-African Convention (q.v.) decided to participate in the structure, and between 1937 and 1946 it regularly passed moderate resolutions calling for the redress of African grievances, which were in turn consistently ignored by the government.

In 1946, the NRC decided to adjourn in protest over the suppression of the mine workers' strike (q.v.). In 1950, shortly after he had become minister of native affairs, H. F. Verwoerd (q.v.) reconvened the NRC to inform it of the need for apartheid (q.v.). It was abolished in 1951 under the Bantu Authorities Act, which provided for the establishment of local, regional, and territorial African councils in the reserves (q.v.).

NDEBELE STATE. A powerful, centralized state created during the mid-1820s in the Transvaal (q.v.) by Mzilikazi (q.v.), the Ndebele had by the early 1830s embraced much of the area between the Limpopo (q.v.), Vaal, Crocodile, and Molopo Rivers and had perhaps 80,000 subjects, the majority of whom were Sotho (q.v.) speakers absorbed through conquest or marriage. The capital moved several times, from close to the Vaal

River, to north of present-day Pretoria (q.v.), to the Marico area in the present North-West Province (q.v.). Regiments were stationed both at the capital and at far-flung military outposts.

In 1832, the Zulu ruler Dingane (q.v.) sent a raiding army to the high veld (q.v.) in an attempt to reduce Ndebele power, but it was repulsed. Challenged by Griqua (q.v.) raiders and then by Voortrekkers (q.v.) from the south and southwest in the mid-1830s, Mzilikazi decided to withdraw and in 1838 moved north across the Limpopo River. He recreated his state in what became known as Matabeleland in southwestern Zimbabwe (q.v.).

NDZUNDZA NDEBELE. Inhabitants of part of what later became the Transvaal (q.v.) long before the arrival there of the Ndebele (q.v.) of Mzilikazi (q.v.), the Ndzundza Ndebele clashed with invaders from Zululand in the 1820s and then in the 1830s and 1840s regrouped under Mabhogo in an area around the capital, Erholweni, on the upper Steelpoort River. Less powerful than the Pedi (q.v.) to the north, they came into conflict with the Voortrekkers (q.v.) over issues of land and labor. A subgroup, the Kekana, were almost entirely wiped out when the trekkers laid siege to a cave in the Waterberg in which they had taken refuge in 1854. The Ndzundza Ndebele nevertheless numbered about 10,000 by the 1860s, and in 1879 they helped the British conquer the Pedi. Then in 1882, Erholweni was besieged by the Boers (q.v.); in the following year their ruler surrendered, and their land was seized and distributed to whites.

Under white rule, the Ndebele struggled to find a new identity: the most striking form this took was the colorful decorations they painted on the walls of their mud homesteads. In the 1970s and early 1980s the government created a new bantustan (q.v.), known as KwaNdebele, but the offer of independence made to it was refused. The struggle to create the bantustan led to much violence between them and neighboring people.

NGQIKA (ca. 1775–1829). Chief of the Rharhabe (q.v.), or western Xhosa (q.v.), from 1786, Ngqika's lengthy and bitter rivalry with Ndlambe, his uncle, was finally resolved in 1818–19. Ngqika was defeated by the combined forces of Ndlambe and Hintsa (q.v.) at the Battle of Amalinde in 1818, after which he enlisted colonial assistance, which was readily given, for the Cape Colony (q.v.) was keen to establish its dominance on the frontier (q.v.). Ndlambe was defeated by Cape (q.v.) forces in 1819, and the Cape then recognized Ngqika as paramount chief. But the colonial authorities forced Ngqika to surrender the land between the Kei and Keiskamma Rivers, comprising much of the Rharhabe land, as a neutral zone between the Xhosa and white settlers. This lost Ngqika the support of many of his followers, and he died an outcast and an alcoholic in 1829.

NGUNI. *Nguni* is the linguistic term for a group of southeast Bantu languages spoken by people living along the coastal belt from Zululand and Swaziland (q.v.) in the north to the Ciskei (q.v.) region in the eastern Cape (q.v.) in the south. The Nguni languages are commonly divided into a northern and a southern group: the northern languages include Zulu (q.v.) and Swazi, while the southern, or Cape, Nguni embrace those spoken by Xhosa (q.v.), Thembu, Mpondo, and Mpondomise. *See also* BANTU-SPEAKING PEOPLE.

Compared with the Sotho (q.v.) languages (q.v.), Nguni languages are distinguished by the number of clicking sounds, an indication of close interaction with Khoisan (q.v.) people over centuries. Extensive intermarriage between Nguni and Khoisan people is further suggested by physical appearance and the incorporation of Khoisan religious and medical ideas into Nguni culture. Nguni speakers practiced both agriculture (q.v.) and pastoralism; cattle ownership played a particularly important part in their economies. From the 15th and 16th centuries, chiefdoms were relatively autonomous, and communities within them were usually small in scale. Segmentation and secession from chiefdoms were conspicuous features of southern Nguni society; political unity seldom occurred.

NKOMATI ACCORD. On 16 March 1984, the Nkomati Accord, a formal nonaggression treaty between South Africa and Mozambique (q.v.), was signed by South African president P. W. Botha (q.v.) and Mozambican president Samora Machel near the town of Komatipoort on the border between the two countries. Both sides undertook to refrain from interference in each other's affairs, to resolve their differences peacefully, and to prohibit the operation of "terrorist organizations" from their territories. At the time, the accord was seen as a breakthrough in the South African government's relations with its neighbor and a major setback for the African National Congress (q.v.), which had to shut down its military operations in Mozambique. But elements in the South African government continued to support RENAMO (the Mozambican National Resistance), and the suspicious death of Machel in a plane crash just within South African territory on 19 October 1986 further served to undermine the accord.

NON-EUROPEAN UNITY MOVEMENT (NEUM). Founded in 1943, the NEUM emerged out of efforts, mainly led by Coloured (q.v.) intellectuals in Cape Town (q.v.), to form a united front of the oppressed against racial discrimination. It brought together those who rejected the Coloured Advisory Council appointed by Jan Smuts (q.v.) and the idea of a separate Coloured Affairs Department, as well as members of the All-African Convention (q.v.). NEUM's policy was noncollaboration and boycott (q.v.) of the institutions of the oppressor. The first of the 10 points on its program was full franchise (q.v.) and citizenship rights for all. In the late 1940s it began to attract considerable support in the rural Transkei (q.v.), but in the early 1950s, when it opposed the Defiance Campaign (q.v.) and the Congress Alliance (q.v.), its main support was in the western Cape (q.v.). By 1959 it had dropped the "Non-European" from its name but was riven by feuds, and it disintegrated in the early 1960s when a number of its leaders were banned (q.v.) or forced into exile. Within South Africa its views continued to be propagated in the *Educational Journal*, a newsletter published by the Teachers' League of South Africa, an affiliate of the Unity Movement.

In April 1985 the organization was revived as the New Unity Movement, based in Cape Town, with two federations of civic organizations (q.v.) as its most important affiliates. It remained strongly critical of what it called liberalism (q.v.) and imperialism, and it regarded the African National Congress (q.v.) as having sold out to imperialism when it began to negotiate with the National Party (q.v.). Its support base remained largely confined to a small group of western Cape intellectuals.

NONGQAWUSE (1841–98). As an adolescent in 1856, the Xhosa (q.v.) prophetess Nongqawuse reputedly had a vision of her ancestors in a pool of water advising the Xhosa to slaughter their cattle. She prophesied that this action would ensure the reestablishment of bonds with the supernatural world and the victory of the Xhosa over the evil forces currently afflicting them: colonial military supremacy, the alienation of their land, the breakdown of traditional custom, and the cattle lung-sickness of 1855–56. Nongqawuse's guardian and uncle, Mhlakaza, was able to convince Sarili (q.v.) of the validity of the prophecy, and he ordered subordinate chiefs, as well as those living under colonial rule in British Kaffraria (q.v.), to slaughter their cattle, with disastrous results. *See also* CATTLE KILLING.

NORTHERN CAPE. The province created in 1994 out of what had been the northern and northwestern Cape (q.v.) Province and parts of the

Bophuthatswana (q.v.) bantustan (q.v.), with its capital at Kimberley (q.v.). Although it covered a very wide geographical area, which comprised fractionally under 30 percent of the country's area, the Northern Cape Province had the smallest population of the country's nine provinces. In the April 1994 election, the African National Congress (q.v.) won 49 percent of the vote, the National Party (q.v.) 41 percent; and Manne Dipico became premier. Mining (q.v.) contributed 45 percent of the region's gross geographic product.

NORTHERN PROVINCE. A new province was created in April 1994 with the transition to democratic rule, with its capital at Pietersburg; initially called Northern Transvaal, it changed its name to the Northern Province in 1995. In the April 1994 election the African National Congress (q.v.) won a large majority in the provincial legislature, taking almost 85 percent of the vote, and Ngoako Ramathlodi became the first provincial premier. The inhabitants of the Bushbuckridge area protested that they did not wish to belong to the poorer Northern Province but instead to Mpumalanga (q.v.); an administrative compromise in 1997 ended the protest. Northern Province, which constituted just over 10 percent of the country's area, was by a considerable margin the poorest of the country's nine provinces, with unemployment estimated at between 30 and 50 percent; it was also beset with serious administrative difficulties, inefficiencies, and corruption inherited from the bantustans (q.v.) of Venda (q.v.) and Lebowa.

NORTH-WEST PROVINCE. Created in April 1994 from areas that were previously part of the Transvaal (q.v.), the Cape (q.v.), and the bantustan (q.v.) of Bophuthatswana (q.v.), the North-West Province constitutes almost 10 percent of the country's area. The town of Mmabatho/Mafeking (q.v.), later called Mafikeng, was chosen as its capital, and Popo Molefe of the African National Congress (ANC) (q.v.) became the first provincial premier, after the ANC won 83 percent of the vote in the election of April 1994. To the surprise of many, the province's white right-wingers did not use force, as they had threatened, to oppose the new order. Mining (at 42 percent) and agriculture (qq.v.) (at 15 percent) contributed most to the province's gross geographic product.

NTSIKANA (ca. 1760–1820). Xhosa (q.v.) prophet, hymn writer, and mystic, Ntsikana was converted to Christianity (q.v.) as a result of the preaching of Johannes van der Kemp (q.v.) of the London Missionary Society (q.v.). He was an adviser to Ngqika (q.v.) and was tolerant of the presence of whites on the western borders of the Xhosa chiefdom. Ntsikana was greatly respected for his prophetic abilities and his skill as a composer of hymns.

NUCLEAR WEAPONS. In 1993, President F. W. de Klerk (q.v.) made public the information that since the late 1970s, at a time when the National Party (q.v.) government felt threatened by the Cuban presence in Angola (q.v.) and the critical attitude of its Western allies, South Africa had, as many had long suspected, been developing nuclear weapons. Six such weapons had been built. De Klerk announced that he had ended the program and the weapons had been destroyed. His announcement opened the way for South Africa to sign the Nuclear Non-Proliferation Treaty and win international credit for being the first country in the world to destroy its nuclear stockpile.

-O-

OIL SUPPLY. The oil-price hikes of 1973, consequent on the formation of OPEC (Organization of the Petroleum Exporting Countries), showed up South Africa's vulnerability and led to the expansion of the production of oil from coal, which had been started in 1955. In 1979 the apartheid (q.v.) regime suffered a severe blow when its close ally, the Shah of Iran, was overthrown, for Iranian oil had accounted for almost 90 percent of South African requirements, and the Ayatollah Khomeini regime immediately cut off supplies. Local production at SASOL (South African Coal, Oil, and Gas Corporation) was again stepped up, but the main plant was damaged when limpet mines planted by Umkhonto weSizwe (q.v.) operatives exploded in 1980. Large quantities of oil were bought to be stored in mine shafts and in a giant underground storage facility built near Saldanha on the west coast.

Because leading multinational oil companies continued to operate in South Africa and oil could be bought on the spot market at relatively high prices, the National Party (q.v.) government was able to circumvent the United Nations (q.v.) embargo against the supply of oil to South Africa, but at vast cost. The search for oil offshore also absorbed great amounts of money, and no suitable finds were made, though a large gas field was discovered off Mossel Bay, and R12 billion was spent in the 1980s to exploit it, making the Mossgas project the largest of P. W. Botha's (q.v.) many white elephants. After the transition to democratic rule began in the 1990s, the selling off of oil stocks brought in revenue for development.

OORLAM. During the 19th century, the term *oorlam* (Malay, "those who are clever") was widely used to refer to a range of mixed groups of Khoikhoi (q.v.), Bastards (q.v.), and Afrikaners (q.v.) renowned for their mastery of firearms and horses. Oorlam groups usually spoke or understood Dutch (q.v.), as some of their members were born among the Dutch colonists in the Cape (q.v.), with whom they maintained ties. They lived in the Cape interior, along the Orange River (q.v.) and northern frontier (q.v.), and in Namibia (q.v.), and they were often feared by indigenous groups for the terror they inflicted through their weaponry.

OPPENHEIMER, ERNEST (1880–1957). An entrepreneur and the founder of South Africa's largest multinational company, the Anglo American Corporation (q.v.), Ernest Oppenheimer arrived in South Africa in 1902 as the representative of a London-based diamond company and soon became involved in amalgamating various diamond (q.v.) interests in South Africa and South West Africa (now Namibia [q.v.]). In the depression of the 1930s, he exploited the De Beers (q.v.) diamond monopoly to keep the diamond industry profitable and then oversaw the opening up of new gold (q.v.) mines in the Orange Free State (q.v.) after World War II (q.v.).

OPPENHEIMER, HARRY (b. 1908). The son of Ernest Oppenheimer (q.v.), Harry Oppenheimer succeeded his father as chairman of the Anglo American Corporation (q.v.) and De Beers Consolidated Mines (q.v.). He served as United Party (q.v.) member of Parliament for Kimberley (q.v.) from 1948 until 1958 and was a founding member and substantial funder of the Progressive Party (q.v.). He retired as head of Anglo American in 1982 and as head of De Beers in 1984.

ORANGE FREE STATE. The territory between the Orange (q.v.) and Vaal Rivers was named the Orange Free State (q.v.) in 1854, when the British formally recognized the independence of white farmers in the area under the terms of the Bloemfontein Convention (q.v.). The region had, however, been settled by Bantu speakers (q.v.) for at least eight centuries prior to this, as the hundreds of stone ruins in the northern parts attest. At the beginning of the 19th century, Sotho (q.v.) speakers lived across virtually the entire region. During the Mfecane (q.v.) of the 1820s, the region experienced considerable turmoil, and two major states emerged on either side of the Caledon River valley: that of Moshoeshoe (q.v.), east of the river, and the Tlokoa state of Sekonyela (ca. 1804–56), to the west. The two rivals finally clashed in 1853, and Moshoeshoe's forces forced most of Sekonyela's followers to flee south of the Orange.

White Voortrekkers (q.v.) passed through the region during the 1830s, en route to the areas across the Vaal River and the Drakensberg (q.v.); many returned to settle as farmers in the region after the British annexation of Natal (q.v.) in 1843. Some began to infiltrate the land of the Griqua (q.v.) around Philippolis in the south, provoking tension and the subsequent proclamation of British sovereignty in the area. The Orange River Sovereignty (q.v.) lasted from 1848 until 1854, when the British recognized Boer independence. A republican constitution, partly modeled on that of the United States, was drawn up, granting the franchise (q.v.) only to white males who had registered for military service.

The Griqua in the south surrendered their land rights to whites in 1861 and moved across the Drakensberg. War had broken out in 1858 in the east, as a result of rivalry between white farmers and the Sotho under Moshoeshoe for control of the fertile lands of the Caledon River valley. Conflict began again in 1865, as whites staked further claims in the region, but ended when Britain, fearing that the Orange Free State was seeking a route to the sea, annexed Basutoland (q.v.) in 1868. In 1884, Thaba Nchu, the largest African settlement in the region, was incorporated into the Orange Free State, thereby finalizing white monopoly of land ownership. The census of 1890 revealed that 77,000 whites and 128,000 Africans resided in what was an overwhelmingly rural and agricultural (q.v.) society. About 15,000 white commercial farmers controlled the land. Blacks were prevented by law from acquiring land, and most entered sharecropping arrangements with white farmers or became squatters (q.v.) and laborers.

Initially, close economic ties with the Cape Colony (q.v.) were forged, with wool (q.v.) as the main export. Orange Free State farmers were slow to respond to the growing demand for agricultural produce from the diamond (q.v.) fields during the 1870s, partly because transportation was extremely undeveloped. Between 1880 and 1891, however, agricultural production doubled, much of it coming from the land in the east conquered from the Sotho. Orange Free State claims to the Kimberley (q.v.) diamond fields failed, but £90,000 was paid in compensation by the British. After the discovery of gold (q.v.) on the Witwatersrand (q.v.) in 1886, the Orange Free State moved into the Transvaal's (q.v.) orbit, weakening ties with the Cape. A growing feeling that Afrikaners (q.v.) should stand together against the British was boosted by the Jameson Raid (q.v.), after which the Orange Free State entered an alliance with the Transvaal that took it into the South African War (q.v.) in 1899. The war brought great conflict and devastation. The capital of Bloemfontein (q.v.) was occupied by the British army in March 1900, and the area became the Orange River Colony. It was incorporated as a province into the Union (q.v.) of South Africa in 1910, reverting to the name Orange Free State; Bloemfontein became the country's judicial capital.

The practice of sharecropping on farms spread rapidly after the South African War, with Africans commonly giving half their crops to white landowners in return for seed and use of the land. Sharecropping was increasingly attacked by white farmers who wished to commercialize and who argued that the practice left them without adequate labor and undermined proper master-servant relations. With the passage of the Natives Land Act (q.v.) of 1913, many Africans were ejected from white-owned farms. Commercial maize farms in the north and northeast, in what became known as South Africa's maize triangle, formed the heart of the regional economy. After World War II (q.v.), the opening of the goldfields brought much new wealth to the north of the province. The region was renamed the Free State (q.v.) after the democratic national elections of 1994.

ORANGE RIVER. The longest of South Africa's rivers, the Orange stretches some 1,200 miles from its source in Lesotho (formerly Basutoland [q.v.]) to the Atlantic Ocean. It is also the least navigable major river, parts of it becoming a mere chain of pools in the dry winter months. It has nonetheless served as an important source of water for various peoples for at least 2,000 years. It was known to the Nama and Korana (q.v.), who lived along its banks from early in the Christian era, as the Gariep (Great) River, and was named Orange River by an employee of the Dutch East India Company (q.v.) in 1779, for the Dutch prince of the House of Orange. In the mid-20th century a vast scheme was undertaken to dam the Orange and divert some of its waters to the eastern Cape (q.v.); the dam, South Africa's largest, was called the Hendrik Verwoerd (q.v.) Dam, after the assassinated prime minister, when it was opened at the end of the 1960s.

Individual white trekboers (q.v.) began to cross the Orange in the 1760s, and they were followed by missionaries (q.v.) and traders. It became the northern boundary of the Cape in stages (1835, 1847). In 1868, war broke out along the middle Orange River, between Korana pastoralists living in loosely organized bands and white farmers encroaching on their land from the south. Conflict again occurred in 1878–79, during which white farmers supported by Cape mounted forces suppressed Korana resistance with great brutality. From 1880, with its annexation of Griqualand West (q.v.), the Cape gained considerable territory north of the Orange and extended its area of influence yet further when it annexed British Bechuanaland (q.v.) in 1895. As the result of an agreement with the Germans, the border with South West Africa (now Namibia [q.v.]) ran along the northern bank of the river.

ORANGE RIVER SOVEREIGNTY (1848–54). In February 1848, Sir Henry Smith (q.v.), governor of the Cape Colony (q.v.) and high commissioner for South Africa, proclaimed British sovereignty over the land between the Orange River (q.v.) and its major tributary, the Vaal River. Smith wished to create stability on the northern border of the Cape (q.v.), where Griqua (q.v.) and white farmers had clashed for some years. Frequent disputes between white farmers and the Sotho (q.v.) people under Moshoeshoe (q.v.) in the region wearied the British, as did the administrative burden and expense of running the territory. In 1854 the sovereignty was ended when Britain formally recognized the independence of the white colonists under the terms of the Bloemfontein Convention (q.v.).

ORDINANCE 50. Legislation promulgated by Cape Colony (q.v.) authorities in 1828 sought to remedy legal inequalities suffered by the Khoikhoi (q.v.) and others—in the words of the legislation, the "Hottentots and other free persons of colour." It guaranteed the legal right of Khoisan (q.v.) people to own land, lifted restrictions on their freedom of movement by removing the requirement that they carry passes (q.v.), and stressed the need for employers to give service contracts to their laborers.

Its origins lie in part in pressure from humanitarians such as John Philip (q.v.), who used his influence with prominent British politicians to achieve the extension of legal equality between Khoisan and whites. For their part, Cape officials wished to create a freer labor market and foster the emergence of a Khoisan or Coloured (q.v.) elite. Apart from the establishment of the Kat River Settlement (q.v.), however, virtually nothing was done to enable Coloured people to escape their inferior and servile position. Although Ordinance 50 had little effect on master-servant relations, particularly in the frontier (q.v.) districts where distances rendered the legislation ineffective, white farmers in general felt that the ordinance removed controls over vagrancy, and it was thus a source of considerable grievance against the British and Cape authorities during the 1830s.

OSSEWA BRANDWAG. Founded in February 1939 as an Afrikaner (q.v.) cultural organization in the wake of celebrations of the centenary of the Great Trek (q.v.), the Ossewa Brandwag (Afrikaans, "ox-wagon sentinel") became, in the early years of World War II (q.v.), a paramilitary body propagating national socialist ideas. It embarked on sabotage against the war effort, but D. F. Malan (q.v.), leader of the Purified National Party, was able to prevent it from dominating or splitting the Afrikaner nationalist (q.v.) movement. *See also* NATIONAL PARTY.

-P-

PACT GOVERNMENT (1924–33). In the 1924 election campaign, J. B. M. Hertzog (q.v.), leader of the National Party (q.v.), entered a pact with the white Labour Party (q.v.), and once the election was won, the two parties formed a coalition government. The pact gradually fell apart and was finally destroyed by the Great Depression and Hertzog's decision to remain on the gold standard.

PAN AFRICANIST CONGRESS OF AZANIA (PAC). In the 1940s a small group of men within the African National Congress (ANC) (q.v.) began calling themselves Africanists. Led by Anton Lembede (q.v.) until his death in 1947, this group included Robert Mangaliso Sobukwe (q.v.), Potlako Leballo, A. P. Mda, and others who became increasingly unhappy with ANC policy in the 1950s. They opposed the multi-racialism of the Congress Alliance (q.v.), fearing that leadership of the struggle for liberation would be taken over by white and Indian (q.v.) communists, and they rejected the Freedom Charter, particularly those sections guaranteeing minority interests, as well as its declaration that South Africa belonged to all who live in it, black and white. They believed in the slogan "Africa for the Africans" and although their definition of Africans could include whites, they saw most whites as settlers without valid claim to the land they owned.

The Africanists believed that the fostering of a racially assertive nationalism was necessary in order to mobilize the masses, and advocated a militant strategy of mass action involving boycotts (q.v.), strikes (q.v.), civil disobedience, non-cooperation, and taking advantage of opportunities presented by popular protests. They identified their struggle for freedom with that of blacks throughout the African continent, spoke of seeking a United States of Africa, and were inspired by the socialist, anti-imperialist leadership of Kwame Nkrumah of Ghana and Tom Mboya of Kenya. In 1958 they broke away from the ANC, and in April the following year they formally established the PAC. Sobukwe, the leading theoretician among them and a lecturer at the University of the Witwatersrand, was elected its president. The new organization stood for government of the country by Africans for Africans, and the establishment of an Africanist social democracy.

One of the PAC's first acts was organizing a campaign against pass laws in March 1960. Within hours of the launch of the campaign, the Sharpeville massacre (q.v.) occurred. The PAC was then banned (q.v.) on 8 April 1960. Some of its members formed Poqo (meaning *pure*) to promote change by violence, but harsh repression and lack of leadership brought the organization to the brink of disintegration by the end of the 1960s. Internecine rivalries continued among the exiled leadership, based at Dar-es-Salaam in Tanzania. In the mid-1960s the PAC absorbed members of the Coloured People's Congress who rejected the ANC's approach as reformist. For a time, the controversial Potlako Leballo, who had taken over the leadership when Sobukwe was jailed, hoped to wage an armed struggle from Lesotho (*see* BASUTOLAND), and he worked closely with the Lesotho Liberation Army. He was effectively sidelined at a conference in Arusha in 1978, and a rival, David Sibeko, was shot by members of the PAC's armed wing, the Azanian People's Liberation Army (APLA), in Dar-es-Salaam. John Pokela then became leader, but proved weak and ineffective. The PAC in exile failed to win the international support given to the ANC, and APLA achieved little before the 1990s.

When unbanned in February 1990, the PAC continued to refuse to suspend its armed struggle. In 1993 APLA conducted a number of terrorist attacks aimed at white civilians. Members of a church congregation were fired upon in Kenilworth in Cape Town, and shots were fired into a pub in the Cape Town (q.v.) suburb of Observatory. Though the party finally decided to participate in the democratic election of April 1994, many of its members did not support that decision and in the election it received only 1.8 percent of the total vote. At the end of 1996, the lackluster Clarence Makwetu, whose support came mainly from the Eastern Cape (q.v.), was replaced as leader by the former head of the Methodist Church, Stanley Mogoba, and it seemed possible that the PAC might revive itself. In 1997 one of its parliamentarians, Patricia de Lille, read out a list of ANC leaders who the PAC claimed had worked for the apartheid (q.v.) regime as spies.

PASS LAWS. Laws designed to control the movement of blacks; they achieved special notoriety during the apartheid (q.v.) era. Their origins lay in the early 18th-century Cape (q.v.) when slaves (q.v.) were required to carry passes. Such a requirement was extended to Khoikhoi (q.v.) laborers by the end of the century, tying them to the farms. These early provisions were consolidated by the new British administration in 1809, but the Khoikhoi were freed from them by Ordinance 50 (q.v.) in 1828. From the mid-19th century Africans entering the Cape Colony (q.v.) from the east were required to carry passes.

With the growth of the country's first industrial center at Kimberley (q.v.) in the 1870s, a more rigid pass system was introduced by a Griqualand West (q.v.) proclamation in 1872. Though it made no direct mention of race, this system served both to control the flow of African labor to the diamond (q.v.) fields and to regiment the African workers already there. In 1895 the Transvaal (q.v.) enacted similar, more overtly racial legislation: Africans were liable for arrest and imprisonment if they failed to carry passes indicating their employment or authorizing them to seek employment. Pass laws were also used to try to stem the high rate of desertion among African workers in the gold (q.v.) mines (in 1910, 15 percent of all workers deserted). Shortly after Union (q.v.), the Native Labour Regulation Act of 1911 required all male African workers, including foreigners, to carry passes. The pass system helped to keep labor cheap by directing labor where employers required it.

In 1952, the most comprehensive legislation yet was enacted: all Africans over the age of 16 were compelled to produce a pass (renamed *reference book*) on request by any member of the police or any administrative official at any time. The pass carried personal data and details of employment. Parallel to the main police force and law courts, a special police and court system emerged to enforce the pass laws. People appearing before these courts, which came to be known as *commissioners' courts*, were deemed guilty until they proved their innocence; the vast majority of cases regarding pass laws were undefended and often dealt with at the rate of over thirty cases per hour. About 500,000 Africans were arrested each year during the 1960s and 1970s, and in the early 1980s many of these were deported to independent bantustans (q.v.) instead of being tried and imprisoned, in terms of an act of 1972 allowing for the summary deportation of foreigners.

By the early 1980s attempts to enforce the pass laws and control the urbanization of Africans were failing, and in 1986 the government repealed the pass laws. By then an estimated 15 to 20 million people had been arrested, fined, imprisoned, or deported. (For protest against the pass laws, *see* ANTI-PASS CAMPAIGNS.)

PATON, ALAN STEWART (1903–1988). Novelist and liberal politician. Born and educated in Natal (q.v.), Paton was principal of Diepkloof Reformatory for Africans in Johannesburg (q.v.) between 1935 and 1948. His famous novel, *Cry, the Beloved Country* (1948), was begun while he was touring Norway in 1946. Its story of a rural African clergyman searching for his son in the urban environment of Johannesburg amid racial and social tension won international renown, though some critics dismissed the novel as sentimental. Other important novels were *Too Late the Phalarope* (1953) and *Ah, But Your Land Is Beautiful* (1981). Paton wrote two significant biographies, *Hofmeyr* (about J. H. Hofmeyr, Jan Smuts's [q.v.] liberal deputy prime minister, published in 1964) and *Apartheid and the Archbishop* (about Archbishop of Cape Town Geoffrey Clayton, published in 1973), as well as short stories, poetry, and an autobiography, *Towards the Mountain* (1980).

Paton was a founder member of the Liberal Party (q.v.) and became its most prominent member and chairman from the late 1950s until it was disbanded in 1968 following goverment legislation against nonracial political parties. His political views were strongly held and passionately and eloquently argued; he was respected by political leaders across the anti-apartheid spectrum, but he adopted more conservative views in his old age.

PEDI. In the mid-17th century, a Kgatla group called the Pedi moved from the region around modern Pretoria (q.v.) to the Steelpoort River valley, where it gained control of trade routes running from the interior to the Mozambique (q.v.) coast, and established its supremacy over other Sotho-speakers (q.v.) in the area. By the beginning of the 19th century, the Pedi had built up considerable power under Thulare (ca. 1780-1820).

Pedi power was severely disrupted during the Mfecane (q.v.), as well as by internal succession disputes. Their influence was stabilized under Sekwati (ca. 1780-1861), who attracted refugees to a new capital called Phiring, situated in a good defensive position between the Steelpoort and Olifants rivers. Sekwati managed to forge friendly ties with the Zulu (q.v.), but relations with the Swazi remained tense. During the 1840s and 1850s, he also had to deal with hostile Voortrekkers (q.v.) who were encroaching on his territory; their capital at Lydenburg was later subsumed within the South African Republic (q.v.).

Sekwati's successor, Sekhukhune, initially consolidated the power of the Pedi, but years of drought and a series of attacks from the South African Republic and the Swazi chiefdom weakened the Pedi during the 1870s. In 1879, the British broke Pedi power and ended their independence; the Transvaal (q.v.) government then expropriated much of their land and forced many to work as apprentices on white-owned farms.

In the 1950s a Pedi migrant workers' organization (Sebatakgomo) tried to oust chiefs, headmen, and others who accepted Bantu authorities and rural betterment programs. In 1958 a major protest took place in Sekhukhuneland in which those who sought to defend the chieftainship were challenged by the new forces. Conflict broke out again in 1986 in what had by then become the bantustan (q.v.) of Lebowa. Members of the United Democratic Front (q.v.) and the underground African National Congress (q.v.) were involved in this youth revolt.

PHILIP, JOHN (1777–1851). A Congregationalist minister from Aberdeen, Scotland, who arrived at the Cape (q.v.) in 1819, John Philip became the influential superintendent of the London Missionary Society (LMS) (q.v.) until his resignation in 1849. He consolidated and expanded the work of the LMS and campaigned for full legal equality for the colonial Khoikhoi (q.v.). A vigorous polemicist, he published his *Researches in South Africa* in 1828 in England, having returned there to use his influence to lobby British politicians and philanthropists. His lobbying resulted in the recommendation of the House of Commons that free people of color should enjoy equal status with whites (q.v.) and the subsequent passage of Ordinance 50 (q.v.) at the Cape. Philip was also responsible for preventing the implementation of a draft vagrancy law at the Cape in 1834, which would have reimposed many former restrictions on the Khoikhoi. During the 1830s and 1840s, he worked hard to persuade the Cape government to develop a new approach to the frontier (q.v.) through a system of treaties with African and Griqua (q.v.) leaders. He approved the extension of British authority but envisaged that Christianized (q.v.) Coloureds (q.v.) and Africans (q.v.), retaining possession of their land, would live harmoniously with the British on both sides of the colonial borders.

Philip's campaigns and writings alienated white settlers, who demonized him as an interfering cleric. Much historical writing, particularly in the settler and Afrikaner (q.v.) traditions, similarly vilified him, but two classic books by the historian W. M. Macmillan (q.v.) in the 1920s, based on Philip's papers, confirmed his stature. *See also* CORY, GEORGE EDWARD; HISTORIOGRAPHY; THEAL, GEORGE MCCALL.

PIETERMARITZBURG. Named after the Voortrekker (q.v.) leaders Piet Retief (q.v.) and Gerrit Maritz, Pietermaritzburg was founded in 1838 as the capital and seat of government of the Boer Republic of Natalia (now Natal [q.v.]). In the decade after the British annexation in 1843, the immigration of English speakers (q.v.) was encouraged, and a significant proportion of them settled in Pietermaritzburg, which became capital of the crown colony of Natal in 1856. It enjoyed considerable commercial prosperity in the 19th century because of its geographical situation between the interior of southern Africa and the coastal port of Durban (q.v.). Its economic importance declined markedly in relation to that of Durban during the 20th century, but it remained the provincial capital and seat of the Natal division of the Supreme Court. From 1994 it was capital of KwaZulu-Natal (q.v.), one of South Africa's nine provinces in the new democratic dispensation.

PLAATJE, SOLOMON TSHEKISHO (1876–1932). Linguist, writer, journalist, and politician, Sol Plaatje, despite a lack of formal education, mastered eight languages, worked as an interpreter and magistrate's clerk in Mafeking (q.v.) during the South African War (q.v.), and subsequently became editor of three newspapers, including the English-Tswana *Bechuana Gazette*. He was a founder of the South African Native National Congress (later the African National Congress [q.v.]) and served as its first general secretary. He spent several years campaigning against the Natives Land Act (q.v.) of 1913, and his closely researched and powerful attack on the act, *Native Life in South Africa*, was published in 1916. His novel *Mhudi*, written in about 1917, also dealt with dispossession; when it appeared in 1930 it was the first novel in English (q.v.) to be published by a black South African.

POLICE. The South African Police force was formed in 1913 out of various colonial and city police forces that had existed prior to creation of the Union (q.v.) of South Africa. The colonial police model—in which policing was centralized under state control in order to maintain the authority of the government and police were regularly called upon to exercise paramilitary duties—heavily influenced the structure and organization of the force. Another force, the South African Mounted Rifles, was simultaneously established alongside the South African Police; although intended as a regular military force, its peacetime duties chiefly comprised policing among blacks in the rural areas. This body was disbanded in 1920, and its members and areas of concern were incorporated into the South African Police.

Throughout the 20th century, and particularly during the years of apartheid (q.v.), the South African Police portrayed itself as an independent servant of the law, whose duties involved the maintenance of law and order, the protection of life and property, and the investigation and prevention of crime. The police motto, Servamus et Servimus ("We protect and we serve"), was central to the creation of an official image of a civil police force above political manipulation and control. In reality, however, the political, legal, and social circumstances of South Africa ensured that the police played a central role in the maintenance of white political power. Its regulation of the edifice of racial segregationist (q.v.) and apartheid laws undermined the public image of the police as an apolitical nonpartisan body; rather, it was a key institution of the state, which operated to maintain state authority. Given the nature of police activities during the 1970s and 1980s, it is not surprising that critics of apartheid referred with increasing frequency to South Africa as a police state.

The police force comprised almost 6,000 members in 1913, just under half of whom were black; in 1972, it totaled just over 32,000 people, with the same proportion of black recruits. There were only 20 black commissioned officers out of almost 1,800 in 1972, the year in which women (q.v.) were first recruited into the force. The ratio of police per thousand head of population barely changed between 1913 and the mid-1970s; it was only after the Soweto uprising (q.v.) of 1976 that its ranks were significantly boosted, as the state was obliged to rely more heavily on the police to enforce social control. The police force nonetheless experienced considerable difficulty in countering opposition to the state and, despite ever greater allocations in the national budget, remained underresourced and unsophisticated, to the extent that in 1984 the state was obliged to begin using the South African Defence Force (SADF) (q.v.) and citizen reserve forces to police the townships and counter mass opposition to apartheid.

Despite criticisms of the police for its inefficiency, some sections operated with considerable effectiveness. Most notable was the Special Branch, established in 1960 to counter sabotage and other activities subversive of the state. The security police were granted greatly enhanced powers by B. J. Vorster (q.v.), minister of justice in the early 1960s, and gained notoriety because of their pursuit and torture of opponents of apartheid. The underground South African Communist Party (q.v.) was infiltrated, and in the 1970s Craig Williamson, a police spy who had been a student leader at the University of the Witwatersrand, became assistant director of the International University Exchange Fund in Geneva, where he gathered information on anti-apartheid activities. From 1963 to the early 1980s a number of political activists, held under detention-without-trial provisions, died while in police custody. In the mid-1980s some members of the security police abducted and assassinated anti-apartheid activists.

In 1969 the government created a Bureau of State Security (q.v.), popularly known as BOSS even after the name was changed to the National Intelligence Service. It gathered intelligence and undertook covert operations, the budget for which was greatly increased in the mid-1970s. It clashed with the Military Intelligence section of the SADF on a number of occasions in the 1970s, but until the uncovering of the Information scandal (q.v.) revealed something of BOSS's role and power, the Military Intelligence section was subordinated to it.

Widely despised and enormously controversial as the South African police was for its role during the 1970s and 1980s, its reform posed difficult problems during the period of transformation in the 1990s. Steps were taken in 1995 and 1996 to demilitarize the force, with military ranks, for example, being replaced by civilian ones. More intractable problems involved the racial composition of the force (mainly in regard to the lack of senior black appointments), the allocation of resources, the provision of adequate training, and the boosting of police morale as well as widespread public perceptions of its inefficiency and its inability to cope with mainstream policing tasks such as the combating of crime.

POLITICAL VIOLENCE. Political violence has taken many forms in South African history, but in the early 1990s politically related violence reached new proportions. Unlike the Soweto (q.v.) and township (q.v.) revolts of 1976–77 and 1984–87, the violence of the late 1980s and early 1990s was more random and sporadic, involving the occasional massacre, attacks on commuters in trains, and a large number of individual shootings and murders. Beginning in Natal (q.v.), where it became a kind of low-intensity civil war between United Democratic Front (q.v.) and Inkatha (q.v.) supporters, this violence moved to the Witwatersrand (q.v.) in mid-1990. In each year in the early 1990s, on average almost 2,000 people were killed, though such statistics must be viewed with caution.

There is no doubt that criminal elements participated in the violence, and some of what was called political violence was the product of an environment in which law and order had broken down. The African National Congress (q.v.) had called for the townships to be made ungovernable. In Natal especially, local warlords sought to retain control of their areas, and one instance of violence often provoked another, producing a cycle of violence. But much of the violence was also deliberately fomented by members of the security forces. In the early 1990s violence flared up when negotiations reached sensitive phases, and it was clearly designed to throw those negotiations off track. Details of who was responsible emerged slowly. In 1989, Dirk Coetzee, former head of the South African Police's (q.v.) Vlakplaas base outside Pretoria (q.v.), told the newspaper *Vrye Weekblad* of assassinations and other dirty tricks carried out by the police in the 1980s. A commission headed by Judge Louis Harms heard disclosures about the activities of the Civil Cooperation Bureau (q.v.) in 1990, and the Commission of Enquiry Regarding the Prevention of Public Violence and Intimidation (the Goldstone Commission [q.v.]) uncovered evidence of covert operations conducted by a body linked to Military Intelligence. In 1996, General Magnus Malan, the former minister of defense, and others went on trial for the training of an Inkatha hit squad, but they were acquitted. It was the Truth and Reconciliation Commission (q.v.) that did most to uncover information concerning some of the killings in the period to 1994. After the April 1994 election, political violence subsided except in KwaZulu-Natal (q.v.), where it continued at a high level for another 18 months.

PONDOLAND REVOLT (1960–61). The Pondoland Revolt was perhaps the most important of a series of rural revolts that occurred in the late 1950s and early 1960s. The Xhosa (q.v.) people of Pondoland resented the interference of the state in their affairs, and an anti-dipping rebellion culminated in a revolt, during which the police (q.v.) opened fire on protesters at Ngquza Hill. The government declared a state of emergency through Proclamation 400, and as a result thousands of men and women went to jail for indefinite periods. About 20 people from Eastern Pondoland were sentenced to death for the role they played during the revolt.

PORT ELIZABETH. A coastal city in the eastern Cape (q.v.), founded in 1820 and named after the wife of Sir Rufane Donkin, then acting governor of the Cape, Port Elizabeth was the debarkation point for the British settlers of 1820. It developed as the major port in the eastern Cape, second in size only to Cape Town (q.v.), and the chief outlet for the export of wool (q.v.). During the 20th century, it became an important industrial and commercial center, a major base for South Africa's automobile industry, but with the collapse of this industry unemployment in the city soared.

POTCHEFSTROOM. Founded in 1838 by the Voortrekker (q.v.) leader Andries Pretorius, Potchefstroom was the capital of the Transvaal (q.v.) until 1860, when it was superseded as the center of government by the newly founded and more centrally situated Pretoria (q.v.). It then remained an important educational and ecclesiastical center for Afrikaners (q.v.). It is today situated in the North-West Province (q.v.).

PRESS. In the first decades of the 19th century, the only regular publication at the Cape (q.v.) was the *Cape Town Gazette and African Advertiser*. The first newspaper, the *South African Commercial Advertiser*, appeared in 1824 but was closed by Governor Charles Somerset (q.v.). It resumed publication in 1828 with the promise of freedom to publish subject only to the law of libel. Thereafter, a number of English (q.v.) and Dutch (q.v.) newspapers appeared, including the bilingual *De Zuid-Afrikaan* (1830) based in Cape Town (q.v.) and the *Grahams Town Journal* (1831) in the eastern Cape.

Many leading English-language newspapers were established in the second half of the 19th century. The formation of the Argus Printing and Publishing Company in 1866 began the era of managerial newspapers. The two leading newspapers in the Argus stable were the *Cape Argus* (first published in 1857) and the *Star* (1889) in Johannesburg (q.v.). The *Rand Daily Mail* (1902) and the *Sunday Times* (1906), both based in Johannesburg, became part of the South African Associated Newspapers (SAAN) group in 1955. Other important newspapers established toward the end of the 19th century were the country's first daily, the *Cape Times* (1876), and the *Natal Witness* (1881). The first Afrikaans-language newspaper, *Die Patriot* (1876), aimed to promote nascent Afrikaner (q.v.) culture and the Afrikaans (q.v.) language (q.v.). In 1915, Nasionale Pers was established and began to publish the Cape Town–based *De Burger*, a mouthpiece of the National Party (q.v.); the first editor was D. F. Malan (q.v.). The National Party later acquired another voice in the Transvaal (q.v.), in the form of *Die Transvaler* (1937), edited by H. F. Verwoerd (q.v.).

The first journals aimed at a black readership emerged from the missions (q.v.) of the eastern Cape in the mid-19th century and appeared in both English and Xhosa (q.v.). An independent black-controlled press began with the establishment in King William's Town in 1884 of *Imvo Zabantsundu* (q.v.), under the editorship of J. T. Jabavu (q.v.). Another prominent newspaper was *Ilanga lase Natal* (1903), founded by J. L. Dube (q.v.). *Indian Opinion* (1903), a weekly founded by Mohandas Gandhi (q.v.) in 1903 to serve an Indian (q.v.) readership, remained financially independent, but from the 1920s most of the black press was taken over by white business interests, who were attracted by the market it served, as well as by some concern about the potential consequences of independent black journalism.

During the apartheid (q.v.) era, newspapers and magazines had to cope with increasing numbers of laws affecting press freedom. The most prominent newspaper to cease publication in the 1950s was the *Guardian*, an organ of the Communist Party of South Africa (q.v.), which was banned (q.v.) in 1950, but re-emerged sporadically under different names until 1963. The *World*, a newspaper that had more than 150,000 black readers, was banned in 1977, and the *Post*, which took its place, was closed in 1981. By this time, more than a hundred laws and regulations restricted press freedom, particularly in the reporting of matters concerning the military, the police (q.v.), the prisons, black politics (particularly exile politics), and issues affecting national security. Some English-language newspapers, of which the *Rand Daily Mail* was the most prominent, were outspoken critics of government policy, but the closure of this newspaper by the management of SAAN in 1985, on the grounds that it was no longer commercially viable, provoked considerable controversy, and its owners stood accused of capitulating to government pressure and fears about the consequences of editorial independence. An independent newspaper, the *Weekly Mail* (1985), founded by former *Rand Daily Mail* journalists, managed to survive as the flagship publication of an embattled alternative press during the late 1980s.

Many of the draconian laws governing freedom of the press were withdrawn or were disregarded by the authorities after 1990. Faced with increasing competition from other media, the press underwent major changes, with the Argus Group becoming Independent Newspaper Holdings and the SAAN group Times Media Ltd.

PRETORIA. Now in Gauteng Province (q.v.), Pretoria was founded in 1855 by Marthinus Pretorius, son of the Voortrekker (q.v.) leader Andries Pretorius, after whom it is named. It became the capital of the Transvaal (q.v.) in 1860 and the administrative capital of the Union (q.v.) of South Africa in 1910. As headquarters of numerous government departments and South Africa's civil service, it became the political heart of the country, although from 1910 the national Parliament sat in Cape Town (q.v.). After 1948, when the government fell under the control of Afrikaner nationalists (q.v.), the word "Pretoria" became synonymous with the South African government and apartheid (q.v.), but it was here, on 10 May 1994, at the Union Buildings, that Nelson Mandela was sworn in as South Africa's first democratically elected president.

PRETORIA MINUTE. An agreement between the National Party (q.v.) government and the African National Congress (ANC) (q.v.), known as the Pretoria Minute, was signed on 6 August 1990. According to the document, "In the interest of moving as speedily as possible toward a negotiated political settlement and in the context of the agreement reached, the ANC announced that it was now suspending all armed actions with immediate effect. As a result of this, no further armed actions and related activities by the ANC and its military wing Umkhonto weSizwe (MK) [q.v.] will take place." This major concession by the ANC did not win any significant immediate reward but was an essential preliminary to formal negotiations. The ANC subsequently made it clear that MK had not disbanded, and it refused to disclose the whereabouts of its arms caches.

PRINGLE, THOMAS (1789–1834). The Scottish-born librarian, journalist, and poet Thomas Pringle, who settled in Cape Town (q.v.) in 1820, published and edited the *South African Journal* and the *South African Commercial Advertiser* during the 1820s. He clashed with Governor Charles Somerset (q.v.) over issues relating to freedom of the fledgling Cape press (q.v.). He is also recognized for his poetry, in particular his *African Sketches* (1834).

PROGRESSIVE PARTY. In 1959, 11 liberal members of Parliament from the United Party (UP) (q.v.) broke with that party over its refusal to challenge more effectively the apartheid (q.v.) policies of the National Party (q.v.) government. They then established the Progressive Party. Although it rejected all forms of racial discrimination, the party decided in 1968, in the face of new legislation barring mixed-race political parties, to carry on as a whites-only party, effectively ditching its few black members. Initially, like the Liberal Party (q.v.) before it, it advocated a qualified franchise (q.v.), on the recommendation of a commission under the chairmanship of a lawyer and former member of Parliament, Donald Molteno (1908–72).

Helen Suzman (q.v.), a doughty fighter for human rights, was for 13 years the only Progressive member of Parliament. From 1974 the party's parliamentary strength began to grow, helped by the disintegration of the UP. In 1975 it amalgamated with the small Reform Party, and after it was joined by a further breakaway from the UP, it was renamed the Progressive Federal Party (PFP). After the general election of 1977 it became the official parliamentary opposition. Under the influence of the charismatic Frederik van Zyl Slabbert (b. 1942), a former professor of sociology at the University of Stellenbosch, who was returned for the Rondebosch constituency in 1974, it adopted universal suffrage as its policy. In 1979, Slabbert took over as leader. In February 1986, however, angered by the refusal of P. W. Botha (q.v.) to give ground, Slabbert suddenly announced that he was leaving the tricameral Parliament (q.v.) because he had come to realize it was incapable of fundamental change. The loss of Slabbert and Alex Boraine (b. 1931) weakened the party, which in 1987 lost its position as official opposition to the right-wing Conservative Party (q.v.). Early in 1989, the PFP merged with other parties to the left of the government to form the Democratic Party (q.v.). *See also* TRUTH AND RECONCILIATION COMMISSION.

PURIFIED NATIONAL PARTY. *See* NATIONAL PARTY.

-Q-

QWAQWA. The bantustan (q.v.) Qwaqwa (formerly Witzieshoek) was created in 1974 for the southern Sotho (q.v.) from a reserve (q.v.) in the Orange Free State (q.v.), which had originally been granted by President J. H. Brand (q.v.) to a southern Sotho group headed by a relative of Moshoeshoe (q.v.). It bordered Lesotho (formerly Basutoland [q.v.]). As squatters (q.v.) were evicted in the Orange Free State with the implementation of the Natives Land Act (q.v.) of 1913, the population increased, but the land was mountainous and barren, and most men had to work as migrants (q.v.). Discontent grew until in early 1950 a series of skirmishes, later called a rebellion, took place. The reserve housed 20,000 people in 1960, but there were 300,000 in the bantustan by 1980 and well over a million by 1990, as those classified Sotho were forcibly relocated there. Most lived in the capital, Phuthaditjhaba, and their main source of income was the remittances of migrant laborers working on the Witwatersrand (q.v.) or in the Orange Free State. In April 1994 the area again fell under the Free State (q.v.) administration.

-R-

RACIAL INEQUALITY. South Africa remained throughout the 20th century one of the most unequal societies on earth. In 1995, the poorest 40 percent of households earned less than 6 percent of total income, while the richest 10 percent earned more than half the total income. This inequality was largely related to race. Africans made up 76 percent of the population, but the African share of income amounted to only 29 percent of the total. Whites, who made up less than 13 percent of the population, received 58.5 percent of total income. Per capita, whites earned 9.5 times the income of blacks and lived, on average, 11.5 years longer. In 1992, the average monthly income per capita was R1,572 for whites, R523 for Indians (q.v.), R325 for Coloureds (q.v.), and R165 for Africans.

By the 1950s white poverty had largely been eliminated, and only in the 1990s did it again emerge as a noticeable phenomenon. In the 1990s, the gap between white and black narrowed, but the gap between a new black elite and the African poor widened. Although class became more important than race, the threat of race conflict remained because of the close correlation between race and class.

RACIAL SEGREGATION. Some historians trace the origins of racial segregation to the first white settlers, but others have highlighted the importance of ideas that came from Britain in the 19th century or have pointed to Theophilus Shepstone (q.v.) in Natal (q.v.) as the first to put segregationist policies into practice. Most scholars now agree that an ideology of racial separation did not develop until the early 20th century, that a full-scale set of segregationist policies was not implemented until after the creation of the Union (q.v.) of South Africa, and that apartheid (q.v.) was a more developed and comprehensively applied form of the racial segregation already in place before 1948.

RACISM. The Europeans who settled at the Cape Colony (q.v.) in the 17th century, like those who went to other parts of the world, looked down upon the indigenous people as inferior, heathen, and barbarous. Scholars have suggested that because the Dutch, and the British settlers who followed them, came from Protestant, bourgeois, and northern European backgrounds, they were more racially prejudiced than southern Europeans would have been. At the Cape, the Dutch found people, Khoikhoi (q.v.), and San (q.v.), whom they regarded as among the lowest forms of human life and sometimes as not truly human at all. Although cohabitation between whites and people of color frequently took place in the Dutch East India Company (q.v.) period, there were few mixed marriages, and the offspring of mixed unions joined the nonwhite groups. Racial prejudice imported from Europe was reinforced by the system of racially based slavery (q.v.) at the Cape and by the conflict between white and black on the eastern frontier (q.v.). The weight some writers once attached to the Calvinism of the Dutch as a cause of racism can be discounted.

Although racially prejudiced, the early white settlers did not develop a systematic racial ideology. This emerged as the social order was challenged by the ideas of British humanitarians in the early 19th century. Racism was then used to justify dispossession of blacks and their subordination and oppression. With the creation of an industrial society, first at Kimberley (q.v.) and then on the Witwatersrand (q.v.), a vast array of discriminatory measures came into being to provide a cheap African labor force, and these were buttressed by a racist ideology. In the 20th century racism was perhaps most blatantly expressed by those whites who were threatened by African competition for jobs in the urban areas.

By the late 1970s, Afrikaner (q.v.) leaders had to some extent dropped their ideological commitment to racial discrimination, because the cooptation of some blacks (especially Coloureds [q.v.] and Indians [q.v.]) was seen as necessary for the continued maintenance of white supremacy. Conservative Afrikaners, and perhaps a majority of the white electorate, remained firmly committed to racist beliefs. With the collapse of apartheid (q.v.) and the transition to democracy, blatant white racism largely went underground, and the extent to which racist beliefs and practices continued became more difficult to assess. It did seem, however, that the advent of African majority rule made anti-African racism in the Coloured community, especially in the Western Cape (q.v.), more overt.

RAILWAYS. Construction of the country's first railway, which linked Cape Town (q.v.) to Stellenbosch and Wellington, began in 1859, and in 1860 a line of two miles was opened in Durban (q.v.). After 1870, with the growth of Kimberley (q.v.), major construction began. Because of the distance from the coast to the diamond (q.v.) fields and the absence of intermediate traffic, the new lines were state ventures. Competition between the coastal towns for the interior trade led to the building of separate lines from Cape Town, Port Elizabeth (q.v.), and East London to the diamond fields. After the discovery of gold (q.v.) in the Transvaal (q.v.) in 1886, both the Cape Colony (q.v.) and Natal (q.v.) extended their lines to the Witwatersrand (q.v.). The link with the Cape was completed in 1892, that with Natal in 1895. The Transvaal government was keen to develop a rail link with the non-British port of Delagoa Bay (q.v.), and although the Netherlands–South African Railway Company responsible for construction experienced financial difficulties, the line was completed in 1894. In the same year, a line from the Cape, which bypassed the

Transvaal and headed for Central Africa through Bechuanaland (q.v.), had reached Mafeking (q.v.). By the end of the century, a considerable portion of the country's present rail network had been completed.

After the South African War (q.v.), a single central South African Railways was established, in 1903; this underpinned the political union (q.v.) of the country in 1910 and provided an essential infrastructure for the later development of the manufacturing (q.v.) industry.

RAMAPHOSA, CYRIL (b. 1953). A lawyer by training and a supporter of black consciousness (q.v.) in the 1970s, Cyril Ramaphosa was imprisoned a number of times and on one occasion spent 17 months in solitary confinement. In 1982 he became the first general secretary of the National Union of Mineworkers. He took the union into the charterist Congress of South African Trade Unions (q.v.) in 1985 and called his members out on strike in 1985 and 1987. The negotiation and settlement skills he learned in the union proved useful in the early 1990s, following his election as secretary-general of the African National Congress (ANC) (q.v.) in July 1991, when he became that organization's chief negotiator at the Convention for a Democratic South Africa (q.v.) and then the Multi-Party Negotiating Forum (q.v.).

Ramaphosa and Roelf Meyer (q.v.), who became the chief negotiator for the National Party (q.v.) in 1992, established a bond of trust, which began, it is said, when the two men were trout fishing in August 1991 and Ramaphosa removed a fishhook that had been embedded in Meyer's finger. He and Meyer met more than 40 times between June and September 1992 in an effort to get their parties talking again when negotiations threatened to break down. He remained the chief ANC negotiator until the agreement on the interim constitution was reached in November 1993, and he then became head of the Constitutional Assembly (q.v.) in 1994 and continued in that post until the successful completion of the final constitution. In 1997 he moved into the business world, taking a top post in the leading black-empowerment consortium, New Africa Investments.

RAMPHELE, MAMPHELA (b. 1947). While training as a medical doctor at the University of Natal, Mamphela Ramphele worked closely with Steve Biko (q.v.). She later bore his son after he was murdered by the security police. One of the first black consciousness (q.v.) activists to be detained, she was banished to a remote part of the northern Transvaal (q.v.), where she started the Ithuseng health clinic. After her banning (q.v.) order was lifted, she moved to Cape Town (q.v.), first to help with the Carnegie inquiry into the roots of poverty—she became coauthor, with Francis Wilson, of the final report, entitled *Uprooting Poverty* (1989)—and then as a researcher at the University of Cape Town. There she gained a doctorate in anthropology and was appointed a deputy vice chancellor. In 1995 she was elected the university's principal and vice chancellor.

RAND REVOLT (1922). The 1922 rebellion of white miners and others against the government of Jan Smuts (q.v.) began as a strike on the coal and gold (q.v.) mines, at a time of depression, against the relaxation of the job color bar (q.v.) that would have given jobs to blacks instead of whites. The strike (q.v.) escalated into a large-scale uprising, and Smuts used the full might of the state to suppress it. About 200 people were killed. The brutal way in which the revolt was put down was a factor in Smuts's defeat in the 1924 election.

RANDLORDS. Men of diverse class and national origins made fortunes from their control of the gold (q.v.) mines of the Witwatersrand (q.v.). By the mid-1890s, some of these randlords believed that their collective interests were being thwarted by the Transvaal (q.v.) government. They resented its failure to provide an adequate and stable labor force, as well as its monopolistic control of dynamite, its concessions to the Netherlands–South African Railway Company, and its sales of liquor to African laborers. *See also* RAILWAYS.

Writing in 1900, J. A. Hobson blamed the randlords for both the Jameson Raid (q.v.) and the South African War (q.v.). But while many randlords aligned themselves with British imperial objectives, some supported Paul Kruger (q.v.), and most did not want the mines disrupted by conflict. The view that the randlords determined British policy and exerted major influence on Sir Alfred Milner (q.v.) between 1895 and 1899 is now discredited. That the interests of the randlords came largely to coincide with those of British imperial policy makers did not mean that the mining magnates were able to dictate imperial policy.

RECONSTRUCTION AND DEVELOPMENT PROGRAMME (RDP). The major policy initiative of the government of National Unity (q.v.), the RDP, created in 1994, emerged from discussion documents put together by the Congress of South African Trade Unions (q.v.). The African National Congress (q.v.) then advocated such a program as part of its election manifesto for the April 1994 election.

Accepted by all parties in Parliament in 1994, the RDP was an integrated, socioeconomic plan to meet basic needs and develop potential and was a vision for the fundamental restructuring of society. A separate ministry was set up under Jay Naidoo. In the first year, free health care was provided for children and pregnant mothers, as were free meals for children at primary schools, and electrification and provision of water advanced rapidly. Major delivery problems were soon experienced, however, and there was much criticism of unnecessary bureaucracy. In 1996, when Naidoo's separate ministry was closed down, responsibility for coordinating RDP spending shifted to Deputy President Thabo Mbeki's (q.v.) office. This went with a new recognition of the importance of economic growth for the achievement of the RDP's goals. The government's Growth, Employment, and Redistribution policy (q.v.), with its emphasis on fiscal discipline as a way to promote foreign investment, then became the main focus of government policy, rather than the RDP itself.

RECORD OF UNDERSTANDING. Perhaps the most important single event in the transition period after 1990 was the signing of a Record of Understanding on 26 September 1992 between the National Party (q.v.) government and the African National Congress (ANC) (q.v.), which followed the Bisho massacre (q.v.) and enabled negotiations to be resumed. One of the preconditions the ANC set for such an agreement was the release of political prisoners, including three who had been convicted of murder. F. W. de Klerk (q.v.) was especially reluctant to accede to this demand, particularly the release of Robert McBride, whose bomb placed in Magoo's bar on the Durban (q.v.) beachfront in 1985 had killed three people, but he agreed to it in the interests of further negotiation. The agreement was angrily repudiated by Mangosuthu Buthelezi (q.v.), who was annoyed at the way he had been sidelined and at the provisions for the fencing of hostels and a ban (q.v.) on the carrying of "traditional" weapons in public, two measures that appeared to him to be directed against the interests of his Inkatha (q.v.) Freedom Party.

REITZ, FRANCIS WILLIAM (1844–1934). A lawyer by training, Francis Reitz was president of the Orange Free State (q.v.) from 1889 until 1895, when he moved to the Transvaal (q.v.) to serve as a judge and as state secretary in Paul Kruger's (q.v.) government. He was the first president of the Senate of the Union (q.v.) of South Africa.

REPUBLIC. Following World War I, Jan Smuts (q.v.) accepted South Africa's position as a dominion in the British Empire and then the Commonwealth (q.v.), and he realized that many English-speaking (q.v.) South Africans had deep ties with Britain and other parts of the Empire and the Commonwealth. During World War II (q.v.), some Afrikaners (q.v.), H. F. Verwoerd (q.v.) among them, advocated the establishment of a Boer (q.v.) republic, which would be Christian-National in character and in which English (q.v.) would be only a second language (q.v.). After the war, realizing that achieving such a republic was impractical, republicans argued for a democratic republic in which English speakers would have full rights. After being elected in 1948, D. F. Malan's (q.v.) priority was to consolidate the National Party (NP) (q.v.) in power. He said that a republic would come about only after a referendum of whites, and throughout the 1950s the NP had too precarious a hold on power for them to risk a referendum defeat.

In January 1960, Verwoerd announced in Parliament that the time to establish a republic had arrived. The republic would be democratic and Christian, and the equality of the two official languages would remain. There would be no drastic constitutional change: the governor-general would be replaced by a state president, chosen by Parliament, who would be the constitutional head of state and above politics. Verwoerd deliberately played down the changes that a republic would bring in order to gain votes in the referendum on the issue. He accepted the idea that the new republic would be a member of the Commonwealth, though he preferred one outside that body.

Verwoerd gained support from his forthright reply to Harold Macmillan's (q.v.) Wind of Change speech (q.v.), from his handling of the Sharpeville (q.v.) crisis, and by the fact that he survived an assassination attempt at the Rand Easter Show in Johannesburg (q.v.) in April: some attributed his remarkable recovery, after he was shot in the face by a deranged farmer, David Pratt, to divine providence. The chaos, which erupted when the Belgian Congo obtained its independence at the end of June 1960, encouraged whites to support the strong South African prime minister. In the referendum campaign held in October 1960, Verwoerd appealed to English-speaking whites (q.v.) to support a republic as a way to bring about white unity; the NP warned that the chaos of the Congo would come to South Africa if it did not become a republic. Of the whites who participated in the referendum, 52 percent—a majority of 74,580 votes—voted for a republic. Verwoerd had all along said that a simple majority would be sufficient. Few English speakers voted for the republic, fearing that it might mean leaving the Commonwealth and cause South Africa to become isolated in the world. Some in Natal (q.v.) spoke of secession, but, as it had been in 1909, that was a pipe dream.

Verwoerd had promised to do everything he could to retain South Africa's membership in the Commonwealth, but when he attended a meeting of Commonwealth prime ministers in London in March 1961, he came under pressure over his government's apartheid (q.v.) policies. When it seemed that South Africa's application to remain in the Commonwealth as a republic might be rejected, he withdrew it and remarked, "No self-respecting member of any voluntary organization could, in view of . . . the degree of interference shown in what are South Africa's domestic affairs, be expected to wish to retain membership in what is now becoming a pressure group." He predicted the breakup of the Commonwealth. On his return to South Africa, his supporters welcomed him back and proclaimed that his journey had ended in triumph and that providence had produced a miracle. The Republic of South Africa came into being on Union Day, 31 May 1961, with C. R. Swart, a former minister of justice, the first president.

RESERVES. As whites conquered more and more territory in the 19th century, small portions were set aside for various black groups. In Natal (q.v.), Theophilus Shepstone (q.v.) was the first to implement a comprehensive reserve policy. Reserves in Natal and elsewhere became reservoirs of labor, from which migrant (q.v.) laborers departed for the white cities and farms to work. In the 1950s and after, the reserves were incorporated into the bantustan policy (q.v.) of the apartheid (q.v.) regime.

RETIEF, PEITER (1780–1838). An unsuccessful businessman in Grahamstown (q.v.), Piet Retief left the Cape Colony (q.v.) in 1837 and became leader of the Voortrekkers (q.v.), advising them to move into Natal (q.v.). Offered land there by Dingane (q.v.), the Zulu (q.v.) king, he and his party were being entertained at the Zulu capital when the king suddenly ordered that the white visitors be killed. Other trekkers avenged Retief's death at the Battle of Blood River (q.v.).

RHARHABE (ca. 1722–82). A Xhosa (q.v.) leader and the son of the paramount chief Phalo, Rharhabe lost a dispute for succession with his brother Gcaleka during the 1770s and moved to the west of the Kei River with his followers, where he consolidated his power. This rift among the Xhosa people weakened them as whites began to encroach upon their land toward the end of the 18th century.

RHODES, CECIL JOHN (1853–1902). Imperialist, mining magnate, and politician, Cecil Rhodes, the son of an English parson, arrived in Natal (q.v.) in 1870 to join his brother Herbert on a cotton farm, but at the end of 1871 he moved to Kimberley (q.v.), where he began to work as a speculative digger on the diamond (q.v.) fields. He built his initial wealth through a pumping contract for the removal of water from submerged claims, some of which he was then able to buy. With the goal of controlling the entire production of diamonds at Kimberley, in 1880 he established the De Beers (q.v.) Mining Company, which owned 90 claims to the De Beers mine, and by 1887 had secured ownership of the entire De Beers mine. In 1888 he formed De Beers Consolidated Mines, which had the monopoly he desired and which brought him vast profits. The same year, he acquired an important stake in the gold (q.v.) mines of the Witwatersrand (q.v.), and by 1895 his Consolidated Gold Fields of South Africa Company had become an even larger source of income than De Beers, though he was personally less involved in its operation.

Rhodes used his base in Kimberley to further a political career: from 1880, when Griqualand West (q.v.) was incorporated into the Cape Colony (q.v.), until his death, he served as a Cape parliamentarian and devoted much of his time to attempting to limit Transvaal (q.v.) influence in the subcontinent. He secured an alliance with Jan Hofmeyr's (q.v.) Afrikaner Bond (q.v.) and was thus able to become prime minister of the Cape in 1890 with the backing of Cape agrarian interests as well as his traditional mining allies. As prime minister, he was responsible for the passage of the Glen Grey Act (q.v.) (1894), designed in part to provide labor for the mines, as well as the takeover of Pondoland, the last independent area between the Cape and Natal, which completed the annexation of the Transkeian (q.v.) territories by the Cape. In 1895 he plotted to overthrow the Transvaal government, but the failure of the Jameson Raid (q.v.) forced him to resign as prime minister and alienated him from much of his former Cape Afrikaner (q.v.) support. Although he retained the support of English speakers (q.v.) in the Cape, his political career was effectively over, particularly as his health deteriorated after 1897.

From the late 1880s much of Rhodes's time was occupied with promoting white settlement in the area north of the Transvaal, which was to bear his name for more than 80 years. His chief instrument in settling what became known as Rhodesia was his British South Africa Company (q.v.).

RIVONIA TRIAL (1963–64). The High Command of Umkhonto weSizwe (q.v.), which comprised those who were arrested at Lilliesleaf farm in Rivonia, outside Johannesburg (q.v.), were tried for high treason, along with Nelson Mandela (q.v.), who was already in jail when the others were arrested. They faced a possible death sentence, but in the event, eight were found guilty of sabotage and sentenced to life imprisonment. The black prisoners were taken from the courtroom to Robben Island (q.v.). In his famous statement from the dock, Mandela spoke of being prepared to die for the ideal of a democratic and free society.

ROAD TO THE NORTH. Also called the missionaries' (q.v.) road, the Road to the North was the corridor linking the Cape Colony (q.v.) to Central Africa through the territory annexed by Britain as Bechuanaland (q.v.) in 1885. It lay on the outer western limits of the pastoral farming region, just within the rainfall belt averaging 15 inches or more per year; further west lay the Kalahari Desert. Transvaal (q.v.) farmers moved into the area during the 1880s, when two small republics, Stellaland and Goshen, were formed on the western border of the Transvaal. Cecil Rhodes (q.v.) feared that, were the Transvaal to secure a hold over the road, further British expansion would be checked, the route used by migrant (q.v.) laborers to Kimberley (q.v.) would be threatened, and territory that might include undiscovered diamonds (q.v.) would be lost to his control. British officials were persuaded that the Transvaal's westward expansion should be halted in order to prevent a possible linkup with the territory that Germany had acquired in South West Africa (now Namibia [q.v.]) in 1884. A British protectorate was thus established in Bechuanaland in 1885. During the 1890s, Rhodes built a railway (q.v.) along the route from Kimberley (q.v.) to the north, skirting the Transvaal.

ROBBEN ISLAND. A flat island guarding the entrance to Table Bay at Cape Town (q.v.), Robben Island is known especially as a political prison—South Africa's Alcatraz—that housed Nelson Mandela (q.v.) and others. Before 1652 it was used as a place to leave letters and occasionally as a prison for sailors; during Dutch and British rule at the Cape (q.v.) it continued to be used as a prison for both criminals and political prisoners, housing, among others, a number of leading Xhosa (q.v.) chiefs in the 1860s. From 1846 until 1931, however, it was used mainly to accommodate chronic sick, those who were insane, and lepers. During World War II (q.v.), troops were stationed there, and it was used by the South African Navy until 1961.

For 30 years thereafter, Robben Island housed political prisoners of the apartheid (q.v.) government. A brutal hellhole, it was also an improvised university, where the prisoners taught each other and their warders. After a hunger strike by prisoners in 1966, conditions began to improve. African National Congress (ANC) (q.v.) and Pan Africanist Congress (q.v.) prisoners were able to discuss ideology and policy, and a number of those who arrived after 1976 on the island as black consciousness (q.v.) sympathizers left as ANC supporters. In 1982, Mandela and a few of his colleagues were moved from Robben Island to Pollsmoor prison on the mainland. The last criminal prisoners left in 1996, and the island then became a heritage site, visited by tourists in large numbers. It was presented as a symbol of both oppression and resistance to oppression.

ROCK ART. Southern Africa is perhaps the richest storehouse of prehistoric art in the world; on the eastern slopes of the Drakensberg (q.v.) alone, there are more than 30,000 individual paintings. Most paintings on rock are to be found either in the mountainous regions of the southwestern and eastern Cape (q.v.) or in the Drakensberg; engravings are more common in the central interior plateau, on rocks and boulders of various sizes in the open veld (q.v.). The oldest known painting (from a site in Namibia [q.v.]) dates from about 26,000 years ago; the earliest engraving is about 10,000 years old. The most recent paintings date from the second half of the 19th century. Subject matter varies greatly, and a multiplicity of human activities are depicted, as well as animal characterizations and geometric patterns. Later paintings reveal a greater range of color, more detail, and a wider variety of subject matter than earlier ones.

This rock art, distinguished by its quantity, excellence, and detail, provides an indispensable record of San (q.v.) life, history, and, particularly, religious belief. It was once believed to comprise mere artistic representations of the immediate environment, but scholars have now shown that it is closely associated with the trance experiences of shamans, or medicine people, who were the bridge between the physical and spiritual worlds. They played a central role in using spiritual power to resolve social conflict, cure the sick, and control rain and the movement of game. Their insights into the spiritual realm were painted or engraved for members of the hunting communities to see, giving people visual reminders of the power that links people, animals, and the environment, particularly during times of change and stress.

ROLONG. The name *Rolong*, which denotes a Tswana-speaking (q.v.) Sotho (q.v.) group, is derived from the group's legendary chief, Morolong. In the early 18th century, under their powerful ruler Tau, the Rolong dominated the northern Cape (q.v.) and southwestern Transvaal (q.v.) regions. Their power was built through alliances with other groups, exploitation of herding and hunting opportunities, and the creation of extensive trading networks, which stretched as far as present-day Namibia (q.v.). They built large stone-walled towns, including Taung (q.v.), their capital, and Dithakong (q.v.), later a center of Tlhaping (q.v.) power. After Tau's death, Rolong power was eclipsed: they split into four groups, all of which experienced disruption during the 1820s. Many sought refuge at Thaba Nchu, on land that was to become part of the eastern Orange Free State (q.v.).

ROMAN CATHOLIC CHURCH. Roman Catholics were prohibited from public worship at the Cape (q.v.) until the Church Ordinance of 1804, which established religious toleration. The authorities remained ambivalent toward Roman Catholicism, however, even after the appointment in 1837 of the first vicar apostolic for South Africa, Father Raymund Griffith. The spread of Catholicism was slow in the face of Protestant hostility; in particular, mission (q.v.) work among Africans was delayed until the late 19th century because of Protestant opposition. The most famous Catholic mission center, Mariannhill, outside Durban (q.v.), was founded in 1882 by contemplative Trappist monks, who later established daughter houses throughout Natal (q.v.).

During the 20th century, Catholicism experienced significant growth, among both whites (q.v.) and Africans (q.v.), despite the antagonism of the Dutch Reformed Church (q.v.) and the National Party (q.v.) government. The hierarchy of the church was often cautious in its confrontation with state authorities during the apartheid (q.v.) era, although from 1952 the South African Catholic Bishops' Conference was critical of apartheid policies. From the 1970s protests grew stronger, and the Catholic Church took the lead among the churches in opening schools to children of all races despite laws forbidding it.

By the 1980s, the Roman Catholic Church had more than 2.5 million adherents in South Africa, making it the largest single Christian denomination in the country (although it was the third-largest Christian grouping after the African independent churches [q.v.] and the Dutch Reformed Church [q.v.]). More than 80 percent of the church's members were black people. *See also* CHRISTIANITY.

RUBICON SPEECH. Major reforms were widely expected in the speech President P. W. Botha (q.v.) was to make to the Natal (q.v.) congress of the National Party (q.v.) in Durban (q.v.) on 15 August 1985, and Botha himself spoke of his speech as "crossing the Rubicon." But the address as delivered ruled out significant concessions to South Africa's black population, and Botha explicitly rejected demands that apartheid (q.v.) be abandoned. Dashing hopes, the speech led directly to the imposition of economic sanctions (q.v.), and there was an immediate flight of capital from the country. Foreign banks, led by Chase Manhattan, refused to roll over their loans. The rand fell sharply in value. The country had to wait until 2 February 1990 for the speech that did mark a major change of direction and, hence, a real "crossing of the Rubicon": that given by F. W. de Klerk (q.v.) unbanning the African National Congress (q.v.) and other organizations.

-S-

SAN. The earliest people who lived in southern Africa were hunter-gatherers. They were widely dispersed across the subcontinent, in a variety of habitats, with the probable exception of areas that were thickly forested. Their lifestyle has often been characterized as precarious, but it was probably relatively stable and secure. Hunter-gatherers had an extensive and profound knowledge of their immediate environment, which they systematically exploited for their survival. They utilized an enormous number of plants (probably more than 60 percent of their diet was gathered) as well as game, smaller animals, and some insects. They lived in small, loosely knit bands, based on the family unit, which facilitated nomadic behavior. During the 18th and 19th centuries, however, they were mercilessly hunted down by white settlers, and large numbers were exterminated. As they came under pressure, they retreated to the deserts and the mountains. From the Drakensberg (q.v.), in particular, they launched raids on cattle-keeping people and their stock in the 19th century, before being overpowered and eliminated. Those who survived were increasingly threatened by new forms of economic activity, and only in the remoteness of the deserts on the fringes of South Africa have a small number of people been able to sustain a mainly hunter-gatherer way of life.

The word *San,* used by Khoikhoi (q.v.) herders at the Cape (q.v.) to describe their hunter-gatherer neighbors, was probably never used by the hunter-gatherers to describe themselves, for they had no need to distinguish themselves from pastoralists or agriculturists. *Sa* ("to inhabit") probably implied a recognition of the San as the original inhabitants of the land. As *sab* means "bush," it is possible that *San* was translated literally as "Bushman." In the 1650s, the Dutch settlers at the Cape heard the term *Sonqua,* which probably meant "poor people," used by herders to describe hunter-gatherer groups who lived without domesticated animals in the mountains to the north of Table Bay. By the 1680s, colonists spoke of "Bosjesmanne" or variants, later "Boesmanne" and "Bushmen," a term frequently used, in a derogatory sense, to describe any marginal community, including dispossessed herders and even runaway slaves (q.v.).

The word *San* came into use again during the 1960s, when historians, anthropologists, and ethnographers wanted an alternative to the belittling *Bushman*. Recently, it has been recognized that *San* barely differs from *Bushman*, in that it is probably no more than a translation and was most likely as disparaging; hence the word *Bushman* has come back into usage.

SANCTIONS. Many different kinds of sanctions were imposed on South Africa under the apartheid (q.v.) regime between 1960 and 1990. Among the most important were the mandatory United Nations (q.v.) arms embargo (q.v.) of November 1977, the financial sanctions that followed P. W. Botha's (q.v.) Rubicon speech (q.v.) in August 1985, and those in the United States (U.S.) Comprehensive Anti-Apartheid Act (CAAA) of 1986, passed over the veto of President Ronald Reagan. There was a lively debate within South Africa on the efficacy of sanctions: Desmond Tutu (q.v.), archbishop of Cape Town, was a leading proponent of sanctions as an alternative to violence, but Helen Suzman (q.v.) of the Progressive Party (q.v.) and Mangosuthu Buthelezi (q.v.) of Inkatha (q.v.), among others, argued that sanctions would only strengthen white resolve not to change and would hurt the poor and create further unemployment. There is no doubt that the sanctions imposed did help persuade the government to accept the need to negotiate with the African National Congress (ANC) (q.v.), but their precise role in bringing about negotiations remains open to debate.

From 1990 the ANC used the removal of sanctions as a way of keeping pressure on the F. W. de Klerk (q.v.) government, arguing that there should be no lifting of sanctions until change was irreversible. But there was a gradual relaxation of sanctions: the CAAA was terminated in July 1991 after U.S. president George Bush agreed that the de Klerk government had met the conditions laid down in the law. Nevertheless, 139 state and local sanctions remained in place in the United States. Then in November 1993, U.S. president Bill Clinton removed further sanctions, including the ban on the United States's voting for an International Monetary Fund loan for South Africa. Other sanctions, including the United Nations arms embargo, were not lifted until after the election of the democratic government in April 1994.

SANDILE (1820–78). Sandile was the son of Ngqika (q.v.) and chief of the Rharhabe (q.v.) Xhosa (q.v.) from 1840. His position was eroded by the frontier (q.v.) wars of 1846–47 and 1850–53 and most particularly by the cattle killing (q.v.) of 1856–57, when he accepted the prophecies and ordered his people to slaughter their cattle. He died during the last frontier war of 1878–79, while resisting British forces in the Ciskei (q.v.).

SARILI (ca. 1814–92). Paramount chief of the Xhosa (q.v.) from 1835 and the head of the Gcaleka Xhosa, Sarili, the son of Hintsa (q.v.), was forced by the colonial authorities to pay reparations after the frontier war of 1846–47, despite the 1844 treaty of friendship with the Cape Colony (q.v.). Cape forces expelled him from much of his land east of the Kei River after the cattle killing (q.v.), and he and his followers clashed several times thereafter with the Mfengu (q.v.) who were settled by the colonial authorities on what had been his land. After the frontier war of 1878–79, he lost what remained of his power. Forced to flee north to Bomvanaland in the Transkei (q.v.), he died there in exile.

SCHOOL PEOPLE. Xhosa (q.v.) who accepted Christianity (q.v.) and attended mission schools were named "school people," in contrast with "red" people, who continued to practice traditional customs. The cleavage between the two groups dates back to the mid-19th century and ran deep within the traumatized Xhosa society from the time of the cattle killing (q.v.) and the success of missionaries (q.v.) in its aftermath.

SCHREINER, OLIVE (1855–1920). Olive Schreiner's novel, *The Story of an African Farm* (1883), written while she was a governess on Karoo (q.v.) farms, won her fame in Europe and the United States. An eloquent opponent of Cecil Rhodes's (q.v.) imperial ambitions and of British imperialism, she was an early advocate of equal rights for women (q.v.), and her *Woman and Labour* (1911) formed a powerful feminist tract.

SECURITY POLICE. *See* POLICE.

SEKHUKHUNE (ca. 1810–82). For most of his period of leadership, Sekhukhune, paramount chief of the Pedi (q.v.) from 1861, was engaged in a struggle with the Boers (q.v.) of the Transvaal (q.v.) to retain his land and independence. After the British annexation of the Transvaal in 1877, Pedi power was finally broken by British forces and their allies in 1879, and Sekhukhune was taken prisoner.

SEME, PIXLEY kaISAKA (1881–1951). A lawyer and founder of the South African Native National Congress (SANNC), later the African

National Congress (ANC) (q.v.), Pixley Seme studied law in the United States and Britain. He returned to South Africa convinced of the need for Africans (q.v.) to unite in the face of the newly created Union (q.v.) of South Africa. He therefore called the founding meeting of SANNC at Bloemfontein (q.v.) in January 1912, and he became the new organization's first treasurer. A conservative and ambiguous figure, he sought to avoid conflict with the authorities and stayed out of the limelight during the 1920s. He became president of the ANC in 1930 but was a weak leader and did nothing to reverse the decline in the organization's fortunes. He remained an elder statesman of African politics, however, and one of those he helped was Anton Lembede (q.v.).

SEPARATE DEVELOPMENT. *See* APARTHEID; BANTUSTAN POLICY.

SHAKA (ca. 1787–1828). Shaka kaSenzangakhona was the creator of the Zulu kingdom (q.v.). Between ca. 1810 and ca. 1816, he was a tributary chief and military commander in the Mthethwa confederacy, during which time he built up a formidable fighting force by equipping his followers with a short stabbing spear and a large shield to make close fighting possible. After Dingiswayo (q.v.), leader of the Mthethwa, was defeated by the Ndwandwe under Zwide (q.v.), Shaka routed Zwide at Gqokoli Hill in ca. 1819. He subsequently consolidated his power, bringing all northern Nguni (q.v.) people living between the Pongola and Thukela Rivers within his control. His militarized and centralized state was the greatest power in southeast Africa during the 1820s; it was surrounded by vassal communities in varying degrees of subordination, who paid him tribute. Shaka was murdered by his half brother Dingane (q.v.) in 1828.

Shaka's personality and life have been the subject of considerable historical and popular writing. He has been portrayed as a ruthless villain and a violent psychopath as well as a brilliant strategist, visionary, and statesman. His symbolic importance is frequently recalled in speeches by Mangosuthu Buthelezi (q.v.) and other Zulu politicians.

SHARPEVILLE MASSACRE. On 21 March 1960, nervous police (q.v.), faced with a crowd of unarmed antipass campaigners of the Pan Africanist Congress (PAC) (q.v.), panicked and opened fire outside a police station in Sharpeville, near Vereeniging (q.v.) south of Johannesburg (q.v.). This resulted in the deaths of 69 people, many of them shot in the back. In the crisis that followed, the African National Congress (q.v.) and the PAC were banned (q.v.), and the decision was made to launch the armed struggle. But the crisis of legitimacy for the regime passed, and in the 1960s apartheid (q.v.) was applied with new determination and far greater repression. The massacre opened a new era, however, and remained symbolically important: it was therefore appropriate that Nelson Mandela (q.v.) went to Sharpeville on 10 December 1996 to pay tribute to those who had died and to announce the signing of South Africa's new democratic constitution.

SHEPSTONE, THEOPHILUS (1817–93). Colonial administrator and secretary for native affairs in Natal (q.v.) from 1856 to 1876, Theophilus Shepstone believed that Africans (q.v.) should be governed separately and coerced two-thirds of Natal's African inhabitants into reserves (q.v.), where they were ruled either through their traditional authorities or by appointed chiefs loyal to him. Customary law was recognized, but the governor, as supreme chief, was given extensive powers, which were exercised by Shepstone on his behalf. Some of the origins of later racial segregationist (q.v.) practices lie in the system Shepstone elaborated in Natal.

In 1877, Shepstone was sent by Lord Carnarvon (q.v.) to annex the Transvaal (q.v.), and he then administered that territory for two years. He urged Sir Henry Bartle Frere (q.v.) to deal with the Zulu kingdom (q.v.) and so helped to precipitate the Anglo–Zulu War (q.v.) of 1879. He retired in 1880 but remained influential in directing policy toward Africans in Natal for another decade.

SIMON'S TOWN. South Africa's principal naval base, Simon's Town was a safe anchorage on the eastern side of the Cape peninsula, 30 miles south of Cape Town (q.v.). From 1743, the Dutch East India Company (q.v.) made it their official winter base, because of the damage that winter storms in Table Bay caused to shipping. British forces landed in Simon's Town when they captured the Cape (q.v.) in June 1795. It became the headquarters of the British South Atlantic Naval Squadron in 1814, and it remained an important naval base during the 19th century, being used chiefly to protect the Cape sea route. The South African government took over the land defenses of the port from the British in 1921. Simon's Town served as a base for Allied vessels operating in the South Atlantic and Indian Oceans during World War II (q.v.). In 1957, Britain handed over control of the port to the South African authorities, and it became the headquarters of the South African Navy. The terms of the Simon's Town agreement gave Britain the right to use the base in peacetime and in war, whether or not South Africa was also at war. The agreement was suspended during the 1960s by Britain in protest against South Africa's apartheid (q.v.) and racial segregationist (q.v.) policies.

SISA. Among both Nguni (q.v.) and Sotho (q.v.), *sisa* (a Bantu word; also *mafisa; ngoma*) was the practice of loaning out cattle. The cattle themselves, or their milk, could be claimed at any time, for the person entrusted with the cattle had the use of them but did not obtain ownership. The *sisa* arrangement was a way of acquiring dependents. Moshoeshoe (q.v.) of Basutoland (q.v.) in particular used it extensively in the aftermath of the Mfecane (q.v.) to build up a large following.

SISULU, WALTER MAX ULYATE (b. 1912). A trade unionist (q.v.), Walter Sisulu joined the African National Congress (ANC) (q.v.) in 1940, opposed black involvement in World War II (q.v.), and became a member of the Transvaal (q.v.) executive of the ANC and a founding member of the African National Congress Youth League (q.v.). He was arrested and banned (q.v.) under the Suppression of Communism Act. After a tour of Eastern-bloc countries, Israel, China, and Great Britain, he modified his views and came to support the multiracial Congress Alliance (q.v.). One of the leading Rivonia trialists (q.v.), he was sent to Robben Island (q.v.) in 1964 and released in October 1989, after which he was active as an elder statesman in the ANC.

SLAGTER'S NEK REBELLION. A rebellion in 1815 of white frontier farmers against the British authorities in the eastern Cape Colony (q.v.) following the refusal of Frederik Bezuidenhout to appear before a tribunal investigating charges of his ill-treatment of a Khoikhoi (q.v.) servant. Bezuidenhout was shot dead while resisting arrest; the subsequent rebellion was put down by British and Khoikhoi soldiers at Slagter's Nek, and the leaders were executed. The event was long commemorated by Afrikaner nationalists (q.v.) as an example of British oppression.

SLAVERY. Slaves were introduced by Jan van Riebeeck (q.v.), the first Dutch East India Company (VOC) (q.v.) commander at the Cape (q.v.). Slave labor was to form the backbone of the Cape economy for a century and a half and so played a major role in shaping Cape society. Initially, imports of slaves were sporadic. Some slaves came from Angola (q.v.), Mozambique (q.v.), and Madagascar, but most slaves were imported from Asia. From about 1720, the number of slaves at the Cape exceeded that of white colonists. Slaves were employed mainly on the arable farms of the southwestern Cape; although some pastoral trekboer (q.v.) farmers in the interior owned slaves, they more commonly used Khoisan (q.v.) labor. Slaves were also employed by the VOC itself on public works projects and on its farms. In Cape Town (q.v.), semiskilled slaves were to be found working as artisans. Most settlers came to associate slaves with menial and manual labor, and thus a close correlation developed at the Cape between class and race. Slave manumission rates at the Cape were extremely low, and the free black (q.v.) community in Cape Town remained small.

Cape slavery has often been described as "mild," mainly because of some contemporary observations and a largely uncritical historiography (q.v.) before the 1970s. In reality, conditions for many slaves were as harsh as in any other slave society, even though the Cape lacked large plantations like those in North America. Company laws and the direct supervision of masters kept slaves firmly in check; physical punishment was frequent; freedom of movement and association were strictly curtailed; and the theoretical right of slaves to seek the protection of the courts could seldom be claimed in practice. Many slaves were incorporated into the paternalistic households of the farmers, which either prevented them from questioning their position or made them unwilling to do so. Apart from two small slave rebellions, in 1808 and 1825, slave resistance tended to take individual forms. Numerous escapes occurred, and some slaves fled to the frontier (q.v.) areas, where toward the end of the 18th century they linked up with Oorlam (q.v.) and Griqua (q.v.) groups. Others joined a community of escaped slaves who had resided at Hangklip, on False Bay, for almost a century. Other forms of resistance, such as inefficient work and damage to the property of owners, regularly occurred.

Because slaves came from many places, spoke different languages (q.v.), and were scattered widely on farms, and because until the 19th century few were Cape-born, a strongly distinctive slave culture, similar to that in North America, did not emerge. Slaves nonetheless contributed to a broader popular culture that emerged at the Cape out of the mix of indigenous and settler communities. Slave languages fed into the creole that later became Afrikaans (q.v.). There was a thriving Muslim community made up mostly of slaves in Cape Town, particularly after the end of the 18th century. *See also* ISLAM.

In 1808, the slave trade was abolished. Humanitarian campaigns in Britain and the Cape became more vociferous in their protests against the continuing enslavement of people, and economic shifts in the colony during the 1820s also resulted in growing doubts about the desirability of slave labor. Wine (q.v.) farming experienced a decline, and wool (q.v.) production was far less dependent on slaves. Farmers and merchants in the eastern Cape began to argue that a cheaper and more mobile labor force was required. The British Parliament abolished slavery in 1834 but provided for a four-year apprenticeship (q.v.) period until 1838, the year of final emancipation for the Cape's 36,000 slaves. Most of the former slaves remained on the farms as laborers, although some settled on mission (q.v.) stations or moved to towns. The legacy of slavery lasted, both in the frontier districts, where it set the pattern for labor relations, and in the interior, where indentured labor was commonly practiced.

SLOVO, JOE (1926–95). The African National Congress (ANC) (q.v.) and communist activist Joe Slovo, born in Lithuania, was brought up in Johannesburg (q.v.), where he became a lawyer and member of the Communist Party of South Africa (q.v.). He married Ruth First (q.v.) in 1949, helped draft the Freedom Charter of 1955, was one of the founders of Umkhonto weSizwe (MK) (q.v.), and fled the country before the arrests that led to the Rivonia trial (q.v.). In exile, he helped draft the ANC's strategy document of 1969 and emerged as the organization's main theoretician. He was also the mastermind behind some of MK's main operations while he was based at Maputo (formerly Delagoa Bay [q.v.]) in Mozambique (q.v.), between 1977 and 1984. He rose to become general secretary of the South African Communist Party (q.v.) in 1986 and commander of MK in 1987. Although in his work, *Has Socialism Failed?* (1989), he admitted the errors of Stalinism, he continued to believe in the socialist dream. He returned to the country in 1990 and became a key figure in the negotiations that followed. He adopted a pragmatic position, and the "sunset clauses" he advocated led to the ANC accepting a form of power sharing with the National Party (q.v.). He served as minister of housing in the government of National Unity (q.v.), which came into office after the first democratic election, until his death.

SMALLPOX. The virulent form of smallpox introduced from abroad after white settlement played a major role in destroying Khoikhoi (q.v.) societies. Epidemics in the early 18th century, in particular, caused enormous loss of life. A less virulent form, *variola minor*, commonly known as "amaas," existed among African societies as an endemic form of the disease and protected Africans from the more virulent forms introduced by white settlers.

SMITH, SIR HENRY (HARRY) GEORGE WAKELYN (1787–1860). The egocentric and bombastic British governor of the Cape Colony (q.v.) and high commissioner from 1847 to 1852, Sir Henry Smith extended British rule northward to the Vaal River and east to the Kei River. He led the colony into war with the Xhosa (q.v.) in 1850 and, largely as a result, was recalled in 1852.

SMUTS, JAN CHRISTIAAN (1870–1950). A soldier, intellectual, and statesman, Jan Smuts was prime minister of South Africa from 1919 to 1924 and from 1939 to 1948. He grew up on a farm north of Cape Town (q.v.), read law at Cambridge University, and was appointed state attorney of the Transvaal (q.v.) in 1898. During the South African War (q.v.) he acquired fame as a commando (q.v.) leader. A minister in the Transvaal government from 1907, he played an important role in the making of the Union (q.v.) of South Africa. A member of the first Union government, he served during World War I (q.v.) in East Africa and was a member of the imperial war cabinet. Louis Botha's (q.v.) right-hand man, he succeeded him as prime minister in 1919.

His first term as prime minister ended when he lost the 1924 election to J. B. M. Hertzog (q.v.), but as a result of the depression crisis he became deputy prime minister under Hertzog in 1933 and prime minister again when Hertzog desired South Africa's neutrality in World War II (q.v.). During the war, Smuts served as adviser to British prime minister Winston Churchill. His activities as an international statesman—he helped found both the League of Nations (q.v.) and the United Nations (q.v.)—led him to neglect his domestic constituency, and in 1948 he lost the general election to the National Party (q.v.) under D. F. Malan (q.v.). He became leader of the parliamentary opposition until his death. For all his intellectual brilliance, Smuts failed to recognize the injustice of racial segregation (q.v.) and so did little to wean the white electorate from racism (q.v.). Among his many intellectual interests was philosophy; he published *Holism and Evolution* in 1926.

SOBUKWE, ROBERT MANGALISO (1924–78). A modest but charismatic man who became a student leader at the University of Fort Hare (q.v.), where he was active in African National Congress (ANC) (q.v.) politics, Robert Sobukwe then taught, becoming lecturer in African languages (q.v.) at the University of the Witwatersrand in Johannesburg (q.v.) in 1954. He came increasingly to question ANC strategy, believing its involvement with non-Africans, especially communists in the Congress of Democrats, weakened it. In 1958 he urged those who thought as he did—they were known as Africanists—to break away. In 1959 he was elected first president of the newly formed Pan Africanist Congress (PAC) of Azania (q.v.). He gave up his lecturing post to lead the mass protest of the PAC against the pass laws (q.v.) in March 1960. Arrested and imprisoned on Robben Island (q.v.), he was detained there, under special legislation, for another six years after serving his sentence. On his release, he was allowed to settle in Kimberley (q.v.), where he opened a law practice despite being under severe restrictions. His funeral in Graaff-Reinet, the place of his birth, was disrupted when some members of the PAC threatened Mangosuthu Buthelezi (q.v.), whom they regarded as a sellout because he worked within the bantustan (q.v.) system.

SOGA, TIYO (1829–71). The Xhosa (q.v.) writer, linguist, and composer Tiyo Soga trained as a missionary (q.v.) in Scotland between 1846 and 1848 and, after being ordained in the Presbyterian Church in 1856, was the first Xhosa Christian (q.v.) minister of religion. He married a Scottish woman, Janet Burnside, and had seven children, in whom he instilled pride in their African (q.v.) heritage. He translated the four gospels and John Bunyan's *Pilgrim's Progress* into Xhosa and wrote several hymns before his death at the age of 42.

SOMERSET, LORD CHARLES HENRY (1767–1831). Governor of the Cape Colony (q.v.) from 1814 until 1826, Charles Somerset was a conservative and autocratic man with a military background and aristocratic connections. His name is associated with his attacks on the fledgling colonial press (q.v.) during the 1820s. He adopted a firm frontier (q.v.) policy against the Xhosa (q.v.), attempting to enforce a neutral territory between white and black and encouraging the settlement of some 5,000 English-speaking (q.v.) immigrants to close the frontier against Xhosa intrusion. He sponsored the establishment of several colonial institutions, such as the South African Public Library and the South African Museum, and also strove to improve agricultural (q.v.) practices and livestock farming.

SOTHO (or SESOTHO). *Sotho* is the name used to denote a group of Bantu-speaking (q.v.) people (and a corresponding subgroup of Bantu languages) on the high veld (q.v.). This group is usually divided into three subclusters: the northern Sotho lived in what became known as the Transvaal (q.v.) and included, in the northeast, the Pedi (q.v.); the western Sotho or Tswana (q.v.); and the southern Sotho, some of whom became known as the BaSotho.

The southern Sotho trace their origins to the 15th and 16th centuries, when their ancestors settled south of the Vaal River, mostly in small villages, in contrast with the much larger settlements to be found among the Tswana. The most prominent chiefdoms in the region were the Fokeng, Kwena, Tlokoa, and Phuting. In the 1820s during the Mfecane (q.v.), the southern Sotho were attacked by Nguni-speaking (q.v.) refugees from across the Drakensberg (q.v.), and the area experienced considerable upheaval. Thereafter, Moshoeshoe (q.v.) was able to establish hegemony in the region. By the late 1830s he had attracted a large number of followers by offering protection to displaced people at his secure mountain base of Thaba Bosiu, building up his cattle herds, and showing tolerance to his enemies. Moshoeshoe was obliged to spend much of his time after the 1830s defending his land from British and Boer (q.v.) claims, alternately using military and diplomatic means in attempting to secure his chiefdom. In 1868, he was forced to give up valuable land to the Orange Free State (q.v.). Many southern Sotho continued to live outside Basutoland, the country Moshoeshoe created.

SOUTH AFRICAN COMMUNIST PARTY (SACP). The legal life of the Communist Party of South Africa (q.v.) ended in 1950 with the passage of the Suppression of Communism Act, under which it would have been declared unlawful, though its newspaper, the *Guardian* (then published under other names), continued until finally extinguished in 1963. The underground SACP was born in 1953. Many members of the earlier Communist Party of South Africa were active in the Congress of Democrats, formed as part of the Congress Alliance (q.v.) in the 1950s. In the early 1960s the security police (q.v.) infiltrated the leadership of the underground SACP, and a number of its officials were tried and convicted, the most notable being Bram Fischer (q.v.).

In exile, leading members of the tightly knit party, which continued to adopt a strongly pro-Soviet line, served on the executive of Umkhonto weSizwe (MK) (q.v.) and helped coordinate the military strategy of the African National Congress (ANC) (q.v.). Its members participated in MK structures. At the Morogoro conference of 1969, the SACP backed the "Strategy and Tactics" document, which endorsed the struggle for a national democratic revolution. From its exile base in London, the party published the *African Communist*. In June 1989 its congress in Havana, Cuba, accepted the idea of a negotiated settlement and adopted a new policy, which it called "The Path to Power." South Africa, the party had long argued, represented colonialism of a special type, in that colony and metropolis were one, and revolution in such a territory must unite class and national forces. Although the SACP had long taken a firmly Stalinist line, in 1989 its leading theoretician, Joe Slovo (q.v.), began a self-critical evaluation in *Has Socialism Failed?*

The party was unbanned by F. W. de Klerk (q.v.) in February 1990. In July of that year it launched itself openly in South Africa, though it did not reveal the names of all its members. Some SACP members played an important role in the negotiations that followed, in which the party endorsed a liberal multiparty democracy as a first step to the goal of socialism. In 1992 it supported mass action to get the negotiations restarted. Its tripartite alliance with the ANC and the Congress of South African Trade Unions (q.v.) tended to blur its independent role, and the assassination of its general secretary, Chris Hani (q.v.), in April 1993 deprived it of its most charismatic figure. Up to half the members of the ANC's National Executive Committee were thought to be members of the SACP.

In the April 1994 election the party supported ANC candidates rather than fielding its own. There was speculation that after the 1999 election it might establish its independence of the ANC.

SOUTH AFRICAN CONGRESS OF TRADE UNIONS (SACTU). Founded in 1955 by people critical of the decision by the Trade Union Congress of South Africa (q.v.) to restrict its membership to registered (non-African) unions, SACTU joined the Congress Alliance (q.v.) as its trade-union wing. By 1961 it claimed 46 affiliated unions and 53,000 members, the vast majority of whom were Africans. In the aftermath of the Sharpeville massacre (q.v.), its leadership was banned (q.v.), and it was driven underground.

SOUTH AFRICAN DEFENCE FORCE (SADF). The SADF was established in 1913 to bring together Boer (q.v.) and British in the armed forces of the four former colonies. The army comprised a relatively small permanent force, which grew to 60,000 in the 1980s, and a much larger citizen force of national servicemen, a part-time citizen army. In World War I (q.v.), 231,000 South Africans volunteered; in World War II (q.v.), almost 400,000. African (q.v.) volunteers served in both world wars in noncombatant roles and as soldiers in the regular army from the late 1970s. In the Korean War, the South African Air Force lost 74 aircraft and 34 pilots. In the Namibian (q.v.) border war, conscripts were sent into Angola (q.v.); in 1975, SADF troops came within sight of the Angolan capital, Luanda, before they withdrew. Between 1966 and 1989, some 788 servicemen (police and military) lost their lives in Namibia (q.v.) and Angola, excluding those who died as members of the South West African Territory Force or in 32 Battalion, most members of which were non–South Africans. Soon after a new national service scheme was introduced in 1993, compulsory service was abandoned.

The transition from apartheid (q.v.) in the 1990s allowed a vast cutback in defense expenditure. Some in Umkhonto weSizwe (MK) (q.v.) and the Azanian People's Liberation Army (APLA) had called for the

SADF to be dissolved and a new force created, but in negotiations from 1992 a process was agreed that provided for continuity, and in effect the SADF absorbed the forces of the MK and the APLA, under the new name of the South African National Defence Force (SANDF). The SANDF was born with the new order in April 1994. Before the election of that month, the Transitional Executive Council's (q.v.) subcouncil on defense had established a national peacekeeping force, which proved a disastrous and short-lived experiment.

SOUTH AFRICAN INSTITUTE OF RACE RELATIONS (SAIRR). A liberal (q.v.) research body concerned with improving black-white relations, the SAIRR was founded in 1929 by a small group of intellectuals led by J. D. Rheinallt-Jones. The institute acted as a critical pressure group on the National Party (q.v.) government, and though accused by the government after 1948 of acting in an unpatriotic manner, it continued to collect and publish material on the effects of racial segregation (q.v.) and discrimination. Its single most influential publication was its annual *Survey of Race Relations*. In the early 1990s, no longer the target of government attack, it came under criticism from the left for its links with Inkatha (q.v.) and because it seemed to blame the African National Congress (q.v.) for the continuing violence.

SOUTH AFRICAN NATIVE AFFAIRS COMMISSION. *See* LAGDEN COMMISSION.

SOUTH AFRICAN NATIVE NATIONAL CONGRESS (SANNC). *See* AFRICAN NATIONAL CONGRESS.

SOUTH AFRICAN PARTY (SAP) (1911–34). The South African Party was established in November 1911, after the achievement of union (q.v.), through the amalgamation of various parties represented in the cabinet of Louis Botha (q.v.). These included the Afrikaner Bond (q.v.), in the Cape (q.v.), and Het Volk (q.v.), in the Transvaal (q.v.). Under Botha and Jan Smuts (q.v.), the SAP stood for conciliation between Afrikaners (q.v.) and English speakers (q.v.) on the basis of a common loyalty to South Africa. After the breakaway of J. B. M. Hertzog (q.v.) and the formation of his National Party (q.v.), the SAP found itself increasingly reliant on the jingoistic Unionist Party (q.v.), and an informal alliance led to the SAP absorbing the Unionists in 1920. After winning 79 seats in the 1921 general election, the SAP grew increasingly unpopular, not least because of Smuts's brutal suppression of the Rand Revolt (q.v.). It lost power to the Pact government (q.v.) in 1924. By then the SAP had been depicted as the party of mining capital, with Smuts as the lackey of Hoggenheimer (i.e., Jewish [q.v.] capitalism) and the tool of British imperialism. Many Afrikaners remained *bloedsappe* ("blood South African Party men," i.e., those with a hereditary loyalty to Botha and Smuts). The policy of conciliation took on new life when in 1933, at a time of economic crisis, Hertzog agreed to form a coalition with the SAP. This led to fusion (q.v.) with Hertzog's party the following year and the formation of the United Party (q.v.).

SOUTH AFRICAN REPUBLIC (SAR). The SAR emerged after the independence of the Voortrekkers (q.v.) north of the Vaal River was recognized by Britain in the Sand River Convention of 1852. Also known as the Transvaal (q.v.), the state was politically divided initially, but gradually unity was achieved among the various trekker communities, and it claimed the entire territory from the Vaal to the Limpopo River (q.v.). The constitution of 1860 reserved citizenship, the ownership of land, and the franchise (q.v.) for whites. The SAR lost its independence when annexed by Britain in 1877 but regained it in 1881 after the Battle of Majuba (q.v.). It was conquered by Britain during the South African War (q.v.) in 1900 and became the crown colony of the Transvaal.

SOUTH AFRICAN STUDENTS' ORGANIZATION (SASO). Steve Biko (q.v.) saw that the few African (q.v.) students active in the National Union of South African Students (q.v.) largely left it to white students to articulate black grievances, and so he decided in 1968 to form an all-black student organization. SASO was inaugurated at a conference at Turfloop, the campus of the University of the North, in 1969, with Biko as its president. Biko argued that blacks should work on their own, not under the guidance of white liberals (q.v.). Although critics called SASO racist, the apartheid (q.v.) government tolerated its strong rhetoric for a time, probably because it was all-black. It won strong support on the African campuses and also among Indian (q.v.) students at the University of Durban-Westville and among Coloured (q.v.) students at the University of the Western Cape. It helped establish in 1972 the Black Peoples' Convention (BPC), an umbrella political movement based on black consciousness (q.v.) philosophy, and called for various campus boycotts (q.v.). From 1973 its leaders began to be banned (q.v.) and detained without trial, and in 1975 some were charged under the Terrorism Act. SASO remained active, however, working closely with the BPC, until October 1977, when both organizations were banned.

SOUTH AFRICAN WAR (1899–1902). The most costly war fought by the British between 1815 and 1914, the South African War was popularly known as the Anglo–Boer War but was known to Afrikaner nationalists (q.v.) as the Second War of Independence. For much of the 20th century, its causes were generally sought in Britain's political and strategic objectives: the need to maintain political dominance in the region in order to protect its sea route to India and its anxiety about the ambitions of other foreign imperialist competitors, particularly Germany, in the subcontinent. In the 1970s, historians began to explore the economic circumstances of the war, returning to examine the argument, first advanced by J. A. Hobson (1858–1940) at the time of the war, that it was fought primarily for economic reasons.

The gold (q.v.) mines of the Witwatersrand (q.v.) had by the mid-1890s become the world's largest single producer of gold, responsible for almost one-quarter of the world's supply. With London the financial capital of the world, an efficient gold-mining industry was essential to British world dominance. Mine owners and the British shared a common frustration with the Transvaal (q.v.) government of Paul Kruger (q.v.), which they perceived to be backward, ill prepared, and unwilling to develop the mines. The abortive Jameson Raid (q.v.) aroused the worst fears of the Transvaal about the converging interests of British imperialists and the mining magnates; these were deepened by the later demands of Sir Alfred Milner (q.v.), the British high commissioner, regarding political reform in the Transvaal. In October 1899, the Transvaal and the Orange Free State (q.v.) declared war to preserve their independence.

The British, expecting a rapid and easy war, predicted a victory before Christmas; instead, they suffered a succession of severe defeats during December 1899, particularly in Natal (q.v.). Reinforcements and more competent command, in the form of Lord Roberts (1832–1914) and Lord Kitchener (q.v.), slowly reversed the tide in 1900. The Boers (q.v.) suffered a significant defeat at Paardeberg in February 1900, and by June 1900 both Bloemfontein (q.v.) and Pretoria (q.v.) had fallen to British forces, and Boer field armies were disintegrating. The war, however, was far from over. Boer commandos (q.v.) resorted to guerrilla tactics, which proved highly effective in disrupting enemy supply lines and preventing the consolidation of British military power. Kitchener, in turn, ordered a scorched-earth strategy, burning farms and destroying crops and livestock in an attempt to deny the commandos the means to continue the war. A vast network of blockhouses connected by barbed-wire barricades was created, and civilians were interned in concentration camps (q.v.).

The growing difficulties faced by commandos and the civilian suffering gradually wore down Boer resistance; some 14,000 guerrillas (dubbed *hensoppers,* or "hands-uppers") surrendered to the British, and more than 5,000 impoverished landless Boers joined the British forces as scouts to play an active role against their former comrades.

In May 1902, the war ended with the Treaty of Vereeniging (q.v.), in which the Boers formally surrendered their independence in return for the promise of large-scale British assistance for the reconstruction of the shattered republics. Britain employed some 450,000 soldiers during the war, against 88,000 Boer fighters. More than 100,000 African (q.v.) and Coloured (q.v.) South Africans became directly involved in the military conflict, approximately one-third of whom were armed and saw active service, thus giving the lie to the image of the conflict as a "white man's war." Altogether, 22,000 British troops and 7,000 Boer soldiers lost their lives, in addition to 28,000 Boer civilians and perhaps 20,000 Africans. Given the splits within Boer society between the *hensoppers* and the *bittereinders* (the "bitter-enders" or "diehards"), as well as black involvement on both sides, the war can to some extent be considered a civil war.

Although Britain had asserted its imperial superiority, the securing of its long-term interests depended on the reconciliation of the white inhabitants of the defeated republics and the colonists of the Cape (q.v.) and Natal (q.v.). To this end, African hopes of greater civil and political rights and economic opportunities were sacrificed, leaving a residue of deep bitterness among those who had supported the British cause against the Boers.

SOUTH WEST AFRICA. *See* NAMIBIA.

SOUTHERN AFRICAN DEVELOPMENT COMMUNITY (SADC). Born in August 1992, the SADC replaced the Southern African Development Coordination Conference (SADCC), established in the 1980s to reduce the economic dependence of neighboring states on apartheid (q.v.) South Africa. The SADCC had in turn emerged out of the meetings of the heads of the so-called frontline states, Angola (q.v), Botswana (formerly Bechuanaland [q.v.]), Mozambique (q.v.), Tanzania, and Zambia, from the mid-1970s. South Africa joined the SADC in 1994 and immediately became the most important member of the organization. Nelson Mandela (q.v.) became its chairman in 1997. The organization sought to resolve interstate disputes and to work to promote economic integration and create a regional trade bloc. Negotiations were held on water, banking, investment, and financial agreements between the member states, but South Africa's dominant role in the region made such agreements difficult to reach. When South Africa intervened in Lesotho (formerly Basutoland [q.v.]) in September 1998, it did so in the name of the SADC.

SOWETO. There were no houses for tens of thousands of Africans (q.v.) who went to Johannesburg to work during World War II (q.v.), and most joined the squatter (q.v.) population, living in shanties on the outskirts of the city. After the war, together with the bulk of the remainder of Johannesburg's African population, they were gradually provided with houses in the 28 townships eventually grouped into Soweto (an acronym formed from "southwestern townships"), which in time became a vast, sprawling residential area. Africans living in the suburb of Sophiatown, much closer to the city center, were forced out and relocated to Soweto in the mid-1950s, losing their freehold titles, as also were many from Alexandra township, to the north of the city center, in the 1970s.

The Soweto houses were mostly four-room "matchboxes" with no electricity, ceilings, or running water. The miles and miles of identical houses were laid out to make control by the authorities as easy as possible. As in other African townships, the spartan conditions were partly a product of an unwillingness to spend more money but were also the result of a belief that better conditions might encourage permanent residence and should not be provided for that reason. In 1955 an attempt was made to zone individual townships on an ethnic basis—Nguni (q.v.), Sotho (q.v.), or "other"—and Zulu (q.v.) male migrants lived separately in hostels, but most of Soweto remained polyglot. Because many of its residents were there illegally, its exact population was never known, but in the mid-1970s it was probably more than one million. Soweto had no industries, and a quarter of a million of its people traveled on the single railway (q.v.), which ran into Johannesburg each day to work. The poverty and dreariness of the place attracted adverse publicity during the Soweto uprising (q.v.), and this led the government to announce plans to provide electricity, entertainment, and sporting facilities.

Initially run by the Johannesburg City Council's Non-European Affairs Department, Soweto was taken over by the West Rand Administration Board, a nominated government body, in 1973. Residents of Soweto had served on the Advisory Board, which was replaced by the Urban Council in 1968; this in turn became the Community Council in 1978. Elections to these bodies consistently produced minuscule turnouts, for the vast majority of Sowetans rejected them as powerless institutions of the oppressors. After the transition to democracy, it was proposed that

Soweto be incorporated in a megacity that included the rest of Johannesburg.

SOWETO UPRISING (1976–77). Often viewed as the event that signaled the end of apartheid (q.v.), the Soweto revolt began on 16 June 1976 as a protest by schoolchildren in Soweto (q.v.) township south of Johannesburg against the government's insistence that Afrikaans (q.v.) be used as a medium of instruction in schools. Hector Petersen was the first martyr of the revolt, which soon spread from Soweto across the country. The African National Congress (q.v.) was caught off guard when the revolt began but tried, nonetheless, to capitalize on it. Ideas of black consciousness (q.v.) were undoubtedly important in flaming the resistance and spreading it. Before the revolt was suppressed, at least 600 people, and probably many more, most of them teenagers, had been shot by the security forces. Thousands of others fled abroad and there joined the liberation struggle. The harsh measures taken to suppress the uprising aroused much international condemnation and created a crisis of legitimacy for the apartheid regime that led eventually to the negotiated settlement of the 1990s.

SPORTS AND SPORTS BOYCOTTS. Modern sports—with its emphasis on physical prowess, self-discipline, and individual and collective effort, as well as the various communal identities of local district, province, and nation carried by team competitions—was brought to South Africa in the 19th century by British immigrants. Sports and British cultural values were closely intertwined, and the development of sports reflected the emerging colonial society and its social structures. Although the first recorded cricket match was played in Cape Town (q.v.) in 1808, cricket clubs were slow to form in the Cape (q.v.) before the 1870s. Port Elizabeth (q.v.) saw the establishment of the first cricket club for whites in 1843 and that for blacks in 1869. Cricket took root in English-speaking (q.v.) public schools and in mission (q.v.) schools in the Cape; by the 1870s, the game was popular throughout the Cape and Natal (q.v.), although no official leagues or competitions took place. In 1888, the first tour by an English team saw South Africa join England and Australia as a recognized contestant in international cricket, and further impetus was given to the game in 1890, when Sir Donald Currie donated a trophy, known as the Currie Cup, to promote first-class competitive cricket between the colonies and the republics.

The first rugby match was played in Cape Town in 1862, after which rugby began to spread in schools. During the decade from 1875, organized sports developed rapidly: the first rugby, football, track and field, tennis, golf, horse-racing, and cycling clubs were formed and regular competitions began. From the late 1880s, as the mineral and industrial transformation of South African began, national associations began to be established. In 1891, the South African Rugby Board was founded to ensure uniformity in rules and to organize tournaments and overseas visits; in that year, the first tour by a British team took place. The Currie Cup, which was first competed for in 1892, became the premier interprovincial award. In 1892, the South African Football Association was formed to control the sport.

At the same time, black sportsmen also began to initiate moves to coordinate competition on a national level: the South African Coloured Rugby Board was formed in 1896 and the South African Coloured Cricket Board in 1902, black rugby players competed for the Rhodes Cup from 1897, and cricket players for the Barnato trophy from 1898, for the mining magnates Cecil Rhodes (q.v.) and Barney Barnato were persuaded to donate trophies similar to the Currie Cup. At the beginning of the 20th century, cricket was the most popular sport among the small black middle class, and competition between black and white cricket (as well as rugby) teams occurred regularly, particularly in the Cape.

After 1910, however, with the intensification of racism and segregation that occurred as the century progressed, contests between black and white teams declined, along with the assimilationist ideals of the black middle class. The powerful mining industry began to control the development of black sports, and cricket went into decline in favor of working-class mass sports, in particular soccer, boxing and athletics. Cricket tended to be considered the sport of English-speaking whites, while rugby came to be dominated by Afrikaners (q.v.). After 1948 the apartheid (q.v.) policies of the National Party (q.v.) stretched, not surprisingly, to the sporting arena. In 1955 the government published its official sports policy based on racial differentiation: each race was to have its own sports amenities, controlling bodies, emblems, and local and international competitions.

By the end of the 1950s, this official policy of sports apartheid had influenced almost every sporting code. Between 1959 and 1962, several black federations in cricket, football, tennis and athletics made a transition toward non-racialism; in 1962, the most influential of these, the South African Non-Racial Olympic Committee (SANROC), was formed. Under the leadership of Sam Ramsamy, it established itself in exile in London in 1966 and led campaigns to isolate South Africa on the sports field.

The international boycott of South African sports, although unevenly applied, increasingly affected the white establishment. South Africa was expelled from international football in 1964, from the Olympic Games in 1966 and the Olympic movement in 1969, and from international cricket in 1970; many other sports teams and individuals experienced various degrees of difficulty when playing abroad. The unyielding attitude of the government was symbolized most clearly in its refusal to grant permission to Basil D'Oliveira, a Coloured (q.v.) cricketer of South African birth, to participate in a cricket test series between England and South Africa in 1966. This was the same year in which a Department of Sport and Recreation was established to influence the practice of sports in the country.

In 1973, the South African Council of Sport (SACOS) was formed within the country and, together with SANROC, campaigned for the complete isolation of South African sports, using the slogan "no normal sport in an abnormal society." Considerable division occurred even within government circles about the respective paths of complete international isolation and limited reform to permit some international competition. A policy of multinationalism was introduced in 1976, which rapidly gave way in 1979 to sports autonomy, whereby the government, in a vain attempt to depoliticize sports, began to remove restrictions on the practice and organization of sports, and allowed individual sports bodies to choose for themselves their structures. During the 1980s, the boycott was applied with considerable effectiveness, with only rugby and some individual sports succeeding in evading isolation to any significant degree. Opponents of international tours argued that sports should rather be developed in disadvantaged communities. The hostility of anti-apartheid campaigners toward international competition was most obviously seen in the difficulties faced by the athlete Zola Budd during 1984–1986. She managed to run in British colours in controversial circumstances. In 1990 a tour of rebel English cricketers had to be canceled.

Campaigners had long argued that using a sports boycott to isolate white South Africa was an extremely effective psychological weapon in the broader anti-apartheid struggle, and the termination of the rebel cricket tour was a significant landmark in popular domestic opposition to apartheid. In November 1990, a broad coalition of opposition sporting organizations decided in Harare, Zimbabwe, that the sports boycott should remain in place until apartheid was dismantled. An interim body, the National Olympic Committee of South Africa (NOCSA), under the leadership of Ramsamy, managed the process toward the readmission of South Africa to international competition; in July 1991 the international Olympic Committee recognized NOCSA as the sole controlling body for Olympic sports in South Africa and readmitted the country to the Olympic Games. The isolation of cricket ended in October 1991, with a short tour of the national team to India and an invitation to the World Cup in Australia in March 1992. South African sports players then performed with credit in international competition: the country reached the semifinals of the cricket World Cup in 1992, was victorious in the rugby World Cup in 1995, and won the soccer Africa Cup of Nations in 1996; at the 1996 Olympics, Josiah Thugwane won the gold medal in the men's marathon.

These successes have not disguised considerable challenges facing many sports in the post-apartheid era: the allocation of resources, vastly diverse facilities, and the virtual absence of Africans in many national teams are among the major issues which confront sporting bodies. In 1998 there was a crisis in rugby, when those who controlled that sport tried to have the President Nelson Mandela's (q.v.) decision to appoint a commission of inquiry into the sport overturned.

In 1991, a government survey revealed that soccer was the most popular sport played in South Africa, followed by netball, cricket, squash, rugby, golf, tennis, athletics, bowls, and hockey. Soccer attracted the most spectators, followed by boxing, tennis, athletics, rugby, golf, and cricket.

SQUATTERS. Term used both for Africans who lived on white-owned rural land and for those who lived in informal or irregular settlements in towns. For much of the 20th century, attempts were made to remove rural squatters, many of whom moved to the cities and became urban squatters. The shacks of urban squatters were frequently bulldozed in the 1970s, but by the mid-1980s the government began to tolerate squatting in limited urban areas.

STATE ENTERPRISES. Though critical of socialism, the National Party (q.v.) government, which ruled from 1948, controlled over 50 percent of fixed assets in the country, including the oil-from-coal industry Sasol, the steel-producing company Iscor (founded in 1928), the electricity supplier Escom (founded in 1922), the telephone company that became known as Telkom, the arms-manufacturing companies Armscor and Denel, South African Airways, and many others. In the 1950s and 1960s, control of state enterprises was a way to provide jobs for poor Afrikaners (q.v.) and raise them to the middle class. The African National Congress (q.v.), which had believed in nationalization, moved toward privatization once in office, despite some opposition from trade unions. This new policy began to take off in 1997, when Telkom obtained a foreign strategic equity partner. It was later announced that a similar arrangement would be concluded for South African Airways.

STATE SECURITY COUNCIL (SSC). Established as a permanent cabinet committee in 1972, the SSC was at first little more than an advisory body on intelligence matters, but after P. W. Botha (q.v.) took over as prime minister in 1978, it became a major policy-making body that met before the cabinet and made decisions that the cabinet then rubberstamped. Its operational arm was the secret National Security Management System (NSMS); a network of joint management centers brought together members of the security forces and others, and coordinated the implementation of SSC policies on the ground. Certain townships were identified as target areas for upgrading, but above all the emphasis was on control and security. In November 1989 F. W. de Klerk (q.v.) abolished the NSMS and effectively returned power to the cabinet. The workings of the SSC became known in detail in 1997–1998 when the Truth and Reconciliation Commission (q.v.), which had gained access to its minutes, held a series of hearings relating to its activities.

STAYAWAYS. The stayaway, which involved a general withdrawal of labor, not over a workplace dispute but for political purposes, emerged as a tactic of black resistance in December 1949, when it was one of the forms of action listed in the Programme of Action adopted by the African National Congress (ANC) (q.v.). The first stayaway organized by the ANC took place on the Witwatersrand (q.v.) on 1 May 1950 as a protest against unjust laws, and was followed by a national stayaway on 26 June of that year. The tactic was used, with varying degrees of success, in 1957, 1958, 1960, 1961, 1976, and 1977. In the most successful, 500,000 workers stayed away from work for three days in 1976 during the Soweto uprising (q.v.).

STEYN, MARTHINUS THEUNIS (1857–1916). Attorney general, president of the Orange Free State (q.v.), and Afrikaner nationalist (q.v.). He attempted to promote cooperation between the Boer republics and the Cape (q.v.) but was strongly alienated by the imperial ambitions of Sir Alfred Milner (q.v.) and Joseph Chamberlain (q.v.). He lent military and guerrilla support to the Transvaal (q.v.) during the South African War (q.v.), and remained a convinced Afrikaner nationalist until his death.

STOCKENSTRÖM, ANDRIES (1792–1864). Administrator on the Cape eastern frontier (q.v.), in the roles of landdrost of Graaff-Reinet (1815–1828), commissioner general for the eastern province (1828–1833), and lieutenant governor of the eastern districts (1836–1839). He was independent-minded and rejected several key aspects of British frontier policy. He tried to reduce the incursions mounted by whites on Xhosa (q.v.) land and livestock, supported Ordinance 50 (q.v.) of 1828, and helped to establish the Kat River Settlement (q.v.) in 1829. When he gave evidence to the Select Committee of the British House of Commons on the treatment of Aborigines in 1835, the colonists regarded his criticisms of them as betrayal. In 1836, he returned to be a much-reviled lieutenant governor of the eastern districts. He remained critical of British policy after his dismissal in 1839, arguing for a reduced British role in southern African affairs and advocating representative government for the Cape.

Stockenström played a key role in the frontier war of 1846–1847. After the introduction of representative government in 1853, he gave up retirement on his farm near the modern town of Bedford and served as a member of the Legislative Council for the eastern districts from 1854 until 1856. In the 19th-century Cape no one had greater breadth of vision, and none gained the respect of a wider constituency, black as well as white.

STONE AGE. The term used by archaeologists to describe the period in southern Africa from about 2.5 million years ago, when hominids first began to shape stone tools, until about 2,000 years ago, when iron-using agriculturists first settled in southern Africa (*see* IRON AGE). The Stone Age is separated into Earlier, Middle, and Later periods, the division between the Earlier and Middle periods occurring about 150,000 years ago, and that between the Middle and Later periods taking place 30,000 years ago. Through time, tools became more varied and sophisticated, increasingly designed for more specific tasks and smaller in size. Hunter-gatherers and Khoikhoi (q.v.) herders, who did not smelt metals, continued to belong, technologically, to the Stone Age.

STRIJDOM, JOHANNES GERHARDUS (1893–1958). National Party (NP) (q.v.) leader and prime minister from 1954 to 1958. A dour man, nicknamed "The Lion of the North," he interpreted apartheid (q.v.) as mere *baasskap*, or "domination by whites." A lawyer and farmer, he found himself, when he supported D. F. Malan (q.v.) in his refusal to enter fusion (q.v.), the sole NP member of parliament in the Transvaal (q.v.). He was chosen NP leader, and therefore prime minister, on Malan's retirement in 1954 because he was leader in the Transvaal and had built up the party there. As prime minister he pushed through the removal of the Coloureds (q.v.) from the common voters' roll (*see* FRANCHISE).

STRIKES. Perhaps the earliest strike to be recorded is that by Coloured (q.v.) boatmen and stevedores at the Cape Town (q.v.) harbor in 1854. They struck for an increase in wages to help compensate for higher bread prices. African workers in Port Elizabeth (q.v.) harbor struck in 1856. In the Cape Town docks African and Coloured workers sometimes joined in strikes together, but cross-ethnic strike action was relatively rare.

The period 1907–1922 was one of great militancy among labor on the Witwatersrand (q.v.), marked by a series of major strikes in the mines. The first such strike by white miners took place in 1907 when the mine owners instructed miners to supervise three instead of two drills. More than 4,000 struck and the army was called in. Afrikaners (q.v.) were hired to take the place of strikers, and the strike was broken. In 1913 some 19,000 white miners went on strike over union bargaining rights. Again, strong-arm tactics were used by both soldiers and the police against the strikers. Louis Botha (q.v.) and Jan Smuts (q.v.) intervened and an agreement was reached. Following the strike, the Riotous Assemblies Act (1914) was passed to give the government the power to ban outdoor meetings and picketing. Massive force was used against another strike in 1914 and the strike leaders were deported. The most important strike by whites took place in 1922. Faced with a crisis of profitability in the coal and gold (q.v.) mines, the owners cut wages in the coal mines and announced that they would do the same for the gold mines, and also allow Africans to take over semi-skilled jobs from whites. First the coal miners struck, then there was a general strike of 20,000 white workers in the gold mines. An armed revolt followed, which was put down by the army. White labor was cowed and then co-opted through the Industrial Conciliation Act (1924).

The first strike by Africans in the gold mines took place in 1896. In 1913 some 9,000 African workers on four gold mines struck, and the army was called in to force them back to work. A subsequent commission of inquiry produced certain improvements in compound and work conditions. In 1918 the Johannesburg (q.v.) sanitation workers struck; arrested for breaking their contracts, the strikers were sentenced to two months' hard labor. Then in 1920, at a time of rapid inflation and severe drought in the rural areas, some 71,000 migrant workers on 21 gold mines struck for higher wages. Again the army was called in, and one by one the compounds (q.v.) were forced to resume work. Some working conditions were improved, but the pass laws (q.v.) were also tightened up.

Massive strike action by Africans began again during World War II (q.v.), when labor was in short supply. In 1942 some 8,000 workers in various Witwatersrand industries went out on strike. A war measure then outlawed strikes by Africans and provided severe penalties for strike action. After the war, under the auspices of the African Mine Workers Union, formed in 1941, over 60,000 workers on 19 mines went on strike. The 1946 strike was forcibly broken up by the police, and 12 miners were killed. One of the consequences was closer relations between the African trade union movement and the African National Congress (q.v.).

An Act of 1953 made strikes by Africans illegal, and in the repressive post-Sharpeville (q.v.) decade black labor was largely docile. But from 1973 there was a dramatic change, which in part followed a successful strike by Ovambo workers in Namibia (q.v.) the previous year. Early in 1973, seemingly spontaneously, strikes spread from brickmakers to textile and other workers in Durban (q.v.); over a two-month period more than 61,000 workers were involved, and in most cases they were able to extract increased wages. The government's first response was to try to encourage the creation of liaison committees, but by the mid-1970s, as major strike action continued, it was clear that such committees were no substitute for representative and recognized trade unions. Although Africans were allowed to form and join registered unions in 1979, strike action continued at roughly the 1973 level as South Africa entered the 1980s. Consumer boycotts (q.v.) organized by community associations often supported strikers.

Strike activity in South Africa reached its peak during the early 1990s, and strikes were used by workers to advance both political and economic demands. Labor unrest was particularly serious in 1992 but declined markedly after the democratic general election of 1994. One of the consequences of the worsening economic crisis of 1998 appeared to be an increase in strike activity, with worker militancy sharpening in the face of growing threats of retrenchment.

SUZMAN, HELEN (b. 1917). Born to Lithuanian Jewish (q.v.) immigrant parents, Helen Suzman, a long-serving opposition member of Parliament, was educated in Johannesburg (q.v.). She was lecturer in economics and economic history at the University of the Witwatersrand until 1953, when she became United Party (q.v.) member of Parliament (M.P.) for the Johannesburg constituency of Houghton. On the liberal (q.v.) wing of the party, she resigned in 1959 with 10 other M.P.s and was a founder member of the Progressive Party (q.v.). In the 1961 election, she was the only Progressive M.P. returned to Parliament, and for 13 years she was the party's sole representative, until the party managed to win further white support from 1974 and become the official opposition, as the Progressive Federal Party. During this period, Suzman acquired an international reputation as a staunch and vocal opponent of apartheid (q.v.) and of legislation that undermined the rule of law; she also used her parliamentary privilege to gain access to many African National Congress (q.v.) political prisoners between the 1960s and the 1980s. Her clashes with H. F. Verwoerd (q.v.), B. J. Vorster (q.v.), and P. W. Botha (q.v.), all of whom intensely disliked her influence, regularly attracted attention. The recipient of several honorary doctorates from British, United States, and South African universities (q.v.), as well as the United Nations Award of the International League for Human Rights (1978), she retired in 1989 after 36 years in Parliament. She remained active in the field of human rights, serving as a commissioner on the Human Rights Commission from 1994 until 1998.

SWAZILAND. The Swazi state was constructed at the beginning of the 19th century, when Sobhuza I fled north of the Pongola River after defeat in battle by Zwide (q.v.) of the Ndwandwe in 1815. Sobhuza established his base at Elangeni and won the allegiance of both Nguni (q.v.) and Sotho (q.v.) speakers, some of whom lived south and west of the boundaries of modern Swaziland. He managed to avoid conflict with both Shaka (q.v.) and Dingane (q.v.) of the Zulu kingdom (q.v.). His son Mswati II was thus able to inherit an important chiefdom on Sobhuza's death in 1838. During the mid-1840s, Mswati, faced with continuing threats from the Zulu in the south, entered into treaties with the Voortrekkers (q.v.) in the eastern Transvaal (q.v.). After his death in 1865, the Transvaal claimed virtually all the territory of the Swazi chiefdom. The present western boundaries were demarcated by the British during their occupation of the Transvaal after 1877; as a result many Swazi people were left within the Transvaal. When gold (q.v.) was discovered in the northwest of Swaziland in 1879, the mineral and land concessions white prospectors obtained weakened the chiefdom. The Transvaal took over the administration of the territory in 1895, to be succeeded by Britain during the South African War (q.v.). By this time, only 38 percent of the land remained in Swazi hands, the rest having passed into the control of individual whites.

Swaziland became a High Commission territory (q.v.) in 1907 and remained under British rule until it was granted independence in 1968. A KaNgwane (q.v.) bantustan (q.v.) was created by the South African government for the 500,000 Swazi living within South Africa. Considerable tension existed during the 1970s and 1980s between the South African and Swaziland governments over the fact that African National Congress (q.v.) and Pan Africanist Congress (q.v.) refugees sought shelter in the country, which some used as a base to launch guerrilla attacks on South Africa. A secret nonaggression pact was signed between the two countries in 1982. Negotiations between the two for the interchange of territory, allowing KaNgwane to be incorporated into Swaziland and Swaziland to obtain access to the Indian Ocean, were not concluded.

-T-

TAMBO, OLIVER REGINALD (1917–93). President of the African National Congress (ANC) (q.v.) from 1967 to 1991, Oliver Tambo was a leading member of the African National Congress Youth League (q.v.) in the 1940s. He worked with Nelson Mandela (q.v.) as a lawyer and in politics in the 1950s. When the Sharpeville (q.v.) crisis broke in 1960, he was instructed to continue the fight in exile. He settled first in London and later in Lusaka, Zambia, working tirelessly to promote the ANC's cause. He successfully held the organization together so that by the mid-1980s it had gained considerable international recognition. He was initially skeptical when told that Mandela wished to talk to the government, and he authorized a secret operation to send senior cadres back into South Africa to mobilize underground support for the ANC (Operation Vula). He suffered a stroke in 1989 and returned from exile in poor health after the ANC was unbanned.

TAUNG SKULL. Professor Raymond Dart of the University of the Witwatersrand caused a furor in the international scientific world when he published his analysis of a fossilized skull in the British scientific journal *Nature* in January 1925. Discovered in lime deposits at Taung in the arid northwest region of South Africa in 1924, it was the skull of a child who had died at about the age of four. It possessed both apelike and humanlike features: the child had walked upright, had humanoid teeth, a smooth, vertical forehead, and a small brain with humanoid features. From the skull, Dart identified an extinct ape family with humanlike characteristics, which he called *Australopithecus africanus*, the southern ape-man of Africa. He suggested that the Taung skull was the link between primates and hominids and provided evidence that humans originated in Africa. *See also* MRS. PLES.

THEAL, GEORGE MCCALL (1837–1919). The most prolific, and probably the most influential, of all historians of South Africa, George McCall Theal was born in Canada. He was heading for Australia when he disembarked in South Africa and remained there. He became an editor in British Kaffraria (q.v.) before starting to write a general history of his adopted country. He completed the first version of this while employed as a teacher at the Lovedale school at Alice in the eastern Cape. He was then employed in various capacities by the Cape Native Affairs Department, and it was during that time that he wrote the bulk of his 11-volume *History of South Africa*. Disappointed not to be given charge of the archives in Cape Town (q.v.), he was later named colonial historiographer (q.v.). Among the numerous works he prepared for publication were 36 volumes of the *Records of the Cape Colony* and eight volumes of *Records of South-Eastern Africa*.

While at Lovedale, Theal had shared missionary (q.v.) sympathies for blacks (q.v.), but after moving to Cape Town in the late 1870s he became increasingly racist in his writing. He continued to proclaim his objectivity and continued to pay respect to original materials, which he sought out both in South Africa and abroad. His deliberate search for evidence to justify white claims to occupy the bulk of South Africa's land was later acknowledged, and his writings, which influenced generations of schoolchildren and a general reading public, helped create the mythology that was to underpin apartheid (q.v.) ideology. From the 1920s, the historians W. M. Macmillan (q.v.) and C. W. de Kiewiet (q.v.) began to challenge Theal's view of South African history, but his writings remained influential into the second half of the century.

THONGA. The Thonga (or Tsonga, or Tonga, from a root meaning "east"; therefore, "people from the east") lived in small chiefdoms north of the Zulu kingdom (q.v.) in the hinterland of Delagoa Bay (q.v.). Thonga had hunted for ivory along the Limpopo River (q.v.) from at least the early 18th century and were the chief middlemen in trade between the Portuguese at Delagoa Bay and both the Nguni (q.v.) and the Sotho (q.v.). During the Nguni raids of the early 19th century, many Thonga were forced westward into the Transvaal (q.v.). One of the earliest African people to participate in migrant (q.v.) labor on an extensive scale, they moved through Zululand into Natal (q.v.) from the 1860s to seek work on the sugar plantations and elsewhere in Natal. The Cape (q.v.) tapped this labor source and imported Thonga labor by sea; at the Cape they were known as "Mosbiekers" (i.e., "from Mozambique" [q.v.]). Large numbers traveled overland to the diamond (q.v.) fields in the 1870s, where they were known as Shangaans.

The Thonga chiefdoms were annexed by the British in 1895 to prevent the Transvaal from obtaining access to the sea. Swiss missionaries (q.v.) who worked in the region, particularly the pioneer ethnographer Henri-Alexander Junod (1863–1934), used the term *Thonga* to include both the people of southern Mozambique and many in the eastern Transvaal. It was, to a considerable extent, the Swiss missionaries who helped construct a Thonga identity, a process carried much further by the South African government during the 1960s and 1970s, when they established a separate bantustan (q.v.) for the Transvaal Thonga, called Gazankulu.

THULAMELA. A hilltop settlement near the confluence of the Luvuvhu and Limpopo (q.v.) Rivers, in the extreme north of the Kruger National Park (q.v.), Thulamela was inhabited, from about the 13th to 16th centuries A.D., by people with cultural links with the inhabitants of Mapungubwe (q.v.) to the west and Great Zimbabwe (q.v.) to the north. The site was excavated in the mid-1990s; remains of stone-walled domestic and court enclosures, now reconstructed, made up the residence of a ruler of considerable power and wealth, who is assumed to have had divine status.

TLHAPING. The most southerly chiefdom of the Tswana (q.v.) people, the Tlhaping lived north of the Orange River (q.v.) in the 18th century and possessed considerable wealth in the form of livestock. They formed close ties with the Korana (q.v.) and acted as middlemen in trade between Tswana people to the north of them and Khoikhoi (q.v.) people along the Orange River and in Namibia (q.v.). Because of their geographical position, they were also the first Tswana to meet whites: a party of travelers and government officials from Cape Town (q.v.) visited their capital, Dithakong, in 1801.

The Tlhaping managed to maintain their power and independence through an alliance with the Griqua (q.v.) at the beginning of the 19th century. In 1823, Tlhaping aided the Griqua and the missionary Robert Moffat (q.v.) in repulsing an attack by displaced people at the Battle of Dithakong (q.v.). The Tlhaping slowly surrendered their land and autonomy to the Cape Colony (q.v.) as the century progressed, a process that accelerated after the discovery of diamonds (q.v.) in the late 1860s. Some Tlhaping rebelled against the Cape (q.v.) in 1878, and others in

1896. Many of them found themselves living in the Bophuthatswana (q.v.) bantustan (q.v.) in the 1980s.

TOMLINSON COMMISSION. In 1950, a commission was appointed by Dr. E. G. Jansen, minister of native affairs in the D. F. Malan (q.v.) National Party (q.v.) government, under the chairmanship of F. R. Tomlinson, to examine the socioeconomic situation of the reserves (q.v.) in order to increase their capacity to support black settlement. The commission produced a massive report in 1955. Its major assumption was that a unitary, common society was not possible in South Africa, as white domination would never be abandoned. The reserves needed to be developed to support the African (q.v.) population: the report concluded that just over half of South Africa's blacks could successfully earn a living in the reserves with the proper development of agriculture (q.v.), the introduction of freehold tenure of land, the incorporation of additional land, and the encouragement of the investment of industrial capital within the reserves or on their borders. To achieve this, the government would need to spend almost £105 million over the next 10 years. The commission projected that, by the turn of the century, the reserves would support some two-thirds of Africans, who would by then number 21 million people. Local self-government under "Bantu authorities" would be promoted in the reserves; in the "white areas," Africans would have no political rights, but outside the reserves they would never outnumber whites.

The Tomlinson report formed the basis of the bantustan policy (q.v.) of H. F. Verwoerd (q.v.) and underpinned National Party planning until the mid-1970s; at the same time, however, key recommendations of the report were rejected. The government argued that the proposals were far too expensive to be implemented. Any economic independence of the reserves was not permissible; neither were they to compete with white areas for capital and labor. Thus, a capitalist class of black farmers with individual land tenure was not permitted to emerge; only subsistence agriculture was allowed; and white capital could only be invested outside the reserves. Tomlinson's recommendations were thus never properly implemented. The report's poor population projections, its underestimation of the difficulties of industrial decentralization, and its focus on the reserves in isolation from the rest of the country meant that it was, in any case, fundamentally flawed.

TORCH COMMANDO. Originally instituted as the War Veterans' Action Committee, the Torch Commando, a quasi-political organization of former servicemen, suddenly emerged in opposition to the National Party

(NP) (q.v.) government in 1951. In May of that year, it staged a series of spectacular protests, some of which included torchlight processions, against legislation being introduced to remove Coloured (q.v.) voters from the common voters' roll. It opened its membership to nonveterans and by late 1951 had attracted some 120,000 members in 350 branches. There were a few Afrikaners (q.v.) in the leadership, but most of the members were English-speaking whites (q.v.). Whether Coloureds could become members was never clarified, but they were not welcomed in the organization, which saw itself as white. *See also* FRANCHISE.

Besides opposing the government on the Coloured vote issue, there was no agreement on what the Torch Commando should do. Some members wanted a new National Convention (q.v.) to revise the constitution; others successfully pushed the organization into a united front with the United Party (q.v.) and the (white) Labour Party (q.v.). The NP sought to depict the Torch Commando as dangerous and unconstitutional. After the NP won the general election of 1953, some Torch Commando members joined the new Liberal Party (q.v.), while others argued that the organization had failed and should disband. A narrow majority of those at its June 1953 congress decided to carry on, but by then the Torch Commando was on its deathbed, and attempts to revive it in 1955 came to nothing.

TOTAL STRATEGY. A 1977 Defence White Paper advanced the idea that South Africa was confronting a "total onslaught," instigated by Moscow, and that to meet the challenge a "total strategy" was called for. When P. W. Botha (q.v.) became prime minister in 1978, he promoted the idea to justify apartheid (q.v.) and advocated the use of any means necessary—including destabilization of neighboring countries—to resist those who sought to overthrow the regime by violence. An elaborate National Security Management System, under the State Security Council (q.v.), was put in place to implement the total strategy and coordinate state activities in the interests of defending the country from the "revolutionary forces" opposed to it. In reality, to the extent that there was a coordinated onslaught on the country, it was one directed at apartheid, not a communist-inspired design to control South Africa.

TOWNSHIP REVOLT (1984–86). In September 1984, as the tricameral Parliament (q.v.) was being inaugurated, an uprising began in the Vaal Triangle south of Johannesburg (q.v.). It was in part a response to the imposition of increased service charges on residents by new township authorities, who were rejected as illegitimate. The revolt soon spread countrywide, and for brief periods some townships were beyond police (q.v.) control. The army was called in to aid the police in suppressing the revolt. As a result of harsh repression, including the imposition of a general state of emergency in 1986, the revolt was brought under control, but by then the apartheid (q.v.) regime was condemned internationally as never before, and widespread sanctions (q.v.) had been imposed against it. More than any other single factor, the revolt led the government to rethink its policies and open negotiations with the jailed Nelson Mandela (q.v.).

TRADE UNION CONGRESS OF SOUTH AFRICA (TUCSA). Formed in 1954–55 as a federation of registered trade unions (q.v.), TUCSA was in the early 1980s the largest such body in the country. In 1956 it opposed legislation extending the job color bar (q.v.), though it excluded African unions from its membership, and the South African Congress of Trade Unions (q.v.) was set up as a rival body to mobilize the African working class. In 1962, TUCSA decided to allow African unions to affiliate, but under pressure from both the government and white unions those that had joined were forced to withdraw in the late 1960s. In 1974, TUCSA once again allowed African unions to affiliate. Those that did so were mainly unions organized parallel to the registered unions and under white control. Those on the left criticized TUCSA for its narrow, nonpolitical approach.

TRADE UNIONS. The earliest unions, formed among white immigrant workers, were craft unions. Cape (q.v.) printers made an attempt to organize in 1838. In 1881, typographical workers' and carpenters' unions were established in Cape Town (q.v.). Unionism greatly increased with the mineral revolution. An Artisans' and Engine Drivers' Association came into being on the diamond (q.v.) fields in 1883, and a branch of the British Amalgamated Society of Engineers was formed in 1886, the forerunner of the Amalgamated Engineering Union established in 1920. The Transvaal Miners' Association brought together white miners in 1902, foreshadowing the all-white Mine Workers' Union established in 1913.

As mine owners sought to lower their labor costs by fragmenting craft operations and substituting semiskilled or unskilled Africans for whites, white trade unions were increasingly concerned not only to improve the economic position of their members against employers and win union recognition but also to prevent Africans (or, for a few years, Chinese [q.v.]) from acquiring jobs currently held by whites. The two decades after the South African War (q.v.) were years of great militancy on the part of the white unions. After the suppression of the Rand Revolt (q.v.), however, trade union membership declined markedly, and the state stepped in to control industrial relations through the recognition of non-African unions and the provision of new conciliation machinery.

With more and more Afrikaners (q.v.) joining the urban working class, the Afrikaner Broederbond (q.v.) played a crucial role in detaching them from English-controlled unions or wresting control of unions from English-speaking (q.v.) cliques. In 1933, for example, a new railwaymens' union was set up for Afrikaners. After a long battle, control of the powerful white Mine Workers' Union passed into Afrikaner hands.

The first African trade unions of any significance were formed at the end of World War I (q.v.). The Industrial Workers of Africa emerged out of classes run for Africans by the International Socialist League in Johannesburg (q.v.) in 1917. Its slogan was *Sifuna zonke* (Zulu, "We want all"); it was hoped that it would grow into a large union of the unskilled, along the lines of the American union called the Industrial Workers of the World. But the police (q.v.) infiltrated the union, and it soon fell apart. The first large general union on the African continent was the Industrial and Commercial Workers' Union (ICU) (q.v.), formed by Clements Kadalie in 1919.

In the late 1920s and early 1930s, as the ICU collapsed, a number of short-lived industrial unions began to emerge among African workers, parallel to unions registered under the Industrial Conciliation Act. Some unions—the Garment Workers' Union, most notably—brought together Afrikaner and Coloured (q.v.) workers. It was not until 1956 that an amendment to the Industrial Conciliation Act prevented any further registration of such unions, but long before that many of them had been hard hit by state action.

During World War II (q.v.), when the African workforce in industry grew rapidly and labor was in short supply, African (q.v.) unionism entered a militant phase, culminating in the 1946 strike (q.v.), when the African Mine Workers' Union, formed in 1941, brought out more than 60,000 miners. The brutal suppression of the strike was followed by greater cooperation between the African trade union movement and the African National Congress (ANC) (q.v.). Between 1954 and 1960, some 40 unions affiliated with the South African Congress of Trade Unions (q.v.), part of the Congress Alliance (q.v.). The 1960s was a decade of repression, with minimal union activity. From the early 1970s, however, young whites, with close links to the universities (q.v.), helped organize unregistered unions; some of these organizers suffered detentions and bannings (q.v.) as a result. (The sixth trade unionist to die in detention was a young white trade-union leader, Neil Aggett, who died in February 1982.)

Gradually both employers and the state were converted to the belief that the best way to control African unionism was to recognize it and thereby permit the registration of African unions. This major step, recommended by the Wiehahn Commission (q.v.), was taken in 1979. The new possibility of registration sparked off a fierce debate within the labor movement, with some arguing that because registration meant increased state control, it should therefore be rejected. The Federation of South African Trade Unions (FOSATU)—formally constituted in 1979, though it grew out of attempts to bring together unions formed during the strikes of 1973 and after—sought to create a nonracial labor movement and encouraged the formation and affiliation of broad-based industrial unions. It was prepared to accept registration, so long as its affiliated unions could be nonracial. This was conceded in 1981, and FOSATU made great gains. Of the unregistered unions, the South African Allied Workers' Union grew, especially in the eastern Cape and Ciskei (q.v.), despite great police harassment. In the 1980s, union membership increased at an unprecedented rate, and individual unions combined in large organizations, the most important of which was the Congress of South African Trade Unions (COSATU) (q.v.), launched in 1985, which later allied itself with the ANC. The largest union in COSATU was the National Union of Mineworkers, the successor to the African Mine Workers' Union.

TRANSITIONAL EXECUTIVE COUNCIL (TEC). A key element in the process of transition from apartheid (q.v.) to democratic rule, the TEC was designed by the constitutional negotiators to meet the need for a body to replace the government in the run-up to the April 1994 election. Made up of representatives from the parties in the constitutional negotiations, it was formally constituted by Parliament in December 1993 and served as a joint executive; it was thus a precursor of the government of National Unity (q.v.). The subcouncil on defense, one of the TEC's seven subcouncils, was responsible for establishing the National Peacekeeping Force, which proved a disastrous experiment. The subcouncil's planning for the creation of a new defense force was much more successful. With the inauguration of a new government after the election, the work of the TEC came to an end. *See also* SOUTH AFRICAN DEFENCE FORCE.

TRANSKEI. Iron Age (q.v.) and probably Bantu-speaking (q.v.) people lived on the Transkei (the land "across" the Kei River) coast by the seventh century A.D. From the 16th century, shipwrecked European sailors told of mixed farmers, speaking Nguni (q.v.) languages, living in the region. During the 1820s, the small northern chiefdoms in the Transkei were devastated by Zulu (q.v.) armies. Disruption would probably have been greater had an intrusive group of Ngwane not been defeated at the Battle of Mbholompo in the central Transkei in 1828. Large numbers of refugees from the Mfecane (q.v.) settled in the Transkei at this time, and European missionary (q.v.) and colonial trading networks from the south began to spread across the Kei.

In the mid-19th century, *Transkei* usually meant the land immediately east of the Kei, between that river and the Mbashe. From the 1870s it often referred to the entire area from the Kei to the southern border of Natal (q.v.) and from the Drakensberg (q.v.) to the Indian Ocean. This area, annexed to the Cape Colony (q.v.) in stages between 1879 and 1894, became a separate administrative unit within the colony, one in which a policy of legal differentiation was applied. In the 20th century, it formed the largest African reserve (q.v.) in the country and became the pacesetter in the bantustan (q.v.) scheme of H. F. Verwoerd (q.v.). The Transkeian bantustan, with its capital at Umtata, received self-government in 1963 and independence, recognized only by South Africa, in 1976. In 1987 its civilian prime minister was overthrown by a military coup; Major General Bantu Holomisa (q.v.) emerged as the Transkei's last ruler. In April 1994 the bantustan was reincorporated into South Africa, and the Transkei became part of the Eastern Cape (q.v.) Province.

TRANSORANGIA. A predominantly high-veld (q.v.) grassland region, Transorangia—the area "across the Orange River" (q.v.), also known as the TransGariep (from "Gariep," the Korana [q.v.] word for the Orange River)—had been occupied originally by Khoisan (q.v.) hunters and herders, and parts of it were settled by Bantu-speaking (q.v.) pastoralists and agriculturists (q.v.) as early as A.D. 1000. During the 17th and 18th centuries, the region experienced considerable conflict between competing Sotho-Tswana (qq.v.) groups, a pattern that intensified in the first half of the 19th century with the arrival of new people in the region. The Griqua (q.v.) under Adam Kok III (q.v.) established themselves in the southern parts, and Voortrekkers (q.v.) settled further north during the 1830s. These groups provided fresh challenges to the Rolong (q.v.), Tlokoa, and Sotho peoples of the region. By the 1840s prevailing conditions of unrest threatened the northern frontier (q.v.) of the Cape Colony (q.v.), persuading the governor, George Napier, to try to establish subsidized buffer states as a means of exercising indirect control without heavy military commitment. The strategy failed, and Britain annexed the area between the Orange and Vaal Rivers as the Orange River Sovereignty (q.v.) in 1848.

TRANSVAAL. Evidence of pastoral farming and cultivation in parts of the Transvaal (the land "across [north of] the Vaal River") dates from at least the fifth century A.D. Bantu-speaking (q.v.) farmers were scattered across the region from the 10th century; according to tradition, Sotho-Tswana (qq.v.) peoples claim descent from the farmers of the Greater Magaliesberg area in the 13th and 14th centuries. By the 16th and 17th centuries, Sotho-Tswana speakers had dispersed from this relatively densely populated region across most of the Transvaal. Large portions of the area were disrupted during the 1820s by the Mfecane (q.v.). Mzilikazi (q.v.) incorporated large numbers of Sotho speakers into his Ndebele state (q.v.) and for a brief time had his capital near modern Pretoria (q.v.).

The Voortrekkers (q.v.) founded four separate republics, based in Potchefstroom (q.v.) (which was, from 1838, the largest white settlement north of the Vaal), Utrecht, Lydenburg, and the Soutpansberg. In the Sand River Convention of 1852, Britain recognized the independence of whites living north of the Vaal, but only in 1858 were the scattered groups of whites brought under the central authority of the South African Republic (SAR) (q.v.), as the Transvaal state was called, with its capital at Pretoria (q.v.). For much of the latter half of the 19th century, the SAR was weak, unstable, poorly administered, and bankrupt; whites also struggled to exercise authority over African chiefdoms in the region. Their inability to defeat the Pedi (q.v.) was used by the British, who were investigating the possibility of confederation (q.v.), to justify the annexation of the SAR in 1877. After the British army defeated both the Zulu (q.v.) and the Pedi, the Anglo–Transvaal War (q.v.) broke out as the Transvaal Afrikaners (q.v.) rose up against British rule. The Pretoria Convention of August 1881 returned self-government to the SAR, but Britain, fearing a threat to continued imperial rule in the subcontinent, made sure that the SAR could not form alliances with a foreign power or acquire direct access to the sea.

The discovery of gold (q.v.) on the Witwatersrand (q.v.) in 1886 fundamentally transformed Transvaal history. Britain feared the potential threat to its interests held by the Transvaal's wealth, and political and economic considerations precipitated the South African War (q.v.) of

1899–1902, during which the SAR lost its independence and became a crown colony. After the war, Sir Alfred Milner (q.v.) hoped to introduce thousands of new British immigrants to the territory to outnumber the Afrikaners and undermine their culture through a determined anglicization policy, but his plans were foiled by the devastating economic consequences of the war. Fundamental adjustments to formal black–white relations, however, were not considered. The original SAR constitution had declared there would be no equality in church or state and that only white males could enjoy the benefits of citizenship. In the Treaty of Vereeniging (q.v.), which ended the war in 1902, Britain undertook not to extend the franchise (q.v.) to blacks, and during negotiations for the creation of the Union (q.v.) of South Africa in 1908 and 1909, the Transvaal opposed any extension of the nonracial franchise of the Cape Colony (q.v.).

In 1910, the Transvaal became one of the Union of South Africa's four provinces, and Pretoria became the national administrative capital. During the 20th century, the Transvaal came to play an increasingly dominant political and economic role in the country. Johannesburg (q.v.), situated on the Witwatersrand, in the center of the Transvaal's mineral belt, became the commercial, financial, and industrial heart of the country. Much economic power lay in the hands of English speakers (q.v.) throughout the century, though Afrikaner capital gained strength from the 1950s. Afrikaner nationalism (q.v.), however, was most robust in the Transvaal, in Pretoria and the rich agricultural districts of the province. The increasingly powerful National Party (NP) (q.v.) of the Transvaal largely dictated the pace of the country's political life from the mid-1950s until the 1980s, when Transvaal Afrikanerdom split between those in the NP prepared to entertain some notions of reform and those who moved into more conservative parties to the right.

In the Witwatersrand region, townships housed the labor supply of the mines and industries on which the country's wealth depended. Those events that represent the most powerful symbols of black resistance to apartheid (q.v.) and white oppression—the Sharpeville massacre (q.v.), the Soweto uprising (q.v.), and the township revolt (q.v.)—began here. After the election of 1994, the Transvaal ceased to exist as a province. Four new provinces were created out of it: Gauteng (q.v.), North-West Province (q.v.), Northern Province (q.v.), and Mpumalanga (q.v.).

TRANSVAAL, ANNEXATION OF (1877). To promote the confederation (q.v.) of South Africa, Lord Carnarvon (q.v.) appointed Theophilus

Shepstone (q.v.) to proceed to the Transvaal (q.v.) (i.e., the South African Republic [q.v.]) and annex it, if its citizens were willing. Using the Transvaal's weak government and its inability to defeat the Pedi (q.v.) as an excuse and ignoring clear evidence that the Transvaal Boers (q.v.) did not want to come under British rule, Shepstone raised the Union Jack in April 1878 and became first British administrator of the Transvaal. British rule aroused much resentment among the Boer community, and the Boers rose up in revolt in 1880. *See also* ANGLO–TRANSVAAL WAR.

TREASON TRIAL (1956–61). Following the adoption of the Freedom Charter by the African National Congress (q.v.) at the Congress of the People held at Kliptown, south of Johannesburg (q.v.), in 1955, the police arrested 156 of the people involved and charged them with treason, on the grounds that they were working for revolution. The trial dragged on, and the remaining accused, including Nelson Mandela (q.v.), were finally acquitted in 1961, the state having failed to establish any revolutionary intent behind their actions.

TREKBOERS. The trekboers (Dutch, "frontier farmers"), white semi-nomadic Dutch-speaking (q.v.) sheep and cattle farmers, began to leave the southwestern Cape (q.v.), with its Mediterranean climate, at the end of the 17th century. They moved into the drier interior, where extensive pastoralism and hunting were the only possible modes of production. In the first half of the 18th century, land was plentiful in the interior, and there were few geographical obstacles to expansion in northerly and easterly directions. Khoisan (q.v.) peoples of the region were variously dispossessed of their land, killed, expelled, or permitted to work as squatters (q.v.) or laborers on the 6,000-acre farms that the trekboers allocated to themselves. One main line of advance was eastward, parallel to the mountain ranges, to the Zuurveld (q.v.) area and the Fish River, where the trekboers met Xhosa (q.v.) stock farmers in the 1770s. Others moved their herds and their ox wagons around or across the barren Karoo (q.v.) and beyond the boundaries the colonial authorities tried periodically to fix. Although the life of the trekboers was largely self-sufficient, they maintained irregular contact with Cape markets to ensure that they were supplied with essential commodities such as firearms and ammunition. Most conducted simple, isolated lives, remote from the control of the Cape authorities. Despite this, they continued to regard themselves as colonial subjects, unlike the Voortrekkers (q.v.) of the 1830s, who deliberately sought to free themselves of colonial control.

TRICAMERAL PARLIAMENT (1984–94). One of P. W. Botha's (q.v.) most important reforms, the tricameral Parliament lay at the heart of the new constitution of 1984. Coloureds (q.v.) and Indians (q.v.) were brought into central government in separate houses of Parliament—a House of Representatives for Coloureds and a House of Delegates for Indians—though provision was made for the three houses to meet together under certain circumstances. The exclusion of Africans (q.v.) from this new arrangement helped fuel the township revolt (q.v.), and the failure of the tricameral Parliament to resolve the government's crisis of legitimacy was an important reason for the decision by F. W. de Klerk (q.v.) to negotiate a settlement with the African National Congress (q.v.) and others. These negotiations led to the dissolution of the tricameral Parliament in December 1993, prior to the general election of 1994, but only after it had approved the interim constitution of 1993, drafted by the Multi-Party Negotiating Forum (q.v.), thus providing legislative continuity.

TRUTH AND RECONCILIATION COMMISSION (TRC). The idea for the TRC was put forward in a speech by the new minister of justice, Dullah Omar, to the first democratic Parliament in July 1994. At this time Alex Boraine (b. 1931), former member of Parliament and executive director of the Institute for a Democratic Alternative in South Africa, headed a nongovernmental organization, Justice in Transition, which argued that South Africa should follow other countries in creating such a commission. The aim was to find out what had led to gross violations of human rights and to deal with that past by granting amnesty to those who made full disclosure of what had happened in the past.

The TRC was set up by an act of Parliament, and its 17 members, headed by Archbishop Desmond Tutu (q.v.), were appointed in December 1995. Its Human Rights Violations Committee investigated gross violations of human rights between 1960 and 1994 (the cutoff date was initially December 1993, but it was later extended to the date of Nelson Mandela's [q.v.] inauguration). Numerous public hearings were held in many parts of the country in 1996 and 1997, and more than 20,000 statements by victims of gross violations of human rights were recorded. The Amnesty Committee heard applications for amnesty from more than 7,000 people for offenses committed in those years. If the offenses had been politically motivated, and if full disclosure was made, amnesty was granted. Some of the hearings revealed much about the way certain high-profile murders and assassinations, including the death of Steve Biko (q.v.), had been carried out. A third committee advised the government on reparations and rehabilitation for victims of gross human rights abuses and proposed that a fund of some R3 billion be established to meet those needs. The TRC's final report was presented at the end of October 1998, but the work of its Amnesty Committee will likely extend well beyond that date.

TSWANA. The Tswana were a western Sotho (q.v.) people who, from the 15th to the 18th centuries, gradually occupied most of the central and western area of the high veld (q.v.). Various chiefdoms among the Tswana experienced a shifting pattern of segmentation and amalgamation during this period. The availability of land enabled dissatisfied people and their followers to break away from chiefdoms and settle in new areas; at the same time, powerful chiefdoms were able to consolidate authority through the conquest of neighbors and the control of natural resources. By the end of the 18th century, however, strains within Tswana societies became more acute: they had reached the limits of their westerly expansion as they began to press against the Kalahari Desert, and an extended drought between 1790 and 1810 intensified competition for pastoral and arable land and for control of trading routes.

During the period of the Mfecane (q.v.), these tensions were exacerbated by the arrival of new peoples, both those with aggressive intentions and many displaced refugees. Although some Tswana groups managed to rebuild themselves during the 1830s, the presence of the Griqua (q.v.) and, particularly, white Voortrekkers (q.v.) from the end of that decade prevented many from resuming independent lifestyles. Tswana who lived in the South African Republic (q.v.) established by the Voortrekkers were forced to compete for land and were often subject to demands for tribute and labor. After the discovery of diamonds (q.v.), many Tswana were caught between conflicting British and Boer (q.v.) requirements, causing enormous strains within chiefdoms over alliances and strategies. This was graphically illustrated in the South African War (q.v.), when the Tswana entered the conflict as active participants on both sides.

After 1910, many Tswana shared the experiences of Africans (q.v.) across the country: their economic independence disintegrated through the system of migrant (q.v.) labor and their alienation from their land. In 1977, under the bantustan policy (q.v.) of the apartheid (q.v.) government, the republic of Bophuthatswana (q.v.) was given independence, and it was there that people of Tswana origins were expected to exercize political rights. Like the other independent bantustans, however, Bophuthatswana could not survive without significant financial and military support from the South African government. A crisis there in March 1994 proved an important precursor to the successful democratic elections of April 1994, when Bophuthatswana was reincorporated in South Africa.

TUTU, DESMOND MPILO (1931–). Clergyman and anti-apartheid activist. Ordained in the Anglican Church (q.v.) in 1961, he was employed by the World Council of Churches before becoming the Anglican dean of Johannesburg in 1975. He was then briefly bishop of Lesotho and general secretary of the South African Council of Churches before being elected archbishop of Cape Town in 1986. Throughout the 1980s he played an important role in mobilizing international opinion against apartheid (q.v.), and he was a strong advocate of the imposition of sanctions (q.v.) against the apartheid regime. He was awarded the Nobel Peace Prize in 1984. Once the liberation movements were unbanned in 1990, he deliberately adopted a less overtly political position, but remained an influential figure, promoting the idea of the "rainbow nation" and commentating on events with wit and humour, as well as profound seriousness. In 1995, on the eve of his retirement as Archbishop of Cape Town, he was appointed head of the Truth and Reconciliation Commission (q.v.).

-U-

UITLANDERS. Afrikaans word meaning *foreigners*, which was applied to non-Afrikaner whites in the Transvaal (q.v.) before the South African War (q.v.). Thousands settled on the Witwatersrand (q.v.) after the discovery of gold (q.v.) in 1886, but restrictive franchise (q.v.) laws made it difficult for new immigrants to acquire citizenship and the right to vote. Those associated with the Transvaal government viewed the Uitlanders as brash, materialistic, and culturally alien, and feared that if they obtained the franchise they would upset Afrikaner (q.v.) political dominance and even cause the independence of the Transvaal from Britain to be revoked. Such fears were almost certainly exaggerated, since few Uitlanders wanted Transvaal citizenship. In the aftermath of the Jameson Raid (q.v.), the British government made Uitlander rights a key issue in its relations with the Transvaal. In 1899 President Kruger (q.v.) was prepared to grant the Uitlanders the vote after they had fulfilled a seven-year residence requirement, but this was unacceptable to Sir Alfred

Milner (q.v.). The franchise issue thus contributed to the outbreak of the South African War. After the war, the franchise was extended to Uitlanders, but despite large Boer losses in the war and further immigration from Britain, Afrikaners remained a clear majority of whites, and an Afrikaner political party, Het Volk (q.v.), triumphed in the whites-only election of 1907.

UMKHONTO WESIZWE (MK). Military wing of the African National Congress (ANC) (q.v.), established in 1961 after the banning (q.v.) of the ANC in 1960. It undertook sabotage from 1961 and then, from exile, guerrilla training. Its guerrillas entered Rhodesia (*see* ZIMBABWE) in the 1960s but suffered a major defeat there at the hands of South African security forces. After the Soweto uprising (q.v.) of 1976, its numbers were boosted as thousands of young men and women joined its ranks. Many found themselves in Angola (q.v.), and some died there fighting against UNITA. In the late 1970s MK operatives entered South Africa to perform acts of sabotage. The guerrilla ethos captured the imagination of many township youths and helped promote the cause of the ANC. Of some 1,500 attacks between 1977 and 1989, among the most spectacular were those on the Sasol oil refinery in June 1880, the rocket attack on the South African Defence Force (q.v.) headquarters at Voortrekkerhoogte outside Pretoria (q.v.) in August 1981, the planting of bombs at Koeberg nuclear power station in December 1982, and the car-bomb that exploded outside the air force command center in downtown Pretoria in May 1983 and killed 19 people.

The escalation in conflict in the 1980s played a major role in leading to the negotiated settlement of the early 1990s. But the New York accords of December 1988, providing for a transition to independence in Namibia (q.v.), required MK to leave its Angolan camps, and its cadres found themselves as far from South Africa as Uganda. When the ANC agreed, in the Pretoria Minute (q.v.) of August 1990, to suspend the armed struggle, it did not disband MK, which grew in size through the early 1990s. Following the democratic election of 1994, its members were integrated into the new South African National Defence Force, but with the downscaling of that force many soon left it.

UNION (1910). Several British-led attempts to unite the various South African states were made and subsequently failed during the 19th century (*see* CONFEDERATION). After the South African War (q.v.), when all four of the states were British, Sir Alfred Milner (q.v.) and members of his Kindergarten (q.v.) took steps to promote the idea; among the schemes he initiated to promote closer ties between the South African states were the amalgamation of the railway (q.v.) networks, the formation of an Inter-Colonial Council, and the appointment of a South African Native Affairs Commission under Sir Godfrey Lagden (q.v.) in 1903 to draw up a South Africa–wide "native policy." A South African Customs Union was also created (1903).

Lord Selborne (1859–1942), Milner's successor as high commissioner, hoped that a federated South Africa would attract large-scale British immigration. Louis Botha (q.v.) and Jan Smuts (q.v.) were attracted to the idea of a united South Africa because they thought it would be less subject to British interference. A discussion paper known as the Selborne Memorandum was issued to the colonial governments in 1907 and then published and widely debated. Written by Lionel Curtis at the high commissioner's invitation, it argued that unity would bring political stability and promote economic progress. Unification seemed likely to pull the country out of the recession from which it had suffered since 1903 and eliminate the tensions that disagreements on customs and railway tariffs had produced. The confidence of Natal's (q.v.) whites in their ability to control their large African population had been shaken by the Bambatha Rebellion (q.v.), making closer union more attractive to the other states.

A National Convention (q.v.), made up of representatives from the various parliaments and therefore all white, met in 1908 and 1909 to draw up a new constitution for the united country. It agreed that the four states should unite, and that South Africa should be a unitary state and not a federation. The proposals emanating from the National Convention were approved by the four states, then incorporated in a South Africa Bill, which went through the British parliament. The Union of South Africa was inaugurated on 31 May 1910, eight years to the day after the signing of the Treaty of Vereeniging (q.v.).

A delegation of white liberals and blacks, led by the former Cape prime minister, William Schreiner, traveled to London to protest against the color bar in the Union constitution, but to no avail. Union was widely hailed as a great achievement. It was clearly to Britain's advantage for South Africa to be one large state, able to defend itself, yet within the Empire. Thus, there was hope of an English (q.v.) and Afrikaner (q.v.) reconciliation, as well as the prospect that the interests of finance and mining capital would be promoted. Nor were Africans entirely overlooked. The Liberal government in Britain hoped that a strong Union would be in the interests of Africans and that the Cape's non-racial franchise (q.v.), protected by the entrenched clauses of the constitution, which could be altered only by a vote of two-thirds of both houses of parliament sitting together, would in time be extended to the other provinces. It was made clear that the wish of the people of the high commission territories (q.v.) should be considered when the question of their incorporation arose.

Though liberal historians have condemned the choice of a unitary rather than a federal constitution for so heterogeneous a society, it was believed at the time that a unitary one would prove easier to work and would provide the necessary strong government. Had South Africa not been a close union, white Southern Rhodesians might have agreed to join it in the 1920s.

UNIONIST PARTY. A political party drawing on English-speaking (q.v.) support, it was the main opposition in the first Union (q.v.) parliament. It emerged from the Progressive Party of the pre-Union Cape Colony (q.v.), which took the name Unionist Party shortly before Union came into being. After the formation of the National Party (q.v.), Louis Botha (q.v.) became increasingly dependent on Unionist support, and it was eventually absorbed by the South African Party (q.v.) in 1920. Its lineal successor was the pro-British Dominion Party (q.v.), founded in 1934.

UNITED DEMOCRATIC FRONT (UDF). The most important internal anti-apartheid organization in the 1980s, it was established at a meeting at Mitchell's Plain outside Cape Town (q.v.) on 20 August 1983. This followed a call by the Rev. Allan Boesak (q.v.) for opposition to the tricameral (q.v.) constitution and to proposed legislation for African administration. Standing for a democratic, non-racial order, the UDF was an umbrella body that brought together hundreds of youth, student, and civic organizations in a decentralized structure that was difficult for the apartheid (q.v.) government to suppress. The reformist image the government wanted to present at first allowed the UDF space to organize, but it was hit hard during the states of emergency from 1985 onwards. The government believed it had played a major role in the township revolt (q.v.), and many of its leading office-bearers suffered imprisonment and other forms of harassment. Twenty-two leading activists, including Patrick Lekota and Popo Molefe, were tried on charges of treason and terrorism in the small town of Delmas from 1985; the trial dragged on for years and the accused were found guilty and imprisoned but were set free when the case went on appeal.

Along with other organizations, the UDF was restricted in February 1988. In showing the strength of internal opposition, it played an important role in the process leading to the negotiated settlement of the 1990s. Once the African National Congress (ANC) (q.v.) and the Pan Africanist Congress (q.v.) had been unbanned, however, the UDF lost its reason for existence, and was disbanded in August 1991 on its eighth anniversary. Many of its leaders played important roles in ANC politics thereafter: Allan Boesak became ANC leader in the Western Cape (q.v.) for a time; Lekota became the first premier of the Free State (q.v.) and then chair of the National Council of Provinces; and Molefe became premier of the North-West Province (q.v.).

UNITED DEMOCRATIC MOVEMENT (UDM). New party founded in September 1997 under the leadership of Roelf Meyer (q.v.), who had left the National Party (q.v.), and Bantu Holomisa (q.v.), who had been expelled from the African National Congress (q.v.) for indiscipline. At first there was joint leadership, but at the party's conference held in mid-1998 Holomisa became the leader, with Meyer his deputy and Sifiso Nkabinde, an ex-ANC warlord from Richmond, KwaZulu-Natal (q.v.), as the secretary. One of the main areas of support for the UDM was the Transkei (q.v.) region of the eastern Cape (q.v.), which Holomisa had once ruled and where there was much dissatisfaction with government policy. The UDM was vague on policy, but was critical of the ANC government for failing to deliver on its promises. Not being represented in parliament, the UDM did not qualify for financial support from the state. This was something the party tried, without success, to challenge.

UNITED NATIONS (UN). The South African prime minister Jan Smuts (q.v.) was the main author of the preamble to the UN Charter, and South Africa was a founder member of the world body, yet it was soon the most criticized country of all in that forum. At the inaugural session in 1946, the Indian delegation brought South Africa's treatment of its Indian (q.v.) minority before the General Assembly, which also rejected South Africa's plea for the incorporation of South West Africa (*see* NAMIBIA). From 1952 the whole apartheid (q.v.) system came under regular attack, despite South African objections that it was a domestic matter and fell under article 2(7) of the UN Charter, which had been designed to protect members from interference by others in matters of domestic jurisdiction. After the Sharpeville massacre (q.v.), criticism became much more strident, with a UN Special Committee against Apartheid being appointed in 1962. In that year the General Assembly recommended that member states break all ties with South Africa, including trade links. The following year the Security Council imposed a non-mandatory arms embargo (q.v.). Gradually South Africa left the various UN agencies: UNESCO in 1956, the International Labour Organization in 1961, and the World Health Organization in 1965.

In October 1966 the General Assembly voted to terminate South Africa's mandate over South West Africa. Thereafter, South Africa's continued occupation of the territory and its refusal to acknowledge UN supervision of it became a matter to which the UN devoted much attention. In 1974 the General Assembly rejected the credentials of the South African delegation, preventing them from speaking, but South Africa remained a member of the world body, speaking in the Security Council and having regular discussions with the Secretary General on the Namibian issue in particular.

Calls for mandatory economic sanctions (q.v.) against South Africa came before the Security Council on a number of occasions, but were vetoed by the Western members—the United States, Britain, and France. In 1977, however, after the murder of Steve Biko (q.v.) and the banning of Black Consciousness (q.v.) organizations, the Security Council did impose a mandatory arms embargo against South Africa. But this was as far as UN sanctions went: in the Cold War era, the United States in particular did not want the Soviet Union to have any decisive say in the removal of sanctions, and so vetoed further sanctions proposed in the Security Council.

South African government suspicions of the UN began to dissipate when the UN played a relatively even-handed role in the transition to independence in Namibia in 1989. UN observers also filled a minor role in monitoring the transition to democracy in South Africa in the early 1990s. After the election of a democratic government in April 1994, South Africa resumed its full role in the UN, and again began paying its membership dues. In 1997 the Mandela (q.v.) government began lobbying hard to secure a permanent seat on an enlarged Security Council.

UNITED PARTY (UP) (1934–1977). Governing party until 1948, and thereafter the official parliamentary opposition to the National Party (NP) (q.v.). The United South African National Party emerged from the fusion of J. B. M. Hertzog's (q.v.) NP and the South African Party (q.v.) of General Smuts (q.v.). Its first major crisis came in September 1939, when Hertzog and his supporters left the organization over South Africa's entry into World War II (q.v.). It lost power in 1948, despite winning a majority of votes, because of the urban concentration of its supporters, the weighting of rural constituencies, and the way that the delimitation of constituencies had been applied. This shocking defeat, followed in short succession by the deaths of Jan Hofmeyr (1894–1948), Smuts's deputy, and then of Smuts himself in 1950, left the party in great disarray. It continued to outpoll the NP until the 1961 election, but as it lost seats in successive elections to the NP, it lost confidence in its ability ever to return to power. Committed to white supremacy, it offered only the 1948 pattern of race relations, the possibility of a few whites representing Africans (q.v.) in Parliament, and white leadership with justice. It became, increasingly, a mainly English-speaking (q.v.) party.

In an attempt to make itself more acceptable to the white electorate, the UP moved closer to the NP and even began to attack that party from the right. In response to the separate development vision of Prime Minister H. F. Verwoerd (q.v.) in 1959, the right-wing in the UP saw an opportunity to brand him a negrophile and urged the party congress to oppose the grant of more land for Africans if such land was to be appended to potentially independent bantustans (q.v.). Eleven of the more liberal-minded members of the party, who included many of its most able debaters and intellectuals, could take its conservative drift no longer and broke away to form the Progressive Party (q.v.). The UP then enjoyed greater internal unanimity for a time, but the mediocre leadership of Sir de Villiers Graaff and its ambivalent policies continued to alienate those on both its left and its right. Another breakaway to the left took place in February 1975. The following year, six right-wing members of Parliament split off to form the South African Party, while six others formed the Committee for a United Opposition, which soon merged with the Progressive Party. The remaining UP members formed the New Republic Party, to the right of the Progressive Party, to which de Villiers Graaff gave his support. This finally brought about the demise of the UP. Its central contradiction was its refusal to abandon white supremacy while opposing a government committed to upholding white supremacy in an extreme form. *See also* APARTHEID.

UNIVERSITIES. The origins of the University of Cape Town lie in the South African College, a private venture begun in 1829 to provide education at a wide range of levels. In 1873 a nonteaching University of the Cape of Good Hope was set up to offer examinations for university degrees; by 1910 it administered eight constituent colleges in the four colonies. Cape Town and Stellenbosch were the first of these to receive independent charters (in 1916 and 1918, respectively). The University of the Cape of Good Hope was transformed into the University of South

Africa (UNISA), with headquarters in Pretoria (q.v.). As the colleges gained independence as full universities, Unisa became a teaching university but offered degrees through correspondence only.

The older Afrikaans-medium universities emerged out of what had been English-medium colleges: Stellenbosch, near Cape Town (q.v.); Pretoria, founded after the South African War (q.v.); and Orange Free State (q.v.), at Bloemfontein (q.v.). The Potchefstroom University for Christian Higher Education played an important role in the development of Afrikaner nationalism (q.v.) after 1919. In the mid-1960s, a dual-medium English-Afrikaans university was founded at Port Elizabeth (q.v.), and the Rand Afrikaans University was established for Afrikaners (q.v.) in Johannesburg (q.v.). The four English-speaking universities—Cape Town, Witwatersrand (in Johannesburg), Rhodes (in Grahamstown) and Natal, with its campuses in Durban and Pietermaritzburg—suffered from an emigration of many of their leading staff for political reasons after 1960 and from their inability to attract academics from other countries, owing to South Africa's increasing isolation. They remained, together with the English-speaking (q.v.) churches and the English-language press (q.v.), the main voice of white liberal opposition to the apartheid (q.v.) regime.

Prior to 1960 the universities of Cape Town and the Witwatersrand and the University of Natal Medical School admitted black students on merit. The numbers were never large. In 1959, legislation was passed, over strong opposition from the open universities, providing that blacks could henceforth attend such universities only by permit. Four new ethnic universities were established: the University of the North, for Sotho (q.v.), Tsonga (q.v.), and Venda (q.v.) speakers; the University College of Zululand for Zulu (q.v.) speakers; the University College of the Western Cape, for Coloureds (q.v.); and the University of Durban–Westville (as it became known), for Indians (q.v.). At the same time, Fort Hare (q.v.) was taken over by the government as a university for Xhosa (q.v.) speakers. The nonresidential University of South Africa admitted all races as students, but examinations were given and degrees awarded on a segregated basis. With the "independence" of the bantustans (q.v.) of Transkei (q.v.), Bophuthatswana (q.v.), and Venda, new universities were established in those territories; though nominally nonracial, they had very few non-African students. In 1981 a new university, called Vista, was founded for Africans in urban areas, and it opened campuses in Mamelodi township outside Pretoria, Soweto outside Johannesburg, Port Elizabeth, and elsewhere. Meanwhile, the African "tribal" or "bush" universities, despite the repressive atmosphere on their campuses, became centers of dissidence in the late 1960s and 1970s, with black consciousness (q.v.) finding wide support among their students.

In the late 1970s it became somewhat easier for blacks to obtain permits to attend the universities of Cape Town and the Witwatersrand, and a few blacks were admitted for graduate work at some of the Afrikaans-medium universities. In the 1980s, after the University of Cape Town opened its residences to all, the number of African students began to increase significantly, and the permit system fell away. An attempt by the government to introduce a quota system came to nothing, and the universities regained the right to admit whomever they wished. From the mid-1990s much attention began to be given to transforming the staff composition of universities, at a time when government funding was being cut back.

URBAN FOUNDATION. Following the Soweto uprising (q.v.) in 1976, big business interests in South Africa decided to become actively involved in improving the quality of life for the country's urban African population. The Urban Foundation was then established, and its first director was former judge Jan Steyn. Chiefly occupied with improving black housing, it invested nearly half a billion rands in development and housing loans between 1978 and 1988 and launched more than 800 housing projects in African townships. Another major area of activity was the upgrading of educational and recreational facilities in African areas. In the early 1990s more money became available for such projects through the Independent Development Trust, set up with government money allocated to social development purposes, and the Urban Foundation was disbanded.

URBANIZATION. The first major urban settlement in South Africa was Mapungubwe (q.v.), on the Limpopo River (q.v.), a city-state that flourished in the 13th century, when perhaps 10,000 people lived there. Centuries later, several tens of thousands lived in the largest Tswana (q.v.) settlement, Dithakong, first visited by literate whites in 1801. The Dutch settlement on Table Bay soon developed into a relatively large town, later known as Cape Town (q.v.). As white settlement spread into the interior, small market centers developed, each with a Dutch Reformed church (q.v.). In the trekker republics, towns served security as well as administrative functions. Large towns developed at the new centers of mining activity, above all Kimberley (q.v.) in the early 1870s and Johannesburg (q.v.) after 1886.

Settlement in such urban centers was for whites: by custom, rather than law, Africans (q.v.) had to live on the outskirts. In Grahamstown (q.v.) in the eastern Cape (q.v.), a separate Fingo (Mfengu [q.v.]) location was demarcated in the 1840s, and separate Indian (q.v.) areas were set out in Durban (q.v.) and Johannesburg so as to restrict Indian commercial competition. African locations were provided in Cape Town in 1901 and in Johannesburg and other large cities a few years later. From the 1920s, Afrikaner (q.v.) migration from rural areas increased, in the face of agricultural (q.v.) collapse. African migration (q.v.) to the cities became much more significant in World War II (q.v.), pushed by rural impoverishment and pulled by the prospect of jobs at relatively high wages in the cities. Large squatter (q.v.) settlements developed on the outskirts of the major centers. In response, the National Party (q.v.) government helped build townships like Soweto (q.v.) outside Johannesburg. At the same time, Group Areas (q.v.) legislation further divided cities and towns, and stricter influx control (q.v.) sought to reverse African urbanization, leading to overcrowding in most townships by the 1970s. By 1991, 89 percent of whites and 50 percent of Africans were urbanized, and annual urban growth rates exceeded 3 percent.

The Natives (Urban Areas) Act of 1923 provided that municipalities could fund locations from profits from the sale of beer in municipal beerhalls, but conditions in the townships remained poor, with no electricity and often inadequate sanitation. Transport costs were high, and life insecure. Municipal autonomy was gradually weakened; and in 1972 the central government took over administration of all African urban locations. Finally, in the 1980s, the attempt to reverse the flow of Africans to the cities was abandoned, and African urbanization took place at a greater rate than ever. After the township revolt (q.v.) of the 1980s, however, the culture of nonpayment for services became so deeply entrenched in many townships that even when services were provided they were not paid for. When the townships were merged with the adjacent towns in new local authority structures after 1994, great fiscal and collection problems remained to be solved.

-V-

VAN DER KEMP, JOHANNES THEODORUS (1747–1811). J. T. van der Kemp, of the London Missionary Society (q.v.), was one of the first missionaries (q.v.) at the Cape (q.v.). Upon his arrival in 1799, he ini-

tially lived among the Xhosa (q.v.) on the eastern frontier (q.v.) but later worked among the Khoikhoi (q.v.) at the Bethelsdorp mission, which he established near Algoa Bay in 1803. His severe criticism of the way the colonists treated their Khoikhoi servants and laborers in the eastern districts of the Cape alienated both the authorities and local colonists.

VAN DER STEL, SIMON (1639–1712). Merchant, army officer, and commander and governor of the Cape (q.v.) between 1679 and 1699, Simon van der Stel oversaw the expansion of white settlement into the Stellenbosch and Drakenstein districts after the subjugation of the Khoikhoi (q.v.) there, and he traveled widely beyond the colonial boundaries in search of mineral wealth. He has generally been considered a reformer, particularly for his fiscal discipline, his improvements to the Cape's defenses, and his success in developing the wine (q.v.) industry. He also enriched himself and farmed his prosperous estate, Constantia, outside Cape Town (q.v.), in his retirement. His son Willem Adriaan (1664–1733), who succeeded him as governor of the Cape in 1699, acquired extensive arable land, cattle, and slaves (q.v.). Complaints from colonists concerning what they regarded as corruption eventually led to his removal from office in 1707.

VAN RIEBEECK, JAN ANTHONISZ (1619–77). Ship's surgeon, merchant, and an official of the Dutch East India Company (q.v.), Jan Van Riebeeck established the refreshment station at the Cape of Good Hope in 1652 to supply ships of the company trading between Holland and the East. He served as first commander of the Cape (q.v.) from 1652 until 1662, and many whites have regarded him as the founding father of South Africa. During his rule, agricultural farming among white officials of the company was promoted, the first slaves (q.v.) were imported, a war was fought against the Khoikhoi (q.v.) pastoralists, and a fort was built—the origins of the Castle, which stands in Cape Town (q.v.) today. A large Van Riebeeck festival was held in Cape Town in 1952 to commemorate his arrival.

VEGKOP, BATTLE OF (1836). The first significant battle between Africans and the Voortrekkers (q.v.) in the South African interior was fought in Vegkop in 1836. A Voortrekker force under Hendrik Potgieter successfully defeated the army of the Ndebele (q.v.) king and so opened the way for trekker advance northward.

VELD. The Afrikaans term *veld* was adopted by English speakers (q.v.) for the open grassland country that characterizes much of the interior of

South Africa. The central portion of the interior plateau became the chief pastoral and maize (corn) belt and was known as the high veld. The land east of the Transvaal (q.v.) escarpment and along the Limpopo River (q.v.) valley, a hot, humid region unsuitable for mixed farming, came to be called the low veld.

VENDA. The Venda were a group of Bantu-speaking (q.v.) people living in the far northern region of South Africa, north of the Soutpansberg range, who spoke a distinct language (q.v.) closely related to Shona, the majority language of Zimbabwe (q.v.), as well as to Sotho (q.v.). Venda settlement of this region dates back to the 17th century, when the royal lineage recognized today probably moved south across the Limpopo River (q.v.). Noted as ironworkers and miners of copper, the Venda maintained close relations with people north of the Limpopo. Because of the remoteness of their settlement, they maintained their independence during the period of the Mfecane (q.v.). For much of the 19th century, under their leaders Makhado (d. 1895) and Mphephu (ca. 1868–1924), they offered resistance to white encroachment, particularly after they had obtained large supplies of guns in exchange for ivory. When the Transvaal (q.v.) finally suppressed this resistance in 1898, Mphephu withdrew across the Limpopo River into Zimbabwe with about 10,000 followers but returned after the British took control of the Transvaal in 1900.

In the apartheid (q.v.) era, the bantustan (q.v.) of Venda was led to self-government and then to "independence" in September 1979 under Patrick Mphephu, who installed himself first as paramount and then as president. Although an opposition Venda Independence Party won a majority of the elected seats in the legislature in the 1973 and 1978 elections, Mphephu retained power thanks to support from nominated members and by using emergency powers to imprison opponents. In the 1980s both corruption and oppression increased, and eventually a military ruler took over. Venda was reincorporated into South Africa with the introduction of the interim constitution of April 1994, as part of the Northern Province (q.v.).

VEREENIGING, TREATY OF (1902). The treaty ending the South African War (q.v.) was signed in Pretoria (q.v.) on 31 May 1902. Its terms were initially approved by Boer (q.v.) and British negotiators at Vereeniging, then a small town on the Vaal River. The treaty terminated the independence of the two defeated Boer states, the South African Republic (q.v.) and the Orange Free State (q.v.). Britain, in turn, made some important concessions: no war indemnity was to be levied on the Boers; £3 million was to be paid for war damage; and the former republics were promised that the question of giving the vote to blacks would not be decided until self-government was granted, which meant in effect that blacks would not obtain the vote in those territories. *See also* FRANCHISE.

VERWOERD, HENDRIK FRENSCH (1901–66). Apartheid (q.v.) ideologue and National Party (q.v.) prime minister from 1958 until 1966, H. F. Verwoerd was born in the Netherlands and was brought to South Africa at an early age. He became founding editor of the Afrikaner nationalist (q.v.) newspaper *Die Transvaler*, then entered Parliament in 1948 and was appointed minister of native affairs by Prime Minister D. F. Malan in 1950. This often charming man revealed himself to be a zealot in the application of apartheid in its most extreme and logically consistent form. He realized that to sell this notion abroad, he had to repackage apartheid as separate development, and he therefore decided that the bantustans (q.v.) should be led to self-government and independence. When appointed prime minister, he pledged himself to establish a republic (q.v.), and because of opposition to apartheid from other members of the Commonwealth (q.v.), he withdrew South Africa's membership, shortly before the inauguration of the Republic on 31 May 1961.

Verwoerd survived an assassination attempt in 1960, in the aftermath of the Sharpeville massacre (q.v.), but a second one was successful. Dimitri Tsafendas, the parliamentary messenger who stabbed him to death on the floor of the House of Assembly, insisted that a snake in his intestines had led him to do the deed. Tsafendas was not tried but was confined to mental institutions. As South Africa became democratic and rejected apartheid, Verwoerd's name was removed from public places.

VILJOEN, CONSTAND (b. 1933). Having joined the South African army at the age of 18, Constand Viljoen rose to become its chief in 1976 and was chief of the South African Defence Force (q.v.) from 1980 to 1985. He emerged from retirement in 1993 to become leader of the Afrikaner Volksfront (q.v.). Present in June 1993 when the Afrikaner Resistance Movement (AWB) (q.v.) sacked the World Trade Centre where the new constitution was being negotiated, he won the support of those on the far right who rejected AWB thuggery and benefited when the AWB was forced out of Bophuthatswana (q.v.) in March 1994. After the Volksfront rejected participation in the democratic election, Viljoen registered a new party, the Freedom Front (q.v.), for this purpose, and when the constitutional principles (q.v.) were changed to permit self-determination, he agreed to join the new politics. From May 1994 he served as the leader of the Freedom Front in Parliament, and he continued to advocate the establishment of an Afrikaner *volkstaat* ("Afrikaner people's state").

VOORTREKKERS. The Voortrekkers (Dutch, "those who travel ahead," "pioneers") were those frontier farmers who rebelled against British rule at the Cape (q.v.) between 1834 and 1840 by participating in the migration later called the Great Trek (q.v.). Unlike the earlier trekboers (q.v.), they wished to establish new states in the interior where they could be free from British domination. Some 15,000 Voortrekkers left the Cape during the latter half of the 1830s.

VORSTER, BALTHAZAR JOHANNES (JOHN) (1915–83). National Party (q.v.) prime minister from 1966 to 1978, B. J. Vorster was interned during World War II (q.v.) for his pro-Nazi sympathies. The grim-faced Vorster became H. F. Verwoerd's (q.v.) minister of justice in 1962 and introduced detention without trial to deal with political opposition after the Sharpeville massacre (q.v.). As prime minister he was more pragmatic than Verwoerd: he welcomed diplomats from Malawi and pursued an "outward" policy, which involved an agreement to talk with black African heads of state on condition that apartheid (q.v.) was not discussed. He allowed P. W. Botha (q.v.) to persuade him to sanction (q.v.) the invasion of Angola (q.v.) in 1975 but was prepared to put pressure on the regime in Rhodesia (now Zimbabwe [q.v.]) to accept the principle of majority rule and agreed to a Western plan for Namibia (q.v.), which involved a transition to independence, supervised by the United Nations (q.v.). He fell from office as a result of the Information scandal (q.v.).

-W-

WALVIS BAY. The only large natural harbor on the coast of Namibia (q.v.), Walvis ("Whale") Bay was visited by the Portuguese explorer Bartolomeu Dias (q.v.) in 1486 but was not exploited for a long time because of the lack of fresh water inland. From the late 17th century, whales were hunted off the coast of what became known as South West Africa, and from the 1830s traders, missionaries (q.v.), and collectors of guano increasingly used Walvis Bay. In the 1860s, Britain proclaimed sovereignty over 12 offshore islands, which were annexed to the Cape Colony (q.v.) in 1874. By that time, traders and missionaries at Walvis Bay had requested British protection, and in 1875 the Cape (q.v.) Parliament sent a commissioner, who recommended the annexation of the entire coast. Britain would authorize the annexation only of Walvis Bay itself, which occurred in 1878. Walvis Bay was in turn incorporated into the Cape Colony in 1884. Three weeks later, Germany proclaimed a protectorate over the remainder of the coast of South West Africa. The boundary between Walvis Bay and the German territory was much disputed, and the issue was resolved only in 1911, after Walvis Bay was included in the new Union (q.v.) of South Africa in 1910.

For reasons of administrative convenience, however, Walvis Bay was administered as part of South West Africa from 1922 to 1977. The Western negotiators (the Contact Group), who from 1977 tried to secure the independence of Namibia, agreed to leave Walvis Bay out of the discussions, knowing that the South African government was adamant that it should remain South African territory. In the 1970s, Walvis Bay's fishing industry was devastated by overfishing, mainly by South African companies.

After Namibia gained independence in 1990, its government sought to gain control of the port, through which most of its trade passed. In 1992 an agreement with the South African government was secured whereby Walvis Bay was to be administered jointly. In 1993 negotiators drawing up South Africa's interim constitution agreed to cede control of Walvis Bay to Namibia. Namibia formally took over the enclave from South Africa at the end of February 1994.

WATERBOER FAMILY. Andries Waterboer (ca. 1790–1853), who was of Khoisan (q.v.) origin, was from 1820 the leader of the main body of Griqua (q.v.) in what became known as Griqualand West (q.v.). He strove to end divisions between competing Griqua clans, fought off Sotho and Tswana (qq.v.) attacks, and concluded treaties with the Ndebele (q.v.) and the British. In 1853 he was succeeded by his son Nicholaas Waterboer (1819–96), who is mainly remembered for his claim to the diamond (q.v.) fields in the Kimberley (q.v.) region after 1867. The British annexed Griqualand West in 1871, and Nicholaas, expelled from his territory in 1878, died in Griqualand East (q.v.) in 1896.

WESTERN CAPE. The Western Cape Province was created in April 1994 out of the southern and western parts of the former Cape (q.v.) Province. The provincial capital is Cape Town (q.v.). With the arrival of a democratic order, the majority of Coloureds (q.v.), having long sought to distinguish themselves from Africans (q.v.), gave their allegiance to the National Party (NP) (q.v.) rather than the African National Congress (ANC) (q.v.), in spite of their having suffered under apartheid (q.v.). The result was that the NP won a majority in the new province in the April 1994 election, attracting 56 percent of the vote as opposed to the ANC's 34 percent, and Hernus Kriel of the NP became the province's first premier. The provincial legislature approved a constitution for the province in 1997, which took effect in early 1998. At the beginning of 1998, a Coloured NP leader, Gerald Morkel, succeeded Kriel as prime minister of the Western Cape.

WHEAT INDUSTRY. Wheat was first planted by the Dutch (q.v.) in the southwestern Cape (q.v.) in the 1650s, and wheat farming became one of the main economic activities of whites during the 17th and 18th centuries. Considerable quantities of the crop were exported to the East Indian colonial possessions of the Dutch. In the 19th century, the discoveries of diamonds and gold (qq.v.) in the interior stimulated wheat production. Although the country was forced to import wheat for some decades thereafter, the crop became a significant export item in the late 20th century.

WHITES. The term *white* was used in place of *European* by the Mining Regulations Commission (1910) on the ground that Coloureds (q.v.) might be of European extraction. At the beginning of the apartheid (q.v.) era, segregated amenities were labeled for "Europeans" and "Non-Europeans." From the 1960s, however, as the Afrikaner (q.v.) leadership wished to assert the legitimacy of its claim to Africa, the term *white* replaced *European*.

WIEHAHN COMMISSION. In 1977, a government commission under Professor Nic Wiehahn was appointed to investigate the country's labor legislation. Its appointment came as a response to the labor unrest that began in 1973 and to pressure for change from abroad, mediated in part through the multinational companies active in South Africa, in the wake of the Soweto uprising (q.v.). The first report of the commission, issued in 1979, recommended that the registration of African trade unions (q.v.) be permitted as a way of controlling the new militant African labor movement. It also recommended the abolition of the principle of statutory reservation of jobs, though it suggested that existing work reservation determinations should remain in force until they could be phased out in consultation with relevant white unions. By an amendment to the Industrial Conciliation Act, this major reform was enacted into law.

WIND OF CHANGE SPEECH. Speaking to a joint sitting of both Houses of Parliament in Cape Town (q.v.) on 3 February 1960, the visiting British prime minister, Harold Macmillan, spoke of the growth of African (q.v.) nationalism and of his conviction that an irresistible "wind of change" was blowing across the continent. South Africa, he said, could not remain isolated from it, and therefore political power should be extended to all on the basis of individual merit. Prime Minister H. F. Verwoerd (q.v.) immediately rejected this analysis, telling Macmillan that South Africa was different, that whites would remain in charge, and that ethnic nationalism among Africans could find outlets in the bantustans (q.v.).

WINE INDUSTRY. Dutch East India Company (q.v.) officials planted the first wine-grape vines close to the new settlement on Table Bay in 1655. Although the wine industry grew gradually thereafter, until the 19th century little was exported because of the inferior quality of most Cape wines. In 1813, however, the British reduced tariffs, which led to an immediate boom in exports; by 1822 the value of wine exported from the Cape (q.v.) exceeded all other exports put together. But the withdrawal of preferential tariffs by the British in 1825 and 1831 proved a major blow to the Cape industry. It was again hard hit in the 1880s when the vines were attacked by a pest, phylloxera.

In 1927, the Ko-operatiewe Wijnbouwers Vereeniging was established to supervise and direct the industry's fortunes. In the apartheid (q.v.) era, there was a widespread international boycott (q.v.) of South African wine. With the collapse of apartheid and the removal of sanctions (q.v.) in the early 1990s, South African wines were once again exported in large quantities.

WITWATERSRAND. Also known as Egoli ("place of gold"), the Reef, or merely the Rand, the Witwatersrand (from the Afrikaans [q.v.], meaning "ridge of white waters"), a hilly ridge north of the Vaal River, has produced more gold (q.v.) than any other place on earth. The gold-bearing rock extends for 62 miles and in some places is 23 miles wide. Johannesburg (q.v.), which became South Africa's largest city, grew at the center of the Witwatersrand.

WODEHOUSE, SIR PHILIP EDMOND (1811–87). Despite economic recession, Sir Philip Wodehouse, Cape governor and high commissioner from 1862 to 1870, expanded British influence in southern Africa—most notably by annexing Basutoland (q.v.) in 1868. He resisted pressure to grant responsible government to the Cape (q.v.), believing the colony was not ready for it.

WOMEN. Historical writing on women and gender relations in South Africa expanded rapidly from the mid-1980s and became a major historiographical (q.v.) concern as historians sought to recover the history of women and develop insights into the role of women in the past. Despite sometimes deeply contested theoretical and conceptual debates among historians and the recognition that women of different classes, races, and backgrounds had widely varying experiences, women's history developed into a significant and semiautonomous branch of research.

In precolonial Bantu-speaking (q.v.) societies, which were based on precapitalist agricultural (q.v.) farming, women's reproductive and productive labor, which represented wealth, was controlled by men. Great social value was placed on fertility, and women also played an important role in the cultivation of crops and the production of food; women therefore enjoyed a recognized, though defined, social status. Early settler society in the 18th and 19th centuries, both Boer (q.v.) and British, was similarly patriarchal, although arguably women enjoyed less recognition for their function as workers and in the home. Colonial society offered limited social mobility to some women, in that working-class and lower-middle-class immigrants were able to establish themselves as part of the colonial elite and delegate some domestic responsibilities to servants. Public questioning of the colonial social order was rare, a notable exception being the work of the feminist writer Olive Schreiner (q.v.) at the end of the 19th century.

After the discovery of gold (q.v.) on the Witwatersrand (q.v.) and the development of industry in emerging urban centers from the end of the 19th century, gender relations were reshaped to fit the demands of the new economy. Increasing numbers of women were drawn into work outside the home, although the great majority worked in jobs that carried limited status and remuneration, such as clerical positions, nursing, and teaching. During the 1920s and 1930s, white women entered the garment and food industries, in particular, but began to be replaced by black women in the 1940s as whites moved into new positions in the service sector of the economy. Considerable tensions, exacerbated by official segregationist policies, existed between black and white workers. Urbanization (q.v.) among black women occurred slowly in the early 20th century, for the migrant (q.v.) labor system, which drew men to the mines, depended on women to remain in the rural areas to maintain agricultural productivity and traditional homesteads. Increasing numbers of women were obliged to act as heads of households, which in turn led to considerable social tension within rural African society.

White women obtained the vote in 1930 after a campaign by a white suffrage movement; this in turn paved the way for women's involvement in public life. Black women began to play a prominent role in national public life only in the 1950s, although glimpses of their potential political involvement had been witnessed as early as 1913 in organized protest against the pass laws (q.v.). Demonstrations against the extension of the pass laws proved a focal point for womens' protest during the 1950s, coordinated by the Women's League of the African National Congress (q.v.) and the nonracial Federation of South African Women (q.v.). Pass laws were extended to include African (q.v.) women in 1963, effectively undermining their right to live and work in urban areas. Women played a prominent role in campaigns leading to the abolition of pass laws in 1986. African women were able to exercise the franchise (q.v.) for the first time in 1994, winning it at the same time as African men.

In the 1990s, women's issues enjoyed greater prominence than before, with more women in leadership positions in the economy and in politics and with gender equality written into the 1996 constitution.

WOOL INDUSTRY. Indigenous fat-tailed sheep are associated with early Khoikhoi (q.v.) settlement in South Africa. Merino sheep were first introduced in 1789 and became the basis of the wool industry, which expanded rapidly, so that by the 1840s wool had become the Cape's (q.v.) most important export. In the 1870s, wool was overtaken by diamonds (q.v.) as the colony's main export but remained one of the country's most important agricultural (q.v.) exports.

WORLD WAR I (1914–18). On 4 August 1914, South Africa automatically found itself, as part of the British Empire, at war with Germany. Louis Botha (q.v.), the prime minister, and Jan Smuts (q.v.) both supported the war wholeheartedly. The government's decision to accede to a British request to invade German South West Africa (now Namibia [q.v.]) led to the Afrikaner Rebellion (q.v.) by whites opposed to South Africa's involvement in the war. The rebellion was soon suppressed, and by mid-1915 South African forces had occupied South West Africa. Smuts then took command of the East African campaign against German forces in what is now Tanzania. More than 20,000 South Africans fought in this campaign, and more than 1,500 died.

A South African brigade fought in the battles on the Somme in 1916 and suffered heavy casualties in the Battle of Delville Wood. A South African Native Labour Contingent, made up of more than 20,000 blacks, who were not allowed to bear arms, worked for the Allied armies in France. In February 1917, 615 of these men were drowned at sea when the troopship carrying them, the *Mendi*, sank in the English Channel. Altogether, 12,452 South Africans died on active service in the war as a whole. During the war Smuts was invited to join the imperial war cabinet, and he played an important role in Allied deliberations on how to bring the war to an end.

WORLD WAR II (1939–45). When Britain declared war on Germany on 3 September 1939, the South African cabinet divided on whether or not South Africa should participate. J. B. M. Hertzog (q.v.) and other former National Party (q.v.) members who had entered the fusion (q.v.) agreement with him believed that South Africa should assert its independence of Britain. As Parliament was sitting, the issue was put to the House of Assembly, which voted (on 4 September 1939) 80 to 67 in favor of South Africa's entering the war. Hertzog then asked Sir Patrick Duncan (q.v.), the governor-general, to dissolve the assembly and call a general election. When Duncan refused, Jan Smuts (q.v.) became prime minister for the second time and at once declared war on Germany (6 September).

To many Afrikaner (q.v.) supporters of the United Party (q.v.), this seemed to run counter to the "South Africa first" principle of fusion, and they withdrew their support, making virtually inevitable Smuts's defeat at the polls in 1948. In its first years, however, the war brought enormous dissension within Afrikaner ranks, with some Afrikaners prepared to undertake illegal acts, including sabotage, to oppose it. As late as 1944, many Afrikaner nationalists (q.v.) expected the Germans to win the war and hoped that this would provide the opportunity for the establishment of an Afrikaner republic (q.v.).

During the war some 390,000 men and women volunteers served in the armed forces, far more than in World War I (q.v.). Union forces first took part in the Ethiopian campaign, which led to the capture of Addis Ababa from Italian forces. They also seized Madagascar and participated in the North African campaign. Ten thousand South African troops were trapped by General Rommel at Tobruk in 1942. South African forces then took part in the invasion of Italy in 1944 and fought their way up the Italian peninsula with the Allied forces. South African pilots played an important role in bombing raids on Poland. During the war, 123,000 blacks served in noncombatant roles. Almost 9,000 South Africans died in hostilities.

A great number of Allied ships passed the Cape (q.v.) during the war, and tens of thousands of Allied troops had shore leave at South African ports. The war boosted the South African economy; consequently, large numbers of Africans (q.v.) poured into the towns in search of work.

-X-

XHOSA. Originally, the Xhosa (the name is thought to derive from a Khoikhoi [q.v.] term meaning "angry men") were those who recognized the authority of the Tshawe royal clan, which had established a chiefdom in the northern Transkei (q.v.) during the 16th century. Over the next two centuries, this chiefdom expanded over a wide area through conquest and incorporation of a variety of people, including Khoikhoi willing to accept Tshawe authority. During the time of Phalo (1715–75), two main groups emerged, one under the senior great house of the Gcaleka in the east, the other under the right-hand house of the Rharhabe (q.v.) in the west. It was the latter who first encountered whites moving eastward toward the end of the 18th century, and in 1779 the first in a series of frontier (q.v.) clashes took place, clashes that were to continue sporadically for a century and ultimately lead to Xhosa defeat. More than 20,000 Rharhabe were expelled from the Zuurveld (q.v.) in 1811–12. They divided between the followers of Ngqika (q.v.), who was prepared to cooperate with the colonial authorities, and Ndlambe, who was determined to oppose them. Settler pressure continued. The Xhosa, already suffering severely, were greatly weakened by the cattle killing (q.v.) of 1857. In 1878, the Gcaleka living in the Transkei were also defeated and brought under colonial rule.

In time, all Nguni (q.v.) people who lived in the eastern Cape (q.v.) and Transkei came to be called Xhosa, whether they were Thembu, Mpondo, Mpondomise, Bhaca, or Mfengu (q.v.), and their common language became known as Xhosa. That Xhosa people were exposed to Christianity (q.v.), Western ideas, and education (q.v.) earlier than other Africans (q.v.) helps explain why so many of them took leading roles in protonationalist and nationalist organizations in the 20th century.

XUMA, ALFRED BITINI (ca. 1898–1962). After studying in the United States and Europe, A. B. Xuma returned to practice as a physician in Johannesburg (q.v.) in 1928. His obvious abilities led to his election first as vice president of the All-African Convention (q.v.) in 1935 and then, in 1940, as president-general of the African National Congress (ANC) (q.v.). The ANC was in a sad state of disorganization when he took it over, but under his leadership it became a more efficient and more centralized organization, which began to attract a wider following. He forged an alliance with Indian (q.v.) antisegregationists in 1946 and in that year lobbied successfully at the United Nations (q.v.) against South Africa's plans to incorporate South West Africa (now Namibia [q.v.]). Essentially conservative, Xuma did not welcome pressure from the African National Congress Youth League (q.v.) for more militant action, and he was ousted as president in 1949.

-Y-

YUSSUF (also TJOESSOP), SHEIKH (1626–99). Exiled by the Dutch East India Company (q.v.) from Java, Sheik Yussuf arrived at Cape Town (q.v.) in 1694 and settled outside the city. Although he spent only the last five years of his life at the Cape (q.v.), he had a great influence as a religious leader and teacher. A memorial to his name stands at Faure, on the Cape Flats, and he is now venerated by Muslims as the man who brought Islam (q.v.) to the Cape. The tercentenary of his arrival was marked by festivities and celebrations in Cape Town, immediately prior to the first democratic election in April 1994.

-Z-

ZIMBABWE. Links between South Africa and the land north of the Limpopo River (q.v.) were strong in the precolonial past. In the late 1830s, the Ndebele (q.v.) crossed from the Transvaal (q.v.) into southwestern Zimbabwe (from the Shona, meaning "place of stones"; formerly Southern Rhodesia), where they settled. White hunters, traders, and missionaries (q.v.) soon began to follow them in increasing numbers. In 1890, the British South Africa (BSA) Company (q.v.) occupied part of southern Zambesia and renamed it after Cecil Rhodes (q.v.). Many of the whites who settled in Zimbabwe came from the Cape (q.v.); as late as 1970, more than 20 percent of settlers were South African–born.

When the BSA administration came to an end, the settlers voted in a referendum (in 1922) not to join the Union (q.v.) of South Africa as a fifth province, despite pressure from Jan Smuts (q.v.) and mining interests for incorporation. After the collapse of the Central African Federation in 1963, the Southern Rhodesian government forged closer ties with South Africa, particularly in the field of military cooperation, and the race policies of Rhodesia also came more closely to approximate those of South Africa than they had previously.

After Southern Rhodesia's unilateral declaration of independence in November 1965, South Africa refused to join the rest of the international community in imposing economic sanctions (q.v.). The continued supply of petroleum, fuel, and military hardware from South Africa was crucial to the country's survival. From August 1967, South African paramilitary police were deployed within Rhodesia to assist the Rhodesians in preventing guerrilla incursions aimed at South Africa; in 1967 and 1968, Umkhonto weSizwe (MK) (q.v.) detachments moved into Rhodesia en route to South Africa, but were defeated before they reached their goal. From the mid-1970s, as Angola (q.v.) and Mozambique (q.v.) moved to independence and the Rhodesian bush war increased in intensity, the South African government began to pressure the Rhodesian prime minister, Ian Smith, to forge a settlement with moderate black leaders. When this was done, it failed to win international recognition or end the war. In the election of early 1980 under the Lancaster House agreement, the South African government supported Bishop Muzorewa; Robert Mugabe's victory came as a considerable shock to Pretoria (q.v.).

Although postindependence Zimbabwe was heavily dependent on close economic ties with South Africa (the bulk of the country's imports and exports were transported by South African railways [q.v.] through South African ports), the political paths of the two countries diverged sharply in the 1980s. Zimbabwe gave diplomatic recognition to the African National Congress (q.v.), but was unable to impose sanctions on South Africa or permit MK guerrilla bases to operate from Zimbabwean soil. Most whites who left Zimbabwe during the 1980s settled in South Africa. After the 1994 election in South Africa, close official ties between the two countries were forged for the first time, but Zimbabwe remained concerned about the way South Africa might use its vastly greater economic power. Tensions between the Zimbabwean and South African governments manifested themselves particularly over regional disputes in the subcontinent (*see* SOUTHERN AFRICAN DEVELOPMENT COMMUNITY).

ZULU KINGDOM. In the late 18th century, the Zulu clan was but one of a number of small groups among the northern Nguni (q.v.). By the 1820s, a powerful Zulu state, one of the most dominant polities in southern Africa, had emerged under the control of Shaka (q.v.). Historians continue to debate the reasons for the rise of a militarized and authoritarian Zulu state. It is possible that the expansion of international trade in ivory, cattle, and possibly slaves (q.v.) from Delagoa Bay (q.v.) after the 1760s sparked competition for resources and trade routes, and promoted political centralization among the various northern Nguni chiefdoms. Other reasons advanced by historians to explain the rise of the Zulu state include population growth following the introduction of maize in the 18th century, which put pressure on scarce resources; severe drought and ecological crisis in about 1806; and innovations such as the short stabbing spear, new formations in battle, and the use of the *amabutho* (q.v.) system for military purposes.

It would seem that Shaka took advantage of the conflict between the Ndwandwe and the Mthethwa to consolidate his power between the Thukela and White Mfolozi rivers before 1818, through his skillful use of the *amabutho*. He then extended his domination northward to the Mkhuze River after defeating the Ndwandwe. He built a militarized, centralized state in this region, a core state surrounded by vassal communities in varying degrees of subordination who paid him tribute. His armies raided as far north as the Pongola River area, and to the Mpondo territory in the south. He was assassinated in 1828 by two of his half-brothers, one of whom (Dingane [q.v.]) succeeded him.

The Zulu state remained vulnerable to internal strains between chiefs, which were intensified by growing external pressures in the form of British traders and missionaries (q.v.), as well as Boer Voortrekkers (q.v.). Dingane viewed the trekkers as a threat, and had a group under the leadership of Piet Retief (q.v.) murdered in 1838. His army was then defeated by the trekkers at the Battle of Blood River (q.v.), and he was driven from his kingdom by Mpande (q.v.), one of his disaffected half-brothers who was in league with the trekkers. Mpande took control of the region north of the Thukela, whereas the trekkers laid claim to the land to the south. With the arrival of the British in 1843 and their annexation of the region to the south of the Thukela as the colony of Natal (q.v.), Mpande won from the new colony recognition of the independence of the area north of the Thukela.

By the 1850s, Mpande's authority had weakened and a dispute over the succession to the kingship resulted in civil war in 1856. Mpande favored his son Mbuyazi as his successor, but another son, Cetshwayo (q.v.), emerged victorious. Though he assumed full power only after Mpande's death, he had by then consolidated his control. At that time perhaps 150,000 people between the Thukela and Pongola rivers saw themselves as Zulu, and Cetshwayo was able to put an army of 40,000 men into the field. Despite such resources, Cetshwayo was threatened on two flanks: British and colonial officials in Natal feared his military might and wanted to challenge his independence, while at the same time Boer farmers in the Transvaal (q.v.) wanted to move onto Zulu land. The British high commissioner, Sir Bartle Frere (q.v.), finally decided to move against the Zulu kingdom at the end of 1878, resulting in the outbreak of the Anglo–Zulu War (q.v.) in January 1879.

The war and the subsequent settlement imposed by the British exacerbated tensions between various chiefs and the Zulu royal house, tensions that led to civil war in 1883. Cetshwayo, who had been sent into exile by the British, was permitted to return in order to govern part of his former kingdom, but his capital was sacked in July 1883 and he soon died under mysterious circumstances. His successor, Dinuzulu (q.v.), granted land to a group of Boers from the Transvaal in return for help against his main rival, Zibhebhu (1841–1904). This helped persuade the British, in 1887, to annex what remained of the Zulu kingdom. Dinuzulu then rebelled, was arrested and tried for high treason, and was sent into exile on the Atlantic Ocean island of St Helena. After his return in 1898, he sought to gain recognition as Zulu king, but was unsuccessful; and his ambivalent role in the Bambatha Rebellion (q.v.), taken by whites as evidence of treason, brought him a four-year sentence of imprisonment.

Once the Zulu kingdom had effectively been destroyed as a political unit during the 1880s, Zulu men were increasingly forced into wage labor outside the kingdom's borders. Though the royal family ceased to exert the control it had enjoyed for much of the 19th century, the role of the king and his *inkosi* (chiefs) nevertheless remained very important in 20th-century KwaZulu (q.v.).

ZUURVELD. Also known as Suurveld, the land between the Fish and Bushmans Rivers in the eastern Cape (q.v.). White trekboers (q.v.) first came into substantial contact with the Xhosa (q.v.) in this region. The Zuurveld was ideal for summer grazing, and small Xhosa groups, escaping the domination of those further east, had lived and farmed there for several generations before regular contact with white settlers began in the 1770s. The first armed clash erupted in 1779, but neither then nor in subsequent wars in the late 18th century were the whites able to dislodge the Xhosa. While the Zuurveld was officially part of the Cape Colony (q.v.) from 1780, large numbers of Xhosa remained within it until 1812 when Boer commandos (q.v.), aided by British troops, expelled 20,000 of them. A line of military forts was then built, the chief of which became the city of Grahamstown (q.v.). In 1820, some 5,000 British immigrants (*see* ENGLISH-SPEAKING WHITES) were settled in the Zuurveld to prevent Xhosa from returning to the area. The Zuurveld was then renamed Albany.

ZWIDE (ca. 1790–1825). Little is known for certain about the life of this ruler of a relatively powerful northern Nguni (q.v.) chiefdom. It is thought he ruled from 1805. Through military shrewdness and perhaps use of the *amabutho* (q.v.), he was able to defeat the armies of the Swazi (q.v.) and of the Mthethwa under Dingiswayo in about 1818, making possible the rise of the Zulu under Shaka (q.v.). Shaka then inflicted a heavy defeat on him at the Battle of Gqokoli Hill, thought to have taken place in 1819. Zwide then fled north from what is now northern KwaZulu–Natal (q.v.) with his remaining troops.

Bibliography

CONTENTS

INTRODUCTION

More has been written on South Africa than on any other African country, especially during the early 1990s, when the apartheid government began to crumble and the road to democracy became the subject of international attention. This bibliography therefore represents only a fraction of works useful for the student of South African history. It does not include unpublished theses, and it mostly lists secondary publications by professional historians and other scholars. It also points mainly to material written in English that is reasonably accessible to readers in Britain and the United States.

Since the publication of the first edition of this dictionary, there has been a major shift in South African historical writing away from political and economic history. The field has broadened to include a range of social and cultural topics that were previously given scant attention, especially in the fields of gender, slavery, environment, religion, sports, and the performing arts. This bibliography attempts to reflect this change.

To keep the bibliography a reasonable size, each item is listed under a single heading only. It was not easy to decide in which category to place many items. A useful book or article that does not appear under one subject heading may be found elsewhere. The guides listed in the first section are an entrée to other sources.

ABBREVIATIONS

AYB   *Archives Year Book for South African History*
CSSA   *Collected Seminar Papers. Societies of Southern Africa* (University of London)
JAH   *Journal of African History*
JSAS   *Journal of Southern African Studies*
SAAB   *South African Archaeological Bulletin*
SAHJ   *South African Historical Journal*
SAJE   *South African Journal of Economics*

REFERENCE

Bibliographies and Guides

Belling, V. *Bibliography of South African Jewry*. University of Cape Town, Kaplan Centre for Jewish Studies and Research, 1997.

Boshoff, M., ed. *French Publications on South Africa to the Year 1935*. Pretoria: State Library, 1978.

Chidester, D., J. Tobler, and D. Wratten. *Christianity in South Africa: An Annotated Bibliography*. Westport, Conn.: Greenwood, 1997.

_____. *Islam, Hinduism, and Judaism in South Africa: An Annotated Bibliography*. Westport, Conn.: Greenwood, 1997.

Coetzee, J. C. *South African Newspapers on Microfilm*. 2d ed. Pretoria: State Library, 1991.

Davis, G. V. *South Africa*. Rev. ed. Oxford: Clio, 1994.

Drew, A. *South Africa's Radical Tradition: A Documentary History*. 2 vols. Cape Town: University of Cape Town Press, 1996.

Eales, M. *An Annotated Guide to the Pre-Union Government Publications of the Orange Free State, 1854–1910*. Boston: G. K. Hall, 1976.

Geyser, O., P. W. Coetzer, and J. H. Le Roux. *Bibliographies on South African Political History*. 2 vols. Boston: G. K. Hall, 1979.

Haron, M. *Muslims in South Africa: An Annotated Bibliography*. Cape Town: South African Library, in association with the Centre for Contemporary Islam, University of Cape Town, 1997.

Hofmeyr, J. W., J. H. Rykheer, and J. M. Nel, eds. *A Select Bibliography of Periodical Articles on Southern African Church History.* Vol. 1, *1975–1989.* Pretoria: Unisa Press, 1991.

Index to the Manuscript Annexures and Printed Papers of the House of Assembly, 1910–1961. Pretoria: Government Printer, 1961.

Index to South African Periodicals. Johannesburg: Public Library, 1940–86 (1986 on microfiche); Grahamstown: National Inquiry Service Centre (NISC), post-1986 (on *Southern African Studies* CD-ROM.)

International African Bibliography. London: Mansell, 1971–98.

Kalley, J. A. *South Africa's Road to Change, 1987–1990: A Select and Annotated Bibliography.* New York: Greenwood, 1991.

_____. *The Transkei Region of Southern Africa, 1877–1978: An Annotated Bibliography.* Boston: G. K. Hall, 1979.

Karnik, S. S. "South Africa and the World: A Select Bibliography." *Africa Quarterly* (India) 30, nos. 1–2 (1990).

Kritzinger, J. J., and P. F. Smit. "Missiological Theses Accepted at South African Universities, 1968–1993." *Missionalia* 22, no. 2 (1994).

Liebenberg, B. J., K. W. Smith, and S. B. Spies, eds. *A Bibliography of South African History, 1978–1989.* Pretoria: Unisa Press, 1992.

Limb, P. *The ANC and Black Workers in South Africa, 1912–1992: An Annotated Bibliography.* London: Zell, 1993.

Long, U. *Index to Authors of Unofficial, Privately Owned Manuscripts Relating to the History of South Africa, 1812–1920.* London: Lund Humphries, 1947.

Mendelssohn, S. *South African Bibliography.* 2 vols. London: Kegan Paul, 1910.

_____. *A South African Bibliography to the Year 1925.* 6 vols. London: Mansell, 1979.

Muller, C., F. A. Van Jaarsveld, and T. Van Wijk, eds. *South African History and Historians: A Bibliography.* Pretoria: University of South Africa, 1979.

Musiker, R. *South African Bibliography: A Survey of Bibliographies and Bibliographical Work.* 2d ed. Cape Town: David Philip, 1980.

Musiker, R., and N. Musiker. *Guide to Cape of Good Hope Official Publications, 1854–1910.* Boston: G. K. Hall, 1976.

Pickover, M. *Records of the Federation of South African Trade Unions, 1939–1986.* Johannesburg: University of the Witwatersrand Library, 1991.

Pollak, O., and K. Pollak. *Theses and Dissertations on Southern Africa: An International Bibliography.* Boston: G. K. Hall, 1976.

Potgieter, P. J. *Index to Literature on Race Relations in South Africa, 1910–1975.* Boston: G. K. Hall, 1979.

Radebe, T. *Natal and Zululand History Theses.* 3d ed. Pietermaritzburg, S. Afr.: University of Natal Library, 1992.

Robinson, A. M., ed. *Theses and Dissertations Accepted for Degrees at South African Universities, 1918–1941.* N.p., 1943.

Roussouw, F. *A South African Bibliography to the Year 1925.* Vol. 5, *Supplement.* Cape Town: South African Library, 1991.

Schapera, I. *Select Bibliography of South African Native Life and Problems.* London: Oxford University Press, 1941. Supplements by M. A. Holden and others, University of Cape Town School of Librarianship, 1958–64.

Schoeman, E. *Economic Interdependence in South Africa, 1961–1989: A Select and Annotated Bibliography.* Johannesburg: South African Institute of International Affairs, 1990.

Schoeman, E., J. A. Kalley, and N. Musiker. *Mandela's Five Years of Freedom: South African Politics, Economics, and Social Issues, 1990–1995—A Select and Annotated Bibliography.* Johannesburg: South African Institute of International Affairs, 1996.

Scholtz, P. L., H. C. Bredekamp, and H. F. Heese. *Race Relations at the Cape of Good Hope, 1652–1795: A Select Bibliography.* Boston: G. K. Hall, 1981.

Seekings, J. *South Africa's Townships, 1980–1991: An Annotated Bibliography.* Stellenbosch, S. Afr.: University of Stellenbosch, Research Unit for Sociology of Development, 1992.

Southern African Update. Johannesburg: University of the Witwatersrand Library, Braamfontein, 1986–98.

Standard Encyclopaedia of Southern Africa. 12 vols. Cape Town: Nasou, 1970–76.

Stultz, N. M. *South Africa as Apartheid Ends: An Annotated Bibliography with Analytical Introductions.* Ann Arbor, Mich.: Pierian, 1993.

Switzer, L., and D. Switzer. *The Black Press in South Africa and Lesotho.* Boston: G. K. Hall, 1979.

Theal, G. M. *Catalogue of Books and Pamphlets Relating to Africa South of the Zambesi.* Cape Town: Cape Times, 1912.

Thompson, L. M., I. Jarrick, and R. Elphick. *Southern African History before 1900: A Select Bibliography of Articles.* Stanford, Calif.: Hoover Institution, 1971.

Union Catalogue of Theses and Dissertations of South African Universities. Potchefstroom, S. Afr.: University Library, 1984. Thereafter (1985+) on Sabinet, www.sabinet.co.za.

Union List of South African Newspapers. Cape Town: South African Library, 1950.

Van Warmelo, N. J. *Anthropology of Southern Africa in Periodicals to 1950.* Johannesburg: Witwatersrand University Press, 1977.

Webb, C. *Guide to the Official Records of the Colony of Natal.* Pietermaritzburg, S. Afr.: University of Natal Press, 1965.

Serial Publications

Acta Academica. Bloemfontein, S. Afr., 1969–.

Acta Diurna Historica. Bloemfontein, S. Afr., 1972–80.

Africa Perspective. Johannesburg, 1974–89.

Africa Seminar Collected Papers. Cape Town, 1978–85.

African Affairs. London, 1901–.

African Communist. London, 1962–.
African Studies Review. Waltham, Mass.: African Studies Association, 1957–.
Africana Notes and News. Johannesburg, 1943–93.
Archives Year Book for South African History. Cape Town and Pretoria, 1938–.
Botswana Notes and News. Gaborone, Bots., 1968–.
Cabo. Cape Town, 1971–91.
Canadian Journal of African Studies. Ottawa, 1967–.
Collected Seminar Papers, Societies of Southern Africa. London, 1970–.
Contention: Debates in Society, Culture, and Science. Bloomington, Ind., 1991–.
Contree: Journal for South African Urban and Regional History. Johannesburg, 1977–90, continued as *New Contree*: Mmabatho, S. Afr., 1996–.
The Critic. Cape Town, 1932–36.
Current Writing: Text and Reception in Southern Africa. Durban, S. Afr., 1989–.
Documentatieblad. Leiden, Neth.: Afrika-Studiecentrum, Rijksuniversiteit te Leiden, 1968–.
Familia: Quarterly Journal of the Genealogical Society of South Africa. Cape Town, 1964–.
Historia. Pretoria, 1952–.
Historiese Studies. Pretoria, 1939–49.
History in Africa. Waltham, Mass., 1974–.
Huguenot Society of South Africa: Bulletin. Franschhoek, S. Afr., 1963–.
International Journal of African Historical Studies. Boston, Mass., 1968–.
Janus. Cape Town, 1974–82.
Journal for Contemporary History. Bloemfontein, S. Afr., 1975–.
Journal of African History. London, 1960–.
Journal of Asian and African Studies. Leiden, Neth., 1966–.
Journal of Imperial and Commonwealth History. London, 1972–.
Journal of the Methodist Historical Society of South Africa. Grahamstown, S. Afr., 1952–61.
Journal of Modern African Studies. Cambridge, Eng., 1963–.
Journal of Natal and Zulu History. Pietermaritzburg, S. Afr., 1978–.
Journal of Southern African Affairs. College Park, Md., 1976–80.
Journal of Southern African Studies. London, 1974–.
Kleio. Pretoria, 1969–.
Kronos: Journal of Cape History. Bellville, S. Afr., 1979–.
Looking Back. Port Elizabeth, S. Afr., 1960–.
Militaria: Official Professional Journal of the South African Defence Force. Pretoria, 1969–.
Military History Journal. Johannesburg, 1967–.
Missionalia. Pretoria, 1969–.
Mohlomi. Roma, Botswana, 1976–77.
Natal Museum Journal of Humanities. Pietermaritzburg, 1989–.
Natalia. Pietermaritzburg, S. Afr., 1971–.

Occasional Papers. Centre for African Studies, University of Cape Town, 1979–.
Perspectives in Education. Johannesburg, 1976–.
Politikon: The South African Journal of Political Studies. Pretoria, 1974–.
Quarterly Bulletin of the South African Library. Cape Town, 1946–.
Race Relations Journal. Johannesburg, 1933–50.
Race Relations Survey. Johannesburg, 1984–.
Review of African Political Economy. London, 1974–.
Searchlight South Africa. London, 1988–93.
Social Dynamics. Cape Town, 1975–.
South Africa International. Johannesburg, 1970–.
South African Archaeological Bulletin. Cape Town, 1945–.
South African Archives Journal. Pretoria, 1959–.
South African Cultural History Museum: Annals. Cape Town, 1987–.
South African Geographer. Stellenbosch, S. Afr., 1969–.
South African Geographical Journal. Johannesburg, 1917–.
South African Historical Journal. Pretoria, 1969–.
South African Human Rights and Labour Law Yearbook. Cape Town, 1990–.
South African Journal of Cultural History. Pretoria, 1984–.
South African Journal of Economic History. Johannesburg, 1986–.
South African Journal of Economics. Johannesburg, 1933–.
South African Journal of Ethnology. Johannesburg, 1978–.
South African Journal of International Affairs. Johannesburg, 1993–.
South African Journal of Labour Relations. Pretoria, 1977–.
South African Journal of Science. Johannesburg, 1903–.
South African Journal on Human Rights. Johannesburg, 1985–.
South African Labour Bulletin. Durban, S. Afr., 1974–.
South African Outlook (Kafir Express, Christian Express). Lovedale, Cape Town, 1870–.
South African Review. Johannesburg, 1983–.
South African Statistics. Pretoria, 1968–.
Southern African Review of Books. London, 1987–.
The State. Johannesburg, 1908–12.
Survey of Race Relations in South Africa. Johannesburg, 1946–1983.
Theoria: A Journal of Studies in the Arts, Humanities, and Social Sciences. Pietermaritzburg, S. Afr., 1947–.
Transactions of the Royal Society of South Africa. Cape Town, 1908–.
TransAfrican Journal of History. Nairobi, 1971–.
Transformation: Critical Perspectives on Southern Africa. Durban, S. Afr., 1986–.
Ufahamu. Los Angeles, Calif., 1970–.
Van Riebeeck Society Publications. Cape Town, 1st ser., 50 vols., 1918–69; 2d ser. 1970–.
Women's Studies. Umtata, Transkei, 1989–.
Work in Progress. Johannesburg, 1977–94.

Edited Source Material

Axelson, E., ed. *South African Explorers*. London: Oxford University Press, 1954.

Balme, J. H. *To Love One's Enemies: The Work and Life of Emily Hobhouse, Compiled from Letters and Writings, Newspaper Cuttings, and Official Documents*. Cobble Hill, B.C., Canada: Hobhouse Trust, 1994.

Bird, J., ed. *The Annals of Natal, 1495–1845*. 2 vols. Cape Town: Maskew Miller, 1888.

Brookes, E. H., ed. *Apartheid: A Documentary Study of Modern South Africa*. London: Routledge and Kegan Paul, 1968.

Chase, J. C., ed. *The Natal Papers, 1498–1843*. 2 vols. Grahamstown, S. Afr.: R. Godlonton, 1843.

Comaroff, J. L., ed. *The Boer War Diary of Sol T. Plaatje: An African at Mafeking*. Johannesburg: Macmillan, 1973.

Davenport, T. R. H., and K. Hunt, eds. *The Right to the Land*. Cape Town: David Philip, 1974.

Davies, R., D. O'Meara, and S. Dlamini. *The Struggle for South Africa: A Reference Guide to Movements, Organizations, and Institutions*. Rev. ed. London: Zed, 1988.

Duminy, A. H., and W. R. Guest, eds. *Fitzpatrick, South African Politician: Selected Papers, 1886–1906*. Johannesburg: McGraw-Hill, 1976.

Fouché, L., ed. *The Diary of Adam Tas*. Cape Town: Van Riebeeck Society, 1970.

Fraser, M., and A. Jeeves, eds. *All That Glittered: Selected Correspondence of Lionel Phillips, 1890–1924*. Cape Town: Oxford University Press, 1977.

Geyser, O., ed. *B. J. Vorster: Selected Speeches*. Bloemfontein, S. Afr.: Institute for Contemporary History, 1977.

Gordon, R. E., and C. J. Talbot, eds. *From Dias to Vorster: Source Material on South African History, 1488–1975*. Cape Town: Nasou, 1977.

Hancock, W. K., and J. Van der Poel, eds. *Selections from the Smuts Papers*. 7 vols. Cambridge: Cambridge University Press, 1966–73.

Headlam, C., ed. *The Milner Papers*. 2 vols. London: Cassell, 1931, 1933.

Houghton, D. H., and J. Dagut, eds. *Source Material on the South African Economy*. 3 vols. Cape Town: Oxford University Press, 1972–73.

Hugo, P., ed. *Quislings or Realists?: A Documentary Study of "Coloured" Politics in South Africa*. Johannesburg: Ravan, 1978.

Kruger, D. W., ed. *South African Parties and Policies, 1910–1960: A Selected Source Book*. Cape Town: Human and Rousseau, 1960.

La Guma, A., ed. *Apartheid*. New York: International, 1971.

Le Cordeur, B. A., and C. C. Saunders, eds. *The Kitchingman Papers*. Johannesburg: Brenthurst, 1976.

———. *The War of the Axe*. Johannesburg: Brenthurst, 1981.

Lewsen, P., ed. *Selections from the Correspondence of John X. Merriman*. 4 vols. Cape Town: Van Riebeeck Society, 1960–69.

Mandela, N. *The Struggle Is My Life: His Speeches and Writings, Brought Together* with *Historical Documents and Accounts of Mandela in Prison by Fellow-Prisoners, 1944–1990*. Bellville, S. Afr.: Mayibuye, in association with David Philip, 1994.

Merrett, C. *The Emergency of the State: A Source Guide to South African Political Issues, 1985–1990*. Pietermaritzburg, S. Afr.: University of Natal Library, 1993.

———. *Thesaurus of South African Socio-Political and Economic Terms from an Anti-Apartheid Perspective*. 3d ed. Pietermaritzburg, S. Afr.: University of Natal Library, 1993.

Moodie, D., ed. *The Record, or a Series of Official Papers Relative to the Condition and Treatment of the Native Tribes of South Africa*. Reprint (original publications 1838–41), Amsterdam: Balkema, 1960.

Pelzer, A. N., ed. *Verwoerd Speaks: Speeches, 1948–1962*. Johannesburg: APB, 1966.

Preston, A., ed. *The South African Journal of Sir Garnet Wolseley, 1879–1880*. Cape Town: Balkema, 1973.

Rees, W., ed. *Colenso Letters from Natal*. Pietermaritzburg, S. Afr.: Shuter and Shooter, 1958.

Rose, B., and R. Tunmer, eds. *Documents in South African Education*. Johannesburg: Ad Donker, 1973.

Schoeman, K., ed. *The Wesleyan Mission in the Orange Free State, 1833–1854, as Described in Contemporary Accounts*. Cape Town: Human and Rousseau, 1991.

South African Archival Documents. Pretoria: Government Printer. Cape Series, 1957–98; Natal Series, 1958–98; Orange Free State Series, 1952–98; Transvaal Series, 1949–98.

South African History Archive. *Images of Defiance: South African Resistance Posters of the 1980s*. Johannesburg: Ravan, 1995.

South African Who's Who. Johannesburg: Ken Donaldson, 1908–98.

Theal, G. M. *Basutoland Records, 1833–1868*. 4 vols. Reprint (original publication 1883), Cape Town: Struik, 1964.

———. *Records of the Cape Colony*. 36 vols. London: Government of the Cape Colony, 1897–1905.

———. *Records of South-Eastern Africa*. 8 vols. London: W. Clowes, 1898–1903.

Thom, H. B., ed. *Journal of Jan van Riebeeck, 1651–1662*. 3 vols. Cape Town: Balkema, 1952–58.

Union Statistics for Fifty Years. Pretoria: Government Printer, 1960.

Van der Merwe, H. W. *African Perspectives on South Africa: Reports, Articles, and Documents*. Stanford, Calif.: Hoover Institution, 1978.

Webb, C., and J. Wright, eds. *The James Stuart Archive*. 3 vols. Pietermaritzburg, S. Afr.: University of Natal Press, 1976–82.

Wilson, F., and D. Perrot, eds. *Outlook on a Century: South Africa, 1870–1970*. Lovedale, S. Afr.: Lovedale, 1973.

Wright, H. M., ed. *Sir James Rose Innes: Selected Correspondence, 1884–1902*. Cape Town: Van Riebeeck, 1972.

BIOGRAPHY

Alexander, P. *Alan Paton: A Biography.* Oxford: Oxford University Press, 1994.

Basner, M. *Am I an African? The Political Memoirs of H. M. Basner.* Johannesburg: Witwatersrand University Press, 1993.

Benson, M. *A Far Cry: The Making of a South African.* Reprint (original publication 1989), Johannesburg: Ravan, 1996.

Berger, M. *Chris Hani.* Cape Town: Maskew Miller Longman, 1994.

Binns, C. T. *Dinuzulu: The Death of the House of Shaka.* London: Longman, 1968.

Breytenbach, J. *Eden's Exiles: One Soldier's Fight for Paradise.* Cape Town: Queillerie, 1997.

Cameron, T. *Jan Smuts: An Illustrated Biography.* Cape Town: Human and Rousseau, 1994.

Clingman, S. *Bram Fischer: Afrikaner Revolutionary.* Cape Town: David Philip, 1998.

Cope, R. K. *Comrade Bill: The Life and Times of W. H. Andrews, Workers' Leader.* Cape Town: Stewart, 1944.

Couzens, T. *The New African: A Study of the Life and Work of H. I. E. Dhlomo.* Johannesburg: Ravan, 1985.

———. *Tramp Royal: The True Story of Trader Horn.* Johannesburg: Ravan, 1992.

Davidson, A. *Cecil Rhodes and His Time.* Moscow: Progress, 1988.

De Villiers, R. M., ed. *Better Than They Knew.* 2 vols. Cape Town: Purnell, 1972, 1974.

Deane, D. S. *Black South Africans.* Cape Town: Oxford University Press, 1978.

Dictionary of South African Biography. 5 vols. Pretoria: Human Sciences Research Council, 1976–87.

Doke, C. M. *Trekking in South-Central Africa, 1913–1919.* Johannesburg: Witwatersrand University Press, 1993.

Driver, J. *Patrick Duncan: South African and Pan-African.* London: Heinemann, 1980.

Du Boulay, S. *Tutu: Voice of the Voiceless.* London: Penguin, 1988.

First, R., and A. Scott. *Olive Schreiner.* New York: Shocken, 1981.

Flint, J. *Cecil Rhodes.* Boston: Little, Brown, 1974.

Gilbey, E. *The Lady: The Life and Times of Winnie Mandela.* Johannesburg: Jonathan Ball, 1993.

Graaff, Sir de V. *Div Looks Back: The Memoirs of Sir de Villiers Graaff.* Cape Town: Human and Rousseau, 1993.

Gregory, T. *Ernest Oppenheimer and the Economic Development of Southern Africa.* Cape Town: Oxford University Press, 1962.

Hagemann, A. *Nelson Mandela.* Johannesburg: Fontein, 1996.

Hancock, W. K. *Smuts.* 2 vols. Cambridge: Cambridge University Press, 1962, 1968.

Harington, A. *Sir Harry Smith: Bungling Hero.* Cape Town: Tafelberg, 1980.

Higgs, C. *The Ghost of Equality: The Public Lives of D. D. T. Jabavu of South Africa, 1885–1959.* Athens: Ohio University Press, 1997.

Hocking, A. *Oppenheimer and Son.* Johannesburg: McGraw-Hill, 1973.

Huttenback, R. A. *Gandhi in South Africa.* Ithaca: Cornell University Press, 1971.

Jabavu, D. D. T. *The Life of J. T. Jabavu.* Lovedale, S. Afr.: Lovedale, n.d.

Jessup, E. *Ernest Oppenheimer: A Study in Power.* London: Collings, 1979.

Kadalie, C. *My Life and the ICU.* London: Cass, 1970.

Kenney, H. *Architect of Apartheid, H. F. Verwoerd: An Appraisal.* Johannesburg: Jonathan Ball, 1980.

Kruger, D. W. *Paul Kruger.* 2 vols. Johannesburg: Dagbreek Boekhandel, 1961, 1963.

Lewsen, P. *John X. Merriman.* New Haven: Yale University Press, 1982.

Liebenberg, B. *Andries Pretorius in Natal.* Pretoria: Academica, 1977.

Lockhart, J. G., and C. M. Wodehouse. *Rhodes.* London: Hodder and Stoughton, 1963.

Luthuli, A. *Let My People Go.* New York: McGraw-Hill, 1962.

McCord, M. *The Calling of Katie Makanya.* Cape Town: David Philip, 1995.

Macmillan, W. M. *My South African Years.* Cape Town: David Philip, 1975.

Mali, T. *Chris Hani: The Sun That Set before Dawn.* Johannesburg: Sached, 1993.

Mandela, N. *Long Walk to Freedom: The Autobiography of Nelson Mandela.* Randburg, S. Afr.: Macdonald Purnell, 1994.

Matthews, Z. K. *Freedom for My People: The Autobiography of Z. K. Matthews, Southern Africa, 1901 to 1968.* London: Collins, 1981.

Meer, F. *Higher than Hope: Mandela, the Biography.* Durban, S. Afr.: Madiba, 1989.

Mendelsohn, R. *Sammy Marks: The Uncrowned King of the Transvaal.* Cape Town: David Philip, 1992.

Mokgatle, M. M. N. *The Autobiography of an Unknown South African.* Berkeley: University of California Press, 1971.

Mouton, F. A. *Voices in the Desert: Margaret and William Ballinger, a Biography.* Pretoria: Benedic, 1997.

Mzala. *Gatsha Buthelezi: Chief with a Double Agenda.* London: Zed, 1988.

New Dictionary of South African Biography. Pretoria: HSRC, 1995.

Pallister, D. *South Africa, Inc.: The Oppenheimer Empire.* Johannesburg: Lowry, 1987.

Paton, A. S. *Apartheid and the Archbishop: The Life and Times of Geoffrey Clayton, Archbishop of Cape Town.* Cape Town: David Philip, 1973.

——. *Hofmeyr.* London: Oxford University Press, 1964.

Pirow, O. *James Barry Munnik Hertzog.* Cape Town: Howard Timmins, 1957.

Pogrund, B. *How Can Man Die Better: The Life of Robert Sobukwe.* Johannesburg: Jonathan Ball, 1997.

Ritter, E. A. *Shaka Zulu: The Rise of the Zulu Empire.* Harmondsworth, Eng.: Penguin, 1978.

Rotberg, R. *The Founder: Cecil Rhodes and the Pursuit of Power.* Johannesburg: Southern, 1988.

Roux, E. *S. P. Bunting: A Political Biography.* Bellville, S. Afr.: Mayibuye, 1993.

Rutherford, J. *Sir George Grey, 1812–1898.* London: Cassell, 1961.

Saayman, W. *A Man with a Shadow: The Life and Times of Professor Z. K. Matthews—A Missiological Interpretation in Context.* Pretoria: Unisa Press, 1996.

Sachs, A. *The Soft Vengeance of a Freedom Fighter.* Cape Town: David Philip, 1990.

Sanders, P. *Moshoeshoe: Chief of the Sotho.* London: Heinemann, 1975.

Saunders, C., ed. *Black Leaders in South African History.* London: Heinemann, 1979.

Skota, T. D. M. *The African Who's Who.* 3d ed. Johannesburg: Central News Agency, 1966.

———, ed. *The African Yearly Register.* Johannesburg: R. L. Esson, ca. 1931.

Strangwayes-Booth, J. *A Cricket in the Thorn Tree: Helen Suzman and the Progressive Party.* Johannesburg: Hutchinson, 1976.

Suzman, H. *In No Uncertain Terms: A South African Memoir.* Johannesburg: Jonathan Ball, 1993.

Tabler, E. C. *Pioneers of Natal and South-Eastern Africa, 1552–1878.* Cape Town: Balkema, 1977.

Temkin, B. *Gatsha Buthelezi: Zulu Statesman.* Cape Town: Purnell, 1976.

Thompson, L. M. *Survival in Two Worlds: Moshoeshoe of Lesotho, 1786–1870.* Oxford: Clarendon, 1975.

Van der Heever, C. M. *General J. B. M. Hertzog.* Johannesburg: APB, 1946.

Van Onselen, C. *The Seed Is Mine: The Life of Kas Maine, a South African Sharecropper, 1894–1985.* New York: Hill and Wang, 1996.

Walker, E. A. *W. P. Schreiner: A South African.* London: Oxford University Press, 1937.

Willan, B. *Sol Plaatje: South African Nationalist, 1876–1932.* London: Heinemann, 1984.

Williams, D. *Umfundisi: A Biography of Tiyo Soga, 1829–1871.* Lovedale, S. Afr.: Lovedale, 1978.

———. *When Races Meet: The Life and Times of William Ritchie Thomson.* Johannesburg: APB, 1967.

Woods, D. *Biko.* New York: Paddington, 1978.

CULTURE

Architecture, Art, Music, Theater, and Film

Bailey, J., and A. Seftel, eds. *Shebeens Take a Bow!: A Celebration of South Africa's Shebeen Lifestyle.* Johannesburg: Bailey's African History Archives, 1994.

Ballantine, C. *Marabi Nights: Early South African Jazz and Vaudeville.* Johannesburg: Ravan, 1993.

———. "Music and Emancipation: The Social Role of Black Jazz and Vaudeville in South Africa between the 1920s and the Early 1940s." *JSAS* 17, no. 1 (1991).

Bensusan, A. D. *Silver Images: History of Photography in Africa.* Cape Town: Howard Timmins, 1966.

Berman, E. *Art and Artists of South Africa: An Illustrated Biographical Dictionary and Historical Survey of Painters, Sculptors, and Graphic Artists since 1875.* Halfway House, S. Afr.: Southern, 1993.

———. *The Story of South African Painting.* Reprint (original publication 1975), Cape Town: Balkema, 1993.

Bradlow, F. *Thomas Bowler.* Cape Town: Balkema, 1967.

Bull, M., and J. Denfield. *Secure the Shadow: The Story of Cape Photography.* Cape Town: McNally, 1970.

Carchidi, V. "Representing South Africa: Apartheid from Print to Film." *Film and History* 21, no. 1 (1991).

Carruthers, J., and M. I. Arnold. *The Life and Work of Thomas Baines.* Vlaeberg, S. Afr.: Fernwood, 1995.

Chipkin, C. *Johannesburg Style: Architecture and Society, 1880s–1960s.* Cape Town: David Philip, 1993.

Cooke, C. K. *Rock Art of Southern Africa.* Cape Town: Books of Africa, 1969.

Coplan, D. B. *In the Time of the Cannibals: The Word Music of South Africa's Basotho Migrants.* Chicago: University of Chicago Press, 1994.

Coplan, D. R. *In Township Tonight!: South Africa's City Black Music and Theatre.* Johannesburg: Ravan, 1985.

De Bosdari, C. *Cape Dutch Houses and Farms.* 2d ed. Cape Town: Balkema, 1964.

Dowson, T. *Rock Engravings of Southern Africa.* Johannesburg: Witwatersrand University Press, 1992.

Dowson, T. A., and D. Lewis-Williams, eds. *Contested Images: Diversity in Southern African Rock Art Research.* Johannesburg: Witwatersrand University Press, 1994.

Erlmann, V. "Africa Civilised, Africa Uncivilised: Local Culture, World System and South African Music." *JSAS* 20, no. 2 (1994).

———. *African Stars: Studies in Black South African Performance.* Chicago: University of Chicago Press, 1991.

———. "Migration and Performance: Zulu Migrant Workers' *Isicathamiya* Performance in South Africa, 1890–1950." *Ethnomusicology* 34, no. 2 (1990).

Gordon-Brown, A. *Pictorial Africana.* Cape Town: Balkema, 1975.

Greig, D. E. *A Guide to Architecture in South Africa.* Cape Town: Howard Timmins, 1970.

———. *Herbert Baker in South Africa.* Cape Town: Purnell, 1970.

Grundy, K. W. "The Politics of South Africa's National Arts Festival: Small Engagements in the Bigger Campaign." *African Affairs* 93, no. 372 (1994).

Grut, M. *The History of Ballet in South Africa.* Cape Town: Human and Rousseau, 1981.

Gunner, E., ed. *Politics and Performance: Theatre, Poetry, and Song in Southern Africa*. Johannesburg: Witwatersrand University Press, 1994.

Gutsche, T. *The History and Social Significance of Motion Pictures in South Africa, 1895–1940*. Cape Town: Howard Timmins, 1972.

Hamm, C. "'The Constant Companion of Man': Separate Development, Radio Bantu, and Music." *Popular Music* 10, no. 2 (1991).

James, D. "Musical Form and Social History: Research Perspectives on Black South African Music." *Radical History Review*, issue 46–47 (1990).

Jowett, G. S. "Hollywood Discovers Apartheid: The Depiction of White South Africans in Recent American Films." *Journal of Popular Film and Television* 19, no. 4 (1992).

Keath, M. *Herbert Baker: Architecture and Idealism, 1892–1913: The South African Years*. Cape Town: Ashanti, 1992.

Kirby, P. R. *The Musical Instruments of the Native Races of South Africa*. 2d ed. Johannesburg: Witwatersrand University Press, 1965.

Lewis-Williams, J. D. *Discovering Southern African Rock Art*. Cape Town: David Philip, 1990.

Molefe, Z. B. *A Common Hunger to Sing: A Tribute to South Africa's Black Women of Song, 1950 to 1990*. Cape Town: Kwela, 1997.

Nettleton, A. "Arts and Africana: Hierarchies of Material Culture." *SAHJ* 29 (1993).

Nixon, R. "Cry White Season: Apartheid, Liberalism, and the American Screen." *South Atlantic Quarterly* 90, no. 3 (1991).

———. *Homelands, Harlem, and Hollywood: South African Culture and the World Beyond*. New York: Routledge, 1994.

Peterson, B. "Performing History Off the Stage: Notes on Working-Class Theater." *Radical History Review*, issue 46–47 (1990).

Radford, D. "The Carriage House and Stables in South African Domestic Architecture." *South African Journal of Cultural History* 5, no. 4 (1991).

———. "Popular Architecture in the United States and South Africa: A Case Study of the Late 19th Century." *South African Journal of Cultural History* 7, no. 1 (1993).

Rankin, E., and E. Miles. "The Role of the Missions in Art Education in South Africa." *Africa Insight* 22, no. 1 (1992).

Ross, S. I. *This Is My World: The Life of Helen Martins, Creator of the Owl House*. Cape Town: Oxford University Press, 1997.

Rudner, J., and I. Rudner. *The Hunter and His Art: A Survey of Rock Art in Southern Africa*. Cape Town: Struik, 1970.

Sampson, A. *Drum: A Venture into the New Africa*. London: Collins, 1956.

Schadeberg, J. *Sof'town Blues: Images from the Black '50s*. Pinegowrie: Self-published, 1994.

Skotnes, P., ed. *Miscast: Negotiating the Presence of the Bushmen*. Cape Town: University of Cape Town Press, 1996.

Van der Mescht, H. H. "South African Students at the Conservatory of Music in Leipzig, 1893–1914." *South African Journal of Cultural History* 8, no. 2 (1994).

Viney, G. *Colonial Houses of South Africa*. Cape Town: Struik-Winchester, 1987.

Vinnicombe, P. *People of the Eland*. Pietermaritzburg, S. Afr.: University of Natal Press, 1976.

Walton, J. *Cape Cottages*. Cape Town: Intaka, 1995.

_____. *Double-Storeyed Flat-Roofed Buildings of the Rural Cape*. Cape Town: Saayman and Weber, 1993.

Wilcox, A. R. *The Drakensberg Bushmen and Their Art, with a Guide to the Rock Painting Sites*. Rev. ed. Winterton, S. Afr.: Drakensberg, 1990.

Yates, R., J. Parkington, and T. Manhire. *Pictures from the Past: A History of the Interpretation of Rock Paintings and Engravings of Southern Africa*. Pietermaritzburg, S. Afr.: Centaur, 1990.

Crafts and Costume

Atmore, M. G. *Cape Furniture*. 3d ed. Cape Town: Howard Timmins, 1976.

Davison, P., and P. Harries. "Cotton Weaving in South-East Africa: Its History and Technology." *Textile History* 11 (1980).

Malan, A. "Victorian Brooches in South Africa: A Reflection of European Fashion." *South African Journal of Cultural History* 5, no. 4 (1991).

_____. "Victorian Weddings in South Africa: Evidence from Personal Recollections, Letters, and Photographs." *South African Journal of Cultural History* 7, no. 1 (1993).

Schofield, J. F. *Primitive Pottery*. Cape Town: Rustica, 1948.

Smith, A. H. *Spread of Printing in South Africa*. Amsterdam: Vangerdt, 1971.

Strutt, D. H. *Fashion in South Africa, 1652–1900*. Cape Town: Balkema, 1975.

Telford, A. A. *Yesterday's Dress*. Cape Town: Purnell, 1972.

Welz, S. *Cape Silver and Silversmiths*. Cape Town: Balkema, 1976.

Woodward, C. S. *Oriental Ceramics at the Cape of Good Hope, 1652–1795*. Cape Town: Balkema, 1974.

Language, Literature, and the Press

Antonissen, R. *Die Afrikaanse Letterkunde van Aanvang tot Hede*. 3d ed. Cape Town: Nasou, 1965.

Attridge, D., and R. Jolly, eds. *Writing South Africa: Literature, Apartheid, and Democracy, 1970–1995*. New York: Cambridge University Press, 1997.

Choonoo, R. N. "Fighting with Their Mighty Pens: A Comparison of the Education and Literary Works of the Black Writers of the Sophiatown and Soweto Generations in the Republic of South Africa, 1950–1980." *Africana Journal* 16 (1994).

Chrisman, L. "Colonialism and Feminism in Olive Schreiner's 1890s Fiction." *English in Africa* 20, no. 1 (1993).

Clingman, S. "Literature and History in South Africa." *Radical History Review* 46–47 (1990).

De Lange, M. *The Muzzled Muse: Literature and Censorship in South Africa.* Amsterdam: John Benjamins, 1997.

De Villiers, G. E., ed. *Ravan, 25 Years, 1972–1997: A Commemorative Volume of New Writing.* Randburg, S. Afr.: Ravan, 1997.

Gordimer, N. *The Black Interpreters.* Johannesburg: Ravan, 1973.

Gray, S. *Southern African Literature: An Introduction.* Cape Town: David Philip, 1979.

Gready, P. "Autobiography and the 'Power of Writing': Political Prison Writing in the Apartheid Era." *JSAS* 19, no. 3 (1993).

———. "The Sophiatown Writers of the Fifties: The Unreal Reality of Their World." *JSAS* 16, no. 1 (1990).

Green, M. *Novel Histories: Past, Present, and Future in South African Fiction.* Johannesburg: Witwatersrand University Press, 1997.

Hepple, A. *Censorship and Press Control in South Africa.* Johannesburg: Self-published, 1960.

Hofmeyr, I. *"We Spend Our Years as a Tale That Is Told": Oral Historical Narrative in a South African Chiefdom.* London: James Currey, 1993.

Jackson, G. S. *Breaking Story: The South African Press.* Boulder: Westview, 1993.

Jolly, R. J. *Colonization, Violence, and Narration in White South African Writing: André Brink, Breyten Breytenbach, and J. M. Coetzee.* Athens: Ohio University Press, 1995.

Jones, A. "From Rightest to 'Brightest'?: The Strange Tale of South Africa's *Citizen.*" *JSAS* 24, no. 2 (1998).

Jordaan, K. "The Origins of the Afrikaners and Their Language, 1652–1720: A Study in Miscegenation and Creole." *Race* 15 (1974).

Jordan, A. *Towards an African Literature.* Berkeley: University of California Press, 1973.

Kannemeyer, J. *Geskiedenis van die Afrikaanse Literatuur.* 2d ed. Pretoria: Academica, 1988.

———. *A History of Afrikaans Literature.* Pietermaritzburg, S. Afr.: Shuter and Shooter, 1993.

Le Cordeur, B. A. "International Aspects of the Struggle for the Freedom of the Press at the Cape: New Perspectives." *Acta Academica* 23, no. 3 (1991).

McKenzie, E. "The English-Language Press and the Anglo-American Corporation: An Assessment." *Kleio* 26 (1994).

———. "An Unholy Trinity?: Big Business, the Progressive Federal Party, and the English Press during the 1983 Referendum." *Journal for Contemporary History* 15, no. 3 (1990).

Merrett, C. E. "The Right to Know and the South African State of Emergency, 1986–1989." *Reality* 22, no. 3 (1990).

Olivier, G. "Afrikaans and South African Literature." *Journal of Literary Studies* 11, no. 2 (1995).

Pachai, B. "The History of the *Indian Opinion,* 1903–1914." *AYB* 24 (1962).

Patel, E., ed. *The World of Nat Nakasa*. Johannesburg: Ravan, 1975.

Peck, R. *A Morbid Fascination: White Prose and Politics in Apartheid South Africa*. Westport, Conn.: Greenwood, 1997.

Potter, E. *The Press as Opposition*. London: Chatto and Windus, 1975.

Robinson, A. M. L. *None Daring to Make Us Afraid: A Study of English Periodical Literature in the Cape Colony from its Beginnings in 1824 to 1835*. Cape Town: Maskew Miller, 1962.

Schulze-Engler, F. "Literature and Civil Society in South Africa." *Ariel: A Review of International English Literature* 27, no. 1 (1996).

Shava, P. V. *A People's Voice: Black South African Writing in the 20th Century*. London: Zed, 1989.

Shaw, G. E. *Some Beginnings: The Cape Times, 1876–1910*. Cape Town: Oxford University Press, 1975.

Smit, J. A., J. Van Wyk, and J-P. Wade, eds. *Rethinking Southern African Literary History*. Durban, S. Afr.: Y Press, 1996.

Snyman, J. P. L. *The South African Novel in English, 1880–1930*. Potchefstroom, S. Afr.: University of Potchefstroom, 1952.

Switzer, L. "The Ambiguities of Protest in South Africa: Rural Politics and the Press during the 1920s." *International Journal of African Historical Studies* 23, no. 1 (1990).

———, ed. *South Africa's Alternative Press: Voices of Protest and Resistance, 1880–1960*. Cambridge: Cambridge University Press, 1997.

Switzer, L., and E. C. Jones. "Other Voices: The Ambiguities of Resistance in South Africa's Resistance Press." *SAHJ* 32 (1995).

Trump, M. *Armed Vision: Afrikaans Writers in English*. Johannesburg: Ad Donker, 1987.

Valkhoff, M. F. *New Light on Afrikaans and 'Malayo-Portuguese'*. Leuven, Bel.: Editions Peeters, 1972.

Valkhoff, D. H. *A Short History of the Newspaper Press in South Africa, 1652–1952*. Cape Town: Nasionale Pers, 1952.

Van der Merwe, C. N. *Breaking the Barriers: Stereotypes and the Changing of Values in Afrikaans Writing, 1875–1990*. Amsterdam: Rodopi, 1994.

Voss, A. E. "'The Slaves Must Be Heard': Thomas Pringle and the Dialogue of South African Servitude." *English in Africa* 17, no. 1 (1990).

———. "Sol Plaatje, the 18th Century, and South African Cultural Memory." *English in Africa* 21, nos. 1 and 2 (1994).

Westphal, E. O. J. "The Linguistic Prehistory of Southern Africa." *Africa* 33 (1963).

White, T. "The Lovedale Press during the Directorship of R. H. W. Shepherd, 1930–1955." *English in Africa* 19, no. 2 (1992).

White, W. B. "The United Party's Afrikaans-Language Press, 1948–1953." *Kleio* 24 (1992).

Literature in English

Abrahams, P. *Mine Boy*. London: Faber and Faber, 1946.

_____. *Tell Freedom*. London: Faber and Faber, 1954.

Afrika, T. *The Innocents*. Cape Town: David Philip, 1994.

Botha, W. P. B. *The Reluctant Playwright*. Oxford: Heinemann, 1993.

Breytenbach, B. *And Death White as Words*. London: Rex Collings, 1978.

_____. *Memory of Snow and Dust*. London: Faber and Faber, 1989.

_____. *Season in Paradise*. London: Jonathan Ball, 1980.

Brink, A. P. *Dry White Season*. London: W. H. Allen, 1979.

_____. *An Instant in the Wind*. London: W. H. Allen, 1976.

_____. *Rumours of Rain*. London: W. H. Allen, 1978.

Campbell, R. *Sons of the Mistral*. London: Faber and Faber, 1941.

Coetzee, J. M. *In the Heart of the Country*. Johannesburg: Ravan, 1978.

Cope, M. *Spiral of Fire*. Cape Town: David Philip, 1987.

Dangor, A. *The Z Town Trilogy*. Johannesburg: Ravan, 1990.

De Kock, L., and I. Tromp, eds. *The Heart in Exile: South African Poetry in English, 1990–1995*. London: Penguin, 1996.

Delius, A. *Border*. Cape Town: David Philip, 1976.

Dikobe, M. *The Marabi Dance*. London: Heinemann, 1973.

Ebersohn, W. *Store Up the Anger*. Harmondsworth, Eng.: Penguin, 1984.

Essop, A. *The Emperor*. Johannesburg: Ravan, 1984.

Forman, S., and A. Odendaal, eds. *A Trumpet from the Housetops: The Selected Writings of Lionel Forman*. Cape Town: David Philip, 1992.

Fugard, A. *My Children! My Africa! And Selected Shorter Plays*. Johannesburg: Witwatersrand University Press, 1990.

_____. *Playland—and Other Words*. Johannesburg: Witwatersrand University Press, 1992.

_____. *Selected Plays*. Oxford: Oxford University Press, 1987.

_____. *Three Port Elizabeth Plays*. Cape Town: Oxford University Press, 1974.

_____. *The Township Plays*. Cape Town: Oxford University Press, 1993.

Galgut, D. *The Quarry*. London: Viking, 1995.

Gool, R. *Cape Town Coolie*. Oxford: Heinemann, 1990.

Gordimer, N. *Burger's Daughter*. London: Jonathan Cape, 1979.

_____. *The Conservationist*. London: Jonathan Cape, 1974.

_____. *July's People*. Johannesburg: Ravan, 1981.

_____. *The Lying Days*. London: Victor Gollancz, 1953.

_____. *A World of Strangers*. London: Victor Gollancz, 1958.

Gray, R., and S. Finn, eds. *Sounding Wings: Stories from South Africa*. Cape Town: Maskew Miller Longman, 1994.

Gray, S., ed. *Modern South African Poetry*. Rev. ed. Johannesburg: Ad Donker, 1984.

_____. *The Penguin Book of Contemporary South African Short Stories*. London: Penguin, 1993.

Grosskopf, H. *Artistic Graves*. Johannesburg: Ravan, 1993.

Havemann, E. *Bloodsong and Other Stories of South Africa*. London: Hamish Hamilton, 1988.

Head, B. *Maru*. London: Heinemann, 1972.

_____. *Tales of Tenderness and Power*. Oxford: Heinemann, 1991.

Hirson, D. *The Heinemann Book of South African Short Stories*. Oxford: Heinemann/Unesco, 1994.

_____. *The House Next Door to Africa*. Cape Town: David Philip, 1986.

Jordan, A. C. *The Wrath of the Ancestors*. Lovedale, S. Afr.: Lovedale, 1980.

Joubert, E. *The Long Night of Poppie Nongena*. Johannesburg: Jonathan Ball, 1980.

Kombuis, K. *Paradise Redecorated*. Rondebosch, S. Afr.: Nemesis, 1990.

Kunene, D. P. *From the Pit of Hell to the Spring of Life*. Johannesburg: Ravan, 1986.

Lanham, P., and A. Mopeli-Paulus. *Blanket Boy's Moon*. London: Collins, 1953.

Maseko, B. *Mamlambo and Other Stories*. Johannesburg: Congress of South African Writers (COSAW), 1991.

Matlou, J. *Life at Home and Other Stories*. Johannesburg: COSAW, 1991.

Mda, Z. *Ways of Dying*. Cape Town: Oxford University Press, 1995.

Mphahlele, E. *Down Second Avenue*. London: Faber, 1965.

_____. *The Wanderers*. Cape Town: David Philip, 1984.

Mtshali, O. *Sounds of a Cowhind Drum*. London: Oxford University Press, 1975.

Mzamane, M. *The Children of Soweto*. Harlow, Eng.: Longman, 1982.

Paton, A. *Ah, but Your Land Is Beautiful*. Cape Town: David Philip, 1981.

_____. *Cry the Beloved Country: A Story of Comfort in Desolation*. London: Jonathan Cape, 1948.

_____. *Too Late the Phalarope*. Cape Town: Cannon, 1953.

Plaatje, S. T. *Mhudi*. London: Heinemann, 1977.

Plomer, W. *Turbott Wolfe*. London: Leonard and Virginia Woolf, 1925.

Reader's Digest Association. *The Best of South African Short Stories*. Cape Town: The Association, 1991.

Rive, R. *Buckingham Palace: District Six*. Oxford: Heinemann, 1986.

Schreiner, O. *The Story of an African Farm*. London: Hutchinson, 1883.

Sepamla, S. *Ride on the Whirlwind*. Johannesburg: Ad Donker, 1981.

Smith, P. *The Beadle*. London: Jonathan Cape, 1926.

_____. *The Little Karoo*. London: Jonathan Cape, 1925.

Themba, C. *The Will to Die*. Reprint (original publication 1972), Cape Town: David Philip, 1982.

Wilhelm, P. *The Mask of Freedom*. Johannesburg: Ad Donker, 1994.

Zwelonke, D. M. *Robben Island*. Reprint (original publication 1973), Oxford: Heinemann, 1989.

Sports

Archer, R., and A. Bouillon. *The South African Game: Sport and Racism*. London: Zed, 1982.

Booth, D. *Playing the Game: Desegregating South African Sport.* Durban, S. Afr.: University of Natal, Development Studies Unit, 1988.

———. "The South African Council on Sport and the Political Antinomies of the Sports Boycott." *JSAS* 23, no. 1 (1997).

———. "United Sport: An Alternative Hegemony in South Africa?" *International Journal of the History of Sport* 12, no. 3 (1995).

Bose, M. *Sporting Colours: Sport and Politics in South Africa.* London: Robson, 1994.

Craven, D. *The Legends of Springbok Rugby, 1889–1989: Doc Craven's Tribute.* Pinelands, S. Afr.: K. C. Publications, 1989.

Craven, D., and C. O. Medworth. *History of Natal Rugby, 1870–1964.* Durban, S. Afr.: Howard Timmins, 1964.

Dobson, P. *Doc: The Life of Danie Craven.* Cape Town: Human and Rousseau, 1994.

———. *Rugby in South Africa: A History 1861–1988.* Cape Town: South African Rugby Board (SARB), 1989.

Ferreira, J. T. *Transvaal Rugby Football Union: One Hundred Years.* Johannesburg: Transvaal Rugby Football Union, 1992.

Grundlingh, A., A. Odendaal, and S. B. Spies. *Beyond the Tryline: Rugby and South African Society.* Johannesburg: Ravan, 1995.

Jarvie, G. *Class, Race, and Sport in South Africa's Political Economy.* Boston: Routledge and Kegan Paul, 1985.

Jooste, G. K. *South African Rugby Test Players, 1949–1995.* Johannesburg: Penguin, 1995.

Lapchick, R. E. *The Politics of Race and International Sport: The Case of South Africa.* Westport, Conn.: Greenwood, 1975.

Louw, R., and J. Cameron-Dow. *For the Love of Rugby.* Johannesburg: H. Strydom, 1987.

McGlew, J., and T. Chesterfield. *South Africa's Cricket Captains: From Melville to Wessels.* Johannesburg: Southern, 1994.

Merrett, C. E. "'In Nothing Else Are the Deprivers So Deprived': South African Sport, Apartheid, and Foreign Relations, 1945–71." *International Journal of the History of Sport* 13, no. 2 (1996).

Nauright, J. *Sport, Cultures, and Identities in South Africa.* Cape Town: David Philip, 1997.

Parker, A. C. *Western Province Rugby: Centenary, 1883–1983.* Cape Town: Western Province Rugby Football Union, 1983.

Partridge, T. *A Life in Rugby.* Halfway House, S. Afr.: Southern, 1991.

Ramsamy, S. *Apartheid, the Real Hurdle: Sport in South Africa and the International Boycott.* London: International Defence and Aid Fund for Southern Africa, 1982.

Schnaps, T. *A Statistical History of Springbok Rugby: Players, Tours, and Matches.* Cape Town: Don Nelson, 1989.

Sello, S. *Chiefs' Twenty-one Glorious Years: The Official History of South Africa's Glamour Football Club.* Johannesburg: Skotaville, 1991.

Van der Merwe, F. J. G. "Afrikaner Nationalism in Sport." *Canadian Journal of History of Sport* 22, no. 2 (1991).

Winch, J. *Cricket in Southern Africa: Two Hundred Years of Achievements and Records.* Rossettenville, S. Afr.: Windsor, 1997.

THE ECONOMY

General

Abedian, I., and A. Cronjé. "Government Foreign Borrowing in South Africa." *SAJE* 63, no. 2 (1995).

Bell, T. "The Impact of Sanctions on South Africa." *Journal of Contemporary African Studies* 12, no. 1 (1993).

Christopher, A. J. "The Pattern of Diplomatic Sanctions against South Africa, 1948–1994." *GeoJournal* 34, no. 4 (1994).

Drew, A. "Events Were Breaking above Their Heads: Socialism in South Africa, 1921–1950." *Social Dynamics* 17, no. 1 (1991).

Fine, B., and Z. Rustomjee. *The Political Economy of South Africa: From Minerals–Energy Complex to Industrialisation.* London: Hurst, 1996.

First, R., J. Steele, and C. Gurney. *The South African Connection: Western Investment in Apartheid.* London: Temple Smith, 1972.

Gelb, S., ed. *South Africa's Economic Crisis.* Cape Town: David Philip, 1991.

Houghton, D. H. *The South African Economy.* 4th ed. Cape Town: Oxford University Press, 1976.

Hutt, W. *The Economics of the Colour Bar.* London: Macmillan, 1964.

Jones, S. "Real Growth in the South African Economy since 1961." *South African Journal of Economic History* 5, no. 2 (1990).

———, ed. *Financial Enterprise in South Africa since 1950.* London: Macmillan, 1992.

Jones, S., and A. Muller. *The South African Economy, 1910–1990.* Basingstoke, Eng.: Macmillan, 1992.

Konczacki, Z. A., J. L. Parpart, and T. M. Shaw, eds. *Studies in the Economic History of Southern Africa.* Vol. 2, *South Africa, Lesotho, and Swaziland.* London: Frank Cass, 1991.

Lipton, M. *Capitalism and Apartheid, South Africa, 1910–1986.* Cape Town: David Philip, 1986.

Lumby, A. "Foreign Trade and Economic Growth: South Africa during the Inter-War Years." *South African Journal of Economic History* 5, no. 2 (1990).

Lundahl, M. *Apartheid in Theory and Practice: An Economic Analysis.* Boulder: Westview, 1992.

Macmillan, W. M. *Complex South Africa: An Economic Foot-Note to History.* London: Faber and Faber, 1930.

Magubane, B. *The Political Economy of Race and Class in South Africa.* New York: Monthly Review, 1979.

Moll, T. "Did the Apartheid Economy 'Fail'?" *JSAS* 17, no. 2 (1991).

Morris, M. "The Development of Capitalism in South Africa." *Journal of Development Studies* 12 (1976).

Müller, A. "Black and Coloured Entrepreneurship in Historical Perspective." *South African Journal of Economic History* 5, no. 2 (1990).

Nattrass, J. *The South African Economy: Its Growth and Change.* 2d ed. Cape Town: Oxford University Press, 1988.

Nattrass, N. "Controversies about Capitalism and Apartheid in South Africa: An Economic Perspective." *JSAS* 17, no. 4 (1991).

Nattrass, N., and E. Ardington, eds. *The Political Economy of South Africa.* Cape Town: Oxford University Press, 1990.

Preston-Whyte, E., and C. M. Rogerson, eds. *South Africa's Informal Economy.* Cape Town: Oxford University Press, 1991.

Robertson, H. M. "One Hundred and Fifty Years of Economic Contact between Black and White: A Preliminary Survey." *SAJE* (1934–35).

Rustomjee, Z. "Capital Flight under Apartheid." *Transformation: Critical Perspectives on Southern Africa* 15 (1991).

Schlemmer, L., and E. Webster. *Change, Reform, and Economic Growth in South Africa.* Johannesburg: Ravan, 1977.

Schumann, C. G. W. *Structural Changes and Business Cycles in South Africa, 1806–1936.* London: Staples, 1938.

Shepherd, G. W., ed. *Effective Sanctions on South Africa: The Cutting Edge of Economic Intervention.* New York: Greenwood, 1991.

Singh, H. "Impact of Sanctions and Armed Struggle on the South African Economy." *Africa Quarterly* (India) 32, nos. 1–4 (1992–93).

Smit, B. W., and B. A. Mocke. "Capital Flight from South Africa: Magnitude and Causes." *SAJE* 59, no. 1 (1991).

Stedman, S. J., ed. *South Africa: The Political Economy of Transformation.* Boulder: Lynne Rienner, 1994.

Van der Walt, J. S., and G. L. De Wet. "The Constraining Effects of Limited Foreign Capital Inflow on the Economic Growth of South Africa." *SAJE* 61, no. 1 (1993).

Agriculture and Rural Change

Beavon, K. S. O., and G. Elder. "Formalizing Milk Production in Johannesburg: The Dissolution of White Petty Milk-Producers, 1908–1920." *Contree* 30 (1991).

Beinart, W., P. Delius, and S. Trapido, eds. *Putting a Plough to the Ground: Accumulation and Dispossession in Rural South Africa, 1850–1930.* Johannesburg: Ravan, 1986.

Bradford, H. "Highways, Byways, and Culs-de-Sacs: The Transition to Agrarian Capitalism in Revisionist South African History." *Radical History Review*, issue 46–47 (1990).

———. *A Taste of Freedom: The ICU in Rural South Africa, 1924–1930.* Johannesburg: Ravan, 1988.

Bundy, C. *The Rise and Fall of the South African Peasantry.* 2d ed. Cape Town: David Philip, 1988.

De Klerk, M. "Seasons That Will Never Return: The Impact of Farm Mechanisation on Employment Incomes and Population Distribution in the Western Transvaal." *JSAS* 11, no. 1 (1984).

Denoon, D. *Settler Capitalism: The Dynamics of Dependent Development in the Southern Hemisphere.* Oxford: Clarendon, 1983.

Donovan, P. A., and W. L. Nieuwoudt. "Estimating Technology's Contribution to Productivity in the South African Sugar Industry, 1925–1986." *Agricultural Systems* 39, no. 3 (1992).

Du Toit, A. "The Micro-Politics of Paternalism: The Discourses of Management and Resistance on South African Fruit and Wine Farms." *JSAS* 19, no. 2 (1993).

Duly, L. C. *British Land Policy at the Cape, 1795–1844: A Study of Administrative Procedures in the Empire.* Durham: Duke University Press, 1968.

Duncan, D. "The State Divided: Farm Labour Policy in South Africa, 1924–1948." *SAHJ* 24 (1991).

Greenberg, S. *Race and State in Capitalist Development: South Africa in Comparative Perspective.* Johannesburg: Ravan, 1980.

Hurwitz, N. *Agriculture in Natal, 1860–1950.* Cape Town: Oxford University Press, 1957.

Jeeves, A. "Sugar and Gold in the Making of the South African Labour System: The Crisis of Supply on the Zululand Sugar Estates, 1906–1939." *South African Journal of Economic History* 7, no. 2 (1992).

Jeeves, A. H., and J. Crush, eds. *White Farms, Black Labor: The State and Agrarian Change in Southern Africa, 1910–1950.* Pietermaritzburg, S. Afr.: University of Natal Press, 1997.

Keegan, T. "The Restructuring of Agrarian Class Relations in a Colonial Economy: The Orange River Colony, 1902–1910." *JSAS* 5, no. 2 (1979).

———. *Rural Transformations in Industrializing South Africa: The Southern Highveld to 1914.* London: Ravan, 1987.

Knight, J., and G. Lenta. "Has Capitalism Underdeveloped the Labour Reserves of South Africa?" *Oxford Bulletin of Economics and Statistics* 42 (1980).

Krikler, J. "Agrarian Class Struggle and the South African War." *Social History* 14, no. 2 (1989).

Lees, R. *Fishing for Fortunes: The Story of the Fishing Industry in Southern Africa and the Men Who Made it.* Cape Town: Purnell, 1969.

Lincoln, D. "Flies in the Sugar Bowl: The Natal Sugar Industry Employees' Union in Its Heyday, 1940–1954." *SAHJ* 29 (1993).

Lye, W. F., and C. Murray. *Transformations on the Highveld: The Tswana and Southern Sotho.* Cape Town: David Philip, 1980.

Macmillan, W. M. *The South African Agrarian Problem and Its Historical Development.* Johannesburg: Central News Agency, 1919.

Marks, S., and A. Atmore, eds. *Economy and Society in Pre-Industrial South Africa.* London: Longman, 1980.

Minnaar, A. de V. "The Effects of the Great Depression (1929–1934) on South African White Agriculture." *South African Journal of Economic History* 5, no. 2 (1990).

———. "The Great Depression, 1929–1934: Adverse Exchange Rates and the South African Wool Farmer." *South African Journal of Economic History* 5, no. 1 (1990).

———. "Labour Supply Problems of the Zululand Sugar Planters: 1905–1939." *Journal of Natal and Zulu History* 12 (1991).

———. *"Ushukela!" A History of the Growth and Development of the Sugar Industry in Zululand: 1905 to the Present.* Pretoria: Human Sciences Research Council (HSRC), 1992.

Morris, M. "The Development of Capitalism in South African Agriculture: Class Struggle in the Countryside." *Economy and Society* 5, no. 2 (1976).

Murray, C. "Structural Unemployment, Small Towns, and Agrarian Change in South Africa." *African Affairs* 94, no. 374 (1995).

Palmer, R., and N. Parsons, eds. *The Roots of Rural Poverty in Central and Southern Africa.* London: Heinemann, 1977.

Plaatje, S. T. *Native Life in South Africa.* 2d ed. Johannesburg: Ravan, 1995.

Platzky, L., and C. Walker. *The Surplus People.* Johannesburg: Ravan, 1985.

Schirmer, S. "Reactions to the State: The Impact of Farm Labour Policies in the Mid-Eastern Transvaal, 1955–1960." *SAHJ* 30 (1994).

Simpkins, C. "Agricultural Production in the African Reserves of South Africa, 1918–69." *JSAS* 7 (1981).

Slater, H. "Land, Labour, and Capital in Natal: The Natal Land and Colonisation Company, 1860–1948." *JAH* 16 (1975).

Trapido, S. "Landlord and Tenant in a Colonial Economy." *JSAS* 5, 1 (1978).

Van Onselen, C. "Race and Class in the South African Countryside: Cultural Osmosis and Social Relations in the Sharecropping Economy of the South-Western Transvaal, 1900–1950." *American Historical Review*, 95, 1 (1990).

Wickens, P. "The Natives Land Act of 1913." *SAJE* 49 (1981).

Wilson, F., A. Kooy, and D. Hendrie, eds. *Farm Labour in South Africa.* Cape Town: David Philip, 1977.

Banking, Currency, and Finance

Abedian, I., and A. Cronje. "Government Foreign Borrowing in South Africa." *SAJE* 63, 2 (1995).

Ally, R. *Gold and Empire: The Bank of England and South Africa's Gold Producers, 1886–1926.* Johannesburg: Witwatersrand University Press, 1994.

———. "The South African Pound Comes of Age: Sterling, the Bank of England and South Africa's Monetary Policy, 1914–1925." *Journal of Imperial and Commonwealth History* 22, 1 (1994).

———. "War and Gold—the Bank of England, the London Gold Market and South Africa's Gold, 1914–1919." *JSAS* 17, 2 (1991).

Arndt, E. H. D. *Banking and Currency Development in South Africa 1652–1927*. Cape Town: Juta, 1928.

Breckenridge, K. "'Money With Dignity': Migrants, Minelords and the Cultural Politics of the South African Gold Standard Crisis, 1920–33." *JAH* 36, 2 (1995).

Conradie, B. *The Confidence of the Whole Country: Standard Bank Reports on Economic Conditions in Southern Africa 1865–1902*. Johannesburg: Standard Bank Investment Corp., 1987.

De Kock, G. *A History of the South African Reserve Bank (1920–1952)*. Pretoria: Van Schaik, 1954.

Frankel, S. H. *Capital Investment in Africa: Its Course and Effects*. London: Oxford University Press, 1938.

Henry, J. A. *The First Hundred Years of the Standard Bank*. London: Oxford University Press, 1963.

Jones, S. "From Building Society to Bank: The Allied of South Africa, 1970–1988." *Business and Economic History* 20 (1991).

———. "Origins, Growth and Concentration of Bank Capital in South Africa, 1860–92." *Business History* 36, 3 (1994).

———, ed. *Financial Enterprise in South Africa Since 1950*. London: Macmillan, 1992.

Kantor, B. "The Evolution of Monetary Policy in South Africa." *SAJE* 39 (1971).

Nel, H. "Monetary Control and Interest Rates during the Post-De Kock Commission Period." *SAJE* 62, 1 (1994).

Shaw, E. M. *A History of Currency in South Africa*. Cape Town: South African Museum, 1956.

Commerce and Industry

Adler, G. "From the 'Liverpool of the Cape' to the 'Detroit of South Africa': The Automobile Industry and Industrial Development in the Port Elizabeth-Uitenhage Region." *Kronos* 20 (1993).

Archer, S. "The South African Industrialization Debate and the Tariff in the Inter-War Years." *CSSA* 11 (1981).

Arkin, M. *Storm in a Teacup. The Cape Colonists and the English East India Company*. Cape Town: Struik, 1973.

Berger, I. *Threads of Solidarity: Women in South African Industry, 1900–1980*. Bloomington: Indiana University Press, 1992.

Bozzoli, B. "Managerialism and the Mode of Production in South Africa." *South African Labour Bulletin* 3, 8 (1977).

_____. "The Origins, Development and Ideology of Local Manufacturing in South Africa." *JSAS* 1, 2 (1975).

_____. *The Political Nature of a Ruling Class.* London: Routledge, 1981.

Callinicos, L. *Working Life, 1886–1940: Factories, Townships and Popular Culture on the Rand.* Johannesburg: Ravan Press, 1987.

Cartwright, A. P. *Golden Age: The Story of the Industrialisation of South Africa and the Part Played in It by the Corner House Group of Companies, 1910–1967.* Cape Town: Purnell, 1968.

Clark, N. L. *Manufacturing Apartheid: State Corporations in South Africa.* New Haven: Yale University Press, 1994.

Crankshaw, O. "Apartheid and Economic Growth: Craft Unions, Capital and the State in the South African Building Industry, 1945–1975." *JSAS* 16, 3 (1990).

Cross, T. "Afrikaner Nationalism, Anglo American and Iscor: The Formation of the Highveld Steel and Vanadium Corporation, 1960–70." *Business History* 36, 3 (1994).

Dix, K. A. "The Motor Car Assembly/Manufacturing Industry in South Africa: Phases I to V." *South African Journal of Economic History* 10, 1 (1995).

Duncan, D. "Foreign and Local Investment in the South African Motor Industry 1924–1992." *South African Journal of Economic History* 7, 2 (1992).

_____. *We Are Motor Men: The Making of the South African Motor Industry.* Latheron: Whittles, 1997.

Fedderke, J. W. "Pricing Behaviour in the South African Manufacturing Industry 1945–1982." *SAJE* 60, 2 (1992).

Jordan, N. "The Informal Sector: Its Historical Context for African Women." *Women's Studies* 6 (1994).

Julius, A. B., and A. Lumby. "Labour and Industry: Job Reservation in the Eastern Cape Motor Industry in the 1960s." *Contree* 33 (1993).

Kaplan, D. "The Politics of Industrial Protection in South Africa." *JSAS* 13, 1 (1976).

Lumby, A. "A Comment on the Real Forces in South Africa's Industrial Growth Prior to 1939." *South African Journal of Economic History* 5, 1 (1990).

Marks, S., and R. Rathbone, eds. *Industrialisation and Social Change: African Class Formation, Culture and Consciousness, 1870–1930.* New York: Longman, 1982.

Martin, W. G. "The Making of an Industrial South Africa: Trade and Tariffs in the Interwar Period." *International Journal of African Historical Studies* 23, 1 (1990).

Müller, A. "Black and Coloured Entrepreneurship in Historical Perspective." *South African Journal of Economic History* 5, 2 (1990).

Myers, D., et al. *United States Business in South Africa.* Bloomington: Indiana University Press, 1980.

Rich, P. B. "Bernard Huss and the Experiment in African Cooperatives in South Africa, 1926–1948." *International Journal of African Historical Studies* 26, 2 (1993).

Rogerson, C. M. "'Unnecessarily Draining the Consumer's Pocket': An Historical Geography of Advertising in South Africa's Black Urban Townships." *South African Geographical Journal* 76, 1 (1994).

Seidman, A. and N. *South Africa and U.S. Multinational Corporations.* Westport: Lawrence Hill, 1978.

Trapido, S. "South Africa in a Comparative Study of Industrialization." *Journal of Development Studies* 7 (1971).

Van der Horst, S. T. "The Economics of Decentralisation of Industry." *SAJE* 33, (1965).

Van Duin, P. "White Building Workers and Coloured Competition in the South African Labour Market, c.1890–1940." *International Review of Social History* 37, 1 (1992).

Van Eyk, H. J. *Some Aspects of the South African Industrial Revolution.* 2d ed. Johannesburg: Institute of Race Relations, 1953.

Van Sittert, L. "'Making Like America': The Industrialisation of the St. Helena Bay Fisheries c.1936–c.1956." *JSAS* 19, 3 (1993).

Van Walbeek, C. P. "The Consequences of Export Instability: South Africa, 1971–1988." *SAJE* 61, 3 (1993).

Wood, B. "Industrializing Twentieth Century South Africa." *International Journal of African Historical Studies* 24, 3 (1991).

Labor, Strikes, and Trade Unions

Adler, G., and E. Webster. "Challenging Transition Theory: The Labor Movement, Radical Reform and Transition To Democracy in South Africa." *Politics and Society* 23, 1 (1995).

Arkin, M. "Strikes, Boycotts—And the History of Their Impact on South Africa." *SAJE* 28 (1960).

Backer, W., and G. J. Oberholzer. "Strikes and Political Activity: A Strike Analysis of South Africa for the Period 1910–1994." *South African Journal of Labour Relations* 19, 3 (1995).

Baines, G. "From Populism to Unionism: The Emergence and Nature of Port Elizabeth's Industrial and Commercial Workers' Union, 1918–1920." *JSAS* 17, 4 (1991).

Ballard, C. C. "Migrant Labour in Natal 1860–1879: With Special Reference to Zululand and the Delagoa Hinterland." *Journal of Natal and Zulu History* 1 (1978).

Baskin, J. *Striking Back: A History of Cosatu.* Johannesburg: Ravan Press, 1991.

Beinart, J. "*Joyini Inkomo*: Cattle Advances and the Origins of Migrancy from Pondoland." *JSAS* 5, 2 (1979).

———. "Transkeian Migrant Workers and Youth Labour on the Natal Sugar Estates, 1918–1948." *JAH* 32, 1 (1991).

Beittel, M. "Labor Unrest in South Africa, 1870–1990." *Review: Ferdinand Braudel Center* 18, 1 (1995).

Berger, I. "Gender, Race and Political Empowerment: South African Canning Workers, 1940–1960." *Gender and Society* 4, 3 (1990).

Bonner, P. "The Decline and Fall of the ICU—a Case of Self-Destruction." *South African Labour Bulletin* 1, 6 (1974).

Cock, J. *Maids and Madams: Domestic Workers under Apartheid.* Rev. ed. London: Women's Press, 1989.

Dekker, L. D., et al. "Case Studies in African Labour Action in South Africa and Namibia" in R. Sandbrook and R. Cohen, eds. *The Development of an African Working Class.* London: Longman, 1975.

Denoon, D. J. N. "The Transvaal Labour Crisis 1900–6." *JAH* 7 (1967).

Dollery, B. "Government Failure as an Explanation for the Asymmetric Effects of Labour Apartheid in South Africa." *South African Journal of Economic History* 10, 1 (1995).

Doxey, G. V. *The Industrial Colour Bar in South Africa.* Cape Town: Oxford University Press, 1961.

Duncan, D. *The Mills of God: The State and African Labour in South Africa, 1918– 1948.* Johannesburg: Witwatersrand University Press, 1995.

———. "The Regulation of Working Conditions for Africans in South Africa, 1918–1948." *African Studies* 52, 1 (1993).

———. "The State and African Trade Unions, 1918–1948." *Social Dynamics* 18, 2 (1992).

Du Toit, D. *Capital and Labour in South Africa. Class Struggles in the 1970s.* London: Kegan Paul International, 1981.

Etherington, N. "Labour Supply and the Genesis of South African Confederation." *JAH* 20 (1979).

Fortescue, D. "The Communist Party of South Africa and the African Working Class in the 1940s." *International Journal of African Historical Studies* 24, 3 (1991).

Friedman, S. *Building Tomorrow Today: African Workers in Trade Unions, 1970– 1985.* Johannesburg: Ravan Press, 1987.

Harries, P. "Capital, State and Labour on the 19th Century Witwatersrand: A Reassessment." *SAHJ* 18 (1986).

———. *Work, Culture, and Identity: Migrant Laborers in Mozambique and South Africa, c.1860–1910.* Johannesburg: Witwatersrand University Press, 1994.

Hemson, D. "Dock Workers, Labour Circulation and Class Struggles in Durban, 1940–1959." *JSAS* 4 (1977).

Hirson, B. *Yours for the Union: Class and Community Struggles in South Africa, 1930–1947.* London: Zed, 1989.

Hofmeyr, J. F. "The Rise in African Wages: 1975–1985." *SAJE* 62, 3 (1994).

Horrell, M. *South African Trade Unionism.* Johannesburg: Institute of Race Relations, 1961.

Jeeves, A. H. "The Control of Migratory Labour on the South African Gold Mines in the Era of Kruger and Milner." *JSAS* 2, 1 (1975).

Jeeves, A. H., and J. Crush. "The Failure of Stabilization Experiments and the Entrenchment of Migrancy to the South African Gold Mines." *Labour, Capital and Society* 1 (1992).

Johns, S. "The Birth of Non-White Trade Unionism in South Africa." *Race* 8 (1967).

Katz, E. N. *A Trade Union Aristocracy: The Transvaal White Working Class and the General Strike of 1913.* Johannesburg: Witwatersrand University Press, 1976.

Kirkwood, M. "The Mineworkers Struggle." *South African Labour Bulletin* 1, 8 (1975).

Kraak, G. *Breaking the Chains: Labour in South Africa in the 1970s and 1980s.* London: Pluto, 1993.

Kritzinger, A. S. "The Establishment and Role of the Institute of Industrial Relations: 1976–1991." *South African Journal of Labour Relations* 18, 4 (1994).

Levy, N. *The Foundations of the South African Cheap Labour System.* Boston: Routledge and Kegan Paul, 1982.

Lewis, J. *Industrialisation and Trade Union Organisation in South Africa, 1924–1955.* Cambridge: Cambridge University Press, 1984.

Luckhardt, K., and B. Wall. *Organize or Starve!: The History of the South African Congress of Trade Unions.* London: Lawrence and Wishart, 1980.

Maree, J., ed. *The Independent Trade Unions, 1974–1984: Ten Years of the "South African Labour Bulletin."* Johannesburg: Ravan, 1987.

Minnaar, A. de V. "Unemployment and Relief Measures during the Great Depression, 1929–1934." *Kleio* 26 (1994).

Moodie, T. D., and V. Ndatshe. *Going for Gold: Men, Mines, and Migration.* Johannesburg: Witwatersrand University Press, 1994.

Murray, M. *South Africa: Time of Agony, Time of Destiny.* London: Verso, 1987.

Nattrass, J. "Migrant Labour and South African Economic Developments." *SAJE* 44, no. 1 (1976).

Nuttall, T. A. "'Do Not Accept Kaffir Standards': Trade Unions and Strikes among African Workers in Durban during the Second World War." *SAHJ* 29 (1993).

O'Meara, D. "The 1946 African Mine Workers' Strike and the Political Economy of South Africa." *Journal of Commonwealth and Comparative Politics* 13, no. 2 (1975).

———. "White Trade Unions, Political Power, and Afrikaner Nationalism." *South African Labour Bulletin* 1, no. 10 (1975).

Plaut, M. "Debates in a Shark Tank: The Politics of South Africa's Non-Racial Trade Unions." *African Affairs* 91, no. 364 (1992).

Ramphele, M. *A Bed Called Home: Life in the Migrant Labour Hostels of Cape Town.* Cape Town: David Philip, 1993.

Roberts, M. *Labour in the Farm Economy.* Johannesburg: Institute of Race Relations, 1959.

Seidman, G. W. *Manufacturing Militance: Workers' Movements in Brazil and South Africa, 1970–1985.* Berkeley: University of California Press, 1993.

Tayal, M. "Indian Indentured Labour in Natal, 1890–1911." *Indian Economic and Social History Review* 14 (1979).

Thomas, W. H., ed. *Labour Perspectives on South Africa.* Cape Town: David Philip, 1974.

Van der Horst, S. T. *Native Labour in South Africa.* Cape Town: Oxford University Press, 1942.

Walker, I. D., and B. Weinbren. *Two Thousand Casualties: A History of the Trade Unions and the Labour Movement in the Union of South Africa.* Johannesburg: South African Trade Union Council, 1961.

Webster, E. *Cast in a Racial Mould: Labour Process and Trade Unionism in the Foundries.* Johannesburg: Ravan, 1985.

_____, ed. *Essays in Southern African Labour History.* Johannesburg: Ravan, 1978.

Wickins, P. L. *The Industrial and Commercial Workers' Union of Africa.* Cape Town: Oxford University Press, 1978.

Wilson, F. *Labour in the South African Gold Mines, 1911–1969.* Cambridge: Cambridge University Press, 1972.

Wolpe, H. "Capitalism and Cheap Labour Power in South Africa." *Economy and Society* 1, no. 4 (1972).

_____. "The 'White Working Class' in South Africa." *Economy and Society* 5, no. 2 (1976).

Wood, G. "The 1973 Durban Strikes: Of Local and National Significance." *Contree* 31 (1992).

Zania, T. "The ICU and the White Parliamentary Parties, 1921–24." *African Communist*, no. 120 (1990).

_____. "The ICU Reaches Its Peak and Begins to Break up." *African Communist*, no. 123 (1990).

Mining

Callinicos, L. *Gold and Workers, 1886–1924.* Johannesburg: Ravan, 1981.

Cartwright, A. P. *The Corner House: The Early History of Johannesburg.* Cape Town: Purnell, 1965.

_____. *The Gold Miners.* Cape Town: Purnell, 1962.

_____. *Gold Paved the Way: The Story of the Gold Fields Group of Companies.* London: Macmillan, 1967.

Crush, J., A. Jeeves, and D. Yudelman. *South Africa's Labour Empire: A History of Black Migrancy to the Gold Mines.* Cape Town: David Philip, 1991.

Henshaw, P. J. "Britain, South Africa, and the Sterling Area: Gold Production, Capital Investment, and Agricultural Markets, 1931–1961." *Historical Journal* 39, no. 1 (1996).

Horner, D., and A. Kooy. *Conflict on South African Mines, 1972–1979.* Cape Town: Southern African Labour and Development Research Unit (SALDRU), 1980.

Innes, D. *Anglo American and the Rise of Modern South Africa*. London: James Currey, 1984.

_____. "The Mining Industry in the Context of South Africa's Economic Development." *CSSA* 7 (1977).

James, W. "Capital, African Labour, and Housing at South Africa's Gold Mines." *Labour, Capital, and Society* 25, no. 1 (1992).

Jeeves, A. H. *Migrant Labour in South Africa's Mining Economy: The Struggle for the Gold Mines' Labour Supply, 1890–1920*. Kingston, Can.: McGill-Queen's University Press, 1985.

Johnstone, F. *Class, Race, and Gold: A Study of Class Relations and Racial Discrimination in South Africa*. Boston: Routledge and Kegan Paul, 1976.

Kanfer, S. *The Last Empire: De Beers, Diamonds, and the World*. New York: Farrar, Straus and Giroux, 1993.

Katz, E. "Miners by Default: Afrikaners and the Gold Mining Industry before Union." *South African Journal of Economic History* 6, no. 1 (1991).

Kubicek, R. V. *Economic Imperialism in Theory and Practice: The Case of South African Gold Mining Finance, 1886–1914*. Durham: Duke University Press, 1979.

Moodie, T. D. "Collective Violence on the South African Gold Mines." *JSAS* 18, no. 3 (1992).

_____. "The Moral Economy of the Black Miners' Strike of 1946." *JSAS* 13, no. 1 (1986).

Nattrass, G. "The Tin-Mining Industry in the Transvaal, 1905–1914: Some Social and Economic Implications and Perspectives." *South African Journal of Economic History* 6, no. 1 (1991).

Newbury, C. *The Diamond Ring: Business, Politics, and Precious Stones in South Africa, 1867–1947*. Oxford: Clarendon, 1989.

O'Meara, D. "The 1946 African Mineworkers' Strike and the Political Economy of South Africa." *Journal of Commonwealth and Comparative Politics* 13, no. 2 (1975).

Packard, R. M. "The Invention of the 'Tropical Worker': Medical Research and the Quest for Central African Labor in the South African Gold Mines, 1903–1936." *JAH* 34, no. 2 (1993).

Sampson, A. *Black and Gold: Tycoons, Revolutionaries, and Apartheid*. London: Hodder and Stoughton, 1987.

Smalberger, J. M. *Aspects of the History of Copper Mining in Namaqualand, 1846–1931*. Cape Town: Struik, 1975.

Smith, M. "'Walking in the Grave': Mining Accidents on the Witwatersrand Gold Mines, ca. 1990–1940." *South African Journal of Economic History* 7, no. 2 (1992).

Turrell, R. *Capital and Labour on the Kimberley Diamond Fields, 1871–1890*. Cambridge: Cambridge University Press, 1987.

_____. "Rhodes, De Beers, and Monopoly." *Journal of Imperial and Commonwealth History* 10, no. 3 (1982).

Wheatcroft, G. S. A. *The Randlords: South Africa's Robber Barons and the Mines That Forged a Nation*. London: Weidenfeld and Nicolson, 1985.

Wilson, F. *Labour in the South African Gold Mines, 1911–1969*. Cambridge: Cambridge University Press, 1972.

Worger, W. *South Africa's City of Diamonds: Mine Workers and Monopoly Capitalism in Kimberley, 1867–1895*. New Haven: Yale University Press, 1987.

Yudelman, D. *The Emergence of Modern South Africa: State, Capital, and the Incorporation of Organized Labor on the South African Gold Fields, 1902–1939*. Westport, Conn.: Greenwood, 1983.

Transport and Communications

Berridge, G. *The Politics of the South African Run: European Shipping and Pretoria*. Oxford: Clarendon, 1987.

Cockbain, T. G. E. "Early History of Aviation in the Eastern Province." *Militaria* 24, no. 1 (1994).

Frankel, S. H. *The Railway Policy of South Africa*. Johannesburg: Hortors, 1928.

Harris, C. J., B. D. Ingpen, and P. G. Bilas. *Mailships of the Union–Castle Line*. Vlaeberg, S. Afr.: Fernwood, 1994.

Heydenrych, H. *The Natal Main Line Story*. Pretoria: Human Sciences Research Council (HSRC), 1992.

Hodson, N. *The Race to the Cape: A Story of the Union–Castle Line, 1857–1977*. Ringwood, Austl.: Navigator, 1995.

Khosa, M. "Accumulation and Labour Relations in the Taxi Industry." *Transformation: Critical Perspectives on Southern Africa* 24 (1994).

———. "Changing Patterns of 'Black' Bus Subsidies in the Apartheid City, 1944–1986." *GeoJournal* 22, no. 3 (1990).

Mallett, A. S. *The Castle–Union Line: A Celebration in Photographs and Company Postcards*. Coltishall, U.K.: Ship Pictorial, 1990.

McCormack, M. C. "Man with a Mission: Oswald Pirow and South African Airways, 1933–1939." *JAH* 20 (1979).

Mitchell, W. H., and L. A. Sawyer. *The Cape Run: The Story of the Union–Castle Service to South Africa and of the Ships Employed*. Lavenham, U.K.: T. Dalton, 1984.

Mossop, E. E. *Old Cape Highways*. Cape Town: Maskew Miller, 1928.

Murray, M. *Union–Castle Chronicle, 1853–1953*. London: Longmans, Green, 1953.

Nock, O. S. *Railways of Southern Africa*. London: Black, 1971.

Pirie, G. H. "Aviation, Apartheid, and Sanctions: Air Transport to and from South Africa, 1945–1989." *GeoJournal* 22, no. 3 (1990).

———. "Dismantling Railway Apartheid in South Africa, 1975–1988." *Journal of Contemporary African Studies* 8–9, nos. 1–2 (1989–90).

———. "Law, Lawyers, and Racially Segregated Public Transport in South Africa." *African Studies* 51, no. 2 (1992).

_____. "Race, Class, and Comfort on Rural Buses, 1925–1955." *Contree* 27 (1990).

_____. "Railways and Labour Migration to the Rand Mines: Constraints and Significance." *JSAS* 19, no. 4 (1993).

_____. "Rolling Segregation into Apartheid: South African Railways, 1949–53." *Journal of Contemporary History* 27, no. 4 (1992).

Porter, A. N. *Victorian Shipping, Business, and Imperial Policy: Donald Currie, the Castle Line, and Southern Africa.* New York: St. Martin's, 1986.

Tayler, J. "Building Railways and 'Building Character': The Model Villages in Northern Natal." *Contree* 35 (1994).

Twyman, L. "Port Natal Harbour and the Colonial Politics of Natal." *Historia* 36, no. 2 (1991).

Van der Poel, J. *Railway and Customs Policies in South Africa, 1885–1910.* London: Longmans, Green, 1933.

Van Helten, J. J. "German Capital, the Netherlands Railway Company, and the Political Economy of the Transvaal." *JAH* 19 (1978).

HISTORY

General

Adler, T., ed. *Perspectives on South Africa.* Johannesburg: University of the Witwatersrand, 1977.

Agar-Hamilton, J. A. I. *The Road to the North: South Africa, 1852–1886.* London: Longman, 1937.

Atmore, A., and S. Marks. "The Imperial Factor in South Africa: Towards a Reassessment." *Journal of Imperial and Commonwealth History* 3, 1 (1974).

Beinart, W. *Twentieth Century South Africa.* New York: Oxford University Press, 1994.

Benyon, J. A. *Pro-Consul and Paramountcy in South Africa.* Pietermaritzburg: University of Natal Press, 1980.

_____. *Working Papers in Southern African Studies.* Johannesburg: University of the Witwatersrand, 1977.

Bonner, P., ed. *Working Papers in Southern African Studies.* vol. 2. Johannesburg: Ravan Press, 1981.

Cameron, T., and S. B. Spies, eds. *A New Illustrated History of South Africa.* 2d rev.ed. Johannesburg: Southern, 1991.

Cory, G. E. *The Rise of South Africa.* 6 vols. 1910–1939. repr. Cape Town: Struik, 1964.

Davenport, T. R. H. *South Africa: A Modern History.* 4th ed. Basingstoke: Macmillan, 1991.

Deacon, H., ed. *The Island: A History of Robben Island.* Cape Town: David Philip, 1996.

Deacon, R. "Hegemony, Essentialism and Radical History in South Africa." *SAHJ* 24 (1991).

De Kiewiet, C. W. *A History of South Africa Social and Economic.* London: Oxford University Press, 1957.

_____. *The Imperial Factor in South Africa: A Study in Politics and Economics.* Cambridge: Cambridge University Press, 1937.

Denoon, D., with B. Nyeko. *Southern Africa since 1800.* New ed. London: Longman, 1984.

Hattersley, A. F. *An Illustrated Social History of South Africa.* Cape Town: Balkema, 1969.

Huttenback, R. *Gandhi in South Africa: British Imperialism and the Indian Question, 1860–1914.* Ithaca: Cornell University Press, 1971.

Keppel-Jones, A. *South Africa: A Short History.* 5th ed. London: Hutchinson, 1975.

Kruger, H. *The Making of a Nation.* Johannesburg: Macmillan, 1972.

Lamar, H., and L. M. Thompson, eds. *The Frontier in History: North America and Southern Africa Compared.* New Haven: Yale University Press, 1981.

Lincoln, D. "Mauritian Settlers in South Africa: Ethnicity and the Experience of 'Creole' emigrés." *Immigrants and Minorities* 13, 1 (1994).

McCracken, D. P., ed. *The Irish in Southern Africa 1795–1910.* Durban: University of Durban-Westville, 1992.

Muller, C. F. J., ed. *Five Hundred Years: A History of South Africa.* 5th ed. Pretoria: Academica, 1986.

Murray, B. K. *Wits: The "Open" Years. A History of the University of the Witwatersrand, Johannesburg, 1939–1959.* Johannesburg: Witwatersrand University Press, 1997.

Norwich, O. I. *Maps of Southern Africa.* Johannesburg: Ad Donker, 1993.

Nuttall, S., and Coetzee, C., eds. *Negotiating the Past: The Making of Memory in South Africa.* Cape Town: Oxford University Press, 1998.

Oberholster, J. J. *The Historical Monuments of South Africa.* Cape Town: National Monuments Council, 1972.

Oliver, R., and J. Fage, gen. eds. *The Cambridge History of Africa.* 8 vols. Cambridge: Cambridge University Press, 1975–86.

Omer-Cooper, J. D. *History of Southern Africa.* 2d ed. Cape Town: David Philip, 1994.

Pampallis, J. *Foundations of a New South Africa.* London: Zed, 1991.

Parsons, N. *A New History of Southern Africa.* 2d ed. Basingstoke: Macmillan, 1993.

Perspectives on the Southern African Past. Cape Town: University of Cape Town: 1979.

Reader's Digest Association. *Illustrated History of South Africa: The Real Story.* 3d ed. Cape Town: The Association, 1994.

Roberts, M. *A History of South Africa.* London: Longman, 1990.

Ross, R. *Beyond the Pale: Essays On the History of Colonial South Africa.* Hanover: Wesleyan University Press, 1993.

Sani, G. *History of the Italians in South Africa 1498–1989*. Johannesburg: Zonderwater Block, 1992.

Saunders, C. C., ed. *An Illustrated Dictionary of South African History*. Sandton: Ibis Books, 1994.

Schreuder, D. M. *The Scramble for Southern Africa*. Cambridge: Cambridge University Press, 1980.

Sookdeo, A. "Ethnic Myths From South Africa: Bigoted Boer and Liberal Briton." *Journal of Ethnic Studies* 18, 4 (1991).

Spiegel, A. D. and P. A. McAllister, eds. *Tradition and Transition in Southern Africa: Festschrift for Philip and Iona Mayer*. Johannesburg: Witwatersrand University Press, 1992.

Theal, G. M. *History of South Africa*. 11 vols. 1888–1919. repr. Cape Town: Struik, 1964.

Thompson, L. M. *A History of South Africa*. Rev. ed. New Haven: Yale University Press, 1995.

_____. *The Unification of South Africa, 1902–1910*. Oxford: Clarendon Press, 1960.

Troup, F. *South Africa: An Historical Introduction*. London: Eyre Methuen, 1972.

Tsotsi, W. M. *From Chattel to Wage Slavery: A New Approach to South African History*. Maseru: Lesotho Printing, 1981.

Van Aswegen, H. J. *History of South Africa to 1854*. Pretoria: Academica, 1990.

Walker, E. A., ed. *Cambridge History of the British Empire, VIII: South Africa*. 2d ed. Cambridge: Cambridge University Press, 1963.

_____. *The Great Trek*. London: A. and C. Black, 1934.

_____. *Historical Atlas of South Africa*. Cape Town: Oxford University Press, 1922.

_____. *A History of Southern Africa*. 3d ed. London: Longman, 1957.

Wilson, M., and L. M. Thompson, eds. *The Oxford History of South Africa*. 2 vols. Oxford: Clarendon Press, 1969, 1971.

Worden, N. *The Making of Modern South Africa: Conquest, Segregation and Apartheid*. Oxford: Blackwell, 1994.

Yap, M., and D. L. Man. *Colour, Confusion and Concessions: The History of the Chinese in South Africa*. Hong Kong: Hong Kong University Press, 1996.

Historiography

Atmore, A., and N. Westlake. "A Liberal Dilemma: A Critique of *The Oxford History of South Africa*." *Race* 14 (1972).

Bank, A. "The Great Debate and the Origins of South African Historiography." *Journal of African History* 38, 2 (1997).

Beinart, W. "Agrarian Historiography and Agrarian Reconstruction." In J. Lonsdale, ed. *South Africa in Question*. London: James Currey, 1988.

_____. "Political and Collective Violence in Southern African Historiography." *JSAS* 18, 3 (1992).

Brown, J., ed. *History from South Africa: Alternative Visions and Practices*. Philadelphia: Temple University Press, 1991.

Bundy, C. *Re-Making the Past: New Perspectives in South African History*. Cape Town: University of Cape Town, Department of Adult Education and Extra-Mural Studies, 1986.

Callinicos, L. "Popularising History in a Changing South Africa." *SAHJ* 25 (1991).

Cornevin, M. *Apartheid: Power and Historical Falsification*. Paris: Unesco, 1980.

Cuthbertson, G. "Racial Attraction: Tracing the Historiographical Alliances between South Africa and the United States." *Journal of American History* 81, 3 (1994).

Furlong, P. J. "Fascism, the Third Reich and Afrikaner Nationalism: An Assessment of the Historiography." *SAHJ* 27 (1992).

Gann, L. H. "Liberal Interpretations of South African History." *Rhodes-Livingstone Journal* 25 (1959).

Grundlingh, A. "Politics, Principles and Problems of a Profession: Afrikaner Historians and Their Discipline, c.1920–c.1965." *Perspectives in Education* 12, 1 (1990/1).

Johnstone, F. "'Most Painful to Our Hearts': South Africa through the Eyes of the New School." *Canadian Journal of African Studies* 16 (1982).

Jones, S. "On Economic History in General and the Economic History of South Africa in Particular." *Perspectives in Economic History* 1 (1982).

Legassick, M. C. "Context, Historiography, Sources and Significance." *Kronos* 21 (1994).

————. "The Dynamics of Modernisation in South Africa." *JAH* 13 (1972).

Marks, S. "African and Afrikaner History." *JAH* 11 (1970).

————. "Liberalism, Social Realities and South African History." *Journal of Commonwealth Political Studies* 10 (1972).

————. "Towards a People's History of South Africa? Recent Developments in the Historiography of South Africa." In R. Samuel, ed. *People's History and Socialist Theory*. London: Routledge, 1981.

Saunders, C. C. *The Making of the South African Past: Major Historians on Race and Class*. Cape Town: David Philip, 1988.

————. "Radical History—the Wits Workshop Version—reviewed." *SAHJ* 24 (1991).

Smith, K. *The Changing Past: Trends in South African Historical Writing*. Johannesburg: Southern, 1988.

Thompson, L. M. "Afrikaner Nationalist Historiography and the Policy of Apartheid." *JAH* 3 (1962).

Trapido, S. "South Africa and the Historians." *African Affairs* 71 (1972).

Van Jaarsveld, F. A. *The Afrikaner's Interpretation of South African History*. Cape Town: Simondium, 1964.

————. "Recent Afrikaner Historiography." *Itinerario* 26, 1 (1992).

Wright, H. M. "*The Burden of the Present* and Its Critics." *Social Dynamics* 6 (1980).

Slavery

Boëseken, A. J. *Slaves and Free Blacks at the Cape, 1658–1700*. Cape Town: Tafelberg, 1977.

Carter, G. E. "A Review of Slavery, Emancipation and Abolition in South Africa and the United States in the 18th Century." *American Studies International* 29, 2 (1991).

Crais, C. "Slavery and Freedom along a Frontier: The Eastern Cape, South Africa, 1770–1838." *Slavery and Abolition* 11, 2 (1990).

Cuthbertson, G. "Cape Slave Historiography and the Question of Intellectual Independence." *SAHJ* 27 (1992).

Edwards, I. E. *Towards Emancipation: A Study in South African Slavery*. Cardiff: University of Wales Press, 1942.

Elbourne, E. "Freedom At Issue: Vagrancy Legislation and the Meaning of Freedom in Britain and the Cape Colony, 1799–1842." *Slavery and Abolition* 15, 2 (1994).

Eldredge, E. A., and F. Morton, eds. *Slavery in South Africa: Captive Labor on the Dutch Frontier*. Pietermaritzburg: University of Natal Press, 1994.

Greenstein, L. J. "Slave and Citizen: The South African Case." *Race* 15 (1973).

Morton, F. "Slave-Raiding and Slavery in the Western Transvaal After the Sand River Convention." *African Economic History* 20 (1992).

Ross, R. *Cape of Torments: Slavery and Resistance in South Africa*. London: Routledge, 1983.

———. "Emancipation and the Economy of the Cape Colony." *Slavery and Abolition* 14, 1 (1993).

———. "Oppression, Sexuality and Slavery in the Cape of Good Hope." *Historical Reflections* 6 (1975).

Shell, R. C.-H. *Children of Bondage: A Social History of the Slave Society at the Cape of Good Hope, 1652–1838*. New Hanover: University Press of New England, 1994.

———. "A Family Matter: The Sale and Transfer of Human Beings at the Cape, 1658 to 1830." *International Journal of African Historical Studies* 25, 2 (1992).

———. "Religion, Civic Status and Slavery From Dordt to the Trek." *Kronos* 19 (1992).

Southey, N. "From Periphery to Core: The Treatment of Cape Slavery in South African Historiography." *Historia* 37, 2 (1992).

Van der Spuy, P. "Slave Women and the Family in Nineteenth-Century Cape Town." *SAHJ* 27 (1992).

Watson, R. L. *The Slave Question: Liberty and Property in South Africa*. Johannesburg: Witwatersrand University Press, 1992.

Worden, N. "The Distribution of Slaves in the Western Cape during the Eighteenth Century." *African Seminar: Collected Papers* 2 (1981).

———. *Slavery in Dutch South Africa*. Cambridge: Cambridge University Press, 1985.

_____. "Diverging Histories: Slavery and Its Aftermath in the Cape Colony and Mauritius." *SAHJ* 27 (1992).

_____. *The Chains That Bind Us: A History of Slavery at the Cape*. Cape Town: University of Cape Town, Department of Extra-Mural Studies, 1994.

Worden, N., and C. Crais, eds. *Breaking the Chains: Slavery and Its Legacy in the Nineteenth-Century Cape Colony*. Johannesburg: Witwatersrand University Press, 1994.

Before White Settlement

Argyle, J., and E. Preston-Whyte, eds. *Social System and Tradition in Southern Africa*. Cape Town: Oxford University Press, 1978.

Avery, D. M. "Micromammals and the Environment of Early Pastoralists at Spoeg River, Western Cape Province, South Africa." *SAAB* 47, 156 (1992).

Axelson, E. V. *South-East Africa 1488–1530*. London: Longmans, Green, 1940.

Bergh, J. S., and A. P. Bergh. *Tribes and Kingdoms*. Cape Town: Don Nelson, 1984.

Conroy, G. C. *Squeezing Blood from a Stone: Computed Tomography of the South African Australopithecus*. Johannesburg: Witwatersrand University Press for the Institute for the Study of Man in Africa, 1993.

Deacon, H. J. *Where Hunters Gathered*. Cape Town: South African Archaeological Society, 1976.

Deacon, J. "Archaeological Sites as National Monuments in South Africa: A Review of Sites Declared Since 1936." *SAHJ* 29 (1993).

Derricourt, R. M. *Prehistoric Man in the Ciskei and Transkei*. Cape Town: Struik, 1977.

Ehret, C. "Agricultural History in Central and South Africa ca. 1000 B.C. to A.D. 500." *TransAfrican Journal of History* 4 (1974).

Fagan, B. M. *Southern Africa during the Stone Age*. London: Thames and Hudson, 1965.

Fortes, M., and E. E. Evans-Pritchard, eds. *African Political Systems*. London: KPI, 1940.

Guy, J. "Analysing Pre-Capitalist Societies." *JSAS* 14 (1987).

Hall, M. *Farmers, Kings and Traders: The People of Southern Africa, 200–1860*. Chicago: University of Chicago Press, 1990.

_____. *Settlement Patterns in the Iron Age of Zululand: An Ecological Interpretation*. Oxford: British Archaeological Reports, 1981.

Hamilton, C. A., and J. Wright. "The Making of the *amaLala*: Ethnicity, Ideology and Relations of Subordination in a Precolonial Context." *SAHJ* 22 (1990).

Hammond-Tooke, W. D., ed. *The Bantu Speaking Peoples of Southern Africa*. 2d ed. repr. Boston: Routledge and Kegan Paul, 1980.

_____. "Kinship Authority and Political Authority in Precolonial South Africa." *African Studies* 50, 1/2 (1991).

Huffman, T. N. "The Early Iron Age and Spread of the Bantu." *SAAB* 25, 1 (1970).

Inskeep, R. R. *The Peopling of Southern Africa*. Cape Town: David Philip, 1978.

Klein, R. G., ed. *Southern African Prehistory and Paleoenvironments*. Boston: Balkema, 1984.

Klein, M. A., and Johnson, G. W., eds. *Perspectives on the African Past*. Boston: Little Brown, 1972.

Maggs, T. *Iron Age Communities of the Southern Highveld*. Pietermaritzburg: Natal Museum, 1976.

———. "Metalwork from the Iron Age Hoards as a Record of Metal Production in the Natal Region." *SAAB* 46, 154 (1991).

———. "Three Decades of Iron Age Research in South Africa: Some Personal Reflections." *SAAB* 48, 158 (1993).

Mason, R. J. *Prehistory of the Transvaal*. Johannesburg: Witwatersrand University Press, 1962.

Maylam, P. *A History of the African People of South Africa: From the Early Iron Age to the 1970s*. Cape Town: David Philip, 1987.

Mazel, A. D. "Early Pottery from the Eastern Part of Southern Africa." *SAAB* 47, 155 (1992).

Mazel, G. D. "Gender and the Hunter-Gatherer Archaeological Record: A View from the Thukela Basin." *SAAB* 47, 156 (1992).

Parkington, J. "The Neglected Alternative: Historical Narrative Rather Than Cultural Labelling." *SAAB* 48, 158 (1993).

———. "Southern Africa: Hunters and Gatherers." In G. Mokhtar, ed. *General History of Africa*. Vol. 2. Paris: Unesco, 1981.

Phillipson, D. W. *The Later Prehistory of Eastern and Southern Africa*. London: Heinemann Educational Books, 1977.

Raven-Hart, R. *Before Van Riebeeck: Callers at South Africa from 1488 to 1652*. Cape Town: Struik, 1967.

Sampson, C. G. *The Stone Age Archaeology of Southern Africa*. New York: Academic Press, 1974.

Schapera, I., and J. L. Comaroff. *The Tswana*. Rev. ed. London: Kegan Paul International, 1991.

Schrire, C. "The Archaeological Identity of Hunters and Herders at the Cape over the Last 2000 Years: A Critique." *SAAB* 47, 155 (1992).

———. *Digging through Darkness: Chronicles of an Archaeologist*. Johannesburg: Witwatersrand University Press, 1995.

Smith, A. B. "On Becoming Herders: Khoikhoi and San Ethnicity in Southern Africa." *African Studies* 49, 2 (1990).

———. *Pastoralism in Africa: Origins and Development Ecology*. Athens: Ohio University Press, 1992.

———. "On Subsistence and Ethnicity in Precolonial Southern Africa." *Current Anthropology* 34, 4 (1993).

———. "The Origins and Demise of the Khoikhoi: The Debate." *SAHJ* 23 (1990).

Sperber, G. H., ed. *From Apes to Angels: Essays in Anthropology in Honor of Phillip V. Tobias*. New York: Wiley-Liss, 1990.

Steyn, H. P. *Vanished Lifestyles: The Early Cape Khoi and San*. Pretoria: Unibook, 1990.

Thompson, L. M., ed. *African Societies in Southern Africa: Historical Studies.* Berkeley: University of California Press, 1969.

Tobias, P.V., ed. *The Bushmen: San Hunters and Herders of Southern Africa.* Cape Town: Human and Rousseau, 1978.

———. *Images of Humanity: The Selected Writings of Phillip V. Tobias.* Rivonia: Ashanti, 1991.

Van Wyk Smith, M. "'The Most Wretched of the Human Race': The Iconography of the Khoikhoin (Hottentots) 1500–1800." *History and Anthropology* 5, 3/4 (1992).

Wet-Bronner, E. "Late Iron Age Cattle Herd Management Strategies of the Soutpansberg Region." *SAAB* 49, 160 (1994).

Whitelaw, G. "Precolonial Iron Production around Durban and in Southern Natal." *Natal Museum Journal of Humanities* 3 (1991).

Willcox, A. R. *Southern Land: The Prehistory and History of Southern Africa.* Cape Town: Purnell, 1976.

Wilson, M. *Reaction to Conquest: Effects of Contact with Europeans on the Pondo of South Africa.* London: Oxford University Press, 1936.

———. *The Thousand Years before Van Riebeeck.* Johannesburg: Institute for the Study of Man, 1970.

Wilson, M. L. "The 'Strandloper' Concept and Its Relevance to the Study of the Past Inhabitants of the Southern African Coastal Region." *Annals of the South African Museum* 103, 6 (1993).

Wood, B. A. *Patterns of Hominid Evolution in Africa.* Johannesburg: Witwatersrand University Press for the Institute for the Study of Man in Africa, 1993.

Wright, J. B. "Hunters, Herders and Early Farmers in Southern Africa." *Theoria* 8 (1977).

The Cape

Bassani, E. "The Image of the Hottentot in the Seventeenth and Eighteenth Centuries: An Iconographic Investigation." *Journal of the History of Collections* 2, 2 (1990).

Beinart, W. *The Political Economy of Pondoland 1860–1930.* Cambridge: Cambridge University Press, 1982.

Beinart, W., and C. Bundy. *Hidden Struggles in Rural South Africa: Politics and Popular Movements in the Transkei and Eastern Cape, 1890–1930.* Johannesburg: Ravan Press, 1987.

Bickford-Smith, V. *Ethnic Pride and Racial Prejudice in Victorian Cape Town.* Johannesburg: Witwatersrand University Press, 1995.

Bickford-Smith, V., E. Van Heyningen, and N. Worden. *Cape Town: A History.* Cape Town: David Philip, 1998.

Blom, I. "Defence in the Cape Colony under Batavian Rule, 1803–1806." *Kronos* 17 (1990).

Bouch, R. "Glen Grey before Cecil Rhodes: How a Crisis of Local Colonial Authority Led to the Glen Grey Act of 1894." *Canadian Journal of African Studies* 27, 1 (1993).

Bradlow, E. "The Anatomy of an Immigrant Community: Cape Town Jewry from the Turn of the Century to the Passing of the Quota Act." *SAHJ* 31 (1994).

———. "The Cape Government Rule of Basutoland, 1871–1883." *AYB* 31, 2 (1968).

Burman, S. B. *Chiefdom Politics and Alien Law*. London: Macmillan, 1981.

Butler, G. *The 1820 Settlers: An Illustrated Commentary*. Cape Town: Human and Rousseau, 1974.

Crais, C. C. *The Making of the Colonial Order: White Supremacy and Black Resistance in the Eastern Cape, 1770–1865*. Johannesburg: Witwatersrand University Press, 1992.

———. "The Vacant Land: The Mythology of British Expansion in the Eastern Cape, South Africa." *Journal of Social History* 25, 2 (1991).

Duly, L. "A Revisit with the Cape's Hottentot Ordinance of 1828." In M. Kooy, ed. *Studies in Economics and Economic History*. London: Macmillan, 1972.

Duminy, A. H. "The Role of Sir Andries Stockenstrom in Cape Politics." *AYB* 23, 11 (1960).

Du Pré, R. H. *Separate but Unequal: The 'Coloured' People of South Africa—A Political History*. Johannesburg: Jonathan Ball, 1994.

Du Toit, A. E. "The Cape Frontier: A Study of Native Policy with Special Reference to the Years 1847–1866." *AYB* 17, 1 (1954).

Edgecombe, D. R. "The Non-Racial Franchise in Cape Politics, 1853–1910." *Kleio* 10 (1978).

Elphick, R. *Kraal and Castle: Khoikhoi and the Foundation of White South Africa*. New Haven: Yale University Press, 1977.

Elphick, R., and H. Giliomee, eds. *The Shaping of South African Society, 1652–1840*. 2d ed. Cape Town: Maskew Miller Longman, 1989.

Forbes, V. S. *Pioneer Travellers of South Africa*. Cape Town: Balkema, 1965.

Freund, W. "The Eastern Frontier of the Cape Colony during the Batavian Period." *JAH* 13 (1972).

Freund, W. M. "Race in the Social Structure of South Africa, 1652–1836." *Race and Class* 17 (1976).

Galbraith, J. S. *Reluctant Empire: British Policy on the South African Frontier, 1834–1854*. Berkeley: University of California Press, 1963.

Goldin, I. *Making Race: The Politics and Economics of Coloured Identity in South Africa*. Harlow: Longman, 1987.

Guelke, L. "Frontier Settlement in Early Dutch South Africa." *Association of American Geographers Annals*, 66 (1976).

Idenburg, P. J. *The Cape of Good Hope at the Turn of the Eighteenth Century*. Leiden: Leiden University Press, 1963.

James, W., and M. Simons, eds. *The Angry Divide: Social and Economic History of the Western Cape*. Cape Town: David Philip, 1989.

Kallaway, P. "Tribesman, Trader, Peasant and Proletarian." *Africa Perspective* 10 (1979).

Kirk, T. E. "Progress and Decline in the Kat River Settlement, 1829–1854." *JAH* 14 (1973).

Lancaster, J. C. S. *The Governorship of Sir Benjamin D'Urban at the Cape of Good Hope, 1834–1838*. Pretoria: Government Printer, 1991.

Le Cordeur, B. A. *The Politics of Eastern Cape Separatism*. Cape Town: Oxford University Press, 1981.

Lewis, J. "Materialism and Idealism in the Historiography of the Xhosa Cattle-Killing Movement 1856–7." *SAHJ* 25, (1991).

Lewsen, P. "The Cape Liberal Tradition: Myth or Reality? *Race* 13 (July 1971).

MacCrone, I. D. *Race Attitudes in South Africa*. London: Oxford University Press, 1937.

Macmillan, W. M. *Bantu, Boer, and Briton: The Making of the South African Native Problem*. Rev.ed. Oxford: Clarendon Press, 1963.

_____. *The Cape Colour Question: A Historical Survey*. London: Faber and Gwyer, 1927.

Marais, J. S. *The Cape Coloured People, 1652–1937*. 2d ed. Johannesburg: Witwatersrand University Press, 1957.

_____. *Maynier and the First Boer Republic*. Repr. Cape Town: Maskew Miller, 1962.

Marks, S. "Khoisan Resistance to the Dutch in the Seventeenth and Eighteenth Centuries." *JAH* 13, (1972).

McCracken, J. L. *The Cape Parliament, 1854–1910*. Oxford: Clarendon Press, 1967.

_____. *New Light at the Cape of Good Hope: William Porter, the Father of Cape Liberalism*. Belfast: Ulster Historical Foundation, 1993.

Mostert, N. *Frontiers: The Epic of South Africa's Creation and the Tragedy of the Xhosa People*. London: Cape, 1992.

Neumark, S. D. *Economic Influences on the South African Frontier, 1652–1836*. Stanford: Hoover Institution, 1957.

Newton-King, S., and C. Malherbe. *The Khoikhoi Rebellion in the Eastern Cape (1799–1803)*. Cape Town: University of Cape Town, 1981.

Peires, J. B. *The Dead Will Arise: Nongqawuse and the Great Cattle Killing of 1856–7*. Johannesburg: Ravan Press, 1989.

_____. *The House of Phalo: A History of the Xhosa People in the Days of Their Independence*. Johannesburg: Ravan Press, 1981.

Ross, R. *Adam Kok's Griquas*. Cambridge: Cambridge University Press, 1976.

_____. "The 'White' Population of the Cape in the Eighteenth Century." *Population Studies* 29 (1975).

Saunders, C. C., and R. M. Derricourt, eds. *Beyond the Cape Frontier: Studies in the History of the Transkei and Ciskei*. London: Longman, 1974.

Scully, P. *The Bouquet of Freedom*. Cape Town: University of Cape Town, Centre for African Studies, 1990.

Stapleton, T. J. *Maqoma: Xhosa Resistance to Colonial Advance, 1798–1873.* Johannesburg: Jonathan Ball, 1994.

_____. "'They Are Depriving Us of Our Chieftainship': The Decline and Fall of the Traditional Xhosa Aristocracy (1846–1857)." *Historia* 38, 2 (1993).

Strauss, T. *War along the Orange. The Korana and the Northern Border Wars of 1868–9 and 1878–9.* Cape Town: University of Cape Town, 1979.

Switzer, L. *Power and Resistance in an African Society: The Ciskei Xhosa and the Making of South Africa.* Pietermaritzburg: University of Natal Press, 1993.

Trapido, S. "African Divisional Politics in the Cape Colony, 1854–1910." *JAH* 9 (1968).

_____. "From Paternalism to Liberalism: The Cape Colony 1800–1834." *International History Review* 12, 1 (1990).

Van der Merwe, P. J. *The Migrant Farmer in the History of the Cape Colony, 1657–1842.* Athens, Ohio: Ohio University Press, 1995.

Van Heyningen, E. "Poverty, Self-Help and Community: The Survival of the Poor in Cape Town, 1880–1910." *SAHJ* 24 (1991).

Ward, K. "The Road to Mamre: Migration and Community in Countryside and City in the Early Twentieth Century." *SAHJ* 27 (1992).

Warren, D. "Class Rivalry and Cape Politics in the Mid-Nineteenth Century: A Reappraisal of the Kirk Thesis." *SAHJ* 24 (1991).

Wilson, M. "The Early History of the Transkei and Ciskei." *African Studies* 18 (1959).

Winer, M., and J. Deetz. "The Transformation of British Culture in the Eastern Cape, 1820–1860." *Social Dynamics* 16, 1 (1990).

Natal and Zululand

Ballard, C. "John Dunn and Cetshwayo: The Material Foundations of Political Power in the Zulu Kingdom, 1857–1878." *JAH* 21 (1980).

Baskerville, B. "The Problem Lies in the Reserves: Towards a History of 'Political Ecology' in Southern Africa." *Journal of Natal and Zulu History* 15 (1994/5).

Bhana, S. *Gandhi's Legacy: The Natal Indian Congress 1894–1994.* Pietermaritzburg: University of Natal Press, 1997.

Bhana, S., and B. A. Pachai. *Documentary History of Indian South Africa.* Cape Town: David Philip, 1984.

Brookes, E. H., and C. Webb. *A History of Natal.* 2d ed. Pietermaritzburg: Natal University Press, 1987.

Bryant, A. T. *The Zulu People as They Were Before the White Man Came.* 2d ed. Pietermaritzburg: Shuter and Shooter, 1967.

Cope, N. *To Bind the Nation: Solomon kaDinuzulu and Zulu Nationalism 1913–1933.* Pietermaritzburg: University of Natal Press, 1993.

_____. "The Zulu *petit bourgeoisie* and Zulu Nationalism in the 1920s: Origins of Inkatha." *JSAS* 16, 3 (1990).

Cope, R. L. "Written in Characters of Blood? The Reign of King Cetshwayo ka Mpande, 1872–9." *Journal of African History* 36, 2 (1995).

Dangor, S. E. "The Myth of the 1860 Settlers." *Africa Quarterly* (India) 32, 1–4 (1992/3).

Daniel, J. B. M. "A Geographical Study of Pre-Shakan Zululand." *South African Geographical Journal* 55, 1 (1973).

Dominy, G. "'Frere's War?': A Reconsideration of the Geopolitics of the Anglo-Zulu War of 1879." *Natal Museum Journal of the Humanities* 5 (1993).

Duminy, A., and C. C. Ballard, eds. *The Anglo-Zulu War: New Perspectives.* Pietermaritzburg: University of Natal Press, 1981.

Duminy, A., and B. Guest. *Natal and Zululand From the Earliest Times to 1910: A New History.* Pietermaritzburg: University of Natal Press, 1989.

Eldredge, E. A. "Sources of Conflict in Southern Africa, ca.1800–30: The 'Mfecane' Reconsidered." *Journal of African History* 33, 1 (1992).

Etherington, N. A. "The Origin of 'Indirect Rule' in Nineteenth Century Natal." *Theoria* 47 (1976).

Freund, B. *Insiders and Outsiders: The Indian Working Class of Durban, 1910–1990.* Pietermaritzburg: University of Natal Press, 1994.

Freund, W. "The Rise and Decline of an Indian Peasantry in Natal." *Journal of Peasant Studies* 18, 2 (1991).

Golan, D. "Inkatha and Its Use of the Zulu Past." *History in Africa* 18 (1991).

_____. *Inventing Shaka: Using History in the Construction of Zulu Nationalism.* Boulder: Lynne Rienner, 1994.

Guest, B. "Gandhi's Natal: The State of the Colony in 1893." *Natalia* 23/24 (1993/4).

_____. *Langalibalele: The Crisis in Natal 1873–1875.* Durban: University of Natal, 1976.

_____. "The Natal Regional Economy 1910–1960 in Historical Perspective." *South African Journal of Economic History* 5, 2 (1990).

Guest, B., and J. M. Sellers, eds. *Receded Tides of Empire: Aspects of the Economic and Social History of Natal and Zululand since 1910.* Pietermaritzburg: University of Natal Press, 1994.

Gump, J. O. *The Dust Rose like Smoke: The Subjugation of the Zulu and the Sioux.* Lincoln: University of Nebraska Press, 1994.

_____. *The Formation of the Zulu Kingdom in South Africa, 1750–1840.* San Francisco: E.M. Texts, 1991.

Guy, J. *The Destruction of the Zulu Kingdom: The Civil War in Zululand, 1879–1884.* Repr. Pietermaritzburg: University of Natal Press, 1994.

_____. *The Heretic: A Study of the Life of John William Colenso 1814–1883.* Johannesburg: Ravan Press, 1983.

_____. "Production and Exchange in the Zulu Kingdom." *Mohlomi* 2 (1978).

Hamilton, C., ed. *The Mfecane Aftermath: Reconstructive Debates in Southern African History.* Johannesburg: Witwatersrand University Press, 1995.

_____. *Terrific Majesty: The Powers of Shaka Zulu and the Limits of Historical Intervention.* Cape Town: David Philip, 1998.

Hattersley, A. F. *The British Settlement of Natal*. Cambridge: Cambridge University Press, 1950.

———. *More Annals of Natal*. London: Warne, 1936.

Henning, C. G. *The Indentured Indian in Natal (1860–1917)*. New Delhi: Promilla, 1993.

Herd, N. *The Bent Pine: The Trial of Langalibalele*. Johannesburg: Ravan Press, 1976.

Jeffery, A. *The Natal Story: 16 Years of Conflict*. Johannesburg: South African Institute of Race Relations, 1997.

Laband, J. P. C. *Kingdom in Crisis: The Zulu Response to the British Invasion of 1879*. Pietermaritzburg: University of Natal Press, 1991.

———. *Rope of Sand: The Rise and Fall of the Zulu Kingdom in the Nineteenth Century*. Johannesburg: Jonathan Ball, 1995.

Laband, J. P. C., and P. S. Thompson. *Kingdom and Colony at War: Sixteen Studies on the Anglo-Zulu War of 1879*. Pietermaritzburg: University of Natal Press, 1990.

La Hausse, P. "The Cows of Nongoloza: Youth, Crime and *Amalaita* Gangs in Durban, 1900–1936." *JSAS* 16, 1 (1990).

Lambert, J. *Betrayed Trust: Africans and the State in Colonial Natal*. Pietermaritzburg: University of Natal Press, 1995.

———. "Violence and the State in Colonial Natal: Conflict between and within Chiefdoms." *SAHJ* 31 (1994).

Le Cordeur, B. A. "The Relations between the Cape and Natal 1846–1879." *AYB* 28, 2 (1965).

Maré, G. *Brothers Born of Warrior Blood: Ethnicity and Politics in South Africa*. Johannesburg: Ravan Press, 1992.

Maré, G., and G. Hamilton. *An Appetite for Power: Buthelezi's Inkatha and South Africa*. Johannesburg: Ravan Press, 1987.

Marks, S. "Natal, the Zulu Royal Family and the Ideology of Segregation." *JSAS* 4, 2 (1978).

———. *The Ambiguities of Dependence in South Africa: Class, Nationalism, and the State in Twentieth Century Natal*. Johannesburg: Ravan Press, 1986.

Morris, D. R. *The Washing of the Spears: A History of the Rise of the Zulu Nation under Shaka and its Fall in the Zulu War of 1879*. repr. London: Pimlico, 1994.

Omer-Cooper, J. D. *The Zulu Aftermath: A Nineteenth Century Revolution in Bantu Africa*. London: Longman, 1966.

Peires, J. B., ed. *Before and After Shaka. Studies in Nguni History*. Grahamstown: Rhodes University, 1981.

———. "Paradigm Deleted: The Materialist Interpretation of the *Mfecane*." *JSAS* 19, 2 (1993).

Taylor, S. *Shaka's Children: A History of the Zulu People*. London: HarperCollins, 1994.

Thompson, P. S. *Natalians First: Separation in South Africa 1909–1961*. Johannesburg: Southern, 1990.

Welsh, D. *The Roots of Segregation: Native Policy in Natal (1835–1910)*. Cape Town: Oxford University Press, 1971.

White, B. "The United Democratic Front in Natal, 1952–1953." *Journal of Natal and Zulu History* 13 (1990/1).

Wright, J. "A.T. Bryant and the 'Wars of Shaka.'" *History in Africa* 18 (1991).

———. *Bushmen Raiders of the Drakensberg, 1840–1870*. Pietermaritzburg: University of Natal Press, 1971.

Wyley, C. "A Bibliography of Contemporary Writings on the Natural History of Natal and Zululand in the Late 19th and Early 20th Centuries." *Journal of Natal and Zulu History* 13 (1990/1).

Wylie, D. "Autobiography as Alibi: History and Projection in Nathaniel Isaac's *Travels and Adventures in Eastern Africa (1836)*." *Current Writing* 3, 1 (1991).

———. "A Dangerous Admiration: E. A. Ritter's *Shaka Zulu*." *SAHJ* 28 (1993).

———. "Textual Incest: Nathaniel Isaacs and the Development of the Shaka Myth." *History in Africa* 19 (1992).

Orange Free State and Transvaal

Allen, G. R. "F. J. Bezuidenhout's Doornfontein: A Case Study in White Farmland Alienation on the 19th Century Witwatersrand." *Contree* 36 (1994).

Baylen, J. O. "W. T. Stead's *History of the Mystery* and the Jameson Raid." *Journal of British Studies* 4 (1964).

Blainey, G. "Lost Causes of the Jameson Raid." *Economic History Review* 2d series, 18 (1965).

Bonner, P. "Factions and Fissions: Transvaal/Swazi Relations in the Mid Nineteenth Century." *JAH* 19 (1978).

Bozzoli, B., ed. *Town and Countryside in the Transvaal: Capitalist Penetration and Popular Response*. Johannesburg: Ravan Press, 1983.

Butler, J. "The German Factor in Anglo-Transvaal Relations." In P. Gifford and W. R. Louis, eds. *Britain and Germany in Africa*. New Haven: Yale University Press, 1967.

———. *The Liberal Party and the Jameson Raid*. London: Oxford University Press, 1968.

Callinicos, L. *A Place in the City: The Rand on the Eve of Apartheid*. Johannesburg: Ravan Press, 1993.

Cope, R. L. "Shepstone, the Zulus and the Annexation of the Transvaal." *SAHJ* 4 (1972).

De Kiewiet, C. W. *British Colonial Policy and the South African Republic, 1848–1872*. London: Longmans, Green, 1929.

Delius, P. *The Land Belongs to Us: The Pedi Policy, the Boers and the British in Nineteenth Century Transvaal*. Johannesburg: Ravan Press, 1983.

———. "Migrants, Comrades and Rural Revolt: Sekhukhuneland 1950–1987." *Transformation: Critical Perspectives on Southern Africa* 13 (1990).

_____. "Sebatakgomo and the Zoutpansberg Balemi Association: The ANC, the Communist Party and Rural Organization, 1939–55." *JAH* 34, 2 (1993).

_____. *A Lion amongst the Cattle: Reconstruction and Resistance in the Northern Transvaal.* Johannesburg: Ravan Press, 1996.

Eldredge, E. A. *A South African Kingdom: The Pursuit of Security in Nineteenth-Century Lesotho.* Johannesburg: Witwatersrand University Press, 1993.

Ellenberger, D. F. *History of the Basuto Ancient and Modern.* Morija: Morija Museum & Archives, 1992.

Garson, N. G. "The Swaziland Question and a Road to the Sea, 1887–1895." *AYB* 20, 2 (1957).

Gordon, C. T. *The Growth of Boer Opposition to Kruger, 1890–1895.* Cape Town: Oxford University Press, 1970.

Harris, K. "Rand Capitalists and Chinese Resistance." *Contree* 35 (1994).

Keegan, T. *Facing the Storm: Portraits of Black Lives in Rural South Africa.* Cape Town: David Philip, 1988.

Krikler, J. *Revolution from Above, Rebellion from Below: The Agrarian Transvaal at the Turn of the Century.* Oxford: Clarendon Press, 1993.

Kubicek, R. V. "The Randlords in 1895: A Reassessment." *Journal of British Studies* 11 (1972).

Lehmann, J. H. *The First Boer War.* London: Jonathan Cape, 1972.

Lye, W. "The Ndebele Kingdom South of the Limpopo River." *JAH* 10 (1969).

Lye, W., and C. Murray. *Transformations on the Highveld.* Cape Town: David Philip, 1980.

Manson, A. "The Hurutshe and the Formation of the Transvaal, 1835–1875." *International Journal of African Historical Studies* 25, 1 (1992).

Marais, J. S. *The Fall of Kruger's Republic.* Oxford: Clarendon Press, 1961.

Mason, R. *Prehistory of the Transvaal: A Record of Human Activity.* Johannesburg: Witwatersrand University Press, 1969.

Mendelsohn, R. "Blainey and the Jameson Raid: The Debate Reviewed." *JSAS* 6 (1980).

Midgley, J. F. "The Orange River Sovereignty, 1848–1854." *AYB* 12 (1949).

Murray, C. *Black Mountain: Land, Class and Power in the Eastern Orange Free State, 1880s to 1980s.* Edinburgh: Edinburgh University Press, 1992.

Pakenham, E. *Jameson's Raid.* London: Weidenfeld and Nicolson, 1960.

Phimister, I. R. "Rhodes, Rhodesia and the Rand." *JSAS* 1, 1 (1974).

_____. "Unscrambling the Scramble for Southern Africa: The Jameson Raid and the South African War Revisited." *SAHJ* 28 (1993).

Pillay, B. *British Indians in the Transvaal: Trade, Race Relations and Imperial Policy in Republican and Colonial Transvaal, 1885–1906.* London: Longman, 1976.

Rasmussen, R. K. *Migrant Kingdom: Mzilikazi's Ndebele in South Africa.* London: Rex Collings, 1978.

Schapera, I. *The Tribal Innovators: Tswana Chiefs and Social Change, 1795–1940.* London: Athlone Press, 1970.

Schirmer, S. "Removals and Resistance: Rural Communities in Lydenburg, South Africa, 1940–1961." *Journal of Historical Sociology* 9, 2 (1996).

Schoeman, K. *The British Presence in the TransOrange, 1845–1854*. Cape Town: Human and Rousseau, 1992.

Schreuder, D. M. *Gladstone and Kruger*. London: Routledge, 1969.

Shillington, K. *The Colonisation of the Southern Tswana, 1870–1900*. Johannesburg: Ravan Press, 1985.

Trapido, S. "Landlord and Tenant in a Colonial Economy: The Transvaal 1880–1910." *JSAS* 5, 1 (1978).

Van der Poel, J. *The Jameson Raid*. London: Oxford University Press, 1951.

Van Onselen, C. "The Social and Economic Underpinning of Paternalism and Violence on the Maize Farms of the South-Western Transvaal, 1900–1950." *Journal of Historical Sociology* 5, 2 (1992).

Williams, D. "Sir George Russell Clerk and the Abandonment of the Orange River Sovereignty, 1853–1854: Room for Another View." *Historia* 36, 1 (1991).

Wylie, D. *A Little God: The Twilight of Patriarchy in a Southern African Chiefdom*. Hanover: University Press of New England, 1990.

South Africa 1899–1910

Barnes, J. *Filming the Boer War*. London: Bishopsgate, 1992.

Cammack, D. *The Rand At War 1899–1902*. London: James Currey, 1990.

Davey, A. M. *The British Pro-Boers, 1877–1902*. Cape Town: Tafelberg, 1978.

Denoon, D. "'Capitalist Influence' and the Transvaal Crown Colony Government." *Historical Journal* 12 (1969).

———. *A Grand Illusion: The Failure of Imperial Policy in the Transvaal Colony during the Period of Reconstruction*. London: Longman, 1973.

Duminy, A. H. *The Capitalists and the Outbreak of the Anglo-Boer War*. Durban: University of Natal, 1977.

Garson, N. G. "'Het Volk': The Botha-Smuts Party in the Transvaal, 1904–11." *Historical Journal* 9 (1966).

Hackett, R. G. *South African War Books: An Illustrated Biography of English Language Publications Relating to the Boer War of 1899–1902*. London: Printed for PG de Lotz, 1994.

Hyam, R. "African Interests and the South Africa Act, 1908–1910." *Historical Journal* 13 (1970).

Le May, G. H. L. *British Supremacy in South Africa, 1899–1907*. Oxford: Clarendon Press, 1965.

Lewsen, P. *John X. Merriman: Paradoxical South African Statesman*. Johannesburg: Ad Donker, 1982.

Marks, S., and S. Trapido. "Lord Milner and the South African State." *History Workshop* 8 (1979).

Mawby, A. A. "Capital, Government and Politics in the Transvaal, 1900–1907." *Historical Journal* 17 (1974).

Nasson, B. *Abraham Esau's War: A Black South African's War in the Cape, 1899–1902*. Cape Town: David Philip, 1991.

Ngcongco, L. D. "Jabavu and the Boer War." *Kleio* 2 (1970).

Pakenham, T. *The Boer War*. Illus. ed. London: Weidenfeld and Nicolson, 1993.

Plaatje, S. T. *Mafeking Diary: A Black Man's View of a White Man's War*. London: James Currey, 1990.

Porter, A. N. "The South African War (1899–1902): Context and Motive Reconsidered." *Journal of African History* 31, 1 (1990).

_____. *The Origins of the South African War: Joseph Chamberlain and the Diplomacy of Imperialism 1895–1899*. Manchester: Manchester University Press, 1980.

Schoeman, K. *Only an Anguish to Live Here: Olive Schreiner and the Anglo-Boer War 1899–1902*. Johannesburg: Human and Rousseau, 1992.

Schreuder, D. "British Imperialism and the Politics of Ethnicity: The 'Warring Nations' of the African Highveld." *Journal of Canadian Studies* 25, 1 (1990).

Smith, I. R. *The Origins of the South African War, 1899–1902*. London: Longman, 1996.

Spies, S. B. *Methods of Barbarism? Roberts and Kitchener and Civilians in the Boer Republics, January 1900–May 1902*. Cape Town: Human and Rousseau, 1977.

Surridge, K. T. *Managing the South African War, 1899–1902: Politicians v Generals*. Woodbridge: Boydell & Brewer, 1998.

Thompson, L. M. *The Unification of South Africa*. Oxford: Clarendon Press, 1960.

Van Onselen, C. "The Randlords and Rotgut, 1886–1903." *History Workshop* 2 (1976).

_____. "'The Regiment of the Hills': South Africa's Lumpenproletarian Army, 1890–1920." *Past and Present* 80 (1978).

_____. *Studies in the Social and Economic History of the Witwatersrand, 1886–1914*. 2 vols. London: Longman, 1982.

_____. "The World the Mine Owners Made." *Review* 3 (1979).

Warwick, P. *Black People and the South African War 1899–1902*. Johannesburg: Ravan Press, 1983.

_____, ed. *The South African War: The Anglo-Boer War, 1899–1902*. London: Longman, 1980.

South Africa 1910–1976

Ballinger, M. *From Union to Apartheid: A Trek to Isolation*. Cape Town: Juta, 1969.

Beinart, L., and C. Bundy. "State Intervention and Rural Resistance: The Transkei, 1900–1965." In M. Klein, ed. *Peasants in Africa*. Beverly Hills: Sage, 1980.

Bozzoli, B. "Capital and the State in South Africa." *Review of African Political Economy* 11 (1978).

_____. *The Political Nature of a Ruling Class: Capital and Ideology in South Africa, 1890–1933*. London: Routledge, 1981.

Brown, J. A. *Retreat to Victory. A Springbok's Diary in North Africa: Gazala to El Alamein, 1942*. Rivonia: Ashanti, 1991.

_____. *They Fought for King and Kaiser: South Africans in German East Africa, 1916*. Rivonia: Ashanti, 1991.

Crwys-Williams, J. *A Country at War, 1939–1945: The Mood of a Nation*. Rivonia: Ashanti, 1992.

Clarke, S. "Capital, 'Fractions' of Capital and the State: 'Neo-Marxist' Analyses of the South African State." *Capital and Class* 5 (1978).

Davenport, T. R. H. "The South African Rebellion, 1914." *English Historical Review* 78 (1963).

Davies, R. *Capital, State and White Labour in South Africa 1900–1960*. Brighton: Harvester, 1979.

_____. "Mining Capital, the State and Unskilled White Workers in South Africa, 1901–1913." *JSAS* 3, 1 (1976).

Digby, P. K. A. *Pyramids and Poppies: The 1st SA Infantry Brigade in Libya, France and Flanders 1915–1919*. Rivonia: Ashanti, 1993.

Edgar, R. "Garveyism in Africa: Dr Wellington and the American Movement in the Transkei." *Ufahamu* 6 (1976).

Gleeson, I. *The Unknown Force: Black, Indian and Coloured Soldiers through Two World Wars*. Rivonia: Ashanti, 1994.

Grundlingh, A. M. *Fighting Their Own War: South African Blacks and the First World War*. Johannesburg: Ravan Press, 1987.

Grundlingh, L. "'Non-Europeans Should Be Kept Away from the Temptations of Towns': Controlling Black South African Soldiers during the Second World War." *International Journal of African Historical Studies* 25, 3 (1992).

_____. "Soldiers and Politics: A Study of the Political Consciousness of Black South African Soldiers during and after the Second World War." *Historia* 36, 2 (1991).

Grundy, K. W. *Confrontation and Accommodation in Southern Africa: The Limits of Independence*. Berkeley: University of California Press, 1973.

Harris, C. J. *War at Sea: South African Maritime Operations during World War II*. Rivonia: Ashanti, 1991.

Kallaway, P. "F. S. Malan, the Cape Liberal Tradition and South African Politics." *JAH* 15 (1974).

Kros, J. *War in Italy: With the South Africans from Taranto to the Alps*. Rivonia: Ashanti, 1992.

Kuper, L. *Passive Resistance in South Africa*. New Haven: Yale University Press, 1967.

Lacey, M. *Working for Boroko. The Origins of a Coercive Labour System in South Africa*. Johannesburg: Ravan Press, 1981.

L'Ange, G. *Urgent Imperial Service: South African Forces in German South West Africa, 1914–1915*. Rivonia: Ashanti, 1991.

Leftwich, A., ed. *South Africa: Economic Growth and Political Change*. London: Allison and Busby, 1974.

Legassick, M. "Legislation, Ideology and Economy in Post-1948 South Africa." *JSAS* 1, 1 (1974).

_____. "South Africa: Capital Accumulation and Violence." *Economy and Society* 3 (1974).

_____. "Race, Industrialisation and Social Change in South Africa: The Case of R.F.A. Hoernlé." *African Affairs* 75 (1976).

Leigh, M. *Captives Courageous: South African Prisoners of War, World War II*. Rivonia: Ashanti, 1992.

McKenzie, E. R. "From Obscurity to Official Opposition: The Progressive Federal Party, 1959–1977." *Historia* 39, 1 (1994).

Moore, D. M. *South Africa's Flying Cheetahs in Korea*. Rivonia: Ashanti, 1991.

Muthien, Y. *State and Resistance in South Africa, 1939–1965*. Aldershot: Avebury, 1994.

Nasson, B. "A Great Divide: Popular Responses to the Great War in South Africa." *War and Society* 12, 1 (1994).

Oosthuizen, F. "Changes and Expectations: The White Union Defence Force Soldier Prior to and during the Second World War." *Militaria* 23, 3 (1993).

_____. "Demobilisation and Post-War Employment of the White Union Defence Force's Soldier." *Militaria* 23, 4 (1993).

_____. "Soldiers and Politics: The Political Ramifications of the White Union Defence Forces Soldiers' Demobilisation Experience after the Second World War." *Militaria* 24, 1 (1994).

Orpen, N., et al. *South African Forces in World War II*. 7 vols. Cape Town: Purnell, 1968–79.

Rich, P. "Liberalism and Ethnicity in South African Politics, 1921–1948." *African Studies* 35 (1976).

Roberts, M., and A. Trollip. *The South African Opposition, 1939–1945*. London: Longmans, Green, 1947.

Robertson, J. *Liberalism in South Africa, 1948–1963*. London: Oxford University Press, 1971.

Saker, H. *The South African Flag Controversy*. Cape Town: Oxford University Press, 1980.

Sampson, A. *The Treason Cage: The Opposition on Trial in South Africa*. London: Heinemann, 1958.

Ticktin, D. "The War Issue and the Collapse of the South African Labour Party 1914–15." *SAHJ* 1 (1969).

White, W. B. "The United Party and the 1948 General Election." *Journal for Contemporary History* 17, 2 (1992).

_____. "The United Party and the 1953 General Election." *Historia* 36, 2 (1991).

_____. "The United Party and the 1950 General Election in South-West Africa." *Historia* 39, 1 (1994).

Witz, L. " 'n Fees vir die Oog': Looking in on the 1952 Jan van Riebeeck Tercentenary Festival Fair in Cape Town." *SAHJ* 29 (1993).

South Africa 1976–1990

Beinart, W., R. Turrell, and T. O. Ranger, eds. "Political and Collective Violence in Southern Africa." *JSAS* (Special issue) 18, 3 (1992).

Carter, G. M., and P. O'Meara, eds. *Southern Africa: The Continuing Crisis.* Bloomington: Indiana University Press, 1979.

Du Pré, R. H. "The Great *Volte Face* of 1983? The Labour Party and the Tricameral System." *Historia* 39, 2 (1994).

Johnson, R. W. *How Long Will South Africa Survive?* London: Macmillan, 1977.

Kane-Berman, J. *Soweto: Black Revolt, White Reaction.* Johannesburg: Ravan Press, 1978.

Karis, T., and G. Gerhart. *From Protest to Challenge*, vol. 5. Pretoria: Unisa Press, 1997.

Marks, S., and S. Trapido, eds. "Social History of Resistance in South Africa." *JSAS* (Special issue) 18, 1 (1992).

Murray, M. *Revolution Deferred: The Painful Birth of Post-Apartheid South Africa.* London: Verso, 1994.

Price, R. M. *The Apartheid State in Crisis: Political Transformation in South Africa, 1975–1990.* New York: Oxford University Press, 1991.

Saunders, C. "South Africa's War in Southern Angola (1987–1988) and the Independence of Namibia." *Journal for Contemporary History* 18, 1 (1993).

Schrire, R. *Adapt or Die: The End of White Politics in South Africa.* Cape Town: David Philip, 1992.

Sparks, A. *Tomorrow Is Another Country: The Inside Story of South Africa's Negotiated Revolution.* Sandton: Struik Book Distributors, 1994.

Spence, J. E. *Change in South Africa.* London: Pinter, 1994.

South Africa post-1990

Arthur, P. "Some Thoughts on Transition: A Comparative View of the Peace Process in South Africa and Northern Ireland." *Government and Opposition* 30, 1 (1995).

Barnard, S. L. "The Election Campaign of the General Election in South Africa in 1994." *Journal for Contemporary History* 19, 2 (1994).

Boraine, A., J. Levy, and R. Scheffer, eds. *Dealing with the Past: Truth and Reconciliation in South Africa.* Cape Town: Institute for a Democratic Alternative for South Africa, 1997.

Brewer, J. D., ed. *Restructuring South Africa.* Basingstoke: Macmillan, 1994.

Coetzer, P. W. "Opinion Polls and Opinions on the Results of the Election of 1994." *Journal for Contemporary History* 19, 2 (1994).

Davenport, T. R. H. *The Transfer of Power in South Africa.* Cape Town: David Philip, 1998.

Du Toit, P. *State-Building and Democracy in Southern Africa: A Comparative Study of Botswana, South Africa and Zimbabwe.* Pretoria: Human Sciences Research Council, 1995.

Friedman, S., ed. *The Long Journey: South Africa's Quest for a Negotiated Settlement*. Johannesburg: Ravan Press, 1993.

Friedman, S., and D. Atkinson, eds. *The Small Miracle: South Africa's Negotiated Settlement*. Johannesburg: Ravan Press, 1994.

Geldenhuys, D. "The Foreign Factor in South Africa's 1992 Referendum." *Politikon* 19, 3 (1992).

Giliomee, H., L. Schlemmer, and S. Hauptfleisch, eds. *The Bold Experiment: South Africa's New Democracy*. Halfway House: Southern, 1994.

Goodwin, J., and B. Schiff. *Heart of Whiteness: Afrikaners Face Black Rule in the New South Africa*. New York: Scribner, 1995.

Henning, L., and J. A. Coetzer. "The Independent Electoral Commission." *Journal for Contemporary History* 19, 2 (1994).

Karis, T. G. "'A Small Miracle' Continues: South Africa, 1994–99." *Round Table* 334 (1995).

Kitchen, H., and J. C. Kitchen, eds. *South Africa: Twelve Perspectives on the Transition*. Westport: Praeger, 1994.

Krog, A. *Country of My Skull*. Bergvlei: Random House, 1998.

Le Roux, J. H. "Violence and Intimidation During the Election Campaign—A Review." *Journal for Contemporary History* 19, 2 (1994).

Johnson, R. W., and L. Schlemmer, eds. *Launching Democracy in South Africa: The First Open Election, April 1994*. New Haven: Yale University Press, 1996.

Lodge, T. "SA '94: Election of a Special Kind." *Southern African Review of Books* 6, 2 (1994).

Martin, M. *South Africa's New Era: The 1994 Election*. London: Mandarin, 1994.

Michie, J. D., and V. Padayachee. *The Political Economy of South Africa's Transition: Policy Perspectives in the Late 1990s*. London: Dryden Press, 1997.

Ottaway, D. *Chained Together: Mandela, De Klerk and the Struggle to Remake South Africa*. New York: Times Books, 1993.

Pollard, A. B. "The Dawn of Freedom—A South African Diary." *Africa Today* 41, 1 (1994).

Rantete, J. M. *The African National Congress and the Negotiated Settlement in South Africa*. Pretoria: J. L. Van Schaik, 1998.

Reynolds, A., ed. *Election '94 South Africa: The Campaigns, Results and Future Prospects*. Cape Town: David Philip, 1994.

Roberts, M. "The Ending of Apartheid: Shifting Inequalities in South Africa." *Geography* 79, 1 (1994).

Schoeman, E. "South African Elections 1994." *Southern African Update* 9, 2 (1994).

Southall, R. "South Africa's 1994 Election in an African Perspective." *Africa Insight* 24, 2 (1994).

Strauss, A. C. P. "The 1992 Referendum in South Africa." *Journal of Modern African Studies* 31, 2 (1993).

———. "Reaction to the 1994 South African General Election." *Journal for Contemporary History* 19, 2 (1994).

Teer-Tomaselli, R. "Moving Toward Democracy: The South African Broadcasting Corporation and the 1994 Election." *Media, Culture and Society* 17, 4 (1995).

Van Rooyen, J. *Hard Right: The New White Power in South Africa.* London: Tauris, 1994.

Waldmeir, P. *Anatomy of a Miracle: The End of Apartheid and the Birth of the New South Africa.* New York: W.W. Norton, 1997.

Welsh, D. "Liberals and the Future of the New Democracy in South Africa." *Optima* 40, 2 (1994).

Wessels, A. "In Search of Acceptable National Symbols for South Africa." *Journal for Contemporary History* 19, 2 (1994).

Wessels, D. P. "Electoral System and System of Representation: Election of 27 April 1994." *Journal for Contemporary History* 19, 2 (1994).

POLITICS

General

Bissell, R. E., and C. Crocker, eds. *South Africa into the 1980s.* Boulder: Westview Press, 1979.

Brotz, H. M. *The Politics of South Africa: Democracy and Racial Diversity.* London: Oxford University Press, 1977.

Carter, G. M. *The Politics of Inequality: South Africa since 1948.* 2d ed. New York: Praeger, 1962.

_____. *Which Way Is South Africa Going?* Bloomington: Indiana University Press, 1980.

Carter, G. M., and P. O'Meara, eds. *Southern Africa: The Continuing Crisis.* Bloomington: Indiana University Press, 1979.

Cervenka, Z., and B. Rogers. *The Nuclear Axis. Secret Collaboration between West Germany and South Africa.* London: Julian Friedman, 1978.

Debroey, S. *South Africa under the Curse of Apartheid.* Lanham: University Press of America, 1990.

De St. Jorre, J. *A House Divided: South Africa's Uncertain Future.* New York: Carnegie Endowment for International Peace, 1977.

Gann, L., and P. Duignan. *Why South Africa Will Survive.* London: Croom Helm, 1981.

Manganyi, N. C., and A. Du Toit, eds. *Political Violence and the Struggle in South Africa.* Halfway House: Southern, 1990.

Gastrow, S. *Who's Who in South African Politics.* 5th ed. Johannesburg: Ravan Press, 1995.

Hanf, T., et al. *South Africa: The Prospects of Peaceful Change.* London: Rex Collings, 1981.

Heard, K. *General Elections in South Africa 1943–1970*. London: Oxford University Press, 1974.

Hellman, E., and H. Lever, eds. *Conflict and Progress. Fifty Years of Race Relations in South Africa*. Johannesburg: Macmillan, 1979.

Lawrence, J. C. *Race, Propaganda and South Africa*. London: Gollancz, 1979.

Lonsdale, J., ed. *South Africa in Question*. Cambridge: Cambridge University Press, 1988.

Magubane, B. *The Political Economy of Race and Class in South Africa*. New York: Monthly Review Press, 1980.

Maguire, K. *Politics in South Africa: From Vorster to De Klerk*. Edinburgh: W. and R. Chambers, 1991.

Marks, S., and S. Trapido, eds. *The Politics of Race, Class and Nationalism in Twentieth Century South Africa*. New York: Longman, 1987.

Merrett, C. E. "Detention without Trial in South Africa: The Abuse of Human Rights as State Strategy in the Late 1980s." *Reality* 23, 1 (1991).

Moll, P. G. "The Decline of Discrimination against Colored People in South Africa, 1970 to 1980." *Journal of Development Economics* 37 (1992).

Molteno, F. "The Coloured Persons' Representative Council." *Africa Perspective* 10 (1979).

Price, R. M., and C. G. Rosberg, eds. *The Apartheid Regime: Political Power and Racial Domination*. Berkeley: University of California, Institute of International Studies, 1980.

Rees, M., and C. Day. *Muldergate*. Johannesburg: Macmillan, 1981.

Rotberg, R. *Suffer the Future. Policy Choices in Southern Africa*. Cambridge, Mass.: Harvard University Press, 1980.

Sarakinsky, I. "The Impulses to Reform: The South African State from Vorster to Botha." *Journal for Contemporary History* 17, 1 (1992).

Schrire, R., ed. *South Africa. Public Policy Perspectives*. Cape Town: Juta, 1982.

Shain, M., and S. Frankental. "South African Jewry, Apartheid and Political Change." *Patterns of Prejudice* 25, 1 (1991).

Shepherd, G. W. "*Africa Today* in the Early Years: The Debate over Strategy for the Liberation of South Africa." *Africa Today* 41, 1 (1994).

Simons, H. J., and R. Simons. *Class and Colour in South Africa 1850–1950*. London: International Defence and Aid Fund, 1983.

Thompson, L. M., and J. Butler, eds. *Change in Contemporary South Africa*. Berkeley: University of California Press, 1975.

Thompson, L. M., and A. Prior. *South African Politics*. New Haven: Yale University Press, 1982.

Van den Berghe, P., ed. *The Liberal Dilemma in South Africa*. London: Croom Helm, 1979.

Vigne, R. *Liberals against Apartheid: A History of the Liberal Party of South Africa 1953–68*. Basingstoke: Macmillan, 1997.

Segregation and Apartheid

Baldwin, A. "Mass Removals and Separate Development." *JSAS* 1 (1975).

Beinart, W., and S. Dubow, eds. *Segregation and Apartheid in Twentieth-Century South Africa.* London: Routledge, 1995.

Bonner, P., P. Delius, and D. Posel, eds. *Apartheid's Genesis, 1935–1962.* Johannesburg: Ravan Press, 1993.

Brookes, E. H. *Apartheid: A Documentary Study of Modern South Africa.* London: Routledge and K. Paul, 1968.

———. *White Rule in South Africa, 1830–1910.* Pietermaritzburg: University of Natal Press, 1974.

Carter, G. M. *The Politics of Inequality: South Africa since 1948.* Repr. New York: Octagon Books, 1977.

Christopher, A. J. "Apartheid and Urban Segregation Levels in South Africa." *Urban Studies* 27, 3 (1990).

———. *The Atlas of Apartheid.* Johannesburg: Witwatersrand University Press, 1994.

———. "Before Group Areas: Urban Segregation in South Africa in 1951." *South African Geographer* 18, 1–2 (1990/1).

———. "Changing Patterns of Group-Area Proclamations in South Africa, 1950–1989." *Political Geography Quarterly* 10, 3 (1991).

———. "Segregation Levels in South African Cities, 1911–1985." *International Journal of African Historical Studies* 25, 3 (1992).

———. "Segregation Levels in the Late-Apartheid City 1985–1994." *Tijdschrift Voor Economische en Sociale Geografie* 85, 1 (1994).

———. "Urban Segregation Levels in South Africa under Apartheid." *Sociology and Social Research* 75, 2 (1991).

Davenport, T. R. H. *The Beginnings of Urban Segregation in South Africa.* Grahamstown: Rhodes University, 1971.

Desmond, C. *The Discarded People: An Account of African Resettlement in South Africa.* Harmondsworth: Penguin, 1971.

Dubow, S. *Illicit Union: Scientific Racism in Modern South Africa.* Johannesburg: Witwatersrand University Press, 1995.

———. *Racial Segregation and the Origins of Apartheid in South Africa, 1919–1936.* Basingstoke: Macmillan, 1989.

Edgecombe, D. R. "The Glen Grey Act." In J. Benyon, et al., eds. *Studies in Local History.* Cape Town: Oxford University Press, 1976.

Engels, D., and S. Marks, eds. *Contesting Colonial Hegemony: State and Society in Africa and India.* London: British Academic Press, 1994.

Evans, I. *Bureaucracy and Race: Native Administration in South Africa.* Berkeley: University of California Press, 1997.

Feinberg, H. M. "The 1913 Natives Land Act in South Africa: Politics, Race and Segregation in the Early 20th Century." *International Journal of African Historical Studies* 26, 1 (1993).

_____. "Pre-Apartheid African Land Ownership and the Implication for the Current Restitution Debate in South Africa." *Historia* 40, 2 (1995).

Fredrickson, G. M. *The Comparative Imagination: On the History of Racism, Nationalism and Social Movements.* Berkeley: University of California Press, 1997.

Hammond-Tooke, W. D. *Command or Consensus: The Development of Transkeian Local Government.* Cape Town: David Philip, 1975.

Hindson, D. *Pass Controls and the Urban African Proletariat in South Africa.* Johannesburg: Ravan Press, 1987.

Keegan, T. *Colonial South Africa and the Origins of the Racial Order.* Cape Town: David Philip, 1996.

Legassick, M. "The Making of South African 'Native Policy', 1902–23: The Origins of Segregation." *Collected Seminar Papers on the Societies of Southern Africa in the 19th and 20th Centuries* (University of London, Institute of Commonwealth Studies) 17, 1972.

Lemon, A., ed. *Homes Apart: South Africa's Segregated Cities.* Bloomington: Indiana University Press, 1991.

Mabin, A. "A Comprehensive Segregation: The Origins of the Group Areas Act and Its Planning Apparatuses." *JSAS* 18, 2 (1992).

Maré, G. *African Population Relocation in South Africa.* Johannesburg: Institute of Race Relations, 1980.

Marx, A. *Making Race and Nation: A Comparison of Race Relations in the United States, South Africa and Brazil.* New York: Cambridge University Press, 1998.

Mesthrie, U. S. "Tinkering and Tampering: A Decade of the Group Areas Act (1950–1960). *SAHJ* 28 (1993).

_____. "The Tramway Road Removals, 1959–61." *Kronos* 21 (1994).

Moleah, A. T. *South Africa: Colonialism, Apartheid and African Dispossession.* Wilmington: Disa Press, 1993.

Murray, C., and C. O'Regan, eds. *No Place to Rest: Forced Removals and the Law in South Africa.* Cape Town: Oxford University Press, 1990.

Nel, E. "Racial Segregation in East London, 1836–1948." *South African Geographical Journal* 73, 2 (1991).

Norval, A. J. *Deconstructing Apartheid Discourse.* London: Blackwell, 1996.

Parnell, S. "Sanitation, Segregation and the Native (Urban Areas) Act: African Exclusion from Johannesburg's Malay Location, 1897–1925." *Journal of Historical Geography* 17, 3 (1991).

Perry, C., and J. Perry. *Apartheid: A History.* Melbourne: Longman, 1992.

Posel, D. *The Making of Apartheid 1948–61: Conflict and Compromise.* Oxford: Clarendon Press, 1991.

Redding, S. "South African Blacks in a Small Town Setting: The Ironies of Control in Umtata, 1878–1955." *Canadian Journal of African Studies* 26, 1 (1992).

Robinson, J. "Administrative Strategies and Political Power in South Africa's Black Townships 1930–1960." *Urban Forum* 2, 2 (1991).

————. "'A Perfect System of Control?' State Power and 'Native Locations' in South Africa." *Environment and Planning. D* 8, 2 (1990).

Sapire, H. "Apartheid's 'Testing Ground': Urban 'Native Policy' and African Politics in Brakpan, South Africa, 1943–1948." *JAH* 35, 1 (1994).

Smalberger, J. M. "The Role of the Diamond Mining Industry in the Development of the Pass Law System in South Africa." *International Journal of African Historical Studies* 9 (1976).

Smith, D. M. *Apartheid in South Africa.* 3d ed. Cambridge: Cambridge University Press, 1990.

Southworth, H. "Strangling South Africa's Cities: Resistance to Group Areas in Durban during the 1950s." *International Journal of African Historical Studies* 24, 1 (1991).

Stadler, H. D. *The Other Side of the Story: A True Perspective.* Pretoria: Contact, 1997.

Swanson, M. W. "The Urban Origins of Separate Development." *Race* 10, (1969).

Tatz, C. M. *Shadow and Substance in South Africa: A Study in Land and Franchise Policies Affecting Africans, 1910–1960.* Pietermaritzburg: University of Natal Press, 1962.

Taylor, B. "Local Government and 'Coloured' Residential Segregation in Port Elizabeth, 1964–1976." *South African Geographical Journal* 76, 1 (1994).

Ticktin, H. *The Politics of Race: Discrimination in South Africa.* London: Pluto, 1991.

Welsh, D. *The Roots of Segregation. Native Policy in Colonial Natal, 1845–1910.* Cape Town: Oxford University Press, 1971.

Wolpe, H. *Race, Class and the Apartheid State.* London: James Currey, 1988.

Resistance to Segregation and Apartheid

Adam, H. "The Rise of Black Consciousness in South Africa." *Race* 15, 2 (1973).

Adhikari, M. "Protest and Accommodation: Ambiguities in the Racial Policies of the APO, 1909–1923." *Kronos* 20 (1993).

African National Congress. *Unity in Action: A Photographic History of the African National Congress South Africa 1912–1982.* London: ANC, 1982.

Alexander, N. *Robben Island Prison Dossier, 1964–1974.* Cape Town: University of Cape Town Press, 1993.

Arnold, M., ed. *Steve Biko: Black Consciousness in South Africa.* New York: Random House, 1978.

Benson, M. *The Struggle for a Birthright.* Harmondsworth: Penguin, 1966.

Biko, S. *I Write What I Like.* London: Bowerdean Press, 1978.

Bonner, P., ed. *Holding Their Ground: Class, Locality and Culture in 19th and 20th Century South Africa.* Johannesburg: Ravan Press, 1983.

Bozzoli, B., ed. *Labour, Townships and Protest: Studies in the Social History of the Witwatersrand.* Johannesburg: Ravan Press, 1979.

Charney, C. "Vigilantes, Clientelism, and the South African State." *Transformation: Critical Perspectives on Southern Africa* 16, (1992).

Cobbett, W., and R. Cohen, eds. *Popular Struggles in South Africa*. London: James Currey, 1988.

Cohen, R., Y. Muthien, and A. Zageye, eds. *Repression and Resistance: Insider Accounts of Apartheid*. London: Hans Zell, 1990.

Cole, J. *Crossroads: The Politics of Reform and Repression, 1976–1987*. Johannesburg: Ravan Press, 1987.

Davis, S. M. *Apartheid's Rebels: Inside South Africa's Hidden War*. New Haven: Yale University Press, 1987.

Deacon, H. *The Island: A History of Robben Island 1488–1990*. Cape Town: David Philip, 1996.

Ellis, S., and T. Sechaba. *Comrades against Apartheid: The ANC and the South African Communist Party in Exile*. Bloomington: Indiana University Press, 1991.

Everatt, D. "Alliance Politics of a Special Type: The Roots of the ANC/SACP Alliance, 1950–1954." *JSAS* 18, 1 (1992).

Feit, E. *African Opposition in South Africa: The Failure of Passive Resistance*. Stanford: Hoover Institution, 1967.

_____. *South Africa: The Dynamics of the African National Congress*. London: Oxford University Press, 1962.

_____. *Urban Revolt in South Africa, 1960–1964: A Case Study*. Evanston: Northwestern University Press, 1971.

Gerhart, G. M. *Black Power in South Africa: The Evolution of an Ideology*. Berkeley: University of California Press, 1978.

Gready, P. "Autobiography and the 'Power of Writing': Political Prison Writing in the Apartheid Era." *JSAS* 19, 3 (1993).

Haysom, N. *Mabangalala: The Rise of Right-Wing Vigilantes in South Africa*. Johannesburg: University of the Witwatersrand, Centre for Applied Legal Studies, 1986.

Hirschman, D. "The Black Consciousness Movement in South Africa." *Journal of Modern African Studies* 28, 1 (1990).

Hirson, B. "Rural Revolt in South Africa, 1937–51." Institute of Commonwealth Studies, Collected Seminar Papers, volume 8 (1977).

_____. *Year of Fire, Year of Ash—The Soweto Revolt*. London: Zed, 1979.

Jabavu, D. D. T. *The Black Problem: Papers and Addresses on Various Native Problems*. Repr. New York: Negro Universities Press, 1969. ed.

Johnson, S., ed. *South Africa: No Turning Back*. Basingstoke: Macmillan, 1988.

Juckes, T. J. *Opposition in South Africa: The Leadership of Z. K. Matthews, Nelson Mandela and Stephen Biko*. London: Greenwood Press, 1995.

Karis, T., and G. M. Carter, eds. *From Protest to Challenge: A Documentary History of African Politics in South Africa, 1882–1964*. 4 vols. Stanford: 1972–1977.

Kirk, J. F. *Making a Voice: African Resistance to Segregation in South Africa*. Boulder: Westview Press, 1998.

La Hausse, P. *Brewers, Beerhalls and Boycotts: A History of Liquor in South Africa*. Johannesburg: Ravan Press, 1988.

Lazerson, J. N. *Against the Tide: Whites in the Struggle against Apartheid*. Boulder: Westview Press, 1994.

Le Roux, C. J. P. "Umkhonto We Sizwe and the SACP Alliance: A Critical Assessment of the Dominant Role That the SACP Played in the Development of the Armed Struggle in South Africa since 1961." *Journal for Contemporary History* 18, 1 (1993).

Lerumo, A. *Fifty Fighting Years: The Communist Party of South Africa 1921–1971*. London: Inkululeko, 1971.

Liebenberg, I., F. Lortan, B. Nel, and G. Van der Westhuizen, eds. *The Long March: The Story of the Struggle for Liberation in South Africa*. Pretoria: HAUM, 1994.

Lobban, M. *White Man's Justice: South African Political Trials in the Black Consciousness Era*. Oxford: Clarendon Press, 1996.

Lodge, T., and B. Nasson, eds. *All, Here, and Now: Black Politics in South Africa in the 1980s*. Cape Town: David Philip, 1991.

Lötter, H. P. P. "The Intellectual Legacy of Stephen Bantu Biko (1946–1977)." *Acta Academica* 24, 3 (1992).

Mafeje, A. "Soweto and Its Aftermath." *Review of African Political Economy* 11 (1978).

Marx, A. W. *Lessons of the Struggle: South African Internal Opposition, 1960–1990*. New York: Oxford University Press, 1992.

Mbeki, G. *Learning from Robben Island: The Prison Writings of Govan Mbeki*. Cape Town: David Philip, 1991.

———. *The Struggle for Liberation in South Africa: A Short History*. Cape Town: David Philip, 1992.

———. *Sunset at Midday: Latshon'ilang'emini*! Braamfontein: Nolwazi Educational Publishers, 1996.

McKinley, D. T. *The ANC and the Liberation Struggle: A Critical Political Biography*. London: Pluto, 1997.

Meli, F. *South Africa Belongs to Us: A History of the ANC*. London: James Currey, 1989.

Michelman, C. *The Black Sash of South Africa: A Case Study in Liberalism*. Oxford: Oxford University Press, 1975.

Moodie, D. "Social Existence and the Practice of Personal Integrity: Narratives of Resistance on the South African Gold Mines." *African Studies* 50, 1/2 (1991).

Mothlabi, M. *The Theory and Practice of Black Resistance to Apartheid: A Social-Ethical Analysis*. Johannesburg: Skotaville, 1984.

Murray, M. J., ed. *South African Capitalism and Black Political Opposition*. Cambridge: Schenkman, 1982.

Nasson, B. "The Unity Movement: Its Legacy in Historical Consciousness." *Radical History Review* 46–47 (1990).

Nolutshungu, S. *Changing South Africa: Political Considerations.* Manchester: Manchester University Press, 1982.

Odendaal, A. "'Even White Boys Called Us "Boy"': Early Black Organisational Politics in Port Elizabeth." *Kronos* 20 (1993).

_____. *Vukani Bantu! The Beginnings of Black Protest Politics in South Africa to 1912.* Cape Town: David Philip, 1984.

Orkin, M. "'Democracy Knows No Colour': Rationales for Guerrilla Involvement among Black South Africans." *JSAS* 18, 3 (1992).

Pityana, B., et al., eds. *Bounds of Possibility: The Legacy of Steve Biko and Black Consciousness.* Cape Town: David Philip, 1991.

Plaatje, S. T. *Native Life in South Africa before and since the European War and the Boer Rebellion.* 2d ed. Johannesburg: Ravan Press, 1995.

Pogrund, B. *Sobukwe and Apartheid.* Johannesburg: Jonathan Ball, 1990.

Ramamurthi, T. G. *Non-Violence and Nationalism: A Study of Gandhian Mass Resistance in South Africa.* Delhi: Amar Prakashan, 1993.

Rathbone, R. "The People and Soweto." *JSAS* 6, 1 (1979).

Reddy, E.S., ed. *Oliver Tambo, Apartheid and the International Community: Addresses to United Nations Committees and Conferences.* New Delhi: Stirling, 1991.

Rich, P. B. *White Power and the Liberal Conscience: Racial Segregation and South African Liberalism 1921–60.* Johannesburg: Ravan Press, 1984.

Rive, R., and T. Couzens. *Seme: The Founder of the ANC.* Johannesburg: Skotaville, 1991.

Roux, E. *Time Longer than Rope: A History of the Black Man's Struggle for Freedom in South Africa.* Wisconsin: University of Wisconsin Press, 1964.

Sapire, H. "Politics and Protest in Shack Settlements of the Pretoria-Witwatersrand-Vereeniging Region, South Africa, 1989–90." *JSAS* 18, 3 (1992).

Snail, M. L. *The Antecedents and the Emergence of the Black Consciousness Movement in South Africa—Its Ideology and Organisation.* Bayreuth: Reka Druck, 1992.

Sono, T. *Reflections on the Origins of Black Consciousness in South Africa.* Pretoria: HSRC, 1993.

Spink, K. *Black Sash: The Beginning of a Bridge in South Africa.* London: Methuen, 1991.

Suttner, I., ed. *Cutting through the Mountain: Interviews with South African Jewish Activists.* London: Viking, 1997.

Swan, M. *Gandhi: The South African Experience.* Johannesburg: Ravan Press, 1983.

Swart, R. *Progressive Odyssey: Towards a Democratic South Africa.* Cape Town: Human and Rousseau, 1991.

Vale, C. A. "Was Apartheid a Unique Phenomenon? A Discussion on Its Origins in the Light of Recent Research." *Journal of Social, Political and Economic Studies* 17, 1 (1992).

Van Tonder, D. "Gangs, Councillors and the Apartheid State: The Newclare Squatters' Movement of 1952." *SAHJ* 22 (1990).

Walshe, P. *The Rise of African Nationalism in South Africa.* London: Ad Donker, 1987.

Wells, J. *We Have Done with Pleading: The Women's 1913 Anti-Pass Campaign.* Johannesburg: Ravan Press, 1991.

_____. *We Now Demand! The History of Women's Resistance to Pass Laws in South Africa.* Johannesburg: Witwatersrand University Press, 1993.

Wentzel, J. *The Liberal Slideaway.* Johannesburg: South African Institute of Race Relations, 1995.

White, T. R. H. "Formative Years: Early Influences on the Career of Z. K. Matthews (1916–1937)." *Historia* 37, 2 (1992).

Williams, D. "African Nationalism in South Africa. Origins and Problems." *JAH* 11 (1970).

Zylstra, B. "Steve Biko on Black Consciousness in South Africa." *Acta Academica* 25, 2/3 (1993).

White Afrikaner Politics

Adam, H. *Modernizing Racial Domination: South Africa's Political Dynamics.* Berkeley: University of California Press, 1971.

Adam, H., and H. Giliomee. *Ethnic Power Mobilised: Can South Africa Change?* New Haven: Yale University Press, 1979.

Archibald, D. "The Afrikaners as an Emergent Minority." *British Journal of Sociology* 20 (1969).

Bloomberg, C., and S. Dubow. *Christian-Nationalism and the Rise of the Afrikaner Broederbond in South Africa, 1918–1948.* Basingstoke: Macmillan, 1990.

Bunting, B. *The Rise of the South African Reich.* London: International Defence and Aid Fund for Southern Africa, 1986.

Charney, C. "Class Conflict and the National Party Split." *JSAS* 10, 2 (1984).

Davenport, T. R. H. *The Afrikaner Bond: The History of a South African Political Party, 1880–1911.* Cape Town: Oxford University Press, 1966.

De Klerk, W. *The Puritans in Africa: A Story of Afrikanerdom.* Harmondsworth: Penguin, 1976.

Dubow, S. "Afrikaner Nationalism, Apartheid and the Conceptualization of 'Race.'" *JAH* 33, 2 (1992).

Du Toit, A. "No Chosen People: The Myth of the Calvinist Origins of Afrikaner Nationalism and Racial Ideology." *American Historical Review* 88, 4 (1983).

Fredrickson, G. M. *White Supremacy: A Comparative Study in American and South African History.* Oxford: Oxford University Press, 1981.

Furlong, P. *Between Crown and Swastika: The Impact of the Radical Right on the Afrikaner Nationalist Movement in the Fascist Era.* Johannesburg: Witwatersrand University Press, 1991.

_____. "Improper Intimacy: Afrikaans Churches, the National Party and the Anti-Miscegenation Laws." *SAHJ* 31 (1994).

Giliomee, H. "*Broedertwis*: Intra-Afrikaner Conflicts in the Transition from Apartheid." *African Affairs* 91, 364 (1992).

_____. "The Last Trek? Afrikaners in Transition to Democracy." *South Africa International* 22, 3 (1992).

_____. "The Non-Racial Franchise and Afrikaner and Coloured Identities, 1910–1994." *African Affairs* 94, 375 (1995).

_____. "'Survival in Justice': An Afrikaner Debate over Apartheid." *Comparative Studies in Society and History* 36, 3 (1994).

_____. "Western Cape Farmers and the Beginnings of Afrikaner Nationalism, 1870–1915." *JSAS* 14, 1 (1987).

Janse van Rensburg, N. S. "'Coloured' Afrikaans-speakers in Potchefstroom before and after 1950: Identity or Political Ideology." *African Studies* 51, 2 (1992).

Johnstone, F. "White Prosperity and White Supremacy in South Africa Today." *African Affairs* 69, 275 (1970).

Kenney, H. *Power, Pride and Prejudice: The Years of Afrikaner Nationalist Rule in South Africa*. Johannesburg: Jonathan Ball, 1991.

Loubser, J. "Calvinism, Equality and Inclusion: The Case of Afrikaner Nationalism." In S. N. Eisenstadt, eds. *The Protestant Ethic and Modernization: A Comparative View*. New York: Basic Books, 1968.

Malan, R. *My Traitor's Heart: A South African Exile Returns to Face His Country, His Tribe, and His Conscience*. New York: Atlantic Monthly Press, 1990.

Manzo, K., and P. McGowan. "Afrikaner Fears and the Politics of Despair: Understanding Change in South Africa." *International Studies Quarterly* 36, 1 (1992).

Marx, C. "The *Ossewabrandwag* as a Mass Movement, 1939–1941." *JSAS* 20, 2 (1994).

Moodie, T. D. *The Rise of Afrikanerdom: Power, Apartheid and the Afrikaner Civil Religion*. Berkeley: University of California Press, 1976.

Morrell, R. *White but Poor: Essays on the History of Poor Whites in Southern Africa 1880–1940*. Pretoria: Unisa, 1992.

Munro, W. A. "Revisiting Tradition, Reconstructing Identity? Afrikaner Nationalism and Political Transition in South Africa." *Politikon* 22, 2 (1995).

O'Meara, D. "The Afrikaner Broederbond 1927–1948: Class Vanguard of Afrikaner Nationalism." *JSAS* 3, 2 (1977).

_____. "Analysing Afrikaner Nationalism: The 'Christian National' Assault on White Trade Unionism in South Africa 1934–1948." *African Affairs* 77 (1978).

_____. *Volkskapitalisme: Class, Capital and Ideology in the Development of Afrikaner Nationalism, 1934–1948*. Johannesburg: Ravan Press, 1983.

_____. *Forty Lost Years*. Athens: Ohio University Press, 1996.

Rich, P. B. "Race, Science and the Legitimization of White Supremacy in South Africa, 1902–1940." *International Journal of African Historical Studies* 23, 4 (1990).

Schrire, R., ed. *Leadership in the Apartheid State: From Malan to De Klerk*. Cape Town: Oxford University Press, 1994.

Serfontein, J. H. P. *Brotherhood of Power*. London: Rex Collings, 1978.

Simson, H. *The Social Origins of Afrikaner Fascism and Its Apartheid Policy*. Stockholm: Almqvist and Wiksell, 1980.

Stadler, A. W. "The Afrikaner in Opposition, 1910–1948." *Journal of Commonwealth Political Studies* 7, 3 (1969).

Steenkamp, T. "Discrimination and the Economic Position of the Afrikaner." *South African Journal of Economic History* 5, 1 (1990).

Stultz, N. M. *Afrikaner Politics in South Africa, 1934–1948*. Berkeley: University of California Press, 1974.

Tamarkin, M. "Nationalism or 'Tribalism': The Evolution of Cape Afrikaner Ethnic Consciousness in the Late Nineteenth Century." *Nations and Nationalism* 1, 2 (1995).

Tayler, J. "'Our Poor': The Politicisation of the Poor White Problem, 1932–1942." *Kleio* 24 (1992).

Thompson, L. M. *The Political Mythology of Apartheid*. New Haven: Yale University Press, 1985.

Trapido, S. "Political Institutions and Afrikaner Social Structure in the Republic of South Africa." *American Political Science Review* 57 (1963).

Van Jaarsveld, F. A. *The Awakening of Afrikaner Nationalism, 1868–1881*. Johannesburg: Human and Rousseau, 1961.

Welsh, D. "Urbanisation and the Solidarity of Afrikaner Nationalism." *Journal of Modern African Studies* 7 (1969).

Wilkins, I., and H. Strydom. *The Super-Afrikaners: Inside the Afrikaner Broederbond*. London: Corgi Books, 1979.

Bantustans

Bank, L. "Between Traders and Tribalists: Implosion and the Politics of Disjuncture in a South African Homeland." *African Affairs* 93, 370 (1994).

———. "The Failure of Ethnic Nationalism: Land, Power and the Politics of Clanship on the South African High Veld, 1860–1990." *Africa* 65, 4 (1995).

Bauer, C., and Wessels, D. P. "Bophuthatswana—Its Creation and Quest for International Recognition." *Journal for Contemporary History* 17, 1 (1992).

Black, P. A., F. K. Siebrits, and D. H. Van Papendorp. "Homeland Multipliers and the Decentralisation Policy." *SAJE* 59, 1 (1991).

Buthelezi, M. G. *White and Black Nationalism. Ethnicity and the Future of the Homelands*. Johannesburg: Institute of Race Relations, 1974.

Butler, J., R. I. Rotberg, and J. Adams. *The Black Homelands of South Africa: The Political and Economic Development of Bophuthatswana and KwaZulu*. Berkeley: California University Press, 1977.

Carter, G. M., T. Karis, and N. M. Stultz. *South Africa's Transkei: The Politics of Domestic Colonialism*. Evanston: Northwestern University Press, 1967.

Christopher, A. J. "South Africa: The Case of a Failed State Partition." *Political Geography* 13, 2 (1994).

Horrell, M. *The African Homelands of South Africa.* Johannesburg: South African Institute of Race Relations, 1973.

Kotzé, D. A. *African Politics in South Africa, 1964–1974: Parties and Issues.* London: Hurst, 1975.

Lawrence, M., and A. Manson. "The 'Dog of the Boers': The Rise and Fall of Mangope in Bophuthatswana." *JSAS* 20, 3 (1994).

Lawrence, P. *The Transkei: South Africa's Politics of Partition.* Johannesburg: Ravan Press, 1976.

Legassick, M., and H. Wolpe. "The Bantustans and Capital Accumulation in South Africa." *Review of African Political Economy* 7 (1976).

Lelyveld, J. *Move Your Shadow: South Africa, Black and White.* London: Jonathan Ball, 1986.

Maré, G. *African Population Relocation in South Africa.* Johannesburg: South African Institute of Race Relations, 1980.

Molteno, F. "The Historical Significance of the Bantustan Strategy." *Social Dynamics* 3 (1977).

Pickles, J., and J. Woods. "South Africa's Homelands in the Age of Reform: The Case of QwaQwa." Association of American Geographers, *Annals* 82 (1992).

Sharp, J. "A World Turned Upside Down: Households and Differentiation in a South African Bantustan in the 1980s." *African Studies* 53, 1 (1994).

Southall, R. "Buthelezi, Inkatha and the Politics of Compromise." *African Affairs* 80 (1981).

———. *South Africa's Transkei: The Political Economy of an 'Independent' Bantustan.* London: Heinemann, 1982.

Streek, B., and R. Wicksteed. *Render unto Kaiser: A Transkei Dossier.* Johannesburg: Ravan Press, 1981.

Stultz, N. M. *Transkei's Half Loaf: Race Separatism in South Africa.* Cape Town: David Philip, 1980.

Union of South Africa. *Summary Report of the Commission for the Socio-Economic Development of the Bantu Areas within the Union of South Africa.* U.G. 61–1955. (Tomlinson Commission).

Vail, L., ed. *The Creation of Tribalism in Southern Africa.* Berkeley: University of California Press, 1989.

Van der Waal, K. "Developing South Africa's Former Rural Homeland Areas towards Human Dignity." *Acta Academica* 26, 2&3 (1994).

Wilson, F., and M. Ramphele. *Uprooting Poverty: The South African Challenge.* Cape Town: David Philip, 1989.

Constitutional, Legal, and Administrative

Bennum, M., and M. Newitt, eds. *Negotiating Justice: A New Constitution for South Africa.* Exeter: University of Exeter Press, 1995.

Benyon, J., ed. *Constitutional Change in South Africa*. Pietermaritzburg: University of Natal Press, 1978.

De Crespigny, A., and R. Schrire, eds. *The Government and Politics of South Africa*. Cape Town: Juta, 1978.

Dugard, C. J. R. *Human Rights and the South African Legal Order*. Princeton: Princeton University Press, 1978.

Ellman, S. *In a Time of Trouble: Law and Liberty in South Africa's State of Emergency*. Oxford: Clarendon Press, 1992.

Fryer, A. K. "The Government of the Cape of Good Hope, 1825–54." *AYB* 27, 1 (1964).

Hahlo, H. R., and E. Kahn. *The South African Legal System and Its Background*. Cape Town: Juta, 1973.

_____. *South Africa: The Development of Its Laws and Constitution*. Cape Town: Juta, 1968.

Horrell, M. *Laws Affecting Race Relations in South Africa (To the End of 1976)*. Johannesburg: South African Institute of Race Relations, 1978.

Liebenberg, S., ed. *The Constitution of South Africa from a Gender Perspective*. Cape Town: David Philip, 1995.

Matthews, A. S. *Law, Order and Liberty in South Africa*. Berkeley: University of California Press, 1972.

_____. *The Darker Reaches of Government*. Cape Town: Juta, 1976.

Maud, J. P. R. *City Government: The Johannesburg Experiment*. Oxford: Oxford University Press, 1938.

May, H. J. *The South African Constitution*. 3d ed. Cape Town: Juta, 1955.

McCracken, J. L. *The Cape Parliament, 1854–1910*. Oxford: Clarendon Press, 1967.

Ross, R. "The Rule of Law at the Cape of Good Hope in the Eighteenth Century." *Journal of Imperial and Commonwealth History* 9 (1980).

Sachs, A. *Justice in South Africa*. Berkeley: University of California Press, 1973.

Seymour, S. M. *Native Law in South Africa*. 2d ed. Cape Town: Juta, 1960.

Simons, H. J. *African Women: Their Legal Status in South Africa*. London: Hurst, 1968.

Thompson, L. M. "Constitutionalism in the South African Republics." *Butterworths South African Law Review* (1954).

_____. *The Government and Politics of South Africa*. Boston: Little Brown, 1966.

Worrall, D., ed. *South Africa: Government and Politics*. Pretoria: Van Schaik, 1971.

Police, Prisons, and Military

Achmat, Z. "'Apostles of Civilised Vice': 'Immoral Practices' and 'Unnatural Vice' in South African Prisons and Compounds, 1890–1920." *Social Dynamics* 19, 2 (1993).

Alden, C. *Apartheid's Last Stand: The Rise and Fall of the South African Security State*. Basingstoke: Macmillan, 1996.

Becker, D. *On Wings of Eagles: South Africa's Military Aviation History*. Durban: Walker-Ramus Trading Company, 1993.

Bouch, R. J., ed. *Infantry in South Africa 1652–1976*. Pretoria: South African Defence Force, 1977.

Brewer, J. D. *Black and Blue: Policing in South Africa*. New York: Clarendon Press, 1994.

Brinton, W. *History of the British Regiments in South Africa 1795–1895*. Cape Town: University of Cape Town Extra-Mural Studies, 1977.

Cock, J., and L. Nathan, eds. *War and Society: The Militarisation of South Africa*. Cape Town: David Philip, 1989.

Coleman, M. *A Crime against Humanity: Analysing the Repression of the Apartheid State*. Cape Town: David Philip, 1998.

Ellis, S. "The Historiographical Significance of South Africa's Third Force." *Journal of Southern African Studies* 24, 2 (1998).

Frankel, P. *Pretoria's Praetorians: Civil-Military Relations in South Africa*. Cambridge: Cambridge University Press, 1984.

Frederikse, J. *South Africa: A Different Kind of War, From Soweto to Pretoria*. Johannesburg: Ravan Press, 1986.

Goodhew, D. "The People's Police-Force: Communal Policing Initiatives in the Western Areas of Johannesburg, circa 1930–62." *JSAS* 19, 3 (1993).

Griffiths, R. J. "South Africa Civil-Military Relations in Transition: Issues and Influences." *Armed Forces and Society* 21, 3 (1995).

Gutteridge, W. "The Military in South African Politics: Champions of National Unity?" *Conflict Studies* 271 (1994).

_____, ed. *South Africa's Defence and Security Into the 21st Century*. Aldershot: Dartmouth, 1996.

Hattersley, A. F. *The First South African Detectives*. Cape Town: Howard Timmins, 1960.

Howe, H. M. "The South African Defence Force and Political Reform." *Journal of Modern African Studies* 32, 1 (1994).

Johns, S. "Obstacles to Guerrilla Warfare: A South African Case Study." *Journal of Modern African Studies* 11 (1973).

Le Roux, C. J. B. "The ANC-SACP's Political Military Council: A Brief Profile of Its Origin and Leadership." *Journal for Contemporary History* 19, 1 (1994).

_____. "*Umkhonto We Sizwe's* Military High Command (HC). A Profile of its Exile Leadership in the Late 1980s." *Journal for Contemporary History* 19, 3 (1994).

Marks, S., and A. Atmore. "Firearms in Southern Africa: A Survey." *JAH* 12 (1971).

Mathews, M., P. B. Heymann, and A. S. Mathews, eds. *Policing the Conflict in South Africa*. Gainesville: University of Florida Press, 1993.

Nasson, B. "'Messing with Coloured People': The 1918 Police Strike in Cape Town, South Africa." *Journal of African History* 33, 2 (1992).

Nathan, L. *The Changing of the Guard: Armed Forces and Defence Policy in a Democratic South Africa*. Pretoria: HSRC, 1994.

Rogerson, C. M. "Defending Apartheid: Armscor and the Geography of Military Production in South Africa." *GeoJournal* 22, 3 (1990).

Seegers, A. *The Military in the Making of Modern South Africa*. London: Tauris, 1996.

_____. "One State, Three Faces: Policing in South Africa (1910–1990)." *Social Dynamics* 17, 1 (1991).

———. "South Africa's National Security Management System, 1972–90." *Journal of Modern African Studies* 29, 2 (1991).

Tylden, G. *The Armed Forces of South Africa*. Johannesburg: Africana Museum, 1954.

_____. "The Development of the Commando System in South Africa 1715–1922." *Africana Notes and News* 13, 8 (1959).

Uys, I. *South African Military Who's Who, 1452–1992*. Germiston: Fortress, 1992.

Van der Waag, I. J. "A Bibliographical Guide to Secondary Sources on the History of the South African National Defence Force, 1912–1995." *Militaria* 25, 2 (1995).

_____. "A History of the South African Defence Force Institution (SADFI) 1916–1991." *Militaria* 21, 3 (1991).

Willan, B. "The South African Native Labour Contingent, 1916–1918." *JAH* 19 (1978).

Young, P. J. *Boot and Saddle: A Narrative Record of the Cape Regiment, the British Cape Mounted Riflemen, the Frontier Armed and Mounted Police and the Colonial Mounted Riflemen*. Cape Town: Maskew Miller, 1955.

South Africa and the Wider World

Alden, C. "Solving South Africa's Chinese Puzzle: Democratic Foreign Policy Making and the 'Two China's' Question." *South African Journal of International Affairs* 5, 2 (1998).

Austin, D. *Britain and South Africa*. London: Oxford University Press, 1966.

Barber, J. *South Africa's Foreign Policy, 1945–1970*. London: Oxford University Press, 1973.

Barber, J., and J. Barrat. *South Africa's Foreign Policy: The Search for Status and Security 1945–1988*. Cambridge: Cambridge University Press, 1990.

Baynham, S. "South Africa and the World in the 1990s." *South Africa International* 23, 3 (1993).

Birmingham, D. *Frontline Nationalism in Angola and Mozambique*. London: James Currey, 1991.

Borstelmann, T. *Apartheid's Reluctant Uncle: The United States and Southern Africa in the Early Cold War*. New York: Oxford University Press, 1993.

Chan, S. *Exporting Apartheid: Foreign Policies in Southern Africa 1978–1988*. London: Macmillan, 1980.

Chanock, M. *Unconsummated Union: Britain, Rhodesia and South Africa 1900–45*. Manchester: Manchester University Press, 1977.

Cliffe, L. *The Transition to Independence in Namibia.* Boulder: Lynne Rienner, 1994.

Clifford-Vaughan, F. M., ed. *International Pressure and Political Change in South Africa.* Cape Town: Oxford University Press, 1978.

Coetzer, P. W. "Relations between South Africa and the Soviet Bloc." *Journal for Contemporary History* 16, 2 (1991).

Cooper, A. D. *The Occupation of Namibia: Afrikanerdom's Attack on the British Empire.* Lanham: University Press of America, 1991.

Crawford, N. C. "South Africa's New Foreign and Military Policy: Opportunities and Constraints." *Africa Today* 42, 1&2, (1995).

Culverson, D. R. "The Politics of the Anti-Apartheid Movement in the United States, 1969–1986." *Political Science Quarterly* 111, 1 (1996).

Custy, M. C., and J. J. Van Wyk. "*Seikei Bunri* and Apartheid: An Analysis of the Japanese-South African Relationship 1985–1991." *Politikon* 21, 2 (1994).

Dodds, K. "South Africa, the South Atlantic and the International Politics of Antarctica." *South African Journal of International Affairs* 3, 1 (1995).

Dreyer, R. *Namibia and Southern Africa: Regional Dynamics of Decolonization, 1945–90.* London: Kegan Paul International, 1994.

Dunn, D. J. "International Relations and the New South Africa." *South African Journal of International Affairs* 3, 1 (1995).

Ellis, S. "Africa and International Corruption: The Strange Case of South Africa and Seychelles." *African Affairs* 95, 379 (1996).

Finnegan, W. *A Complicated War: The Harrowing of Mozambique.* Berkeley: University of California Press, 1992.

Geyser, O. "South Africa Rejoins the Commonwealth." *Round Table* 331 (1994).

Guimaraes, F. A. *The Origins of the Angolan Civil War: Foreign Intervention and Domestic Political Conflict.* Basingstoke: Macmillan, 1998.

Hailey, Lord. *The Republic of South Africa and the High Commissioner Territories.* London: Oxford University Press, 1963.

Hallett, R. "South Africa's Involvement in Angola, 1975–76." *African Affairs* 77 (1978).

Hanlon, J. *Beggar Your Neighbours: Apartheid Power in Southern Africa.* London: James Currey, 1986.

Hayes, P. et al., eds. *Namibia under South African Rule: Mobility and Containment, 1915–46.* Athens: Ohio University Press, 1998.

Henshaw, P. J. "Britain and South Africa at the United Nations: 'South West Africa', 'Treatment of Indians' and 'Race Conflict', 1946–1961." *SAHJ* 31 (1994).

———. "The Transfer of Simonstown: Afrikaner Nationalism, South African Strategic Dependence and British Global Power." *Journal of Imperial and Commonwealth History* 20, 3 (1992).

Hoskins, L. A. "Apartheid South Africa: The Commonwealth Stand and US-British Collusion." *Current Bibliography on African Affairs* 22, 1 (1990).

Hyam, R. *The Failure of South African Expansion, 1908–1948.* London: Macmillan, 1972.

Irogbe, K. *The Roots of United States Foreign Policy toward Apartheid South Africa, 1969–1985*. Lewiston: Edwin Mellen Press, 1997.

James, W. M. *A Political History of the Civil War in Angola 1974–1990*. New Brunswick: Transaction, 1991.

Jervis, D. "After the Euphoria: The United States and South Africa in the 1990s." *South African Journal of International Affairs* 3, 1 (1995).

Keto, C. T. *American-South African Relations, 1784–1980: Review and Select Bibliography*. Athens, Ohio: Ohio University, Center for International Studies, Africa Studies Program, 1985.

Kline, B. "The United States and South Africa during the Bush Administration: 1988–91." *Journal of Asian and African Affairs* 4, 2 (1993).

Kruchem, T. "The Foreign Policy of the Federal Republic of Germany towards South Africa." *South Africa International* 20, 3 (1990).

Lemarchand, R., ed. *American Policy in Southern Africa: The Stakes and the Stance*. Washington, D.C.: University Press of America, 1978.

Leys, C., and J. S. Saul, et al. *Namibia's Liberation Struggle: The Two Edged Sword*. London: James Currey, 1994.

Lloyd, L. "'A Most Auspicious Beginning': The 1946 United Nations General Assembly and the Question of Treatment of Indians in South Africa." *Review of International Studies* 16, 2 (1990).

Massie, R. K. *Loosing the Bonds: The United States and South Africa in the Apartheid Years*. New York: Doubleday, 1997.

Mills, G., ed. *From Pariah to Participant: South Africa's Evolving Foreign Relations, 1990–1994*. Johannesburg: South African Institute of International Affairs, 1994.

Minter, W. *Apartheid's Contras: An Inquiry into the Roots of War in Angola and Mozambique*. Johannesburg: Witwatersrand University Press, 1994.

Nolutshungu, S. *South Africa: A Study of Ideology and Foreign Policy*. New York: Africana Pub. Co., 1975.

Nwokedi, E. "South Africa and the United Nations: The Dynamics of Duplicity and Defiance." *Quarterly Journal of Administration* 25, 1 (1990/1).

Pachai, B. *The International Aspects of the South African Indian Question, 1860–1971*. Cape Town: Struik, 1971.

Potholm, C., and Dale, R., ed. *Southern Africa in Perspective*. New York: Free Press, 1972.

Ramamurthi, T. G. "India's South Africa Policy." *Africa Quarterly* (India) 32, 1/4 (1992/3).

Sawant, A. B. "India's Policy towards South Africa." *Africa Quarterly* (India) 31, 1/2 (1991).

Schoeman, C., and E. Schoeman. *South Africa's Foreign Relations in Transition 1985–1992: A Chronology*. Johannesburg: South African Institute of International Affairs, 1993.

Sole, D. "South African Foreign Policy Assumptions and Objectives from Hertzog to De Klerk." *South African Journal of International Affairs* 2, 1 (1994).

Spence, J. E. *Republic under Pressure*. London: Oxford University Press, 1965.

Study Commission on U.S. Policy Toward Southern Africa. *South Africa: Time Running Out*. Berkeley: University of California Press, 1981.

Thomas, A. M. *The American Predicament: Apartheid and United States Foreign Policy*. Aldershot: Ashgate, 1997.

Thomas, S. *The Diplomacy of Liberation: The Foreign Relations of the African National Congress since 1960*. London: Tauris Academic Studies, 1996.

Thompson, A. "Incomplete Engagement: Reagan's South Africa Policy Revisited." *Journal of Modern African Studies* 33, 1 (1995).

Vandenbosch, A. *South Africa and the World*. Lexington: University Press of Kentucky, 1970.

Van Wyk, K. "Foreign Policy Orientation of the P.W. Botha Regime: Changing Perceptions of State Elites in South Africa." *Journal of Contemporary African Studies* 10, 1 (1991).

Van Wyk, K., and S. Radloff. "Symmetry and Reciprocity in South Africa's Foreign Policy." *Journal of Conflict Resolution* 37, 2 (1993).

Wood, B. "Canada and South Africa: A Return to Middle Power Activism." *Round Table* 315, (1990).

RELIGION

Baines, G. "'In the World but Not of It': Bishop Limba and the Church of Christ in New Brighton, c.1929–1949." *Kronos* 19 (1992).

Balia, D. M. "'Insurrection of Subjugated Knowledge': Rewriting 'Mission' History in South Africa." *Missionalia* 21, 3 (1993).

Batts, H. J. *The Story of a Hundred Years, 1820–1920: Being the History of the Baptist Church in South Africa*. Cape Town: Maskew Miller, n.d.

Boas, J. "The Activities of the London Missionary Society in South Africa, 1806–1836: An Assessment." *African Studies Review* 16 (1973).

Bourquin, S. *Wilhelm Posselt: A Pioneer Missionary among the Xhosa and Zulu and the First Pastor of New Germany, Natal. His Own Reminiscences*. Westville: Bergtheil Museum, 1994.

Bredekamp, H., and R. Ross, eds. *Missions and Christianity in South African History*. Johannesburg: Witwatersrand University Press, 1995.

Briggs, D. N., and J. Wing. *The Harvest and the Hope: The Story of Congregationalism in Southern Africa*. Johannesburg: United Congregational Church of South Africa, 1970.

Brown, W. E. *The Catholic Church in South Africa*. London: Burns and Oates, 1960.

Campbell, J. "'Like Locusts in Pharaoh's Palace': The Origins and Politics of African Methodism in the Orange Free State, 1895–1914." *African Studies* 53, 1 (1994).

———. *Songs of Zion*. New York: Oxford University Press, 1995.

Chidester, D. *Religions of South Africa.* London: Routledge, 1992.

———. *Shots in the Streets: Violence and Religion in South Africa.* Cape Town: Oxford University Press, 1992.

Cobley, A. G. "The 'African National Church': Self-Determination and Political Struggle Among Black Christians in South Africa to 1948." *Church History* 60, 3 (1991).

Comaroff, J. *Body of Power, Spirit of Resistance.* Chicago: University of Chicago Press, 1985.

———. "Missionaries and Mechanical Clocks: An Essay on Religion and History in South Africa." *Journal of Religion* 71, 1 (1991).

Comaroff, J., and J. Comaroff. *Of Revelation and Revolution: Christianity, Colonialism, and Consciousness in South Africa.* Chicago: University of Chicago Press, 1991.

———. *Of Revelation and Revolution. Volume 2: The Dialectics of Modernity on a South African Frontier.* Chicago: University of Chicago Press, 1997.

Cook, C. W. "The Writing of South African Church History." *SAHJ* 2 (1970).

Cuthbertson, G. "'Cave of Adullam': Missionary Reaction to Ethiopianism at Lovedale, 1898–1902." *Missionalia* 19, 1 (1991).

Davenport, T. R. H. "Christian Mission and the South African Melting Pot in the Nineteenth Century." *Studia Historiae Ecclesiasticae* 18, 2 (1992).

Davids, A. *The Mosques of Bo-Kaap. A Social History of Islam at the Cape.* Athlone, Cape: Arabic and Islamic Research, 1980.

———. "Muslim-Christian Relations in Nineteenth Century Cape Town, 1825–1925." *Kronos* 19 (1992).

De Gruchy, J. W. *The Church Struggle in South Africa.* 2d ed. Cape Town: David Philip, 1986.

De Kock, L. *Civilising Barbarians: Missionary Narrative and African Textual Response in Nineteenth-Century South Africa.* Johannesburg: Witwatersrand University Press, 1996.

———. "'Drinking at the English Fountains': Missionary Discourse and the Case of Lovedale." *Missionalia* 20, 2 (1992).

———. "'History', 'Literature' and 'English': Reading the Lovedale Missionary Record within South Africa's Colonial History." *EAR (English Academy Review)* 9 (1992).

Donaldson, M. "Nineteenth-Century Missionaries: The Need for a Contextualised History." *Studia Historiae Ecclesiaticae* 18, 2 (1992).

Dubb, A. *Community of the Saved: An African Revivalist Church in the Eastern Cape.* Johannesburg: Witwatersrand University Press, 1976.

Dubb, A. A., and A. G. Schutte, eds. *Black Religion in South Africa.* Johannesburg: Witwatersrand University Press, 1974.

Du Plessis, J. *A History of Christian Missions in South Africa.* London: Longman, 1911.

Edgar, R. *Because They Chose the Plan of God: The Story of the Bulhoek Massacre.* Johannesburg: Ravan Press, 1988.

Elbourne, E. "Early Khoisan Uses of Mission Christianity." *Kronos* 19 (1992).

Elphick, R., and R. Davenport, eds. *Christianity in South Africa: A Political, Social and Cultural History.* Cape Town: David Philip, 1997.

Etherington, N. *Preachers, Peasants and Politics in Southeast Africa, 1835–1880: African Christian Communities in Natal, Pondoland and Zululand.* London: Royal Historical Society, 1978.

Fast, H. F. "'In One Ear and Out at the Other': African Response to the Wesleyan Message in Xhosaland 1825–35." *Journal of Religion in Africa* 23, 2 (1993).

Gerdener, G. B. A. *Studies in the Evangelisation of South Africa.* London: Longman, 1911.

Gunn, A. M. "From Assent to Dissent: Apartheid and the Dutch Reformed Church." *South Africa International* 22, 1 (1991).

Hexham, I., ed. *The Scriptures of the AmaNazaretha of Ekuphakameni: Selected Writings of the Zulu Prophets Isaiah and Londa Shembe.* Calgary: University of Calgary Press, 1994.

Hinchliff, P. B. *The Anglican Church in South Africa.* London: Darton: Longman and Todd, 1963.

———. *John William Colenso, Bishop of Natal.* London: Nelson, 1964.

———. *The Church in South Africa.* London: Society for Promoting Christian Knowledge, 1968.

Hodgson, J. *Ntsikana's Great Hymn.* Cape Town: University of Cape Town, 1980.

Hofmeyr, J. W., and G. J. Pillay, eds. *A History of Christianity in South Africa: Vol. 1.* Pretoria: HAUM Tertiary, 1994.

Holt, B. *Joseph Williams and the Pioneer Mission to the South-Eastern Bantu.* Lovedale: Lovedale Press, 1954.

Hulley, L. "The Churches and Civil Disobedience in South Africa." *Missionalia* 21, 1 (1993).

Kennedy, B. "Missionaries, Black Converts and Separatists on the Rand, 1886–1910: From Accommodation to Resistance." *Journal of Imperial and Commonwealth History* 20, 2 (1992).

Khandela, R. S. "The Trappists in South Africa: A Short Overview." *Kleio* 27 (1995).

Kinghorn, J. "Social Cosmology, Religion and Afrikaner Ethnicity." *JSAS* 20, 3 (1994).

Kretzschmar, L. "The Neglected Heritage: An Examination of the Anabaptist Roots of the South African Baptist Churches." *Studia Historiae Ecclesiasticae* 16, 2 (1990).

Kritzinger, J. J. "The Past 25 Years of Missiology in South Africa: A Stock-Taking Exercise." *Missionalia* 22, 2 (1994).

———. "The Witness of the Reformed Churches in South Africa—A Certain Past and Uncertain Future." *International Review of Mission* 83, 328 (1994).

Kruger, B. *The Pear Tree Blossoms: A History of Moravian Mission Stations in South Africa, 1737–1869.* Genadendal: Moravian Church, 1966.

Lewis, C., and G. B. Edwards. *Historical Records of the Church of the Province of South Africa.* London: Society for Promoting Christian Knowledge, 1934.

Loubser, J. A. *A Critical Review of Racial Theology in South Africa: The Apartheid Bible*. Lewiston: Edwin Mellen Press, 1987.

Mahida, E. M. *History of Muslims in South Africa: A Chronology*. Durban: Arabic Study Circle, 1993.

Maloka, T. "Missionary Work and the Sotho in the Gold Mine Compounds, 1920–1940." *SAHJ* 32 (1994).

Moore, B., ed. *Black Theology: The South African Voice*. London: Hurst, 1973.

Nel, M., B. Njumbuxa, and H. Pieterse. "The Role of Christian Church Leaders in the Peace Process in South Africa." *R&T (Religion and Theology)* 1, 1 (1994).

Norman, E. R. *Christianity in the Southern Hemisphere: The Churches in Latin America and South Africa*. Oxford: Clarendon Press, 1981.

Oosthuizen, G. C. "The Use of Oral Information in the Writing of the History of African Indigenous Churches." *Studia Historiae Ecclesiasticae* 19, 1 (1993).

Pauw, B. A. *Christianity and Xhosa Tradition*. Cape Town: Oxford University Press, 1975.

Pillay, G. J. "The Problem of Interpreting the History of Black Churches and Writing the History of Christianity in South Africa." *Studia Historiae Ecclesiasticae* 18, 2 (1992).

Pillay, G. J., and J. W. Hofmeyr, eds. *Perspectives on Church History*. Pretoria: De Jager-Haum, 1991.

Pretorius, H. L. *Historiography and Historical Sources Regarding African Indigenous Churches in South Africa: Writing Indigenous Church History*. Lewiston: Edwin Mellen Press, 1995.

Prior, A., ed. *Catholics in an Apartheid Society*. Cape Town: David Philip, 1982.

Prozesky, M. H., ed. *Christianity in South Africa*. Bergvlei: Southern, 1990.

Robert, D. L. "Mount Holyoke Women and the Dutch Reformed Missionary Movement." *Missionalia* 21, 2 (1993).

Ross, A. *John Philip (1775–1851): Missions, Race and Politics in South Africa*. Aberdeen: University of Aberdeen Press, 1986.

Ryan, C. *Beyers Naude: Pilgrimage of Faith*. Cape Town: David Philip, 1990.

Saayman, W. "Christian Mission in South Africa: A Historical Reflection." *International Review of Mission* 83, 328 (1994).

Sales, J. M. *Mission Stations and the Coloured Communities of the Eastern Cape, 1800–1852*. Cape Town: Balkema, 1975.

———. *The Planting of the Churches in South Africa*. Grand Rapids: Eerdmans, 1971.

Saron, G., and L. Hotz, eds. *The Jews in South Africa: A History*. Cape Town: Oxford University Press, 1955.

Shain, M. "Anti-Semitism and South African Society: Reappraising the 1930s and 1940s." *SAHJ* 27 (1992).

———. *The Roots of Antisemitism in South Africa*. Charlottesville: University Press of Virginia, 1994.

Shimoni, G. *Jews and Zionism: The South African Experience 1910–1967*. Cape Town: Oxford University Press, 1980.

Strassberger, B. *The Rhenish Mission Society in South Africa, 1830–1950.* Cape Town: Struik, 1969.

Stuart, D. "'For England and For Christ': The Gospel of Liberation and Subordination in Early Nineteenth Century South Africa." *Journal of Historical Sociology* 6, 4 (1993).

Sundermeier, T., ed. *Church and Nationalism in South Africa.* Johannesburg: Ravan Press, 1975.

Sundkler, B. G. M. *Bantu Prophets in South Africa.* 2d ed. London: Oxford University Press, 1961.

Thom, G. "Between Priestly Identification and Prophetic Confrontation: The Roots of the *volkskerk* in Afrikaner History." *Studia Historiae Ecclesiasticae* 18, 2 (1992).

Tingle, R. *Revolution or Reconciliation? The Struggle in the Church in South Africa.* London: Christian Studies Centre, 1992.

Van den Bergh, E. "Between Resistance and Reconciliation: A Bibliographical Essay on Church and Theology in a Changing South Africa." *Exchange: A Journal of Missiological and Ecumenical Research* 23, 3 (1994).

Van der Geest, S., and J. P. Kirby. "The Absence of the Missionary in African Ethnography, 1930–65." *African Studies Review* 35, 3 (1992).

Villa-Vicencio, C. *Civil Disobedience and Beyond: Law, Resistance and Religion in South Africa.* Cape Town: David Philip, 1990.

Watt, P. *From Africa's Soil: The Story of the Assemblies of God in Southern Africa.* Cape Town: Struik Christian Books, 1992.

West, M. *Bishops and Prophets in a Black City: African Independent Churches in Soweto, Johannesburg.* Cape Town: David Philip, 1979.

Whiteside, J. *History of the Wesleyan Methodist Church of South Africa.* London: Stock, 1906.

Worsnip, M. E. *Between the Two Fires: The Anglican Church and Apartheid 1948–1957.* Pietermaritzburg: University of Natal Press, 1991.

SCIENCES

General, Geography, and the Environment

Beinart, W., and P. Coates. *Environment and History: The Taming of Nature in the United States of America and South Africa.* London: Routledge, 1995.

Brown, A. C., ed. *A History of Scientific Endeavour in South Africa.* Cape Town: Royal Society of South Africa, 1977.

Carruthers, J. *The Kruger National Park: A Social and Political History.* Pietermaritzburg: University of Natal Press, 1995.

Christopher, A. J. *Southern Africa.* Folkestone, Kent: Dawson, 1976.

Cole, M. M. *South Africa.* 2d ed. New York: E. P. Dutton, 1966.

Ellis, B. "Game Conservation in Zululand 1824–1947: Changing Perspectives." *Natalia* 23/24 (1993/4).

Ellis, S. "Of Elephants and Men: Politics and Nature Conservation in South Africa." *JSAS* 20, 1 (1994).

Griffiths, T., and L. Robin, eds. *Ecology and Empire: Environmental History of Settler Societies*. Pietermaritzburg: University of Natal Press, 1997.

Gunn, M., and L. E. Codd. *Botanical Exploration of Southern Africa*. Cape Town: Balkema, 1981.

Khan, F. "Rewriting South Africa's Conservation History: The Role of the *Native Farmers Association*." *JSAS* 20, 4 (1994).

McCracken, D. P. "Kirstenbosch: The Final Victory of Botanical Nationalism." *Contree* 38 (1995).

McDonald, D. A. "Neither from Above Nor from Below: Municipal Bureaucrats and Environmental Policy in Cape Town, South Africa." *Canadian Journal of African Studies* 31, 2 (1997).

Müller, J. J. "A Greener South Africa? Environmentalism, Politics and the Future." *Politikon: South African Journal of Political Studies* 24, 1 (1997).

Plug, C. "Early Scientific and Professional Societies in the Transvaal: Barberton 1887–1889." *South African Journal of Cultural History* 4, 3 (1990).

————. *Publications on the History of South African Science: Annotated Bibliography to the End of 1987*. Pretoria: Unisa, 1990.

————. "Scientific Societies in South Africa to the End of the Nineteenth Century." *South African Journal of Science* 88, 5 (1992).

Pollock, N. V., and S. Agnew. *An Historical Geography of South Africa*. London: Longman, 1963.

Raper, P. E. *Dictionary of Southern African Place Names*. 2d ed. Johannesburg: Jonathan Ball, 1989.

————. *Source Guide for Toponymy and Topology*. Pretoria: Human Sciences Research Council, 1975.

Stevenson-Hamilton, J. *South African Eden: The Kruger National Park 1902–1946*. Rev. ed. Cape Town: Struik, 1993.

Summers, R., comp. *A History of the South African Museum, 1825–1975*. Cape Town: Balkema, 1975.

Talbot, A. M., and W. J. Talbot. *Atlas of the Union of South Africa*. Pretoria: Government Printer, 1960.

Truswell, J. F. *Geological Evolution of South Africa*. Cape Town: Purnell, 1977.

Warner, B. *Astronomers at the Royal Observatory, Cape of Good Hope: A History with Emphasis on the Nineteenth Century*. Cape Town: Balkema, 1979.

Wellington, J. H. *Southern Africa: A Geographical Study*. 2 vols. Cambridge: Cambridge University Press, 1955.

Health, Disease, and Medicine

Bell, M. "The Pestilence That Walketh in Darkness—Imperial Health, Gender and Images of South Africa c.1880–1910." *Transactions of the Institute of British Geographers* 18, 3 (1993).

Brain, J. B. "'But Only We Black Men Die': The 1929–1933 Malaria Epidemics in Natal and Zululand." *Contree* 27, (1990).

Burrows, E. H. *A History of Medicine in South Africa Up to the End of the Nineteenth Century*. Cape Town: Balkema, 1958.

Caldwell, S. "Segregation and Plague: King William's Town and the Plague Outbreaks of 1900–1907." *Contree* 29 (1991).

Cluver, E. H. *Public Health in South Africa*. 4th ed. Johannesburg: Central News Agency, 1944.

Grobler, V. *History of Dentistry in South Africa, 1652–1900*. Cape Town: HAUM, 1977.

Katz, E. *The White Death: Silicosis on the Witwatersrand Gold Mines, 1886–1910*. Johannesburg: Witwatersrand University Press, 1994.

Laidler, P. W., and N. Gelfand. *South Africa: Its Medical History, 1652–1808*. Cape Town: Struik, 1971.

Le Sueur, D., B. L. Sharp, and C. C. Appleton. "Historical Perspective of the Malaria Problem in Natal with Emphasis on the Period 1928–1932." *South African Journal of Science* 89, 5 (1993).

Marks, S. *Divided Sisterhood: Race, Class and Gender in the South African Nursing Profession*. Johannesburg: Witwatersrand University Press, 1994.

Packard, R. M. *White Plague, Black Labor: Tuberculosis and the Political Economy of Health and Disease in South Africa*. Berkeley: University of California Press, 1989.

Parnell, S. "Creating Racial Privilege: The Origins of South African Public Health and Town Planning Legislation." *JSAS* 19, 3 (1993).

Phillips, H. *'Black October': The Impact of the Spanish Influenza Epidemic of 1918 on South Africa*. *AYB* 53, 1 (1990).

Phoofolo, P. "Epidemics and Revolutions: The Rinderpest Epidemic in Late Nineteenth-Century South Africa." *Past and Present* 138 (1993).

Searle, C. *History of the Development of Nursing in South Africa, 1652–1960*. Cape Town: Struik, 1965.

Swart, S. "The Black Insane in the Cape, 1891–1920." *JSAS* 21, 3 (1995).

Van Onselen, C. "Reactions to Rinderpest in Southern Africa, 1896–1897." *JAH* 13 (1972).

Westcott, G., and F. Wilson, eds. *Economics of Health in South Africa*. 2 vols. Johannesburg: Ravan Press, 1979.

SOCIETY

General

Adam, H., ed. *South Africa: Sociological Perspectives*. London: Oxford University Press, 1976.

Burman, S., and M. Huvers. "Church versus State: Divorce Legislation and Divided South Africa." *JSAS* 12, 1 (1985).

De Villiers, A., ed. *English-Speaking South Africa Today*. Cape Town: Oxford University Press, 1976.

Fleisch, B. D. "Social Scientists as Policy Makers: E.G. Malherbe and the *National Bureau for Educational and Social Research, 1929–1943*. *JSAS* 21, 3 (1995).

Greenberg, S. *Race and State in Capitalist Development*. New Haven: Yale University Press, 1980.

Hare, A. P., et al., eds. *South Africa: Sociological Analyses*. Cape Town: Oxford University Press, 1979.

Kuper, L. *An African Bourgeoisie: Race, Class and Politics in South Africa*. New Haven: Yale University Press, 1965.

Lever, H. *South African Society*. Johannesburg: Jonathan Ball, 1976.

Mayer, P., ed. *Black Villagers in an Industrial Society*. Cape Town: Oxford University Press, 1980.

Murray, C. *Divided Families*. Cambridge: Cambridge University Press, 1981.

Orpen, C., and S. J. Moore, eds. *Contemporary South Africa: Social and Psychological Perspectives*. Cape Town: Juta, 1975.

Posel, D. "State, Power and Gender: Conflict over the Registration of African Customary Marriage in South Africa, 1910–1970." *Journal of Historical Sociology* 8, 3 (1995).

Preston-Whyte, E., and S. Burman. *Questionable Issue: Illegitimacy in South Africa*. Cape Town: Oxford University Press, 1992.

Rex, J. "The Compound, the Reserve and the Urban Location: The Essential Institutions of Southern African Labour Exploitation." *South African Labour Bulletin* 1, 4 (1974).

Stone, J. *Colonist or Uitlander? A Study of the British Immigrant in South Africa*. Oxford: Oxford University Press, 1973.

Van der Merwe, N. J., and M. West, eds. *Perspectives on South Africa's Future*. Cape Town: University of Cape Town, 1973.

Yap, M., and D. L. Man. *Colour, Confusion and Concessions: The History of the Chinese in South Africa*. Hong Kong: Hong Kong University Press, 1996.

Education

Adhikari, M. "Coloured Identity and the Politics of Coloured Education: The Origin of the Teachers' League of South Africa." *International Journal of African Historical Studies* 27, 1 (1994).

———. *'Let Us Live For Our Children': The Teachers' League of South Africa, 1913–1940*. Cape Town: University of Cape Town Press, 1993.

Auerbach, F. E. *The Power of Prejudice in South African Education. An Enquiry into History Textbooks*. Cape Town: Balkema, 1965.

Behr, A. L. *New Perspectives in South African Education*. Durban: Butterworth, 1978.

Behr, A. L., and R. G. Macmillan. *Education in South Africa*. 2d ed. Pretoria: Van Schaik, 1971.

Boucher, M. *Spes in Arduis: A History of the University of South Africa.* Pretoria: University of South Africa, 1973.

———. "The University of the Cape of Good Hope and the University of South Africa, 1873–1946." *AYB* 35, 1 (1972).

Bradlow, E. "Women and Education in Nineteenth-Century South Africa: The Attitudes and Experiences of Middle-Class English-Speaking Females at the Cape." *SAHJ* 28 (1993).

Brook, D. L. "From Exclusion to Inclusion: Racial Politics and South African Educational Reform." *Anthropology and Education Quarterly* 27, 2 (1996).

Brookes, E. H. *A History of the University of Natal.* Pietermaritzburg: University of Natal Press, 1966.

Burchell, D. E. "African Higher Education and the Establishment of the South African Native College, Fort Hare." *SAHJ* 8 (1976).

Davis, R. H. "Charles T. Loram and an American Model for African Education in South Africa." *African Studies Review* 19 (1976).

———. "Elijah Makiwane and the Cape School Community." *African Affairs* 78 (1979).

Diseko, N. "The Origins and Development of the South African Students' Movement (SASM): 1968–1976." *JSAS* 18, 1 (1992).

Harley, K. "African Education and Social Control in Colonial Natal." *Perspectives in Education* 13, 2 (1992).

Horrell, M. *Bantu Education to 1968.* Johannesburg: Institute of Race Relations, 1968.

———. *The Education of the Coloured Community in South Africa.* Johannesburg: Institute of Race Relations, 1970.

Horton, J. W. *The First Seventy Years, 1895–1965: Being an Account of the Growth of the Council of Education, Witwatersrand.* Johannesburg: Witwatersrand University Press, 1968.

Hyslop, J. "State Education Policy and the Social Reproduction of the Urban African Working Class: The Case of the Southern Transvaal, 1955–1976." *JSAS* 14, 3 (1988).

Johnson, D. "Aspects of a Liberal Education: Late Nineteenth Century Attitudes to Race, from Cambridge to the Cape Colony." *History Workshop* 36 (1993).

Kallaway, P., ed. *Apartheid and Education: The Education of Black South Africans.* Johannesburg: Ravan Press, 1984.

Kerr, A. *Fort Hare, 1915–1948: The Evolution of an African College.* Pietermaritzburg: Shuter and Shooter, 1968.

Krige, S. C. "'Should Education Lead or Follow the Social Order': The Welsh Report and the Policy of Segregation, 1935–1940." *SAHJ* 28 (1993).

Kros, C. "'Deep Rumblings': Z. K. Matthews and African Education Before 1955." *Perspectives in Education* 12, 1 (1990/1).

Lemon, A. "Desegregation and Privatisation in White South African Schools: 1990–1992." *Journal of Contemporary African Studies* 12, 2 (1994).

Love, J., and P. C. Sederberg. "Black Education and the Dialects of Transformation in South Africa, 1982–8." *Journal of Modern African Studies* 28, 2 (1990).

Mager, A. "Girls' Wars, Mission Institutions and Reproduction of the Educated Elite in the Eastern Cape, 1945–1959." *Perspectives in Education* 14, 1 (1992/3).

Malherbe, E. G. *Education in South Africa.* 2 vols. Cape Town: Juta, 1925, 1977.

Maseko, S. S. "Student Power, Action and Problems: A Case Study of UWC SRC, 1981–92." *Transformation: Critical Perspectives on Southern Africa* 24 (1994).

Merrett, C. E. *A Culture of Censorship: Secrecy and Intellectual Repression in South Africa.* Cape Town: David Philip, 1994.

Mugomba, A., and M. Nyaggah, eds. *Independence without Freedom. The Political Economy of Colonial Education in Southern Africa.* Santa Barbara: ABC-Clio, 1980.

Murray, B. K. "Wits as an 'Open' University 1939–1959: Black Admissions to the University of the Witwatersrand." *JSAS* 16, 4 (1990).

Nasson, B., and J. Samuel, eds. *Education: From Poverty to Liberty.* Cape Town: David Philip, 1990.

Phillips, H. *The University of Cape Town 1918–1948: The Formative Years.* Cape Town: University of Cape Town Press, 1993.

Ritchie, W. *The History of the South African College, 1829–1918.* 2 vols. Cape Town: Maskew Miller, 1918.

Rose, B., ed. *Education in Southern Africa.* Johannesburg: Collier-Macmillan, 1970.

Shepherd, R. H. W. *Lovedale, South Africa: The Story of a Century, 1841–1941.* Lovedale: Lovedale Press, n.d.

Soudien, C. A. "Violence and the Discourse of Apartheid in Education." *Acta Academica* 27, 1 (1995).

Spro-Cas. *Education beyond Apartheid.* Johannesburg: Spro-Cas, 1971.

Unterhalter, E. "The Impact of Apartheid on Women's Education in South Africa." *Review of African Political Economy* 48 (1990).

Unterhalter, E., et al., eds. *Apartheid Education and Popular Struggles.* Johannesburg: Ravan Press, 1991.

Van der Merwe, H. W. *The Future of the University in South Africa.* Cape Town: David Philip, 1977.

Van der Merwe, H. W., and D. Welsh, eds. *Student Perspectives in South Africa.* Cape Town: David Philip, 1972.

White, T. R. H. "An Historical Study of Vocational Education at Lovedale Missionary Institute 1930–1955." *Acta Academica* 22, 2 (1990).

Wilson, D. M. *Against the Odds: The Struggle of the Cape African Night Schools 1945–1967.* Cape Town: University of Cape Town, Centre for African Studies, 1991.

Gender Studies

Bank, L. "Angry Men and Working Women: Gender, Violence and Economic Change in Qwaqwa in the 1980s." *African Studies* 53, 1 (1994).

Bozzoli, B. "Marxism, Feminism and South African Studies." *JSAS* 9, 2 (1983).
_____. *Class Community and Conflict*. Johannesburg: Ravan Press, 1987.
Bozzoli, B., and M. Nkotsoe. *Women of Phokeng: Consciousness, Life Strategy and Migrancy in South Africa, 1900–83*. Johannesburg: Ravan Press, 1991.
Bradford, H. "Women, Gender and Colonialism: Rethinking the History of the British Cape Colony and Its Frontier Zones, c.1806–1870." *JAH* 37, 3 (1996).
Chisholm, L. "Class, Colour and Gender in Child Welfare in South Africa, 1902–1918." *SAHJ* 23 (1990).
Clayton, C. *Women and Writing in South Africa: A Critical Anthology*. Johannesburg: Heinemann, 1989.
Cock, J. *Women and War in South Africa*. London: Open Letters, 1992.
Daymond, M. T. "Gender and 'History': 1980s South African Women's Stories in English." *Ariel: A Review of International English Literature* 27, 1 (1996).
Glaser, C. "The Mark of Zorro: Sexuality and Gender Relations in the Tsotsi Subculture on the Witwatersrand." *African Studies* 51, 1 (1992).
Golan, D. "The Life Story of King Shaka and Gender Tensions in the Zulu State." *History in Africa* 17 (1990).
Hansson, D. "South African Feminism and the Patchwork Quilt of Power Relations." *Women's Studies* 6 (1994).
Harries, P. "Symbols and Sexuality: Culture and Identity on the Early Witwatersrand Gold Mines." *Gender and History* 2, 3 (1990).
Heatherington, P. "Women in South Africa: The Historiography in English." *International Journal of African Historical Studies* 26, 2 (1993).
Krebs, P. M. "'The Last of the Gentlemen's Wars': Women in the Boer War Concentration Camp Controversy." *History Workshop* 33 (1992).
Landman, C. *The Piety of Afrikaans Women: Diaries of Guilt*. Pretoria: University of South Africa, 1994.
Manicom, L. "Ruling Relations: Rethinking State and Gender in South African History." *JAH* 33, 3 (1992).
Moodie, T. D. "Migrancy and Male Sexuality on the South African Gold Mines." *JSAS* 14, 2 (1988).
Murray, C. M., and T. W. Bennett. *Gender and the New South African Legal Order*. Kenwyn: Juta, 1994.
Mzamane, M. V. "Gender Politics and the Unfolding Culture of Liberation in South Africa." *Women's Studies* 6 (1994).
Seidman, G. W. "'No Freedom without the Women': Mobilization and Gender in South Africa, 1970–1992." *Signs* 18, 2 (1993).
Southey, N. "Uncovering Homosexuality in Colonial South Africa: The Case of Bishop Twells." *SAHJ* 36 (1997).
Swaisland, C. *Servants and Gentlewomen to the Golden Land: The Emigration of Single Women from Britain to Southern Africa, 1820–1939*. Pietermaritzburg: University of Natal Press, 1993.
Tisani, N. "The Shaping of Gender Relations in Mission Stations." *Kronos* 19 (1992).

Todes, A., and N. Walker. "Women and Housing Policy in South Africa: A Discussion of Durban Case Studies." *Urban Forum* 3, 2 (1992).

Walker, C. *Women and Gender in Southern Africa to 1945*. Cape Town: David Philip, 1990.

_____. *Women and Resistance in South Africa*. 2d ed. Cape Town: David Philip, 1991.

_____. *Women's Suffrage Movement in South Africa*. Cape Town: University of Cape Town, 1979.

Urbanization

Baines, G. "The Origins of Urban Segregation: Local Government and the Resistance of Africans in Port Elizabeth, c.1835–1865." *SAHJ* 22 (1990).

Bickford-Smith, V. "South African Urban History, Racial Segregation and the 'Unique' Case of Cape Town." *JSAS* 2, 1 (1995).

Bonner, P. "African Urbanisation on the Rand between the 1930s and 1960s: Its Social Character and Political Consequences." *JSAS* 21, 1 (1995).

_____. "The Politics of Black Squatter Movements on the Rand, 1944–1952." *Radical History Review* 46–47 (1990).

Crankshaw, O. "Squatting, Apartheid and Urbanisation on the Southern Witwatersrand." *African Affairs* 92, 366 (1993).

Davenport, T. R. H. "African Tribesmen? South African Natives (Urban Areas) Legislation Through the Years." *African Affairs* 68, 1969.

_____. "The Triumph of Colonel Stallard: The Transformation of the Natives (Urban Areas) Act between 1923 and 1937." *SAHJ* 2 (1970).

Elder, G. "The Grey Dawn of South African Racial Residential Integration." *GeoJournal* 22, 3 (1990).

Ellis, G., et al. *The Squatter Problem in the Western Cape*. Johannesburg: Institute of Race Relations, 1977.

Gluckman, M. "Tribalism, Ruralism and Urbanism in South and Central Africa." In V. Turner, ed. *Colonialism in Africa*. Vol. 3. Cambridge: Cambridge University Press, 1971.

Hendler, P. "Living in Apartheid's Shadow: Residential Planning for Africans in the PWV Region 1970–1990." *Urban Forum* 3, 2 (1992).

Lemon, A., ed. *Homes Apart: South Africa's Segregated Cities*. Bloomington: Indiana University Press, 1991.

Maasdorp, G., and A. S. B. Humphreys, eds. *From Shantytown to Township: An Economic Study of African Poverty and Rehousing in a South African City*. Cape Town: Juta, 1975.

Mabin, A., and D. Smit. "Reconstructing South Africa's Cities? The Making of Urban Planning 1900–2000." *Planning Perspectives* 12, 2 (1997).

Mayer P., and I. Mayer. *Townsmen or Tribesmen: Conservatism and the Process of Urbanization in a South African City*. 2d ed. Cape Town: Oxford University Press, 1971.

Maylam, P. "Explaining the Apartheid City: 20 Years of South African Urban Historiography." *JSAS* 21, 1 (1995).

————. "The Rise and Decline of Urban Apartheid in South Africa." *African Affairs* 89, 354 (1990).

Parnell, S. M. "The Ideology of African Home-Ownership: The Establishment of Dube, Soweto, 1946–1955." *South African Geographical Journal* 73, 2 (1991).

Parnell, S., and A. Mabin. "Rethinking Urban South Africa." *JSAS* 21, 1 (1995).

Robinson, J. *The Power of Apartheid: State, Power and Space in South African Cities*. Boston: Butterworth Heinemann, 1995.

Sapire, H., and J. Beall. "Urban Change and Urban Studies in Southern Africa." *JSAS* 21, 1 (1995).

Saunders, C. C. *Writing History: South Africa's Urban Past and Other Essays*. Pretoria: HSRC, 1992.

Saunders, C. C., et al., eds. *Studies in the History of Cape Town*. 6 vols. Cape Town: University of Cape Town: 1978–84.

Smith, D. M., ed. *The Apartheid City and Beyond: Urbanization and Social Change in South Africa*. Johannesburg: Witwatersrand University Press, 1992.

Stadler, A. "Birds in a Cornfield: Squatter Movements in Johannesburg, 1944–1947." *JSAS* 6, 1 (1979).

Swanson, M. W. "The Durban System: Roots of Urban Apartheid in Colonial Natal." *African Studies* 35, (1976).

————. "The Sanitation Syndrome." *JAH* 17 (1977).

Swilling, M., et al., eds. *Apartheid City in Transition*. Cape Town: Oxford University Press, 1991.

Van Heyningen, E., ed. *Studies in the History of Cape Town*. Vol. 7: Cape Town: University of Cape Town Press, 1995.

Van Tonder, D. "Boycotts, Unrest and the Western Areas Removal Scheme, 1949–1952." *Journal of Urban History* 20, 1 (1993).

West, M. *Divided Community*. Cape Town: Balkema, 1971.

Western, J. *Outcast Cape Town*. New ed. Berkeley: University of California Press, 1996.

About the Authors

Christopher Saunders is an associate professor of history at the University of Cape Town. He was the author of the first edition of this dictionary, published in 1983. He is a former head of the history department at the University of Cape Town, and has published widely in South African history. He has also written on recent Namibian history.

Nicholas Southey is a senior lecturer in the history department at the University of South Africa. His special areas of interest include the history of missions and the Anglican church, the history of slavery, and the history of sexuality in South Africa.

Mary-Lynn Suttie is a senior librarian at the University of South Africa. She is well known for the select bibliographies of South African history she contributes regularly to the *South African Historical Journal*.